Treat this book with care and respect.

It should become part of your personal and professional library. It will serve you well at any number of points during your professional career.

JAMES B. HOBBS, D.B.A.

Professor of Accounting and Management
College of Business and Economics
Lehigh University

CARL L. MOORE, M.A., C.P.A.

Chairman, Department of Accounting and Law
College of Business and Economics
Lehigh University

Financial Accounting

concepts · valuation · analysis

second edition

Published by

A21   **SOUTH-WESTERN PUBLISHING CO.**

CINCINNATI   WEST CHICAGO, ILL.   DALLAS   PELHAM MANOR, N.Y.   PALO ALTO, CALIF.

ISBN: 0-538-01210-2

Library of Congress Catalog Card Number: 77-88318

2 3 4 5 6 D 4 3 2 1 0

Printed in the United States of America

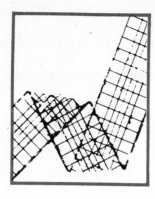

Preface

*The miracle of the mind is its capacity for
organizing confusion into sanity.*
. . . Albert Einstein

This preface to the second edition of *Financial Accounting* provides a brief overview of the text by highlighting the following topics:

- Central thrust of the text.
- Intended audience.
- Organization of material.
- Significant changes in the second edition.
- End-of-chapter and supplementary material.

Central Thrust of the Text

A student's initial exposure to accounting at the college and university level should encompass more than mere procedural format and bookkeeping routines. This text is designed to achieve the following *objectives*:

(1) Examine the basic concepts and procedures of financial accounting.
(2) Develop an awareness of accounting as "the language of business" and of the environment in which it operates.
(3) Encourage an appreciation of how the accounting methodology and discipline can be used to organize great masses of financial data into coherent and meaningful information.
(4) Strengthen student capacity to approach problems in a disciplined, logical, and sequential step-by-step manner.

In a broader perspective, this text encompasses fundamental aspects of the accounting discipline by focusing on significant financial accounting issues and problems that confront the modern business executive.

Intended Audience

Financial Accounting is designed for use in the first course in accounting, whether the student is a nonaccounting major or intends to pursue the discipline in greater depth in subsequent course work. Because the emphasis throughout the text is on logical reasoning and a disciplined approach to problem solving, it is particularly useful to undergraduates enrolled in strong liberal arts and sciences, business, economics, and engineering curricula. Because of the text's pragmatic and managerial orientation, it is particularly suitable as a teaching vehicle in the first accounting course in MBA and related graduate programs.

Organization of Material

The text is organized into three parts:

PART I: Concepts and Procedures............................ Chapters 1–5
PART II: Valuation Alternatives and Refinements........ Chapters 6–12
PART III: Analysis and Interpretation......................... Chapters 13–16

Chapter 1 is a "working chapter" which provides useful background material for the examination of accounting, rather than merely an introduction to be lightly scanned or ignored. The essence and attributes of double-entry accounting, namely balance and duality, are introduced in Chapter 2 by means of the balance-sheet-related accounts and are subsequently integrated with revenue and expense recognition in Chapter 3. Considerable attention is devoted in these two chapters to clarifying the critical linkage between the income statement and the balance sheet. The last two chapters of Part I serve as a review and extension of material covered in the preceding three chapters within the context of the accrual concept and the accounting cycle.

The perplexing and challenging problem of "value" is introduced in Chapter 6 and expanded in considerable detail throughout Part II. Alternative methods of valuation are considered in Chapter 6, with particular emphasis on the relevance to accounting of the present value concept and the discounting process. The present value concept is subsequently integrated into material presented in Chapters 7 (Liquidity), 9 (Plant assets, Natural Resources, and Intangibles), and 10 (Long-Term Liabilities). The concept of holding (or unrealized) gains and losses is examined in Chapters 7 and 8 (Inventory); and a brief exposure to current replacement costing is included near the end of both Chapters 8 and 9. Problems and issues associated with Owners' Equity and Consolidations are covered in Chapters 11 and 12, respectively.

Part III focuses on the analysis and interpretation of financial statements. Chapter 13 deals with the analysis of net working capital. Funds flow analysis is extended to cash flow in Chapter 14. Successful preparation of the statement of changes in financial position from either the net working capital or cash flow perspective requires a thorough understanding of both the material and methodology presented in the preceding chapters of Parts I and II. Chapter 15 covers financial statement and ratio analysis within a framework of liquidity, profitability, and leverage measures. Chapter 16 focuses on the as yet unresolved issues surrounding the means of accounting for the impact of inflation and changing price levels on financial statements.

Significant Changes in the Second Edition

Although the fundamental orientation and general organization of the text remain substantially unaltered, approximately 95% of the material presented in the first edition has been entirely reworked and rewritten. Chapter 2 now deals solely with balance-sheet-related accounts, with the introduction to the revenue/expense recognition process being deferred until Chapter 3. This improvement allows the student to grasp more fully the essential attributes of the balance sheet equation, duality, and the double-entry accounting system before being exposed to the income-earning process.

Service, retail, and wholesale establishments are emphasized throughout this edition in illustrations and end-of-chapter material. Other than to mention the existence of the three-stage inventory process (raw materials, work in process, and finished goods) in manufacturing entities, the concept has been deleted from this edition.

Relevant portions of recent Statements of Financial Accounting Standards have been integrated into appropriate chapters. The chapter on accounting for price-level changes and inflation has been expanded to include examination of current replacement costing as an alternative to price-level indexing in accounting for changes in the price level.

Of considerable importance in this edition is the inclusion of a broader selection of exercises and problems at the end of each chapter. Exercises and problems have been designed which cover the range from simpler, more straightforward material, through the middle-range of difficulty, to problems and decision cases that are more complex and comprehensive in scope. In short, more assignment material is made available from the 389 questions, 180 exercises, 123 problems, and 19 decision cases to accommodate a much wider variety of student competencies and expertise than was available in the previous edition. One particular innovation, beginning with Chapter 4, in this second edition, is the inclusion among the end-of-chapter material of at least one decision case per chapter. These decision cases require a grasp of selected material presented in a particular chapter and application of that material within the context of the pragmatic decision-making environment of business.

End-of-Chapter and Supplementary Material

Questions at the end of each chapter provide a detailed and comprehensive review and summary of the principal ideas and essential points covered in the chapter and are presented generally in the order that material was covered in the chapter. Exercises usually focus on a single topic or specific point developed in the chapter, again in the approximate order that these points were presented in the chapter. Problems and decision cases normally require integration of several topics or areas presented in the chapter, and hence are more complex and comprehensive in scope. Problems are generally presented in the order of comprehensiveness, complexity, or level of difficulty, with the less advanced problems presented first.

Finally, we deeply appreciate and wish to acknowledge the constructive criticisms, and many suggestions received from several of our colleagues during the preparation of this second edition. These colleagues include: Professors John Gehman and Mayo W. Lanning of Moravian College; Professors D. Raymond Bainbridge, Jon T. Innes, Alfred P. Koch, Frank S. Luh, Robert H. Mills, John W. Paul, Eli Schwartz, Kenneth P. Sinclair, John L. Tucker, and Stuart K. Webster of Lehigh University; Professor Douglas R. Haines and his staff at Rutgers University; Professors Bevan J. Clarke, Frank Devonport, and C. Roy Hasseldine of the University of Canterbury, New Zealand; H. Louis Thompson of the Lehigh Coal and Navigation Company; and Dale F. Falcinelli, management consultant.

JAMES B. HOBBS
CARL L. MOORE

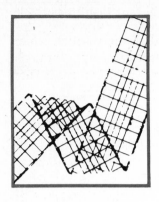

Contents

PART III   Analysis and Interpretation

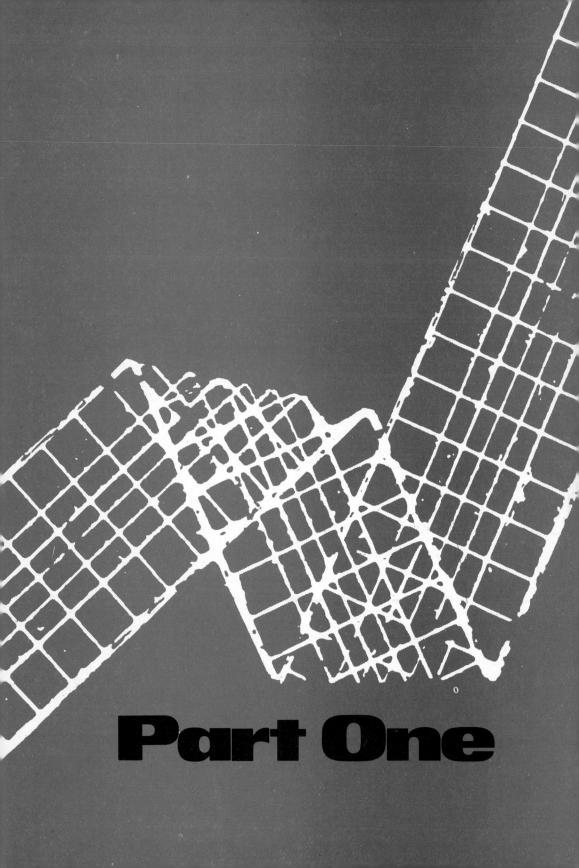

Part One

Concepts and Procedures

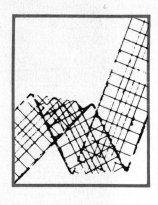

1
Perspective

In this "age of accounts," some literacy in accounting has become a necessity.

Paul Samuelson

Virtually every organization during its life faces moments of reckoning in terms of dollars and cents. Whether the organization is a profit-seeking business, an individual household, or an educational, religious, or government institution, questions of money arise repeatedly which must be answered. For example, does the organization possess sufficient cash with which to pay its bills? Has management overextended the organization's capacity to retire its short- or long-term financial obligations on their due dates? Does the organization's ability to generate income suggest growth, stability, or stagnation? On the basis of past performance and future projections, should current operations be continued, expanded, curtailed, or abandoned?

Constant monitoring by managerial personnel of an organization's financial status is essential to detect shortcomings and to identify opportunities for improvement. In addition, a large number of individuals and groups outside the organization rely on relevant and timely financial information to support their decision-making activities. Continuous review is of particular sig-

3

nificance in operating a business enterprise, which is the organization that is emphasized in this text. At the hub of this information-gathering and decision-making process will usually be found the professional accountant.

THE FOCAL POINT OF ACCOUNTING

During the past 500 years, accountants have developed a framework of concepts and procedures that facilitates the administration of financial activity. Knowledge of this framework is an essential first step toward understanding the financial language of business organizations. An examination of this framework will begin by defining the discipline of accounting, identifying its objectives, and outlining briefly its approach to organizing financial data into useful information.

Definition and Objectives of Accounting

Accounting has been concisely defined as the art of recording, classifying, and summarizing financial transactions and events that occur in an organization, and interpreting the results of those activities for various interested groups.[1] Restated, the accountant attempts to accomplish the following four objectives:

(1) Identify financial events and transactions that occur in an organization.
(2) Measure the value of these occurrences in terms of money.
(3) Organize the accumulated financial data into meaningful information.
(4) Analyze, interpret, and communicate that information to a broad range of persons and groups, both within and outside the organization.

A preliminary overview of how the accountant proceeds to accomplish these objectives will assist in introducing several basic terms with which accounting is involved.

A Glance at the Accounting Approach

The accountant's initial task is to identify financial transactions and events that occur in the business enterprise. These occurrences may be described briefly as those which affect the company's financial resources, obligations, and rights of the owners in the business. The *financial resources* of a business include: cash; inventories of goods, either for sale direct to customers or for con-

---

[1] *Accounting Research and Terminology Bulletins — Final Edition*, "Accounting Terminology Bulletins, No. 1, Review and Resumé" (New York: American Institute of Certified Public Accountants, 1961), par. 9.

version into other products for subsequent sale; and plant facilities such as land, buildings, machinery, and equipment. Accountants have coined the technical term _assets_ to describe these financial resources.

Financial obligations of a company include monetary amounts that are owed to other individuals or organizations, such as suppliers (called vendors) of goods and services and banks. Individuals and organizations to whom the firm owes money are called _creditors_, and the amounts owed to the various creditors are _liabilities_. In effect, a _liability_ represents a creditor's specific claim or right in the total assets of the company. Another important type of financial right or claim in the total assets of the business is possessed by the owners of the business. These rights or claims of owners are called _owners' equity_.

Restated, the financial resources of a company are called assets, its financial obligations to individuals and groups outside the company are liabilities, and the rights or claims possessed by the owners in the company's total assets are its owners' equity.

To illustrate the accounting approach and the above terminology, assume that a company **(1)** borrowed $1,000 from a bank, and **(2)** received an additional investment of $4,000 from an owner. Two identifiable financial events affected the financial composition of the company. In the first instance, the company obtained a financial resource or asset ($1,000 cash) by incurring a financial obligation or liability to the bank. In effect, the bank became a creditor of the company and acquired a $1,000 claim or right in the total financial resources of the company. In the second instance, the company obtained an asset ($4,000 cash) from an owner, who in return acquired an ownership right, claim, or equity in the amount of $4,000 in the company's total assets.

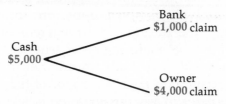

The value associated with each of the preceding events is, in this instance, clearly measurable in terms of money. The basis for this value-measurement is usually established by the _exchange price_ at which assets or property rights are transferred between two parties, such as creditor and borrower, owner and company, or seller and buyer. This exchange price mechanism is directly associated with the _arms-length_ bargaining process. The accountant presumes that the parties involved in a financial transaction are bargaining on behalf of their own best economic interest, in other words at arms length, so that the exchange price ultimately agreed on by both parties establishes a valid basis by which to measure the monetary value involved in that particular event. For example, assume that a truck was advertised for sale by a dealer for $11,000. An interested buyer offered to purchase that truck for $9,000, and the dealer accepted the offer. An accountant would enter $9,000 in the accounting records of the buyer to reflect the monetary value of the truck, rather than the $11,000 advertised price.

Following identification and measurement, each financial event is recorded and subsequently organized by means of the _accounting process_. Finally, the accountant summarizes and communicates large volumes of financial detail to a broad spectrum of interested persons for their review and decision-making purposes. In short, the accountant's key mission is to organize great masses of financial data into meaningful information so that users will be better able to make prudent decisions.

The Role of Accounting in Decision-Making

Accounting plays a critical role in the decision-making activities of individuals and groups. The two-pronged function of the profession is to provide financial information:

(1) As a record of past activity, and
(2) As a guide to future action.

In effect, the accountant's task is to assemble and manage an information system that contains a complex assortment of financial data. The output of that system takes the form of financial reports, which in turn are used, not only to appraise and monitor the past performance of individuals and groups, but to design and make decisions affecting the future. Few intelligent financial and economic decisions can be made in the absence of that information reservoir. Involvement with both time dimensions, past and future, places the accountant near the center of the control and decision-making processes in any organization.

In recent years, accounting has become compartmentalized into two branches: managerial accounting and financial accounting. This compartmentalization has to some degree arisen in response to two segments in the business community which make different demands on the accounting profession. _Managerial accounting_ is oriented primarily toward managerial control and other decision-making groups inside the organization. These personnel require timely financial information that deals with all aspects of the firm, ranging from special-purpose reports of a specific department's operating performance to the preparation of annual budgets and forecasts which encompass the entire business. *Financial accounting*, on the other hand, is oriented more toward those individuals and groups outside the organization, such as prospective investors, government regulatory agencies, creditors, and the general public. Accountants prepare general purpose reports for these external constituencies, such as the financial statements that are contained in a firm's annual stockholder reports. The format and content of these external reports are rather well prescribed and formalized by various professional accounting and governmental bodies, as opposed to the relatively flexible format and content of financial reports and documents that are prepared for internal management's use. To summarize, the primary distinction between these two branches of accounting concerns orientation: managerial accounting is internally oriented with respect to the business enterprise; whereas financial accounting is externally oriented.

This compartmentalization is somewhat artificial and misleading, however, since both branches usually draw from a common pool of financial data in preparing reports for groups who are often involved in making a variety of interdependent decisions. Although the financial accounting branch will be stressed in this text, instances will frequently arise where specific topics blend into the managerial area, particularly in Chapters 8 and 9 which deal with inventory costing and depreciation alternatives.

THE ENVIRONMENT OF ACCOUNTING

Accountants generate a continuous stream of financial information within a society that contains a variety of business enterprises. Examination of this environment will begin by focusing briefly on the early development of the art of accounting.

Early Development of Accounting

Some form of accounting probably originated when society first recognized the need to count and maintain records of personal and group possessions, such as livestock, grain, or ships. Scribes of ancient Egypt maintained comprehensive records of the wealth accumulated by each pharaoh. Clerks employed by merchants and government tribunals in the Greek and Roman empires recorded the daily financial activities undertaken by these managers and organizations. It appears, however, that the system of accounting as known today was not developed or communicated until the late 15th Century.

Accounting historians often cite five prerequisites for the emergence of our modern accounting system:

   (1) A written language.
   (2) Arithmetic.
   (3) A common monetary standard.
   (4) Extensive commerce.
   (5) A developer or synthesizer of the art.

The Italian city-states during the Renaissance provided the environment in which these elements meshed.

The first two requirements were so clearly present during that period that their importance to the accounting process tends to be ignored. Until some medium of exchange became generally accepted, an accountant experienced serious difficulty in totaling the assets of a company that consisted of 40 silver ingots, 2 ships purchased for 600 head of cattle, and a warehouse filled with 400 sacks of salt. The primary standard of money that emerged in the Mediterranean area during the latter 15th Century was the gold florin of Florence.

As a result of the Holy Crusades (approximately 1096–1272), major trade routes between Europe and Middle East developed throughout the Mediterranean in Milan, Genoa, Naples, Venice, and Florence. Large numbers of merchants and other entrepreneurs from many cultural and economic backgrounds gathered in these areas to engage in commercial activity, creating pressures that forced the development of a more uniform and efficient system by which to account for exchanges of wealth.

The scholar-priest Luca Paciolo (1445–1515) is usually credited with synthesizing accounting as then practiced into the comprehensive system which serves as the foundation of modern accounting. Paciolo, an eminent mathematician and logician, was disturbed by the frantic pace of economic activity and the often haphazard, incoherent manner in which financial records were maintained. Paciolo applied mathematics and logical reasoning to the solution of these practical problems and constructed the foundation for accounting in his mathematical treatise, *Summa de Arithmetica, Geometria, Proportioni et Proportionalita* in 1494.[2]

---

[2]A free translation of the title is *A Comprehensive Summary of Arithmetic, Geometry, Proportions, and Proportionality*. A vignette of Luca Paciolo, and a reproduction of the *Summa* tract in Latin, are in R. Gene Brown and Kenneth S. Johnson, *Paciolo on Accounting* (New York: McGraw-Hill Book Company, 1963). Whether his name should be spelled Paciolo or Pacioli is a matter of controversy among accounting historians. Most scholars agree, however, to permit either spelling.

Accounting evolved from this point into a socially useful discipline, the purpose of which is to coherently and systematically organize an otherwise chaotic assortment of financial detail. This text will stress that facet of accounting, namely, that it is a time-tested system through which unorganized financial data are converted into useful financial information.

Although certain aspects of present-day accounting closely resemble the process described by Paciolo, several environmental changes have altered the scope and complexity of accounting:

(1) The Industrial Revolution required that accounting extend itself into new and complex areas of mass production and distribution of goods and services.

(2) The accelerated pace of business activity and technological change compelled accountants to develop improved techniques of accumulating and analyzing financial information.

(3) The increased role of governments in the taxation of income and property, and the regulation of competition necessitated that accounting departments prepare numerous technical and comprehensive financial reports for these government agencies.

(4) The emergence and growth of the corporate form of business, first in England and later in America, required the accounting profession to extend its methodology and procedures to accommodate this more complicated and sophisticated form of business organization.

(5) A wider range of individuals and organizations required financial information, thus forcing accountants to interpret and communicate the information in a manner that each group could understand.

Forms of Business Organization

With few exceptions, business activity is organized under one of the following arrangements: (1) proprietorship; (2) partnership; and, (3) corporation. Of the approximately 13½ million business establishments in the United States in 1973, less than 2 million (or 14 percent) were organized as corporations. Surprisingly however, this relatively small portion of total businesses was responsible for generating slightly more than 85 percent of total sales made by all American firms. From another perspective, less than 15 percent of total sales was generated by approximately 85 percent of business establishments that were organized as proprietorships and partnerships.[3] An examination of several features of each organizational arrangement will reveal some explanations for this heavy concentration of business activity among corporations.

Proprietorship. The proprietorship is the oldest, simplest, and most convenient form of business organization. An individual

[3]*Statistical Abstract of the United States — 97th Edition* (Washington, D.C.: U.S. Bureau of the Census, 1976).

possessing limited financial resources may begin business at a
moment's notice with little government restriction or legal paperwork. The owner-proprietor may immediately incur debts, sell
goods or services, and perhaps enjoy profits from the business.
However, the proprietorship form of organization possesses the
following major disadvantages:

(1) The owner is liable for all debts incurred by the business. This means
that personal assets held by the owner, such as a home or investments,
may be seized or attached by creditors of the business to satisfy their
financial claims.

(2) The life of the business is directly tied to that of the owner. Upon the
owner's death, retirement, or sale of the business, the proprietorship
ceases to exist.

Partnership. The partnership is an arrangement, usually
slightly more complicated to form than a proprietorship, whereby
two or more individuals agree to operate a business as co-owners.
Provisions in the agreement regarding authority, responsibility,
and the distribution of net income or loss among the partners may
be complex. Aside from the Uniform Partnership Act which enu-
merates and defines certain partnership activities (currently
adopted by most states and the District of Columbia), state and
federal governments normally exercise minimal control over the
origin and supervision of partnerships. Since at least two persons
are involved, the partnership may have wider access to financial
resources than the proprietorship.

But the partnership form of business contains disadvantages
similar to those previously outlined under the proprietorship organizational form.

(1) Each general partner has unlimited liability for all debts incurred by the
business. Creditors of a partnership may seize or attach the personal
assets of all general partners to satisfy their claims. Although a general
partner is not liable for the personal debts of the other general partners,
each may become dependent upon the ability and integrity of other
partners regarding personal finances.

(2) The partnership is dissolved when any general partner dies, retires, or
sells the partner's interest in the business.

A federal tax is not levied on the net income of proprietorships
or partnerships. Instead, the net income of these businesses is
taxed as part of each owner's individual income, even though income from the business is not withdrawn. In effect, the tax assessment on each owner's total taxable income, which includes business net income plus any income derived from other sources, is
based on the tax rate bracket into which that total taxable income
places the owner. Recent personal income tax rates vary from 14

percent in the lowest tax bracket to a maximum of 70 percent on that portion of taxable income exceeding $200,000. For example, a married couple filing a joint return, consisting of a $50,000 taxable income, would be assessed a federal income tax of $14,060 on the first $44,000 of taxable income, plus 50 percent of that portion exceeding $44,000, or $3,000 [($50,000 − $44,000) × .50].[4] The total tax assessment in this instance would be $17,060, as shown below:

TAXABLE INCOME		TAX ASSESSMENT
$44,000		$14,060
6,000	× 50%	3,000
$50,000		$17,060

Corporation. The corporate form of business organization is a relatively recent legal arrangement originating with the limited (Ltd.) English joint stock company. Owners of a corporation are persons who have invested their financial resources in the business in return for certificates of ownership, commonly called shares of capital stock. Each capital stock certificate represents a pro rata share in the financial resources of the corporation.

A corporate charter may be obtained from any of the fifty Secretaries of State upon declaration of the intent and objectives of the corporation. Obtaining a corporate charter from a state involves considerable paperwork, incorporation fees, registration certificates, and other legal requirements. Nevertheless, the corporate form of organization possesses significant advantages, as shown below:

(1) Continuity of existence.
(2) Limited liability of owners.
(3) Ownership more easily transferred.
(4) Access to wider sources of funds.
(5) Lower federal income tax rates under certain conditions.

Discussion of these advantages will help explain the heavy concentration of sales generated by the corporate form of business.

First, with rare exception, a corporation's life is presumed continuous and separate from any individual owner. Death of a stockholder or transfer of stock certificates to another individual has no impact on the life of the corporation. Although a business organized under any of the three organizational forms is viewed by accounting as an entity that is separate and distinct from its owner, only the corporation is recognized as a legal and taxable entity apart from its ownership group.

---

[4]Since federal income tax rates are subject to frequent change, reference should be made to the most recent tax directives.

Second, and one of the most attractive features of the corporate form, the maximum loss which a stockholder normally can incur on fully paid shares of capital stock is the amount paid for the shares. This provision may be attractive to current and prospective owners, since creditors of the corporation may not seize or attach their personal assets.

Third, each stock certificate is usually transferable to anyone willing to pay the exchange price asked by its owner. Stock of many American corporations is actively traded on one of several national stock exchanges or over-the-counter; and the prices at which shares are currently selling are usually obtainable through stock brokerage offices and daily newspapers. Thus, a stockholder's financial interest in a corporation is often more easily transferred within a wider market than an ownership interest in either a proprietorship or partnership.

Fourth, because of the advantages previously described, the corporation usually has access to wider sources of funds from investors. To some extent, creditors tend to be more willing to lend money to a corporation than to a proprietorship or a partnership. An apparent veil of continuity, solidity, and strength surrounds the corporate form of organization, even though a corporation is not immune to losses or bankruptcy.

Finally, federal and most state income taxes on corporate income are assessed directly against the corporation. Taxable income earned by a corporation may be taxed at a lower rate than that earned by a proprietorship or partnership. The current federal corporation income tax rate as calculated on a U.S. Corporation Income Tax Return (Form 1120) is 20 percent on the first $25,000 of taxable income, 22 percent on the next $25,000, and 48 percent on any amount exceeding $50,000.[5] For example, the total tax assessment on $80,000 of corporate taxable income would be $24,900, as shown below:

$25,000 × 20%	$ 5,000
25,000 × 22%	5,500
30,000 × 48%	14,400
$80,000	$24,900

Any net income that is distributed by a corporation to its stockholders in the form of cash dividends is again taxed to each stockholder according to the tax bracket applicable to the stockholder's total personal taxable income. This feature of the income tax regulations is commonly referred to as *double taxation*. In other words,

---

[5]Footnote 4 is likewise applicable to corporate income tax rates.

that portion of net income that is distributed to stockholders in the form of a cash dividend is taxed twice by the federal governments as well as by many state governments: (1) as taxable net income to the corporation; and (2) as taxable income to the stockholder.

The exhibit on page 14 summarizes the principal attributes discussed previously for each of the three organizational forms.

Proprietorships and partnerships were the dominant forms of business organizations until the mid-19th Century. As the Industrial Revolution expanded, however, the corporation became a more significant business institution. This text emphasizes the corporate form of organization because (1) this form has considerable economic, political, and social importance, and (2) the corporation provides exposure to more complex accounting issues than are normally found in the other two organizational forms.

Consumers of Accounting Information

The audience for whom the accountant prepares financial information comprises an increasing number and variety of concerned individuals and groups. The following groups may be identified among the principal consumers of the financial information provided by accountants:

- (1) Owners.
- (2) Board of directors.
- (3) Managerial personnel.
- (4) Creditors.
- (5) Employees.
- (6) Government agencies.
- (7) Financial analysts.

Owners The ownership group consists of proprietors, partners, and stockholders who have invested their financial resources in a business enterprise. This group requires information periodically on how their investment is performing, and whether or not their continued investment in a particular company is justified. To what extent is the company profitable? How does the company's overall financial condition compare with competing firms? Is the firm expanding, remaining stable, or approaching bankruptcy? Financial statements contained in annual stockholder reports plus other interim accounting reports provide answers to questions such as these.

Board of Directors. The board of directors is a group of individuals elected by stockholders to represent their interests in the

PRINCIPAL ATTRIBUTES OF THE MAJOR FORMS OF BUSINESS ORGANIZATION

	PROPRIETORSHIP	PARTNERSHIP	CORPORATION
EASE OF FORMATION	• Extremely simple. • Little paperwork. • Few government restrictions.	• Less complex than incorporation. • Slightly more involved than forming a proprietorship, particularly if the Uniform Partnership Act is adopted in the state of jurisdiction.	• Incorporation charter must be obtained from state's Secretary of State. • Legal fees, organizational expenses, numerous incorporation, and registration papers add complexity. • Intricate procedures are required by government agencies if stock is sold to general public.
CONTINUITY OF EXISTENCE	• Life of business limited to life of owner. • Death, retirement, or sale of owner dissolves the entity.	• Life of partnership limited to life of any one general partner. • Death, retirement, or sale of any partner's share dissolves the entity.	• Unless otherwise stated, corporation's life is presumed continuous. • Death of any owner or sale of any owner's interest has no effect on the corporation's life.
LIABILITY OF OWNERS	• Owner is liable for all debts incurred by the business. • Business creditors may seize or attach owner's personal assets to satisfy their claims.	• Each general partner is liable for all debts incurred by the partnership. • Business creditors may seize or attach each general partner's personal assets to satisfy their claims.	• The maximum loss which a stockholder can normally incur on fully paid shares of stock is the amount paid for those shares.
TRANSFERABILITY OF OWNERSHIP	• Limited access to potential investors. • Expensive search-and-find program usually required to locate interested buyers of the business.	• Problems similar to a proprietorship, although the more numerous the partners, the wider may be contacts for locating interested buyers.	• If the corporation is listed on a national stock exchange, daily publication of stock prices and a network of stock brokers often expedite transferability. • Unlisted corporations, or those with few owners may encounter difficulties similar to the other two organizational arrangements.
ACCESS TO FINANCIAL RESOURCES IN THE INVESTMENT COMMUNITY	• Often limited to the owner's personal resources. • Creditors may be reluctant to loan funds, depending on the firm's financial history and the reputation of the owner.	• Additional resources may be available, depending on the number of the partners and their personal wealth. • Creditors may be less reluctant to loan funds since they can look to more than one general partner to satisfy their claim.	• Generally, corporations are better able to attract financial resources from a wider community of investors due to several of the above features, particularly continuity, limited liability, and ownership transferability.
RECOGNITION AS A SEPARATE AND DISTINCT ENTITY			

• The lawyer views the corporation as an entity distinct from its ownership. The sole proprietorship and partnership possess no separate legal identity.
• The Internal Revenue Service recognizes only the corporate form as a taxable entity. Net income of the partnership and proprietorship is taxed direct to owners whether withdrawn from the business or not.
• The accountant views each form of business organization as an entity separate and distinct from its owners.

affairs of the corporation. Members of the board may or may not own stock in the particular corporation. In the case of the American Telephone and Telegraph Company, approximately 20 board members represent the interests of about 2.9 million AT & T stockholders who own over 618 million shares of company stock. The board's principal functions are to evaluate the performance of corporate management and establish guidelines and policies with respect to the current and future direction of the firm's activity. In order to effectively fulfill these responsibilities, the board requires timely financial information.

Managerial Personnel. Managers implement the policies and long-range plans developed by the board in corporations, and by the ownership in most unincorporated businesses. However, a manager may, but need not necessarily be an owner in any of the three types of business organizations. In order to plan and control daily operations, each manager, from shop superintendent to president, requires accurate and current financial information pertinent to specific areas of responsibility. A division sales manager must know how sales of specific product lines are progressing in each territory and which sales people are fulfilling their quotas. A production manager often requires daily or hourly financial information in order to control manufacturing costs of various products.

Creditors This group includes money-lending institutions such as banks and insurance companies. They are primarily concerned with the safety of their investment in the borrowing firm, the prompt receipt of interest when due, and the collection of the loan on the scheduled date. When a firm seeks financial resources through borrowing, the lending institution usually investigates the credit standing of the firm, its past and projected earnings, and the size of the requested loan in relation to the firm's financial structure.

The creditor group also includes companies which furnish goods and services to other firms on credit. For example, a household appliance manufacturer may order several tons of sheet steel from a steel mill on 60-day credit terms. The 60-day lag between shipment of the goods to the manufacturer and receipt of payment by the mill is a form of credit. Financial statements and credit agency reports, such as the Dun & Bradstreet published ratings, are useful in evaluating whether or not a customer should be extended a line of credit or a prospective borrower should be loaned money.

Employees Labor union officials and the union membership make frequent use of available financial information about a company to substantiate its claims for higher wages, wider fringe benefits, more vacation time, or to refute management's counterclaims at the bargaining table. Most college and university graduates seeking employment investigate the potential of a prospective employer from its past earnings record and related information that appear in the firm's financial statements.

Government Agencies Federal, state, and local government agencies have become one of the largest groups of consumers of accounting information. Since income is taxable by the federal government, about 44 state governments, many local communities and foreign countries, income must be defined and measured rigorously for today's 86 million U.S. corporate and individual taxpayers. Business establishments, charged with the responsibility of collecting state and local sales taxes, must maintain detailed accounting records to determine and substantiate the percentage of total receipts that must be forwarded to tax collection bodies. School district and county appraisers and tax collectors often determine the value of personal and real property for tax assessment purposes by examining accounting records.

Other government agencies interested in the information generated by the accountant include:

(1) The *Securities and Exchange Commission* (a federal agency), which requires that any corporation intending to sell its capital stock to the public must first provide the public with complete and accurate financial information of past and current activities.

(2) The *Public Utility and Interstate Commerce Commissions*, which formulate and supervise equitable utility and trucking rates after examining the financial conditions of companies in the respective industry. The *Federal Communications Commission* and the *Civil Aeronautics Board* perform similar functions in regulating interstate telephone and telegram rates, and airline fares, respectively.

(3) The *Social Security Administration*, which recommends appropriate tax rates to Congress, and thereafter collects the tax from wage earners and employers at specific intervals to support the medicare, old-age survivors, disability, and supplemental security programs.

Financial Analysts. These individuals assemble and examine volumes of financial information for their own investment decision-making purposes or for use by their clients. Institutional investors, such as insurance firms, mutual investment companies, and trustees of large estates and university endowment funds, normally retain a staff of financial analysts who advise the institution's governing board on how the funds under its control might be profitably invested among various lucrative opportunities. Other analysts receiving accounting information include those members and staff personnel associated with national and regional stock exchanges who facilitate the daily transfer of millions of shares of stock among the general public and institutional investors.

This partial list of consumers of financial information who require different information for different purposes suggests the scope and complexity of accounting. Larger and better trained accounting staffs have been assisted by high-speed electronic data processing equipment in meeting the diverse demands placed on the profession. In addition, the principles of accounting theory undergo continuous modification and refinement to satisfy evolving consumer and business requirements.

FRAMEWORK OF ACCOUNTING

Prior to the twentieth century, the accounting profession lacked a comprehensive, standardized body of theory by which to handle the almost infinite variety of financial transactions that arise during the life of a business enterprise. Up to that time, an accountant often had to consult numerous books that contained specific, yet oftentimes conflicting, rules and complex instructions for recording each event. From such complexity and nonuniformity, there gradually evolved several generally accepted accounting principles, commonly referred to as GAAP, which today constitute the backbone of accounting theory.

Generally Accepted Accounting Principles

This body of knowledge will be referred to in this text as "principles," although they have been referred to in the literature by such terms as "basic standards, guidelines, concepts, precepts, conventions, or fundamental features." The major principles identified and briefly introduced are:

(1) Business entity.	(8) Conservatism.
(2) Monetary measure.	(9) Consistency and comparability.
(3) Historical cost.	(10) Full disclosure.
(4) Going concern.	(11) Materiality and practicality.
(5) Periodicity.	(12) Objectivity and verifiability.
(6) Matching expenses with revenue.	(13) Conformity with the law.
(7) Accrual.	

Business Entity. Accounting is concerned with the financial events that occur in any organization, whether it is a business enterprise or a not-for-profit institution. This text will stress the business organization. Each proprietorship, partnership, or corporation is viewed by the accountant as an entity. In a very real sense, the business is considered an entity, separate and distinct from its owners, which is capable of generating sales, expenses, and income by, of, and for itself. The ownership interests and managerial personnel may be regarded as the brain or communication center which establishes policy, implements decisions, and supervises operations; but they are not considered to be "the business." For example, cash that is invested in a business by an owner becomes separated and divorced from the investor-owner the instant it is invested in the business. Thereafter, that financial resource is considered an asset of the company. The business itself may be viewed as obtaining assets, selling goods and services, incurring costs and financial obligations, and allocating financial resources within the firm on its own behalf.

Monetary Measure. The monetary unit by which accountants measure financial events is standardized. In America the standard is the dollar, in Russia the ruble, and in France the franc. The adoption of a standard monetary baseline, however, confronts the accountant with considerable problems, not the least of which is the tendency of the purchasing power of the dollar to fluctuate. Assume, for example, that two identical pieces of machinery were purchased by a company from the same manufacturer, one at the beginning of the year for $30,000, the other near the end of the year for $35,000. The $5,000 price difference, in this instance, is probably attributable solely to inflation's impact on the dollar; in other words, the purchasing power of the dollar declined during the year. The accounting problem that commonly arises today from this type of situation is not easily solved; namely, the total exchange price of $65,000 that is reflected in the accounting records for two identical machines purchased in the same year contains a mixture of two types of dollars, each reflecting a different purchasing power. This problem and its implications for financial reporting and decision-making purposes are given special attention in Chapter 16.

Historical Cost. Generally, an accountant considers the cost or value of a financial resource to be the cash outlay required to obtain that resource. Even if property other than cash is given up in the exchange, the cost of the asset acquired is the agreed-on cash equivalent of the property given up. This exchange price, which emerges under conditions of arms-length bargaining, establishes the historical cost of the item.

Assume, for example, that John Seguro purchased a used car for $1,250. The cost or value of the car to Seguro is $1,250, and an accountant would enter this amount in Seguro's financial records. For financial reporting purposes, the accountant would disregard each of the following facts: (1) the used car bluebook reflected a suggested price of $1,400; (2) the dealer had previously posted a $1,350 sign on the car's windshield; (3) Seguro could have purchased a similar car elsewhere for $1,200; and (4) Seguro refused an offer of $1,460 for the car the day following its purchase. Recording a monetary amount to reflect cost or value other than the actual exchange price of $1,250 raises questions on which universal agreement is almost impossible. Even though the historical cost principle contains inherent weaknesses, the exchange price established at the time of the transaction is a relatively certain amount on which qualified observers can agree. Accounting has therefore adopted the principle that the exchange price, as measured by cash outlay or its cash equivalent, establishes the historical cost of a specific item.

Going Concern. The going-concern concept presumes, in the absence of other evidence, that the business entity will continue indefinitely. The corporate form of organization best exemplifies this concept since its state charter of incorporation usually expresses or tacitly assumes a perpetual life.

Periodicity. Although the accountant assumes that the business has a continuous life, most consumers of financial information require periodic reports of the firm's financial condition. For example, both owners and management seek information about the firm's "state of financial health" at selected intervals.

Federal income tax regulations require individual and corporate taxpayers to file an annual income tax return. In response to such needs, accountants usually prepare financial statements at yearly intervals during the company's life to reflect the company's financial condition and the results of the past year's operations. This yearly interval, called the *fiscal year*, covers any consecutive 12-month period; it need not coincide with the calendar year.

Matching Expenses with Revenue. In order to determine the *net income* of a business, the expenses that were incurred are matched with, and then subtracted from, the revenue that was generated. For purposes of this introductory discussion, revenue and expense are defined as follows:

(1) *Revenue* is the increase in a financial resource, such as cash or a claim to cash, that results from the sale of goods and services to customers.

(2) *Expense* is the decrease in a financial resource, such as inventory, that results when goods and services are sold to customers.

For example, a retail dress shop manager purchased dresses for cash from a distributor for $700 and subsequently sold them the next month to various customers for a total of $1,200 cash. At the date of purchase from the distributor, the shop's inventory increased by $700, being offset by a $700 decrease in its cash balance. As the dresses were sold during the subsequent month, the firm's cash balance (an asset) reflected an increase of $1,200, whereas its inventory (another asset) reflected a $700 decrease. In technical accounting language, the inventory was matched as an expense with the revenue it helped generate. The net financial impact of this matching process on operations of the dress shop was the realization of $500 net income. A cash flow analysis and the determination of net income for the 2-month period is shown below:

CASH INFLOW (OUTFLOW)		REVENUE (EXPENSE)	
Cash sales	$1,200	Revenue (from cash sales)	$1,200
Cash purchases for inventory	(700)	Expense (cost of dresses sold)	(700)
Net cash inflow	$ 500	Net income	$ 500

One critical aspect of the matching concept is *recognition*. The financial resource or asset received by the seller need not be cash in order for revenue to be recognized and net income to be earned. Generally, the accountant recognizes revenue when services are performed or when legal title to goods is transferred to the customer. The customer may agree to pay cash either at the time of sale or within a specified time after the sale. If cash is transferred to the seller after the sale occurs, the transaction is called a *credit sale*. An *account receivable*, rather than cash, is the financial resource received by the seller at the time the credit sale is transacted. Using the previous example, if all of the dresses had been sold to customers on 30-day credit terms, the accountant would have recognized a $1,200 claim against the customers in the form of an account receivable that would stipulate payment within 30 days from the date of sale. Under this credit sale arrangement, revenue of $1,200 would still be recognized, and an expense of $700 would be matched with the revenue, resulting in $500 of net income. A cash flow analysis and the determination of net income for the 2-month period when merchandise was sold under 30-day credit terms are shown below. It is presumed, in this illustration, that customers have not yet forwarded any cash payment to the seller:

CASH INFLOW (OUTFLOW)		REVENUE (EXPENSE)	
Sales under 30-day credit terms (not yet collected).................	—	Revenue (from credit sales)	$1,200
Cash purchases for inventory....	$(700)	Expense (cost of dresses sold) ..	(700)
Net cash outflow	$(700)	Net income........................	$ 500

In this particular instance, $1,200 of revenue was recognized at the time of the credit sales even though cash collections from the customer would probably not occur until 30 days later.

Accrual. Accrual accounting is closely related to the going-concern, periodicity, and matching principles. The *accrual principle* may be defined at this point, as the recognition of revenue, expense, or liability without regard as to when cash is received or paid by the business enterprise. For example, if an employee earns $20 each day, the employing firm would incur a financial obligation to that employee at a daily rate of $20. Normally, the accountant would not record this liability of $20 at the close of each day. Instead, the obligation that had accumulated during a 5-day period would be removed each Friday with a $100 payment to the employee. However, when financial statements are prepared at the end of each fiscal year, all liabilities incurred by the company as of the end of that year must be reflected on those statements. If the fiscal year ends on a Wednesday, the accountant would have to accrue a $60 obligation to the employee for the final three working days of the year, even though cash payment for services rendered would not occur until the first Friday of the next fiscal year.

Conservatism. To the accountant, *conservatism* means that all losses should be recognized and reflected in financial records if reasonable likelihood exists that they may occur. On the other hand, anticipated gains and other financial benefits should not be reflected in the records until they are realized. Restated: "Don't count your chickens until the eggs hatch." This conservative approach to financial matters has often been called the hallmark of the accounting profession. One danger of applying an overly conservative approach to the firm's financial resources is that it may make the business appear to be in a more unfavorable financial position than is actually the case. On the other hand, the conservative skepticism of the accountant often helps management counterbalance overly optimistic attitudes that may exist elsewhere in the company.

Consistency and Comparability. *Consistency*, as used in accounting, means that the same accounting procedures should be used over a period of years so that *comparable* financial information is furnished to interested parties. For example, if two consecutive fiscal years for a company were to end midweek, the accountant should consistently reflect any unpaid wage and salary obligations as liabilities of the firm at each year end. To reflect a liability for earned but unpaid wages and salaries at December 31, 1979, and to ignore the same item at the end of 1980, would violate both principles of consistency and comparability.

Full Disclosure. *Full disclosure* means that all financial events which occur during the fiscal year should be fully reported in the financial statements. This principle is particularly applicable, for example, when reporting or recording procedures are changed. Unless such modifications are fully disclosed, readers of financial information might easily be misled into misinterpreting financial information. However, application of the full disclosure principle must be tempered by the next two principles.

Materiality and Practicality. What is significantly material in one instance to warrant full disclosure may not justify complete reporting in another circumstance because of practical considerations. The loss of $712.38 in cash or merchandise by the owner of a grocery store might be sufficiently material to warrant full disclosure. However a loss of the same amount of cash in the Coca-Cola Company, whose total assets approximated $2.2 billion at December 31, 1977, would probably not justify disclosure as a separate item on the financial statement. In addition, and unless legally required, most companies are reluctant to disclose detailed cost and related confidential information to their competitors and the general public. Application of the principles of full disclosure, materiality, and practicality to specific situations requires experienced judgment.

Objectivity and Verifiability. Accountants normally insist that each financial event that is recorded should be substantiated with objective and verifiable source documentation, such as sales slips, purchase invoices, employee time cards, or other written evidence. This practice provides better assurance that any qualified accountant, whether or not employed by the company, viewing the same evidence would probably arrive at a similar treatment of the financial event. Retention of source documents also protects the company should legal disputes arise. Adoption of both of these principles is accounting's attempt to ensure that capricious or unsubstantiated judgments do not enter into the financial records of the company.

Conformity with the Law. Every accountant must be aware of legal requirements, such as contract provisions or tax regulations, that impinge on a firm's financial affairs. The accountant must also alert company officials to operating procedures which might be illegal. For example, an accountant may and should assist management in legally minimizing or avoiding corporate income tax payments. But to condone illegal attempts to evade taxation would be in violation of the standards of professional conduct and would also subject the accountant to criminal prosecution as an accomplice.

This brief exposure to several principles of accounting will serve as a point of reference upon which subsequent chapters will expand as specific financial events are discussed. Clear cut application of a few of these principles may on occasion prove difficult because of controversy that surrounds some of them. In addition, each principle is undergoing continued refinement, modification, and clarification as the profession adapts theory to a rapidly changing society. Accountants have learned that they must modify both theory and practice to accommodate evolving social needs.

Groups That Influence the Evolution of Accounting

Several accounting-related organizations are active in defining controversial areas, determining which arguments possess greatest validity, and developing new guidelines. Although no single group can be pinpointed as the ultimate arbiter in accounting issues, nor does space allow insertion of all influential groups, those identified below are among the most dominant.

The American Institute of Certified Public Accountants (AICPA) includes the majority of those individuals who, after successfully completing a rigorous examination and satisfying other professional qualifications, are entitled to practice the profession of public accounting as a CPA. Because the AICPA membership has daily contact with accounting problems in business, government, and other institutions, its opinions, collectively and as individuals, influence significantly the interpretation and development of accounting principles. In addition, most of the larger public accounting firms circulate their views on new or controversial issues through separate in-house publications.[6] An important means whereby CPAs, other accountants, and public accounting firms influence the development and practice of accounting is through its *attest function*. If after examining a firm's financial details and financial statements for the current year, all procedures appear to have been performed satisfactorily, the accountant or public accounting firm will attest that in its opinion:

> The financial statements present fairly the financial position of the firm, the results of its operations and changes in its financial position for the current year, in conformity with generally accepted accounting principles applied on a consistent basis.

Readers of these published financial statements would be forewarned of any significant deviations from GAAP by means of an accompanying explanation made by the certifiying accountant.

Prior to 1972, the eighteen member Accounting Principles Board (APB) was the senior policy-making body of the AICPA. The Board was continuously involved in controversial areas; they issued timely opinions in such areas, for example, as whether or not unrealized gains arising from holding land or buildings during inflationary periods should be disclosed in a firm's financial statements. Although opinions expressed by this Board were not legally binding, they exerted a powerful force on the profession. Publications that contain statements and opinions of the AICPA, APB, and their individual members include the *Accounting Research Bulletin, Accounting Terminology Bulletin,* and the *Journal of Accountancy*.

The accounting profession undertook a major reorganization of its activities during 1972–1973 with the creation of the Financial Accounting Foundation and several related organizational units. The nine trustees of the Foundation, who are appointed by the board of directors of the AICPA, are assigned the responsibility of appointing and obtaining funds for the seven-member Financial Accounting Standards Board (FASB). Membership of the FASB reflects the current diversity within the profession by including former CPA practitioners, corporate financial officers, accounting educators, and financial analysts.

---

[6]The eight largest public accounting firms are frequently identified as the "Big Eight." These firms and their headquarters are:

Arthur Andersen & Co., Chicago	Coopers & Lybrand, New York
Arthur Young & Co., New York	Peat, Marwick, Mitchell & Co., New York
Deloitte Haskins & Sells, New York	Price Waterhouse & Co., New York
Ernst & Whinney, Cleveland	Touche, Ross, and Company, New York

The primary task of the FASB is to establish rules and standards by which companies report their financial results. For the first time, these rules now make it mandatory that CPAs and public accounting firms follow the APB opinions and the FASB statements when they certify and attest to financial statements. The sole exceptions now permitted are "unusual" situations where the use of official opinions would produce misleading results. Relevant portions of APB opinions and FASB statements currently in force will be cited at appropriate points in succeeding chapters.

Membership of the American Accounting Association (AAA) and the National Association of Accountants (NAA) consists of CPAs, financial analysts, vice presidents, controllers, industrial cost specialists, teachers, and government accountants. Varied pronouncements by these associations and their members are contained in *The Accounting Review* (AAA-sponsored) and *Management Accounting* (NAA-sponsored). For example, the AAA recommended in its 1966 publication, *A Statement of Basic Accounting Theory*, the application of the following four guidelines when preparing financial statements:

(1) That statements be relevant to the purposes for which the information is to be used.
(2) That they be verifiable, such that two independent observers viewing the same financial events would reach similar conclusions.
(3) That they be impartially determined and free from bias.
(4) That the data presented be quantifiable.[7]

The Securities and Exchange Commission (SEC) and the Internal Revenue Service (IRS) exert considerable influence on the development, interpretation, and application of accounting principles. For example, in order to receive approval from the SEC, any corporation wishing to sell its stock to the public must submit financial statements based on the historical cost concept for the SEC's inspection. The IRS continuously refines and clarifies federal income tax regulations with respect to what financial items may or may not be included in determining taxable income. Although accountants frequently criticize many government regulations as being unsound accounting practice, few deny the powerful voice these agencies have in influencing the profession.

SUMMARY AND SELECTED REFERENCES

This introductory exposure to the environment in which accounting functions provides perspective and background for an

---

[7]*A Statement of Basic Accounting Theory* (Evanston, Illinois: American Accounting Association, 1966), pp. 8–13.

intensive examination of the discipline. As considerable accounting detail and procedure unfold in subsequent chapters, it may prove beneficial to keep in mind that the three-pronged objective of the profession is to organize, measure, and communicate financial information about business and other organizations. The thread which unifies the several detailed steps necessary to achieve this objective is systematic order. Accounting is a time-tested system of thought through which unorganized financial data is transformed into useful financial information.

QUESTIONS

1. Accounting is the financial language of organizations, whether the organization is profit-seeking, religious, educational, or charitable. Comment.

2. State in your own words the objectives of accounting, and the specific steps an accountant takes to fulfill each of these objectives.

3. Define and distinguish between each of the following accounting terms: (a) financial resources; (b) financial obligations; and (c) financial rights of an owner.

4. Distinguish between the orientation of financial and managerial accounting.

5. Explain how the elements of time, place, and other factors meshed to enable the emergence of modern accounting.

6. How do the three business organizational forms differ with respect to: (a) ease of formation; (b) access to financial resources in the investment and community.

7. Compared to the corporate form of business organization, what disadvantages might the proprietorship and partnership possess with respect to: (a) transferability of ownership interests; (b) continuity of existence.

8. Distinguish between the extent of ownership liability in the three forms of business organization, and explain the importance of these variations for the ownership and creditor groups.

9. In what respect do the accountant, the attorney, and the internal revenue agent differ in their views of each of the three organizational forms of business as an entity that is separate and distinct from its respective ownership group?

10. What is meant by double taxation of a corporation's net income? In what respect is this term applicable to a proprietorship and partnership?

11. How might income tax regulations influence owners in deciding on which business form to organize?

12. If income and property tax legislation were abolished, what sectors or groups within a modern society might continue to require the services provided by an accountant? Suggest reasons for each sector or group identified.

13. Explain the relevance of arms-length bargaining and the exchange price mechanism to the monetary measure and historical cost principles.

14. Explain how the application of the principle of monetary measure to an American firm's financial operations might reflect something less than a perfectly stable and uniform measure of value over a period of years.

15. In what way are the going-concern and periodicity principles related?

16. Define the two components of net income. How is the matching principle related to net income?

17. Must cash be received by a firm which sells merchandise before it can recognize revenue? Explain.

18. Explain the relevance of accrual accounting with respect to: (a) The recognition of revenue during a fiscal year and cash inflow; (b) The recognition of a financial obligation at the end of a fiscal year and cash outflow.

19. Define conservatism, and identify an advantage and a disadvantage that may result from consistently reporting financial information in a conservative manner.

20. What is the linkage between the principles of consistency and comparability?

21. Indicate in what way the accounting principles of full disclosure, materiality, and practicality are interconnected.

22. How might adherence to objectivity and verifiability assist the accountant in conforming with the law?

23. Indicate at least three groups which influence the development and direction of accounting.

24. What are APB opinions and FASB statements; and to what extent must members of the accounting profession adhere to their contents?

25. At this introductory stage of your exposure to accounting, identify what appears to be the critical function or focal point of accounting.

EXERCISES

1. **Identification of financial transactions.** Listed below are transactions which occurred in different firms:

   (1) The owner invested an additional $15,000 cash in the proprietorship, a hardware store.

   (2) The owner of an automobile service station paid $2,200 cash for 4,000 gallons of regular-grade gasoline upon delivery by the national distributor.

   (3) The senior fashion designer for an exclusive dress manufacturer in New York City put the finishing touches on her portfolio of ideas for the firm's new line of wearing apparel. The designer was unable to estimate the exact value of the ideas, except to say that the financial success or failure of the company depended on the portfolio.

(4) An uninsured building which originally cost $80,000 containing various pieces of equipment and machinery worth $470,000 was destroyed by fire.

Required: Indicate whether or not each of the transactions affected the financial composition of the respective company and give reasons for such indication. Use the following format:

<table>
<tr><td>Affected the Firm's
Financial Composition</td><td>Reason</td></tr>
</table>

2. Valuation of a residence. The Monroes were preparing an application for a home improvement and expansion loan on their residence from the local savings and loan association. They were in a quandary as to what value to report their home on the loan application. Jill Monroe suggested $21,800, which was the price they paid for the house in 1966. Jim Monroe, however, believed that about $46,000 was the more appropriate value, citing that several homes of similar design in the same neighborhood were selling at between $42,000 and $47,500.

Required: Which amount would you recommend for purposes of: (a) Objectivity and verifiability in the accounting records of the Monroes. (b) Usefulness to the savings and loan institution. (c) Usefulness for fire and casualty insurance purposes.

3. Asset measurement. The production supervisor of Merimak Industries purchased a precision metal-cutting machine in January for $20,000. The machine was advertised at that time for $22,000 in a widely circulated trade journal, but the dealer gave a $2,000 special sale price reduction. Terms of sale were 25% cash and the balance due within 60 days. Had the transaction been entirely in cash, the dealer would have allowed an additional 5% discount, for a net cash outlay of $19,000. In October of the same year, the supervisor noticed that an identical machine was being advertised for $26,000 in the latest edition of the same trade journal. Only a month before, one of Merimak's competitors offered to buy the machine from Merimak for $24,500. The production supervisor had declined that offer.

Required: At what amount should the machine be reflected in the accounting records of Merimak Industries?

4. Cash flows and net income. Tim Pondalek contracted to paint the Lindhurst residence for $1,900. He rented ladders, drop cloths, scaffolding, and other equipment from a local Rent-All store for $80 cash. Pondalek paid two high school youths $375 each to help him paint. He purchased paint and paint supplies for $260 in cash. The job was completed within 20 days, at which time, Lindhurst paid the agreed amount.

Required: (a) Determine Pondalek's net cash outflow or inflow as a result of the job. (b) Determine his net income from the job.

5. Preliminary exposure to accounting logic. A tourist purchased a used car for $800 by giving a $900 check to the dealer, who in turn persuaded the local bank to cash the check. The dealer kept $800 as payment in full for the car; and the tourist, after receiving $100 in change from the dealer, departed with the car and was never seen again. The dealer had originally paid $600 for the used car. One week later, the tourist's check was found to be worthless, and the dealer had to refund $900 to the bank.

Required: How much did the financial resources of each of the following separate entities change because of this sequence of events: (a) the bank? (b) the dealer? (c) tourist?

PROBLEMS

1-1. **Identification of financial events.** The following are independent events which occurred in various business organizations:

(a) Four owners invested an additional $12,000 each in their small manufacturing partnership.

(b) Employees were paid $3,000 for work performed during the previous week.

(c) The new president of a corporation possessed a personal estate valued at $550,000 plus various rental properties.

(d) A new chemical process was discovered accidentally by a firm's research and development staff. The company, which had not yet incurred any expenditures toward developing the chemical process, anticipated that the process might generate $60,000 net income per year during the next 12 years.

(e) Customers purchased $80,000 worth of merchandise from a department store during November, 40% ($32,000) of which was paid for in cash, and the remainder under 30-day credit arrangements. The department store had paid $64,000 for the merchandise in September.

(f) A corporation's sales manager was transferred from the Denver to the Atlanta sales region. Current annual sales of $15,000,000 in the Atlanta region were forecast to increase by $4,000,000 because of the transfer of the effective sales executive.

(g) A hospital purchased a 4-month supply of medical supplies for inventory on 30-day credit terms.

(h) A loan of $20,000 was obtained from the local bank to finance the construction of a building annex. The borrowing firm received the money upon signing an agreement to repay the loan within one year.

(i) A local wholesaling company donated $15,000 to a nearby community college during the college's annual scholarship fund drive.

Required: Indicate which event would be considered by an accountant as financial or nonfinancial and give reasons for each indication. Use the format as shown below.

Financial	Nonfinancial	Reason

1-2. **Determination of financial wealth.** Bob Kalskag and Jake Noorvik, both members of the Aleut group of Eskimos, resigned from their tool and die-maker jobs with the Osgood Corporation in Anchorage in 1976, and moved to separate locations along the Yukon river in Alaska in an effort to recapture and preserve some of the life and traditions of their ancestors.

Bob and his wife, Betty, built a 2-room cabin on a 750-acre plot of tundra near Beaver. Jake purchased a 1-room shack for $850, plus 50 acres of land for $2,000 near Fort Yukon. On their third summer along the Arctic Circle, Jake decided to take his raft down the Yukon to see the Kalskags for some companionship and to renew their acquaintance. Conversation during their first day included a discussion of their relative financial positions since their departure from Anchorage. The three listed their major possessions as follows:

Bob Kalskag: 750 acres of land, bought in 1976, at $40 per acre.
2-room cabin, for which a neighbor offered 100 acres of land last month.
2,400 reindeer.
1,500 caribou.
$3,600 cash.
$1,200 rent due from a neighbor for ranging 300 head of caribou on the Kalskag's property.

Betty Kalskag: Loom and spinning wheel, purchased for $600 in 1977.
Sewing machine, obtained by trading 2 musk-ox coats that were made by Betty. (An identical sewing machine was available at the nearby trading post for $500.)
6 finished musk-ox coats on hand. These coats were made from the wool of the oxen.

Jake Noorvik: 1-room shack, bought in 1976 for $850.
50 acres of land bought at $40 per acre.
Iron ore mining claim, estimated to contain 50,000 tons of ore at a resale value of $2.50 per ton, net of extraction and delivery costs.
400 reindeer. The reindeer were owed to four other Eskimos who had prospected with Jake.
$1,500 cash.
Owes $300 for a plane he chartered for the return trip to Fort Yukon, via Fairbanks.
A raft, which he intended to abandon in Beaver.

Required: (1) Determine the financial condition of each individual on the date they renewed their friendship. Assume that one reindeer, one caribou, and one-half acre of land are of equivalent value.

(2) State any additional assumptions that you feel are critical before an approximate comparative financial condition can be determined.

1-3. General accepted accounting principles. Refer to Problem 1-2.

Required: (1) Identify those generally accepted accounting principles that are relevant to arriving at a solution to the data presented in that problem.

(2) Indicate specific instances when a particular GAAP can be applied.

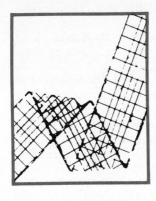

2
The Balance Sheet: Equality and Duality

Two of the most important and widely used financial statements produced by accountants are the balance sheet and the income statement. The *balance sheet* reflects the financial position of
the company at a specified date; whereas the *income statement*
reflects the net income or loss earned by the company during a
specific period of time. Owners and creditors refer to both statements to evaluate the financial security and soundness of their investment. Financial analysts and prospective investors examine
them to detect signs of strength or weakness in a company's competitive position. Various government agencies rely on their content to collect or assess the taxes required to support modern society. Finally, management uses the detailed information from
which the statements are prepared to control and plan daily operations.

Before either the balance sheet or the income statement can be
prepared, however, several requirements must be fulfilled by an

accounting department that has been staffed with competent personnel: a classification system must be developed by which to categorize financial events, and some method must be prescribed whereby every detail of each financial event can be organized, summarized, and analyzed.

The objective of this and the following three chapters is to provide a thorough exposure to accounting methodology, the accounting cycle, and the means whereby the accountant organizes and condenses financial information for presentation in these two basic financial statements. The key procedural elements that will be examined in this chapter within the context of the balance sheet include:

(1) The specific components of the balance sheet.
(2) The debit-credit procedure.
(3) The impact that financial transactions have on various financial resources and obligations of an operating enterprise.

THE BALANCE SHEET

The *balance sheet* lists a company's financial resources and the rights or claims of creditors and owners in those total resources at a specific time. It is often referred to as the statement of financial position or financial condition of the firm.

The Balance Sheet Illustrated

The balance sheet shown on the following page reflects the financial position of the Simplex Corporation as of December 31, 1979. The corporation manufactures navigation and communication equipment for sale to various airplane manufacturers.

Note the following aspects of the balance sheet as shown in the account format:

(1) The heading specifies that the balance sheet was prepared for a particular business entity as of a specific point in time, which in this case is December 31, 1979.
(2) The assets are divided into four major categories: current assets, investments, plant assets, and intangibles.
(3) Equities are divided into three major categories: current liabilities, long-term liabilities, and owners' equity.
(4) Total assets equal total equities.

Other arrangements of the assets and equities on the balance sheet are possible. For example, a single-column report format is frequently used, with the equities section being placed below the assets section.

put in

Simplex Corporation
Balance Sheet
December 31, 1979

equ rep sources of financing of assets

Assets *have resources*		Equities *don't have obligations to outside creditors*	
Current assets:		**Current liabilities:**	
Cash...........................	$ 20,000	Notes payable	$ 40,000
Marketable securities	3,000	Accounts payable...........	82,000
Notes receivable............	8,000	Wages payable.............	5,500
Accounts receivable	56,000	Income taxes payable......	12,500
Inventory	120,000	Total current liabilities..	$140,000
Prepaid expenses...........	13,000		
Total current assets	$220,000	**Long-term liabilities:**	
		Mortgage notes payable	
Investments:		(due 1985)	$ 70,000
Investment in Alpha, Inc. ..	$ 25,000	Bonds payable (due 1983)	130,000
		Total long-term	
Plant assets:		liabilities..............	$200,000
Land............................	$ 15,000		
Building $105,000			
Equipment....... 310,000		**Owners' equity:**	
$415,000		Capital stock, $10 par;	
Less accumulated		17,500 shares issued	
depreciation .. 60,000	355,000	and outstanding	$175,000
Total plant assets	$370,000	Retained earnings..........	105,000
		Total owners' equity.....	$280,000
Intangibles:			
Patents........................	$ 5,000		
Total assets.....................	**$620,000**	**Total equities..................**	**$620,000**

people claim

former

The balance sheet focuses on the financial position of the business entity, rather than on the financial position of the owners or creditors of the business. It is normally prepared at the end of each fiscal year, although it may be prepared more often, such as quarterly or semiannually. The balance sheet is a static financial statement, since it presents the financial position of the firm at only one instant in time. That position changes in some respect each day that the firm operates. For example, any sale of merchandise, any purchase of inventory, or any additional investment by owners could alter the financial position of the firm.

The Balance Sheet Equation

Perhaps the most critical feature of modern accounting is expressed in the balance sheet equation shown below:

$$\text{Total Assets} = \text{Total Equities}$$
or
$$\text{Assets} = \text{Liabilities} + \text{Owners' Equity}$$

This latter statement may be expressed symbolically as follows:

$$A = L + OE$$

The expression of equality is the building block of the modern double-entry accounting system.

The two-sided nature of the firm's financial position is evident from the balance sheet shown on page 33. In general, *assets* are the financial resources, expressed in monetary terms, to which the firm possesses legal title. These resources take various forms, such as cash, receivables, inventory, and equipment. The rights or claims of the creditors and owners in these assets are stated in monetary terms under the *equities* section of the balance sheet. In a sense, the various equities represent the sources of financing of the assets. However, a direct one-for-one relationship between a specific asset and a specific equity cannot normally be identified simply by examining the balance sheet.

For example, the source of the $20,000 cash balance in Simplex Corporation at the end of 1979 may have been a bank loan, an investment by owners, sales either on cash terms or under credit arrangements for which customers subsequently paid cash, or some combination of the foregoing events. In short, the reader of a balance sheet will seldom be able to directly associate a specific asset with its original source; nor will it be any easier to discover in what specific assets a bank loan or the original investment by owners is held at a specific moment. The process of mingling and subsequent loss of direct association between assets and equities begins the instant the firm commences operation.

Regardless of this loss of direct association, however, constant equality must be maintained between the total assets and the total equities. The balance sheet, with its dual nature and constant equilibrium, is similar to a coin in that both sides will always be equal even though each side shows distinctively different features.

CHARACTERISTICS OF THE ASSETS

The following characteristics are associated with the various assets identified on a balance sheet: (1) legal status; (2) valuation basis; and (3) time dimension.

Legal Status

Legal title to a financial resource must normally be held by the firm before that resource may be identified as an asset of the firm.

Evidence of title passage may include such *source documentation* as a bill of sale, invoice, signed contract, property deed, or a patent certificate issued by the federal government. Normally the firm has physical possession of the asset, although this is not mandatory. For example, if the $20,000 cash balance is on deposit in a bank but under control of the management of Simplex Corporation, it should be reported as an asset of the corporation.

Valuation Basis

In general, the monetary amount associated with each asset reflected on the balance sheet is based upon the exchange price, established during a presumed arms-length bargaining process, that the entity either paid or agreed to pay at a future date to obtain legal title to that asset.

Time Dimension

Assets are usually divided into two major categories: current assets and noncurrent assets.

Current assets include cash and other financial resources which are reasonably expected to be converted into cash during the normal operating cycle of the business. The *normal operating cycle* is generally defined as the time between the acquisition of materials and related services such as labor, and their final conversion into cash. For example, the normal time required by a supermarket to convert purchased merchandise into sold merchandise ranges from one to four weeks. The cycle may approximate three to five months in a retail department store, and usually ranges from three to nine months for manufacturing enterprises. In the case of shipbuilders or liquor manufacturers, the cycle may exceed two or more years. High quality scotch or bourbon whiskey may age in the distiller's inventory for fifteen years. Technically, if the normal operating cycle is one year or less, a twelve-month period should be used as the basis for classifying specific assets as current. Where the cycle exceeds twelve months, the longer period should be used. For purposes of subsequent discussion, however, the following simplifying assumption will be used throughout this text: current assets include cash and other financial resources that can reasonably be expected to be converted into cash during the next twelve months.

Noncurrent assets include investments, plant assets, and intangibles which are not expected to be converted into cash within twelve months (or the normal operating cycle, if longer) from the

date of the balance sheet. The investments category reflects ownership rights of the entity in the securities of other business establishments or government units, such as the Simplex Corporation
owning Eastman Kodak Company stock or U.S. Government
bonds. Most plant assets possess certain benefits that will be released and consumed over a long period of time in the process of
generating revenue. For example, the enormous presses used by
automotive manufacturers contain metal-shaping capabilities that
will be used up gradually over several years in the process of
stamping out car bodies and parts. The lives of intangibles such as
patents are regulated by law.

SPECIFIC ASSETS DEFINED

A brief definition of each of the assets commonly reflected on
the balance sheet is provided below.

Current Assets

This major category of assets includes cash, marketable securities, receivables, inventories, and prepaid expenses. Current
assets are generally listed in the order of their liquidity or con-
vertibility into cash.

Cash. The cash balance includes monies within the business
and those on deposit at one or more banks to which the company
has immediate access. Both demand and savings deposits may be
included. Any cash that is restricted for a specific purpose, such as
the repayment of certain long-term liabilities, would normally be
classified separately as restricted cash or under the investments
category of the balance sheet.

Marketable Securities. Excess idle cash is often invested temporarily in short-term business securities, such as notes payable
issued by other firms (commercial paper), or short-term U.S. Government securities, such as 90- and 180-day Treasury bills. These
securities earn interest for their holders. Short-term marketable securities are classified as current assets because they can be easily
and quickly converted into cash should the need arise.

Receivables. The total of accounts and notes receivable represents outstanding claims of the firm against its customers who
purchased goods and services on credit terms. An *account receiv-*

able is documented by an invoice that normally specifies the exact date on which the amount due must be paid. Trade practice usually allows the customer who purchased merchandise under credit terms, such as 30 days, a 5- to 10-day grace period to pay the account. A customer may convert an account receivable into a note receivable or may purchase merchandise under a note receivable arrangement. A *note receivable* is a promissory note in which the customer explicitly promises to pay the obligation plus interest charges to the business on or before a specified date. In effect, a note receivable is considered a stronger legal claim against the customer than is an account receivable. Hence, notes receivable are usually classified above accounts receivable on the balance sheet. The classification of the $64,000 total receivables as current assets of Simplex Corporation implies that they are expected to be collected within the next fiscal year.

Four of the current assets — cash, marketable securities, notes receivable, and accounts receivable — are often called *quick assets* because they represent cash or assets expected to be converted into cash within a very short time.

Inventory. Inventory usually reflects one of the larger amounts among the assets of merchandising and manufacturing firms. Since a merchandiser's inventory ordinarily consists of goods that require little additional labor or other services to prepare them for resale, the balance normally reflects the purchase cost of the merchandise on hand. The inventory of a manufacturer, however, normally includes an assortment of several items in various stages of production. For example, an itemized breakdown of Simplex Corporation's inventory balance of $120,000 would probably disclose that it consists of (1) raw materials, (2) various items in the process of becoming finished products, and (3) some finished goods that are ready for immediate sale. It is often customary to maintain separate inventory subclassifications in the detailed accounting records, such as raw materials, work in process, and finished goods, and then combine these under one inventory classification on the balance sheet for presentation purposes.

Prepaid Expenses. The prepaid expenses balance includes unused supplies and services for which the firm either actually paid in advance or incurred a liability to pay. A detailed inspection of Simplex Corporation's financial records would disclose that the prepaid expenses balance at December 31, 1979, is composed of the following items:

Factory supplies	$ 2,000
Office and clerical supplies	1,400
Prepaid insurance, covering a fire and casualty policy effective during the 12-month period ending December 31, 1980	3,600
Prepaid rent, at $500 per month for the year ending December 31, 1980	6,000
Total	$13,000

Each prepaid item contains either service benefits that will be used up or supplies that will be consumed, usually within twelve months after the balance sheet date. As an example, factory supplies are physically consumed during an accounting period, whereas fire insurance and rent expense expire as time passes. The benefit that is contained in one month's prepaid rent ($500) will expire on January 31, 1980; and this expiration process will continue throughout 1980 until the balance of $6,000 existing at December 31, 1979, is reduced to zero at the end of 1980.

Noncurrent Assets

This major category of assets includes: investments; plant assets (tangibles) such as land, building, and equipment; and intangibles, such as patents, copyrights, franchises, and goodwill.

Investments. The investments category usually reflects rights or claims of the reporting business in the total financial resources of other business establishments. In this instance, the amount invested in Alpha, Inc., represents the financial interest held by Simplex Corporation as a stockholder in Alpha Inc., an aircraft manufacturer. Investments in the securities of other businesses and government entities, which either are held for control purposes or are not intended to be converted into cash during the ensuing 12-month period, are classified as noncurrent assets, separately classified from the previously listed marketable securities.

Plant Assets. This category of assets includes tangible assets such as land, buildings, equipment, and machinery intended for primary use in the normal operations of the business. Plant assets are not intended for sale or disposal until such time as their value to the firm's operations approaches zero.

Land. Land is a plant asset that includes the sites on which the firm's buildings are located plus land acquired for expansion purposes. Like prepaid expenses, the original cost of the land contains service benefits that are used up in the process of generating revenue. However, accountants assume that since land has an infinite life and an unlimited capacity to support buildings and equipment, the periodic consumption of the benefits contained in land is so minute as to be unmeasurable. Hence, the original cost of the land remains on the balance sheet until it is sold.

Buildings and Equipment. Buildings and equipment are assets that have limited useful lives. The benefits contained in these financial resources will be used up over a period of time in the process of producing and marketing the various navigation and communication products of the corporation. As the benefits in these assets are released and consumed, the $415,000 original cost of building and equipment is reduced by means of what is called the *depreciation* process, the details of which are discussed in Chapter 4. At this point, however, note on the balance sheet the $60,000 negative amount classified as Accumulated Depreciation. This amount represents the portion of the original cost of buildings and equipment consumed or used up as of December 31, 1979. Restated, approximately $355,000 of the original cost of these assets awaits consumption during future periods.

Intangibles: Patents. The receipt of a patent from the United States Patent Office confers on the patent holder the right, without competition, to reap the rewards from a discovery for 17 years. No other person or group may copy the essential attributes of the invention during that time. From an accounting viewpoint, the benefits contained in this intangible noncurrent asset will, over a period of the patent's remaining useful life, diminish to zero by means of a process similar to the depreciation of tangible assets mentioned above. This process is called *amortization*.

An overview description of all financial resources of Simplex Corporation that can be measured in monetary terms at the end of 1979 is now complete. Notice, however, that perhaps the most valuable assets and resources possessed by this corporation or any other business are always omitted from the balance sheet, namely: its managerial talent and competence; the creativity and energy of its personnel; and its organizational esprit de corps. The principal reason why these valuable assets are excluded from the firm's balance sheet is because the benefits contained in such assets cannot be objectively measured in monetary terms.

CHARACTERISTICS OF THE EQUITIES

The three characteristics associated with the various assets are also applicable to equities that are identified on the balance sheet: (1) legal status; (2) valuation basis; and (3) time dimension.

Legal Status

Each equity may be viewed as a legal claim by an individual or group in the total assets of the entity. Another way of perceiving the liabilities is to consider them as financial obligations that were incurred to obtain various financial resources whose service benefits are expected to be used up in the process of generating future income. In the case of Simplex Corporation, it has a legal obligation to pay its debts on a specific date to individuals, banks, or other organizations from which it borrowed money (as reflected by a note, bond, or mortgage note payable), or from which it purchased goods and services on credit terms (accounts payable). Unpaid employee compensation and tax assessments to various levels of government are also classified as liabilities.

The legal claims of owners in the total assets of the entity are usually evidenced by stock certificates, partnership agreements, or proprietary rights in the case of a single-owner business. These ownership claims are normally considered to continue in existence during the presumably infinite life of the business. In the extreme case of the firm's complete liquidation, however, owners are normally entitled to any proceeds that remain from the conversion of financial resources into cash after all financial obligations to creditors have been satisfied. In a sense, therefore, owners' equities can be considered as liabilities of the firm which must eventually be repaid to the owners upon discontinuance of operations.

Valuation Basis

With the exception of retained earnings, the monetary value of each equity is derived from the exchange price that was used to establish the value of the various assets. For example, when Simplex Corporation borrowed $40,000 from the bank under a short-term arrangement in the form of a note payable, a $40,000 liability was simultaneously created. In another example, the capital stock balance of $175,000 probably arose from stockholders investing cash and other financial resources in the firm. The monetary amount shown in retained earnings generally represents the cumulative net income earned and retained within the business up to the date of the balance sheet.

Time Dimension

The equities are usually divided into three major categories: (1) current liabilities; (2) long-term liabilities; and (3) owners' equity. *Current liabilities* are financial obligations which are expected to be repaid within the next twelve months or the normal operating cycle, whichever is longer. For example, the $12,500 obligation for income taxes would be classifed as a current liability if that debt is expected to be paid off with cash during the next twelve months. Liabilities that are not expected to be repaid within that time period are classified as *long-term liabilities*. The various *owners' equities* reflect the investment in the firm by owners, plus the earnings that have not yet been either withdrawn by the owners of an unincorporated business in the form of cash, or distributed to stockholders in the form of cash dividends. Normally, these owners' equities or rights are not expected to be liquidated or retired during the life of the business enterprise.

SPECIFIC EQUITIES DEFINED

A brief definition of each of the more common equities reflected on the balance sheet is provided below. Equities, particularly the liabilities, tend to be listed in the order they are expected to be repaid or removed as obligations of the firm.

Current Liabilities

This major equity category includes notes, accounts, wages, and income taxes payable, plus other short-term accrued liabilities.

Notes Payable. The notes payable balance reflects amounts due on short-term loans that were probably obtained from banks and other creditors. Normally, these notes must be paid on or before specified dates during the next fiscal year, plus any interest that may be charged during the period the notes are outstanding. The $40,000 notes payable of Simplex Corporation would be reflected as a note receivable on the bank's balance sheet.

Accounts Payable. These financial obligations arise from the purchase of inventory and various operating items on credit terms. They are classified as current because management expects to remove them as liabilities with cash payment within the next twelve months. An account payable of Simplex Corporation would be reflected as an account receivable on the balance sheet of the vendor who had sold goods and services to Simplex Corporation on credit.

Wages Payable. Amounts owed to employees for services rendered are represented in this balance. An employee who provided labor services to the company for which payment has not yet been received is as much a creditor of Simplex Corporation as a bank which loaned it money. If the corporation were to liquidate the $5,500 liability to employees during January, 1980 (with no other financial events intervening to affect the cash balance), the wages payable balance would be reduced to zero and the cash balance would decrease to $14,500. The balance sheet, however, would remain in perfect balance after this payment, with total assets of $614,500 equaling total equities of $614,500.

Income Taxes Payable. Unpaid taxes assessed by federal, state, and local governments on net income earned during the fiscal year ended December 31, 1979, are included in the $12,500 balance shown on the financial statement. Other taxes payable frequently seen on the balance sheet include unpaid property tax assessments, employee taxes withheld, unemployment compensation, and social security taxes.

Long-Term Liabilities

Mortgage notes payable, bonds payable, and other liabilities that are not expected to be paid off within the next fiscal year comprise this major equity category.

Mortgage Note Payable. In 1970, management of Simplex Corporation borrowed from an insurance company $70,000 with which to pay a large portion of the construction costs incurred on the building that is shown as a plant asset. Under terms of the agreement, the corporation is obligated to repay the principal amount of the loan, $70,000, to the insurance company in 1985, plus interest charges at specified intervals during that period. This financial obligation is classified as a long-term liability as of December 31, 1979, because the principal is not due for payment within the next fiscal year.

In the event that the principal or interest charge is not paid at the respective specified dates, the insurance company could foreclose the mortgage and obtain the property deed and title from Simplex Corporation. The insurance company would then be in a position to sell the building and retain the amount equivalent to any unpaid portion of the mortgage note. In effect, tangible physical property, in this case the building, serves as tangible *collateral* for the mortgage notes payable.

Bonds Payable. The bonds payable balance of $130,000 represents the principal amount of a long-term loan that is due to be repaid in 1983. The money was borrowed from various creditors to purchase certain items of equipment. Each lender would possess one or more bond certificates to evidence the amount that had been loaned to Simplex Corporation. Bondholders normally receive interest payments at specified intervals during which the bonds are outstanding. The specific assets financed from funds obtained through the bond issue may or may not serve as collateral for the loan, depending on provisions in the bond agreement, called the *indenture*. Two significant distinctions between a mortgage note and bond financing are: (1) a mortgage note payable is usually secured by specified tangible assets, whereas a bond issue may or may not be secured; and (2) a mortgage note payable usually evidences a financial obligation to a single creditor, whereas a bond issue is often sold to more than one creditor.

Owners' Equities

The two most common subdivisions of the owners' equity category in the corporate form of organization are (1) capital stock, and (2) retained earnings.

Capital Stock. At the time the state granted the corporation a charter, it also authorized the firm to issue a specified number of shares of capital stock to persons who wish to invest in the firm. Each stock certificate is inscribed with a *par value* of $10, as authorized in the charter. Par values may be established at various amounts, depending upon the amount of money to be raised from investors and the number of shares desired for ultimate issue. For example, an individual investing $1,000 in Simplex Corporation would receive 100 shares of $10 par value capital stock, assuming the market value of the firm's capital stock equaled its par value. Had the par value been stated at $100, that stockholder would have received ten shares of the stock.

Retained Earnings. The accumulated earnings of the corporation that remain in the firm are reflected in retained earnings. Any distribution of these earnings to stockholders in the form of dividends would decrease the retained earnings balance. That is, if a cash dividend were paid to stockholders of the corporation, the firm's cash and retained earnings balances would be decreased by the amount of the dividend paid.

THE ORGANIZATION OF FINANCIAL EVENTS

Financial events and transactions that occurred during the first month of operations in a newly organized corporation will serve to illustrate the methodology and procedures by which accountants record, organize, and communicate financial data. This initial exposure to accounting's framework and terminology is presented within the context of the balance sheet.

The Journal Entry and Debit-Credit Procedure

The Melvin Corporation was chartered on January 1, 1979, as a home appliance wholesale distributor to sell various appliances to retailers in the surrounding area. The principal product lines to be handled included cook tops, wall ovens, free-standing ranges, refrigerators, freezers, and food waste disposers. Each of eight individuals invested $25,000 in the corporation at that date, and in return received 2,500 shares of the corporation's $10 par value capital stock.

The accountant's task began the instant the $200,000 investment became subject to the corporation's control. Specific asset and owners' equity designations, cash and capital stock, were created for Melvin Corporation; and the monetary amount associated with each designation increased from zero to $200,000. Rephrased, a financial resource (cash) was obtained by the corporate entity; and the source of that asset was an investment by owners, reflected in the accounting records as an owners' equity (capital stock). Each of the 2,500 individual stock certificates issued to the investor evidenced a proportionate right or claim to the total financial resources of the corporation. Hence, insofar as each new owner was concerned, the $25,000 cash that was formerly a financial resource of that owner was replaced by 2,500, $10 par value stock certificates as evidence of the owner's right in the total assets of Melvin Corporation. Assuming no other financial events occurred during the first day of operations, a balance sheet prepared as of the end of that day would appear as shown below:

Melvin Corporation
Balance Sheet
January 1, 1979

Assets	Equities
	Capital stock, $10 par; 20,000 shares issued and
Cash.............................. $200,000	outstanding $200,000

The customary framework by which an accountant first enters this financial event in the accounting records of the firm is called a *journal entry*.

Each journal entry is recorded in the *general journal*, which is one of the two permanent accounting records used in almost every business enterprise. Each entry is *journalized* in chronological order. A portion of the general journal for Melvin Corporation is shown below to reflect this first financial transaction that occurred in the company:

	DATE		DESCRIPTION	POST. REF.	DEBIT	CREDIT	
1	1979 Jan.	1	*Dr.* Cash (CA)	100	20 0 0 0 0 00		1
2			*Cr.* Capital Stock (OE)	610		20 0 0 0 0 00	2
3			Initial investment of $25,000 by each of eight				3
4			owners creates Melvin Corporation.				4
5							5

JOURNAL   PAGE 1

Note the following items in the format of the general journal:

(1) The *Date* column. The date of the event is normally included in each entry, but will be shown hereafter only in instances when confusion might otherwise exist.

(2) The *Description* column. The specific asset or equity that is affected by the transaction is located in this column, with the details of the transaction explained below.

(3) The *Posting Reference* column. Notations in this column are numbers that have been assigned by the accounting department to each asset and equity.

(4) The *Debit and Credit* columns. The dollar amounts involved in the transaction are entered in these two columns. In each journal entry, the total debits will always equal the total credits.

Information contained in the description column warrants additional explanation. The accountant increases all assets by debiting them, designated as *Dr.* and increases all equities by crediting them, designated as *Cr.* Conversely, assets are credited and equities are debited to decrease them. This fundamental procedure of double-entry accounting is shown below:

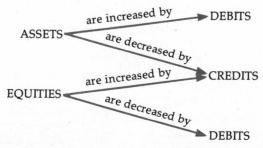

In the preceding entry, *Dr.* merely means to debit or increase Cash, a current asset (CA) account; whereas *Cr.* means to credit or increase Capital Stock, an owners' equity (OE) account. Since the account credited is always indented and shown below the account that is debited in a journal entry, the Dr. and Cr. notations will be deleted hereafter.

It should be emphasized at this point that the debit-credit notation system is simply traditional nomenclature that the accounting profession has adopted for purposes of recording financial transactions. The terms debit and credit should not be viewed as connoting "favorable or unfavorable," "good or bad."

The abbreviations shown in parentheses after each account in the entry will be used as a learning aid throughout Part I to denote the major category into which each account is classified. These abbreviations are shown below:

CA = Current assets
NA = Noncurrent assets (including investments, plant assets, and intangibles)

CL = Current liabilities
LL = Long-term liabilities
OE = Owners' equities

These symbolic notations may be grouped into an expanded version of the balance sheet equation presented previously, as shown below:

$$CA + NA = CL + LL + OE$$

A brief explanation of the transaction or event is usually included beneath the various elements in the entry if the meaning of the entry is not readily apparent.

The Account

Monetary amounts that pertain to a specific financial resource or equity are accumulated in an *account*, the basic classification device in accounting. A shorthand device called the *T account* is frequently used by accountants to convey the essential information contained in financial transactions. This mechanism can be used to illustrate the role of the debit-credit procedure in more detail.

The large T shown at the top of the next page can be viewed as a skeleton balance sheet. The smaller T's represent the two accounts under consideration at this point. Visualize the large T as a weightless free-hanging mobile suspended from its midpoint. In turn, each smaller T is suspended by its center from the midpoint of the respective arm of the large T. As the Cash T account is debited (increased) by $200,000, it becomes unbalanced to the left,

THE BALANCE SHEET T

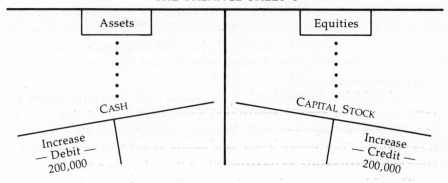

as would the large balance sheet T. When the Capital Stock T account is simultaneously credited (increased) by $200,000, it too goes out of balance, but to the right. However the large T now comes into perfect balance. The fact that each small T account within the overall structure is not balanced is irrelevant. If a small T account is perfectly balanced, it will have a net balance of zero.

The critical point, which warrants constant emphasis, is that the large balance sheet T must always be in balance after the monetary amounts involved in each financial transaction or event have been properly recorded in the relevant accounts. This is the essential feature of the double-entry system of accounting: total assets must always equal total equities.

This physical analogy can be expanded to illustrate the complete debit-credit procedure that is used with respect to all balance-sheet-related accounts:

THE EXPANDED BALANCE SHEET T

Assets		Equities	
CURRENT ASSETS		CURRENT LIABILITIES	
To Increase — Debit —	To Decrease — Credit —	To Decrease — Debit —	To Increase — Credit —
NONCURRENT ASSETS		LONG-TERM LIABILITIES	
To Increase — Debit —	To Decrease — Credit —	To Decrease — Debit —	To Increase — Credit —
		OWNERS' EQUITY	
		To Decrease — Debit —	To Increase — Credit —

To reemphasize the concept: all asset accounts are increased by debiting them and decreased by crediting them; whereas all equities are increased by credits and decreased by debits. The reader is strongly advised to commit either the preceding sentence or the diagram to memory before venturing beyond this point! Also be aware that the normal balance in most asset accounts is a debit, and for most equity accounts the normal balance is a credit.

Transaction Analysis

The identification of every aspect in an event which alters the financial composition of the business enterprise may be referred to as *transaction analysis*. The process of transaction analysis involves the following steps:

(1) Identification of specific accounts involved in the event or transaction.
(2) Determination of the monetary change in each account.
(3) Translation of monetary changes into debit-credit language.
(4) Recording this information in the form of a journal entry.

Ten financial events or transactions which occurred in Melvin Corporation during its first month of operation will be reconstructed and analyzed in the remainder of this chapter. The firm's normal operating cycle varies between three to six months, and its fiscal year ends each December 31. Only balance-sheet-related accounts will receive attention in this illustration.

Event 1

Owners' Investment

The journal entry reflecting the total original investment of $200,000 by the eight owners is repeated here for completeness:

```
Jan. 1    Cash (CA) ........................................ 200,000
             Capital Stock (OE)...........................        200,000
             Initial investment of $25,000 by each of
             eight owners creates Melvin Corpora-
             tion.
```

The current asset account, Cash (CA), was increased by a debit; and the owners' equity account, Capital Stock (OE), was simultaneously increased by a credit.

Event 2

Short-Term Loan

On January 2, the company's president obtained a $20,000 loan from the bank on behalf of the corporation. A promissory note, authorized and signed by the president, was given to the bank. The note stated that the company agreed to pay the $20,000 on demand at the discretion of the bank after September 30, 1979. (Interest charges normally incurred by the firm on any notes, mortgage notes, and bonds payable issued by the firm are ignored in this example.) The cash balance increased by $20,000; and the source of that cash was the incurrence of a financial obligation called notes payable. Since this note is payable at the bank's option any time after September, the liability is considered current. The current asset, Cash, is increased (debited); and the current liability, Notes Payable, is increased (credited) in the following entry:

Jan. 2   Cash (CA) 20,000
              Notes Payable (CL)............................   20,000
              Loan payable at discretion of bank
              after September 30, 1979.

Of the firm's total financial resources of $220,000, at this point, the bank as a creditor, had a claim of $20,000, and the owners had a financial claim of $200,000 as shown below:

Assets	=	Liabilities	+	Owners' Equity
$220,000		$20,000		$200,000
Cash		Notes Payable		Capital Stock

Event 3

Land Mortgage

On the following day, the company purchased land on which a building was to be erected for warehousing, salesrooms, and administrative facilities. The $40,000 cost of the land was financed under a 5-year mortgage note payable arrangement with a local building and loan association. The association paid the $40,000 amount directly to the seller of the land; title to the land which served as collateral for the loan was transferred to Melvin Corporation; and the note signed by an officer of the firm obligated the company to reimburse the association for the amount of the loan on December 31, 1983.

Translated into accounting terminology: a plant asset, land, was obtained; and the source of that financial resource was the incurrence of a long-term mortgage note payable. The entry appears as follows:

Jan. 3   Land (NA)... 40,000
              Mortgage Note Payable (LL).................   40,000
              Purchase of land under mortgage note
              payable arrangement, due December
              31, 1983.

Event 4

Bond Issue

The corporation's cash balance, reflecting $220,000 after journalizing Event 3, consisted of $200,000 invested by the owners plus $20,000 obtained under the short-term bank loan. Since the necessary building and equipment would entail a total cost approximating $400,000, Melvin Corporation's management arranged to sell $250,000 of bonds on January 4. The terms of the bond issue specified: the corporation was required to repay bondholders on December 31, 1985; cash proceeds from the sale of the bond issue were to be used to construct a building and purchase various pieces of equipment; and these plant assets were to serve as collateral for the bond issue. The entry was recorded as shown below:

```
Jan. 4    Cash (CA) ......................................... 250,000
              Bonds Payable (LL) ...........................        250,000
                  Sale of bonds, due December 31, 1985.
```

Event 5

Payment for Building

On January 15, the corporation forwarded $100,000 to the building contractor in payment for the recently constructed prefabricated building. The entry to record payment for this tangible noncurrent plant asset is shown below:

```
Jan. 15   Building (NA) ..................................... 100,000
              Cash (CA) .....................................        100,000
                  Payment for building.
```

Event 6

Equipment Purchase

The company on January 17, paid a total of $300,000 to several vendors for various items of equipment to be used in subsequent operations. These payments may be combined and condensed into one journal entry, called a *summary entry*, as shown below:

```
Jan. 17   Equipment (NA)..................................... 300,000
              Cash (CA) .....................................        300,000
                  Payment to several vendors for various
                  items of equipment.
```

Two observations may be made at the point immediately following Event No. 6 on January 17:

(1) The assets and equities of Melvin Corporation are composed of the following accounts and amounts:

Assets		Equities	
Cash (CA)	$ 70,000	Notes payable (CL)	$ 20,000
Land (NA).................	40,000	Mortgage note payable (LL).	40,000
Building (NA)............	100,000	Bonds payable (LL)............	250,000
Equipment (NA).........	300,000	Capital stock (OE)..............	200,000
Total assets............	$510,000	Total equities................	$510,000

(2) Total assets still equal total equities.   *liabilities are > by credit account*

Event 7   *expenses are > by debit*

Prepaid Rent and Insurance Expense

The treasurer prepared two checks on January 18, in payment for the following items:

(1) Rental charges on several fork lift trucks for the year 1979, at the rate of $300 per month, effective January 1, 1979 .... $3,600
(2) Fire and casualty insurance premium for one year, at the rate of $50 per month, effective January 1, 1979 600

Total.. $4,200

Purchases of this type, in which a payment is made in advance of (1) the expiration, or (2) the consumption of service benefits, are called *prepaid expenses*. They would be reflected as a current asset in the following entries:

Jan. 18	Prepaid Expenses (CA)	3,600	
	Cash (CA)......................................		3,600
	Paid one year rental charges for fork-lifts.		
	Prepaid Expenses (CA)	600	
	Cash (CA)......................................		600
	Paid fire insurance premium for the year.		

Event 8

Inventory Purchases on Credit

Various home appliances costing a total of $155,000 were purchased for inventory on 60-day credit terms from several vendors between January 19 to January 22. At each purchase date, an asset identified as inventory was obtained, and a financial obligation was incurred in the form of an account payable. The following summary entry reflects a consolidation of several entries that might have been made during this four-day period to record these purchases of merchandise for subsequent resale:

```
Jan. 22   Inventory (CA) ...................................... 155,000
              Accounts Payable (CL) .........................         155,000
              Purchase of appliances for inventory on
              60-day credit terms between January
              19–22.
```

Event 9

Prepaid Expenses — Supplies

Various office, warehouse, and administrative supplies, such as cleaning solvents, wrapping paper, stationery, and envelopes, totaling $22,800 were purchased under a variety of credit terms on January 23. These supplies possessed service benefits, which in many instances would probably be paid for in advance of their consumption. This purchase was recorded as shown in the following summary entry:

```
Jan. 23   Prepaid Expenses (CA) .......................... 22,800
              Accounts Payable (CL) .........................         22,800
              Purchased supplies under credit ar-
              rangements.
```

Event 10

Payment for Prepaid Supplies

On January 30, a check for $6,100 was forwarded to a vendor from whom the company had purchased some office supplies on credit (see Event 9). The payment to reflect the simultaneous decrease in a current liability and a current asset was recorded as shown below:

```
Jan. 30   Accounts Payable (CL) ........................... 6,100
              Cash (CA) .......................................         6,100
              Payment for office supplies previously
              purchased on credit.
```

The analysis and recording of all financial events that occurred during Melvin Corporation's first month of operations is now complete.

Tabular Summarization. A convenient way of summarizing the essential financial detail involved in the Melvin Corporation illustration is shown on the following page within the framework of a tabular presentation. This particular viewpoint emphasizes two critical relationships: (1) the *concept of duality* whereby total

MELVIN CORPORATION
TABULAR SUMMARY OF FINANCIAL EVENTS
FOR THE MONTH ENDED JANUARY 31, 1979

Event No.	Current Assets	+	Noncurrent Assets	=	Current Liabilities	+	Long-Term Liabilities	+	Owners' Equity
1	$200,000 Cash			=					$200,000 Capital Stock
2	20,000 Cash			=	$ 20,000 Notes Payable				
3			$ 40,000 Land	=			$ 40,000 Mortgage Note Payable		
4	250,000 Cash			=			250,000 Bonds Payable		
5	− 100,000 Cash		100,000 Building						
6	− 300,000 Cash		300,000 Equipment						
7	+ 4,200 Prepaid Expenses								
	− 4,200 Cash								
8	155,000 Inventory			=	155,000 Accounts Payable				
9	22,800 Prepaid Expenses			=	22,800 Accounts Payable				
10	− 6,100 Cash			=	− 6,100 Accounts Payable				
Total	$241,700	+	$440,000	=	$191,700	+	$290,000	+	$200,000

debits must always equal total credits in each entry; and, (2) the
concept of equality whereby perfect balance is constantly maintained between total assets and total equities.

Posting the Events

The information contained in each of the preceding financial
events that has been recorded in the general journal can now be
transferred, through a process referred to as *posting*, to the second
of the two permanent accounting records, the *general ledger*.

The General Ledger. The general ledger is a book or record
which contains a separate page or section for each account. Pages
or sections associated with each account are usually arranged in
the order that the accounts appear on the balance sheet and the
income statement, with the balance-sheet-related accounts presented first. Each account may be identified by an account number
to facilitate data processing or to assist in cross-referencing. Two
of these accounts with their company number are shown below
for Melvin Corporation:

ACCOUNT NUMBER	ACCOUNT TITLE
100	Cash
610	Capital Stock

The journal entries are posted to the general ledger in the same
order in which they were entered in the journal. The date, item,
posting reference, and amount debited or credited are posted,
after which the account number is placed in the Posting Reference
column of the journal. The two general ledger accounts that were
involved in the first financial transaction of the Melvin Corporation are presented on the following page to illustrate this process.
Note the arrangement and content of each ledger account:

(1) The account title and number at the top.
(2) The date of each transaction.
(3) The Posting Reference column in which is entered the source of the information. GJ1 refers to General Journal, page 1.
(4) The four columns: Debit, Credit, and the two Balance columns.

Three reasons may be advanced for what appears at first glance
to be an unnecessary maintenance of two permanent records, the
general journal and the general ledger.

(1) The general journal reflects every account involved in each financial event
in chronological order. However, the balance in a specific account at any
moment cannot be quickly determined by inspecting only the journal.
(2) When properly posted and updated, the account in the general ledger
provides the balance in a specific account at a particular moment. How-

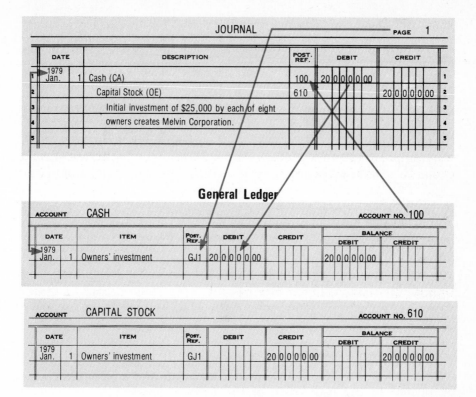

ever, a listing of each complete transaction that gave rise to that balance is not easily discernible from examining only the ledger.

(3) In the event that one of these permanent accounting records is lost, stolen, or damaged, a complete reconstruction of the financial history of the business entity can be accomplished from the other.

Prior to machine accounting and electronic data processing, the journal and ledger were usually maintained as loose-leaf or bound books in the accounting department. Now, both of these accounting records may be contained on tapes, drums, discs, punch cards, or other storage devices. Although this financial information may be physically located in a data processing area removed from the accounting offices, that information is always under the control of the accounting department.

The Master T Structure. The master T structure shown on page 56 is another short-hand device which represents the general ledger that is maintained within the Melvin Corporation. The essential information contained in each of the preceding ten financial transactions have been posted to the relevant T accounts, in much the same manner that the same information would be formally posted to individual accounts in the general ledger.

PART 1   CONCEPTS AND PROCEDURES

Melvin Corporation
Master T Structure
January 31, 1979

Assets		Equities	

CASH (CA)

(1) 200,000	(5) 100,000
(2) 20,000	(6) 300,000
(4) 250,000	(7) 3,600
	600
	(10) 6,100
Bal. 59,700	

INVENTORY (CA)

(8) 155,000	
Bal. 155,000	

PREPAID EXPENSES (CA)

(7) 3,600	
600	
(9) 22,800	
Bal. 27,000	

LAND (NA)

(3) 40,000	
Bal. 40,000	

BUILDING (NA)

(5) 100,000	
Bal. 100,000	

EQUIPMENT (NA)

(6) 300,000	
Bal. 300,000	

NOTES PAYABLE (CL)

	(2) 20,000
	Bal. 20,000

CAPITAL STOCK (OE)

	(1) 200,000
	Bal. 200,000

ACCOUNTS PAYABLE (CL)

(10) 6,100	(8) 155,000
	(9) 22,800
	Bal. 171,700

MORTGAGE NOTE PAYABLE (LL)

	(3) 40,000
	Bal. 40,000

BONDS PAYABLE (LL)

	(4) 250,000
	Bal. 250,000

For example, Event No. 1 requires that $200,000 debit be posted to the left side of the Cash T account, and a $200,000 credit be posted to the right side of the Capital Stock T account. The number in parenthesis beside each amount in each T account denotes the event number designation used in the preceding illustration. Notice throughout the entire posting process that the master T structure remains in perfect balance after all accounts in each entry have been posted.

Balance Sheet Preparation

After determining the ending balance in each T account contained in the preceding master T structure, the balance sheet at January 31, 1979, may now be prepared. The balance sheet shown on the following page presents a snapshot of the firm's financial position at one instant in time, namely January 31, 1979.

An Essential Observation Reemphasized

One critical observation and conclusion can be drawn from the Melvin Corporation illustration: every journal entry must balance. The double-entry accounting system makes perfect balance imperative. Two sides exist in every financial transaction or event. If this fundamental principle of duality is followed consistently, the

Melvin Corporation
Balance Sheet
January 31, 1979

Assets		Equities	
Current assets:		**Current liabilities:**	
Cash...........................	$ 59,700	Notes payable	$ 20,000
Inventory	155,000	Accounts payable...........	171,700
Prepaid expenses...........	27,000	Total current liabilities..	$191,700
Total current assets	$241,700		
		Long-term liabilities:	
Plant assets:		Mortgage note payable ...	$ 40,000
Land...........................	$ 40,000	Bonds payable	250,000
Building	100,000	Total long-term	
Equipment....................	300,000	liabilities..............	$290,000
Total plant assets	$440,000		
		Owners' equity:	
		Capital stock, $10 par;	
		20,000 shares issued	
		and outstanding	$200,000
Total assets.....................	$681,700	Total equities..................	$681,700

general journal, the general ledger or master T structure, and the balance sheet will always maintain perfect balance. This "universal law" of double-entry accounting is akin to Newton's Third Law of Motion: "To every action there is always opposed an equal reaction."

Maintenance of perfect balance does not imply, however, that accounting is a perfect art. For example, erroneous but balancing amounts may be entered in the proper accounts, or correct amounts may be entered in the wrong accounts. The most difficult challenge in accounting is to analyze each transaction correctly, identify the correct accounts, and determine the correct amounts involved!

QUESTIONS

1. "The balance sheet presents a snapshot of the firm's financial position at a specific moment." (a) Explain the meaning of this statement. (b) Explain why the income statement is something other than a "snapshot."

2. How does the balance sheet heading reflect application of the accounting principles of business entity and periodicity?

3. Identify and briefly explain: (a) the four major asset categories, and (b) the three major equity categories into which the balance sheet is usually divided.

4. Why is it difficult to directly associate specific financial resources with specific equities that appear on a firm's balance sheet after operations commence?

5. "Equality is the critical foundation on which the double-entry system of accounting is based." Explain how the journal entry and the balance sheet equation illustrate this concept.

6. Explain how the general characteristic of legal status is related to the assets and equities.

7. Explain how the general characteristic of valuation basis is related to the assets and equities.

8. Distinguish between a firm's fiscal year and its normal operating cycle. How are these terms applied in classifying assets as current or noncurrent, and liabilities as current or long-term?

9. How would an accountant distinguish between categorizing an investment by a company in another business as a marketable security or as an investment?

10. Explain what is meant by the phrase, "many plant assets such as equipment and machinery contain service benefits that will be released or consumed over a period of time in generating revenue."

11. In what respects are accounts and notes receivable different? The same?

12. Explain in what way the prepaid expenses category contains benefits that will expire or be consumed in the future.

13. In what respects might the inventory of a dress manufacturer and a dress retailer be different?

14. Identify several resources of a business establishment that are not reflected on the firm's balance sheet. Explain why these valuable assets are not shown.

15. Under what condition might various accounts included in the owners' equity section be considered a liability of the business entity?

16. How would a creditor's account or note receivable probably be classified in the accounting records of the debtor?

17. How might Income Taxes Payable and Wages Payable that are reflected at the end of a firm's fiscal year be considered an application of the accrual and going-concern principles?

18. Explain how a corporation's own employees and the federal government could be considered creditors of that corporation.

19. In what respects are mortgage notes payable and bonds payable similar? Different?

20. In comparing corporations, the corporation that issued the largest number of stock certificates, regardless of par value per share, would reflect in its capital stock account the largest financial claim of owners in the total resources of the firm. True or false? Explain your answer.

21. A corporation borrowed $400,000 from the bank under a note payable arrangement on July 1, 1979. The loan required repayment on March 31, 1980. Prepare the appropriate journal entry, and explain every detail of the entry.

22. Explain how two or more balance sheet accounts can be out of balance, yet the balance sheet itself would remain in perfect balance.

23. Integrate the following terms into a brief explanation of double-entry accounting: "two sides in every financial transaction"; "perfect balance"; and "total debits must always equal total credits."

24. Indicate how the debit-credit notation system is used to indicate the direction of monetary change in all balance-sheet-related accounts.

25. Identify and illustrate each step involved in transaction analysis, using the following example: a retailer purchased $3,000 of merchandise for its inventory on 30-day credit terms.

26. Prepare separate journal entries to record the following two events: (a) Incurrence of a liability on January 1, 1979, to pay for one year's rent, covering the year 1979 at the rate of $100 per month. (b) Payment and removal of that liability on January 15, 1979.

27. Define: (a) quick assets; and (b) an account.

28. Define: (a) a summary journal entry; and (b) posting.

29. Distinguish between the general journal and the general ledger with respect to what each is designed to accomplish.

30. Since both the general journal and the general ledger contain substantially the same information, only in slightly different format, explain why it is desirable to maintain both records.

31. "An account in the general ledger and its associated T account reflect essentially the same information." Illustrate and explain this statement by comparing the Accounts Payable T account shown on page 56 with the accounts payable account sheet or section that would appear in the general ledger of Melvin Corporation.

EXERCISES

1. **Major category classification.** Indicate in the parentheses below the major category for each of the following balance-sheet-related accounts. The cash account provides a sample format. Use the following symbolic notations for the six major categories:

CA = Current assets   CL = Current liabilities
NA = Noncurrent assets   LL = Long-term liabilities
      (including investments,   OE = Owners' equities
      plant assets, and intangibles)

Accounts Payable .... (CL)
Accounts Receivable .... (CA)
Accumulated Depreciation.. (NA)
Bonds Payable, due four years from date of balance sheet .... (LL)
Building .... (NA)
Capital Stock .... (OE)
Cash .... (CA)
Equipment... (NA)
Income Taxes Payable .... (CL)
Inventory.. (CA)
Investment in Severn Corp. .... (OE)
Land .... (NA)
Marketable Securities... (CA)
Mortgage Note Payable, due nine years from balance sheet date .... (LL)
Mortgage Note Payable, due nine months from balance sheet date. (CL)
Notes Payable, short-term .... (CL)
Notes Receivable.. (CA)
Patents .... (NA)
Prepaid Expenses .... (CA)
Retained Earnings .... (OE)
Wages Payable... (CL)

2. **Quick, current, and total assets.** The balance in each of the following accounts at December 31, 1979, is indicated below:

	BALANCE AT DECEMBER 31, 1979 (CREDIT)
Accounts Payable	$(140,000)
Accounts Receivable	160,000
Building	160,000
Capital Stock	(480,000)
Cash	90,000
Equipment and Machinery	355,000
Federal Income Tax Payable	(50,000)
Inventory	430,000
Investment in Transamerica, Inc.	60,000
Land	90,000
Marketable Securities	40,000
Mortgage Note Payable, due December 31, 1984	(150,000)
Notes Payable, due June 30, 1980	(80,000)
Notes Receivable	10,000
Patents	35,000
Prepaid Expenses	70,000
Wages and Salaries Payable	(16,000)

Required: (a) Determine the total quick assets at December 31, 1979. (b) Determine what percent the quick assets are of total current assets. (c) Determine what percent the quick assets are of total assets.

3. **Debit-credit notation.** Indicate in the column below whether a debit (Dr.) or credit (Cr.) is used to increase each of the following accounts. The cash account provides a sample format.

ACCOUNT TITLE	TO INCREASE
Accounts Payable	
Accounts Receivable	
Bonds Payable	
Building	
Capital Stock	
Cash	Dr.
Equipment	
Inventory	
Investments in Macadamia, Inc.	
Land	
Machinery	
Marketable Securities	
Mortgage Note Payable	
Notes Payable	
Patents	
Prepaid Expenses	
Retained Earnings	
Wages Payable	

4. **Journal entry format.** Translate the following financial transaction data into proper journal entry format. Identify each account title with its appropriate subclassification, for example Cash (CA); and provide a concise explanation of the financial transaction that probably occurred for each entry.

(a) Increase Inventory and Accounts Payable by $3,000 each.
(b) Increase Mortgage Note Payable (due in seven years) and Land by $17,000.
(c) Decrease both Accounts Payable and Cash by $23,000.
(d) Increase Capital Stock and Cash by $9,000 each.
(e) Decrease Cash and Notes Payable (short-term) by $7,000.

5. Journal entry explanation. Using one sentence, explain each of the financial transactions (a) through (e) shown below in the master T structure:

	Assets				Equities	
	CASH (CA)				ACCOUNTS PAYABLE (CL)	
(a)	9,000	(d)	2,000	(e)	3,000 (c)	8,000
	6000	(e)	3,000			
	INVENTORY (CA)				MORTGAGE NOTE PAYABLE (LL)	
(c)	8,000				(b)	6,000
	PREPAID EXPENSES (CA)				CAPITAL STOCK (OE)	
(d)	2,000				(a)	9,000
	LAND (NA)					
(b)	6,000					

6. Sources of cash. Jetspar Corp. was formed on July 14, 1979, when 6,000 shares of capital stock were sold to various investors at an average price of $20 per share. Ten days later, a short-term loan of $65,000 was obtained from a local bank under a note payable arrangement. An $80,000 bond issue, which was due to be repaid on October 31, 1988, was sold to various individuals on October 31, 1979, and $30,000 that had been borrowed in July from the bank under the note payable arrangement was repaid on November 15, 1979.

Required: Prepare a separate journal entry to record each of the four financial transactions described above.

7. Purchase of plant and intangible assets. Quinsips, Inc., purchased a parcel of land for expansion purposes on March 15, 1979, for $75,000 under a 7-year mortgage note payable arrangement. The warehouse that was erected on that parcel of land was completed on October 31, 1979; and its $240,000 cost was financed under another mortgage note payable arrangement which required payment within nine years. Equipment and machinery costing $620,000 were purchased on November 15, 1979, under 90-day credit terms. Three days later, several patents were purchased for $47,000 cash.

Required: Prepare a separate journal entry to record each of the four financial transactions described above.

8. Analysis of inventory transactions. Prepare a summary journal entry to record each of the following inventory-related financial transactions that occurred in a furniture dealer's operations during December:

(a) Various items of furniture totaling $67,000 were purchased from several furniture manufacturers during the month on 60-day credit terms.

(b) Checks amounting to $58,000 were forwarded to various vendors during December in payment for furniture that had been purchased during October and November.

(c) Additional shipments of furniture for inventory were received and paid for during December. Cost of the furniture shipments totaled $49,000.

(d) Determine the balance in the inventory account at December 31, assuming the inventory balance at the beginning of December was $16,000.

9. Analysis of prepaid expense transactions. Priced-Rite Pharmacy, Inc., paid its entire rental charge of $6,000 for one year in advance on January 1. Ten days later, the pharmacy received a bill from its insurance company for a one-year fire, theft, and casualty insurance premium of $2,600, effective January 1. The pharmacy paid the liability on January 31. Various office and cleaning supplies totaling $1,600 were purchased for cash during January and none of these supplies had been used during January.

Required: Prepare a journal entry to record each of the following financial events:

(a) Payment of rent.

(b) Incurrence of liability for the insurance premium on January 11.

(c) Payment for insurance premium on January 31.

(d) Summary entry to reflect cash purchases of office and cleaning supplies.

(e) Determine the balance in Prepaid Expenses at January 31, assuming the debit balance at January 1 was $2,900.

10. Short-term and long-term investments. Pureem Corp. invested $40,000 of its excess cash in some 90-day U.S. Treasury Bills on October 10. Management decided on November 20 to invest an additional $260,000 in the stock of Amalgamated Industries. Management considered this latter investment would be a 4-year commitment of funds, rather than one of short-term duration.

Required: Prepare separate journal entries to record each of the above financial investments.

11. Financial obligation transactions. The following transactions occurred during April in the Rayback Corp.:

(a) Various items costing $28,000 were purchased for inventory on 30-day credit terms on April 4.

(b) Two invoices for office supplies, $3,000, and insurance premiums, $2,400, were received in March and recorded as accounts payable at that time. Both invoices were paid on April 7.

(c) A check for $28,000 was forwarded to the vendor on April 24 for items purchased in item (a) above.

(d) A short-term loan of $17,200 was obtained from a local bank on April 26.

(e) A four-year mortgage note payable totaling $73,000, was paid off on April 29.

Required: Prepare a journal entry to record each of the transactions that occurred during April.

12. Preparation of balance sheet from T account information. Prepare a properly classified balance sheet for Tutmarck Corporation at December 31, 1979, from the 1979 fiscal year-end balance shown in each of the following T accounts:

CASH		ACCOUNTS RECEIVABLE		BUILDINGS, MACHINERY, AND EQUIPMENT	
100,000	33,000	17,000	83,000	130,000	
16,000	32,000	123,000	14,000	250,000	
3,000		54,000		380,000	
54,000		97,000			

INVENTORY		CAPITAL STOCK		MARKETABLE SECURITIES	
26,000			210,000	6,000	
130,000			150,000	2,700	
156,000			360,000	8,700	

PREPAID EXPENSES		WAGES AND SALARIES PAYABLE		RETAINED EARNINGS	
6,000					30,000
7,300			7,900		
13,300				INVESTMENTS	

ACCOUNTS PAYABLE			20,000	12,000
66,000	30,000		38,000	
	120,000		46,000	
	84,000			

NOTES PAYABLE (CL)	
	55,000
	65,000
	120,000

LAND	
196,900	

MORTGAGE NOTE PAYABLE (LL)	
	350,000

PROBLEMS

2-1. Balance sheet preparation. Balances extracted from all accounts in the general ledger of Tristine Corporation at June 30, 1980, are listed below and on the following page. Each account reflects its normal debit or credit balance.

	BALANCE AT JUNE 30, 1980
Land	$ 87,000
Cash	37,000
Retained Earnings	155,000
Prepaid Expenses (rent, supplies, insurance)	14,000
Bonds Payable, due December 31, 1985	200,000
Accounts Payable	209,000

	BALANCE AT JUNE 30, 1980
Bank Loan Payable (short-term)	120,000
Patents	62,000
Accounts Receivable	?
Capital Stock	600,000
Wages and Salaries Payable...........................	17,000
Notes Receivable	8,000
Mortgage Note Payable, due June 30, 1983	150,000
Income Taxes Payable	29,000
Inventory	216,000
Equipment, Machinery, and Fixtures	430,000
Building	228,000
Investment in Bascom, Inc. (long-term investment)	54,000
Marketable Securities (U.S. Treasury bills)	24,000

Required: (1) Prepare a properly classified balance sheet for Tristine Corporation at June 30, 1980. Determine the correct Accounts Receivable balance.

(2) Determine the amount by which quick assets exceed current liabilities.

2-2. **Transaction analysis — journal entry format.** The four Kawickis (three sisters and one brother) decided to devote the month of September to organize and ready their new business venture, Footwear Co., which would begin operations on October 1. Each of the Kawickis is to play an active role in managing the affairs of the company, the prime objective of which is to sell sophisticated casual and sports footwear to an adult clientele. The following financial events occurred during September:

(a) On September 2, each of the four Kawickis invested $10,000 cash to create Footwear Co., in return for which each received 1,000 shares of $10 par value capital stock.

(b) Six-months rent, at the rate of $500 per month effective September 1, for first floor accommodations in a downtown shopping area was paid on September 3, to the landlord.

(c) A shipment of various types of shoes that had been ordered from a manufacturer during the later part of August was received on September 5. The total cost of these items that were purchased for inventory under 20-day credit terms was $60,000.

(d) Angela Kawicki visited the local bank on September 6 to obtain a $20,000 loan which had to be repaid on or before June 30 of the next year.

(e) Various furniture and fixtures, which were to be classified as plant assets, were purchased on 90-day credit terms for $12,000 on September 6.

(f) Two business acquaintances agreed to invest $8,000 cash each, in Footwear Co., on September 10, for which each received 800 shares of capital stock.

(g) On September 10, another business acquaintance contributed a $2,000 billing and accounting machine to the corporation and received 200 shares of stock in return. The machine was classified as a plant asset.

(h) A $500 premium on a fire, theft, and casualty insurance policy was paid on September 20, covering the period ending March 31 of the following year.

(i) A check for the inventory purchased on September 5 was sent to the manufacturer on September 25.

Required: (1) Prepare a journal entry for each financial event that occurred during September. Indicate in each entry the major account category within which each account is classified.

(2) Determine the cash balance available with which to begin operations on October 1.

2-3. Transaction analysis: tabular summary format. Refer to Problem 2-2.

Required: (1) Prepare a tabular summary similar to that on page 53 of the nine financial events that occurred during September in the Footwear Co. Journal entries are not to be prepared.

(2) Prepare a balance sheet for Footwear Co. at September 30.

2-4. Transaction analysis: journal entry format. Balances at January 1, 1979, are shown below for each of the accounts maintained by Wixon Co., a retail sporting goods establishment:

	BALANCE AT JANUARY 1, 1979 (CREDIT)
Accounts Payable	$ (56,300)
Accounts Receivable	38,000
Building and Annex..	50,000
Capital Stock..	(120,000)
Cash..	47,000
Equipment, Furniture, and Fixtures..........................	113,000
Inventory	173,500
Mortgage Note Payable, due September 30, 1985	(155,000)
Prepaid Expenses	4,500
Retained Earnings	(92,000)
Wages and Salaries Payable....................................	(2,700)

The following transactions occurred during January, 1979:

(a) Paid six months rent in advance at the rate of $600 per month on two delivery trucks that were leased by Wixon Co.

(b) Some additional equipment costing $27,000 was purchased on 60-day credit terms on January 5.

(c) Administrative and warehouse supplies (considered as prepaid items) totaling $7,000 were purchased, 50% on cash terms and 50% on 30-day credit terms.

(d) The Wages and Salaries Payable balance that existed at January 1 was paid during January.

(e) Items costing $10,500 were purchased for inventory on 30-day credit terms during January.

(f) Various customers paid $31,000 on their outstanding accounts receivable balances during the month.

(g) A loan amounting to $42,000 was obtained on January 16 from a local bank. Terms of the loan required repayment on or before November 30, 1979.

(h) Various accounts payable totaling $75,600 were paid during the last two weeks of January.

(i) Each of three stockholders invested an additional $5,000 cash in Wixon Co. on January 28.

Required: Prepare separate journal entries to record each of the financial transactions which occurred during January, 1979, in the Wixon Co. Do not post or enter these transactions in T accounts.

2-5. Transaction analysis: T account format and balance sheet preparation. Refer to Problem 2-4.

Required: (1) Set up T accounts including January 1, 1979 balances.

(2) Post each of the transactions to appropriate T accounts. Determine the closing balance at January 31, 1979, in each account.

(3) Prepare a properly classified balance sheet at January 31, 1979.

2-6. Preparation of balance sheet from journal entries. The balance sheet shown below was prepared three days after the creation of Caldwell Corp., but prior to normal operations beginning on June 4, 1979. The accounts payable at June 3 were directly associated with inventory purchases on credit terms; and the plant assets were completely financed by the mortgage note payable.

Caldwell Corp.
Balance Sheet
June 3, 1979

Assets		Equities	
Current assets:		Current liabilities:	
Cash.........................	$ 55,000	Notes payable.............	$ 20,000
Inventory....................	30,000	Accounts payable.........	30,000
Total current assets	$ 85,000	Total current liabilities	$ 50,000
Plant assets:		Long-term liabilities:	
Land.........................	$ 5,000	Mortgage note payable,	
Building and equipment.	35,000	due December 31,	
Total plant assets	$ 40,000	1984......................	40,000
		Owners' equity:	
		Capital stock..............	35,000
Total assets....................	$125,000	Total equities.................	$125,000

The following transactions occurred during the remainder of June, 1979:

(a) Additional inventory was purchased for $17,000 cash.

(b) Advance payments for $2,400 of insurance premiums and $3,700 rental charges on miscellaneous equipment were made during June.

(c) A $3,000 portion of the short-term note payable was paid off.

(d) Additional equipment was purchased for $53,000 under 90-day credit terms.

(e) Supplies costing $14,000 were purchased under 30-day credit arrangements. These supplies were considered a prepaid expense item.

(f) An additional parcel of land costing $23,000 was purchased for expansion purposes under a 60-day credit term arrangement.

(g) Additional capital stock was issued to several stockholders for $75,000 cash.

(h) Excess idle cash totaling $34,000 was temporarily invested in marketable securities on June 28.

(i) In order to reflect a better financial position to prospective creditors and investors, management had paid off all except $55,000 of accounts payable by June 30.

Required: (1) Prepare a journal entry by which to record each of the transactions.

(2) Prepare a balance sheet as of June 30, 1979.

2-7. Preparation of balance sheet from T accounts. The Withee Corporation was created on November 1, 1979, as a lumber wholesaler upon the issuance of 4,000 shares of $20 par value per share capital stock to various investors in return for their $80,000 cash investment. The various activities described below and on page 68 occurred during the firm's two months of operations ending December 31, 1979. At the end of that period, management directed the accountant to prepare a balance sheet in order to determine the financial status of the corporation. The accounts involved in transactions that occurred during November and December are listed below:

Cash	Land	Accounts Payable
Marketable Securities	Buildings	Bonds Payable
Inventory	Equipment	Capital Stock
Prepaid Expenses	Notes Payable	

November and December transactions were as follows:

(a) The corporation was created upon the issuance of stock, as described above.

(b) A $30,000 bond issue was sold on November 2. The bonds required repayment on September 30, 1989.

(c) A large parcel of land containing an office building, warehousing facilities, and storage sheds was purchased for cash on November 3 at a cost of $45,000. Ten percent of that total cost was prorated to the land; and the remainder was allocated to the buildings.

(d) Equipment was purchased during November on 60- and 90-day credit terms from several vendors. This equipment included forklift and delivery trucks, saws, planes, and office machines. Total cost of all equipment amounted to $51,600.

(e) The following prepaid expense items were paid during November:

Rent on a vacant lot for one year at $400 per month, effective November 1, 1979	$ 4,800
Fire, casualty, and public liability insurance policy for one year at $250 per month, effective November 1, 1979.	3,000
Supplies (office, warehouse, and delivery)	7,000
Total prepaid items	$14,800

(f) Timber, lumber, cement, and other building materials were purchased for inventory from various manufacturers and mills dur-

ing the 2-month period at a total cost of $83,000 under 30- to
90-day credit terms.
(g) A short-term loan of $41,000 was obtained during November.
(h) Marketable securities totaling $16,000 were purchased on De-
cember 26 in order to convert some idle cash into a more productive financial resource.
(i) Accounts payable totaling $64,000 were paid off during the two-
month period.

Required: (1) Post each of the transactions to T accounts, indicating the
event "letter" in parentheses alongside each amount posted.
(2) Determine the ending balance in each account at December 31,
1979, and reflect that amount in each T account.
(3) Prepare a properly classified balance sheet at December 31, 1979.

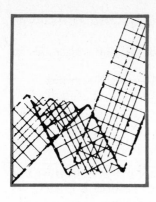

3

The Income Statement: The Matching Process

One of the real problems with profits is that you never really know what they are.

Alan Greenspan

The process of income determination is by no means obvious nor simple. Probably the most significant challenge confronting the accountant is determining the net income or profit earned by a business during a specific period of time. Accurate and timely measurement of net income is essential to enable:

(1) Owners to assess the financial performance of the company.
(2) Creditors to monitor the safety and security of resources they have loaned the firm.
(3) Management to appraise operational performance, implement planning and control devices, and calculate income taxes due various levels of government.
(4) The financial community to evaluate alternate investment opportunities among business enterprises.

The purpose of the next two chapters is to establish several guidelines and procedures by which to determine the amount of revenue that is recognized during a specific time-span and the amount of expenses that are matched with and subtracted from that revenue. Before proceeding directly into these technical aspects, however, a brief look at several interpretations of income may provide deeper appreciation of what accounting income is and what it is not.

VIEWS OF INCOME

Income is generally understood to mean a net inflow of wealth which places an individual, organization, or society in a better position economically than before that inflow occurred. However, in response to the complexity of economic institutions and activities that exist in modern society, the need has arisen to develop sharper, more detailed definitions of income. Three interpretations of which the accountant and users of accounting information should be aware of are briefly outlined below.

Cash Flow Income

The excess of cash receipts over cash disbursements can be regarded as one type of income. An organization or individual whose bank balance increased during the month can be considered as having improved its economic position. Likewise, one way to determine whether or not a business had generated wealth in the form of earned income during its lifetime would be to liquidate the firm and convert all its assets to cash. After subtracting the financial resources in the form of cash that went into the business from the cash that remains upon liquidation after the payment of all debts, the resulting excess cash could be referred to as the overall *profitability* of that firm.

The difficult task confronting the accountant, however, is that the income generated by the firm must be determined periodically at several discrete intervals during its lifetime, rather than only at the termination of activities. In short, any concept of income that encompasses only cash transactions, or which must rely on the liquidation of a business enterprise to adequately determine its income-generating ability, is far too narrow and simplistic to be of any significant benefit to the accountant.

Economic Income

The economist, on the other hand, has adopted an extremely broad interpretation of income. Economists define the total income of society as the wealth received by individuals and organizations from rent, employee compensation, and interest, plus the net income earned by all business enterprises before income taxes.

Restated, a *nation's income* is defined by the economist as rent plus wages plus interest plus profit.

From another perspective, national income may also be defined generally as the aggregate expenditures made by all segments in society, both individuals and organizations. What is considered an expenditure by one segment, is income to another segment. Hence, the total income of society is always equal to its total expenditures, in much the same way that the total assets of a business enterprise always equal its total equities. Although national income is measurable in terms of dollars, this definition of income is too broadly conceived to help the accountant determine the income earned by a specific business.

Psychic Income

Individuals do not always behave as purely rational economic beings, nor are they motivated solely by the objective of monetary profit. A potter, for example, may sell hand-crafted earthenware for very little monetary reward. However, the psychic or emotional income obtained in the form of creative, artistic accomplishment from such craftsmanship may provide sufficient compensation to offset a relatively low monetary income. Psychic income adds a new dimension to financial and economic considerations. But an application of the concept to specific cases is subject to wide variance of interpretation, and it is extremely difficult if not impossible to quantify in terms of dollars. To place a specific value on psychic income earned by an individual or business would probably be as difficult as to agree on the total worth of managerial talent and creativity within a business enterprise.

None of the preceding concepts of income, however valid for specific purposes, benefits the accountant to any great extent in determining the amount of income earned by a firm. The accountant requires a definition of income that can be measured in terms of dollars, one that is not too narrowly nor too broadly conceived.

THE ACCOUNTING CONCEPT OF INCOME

Accounting is primarily concerned with objectively measuring the income earned by separate accounting entities, particularly business organizations, during specific time-frames. Although the accounting profession has no direct responsibility for measuring the broad concept of national income, the financial information that accountants generate is frequently consolidated into national income statistics that are published at periodic intervals by the U.S. Department of Commerce. Neither does the accountant attempt to deal with psychic income, since the concept is too conjectural and is not subject to objective quantification and verification. Cash receipts and cash disbursements as they affect income are of interest to the accountant — but only in a very limited and restricted sense. An introductory exposure to the accounting concept of income will first examine the contents of a relatively simple income statement, then proceed to define several technical terms associated with income statements in general.

The Income Statement Illustrated and Interpreted

The income statement shown below reflects in some detail the total income and deductions from income that were recognized by the Simplex Corporation in carrying out its business activities during the fiscal year ended December 31, 1979. Notice two important aspects of this particular income statement:

Simplex Corporation
Income Statement
For the Year Ended December 31, 1979

Sales...		$460,000
Cost of goods sold..		350,000
Gross margin..		$110,000
Operating expenses:		
Wages and salaries.................................	$44,000	
Office and factory supplies......................	10,000	
Insurance...	7,000	
Rent...	6,000	
Interest...	4,000	71,000
Operating income...................................		$ 39,000
Other income:		
Rental income..		2,000
Income before gains and losses....................		$ 41,000
Gains and losses:		
Gain on sale of land................................	$ 8,000	
Loss on sale of marketable securities...........	(3,000)	5,000
Income before federal income tax...............		$ 46,000
Federal income tax expense (50%)................		23,000
Net income...		$ 23,000

(1) The income statement reflects the income-generating performance of the firm during a specific period of time, in this instance during the fiscal year ended December 31, 1979. In effect, it is a summary of all the income and expense producing activities that were associated with the firm's

operations during that particular time frame. Recall in contrast, that the balance sheet reflects the financial position of the firm at only one instant in time.

(2) The particular arrangement of this income statement is referred to as the *multiple-step* format, chiefly because it divides the information into multiple subcategories. The five subcategories in this instance are:
   (a) Gross margin.
   (b) Operating income.
   (c) Income before gains and losses.
   (d) Income before federal income tax (frequently called pretax income).
   (e) Net income (or after-tax profit). A federal income tax rate of 50 percent was assumed in this example for purposes of simplicity.[1]

Definitions and Terminology

Income is composed of three components: *revenue, other income,* and *gains*.

(1) *Revenue* is the increase in financial resources, such as cash and accounts receivable, that result from the sale of goods and services to customers. This activity is usually considered to be the principal activity of the firm, the financial effect of which is designated on the income statement as sales or selling revenue.

(2) *Other income* includes increases in financial resources, such as cash or a receivable, that arise from transactions which are considered secondary to the firm's main activity. Other income may include rental income, interest or dividends earned on investments, marketable securities, and notes receivable.

(3) A *gain* is a net increase in financial resources resulting from the sale or disposal of assets other than inventory, such as marketable securities, investments, and plant assets, at a price above their purchase cost. Gains may also include the repayment of financial obligations at less than their recorded monetary value or cost.

Other income and gains are normally classified separately from revenue on the income statement.

Deductions from income are usually divided into two components: *expenses* and *losses*.

(1) An *expense* is a decrease in the firm's financial resources that is associated with the sale of goods and services to customers. Expenses commonly reflected on the income statement include cost of goods sold and operating expenses such as employee compensation, insurance, interest, rent, and supplies. These expenses are matched with and deducted from revenue in the process of determining operating income.

(2) A *loss* is an economic sacrifice for which the firm receives no offsetting financial benefit. In technical terms, it is the net decrease in financial resources resulting from either the sale or disposal of an asset below its purchase cost, or the repayment of a financial obligation at a price exceeding its recorded monetary value or cost. Losses are normally shown separately from the operating expense items on the income statement.

---

[1]The technical procedures involved in allocating the federal income tax between (1) income before gains and losses, and (2) income after gains and losses are deferred to more advanced texts.

Net income is the difference between total income and total deductions from income. Restated:

Net Income = Revenue + Other Income + Gains − (Expenses + Losses).

An instance in which expenses plus losses exceed total income is referred to as a *net loss*.

The Income Determination Process

This chapter's primary focus is twofold: (1) to understand the relationship that exists between the income statement and the balance sheet; and (2) to become acquainted with the procedures involved in recognizing revenue and expenses. The bond between the two financial statements will be examined from the following perspectives before the process of income determination is illustrated with specific examples:

(1) Algebraic rearrangement.
(2) Diagrammatic flowchart.
(3) T account format.

Algebraic Rearrangement. The balance sheet equation was defined in the previous chapter as assets equal equities; or in the slightly expanded version as assets (A), equal liabilities (L), plus owners' equity (OE). This equality is expressed symbolically as:

$$A = L + OE \qquad [1]$$

Corporate owners' equity can be divided into two segments, capital stock (CS) and retained earnings (RE), as shown below:

$$OE = CS + RE \qquad [2]$$

By substituting Equation [2] for OE in Equation [1], the balance sheet equation becomes:

$$A = L + CS + RE \qquad [3]$$

Retained earnings normally reflect the accumulation of all net incomes that have been earned by the corporation during its lifetime which have not been distributed to stockholders in the form of dividends.

Equation [3] can be rearranged to read as follows:

$$RE = A - (L + CS) \qquad [4]$$

Net income was defined previously as revenue plus other income and gains, less expenses and losses. This definition will be simplified at this point in order to concentrate on the two principal elements of net income, namely revenue (Rev) and expenses (Exp), as shown below:

$$\text{Net Income} = \text{Rev} - \text{Exp} \qquad\qquad [5]$$

Inclusion of other income, gains, and losses in the above equation would merely extend and formally complete accounting's concept of net income.

Assuming no dividends have been declared during a specific period, such as a fiscal year, any change in retained earnings during that period can be said to equal revenue less expenses: in short, net income.

The algebraic symbol that is customarily used to denote a change in any particular account or item is the *delta notation* Δ. By incorporating this symbol into Equation [5], the change in retained earnings during a period can then be expressed as follows:

$$\Delta RE = \text{Rev} - \text{Exp} = \text{Net Income} \qquad\qquad [6]$$

By placing the Δ notation in front of each element in Equation [4], that equation can be transformed into the following:

$$\Delta RE = \Delta A - (\Delta L + \Delta CS) \qquad\qquad [7]$$

Close examination of Equations [6] and [7] reveals that a change in retained earnings can be viewed from either of two perspectives, as shown below:

$$\Delta RE = \underbrace{\text{Rev} - \text{Exp}}_{(a)} = \underbrace{\Delta A - (\Delta L + \Delta CS)}_{(b)} \qquad\qquad [8]$$

Restated verbally: the change in retained earnings during a specific period may be defined in either of the following ways:

(a) As the excess of revenue recognized during the period over the expenses matched against and deducted from that revenue ($\Delta RE = \text{Rev} - \text{Exp}$), which equals net income.
(b) As the net increase during the period in assets less the net increase in all equities other than retained earnings ($\Delta RE = \Delta A - (\Delta L + \Delta CS)$).

These two ways of perceiving the change in retained earnings are identical. Explanation (a) focuses on items that comprise the income statement; whereas explanation (b) focuses on the accounts upon which the balance sheet is based. When these are clearly seen and understood within the context of the duality concept as merely two views of net income, the critical integration of the two financial statements will have been largely accomplished.

Diagrammatic Flowchart. The preceding discussion may be summarized by diagramming this linkage using two abbreviated balance sheets, one at the beginning and one at the end of the 1979 fiscal year. It is the income statement for the 1979 fiscal year which provides the critical linkage or coupling bond between the two balance sheets, as shown below:

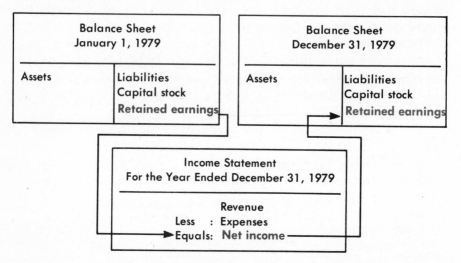

In interpreting the above diagram, recall the simplifying assumption that no dividends or other distribution of earnings were made to stockholders. Notice that this diagrammatic flowchart emphasizes explanation (a) of the change that occurred in retained earnings during fiscal year 1979; that is, the excess of recognized revenue over the expenses that are matched against and deducted from that revenue — $\Delta RE = Rev - Exp$.

T Account Format. The final perspective from which the linkage between the balance sheet and income statement will be examined is the structure of revenue and expense accounts associated with the income statement.

Since such a close relationship exists between the two financial statements, a logical question might arise concerning why the need exists to prepare both a balance sheet and an income statement. Since most consumers of accounting information place considerable emphasis on the income-producing activities of business enterprises, accountants developed the concept of the income statement in order to present income-related information in a concise format apart from the balance sheet. The income statement presented on page 72 accomplishes this objective. Had the income statement not been devised any person interested in obtaining income-related information would have been forced to extract it by laboriously searching among all of the balance-sheet-related accounts: in short, to investigate all the accounts associated with the equation $\Delta RE = \Delta A - (\Delta L + \Delta CS)$. This task would prove most cumbersome and time-consuming. Hence, the income statement is devised as a convenient method of explaining in detail the change that occurs in retained earnings as a result of rendering goods and services to customers.

The actual construction of the income statement and the accounts associated with that document can be illustrated by transforming and exploding the shaded portion of the retained earnings T account, shown below, into a master T structure of the income statement:

INCOME STATEMENT MASTER T

DEBITS are used to: INCREASE EXPENSE and DECREASE REVENUE accounts	CREDITS are used to: INCREASE REVENUE and DECREASE EXPENSE accounts

Which ultimately DECREASE Retained Earnings

RETAINED EARNINGS (OE)

Which ultimately INCREASE Retained Earnings

		Balance at beginning of period
Decrease DEBIT		Increase CREDIT
		Balance at end of period

Revenue and expense accounts appear in the general ledger along with all balance-sheet-related accounts. These income-statement-related accounts are frequently referred to as *temporary*, *nominal*, or *holding* accounts. As transactions occur during the period which affect revenue and expenses, monetary amounts are entered in these accounts by means of journal entries. The income statement is then prepared at the end of the period from the balances in the revenue and expense accounts. Finally, the ending balance in each revenue and expense account is "zeroed out" and transferred to Retained Earnings at the end of the period by what is referred to as the *closing entry* procedure.

The Income Determination Process Illustrated

The Melvin Corporation example that was previously developed within the context of the balance sheet will be expanded to include income-related activities by focusing on several transactions that occurred during the remaining eleven months of the fiscal year ended December 31, 1979.

Event 11

(a) Sale of Merchandise on Credit

Various home appliances were sold to customers during the remaining eleven months of 1979 on 30-day credit terms for $140,000. Financial resources flowed into the firm from these sales in the form of claims against customers for future cash payment, called *accounts receivable*. These revenue-producing activities resulted in a $140,000 increase in Accounts Receivable, a current asset, and a simultaneous increase in the income-statement-related account called Sales. All of the individual entries that were made during 1979 to record these individual credit sales may be condensed into the following summary entry:

```
Accounts Receivable (CA)..................................... 140,000
    Sales (IS)................................................            140,000
        Summary entry to reflect appliances sold under
        30-day credit arrangements during 1979.
```

Notice that the revenue account, Sales, is increased by crediting it, and that the (IS) notation following that account denotes it as an income-statement-related account. This credit to Sales will ultimately result in an increase in Retained Earnings, as shown in the income statement master T structure on page 77.

(b) Sale of Merchandise for Cash

An additional assortment of home appliances were sold during the 11-month period to various customers who paid $30,000 cash. The following summary entry reflects these sales of merchandise on cash terms:

```
Cash (CA)....................................................... 30,000
    Sales (IS)................................................            30,000
        Summary entry to reflect appliances sold for cash
        during 1979.
```

Event 12

Expense Inventory as Cost of Goods Sold

The total cost of appliances that were transferred to customers in these transactions must be matched as an expense against this revenue-generating activity. The total cost at which these particular appliances were carried in inventory was $120,000. The recognition of the expense, called Cost of Goods Sold, that must be matched against these sales is reflected in the following summary entry:

Cost of Goods Sold (IS)...................................... 120,000
decrease the Inventory (CA)... 120,000
    Summary entry to record as an expense the cost of
    appliances sold during 1979.

Notice that this entry results in the simultaneous decrease of a financial resource, Inventory, and an increase in an expense account, Cost of Goods Sold. The latter will ultimately result in a decrease in Retained Earnings.

The net effect of the two preceding entries on Melvin Corporation's income-producing activities during 1979 can be summarized as shown below:

Sales (revenue).. $170,000
Less cost of goods sold (expense)... 120,000
    Gross margin.. $ 50,000

This $50,000 net amount is referred to as the gross margin. *Gross margin* is not an account, but is the difference between sales revenue and the related expense called cost of goods sold. Another way of viewing this gross margin concept is to consider it as a $50,000 net increase in three current assets (cash plus accounts receivable, less inventory). See Equation [8] on page 75.

Event 13

Payments for Employee Compensation

Wages and salaries totaling $21,800 were paid to employees of the firm at various times during 1979, as reflected in the following summary entry:

Wages and Salaries Expense (IS) 21,800
    Cash (CA)... 21,800
    Summary entry to record employee compensation
    paid in cash during the year.

Again, note that this decrease in a current asset is offset by a simultaneous increase in an expense item. This will ultimately result in a decrease to Retained Earnings.

Event 14

Charge Prepaid Rent and Insurance to Expense

Recall that rent for the forklifts of $3,600 and insurance premiums of $600, covering the 12-month period ending December

31, 1979, were prepaid on January 18. Because the service benefits contained in those two financial resources expired during the year, it is customary to recognize this expiration as a normal expense of doing business during the period in which those benefits helped to generate revenue. The charging of these two prepaid items to expense is reflected in the following compound journal entry made at the end of the fiscal year:

```
Dec. 31  Rent Expense (IS) .....................................  3,600
         Insurance Expense (IS)..............................    600
             Prepaid Expenses (CA) ...........................           4,200
             Charge to expense the service benefits
             that expired during 1979 for rent and in-
             surance.
```

A *compound journal entry* is an entry that includes three or more accounts, and is frequently used to expedite the journalizing process. An entry in which only two accounts appear is referred to as a *simple journal entry*.

Event 15

Collection of Accounts Receivable

Several customers who purchased appliances under credit arrangements during 1979 paid their account balances prior to the year-end. These several collections of receivables amounted to $130,000 during the year, and are shown in the following summary entry:

```
Cash (CA).......................................................  130,000
    Accounts Receivable (CA) ...................................          130,000
    Summary entry to record collection of accounts re-
    ceivable during the fiscal year ending December
    31, 1979.
```

The above entry reflects the transformation of one current asset, accounts receivable, into another current asset, cash.

Event 16

Payments for Credit Purchases of Inventory and Supplies

Payments to various vendors from which Melvin Corporation purchased the appliances and supplies on credit terms in Events No. 8 and 9 totaled $163,000, as reflected in the following summary entry:

```
Accounts Payable (CL)........................................  163,000
    Cash (CA)...................................................          163,000
    Summary entry to record payments for credit pur-
    chases of inventory and supplies.
```

Event 17

Recognition of Federal Income Tax Expense

The amount of income tax assessed by and payable to the federal government must be determined at the end of 1979. The revenue and expense items that were recognized during 1979 and which had a direct impact on determining the income tax are summarized below:

Event No.

11	Sales (revenue)		$170,000
	Less expenses:		
12	Cost of goods sold	$120,000	
13	Wages and salaries	21,800	
14	Rent	3,600	
14	Insurance	600	146,000
	Total taxable income		$ 24,000

For purposes of simplicity the federal income tax assessment was 50 percent of taxable income. Hence, $12,000 ($24,000 × 50%) should be assigned as an expense to the income-generating activities of 1979, even though that amount would normally be paid in cash to the federal government during the first quarter of 1980. The entry to reflect the recognition of federal income tax expense is shown below:

```
Dec. 31  Federal Income Tax Expense (IS) ................  12,000
             Federal Income Tax Payable (CL)..............          12,000
             To record income tax expense associated
             with 1979 operations.
```

Restated, this tax assessment, even though payable in a subsequent fiscal period, is directly associated with income-producing activities during 1979 and is chargeable as an expense to the operations of 1979.

Tabular Summarization. The preceding seven events (Nos. 11–17) may now be summarized in the following tabular presentation on page 82, using the format of Equation [8] that was previously developed on page 75. The amounts shown on the first line of this table were rearranged and brought forward from the last line of the tabular summary presented on page 53.

Note the following points with respect to the summary:

(1) Events Nos. 1–10, 15, and 16 directly affected only balance-sheet-related accounts. In other words, changes may occur in asset, liability and capital stock accounts without affecting revenue, expenses, net income, or retained earnings.
(2) The only financial events which directly affected income-statement-related accounts during the fiscal year ended December 31, 1979, were

① of cess of Rev over Expenses
② net in⌐ does not → in equities other than RE

Melvin Corporation
Tabular Summary of Financial Events
For the Year Ended December 31, 1979

EVENT NO.	ΔRE	=	Rev	− Exp	=	Δ A	−(ΔL	+ ΔCS)
1–10		=			=	$681,700	−($481,700	$200,000)
11a	$140,000	=	$140,000 Sales		=	140,000 Accounts Receivable		
b	30,000	=	30,000			30,000 Cash		
12	− 120,000	=		−$120,000 Cost of Goods Sold	=	− 120,000 Inventory		
13	− 21,800	=		− 21,800 Wages and Salaries Expense	=	− 21,800 Cash		
14	− 4,200	=		− 3,600 Rent Expense − 600 Insurance Expense	=	− 4,200 Prepaid Expenses		
15		=			=	+ 130,000 Cash − 130,000 Accounts Receivable		
16		=			=	− 163,000 Cash	−(− 163,000 Accounts Payable	)
17	− 12,000	=		− 12,000	=		−(12,000 Taxes Payable	)
Total	$ 12,000	=	$170,000	−$158,000	=	$542,700	−$330,700	+$200,000)

transactions Nos. 11–14 and 17. In addition, these particular transactions also affected balance-sheet-related accounts.

(3) The increase in Retained Earnings (ΔRE) of $12,000 during this period can be interpreted from either of two perspectives:

(a) As the excess of revenue over expenses, or $170,000 − $158,000, as shown in the Rev-Exp column.

(b) As the net increase in assets less the net increase in all equities other than Retained Earnings [ΔA − (ΔL + ΔCS)], or $542,700 − ($330,700 + $200,000).

Preparation of the Income Statement. Each of the preceding journal entries is posted to its respective accounts in the general ledger. The information contained in these revenue and expense accounts will then be used to prepare an income statement for the particular fiscal period. An income statement, the essential detail of which is reflected in the preceding tabular summary (Rev-Exp column), is shown below for Melvin Corporation's fiscal year ended December 31, 1979, using the multiple-step format:

Melvin Corporation
Income Statement
For the Year Ended December 31, 1979

Sales..		$170,000
Cost of goods sold...		120,000
Gross margin..		$ 50,000
Expenses:		
Wages and salaries...	$21,800	
Rent..	3,600	
Insurance	600	26,000
Income before federal income tax............................		$ 24,000
Federal income tax expense (50%)		12,000
Net income		$ 12,000

The caption "Income before federal income tax" in the above illustration is equivalent to the "Operating income" caption shown on page 72 for the generalized income statement, because no "Other income" or "Gains or losses" occurred in the Melvin Corporation during 1979.

The Closing Entry. The final step involved in the revenue-expense recognition sequence is to transfer the balances of each income-statement-related account to Retained Earnings. This procedure is called the *closing entry* and is initiated at the end of a specific period of time, such as a month, quarter, or more usually at the end of each fiscal year. The closing entry in effect zeroes out the credit balances in all revenue accounts, and the debit balances in all expense accounts. These accounts are then ready to accumulate only those revenue and expenses associated with the next accounting period without intermingling amounts from prior periods.

The difference between total revenue and total expenses, or net income, can be transferred to Retained Earnings by means of the two-step closing procedure shown below:

```
Dec. 31  Sales (IS).............................................. 170,000
              Cost of Goods Sold (IS).........................         120,000
              Wages and Salaries Expense (IS) .............          21,800
              Rent Expense (IS) .................................           3,600
              Insurance Expense (IS)..........................             600
              Federal Income Tax Expense (IS) ..............          12,000
              Income Summary..................................          12,000
                   Zero out and transfer all income-state-
                   ment-related account balances to the in-
                   come summary account.
```

The income summary account is a *suspense account* which momentarily reflects the net income (or net loss) earned by the business during a particular period of time. In effect, the net income (or net loss) is suspended for one instant "in limbo" between the income statement and the balance sheet. Immediately, another entry is made to finally transfer the $12,000 net income from Income Summary to Retained Earnings, as shown below:

```
Dec. 31  Income Summary...................................... 12,000
              Retained Earnings (OE) .........................          12,000
                   Transfer net income from Income Summary
                   to Retained Earnings.
```

Because the income summary account exists for only a moment in time, no parenthetical designation is shown after the account in the above journal entries.

An alternate single-step closing procedure is frequently used by accountants to accomplish the same result as the two-step procedure outlined above:

```
Dec. 31  Sales (IS)............................................. 170,000
              Cost of Goods Sold (IS).........................         120,000
              Wages and Salaries Expense (IS) .............          21,800
              Rent Expense (IS) .................................           3,600
              Insurance Expense (IS)..........................             600
              Federal Income Tax Expense (IS) ..............          12,000
              Retained Earnings (OE) .........................          12,000
                   Single-step closing entry to zero out and
                   transfer all revenue and expense bal-
                   ances directly to Retained Earnings.
```

This single-step procedure dispenses with the income summary account, thereby expediting the closing procedure. In addition, notice that the preceding entry closely resembles the content of the income statement prepared on page 83. In short, the single-step procedure presents the essential content of the income statement in journal entry format, and more clearly shows the ultimate impact of the balances in the revenue and expense accounts on Retained Earnings.

Summary of Financial Events: Master T Structure. The essential information contained in the several transactions (1–17) which occurred in the Melvin Corporation during its entire first fiscal year of operations is summarized on page 86 using a master T structure. Data for events 1–10 were obtained from the master T structure shown on page 53.

Preparation of the Balance sheet. The balance sheet at December 31, 1979, may also be prepared after the closing entry has been recorded. Information that is reflected in the following balance sheet was extracted from the closing balance of each account as shown in the preceding Master T Structure:

Melvin Corporation
Balance Sheet
December 31, 1979

Assets		Equities	
Current Assets:		Current liabilities:	
Cash	$ 34,900	Notes payable	$ 20,000
Accounts receivable	10,000	Accounts payable	8,700
Inventory	35,000	Federal income tax	
Prepaid expenses	22,800	payable	12,000
Total current assets	$102,700	Total current liabilities	$ 40,700
Plant assets:		Long-term liabilities:	
Land	$ 40,000	Mortgage note payable	$ 40,000
Building	100,000	Bonds payable	250,000
Equipment	300,000	Total long-term	
Total plant assets	$440,000	liabilities	$290,000
		Owners' equity:	
		Capital stock	$200,000
		Retained earnings	12,000
		Total owners' equity	$212,000
Total assets	$542,700	Total equities	$542,700

Summary of the Debit-Credit Procedure. A complete summary of the debit-credit procedure is presented on page 87 with respect to all balance sheet and income statement-related accounts:

Melvin Corporation
Master T Structure
December 31, 1979

Assets

CASH (CA)

(1)	200,000	(5)	100,000
(2)	20,000	(6)	300,000
(4)	250,000	(7)	3,600
(11b)	30,000		600
(15)	130,000	(10)	6,100
		(13)	21,800
		(16)	163,000
Bal.	34,900		

ACCOUNTS RECEIVABLE (CA)

(11a)	140,000	(15)	130,000
Bal.	10,000		

INVENTORY (CA)

(8)	155,000	(12)	120,000
Bal.	35,000		

LAND (NA)

(3)	40,000		
Bal.	40,000		

EQUIPMENT (NA)

(6)	300,000		
Bal.	300,000		

PREPAID EXPENSES (CA)

(7)	3,600	(14)	4,200
	600		
(9)	22,800		
Bal.	22,800		

BUILDING (NA)

(5)	100,000		
Bal.	100,000		

Equities

ACCOUNTS PAYABLE (CL)

(10)	6,100	(8)	155,000
(16)	163,000	(9)	22,800
		Bal.	8,700

NOTES PAYABLE (CL)

		(2)	20,000
		Bal.	20,000

WAGES AND SALARIES PAYABLE (CL)

(13)	21,800		
Bal.	21,800		

FEDERAL INCOME TAX PAYABLE (CL)

		(17)	12,000
		Bal.	12,000

MORTGAGE NOTE PAYABLE (LL)

		(3)	40,000
		Bal.	40,000

BONDS PAYABLE (LL)

		(4)	250,000
		Bal.	250,000

CAPITAL STOCK (OE)

		(1)	200,000
		Bal.	200,000

RETAINED EARNINGS (OE)

		(cl)	12,000
		Bal.	12,000

SALES (IS)

(cl)	170,000	(11a)	140,000
		(11b)	30,000
		Bal.	-0-

COST OF GOODS SOLD (IS)

(12)	120,000	(cl)	120,000
Bal.	-0-		

RENT EXPENSE (IS)

(14)	3,600	(cl)	3,600
Bal.	-0-		

INSURANCE EXPENSE (IS)

(14)	600	(cl)	600
Bal.	-0-		

WAGES AND SALARIES EXPENSE (IS)

(13)	21,800	(cl)	21,800
Bal.	-0-		

FEDERAL INCOME TAX EXPENSE (IS)

(17)	12,000	(cl)	12,000
Bal.	-0-		

	ASSETS		EQUITIES	
Balance Sheet Accounts	*DEBIT* to *INCREASE*	*CREDIT* to *DECREASE*	*DEBIT* to *DECREASE*	*CREDIT* to *INCREASE*

	EXPENSES and LOSSES		REVENUE, OTHER INCOME, and GAINS	
Income Statement Accounts	*DEBIT* to *INCREASE*	*CREDIT* to *DECREASE*	*DEBIT* to *DECREASE*	*CREDIT* to *INCREASE*
	which *DECREASES* Retained Earnings	which *INCREASES* Retained Earnings	which *DECREASES* Retained Earnings	which *INCREASES* Retained Earnings

OWNERS' EQUITY IN A PROPRIETORSHIP AND PARTNERSHIP

To this point, the text has stressed the corporate form of business organization. With perhaps two major exceptions, the chart of accounts, account titles, and the arrangement of the balance sheet and income statement are virtually identical with respect to a corporation, partnership, and proprietorship. The first exception is that Income Tax Payable and Income Tax Expense do not appear in the chart of accounts of any unincorporated form of business, since federal and state income taxes are not directly assessed to a proprietorship or partnership. Recall that income tax assessments are levied directly against the respective proprietor or partners.

The other exception to uniform accounting treatment pertains to the owners' equity section of the balance sheet. The principal owners' equity accounts used in unincorporated businesses can be illustrated and compared with the accounts of a corporation, using an example in which John Knight is the sole owner of a proprietorship and Julio Rivas and Diana Junco are co-owners of a partnership:

CORPORATION	PROPRIETORSHIP	PARTNERSHIP
Capital Stock	Capital — John Knight	Capital — Julio Rivas
		Capital — Diana Junco
Retained Earnings	Drawing — John Knight	Drawing — Julio Rivas
		Drawing — Diana Junco

Investment by Ownership Interests

Each investment of financial resources by the various owners in each type of business is credited to Capital Stock under the corporate form, and to Capital — (owner's name) in the unincorporated form. For example, an investment of $10,000 cash in each type of business would be recorded as follows, using a comparative journal entry format, assuming Julio Rivas and Diana Junco invested $5,000 each:

	CORPORATION		PROPRIETORSHIP		PARTNERSHIP	
Cash (CA)............................	10,000		10,000		10,000	
Capital Stock (OE)		10,000				
Capital — John Knight (OE)...				10,000		
Capital — Julio Rivas (OE).....						5,000
Capital — Diana Junco (OE)..						5,000

Investment of $10,000 cash by respective ownership interests in each form of business organization.

Treatment of Net Income

The net income earned in each type of business is transferred from the income-statement-related accounts to Retained Earnings in the case of the corporation, and to each of the owners' capital accounts in the unincorporated forms. For example, the single-step closing procedure under each of the three forms of business organization is shown below, assuming: sales revenue of $15,000; cost of goods sold of $8,000; wages expense of $4,000; and the two partners sharing equally the net income of $3,000. Income taxes are ignored in this example:

	CORPORATION		PROPRIETORSHIP		PARTNERSHIP	
Revenue (IS)...........................	15,000		15,000		15,000	
Cost of Goods Sold (IS)..........		8,000		8,000		8,000
Wages Expense (IS)..............		4,000		4,000		4,000
Retained Earnings (OE)		3,000				
Capital — John Knight (OE)...				3,000		
Capital — Julio Rivas (OE).....						1,500
Capital — Diana Junco (OE) ..						1,500

Transfer balances in revenue and expense accounts to respective ownership interests in each form of business organization.

Distributions to Owners

A distribution of corporate earnings to stockholders in the form of a $1,000 cash dividend would be recorded as follows:

Retained Earnings (OE)	1,000	
Cash (CA)..		1,000

Payment of cash dividend to stockholders.

It should be noted that the distribution of a portion of retained earnings to stockholders in the form of a cash dividend is not an expense of the business, nor is it reflected on the income statement. A cash dividend is merely the distribution of some portion of current or prior-period net income to stockholders as partial compensation for the use of the funds they have invested in the corporation. Notice also that irrespective of the amount of net income generated in the current or prior periods, a sufficient cash balance must exist with which to pay the dividend.

Any withdrawal of cash by a proprietor or partner for whatever reason is normally charged against (debited to) that owner's drawing account. Each drawing account is an owners' equity (OE) account, rather than an income-statement-related account. Assume that $1,000 was withdrawn by the proprietor and $500 by each partner. The entry, in comparative format, would appear as shown below:

	PROPRIETORSHIP	PARTNERSHIP
Drawing — John Knight (OE)	1,000	
Drawing — Julio Rivas (OE)		500
Drawing — Diana Junco (OE)..........		500
Cash (CA)	1,000	1,000

Withdrawal of cash by ownership interests in unincorporated firms.

Any debit balance in a drawing account may be transferred at periodic intervals to the respective owner's capital account by means of the following entry:

	PROPRIETORSHIP	PARTNERSHIP
Capital — John Knight (OE)	1,000	
Capital — Julio Rivas (OE)		500
Capital — Diana Junco (OE)...........		500
Drawing — John Knight (OE)	1,000	
Drawing — Julio Rivas (OE)		500
Drawing — Diana Junco (OE).......		500

Transfer balances in respective owner's drawing accounts to capital accounts.

Note that each owner's capital account is reduced by transferring into it the debit balance from the respective drawing account.

Summary

The owners' equity section for each organizational type of business would appear as shown below after all of the previous transactions have been recorded:

CORPORATION		PROPRIETORSHIP		PARTNERSHIP	
Capital stock................	$10,000	Capital—John Knight	$12,000	Capital—Julio Rivas	$ 6,000
Retained earnings.........	2,000			Capital—Diana Junco	6,000
Total owners' equity ..	$12,000			Total owners' equity ..	$12,000

If debit balances in the proprietor's or either partner's drawing account were not transferred to the respective capital account prior to preparation of the balance sheet, the drawing account and its debit balance would be reflected in the owners' equity segment of the income statement.

The commonly used balance sheet titles that are affected by frequently experienced financial events or transactions in each of the three business forms are summarized in the following table.

Type of Financial Transaction or Event	Commonly Used Balance Sheet Titles		
	Corporation	Proprietorship	Partnership
Investment by owners	Capital Stock CREDIT	Capital—John Knight CREDIT	Capital—Julio Rivas Capital—Diana Junco CREDIT
Net income earned by the business	Retained earnings CREDIT	Capital—John Knight CREDIT	Capital—Julio Rivas Capital—Diana Junco CREDIT
Withdrawal of earnings from the business for distribution to owners	Retained earnings DEBIT	Drawing—John Knight DEBIT	Drawing—Julio Rivas Drawing—Diana Junco DEBIT

TIMING OF REVENUE AND EXPENSE RECOGNITION

Of considerable importance in the income determination process is the identification of the appropriate amounts of revenue and expenses to recognize during a particular accounting period. Several criteria or guidelines have been developed to assist the accountant in determining how much revenue and expense to recognize during a period. Generally, the following conditions should exist before revenue may be recognized:

(1) All costs have been incurred by the seller to make the goods or service transferable to a customer; or any future costs are relatively minor, or can be predicted with reasonable certainty.
(2) The seller's function in providing the goods or service is complete, that is, either the title has been transferred or the service has been performed; or whatever remains to be done by the seller is of relatively minor significance, or can be predicted with reasonable certainty.
(3) The amount to be collected by the seller from a specific customer has been determined.

An automobile dealer, for example, may recognize revenue if: all costs relevant to a transaction were incurred, or reasonably predicted by the dealer; the car is in the possession of the buyer; and the amount that the buyer is to be billed has been specified. A physician engaged to perform a routine appendectomy may recognize revenue if: most or all of the costs of performing the operation were incurred; the cost of post-operative treatment and examinations are of a routine or predictable nature; and the amount that the patient is to be billed has been determined.

Possible Points for Revenue Recognition

The general rule for revenue recognition is the passage of title to the customer. This legal event is usually evidenced either by delivery of goods to, or performance of service for the customer. However, at least six other events which normally occur during a firm's normal operating cycle appear as conceivable points at which revenue might be recognized. The three criteria previously outlined will be applied to each of these possible points shown on the following time-scale to determine the extent to which it fulfills these criteria.

POSSIBLE POINTS FOR REVENUE RECOGNITION

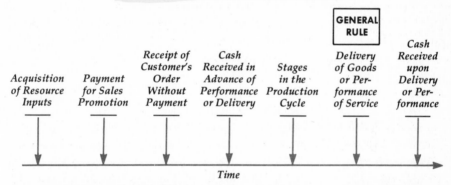

Time

Acquisition of Resource Inputs. Acquisition of materials, labor services, and other production or operating expenditures present a possibility for revenue recognition. Total input costs may have been paid for, and the price to be charged for the finished product or service may have been firmly established. But until the goods or service is in finished form, a particular buyer identified, and title to goods transferred, the accountant would not normally recognize any revenue. The fact that some uncertainty exists with respect to delivery or performance, plus the lack of a specific buyer, eliminates this event as an acceptable point on the time scale for revenue recognition.

Payment for Sales Promotion. Payment by the prospective seller for advertising and sales promotion activities, although a significant event, is normally considered to be merely a solicitation for customer orders. Even though the product or service advertised may be ready for delivery, with all major costs incurred or predictable and the sales price firmly established, specific customers cannot yet be identified. Until a specific customer is identified and the title to goods transferred or service performed for the customer, revenue should not be recognized.

Receipt of Customer's Order Without Payment. If the goods or service is ready for delivery, all major costs incurred, and the price firmly established, the receipt of an order from a specific customer with no accompanying payment might be considered an appropriate time for revenue recognition. However, an accountant would reason that either of two eventualities could occur: the customer might cancel the order; or the seller might be unable to deliver the goods or perform the service. Both eventualities contribute to the accountant's reluctance, founded on the principle of conservatism, to recognize a benefit until it actually occurs.

Cash Received in Advance of Delivery or Performance. It is not uncommon for firms to receive customer orders accompanied by prepayment for subsequent delivery of goods or performance of services. If a delay in filling a customer's order is expected to extend beyond a reasonable time, such as a week or beyond the fiscal year-end, the customary procedure is to create a *performance liability* in the accounting records of the order-receiving firm. Until the delivery or performance aspect of the transaction has occurred, the firm has incurred a financial obligation to either fill the order or return the advance payment. To illustrate, assume that a $4,000 prepayment accompanied an order from a wholesaler for several pieces of merchandise which were temporarily out of stock and the order could not be filled within ten days. An appropriate entry to record this event is as follows:

Cash (CA)..	4,000	
Performance Liability (CL)		4,000
Advance payment received for goods temporarily out of stock.		

Unearned Income is an alternate account title that is frequently used instead of Performance Liability.

When the order is filled, the appropriate entry to record the earning of income is shown below:

Performance Liability (CL)	4,000	
Sales (IS)..		4,000
Recognition of revenue and simultaneous removal of financial obligation to perform.		

In instances where the delay in filling a prepaid order is estimated to entail less than a week, it is customary to recognize revenue immediately upon receipt of the order, rather than create a performance liability that will shortly be eliminated upon performance or delivery.

Stages in the Production Cycle. Recognition of revenue at various stages of production or processing is sometimes mentioned as an appropriate time to recognize revenue. At first glance, revenue recognition during various stages of the production cycle appears justifiable in the case of standardized goods, such as passenger car tires, breakfast foods, and shoes, that are manufactured for stock at reasonably predictable costs and which have a ready market at an established price. As these items move nearer the end of the assembly line, they give the appearance of becoming more salable and thus more valuable products. An economist might argue: why not recognize small increments of the final selling price as revenue, and match the appropriate costs incurred as expenses with these revenue increments as the product moves nearer completion?

Accountants have squarely faced the merits of this issue and its consequences. Although the accumulated value of the product may increase as it moves toward completion and ultimate sale, no monetary amount should be recognized as revenue until the product is actually sold to a customer. Anticipation of a possible sale or benefit is not realization. Again recalling the principle of conservatism: although probable losses are usually recognized before they occur, anticipated gains or benefits generally are never recognized until they are actually realized. Revenue recognition prior to that point would be based on an arbitrary estimate of a benefit that may never occur.

Delivery of Goods or Performance of Service. This is the most frequently adopted time-point at which to recognize revenue. All three criteria are usually met in this instance: (1) most, if not all, costs have been incurred; (2) the seller has delivered the goods or performed the service with legal title to the goods or an equity in the service normally being transferred; and (3) a selling price to a specific customer has been established.

Percentage-of-Completion Contracts. It is sometimes permissible under rigidly specified circumstances for a vendor to recognize revenue prior to complete delivery, performance, or passage of title. For example, revenue may be recognized under enforceable written contracts that contain a firm selling price, plus other agreements, for delivery or completion at a future date. Such contracts often provide that partial payments are to be made to the seller at preselected intervals during the production process. Long-term projects like dams, ships, supersonic aircraft, and large electric turbines are frequently constructed under such arrangements. A percentage-of-completion contract differs significantly from what would otherwise appear to be revenue recognition at various stages in the production cycle; however, the percentage-of-completion contract contains a detailed written contractual statement which specifies particular terms that must be satisfied over an extended period of time.

For example, a written enforceable contract between a state government authority and a highway contractor might contain technical specifications for a particular ten-mile stretch of interstate highway to be constructed at a total price of $50,000,000. Assume the contract stated that the government authority is required to make progress payments of $10,000,000 to the contractor at the completion of each two-mile segment. In effect, partial legal title would be constructively transferred to the government authority under this type of arrangement as each two-mile segment is completed and paid for, even though part of the ten-mile stretch still remains unfinished. The highway contractor would be justified in recognizing revenue upon receipt of $10,000,000 for each two-mile segment completed.

Cash Received upon Delivery or Performance. Revenue would undoubtedly be recognized when cash is received by the seller upon delivery of merchandise or performance of service. But the principal signal that alerts the accountant to recognize revenue is not the receipt of the cash by the seller; rather, it is the delivery, or performance, and title transfer at an agreed price. Revenue recognition is warranted under a credit-term sales arrangement where the customer agrees to pay on or before a reasonable or specified date following delivery. Under such circumstances, an account receivable is the financial resource that is increased.

To summarize, the usual time to recognize revenue is when the product is delivered or the service is performed for the customer; in other words, when title passes from seller to buyer. Upon close inspection, the percentage-of-completion arrangement is merely delivery and title passage in incremental stages rather than all at once. Finally, it is not essential that the seller actually receives cash for revenue to be recognized if the three previously outlined criteria have been satisfied.

Matching Expense with Recognized Revenue

As a general rule, the benefits contained in such assets as inventory and prepaid expense items, and other costs, like wages and salaries are matched with revenue during the accounting period in which those activities helped generate the recognized revenue. This procedure was applied in a straightforward manner with respect to the sale of merchandise in the Melvin Corporation illustration. Revenue was recognized when legal title to merchandise was conveyed to customers, who in turn either paid $30,000 cash or incurred an obligation to pay a total of $140,000 under credit arrangements (Events 11a and 11b). The cost of the merchandise inventory associated with these sales, $120,000, was matched as an expense against revenue as merchandise was transferred to customers (Event 12). The benefits contained in labor services received from employees ($21,800 in Event 13) to help generate that revenue was also matched as an expense with the revenue recognized during the period. Other benefits contained in such items as insurance, rent, and supplies which expire with time or are consumed would also be reflected, along with wages and salaries, as operating expenses on the income statement.

Distinction Between Expense and Cost. The two terms, expense and cost, are considered under normal circumstances to convey a similar meaning. In accounting, however, a sharp distinction is usually made between the two terms. Generally, a *cost* is incurred either by means of cash payment or the creation of a liability. To illustrate, a company incurred a cost at the beginning of the fiscal year for various office supplies totaling $4,000, paying $3,000 cash immediately and incurring a liability to pay the remaining $1,000 within 30 days. This $4,000 total cost could be immediately *capitalized* as an asset, called prepaid expenses, as shown in the following entry:

(1) Prepaid Expenses (CA)................................. 4,000
     Cash (CA) 3,000
     Accounts Payable (CL)................................. 1,000
       Record purchase of various office supplies:
       $3,000 cash payment and balance due in 30
       days. Immediate capitalization of cost as an
       asset.

Some portion, or all, of the cost of these supplies would be charged to the income statement as an *expense* at a subsequent date as they are consumed in the process of helping to generate revenue. Assuming all of these prepaid supplies were consumed during the fiscal year, the entry to record the expiration or expensing of that cost would be as follows:

(2) Office Supplies Expense (IS) 4,000
      Prepaid Expenses (CA)............................... 4,000
        Record consumption of capitalized cost of office supplies during the year.

To summarize, entry (1) would be described as capitalizing a cost as an asset; whereas entry (2) would be referred to as charging a capitalized cost to expense, or expensing a cost. It should be noted that capitalized costs appear only on the balance sheet as assets (such as inventory, prepaid expenses, and plant assets); whereas expenses are expired costs which only appear on the income statement.

Another method of handling outlays for costs is to expense them immediately at the time of purchase. Outlays for advertising and sales promotion activities are usually charged to expense immediately upon payment or the incurrence of a liability for their payment. This treatment is based on the premise that the benefits contained in such outlays are difficult to identify as being directly associated with specific portions of recognized revenue or time frames. For example, a firm which received an $800 bill from the local newspaper for running a full-page advertisement would usually charge this item to expense immediately, as shown below:

Advertising Expense (IS) 800
    Cash (CA)... 800
      Incurrence of liability for advertising in local newspaper. Cost immediately charged to expense.

Percentage-of-Completion Contracts. The general rule concerning the timing of expense recognition is also applicable to percentage-of-completion contracts. For example, various costs associated with a highway construction project might be accumulated in such accounts as Inventory and Prepaid Expenses, where they would be held as capitalized costs pending recognition of revenue as each two-mile segment is completed. The capitalized costs associated with a specific segment of completed highway would then be charged to expense and matched with that portion of revenue which was recognized at the time payment was received from the customer.

To illustrate, assume that the contractor had incurred and capitalized (as assets) total costs of $9,000,000 when the initial $10,000,000 payment was received from the government authority for completion of the first two-mile segment of highway. Of this total, $7,000,000 was directly identifiable with the first segment, as shown below:

Inventory (consisting of construction materials)................... $6,500,000
Prepaid expenses (insurance, rent, and supplies)................   500,000
Total.. $7,000,000

Appropriate entries that might be recorded at the time the first $10,000,000 payment was received are shown below:

Cash (CA)... 10,000,000
   Sales (IS)...   10,000,000
     Recognition of revenue upon completion
     of first two-mile segment of highway.
Cost of Goods Sold (IS)............................ 6,500,000
   Inventory (CA).....................................   6,500,000
     Charging inventory to expense upon re-
     ceipt of payment for first two-mile seg-
     ment.
Insurance, Rent, and Supplies Expense (IS).....   500,000
   Prepaid Expenses (CA)   500,000
     Charging prepaid expenses to expense
     upon receipt of payment for first two-mile
     segment.

Losses and Gains

Certain assets other than inventory may be sold or disposed of during a period, which results in the recognition of a loss or gain. Recall that a loss was described as an event that generates no revenue or offsetting economic benefit, whereas expenses are generally compensated for through the revenue which they help generate. For example, the sale for $23,000 of marketable securities that were originally purchased for $27,000 would result in a recognizable loss of $4,000. The transaction is recorded as shown below:

Cash (CA)... 23,000
Loss on Sale of Marketable Securities (IS) 4,000
   Marketable Securities (CA)...............................   27,000
     Sale at $4,000 loss of marketable securities origi-
     nally costing $27,000.

A loss might also arise from fire, theft, or natural disaster. For example, a loss that was incurred because a new piece of machinery, originally costing $7,000, was totally destroyed by fire would be recorded as shown below:

Fire Loss (IS)... 7,000
   Machinery (NA)...   7,000
     Loss due to fire.

A gain on the sale of an asset may be illustrated by assuming that a company sold land at $5,000 more than its purchase cost of $56,000, as shown below:

Cash (CA)..	61,000	
Land (NA)		56,000
Gain on Sale of Land (IS).....................................		5,000
Sale of land, originally costing $56,000, for $61,000.		

All gains and losses should be reported under the "Gains and losses" caption on the income statement, as shown on page 72.

SUMMARY DEMONSTRATION PROBLEM AND SOLUTION

The following comprehensive problem provides a summary of several key concepts and procedures previously discussed.

Stolpe Furniture Corp. was formed as a retail furniture store on January 1, 1979, when three business associates invested $40,000 each and in return received 400 shares of $100 par value stock. The financial transactions described below occurred during the firm's first fiscal year of operations ended December 31, 1979. Income taxes and dividends are ignored in this summary problem.

(a) The cash investment by the three stockholders created the corporation, as described previously.

(b) Building and land were purchased for $120,000 under a 10-year mortgage note payable arranged at a local bank. Fifteen percent of the $120,000 cost was apportioned to the land.

(c) A large assortment of furniture and fixtures totaling $340,000 was purchased for inventory under 40-day credit terms.

(d) A cash outlay of $3,500 for advertising was immediately charged to expense.

(e) A bill of $12,000 for fire and casualty insurance premiums covering the first twelve months of operations, effective January 1, 1979, was received; and office and clerical supplies totaling $5,000 were purchased. Each of these items was purchased under 30-day credit terms and was capitalized as a prepaid expense.

(f) Sales during the year totaled $320,000, 10% of which were made on cash terms. The remaining portion of sales were made under 30-day credit arrangements. Cost of the furniture and fixtures associated with these sales amounted to $270,000.

(g) Wage and salary payments totaled $29,000.

(h) The entire amount of prepaid insurance was charged to expense on December 31, 1979; and $3,000 of office supplies were determined to have been used up during the year.

(i) Cash payment of accounts payable amounted to $295,000; and collections of accounts receivable totaled $202,000 during the year.

(j) A small fire completely destroyed some furniture in November, the original cost of the furniture was $600. Since the fire insurance policy contained a $1,000-deductible clause for items of inventory, no proceeds were obtained from the insurance company.

Required:

(1) Prepare a journal entry for each financial event. Prepare two entries for each of items (f) and (i). Use the general journal format illustrated on page 45.

(2) Prepare a master T structure, and post each of the financial transactions to individual T accounts. Place a check mark in the Posting Reference column of the general journal as each item is posted to respective T accounts.

(3) Prepare the closing entry, using the single-step method; and post this entry to appropriate T accounts.

(4) Determine the ending balance in each account at December 31, 1979.

(5) Prepare a balance sheet at December 31, 1979, and an income statement for the fiscal year ended December 31, 1979.

Suggested Solution:

(1)   JOURNAL   Page 1

Event	Description	Post. Ref.	Debit	Credit
(a)	Cash (CA)	✓	120,000	
	Capital Stock (OE)	✓		120,000
	Investment of $40,000 by each of 3 persons creates the corporation.			
(b)	Land (NA)..	✓	18,000	
	Building (NA)	✓	102,000	
	Mortgage Note Payable (LL)	✓		120,000
	Purchase of plant assets under Mortgage Note Payable arrangement: Land — $120,000 × .15 = $18,000.			
(c)	Inventory (CA)...	✓	340,000	
	Accounts Payable (CL)...............................	✓		340,000
	Purchase of merchandise for inventory on 40-day credit terms.			
(d)	Advertising Expense (IS)..............................	✓	3,500	
	Cash (CA)	✓		3,500
	Payment for advertising.			
(e)	Prepaid Expenses (CA)	✓	17,000	
	Accounts Payable (CL)...............................	✓		17,000
	Capitalization of insurance premiums and supplies purchased under 30-day credit terms.			
(f)	Cash (CA)	✓	32,000	
	Accounts Receivable (CA)	✓	288,000	
	Sales (IS)	✓		320,000
	Sale of merchandise on credit terms: $320,000 × .9 = $288,000.			

JOURNAL

Event	Description	Post. Ref.	Debit	Credit
(f)	Cost of Goods Sold (IS)............................	✓	270,000	
	Inventory (CA)...	✓		270,000
	Cost of merchandise sold charged to expense.			
(g)	Wages and Salaries Expense (IS)...................	✓	29,000	
	Cash (CA)	✓		29,000
	Payment of employee compensation.			
(h)	Insurance Expense (IS)..............................	✓	12,000	
	Office Supplies Expense (IS)	✓	3,000	
	Prepaid Expenses (CA)..............................	✓		15,000
	Charge to expense the expired or consumed portion of benefits contained in prepaid expenses.			
(i)	Accounts Payable (CL)..............................	✓	295,000	
	Cash (CA)	✓		295,000
	Payment of accounts payable.			
	Cash (CA)	✓	202,000	
	Accounts Receivable (CA).........................	✓		202,000
	Collection of receivables.			
(j)	Fire Loss (IS)...	✓	600	
	Inventory (CA).......................................	✓		600
	Loss due to fire.			

(2) and (4)

CASH (CA)

(a)	120,000	(d)	3,500
(f)	32,000	(g)	29,000
(i)	202,000	(i)	295,000
Bal.	26,500		

ACCOUNTS RECEIVABLE (CA)

(f)	288,000	(i)	202,000
Bal.	86,000		

INVENTORY (CA)

(c)	340,000	(f)	270,000
		(j)	600
Bal.	69,400		

PREPAID EXPENSES (CA)

(e)	17,000	(h)	15,000
Bal.	2,000		

LAND (NA)

(b)	18,000		
Bal.	18,000		

BUILDING (NA)

(b)	102,000		
Bal.	102,000		

ACCOUNTS PAYABLE (CL)

(i)	295,000	(c)	340,000
		(e)	17,000
		Bal.	62,000

MORTGAGE NOTE PAYABLE (LL)

		(b)	120,000
		Bal.	120,000

CAPITAL STOCK (OE)

		(a)	120,000
		Bal.	120,000

RETAINED EARNINGS (OE)

		(3)	1,900
		Bal.	1,900

SALES (IS)		
(3)	320,000	(f) 320,000
		Bal. —0—

ADVERTISING EXPENSE (IS)		
(d)	3,500	(3) 3,500
Bal.	—0—	

COST OF GOODS SOLD (IS)		
(f)	270,000	(3) 270,000
Bal.	—0—	

OFFICE SUPPLIES EXPENSE (IS)		
(h)	3,000	(3) 3,000
Bal.	—0—	

WAGES AND SALARIES EXPENSE (IS)		
(g)	29,000	(3) 29,000
Bal.	—0—	

FIRE LOSS (IS)		
(j)	600	(3) 600
Bal.	—0—	

INSURANCE EXPENSE (IS)		
(h)	12,000	(3) 12,000
Bal.	—0—	

(3) Sales (IS).. 320,000
    Cost of Goods Sold (IS).................................. 270,000
    Wages and Salaries Expense (IS)..................... 29,000
    Insurance Expense (IS).................................. 12,000
    Advertising Expense (IS)................................ 3,500
    Office Supplies Expense (IS).......................... 3,000
    Fire Loss (IS) 600
    Retained Earnings (OE)................................. 1,900
       Close out and transfer income-statement-
       related account balances to Retained Earnings.

(5)

Stolpe Furniture Corp.
Balance Sheet
December 31, 1979

Assets		Equities	
Current assets:		Current liabilities:	
Cash...........................	$ 26,500	Accounts payable...........	$ 62,000
Accounts receivable	86,000		
Inventory	69,400	Long-term liabilities:	
Prepaid expenses...........	2,000	Mortgage note payable ...	$120,000
Total current assets	$183,900		
		Owners' equity:	
		Capital stock.................	$120,000
Plant assets:		Retained earnings..........	1,900
Land...........................	$ 18,000	Total owners' equity.....	$121,900
Building	102,000		
Total plant assets	$120,000		
Total assets....................	$303,900	Total equities..................	$303,900

Stolpe Furniture Corp.
Income Statement
For the Year Ended December 31, 1979

Sales..		$320,000
Cost of goods sold......................................		270,000
Gross margin		$ 50,000
Expenses:		
Wages and salaries.................................	$29,000	
Insurance...	12,000	
Advertising	3,500	
Office supplies.....................................	3,000	47,500
Operating income		$ 2,500
Gains and losses:		
Fire loss		(600)
Net income		$ 1,900

QUESTIONS

1. Identify several reasons why groups who use accounting information would be interested in the accurate measurement of net income that is earned by a business during a particular period.

2. Distinguish between the following interpretations of income: (a) cash flow; (b) economic; (c) psychic; (d) accounting.

3. In what way may the accounting concept of income be considered a subdivision of economic income?

4. Enumerate reasons why the accountant is reluctant to adopt the cash flow, economic, and psychic viewpoints of income as methods by which to measure net income.

5. Distinguish between the income statement and the balance sheet with respect to the time dimension encompassed by each financial statement.

6. Define the following captions that appear on the income statement: (a) gross margin; (b) operating income; (c) income before gains and losses; (d) net income.

7. Identify and define the five components or elements of net income as used by the accountant.

8. Distinguish between an expense and a loss.

9. After defining each symbol in the following set of equations, indicate how this symbolic expression may be used to account for or explain the change in retained earnings during a fiscal period from two perspectives:

$$\Delta RE = Rev - Exp = \Delta A - (\Delta L + \Delta CS)$$

10. Explain how the income statement for a particular period can be used to illustrate the coupling-linkage between two balance sheets, one prepared at the beginning and one at the end of a specific period.

11. Explain the linkage that exists between the income statement and the balance sheet by expanding the Retained Earnings T account into the income statement master T.

12. The net income earned during a period by a business can be determined by noting the change in retained earnings between two balance sheets, one prepared at the beginning and one at the end of that period. Why then has the income statement been developed as a separate financial statement?

13. Why are income-statement-related accounts often called "temporary" or "holding" accounts?

14. A credit to an income-statement-related account ultimately results in an increase in retained earnings or each owner's capital account, whereas a debit to an income-statement-related account ultimately results in a decrease in retained earnings. Explain.

15. Define: (a) a compound journal entry; and (b) the gross margin.

16. A corporation reflected $20,000 sales revenue, $11,000 cost of goods sold, $6,000 wages expense, and $2,500 rent and insurance expense during the fiscal year. Prepare two closing entries: (a) the two-step entry involving the income summary account; and (b) the single-step method.

17. Explain the purpose of the closing procedure.

18. Income Summary can be viewed as a "suspense" account. Explain.

19. Explain in detail how merchandise that was sold by a retailing corporation under cash terms and the related expense, cost of goods sold, ultimately affect retained earnings.

20. Prepare separate journal entries to zero out and transfer $9,000 from Income Summary to appropriate owners' equity accounts in: (a) a corporation; and (b) a partnership involving two persons, each of whom shares equally in the profits.

21. How are the terms debit and credit used to denote an increase or decrease in the following types of accounts:

    (a) Asset   (e) Other Income
    (b) Liability   (f) Gain
    (c) Owners' Equity   (g) Expense
    (d) Revenue   (h) Loss

22. Explain why a cash dividend to stockholders is not an expense that is charged or matched against revenue.

23. Illustrate by using journal entries how a payment of a $4,000 cash dividend to stockholders differs from the withdrawal of the same amount from a proprietorship by its owner.

24. You are handed an assortment of balance sheets, none of which contain any balance sheet heading. How may the organization form of each business be determined?

25. Identify an asset account that contains the term "expense" in its title, and an expense account that contains the term "cost" in its title.

26. Identify and explain three guidelines which assist the accountant in deciding when to recognize revenue.

27. (a) Specify which of seven possible points in the operating cycle of a business is considered the appropriate time to recognize revenue. (b) Explain the principal objection to using each of the other six apparent possibilities.

28. (a) Under what circumstance may a performance liability arise; and (b) what financial event signals the accountant to dispose of that performance liability?

29. Explain the principal reason why revenue is not recognized during various stages in the production cycle.

30. Does revenue recognition under a percentage-of-completion contract contradict the general rule which applies to the recognition of revenue? Explain.

31. (a) Provide an example in which revenue or other income is not recognized even though cash flows into the firm. (b) Provide an example in which revenue is recognized even though the cash balance does not increase.

32. Distinguish a cost from an expense.

33. How are the following terms related: (a) asset; (b) capitalized cost; and (c) expense?

34. Provide an illustration where: (a) an expense is recognized prior to cash outflow; and (b) cash outflow precedes recognition of an expense.

35. Prepare the journal entry under each of the following conditions to record the cash sale of a parcel of land that was originally purchased for $74,000: (a) sale for $84,000; (b) sale for $57,000; (c) sale for $74,000.

EXERCISES

1. **Components of income.** Determine the revenue, total expenses, and net income for the fiscal year ended December 31 from information supplied below, assuming no dividends were paid to stockholders:

Total gains realized during the year	$ 3,000
Total losses incurred during the year	6,000
Other income realized	2,000
Increase in retained earnings during the year	29,000

Revenue exceeded total expenses by 50% for the year.

2. **Gross margin.** Midwestern TV Corporation operated as a retailer of television sets and cabinets. During its first fiscal year of operations ending September 30, the firm billed customers $89,000 for various TV sets and cabinets. Eighty percent of these sales were made under 90-day credit terms, and the remainder was for cash. Credit sales of $19,000 still remained uncollected at September 30. The cost of all TV sets and cabinets purchased during the fiscal year totaled $68,000, of which $57,000 represented the purchase cost of those sold to customers during the year.

Required: Determine the corporation's gross margin for its first fiscal year of operations.

3. **Multiple-step income statement.** From the account balances shown below and on top of page 105, prepare an income statement for Cogswell Corp. for the fiscal year ended December 31, 1979. Use the multiple-step format shown on page 72.

	BALANCE AT DECEMBER 31, 1979 (CREDIT)
Accounts Payable	$(120,000)
Accounts Receivable	50,000

	BALANCE AT DECEMBER 31, 1979 (CREDIT)
Advertising Expense	16,000
Commissions Expense	15,000
Cost of Goods Sold	280,000
Dividend Income	(3,500)
Federal Income Tax Expense	40,000
Gain on Sale of Marketable Securities	(8,000)
General Administrative Expense	20,000
Insurance Expense	5,000
Inventory	210,000
Loss on Disposal of Buildings	4,000
Office Expense	4,000
Rent Expense	10,000
Rental Income	(2,500)
Sales	(480,000)
Wages and Salaries Expense	60,000

4. Transaction analysis: journal entry format. Each of the following financial events occurred during September in Bamberger's Luggage Shoppe:

(1) Rent was prepaid for three months, effective September 1, at the rate of $600 per month.

(2) Various articles of luggage totaling $8,000 were purchased for inventory during the month on 20-day credit terms.

(3) Wages amounting to $1,700 were paid to two employees for services rendered.

(4) Inventory originally costing $3,500 was sold for $5,000 cash.

(5) Seventy percent of the credit purchases in (2) were paid.

(6) Rent expense for September was recognized.

Required: Prepare a journal entry to record each of the above events, using appropriate income-statement-related accounts where necessary. Prepare two entries for transaction (4).

5. Accounts/notes payable and accounts/notes receivable. Sangria Corp. purchased two air-conditioning units from Taylor, Inc., during the year for which Sangria Corp. was billed $47,000. Terms of payment were: $37,000 under a 60-day account payable arrangement; and the remaining $10,000 under a 150-day note payable arrangement. Sangria Corp. paid $37,000 on June 30 and the $10,000 note on October 31. (Interest charges are ignored in this instance.)

Required: Prepare the entry that would be made in the accounting records of: (a) Sangria Corp. on June 30; (b) Taylor, Inc., on June 30; (c) Sangria Corp. on October 31; (d) Taylor, Inc., on October 31.

6. Transaction analysis: T account format. The following events took place during the month of June in Waring's Photo Mart:

(1) Photographic equipment and supplies were purchased for inventory totaling $30,000, 40% of which was paid in cash, the remainder bought under 30-day credit terms.

(2) A fire and casualty insurance premium totaling $6,000 for six months was paid. The policy's effective date was June 1.

(3) The proprietor withdrew $2,500 cash from the business for personal expenses.

(4) Various photographic supplies and equipment costing $14,000 were sold for $25,000. Sixty percent of the sales were made under 30-day credit arrangements, and the balance for cash.

(5) Insurance expense for the month was recognized.

(6) All except $4,000 of accounts receivable had been collected by the end of June.

Required: Prepare necessary T accounts, and enter each of the transactions in those accounts.

7. **Closing entry: single-step procedure.** The following were account balances at the end of a recent fiscal year in the McElhenny Corporation:

	BALANCE AT END OF FISCAL YEAR (CREDIT)
Accounts Payable	$(34,000)
Accounts Receivable	29,000
Advertising Expense	17,000
Cash	28,000
Cost of Goods Sold	55,000
Insurance Expense	7,000
Office Supplies Expense	2,000
Prepaid Expenses	16,000
Rent Expense	4,500
Sales	(97,000)
Wages and Salaries Expense	10,300

Required: Prepare the closing entry, using the single-step procedure, to close out and transfer the balances in income-statement-related accounts to the appropriate owners' equity account.

8. **Closing entry: two-step procedure.** The accounts shown below for Salvatore Construction Company at the end of the 1980 fiscal year reflected the balances indicated:

	DEBIT (CREDIT)
Accounts Receivable	$ 38,000
Advertising Expense	6,500
Capital — J. Salvatore	(84,000)
Capital — N. Salvatore	(61,000)
Cost of Goods Sold	86,000
Drawing — J. Salvatore	12,000
Inventory	69,000
Prepaid Expenses	31,000
Property Tax Expense	1,200
Rent and Insurance Expense	8,300
Salaries and Commissions Expense	28,000
Sales	(135,000)
Supplies Expense	3,000

Required: Prepare the necessary closing entries, using the two-step procedure, to close out and transfer the balances of income-statement-related accounts to the appropriate owners' equity accounts, presuming the net income or net loss is shared equally by each of the two partners.

9. **Cash dividend payment.** After determining that the Frangipani Corporation earned a net income of $65,000 during the current fiscal year, the board of directors decided to pay a $35,000 cash dividend to stockholders.

Required: (a) Prepare a journal entry to record the payment of the cash dividend. (b) To what extent would the $35,000 cash dividend be reflected on the firm's income statement as an expense item?

10. **Partnership equity accounts.** Diane Foltz and Fran Balboa created a children's ready-to-wear shop on January 1. Foltz invested $30,000 cash and Balboa, $20,000. Any profit or loss was to be shared in the same ratio as these initial investments. The net loss incurred during the first fiscal year ending December 31 was $7,000. Foltz and Balboa withdrew cash from the business during the year for personal expenses amounting to $9,000 and $7,500 respectively.

Required: (a) Prepare an entry to close out each owner's drawing account to her respective capital account. (b) Determine the balance in each owner's capital account after all closing entries are presumed to have been made. Show calculations.

11. **Performance liability.** The Langhorne Corporation received an order of $7,500 for specialized hi-fidelity recording equipment on April 10, accompanied by the customer's check for that amount. The shipping manager discovered that various components associated with the order were out of stock, making it necessary to delay shipment until April 28. The total order, which was carried in inventory at a cost of $5,200, was shipped to the customer on April 28.

Required: Prepare whatever journal entry is required to record the following transactions: (a) The receipt of order on April 10. (b) The shipment of equipment on April 28. (Prepare two entries).

12. **Percentage-of completion contract.** The Plattesbury Construction Corp. entered into a written contract with the U.S. Government's Corps of Engineers on February 1 to construct a dam across a river system in a nearby county. The contract price for the entire job was $7,000,000, and completion of the job was expected to entail 22 months.

Terms of the agreement specified that the government would forward payments to the corporation as each 10% of the total project was completed; for example, at the first 10% interval, $700,000 would be received; and an additional $700,000 for each 10% increment thereafter. The construction company intended to charge to expense appropriate amounts of inventoriable supplies and prepaid expenses associated with completed segments of the dam as progress payments were received.

The initial 10% progress payment was received on March 20, at which time the following costs had been incurred by the contractor:

	TOTAL COST INCURRED	PERCENT ASSOCIATED WITH INITIAL 10% SEGMENT
Inventoriable supplies....................	$900,000	80%
Prepaid insurance and rent expense	50,000	60%

Required: (a) Prepare the entry on March 20, to recognize the appropriate amount of revenue. (b) Prepare an entry on the same date to recognize the appropriate amount of expenses to be matched against the revenue. (c) Determine the net income earned or loss incurred on this initial segment of the total dam project.

13. **Cost, expense, and loss distinctions.** The series of activities outlined below occurred in the Palmerston Department Store during August:

(1) A bill was received from a fire and casualty insurance company on August 5 for a one-year $12,000 insurance premium, effective August 1. The payment was capitalized as a cost.

(2) Rent totaling $2,500 was paid for August and immediately recorded in an income-statement-related account.

(3) The cost of inventory associated with sales amounted to $324,000.

(4) A fire destroyed a new annex building, originally costing $56,000.

(5) Inventory totaling $168,000 was purchased on 30-day credit terms.

(6) Prepaid insurance applicable to August expired at the end of the month.

(7) Checks totaling $91,000 were forwarded to various vendors for credit purchases of inventory.

Required: Using the format shown below, classify each of the above activities as indicated:

EVENT NO.	CAPITALIZED COST	EXPENSE	LOSS	COMMENTS

14. **Recognition of loss and gain.** The three events described below occurred outside the range of normal business activities experienced by the Olgivie Corporation:

(1) A portfolio of marketable securities originally purchased at $27,000 was sold for $32,000.

(2) A parcel of land originally costing $86,000 was disposed of for $73,000.

(3) A tornado completely leveled a company warehouse that had been built for $62,000. The insurance company forwarded a check for $48,000 to the company as final payment for the damages.

Required: Prepare a separate journal entry to record each event.

PROBLEMS

3-1. **Account classification and normal balances.** Indicate in which subcategory (CA, NA, CL, LL, OE, IS) each account listed title is classified. Note that some account titles pertain to different organizational forms of business. In addition, indicate whether the normal account balance is debit or credit. The cash account provides a guideline.

ACCOUNT TITLE	SUBCATEGORY	NORMAL BALANCE
Cash...	CA	DR.
Accounts Payable		
Accounts Receivable		
Advertising Expense		
Bonds Payable (due six months from today)....		

Account Title	Subcategory	Normal Balance
Buildings	____	____
Capital — J. T. Bryan	____	____
Cost of Goods Sold	____	____
Drawing — P. Kovacs	____	____
Equipment and Machinery	____	____
Fire Loss	____	____
Gain on Sale of Equipment	____	____
Heat, Light, and Power Expense	____	____
Income Summary	____	____
Insurance Expense	____	____
Inventory	____	____
Land	____	____
Property Tax Expense	____	____
Property Tax Payable	____	____
Loss on Damaged Inventory	____	____
Marketable Securities	____	____
Mortgage Note Payable (due in five years)	____	____
Notes Payable (short-term)	____	____
Notes Receivable	____	____
Office Salaries Expense	____	____
Office Salaries Payable	____	____
Office Supplies Expense	____	____
Other Income	____	____
Patents	____	____
Performance Liability (unearned income)	____	____
Prepaid Expenses	____	____
Rent Income	____	____
Retained Earnings	____	____
Sales	____	____
Wages and Salaries Expense	____	____

3-2. Financial statement preparation. The following account balances appeared in the general ledger of the Corvallis Company immediately prior to closing the account records for the fiscal year ended June 30, 1980:

Account Title	Debit (Credit)
Accounts Payable	$ (55,000)
Accounts Receivable	36,000
Advertising Expense	7,000
Bonds Payable (due 1986)	(80,000)
Buildings	112,000
Capital Stock	(210,000)
Cash	38,000
Cost of Goods Sold	173,000
Equipment and Machinery	191,000
Federal Income Tax Expense	24,000
Fire Loss	12,000
Gain on Sale of Machinery	(14,000)
Insurance Expense	5,000
Inventory	91,000
Land	62,000
Loss from Theft	3,000
Marketable Securities	14,000

ACCOUNT TITLE	DEBIT (CREDIT)
Mortgage Note Payable (due 1987)	(77,000)
Notes Payable (short-term)	(62,000)
Notes Receivable	7,000
Patents	48,000
Prepaid Expenses	16,000
Property Tax Expense	1,000
Rent Expense	6,000
Rental Income	(4,000)
Retained Earnings	?
Salaries Expense	16,000
Sales	(286,000)
Supplies Expense	2,000
Taxes Payable	(19,000)
Unearned Income	(6,000)
Utility Expense	3,000
Wages Expense	28,000

Required: (1) Prepare an income statement in multiple-step format for the year ended June 30, 1980. Note that the Retained Earnings balance must be determined.

(2) Prepare the balance sheet at June 30, 1980.

(3) Prepare the single-step closing entry that would have been recorded at June 30, 1980.

3-3. **Two-sided nature of each transaction.** Each of the financial events described below occurred in the Isomer Corp. during March.

(a) Isomer Corp. issued and sold a $40,000 bond issue to an insurance company, due for repayment in five years. The insurance company forwarded the cash to Isomer Corp. and treated the bonds received as long-term investment in its account records.

(b) Various items were purchased for inventory on 30-day credit terms from a local wholesaler. The invoice price of the goods to Isomer Corp. was $16,000, and the cost of those goods in the records of the wholesaler was $12,000. (Prepare two entries for the wholesaler.)

(c) Isomer Corp. billed Tactite Co. for $20,000 of merchandise, 60% of which was sold under 30-day credit terms, and the balance paid for in cash. Tactite Co. recorded the purchase as an addition to its inventory. The cost at which the merchandise sold to Tactite Co. was carried in Isomer Corp's inventory was $15,500. (Prepare two entries for Isomer Corp.)

(d) A customer forwarded $14,000 in payment of its account for merchandise purchased from Isomer Corp. during the previous month.

(e) Prepaid rent which expired during March totaled $780.

(f) A fire insurance premium for $900 was prepaid. The insurance company treated the receipt of cash as earned revenue.

Required: Prepare two journal entries for each transaction: (1) the entry or entries that would be recorded in the records of Isomer Corp.; and (2) the entry or entries that would appear in the accounting records of any other business or individual who was a party to the transaction.

3-4. Transaction analysis: tabular summary format. Lois Phares received a franchise from Consolidated Motors Corporation in June, 1979, to establish a car dealership. With $50,000 obtained from her personal resources and local business acquaintances, plus a $45,000, 3-year bank loan, Phares installed herself as president and began operations of Phares Wheels Corp. on July 1, 1979. The following financial transactions occurred during the first six months of 1979:

(a) The original investment by Phares and other business associates in exchange for 500 shares of $100 par value capital stock created the corporation. The bank loan was obtained at the same date.

(b) Phares arranged financing terms on July 1 with Valley Savings and Loan Association for the purchase of the following plant assets:

	COST
Land	$ 10,000
Building	30,000
Equipment and Fixtures	70,000
Total	$110,000

The association loaned Phares Wheels Corp. 80% of this total cost under a 4-year mortgage note payable arrangement whereby the $88,000 was to be repaid in four equal installments beginning July 1, 1980. (Interest charges on all loans are ignored in this problem.) The balance of the purchase cost was paid in cash.

(c) Phares Wheels Corp. received from Consolidated Motors Corporation the new car models shown below:

QUANTITY	MODEL	SUGGESTED RETAIL PRICE PER CAR
30	4-door sedan	$6,000
20	2-door sedan	4,500
40	Hardtop	5,000

The cost and terms of sale to Phares Wheels Corp. were 70% of the suggested retail price payable 90 days from delivery date.

(d) The following prepaid items were purchased on 30-day credit terms, 80% of which were paid by December 31, 1979:

Insurance premiums (for one year beginning July 1, 1979)	$ 3,000
Maintenance and repair supplies	5,000
Office supplies	2,000
Service shop supplies	4,000
Spare auto parts	11,000
Total	$25,000

(e) Prepaid expenses consumed and charged directly to appropriate expenses accounts from Prepaid Expenses were:

Maintenance and repair supplies	$2,000
Office supplies	500
Service shop supplies	1,500
Spare auto parts	3,000
Total	$7,000

In addition, one-half year of the prepaid insurance expired and was expensed on December 31.

(f) By December 31, only $40,000 remained to be paid to Consolidated Motors Corporation for the new cars delivered to Phares Wheels Corp. during the year.

(g) During November, one hardtop was stolen and another was completely destroyed by fire. All but $1,600 of the total purchase cost of both hardtops was recovered in cash from the insurance company by November 30. No further settlement was anticipated.

(h) The following cars were sold at their suggested retail price under 90-day credit arrangements:

	QUANTITY
4-door sedan	22
2-door sedan	15
Hardtop	34

By December 31, $200,000 of these accounts receivable had been collected.

(i) Wages and salaries paid to employees, including Phares, totaled $72,000.

(j) Utility expenses totaling $4,000 for heat, light, and power were paid.

Required: (1) Construct a tabular summary (similar to the format shown on page 82) of the events that occurred during the first six months. Journal entries need not be prepared.

(2) Prepare a closing entry at December 31, 1979, using the two-step procedure.

3-5. Transaction analysis: journal entry format and income statement preparation. Landscapers, Inc., was organized as a corporation in the mid-1970's to originate and implement architectural landscaping designs for industrial and residential clients. The following financial events occurred during the fiscal year ending August 31, 1980.

(a) Cash payments for advertising totaling $14,500 were immediately charged to expense upon payment.

(b) Wages and salaries paid during the year amounted to $85,500.

(c) The following prepaid expense items were purchased under the terms indicated below:

	CASH PAYMENT	30-DAY CREDIT PURCHASE
Repair and maintenance supplies	—0—	$ 8,000
Office supplies	—0—	4,000
Insurance premiums (effective January 1, 1980, for 1980 calendar year, at $1,500 per month)	$18,000	—0—
Rent (effective January 1, 1980, for 9-month period ending September 30, 1980, at $3,000 per month)	27,000	—0—
Total	$45,000	$12,000

(d) Clients were billed a total of $397,000 on 40-day credit terms during the fiscal year. Of that amount, $316,000 had been collected by the fiscal year-end. In addition, $34,000 of outstanding accounts receivable at September 1, 1979, were collected during the fiscal year ended August 31, 1980.

(e) Costs of inventoriable goods, such as plantings and construction materials, associated with the current period sales totaled $261,000.

(f) Goods purchased for inventory on 30-day credit terms totaled $314,000, of which $280,000 had been paid by August 31, 1980.

(g) Appropriate amounts of insurance and rent that had been paid during the 1980 calendar year were charged to expense. In addition, $4,800 of insurance premiums and $12,500 of rent that were reflected in the Prepaid Expenses balance on September 1, 1979 were charged to expense.

(h) Repair, maintenance, and office supplies purchased in item (c) were fully paid for as of the end of the fiscal year. Ninety percent of each type of supplies was charged to expense during the fiscal year.

Required: (1) Prepare appropriate journal entries for each of the financial transactions.

(2) Prepare an income statement for the fiscal year ended August 31, 1980.

3-6. Transaction analysis: T account format and closing entries. Jane and Robert Finnegan formed Finest Cleaning in the mid-1960's as a partnership which specialized in laundering and drycleaning expensive wearing apparel and home furnishings. The financial position of the firm at January 1, 1979, can be determined from the balance-sheet-related-accounts shown below:

	DEBIT (CREDIT)
Cash	$ 27,000
Accounts Receivable	47,000
Inventory	28,000
Prepaid Expenses	15,000
Land	30,000
Buildings and Fixtures	81,000
Delivery Equipment	41,000
Machinery	107,000
Accounts Payable	(62,000)
Notes Payable (short term)	(35,000)
Unearned Income (gift certificates)	(6,000)
Mortgage Note Payable (due 1985)	(122,000)
Capital — Jane Finnegan	(88,000)
Capital — Robert Finnegan	(74,000)
Drawing — Jane Finnegan	11,000

The following information summarizes transactions which occurred during the fiscal year ended December 31, 1979. The only items passing through the inventory account were supplies used in cleaning, laundry, and packaging aspects of the business. The partnership agreement contained the provision that any net income or net loss would be shared equally by the two partners.

(a) Sales generated during the year totaled $980,000, of which $870,000 were on cash-and-carry terms, the remainder under 30-day charge-and-deliver arrangement. [Note item (h) below.]

(b) The accounts receivable balance at December 31, 1979, was $31,000.

(c) The following inventory and prepaid expenses were purchased during the year. Only one prepaid expenses account was used.

ITEM	IMMEDIATE CASH PURCHASE	30-DAY CREDIT TERM PURCHASE	TOTAL
Prepaid expense items:			
Delivery and office supplies.......	$ 8,000	$ 25,000	$ 33,000
Liability, fire, and casualty insurance premiums	—0—	14,000	14,000
Rent	20,000	142,000	162,000
Repair and maintenance supplies	—0—	6,000	6,000
Total prepaid expense items ...	$28,000	$187,000	$215,000
Inventory (detergent, solvents, wrappers, etc.)	16,000	404,000	420,000
Total all items	$44,000	$591,000	$635,000

(d) Prepaid expense items were charged to expense in the following amounts:

Delivery and office supplies...	$ 28,000
Insurance premiums	14,000
Rent on numerous shopping center locations	150,000
Repair and maintenance supplies.......................................	7,000
Total..	$199,000

(e) The Inventory balance at December 31, 1979 reflected $36,000. All credit entries to Inventory were offset by debits to Cost of Goods Sold.

(f) Various items of plant and equipment totaling $74,000 were purchased, while others were sold during the year. Amounts shown in the first two columns reflect the original cost of respective assets either purchased or sold during the year:

ITEM	ORIGINAL COST PURCHASED FOR CASH	SOLD	CASH RECEIVED FROM SALE OF ASSETS
Buildings and fixtures............	$25,000	$18,000	$39,000
Delivery equipment..............	17,000	15,000	6,000
Machinery..........................	32,000	48,000	21,000
Total...............................	$74,000	$81,000	$66,000

(g) The Accounts Payable balance at December 31, 1979, was $83,000.

(h) Several customers purchased gift certificates during December for $15,000. These certificates entitled recipients to a specified amount of laundry and cleaning services during 1980. All certificates outstanding at January 1, 1979, had been redeemed in 1979, the offsetting credit being made to Sales in addition to what had previously been recorded in item (a).

(i) Employee wage expenses paid totaled $261,000.

(j) Property tax and utility expenses paid totaled $18,000 and $39,000, respectively.

(k) Jane and Robert withdrew $16,000 and $23,000, respectively, from the business during the year for personal expenses.

Required: (1) Prepare a master T account structure containing all accounts and their respective balances at January 1, 1979. Then post each of the transactions to these accounts, originating new accounts as required. Support any posting with clarifying comments where appropriate.

(2) Determine the balance in each account at December 31, 1979.

(3) Prepare, but do not post, a single-step closing entry to transfer all income-statement-related accounts to respective capital accounts at December 31, 1979.

(4) Prepare, but do not post, the entry to transfer balances in each owner's respective drawing account to the capital account.

3-7. Percentage-of-completion-contract: cash flow and net income. Orion Corp. signed a contract in early 1978 to construct and deliver to Mulvern Oil Corporation a 300,000 deadweight-ton capacity oil tanker at a price of $100,000,000. Anticipated time to completion was 22 months, and the total expenses associated with the project were forecast at $80,000,000. Progress payments were required to be made by the oil company to the shipbuilder at specific intervals according to the following schedule contained in written agreement:

PROGRESS PAYMENT NO.	WHEN THE PERCENTAGE OF THE TOTAL COMPLETED PROJECT EQUALS	THE CUMULATIVE PROGRESS PAYMENTS THAT MUST BE FORWARDED TO ORION CORP. MUST EQUAL THE FOLLOWING PERCENTAGE OF THE TOTAL CONTRACT PRICE OF $100,000,000
1	10%	8%
2	25	22½
3	50	47
4	75	72
5	100	100

When a project entailed a period exceeding 12 months, revenue was recognized in an amount equal to the progress payment received.

Costs incurred by the shipbuilder for inventory, prepaid expense items, and related expenditures associated with this project were capitalized over the 22-month period. As each of the five progress payments were received, the accounting department charged to expense an amount of capitalized costs equal to 80% of the revenue recognized. The amount of costs that were capitalized at the date when each progress payment was received is reflected below:

PROGRESS PAYMENT NO.	CAPITALIZED COSTS EXISTING AT SPECIFIC PROGRESS PAYMENT DATES ($-MILLION)
1	$ 7.8
2	15.4
3	23.0
4	26.3
5	7.5

All capitalized costs were completely paid for by the time each progress payment was received.

Required: Complete the financial summary of operations associated with the 300,000-dwt oil tanker project using the format shown below:

PROGRESS PAYMENT NO.	AMOUNT OF REVENUE RECOGNIZED ($-MILLION)	EXPENSES MATCHED WITH REVENUE ($-MILLION)	NET INCOME ($-MILLION)	CASH FLOW ($-MILLION)
1				
2				
3				
4				
5				
Total				

3-8. **Group transaction analysis — probable occurrences.** Each of the following three groups of T accounts is entirely independent of the other two groups. However, all accounts within each group are interconnected. The closing entry procedure has been ignored in the following group analyses.

GROUP 1: SALES TRANSACTIONS

	CASH (CA)		ACCOUNTS RECEIVABLE (CA)		SALES (IS)
Bal. at Jan. 1	25,000		?		—0—
	?	?	?	?	?
Bal. at Dec. 31	37,000		46,000		312,000

Additional information:
    All sales were made on 30-day credit terms.
    Total credits to Cash during the period amounted to $281,000.
    The only increases in Cash during the period arose from collections of accounts receivable.

GROUP 2: INVENTORY TRANSACTIONS

	CASH (CA)		INVENTORY (CA)		ACCOUNTS PAYABLE (CL)		COST OF GOODS SOLD (IS)
Bal. at Jan. 1	74,000		53,000		124,000		—0—
	418,000	?	?	684,000	?	?	?
Bal. at Dec. 31	23,000		87,000		?		?

Additional information:
    No additional increase to Cash occurred during the period other than as shown above; and the only decreases in the cash account arose from payments of Accounts Payable.
    All inventory was purchased under 30-day credit terms.

GROUP 3: PREPAID EXPENSES

	Cash (CA)		Prepaid Expenses (CA)		Accounts Payable (CL)		Various Expenses (IS)
Bal. at Jan. 1	6,000		28,000			87,000	—0—
	?	?	?	?	?	?	?
Bal. at Dec. 31	?		9,000			34,000	?

Additional information:

Total debits to Cash during the period was $216,000.

All prepaid items were purchased on 30-day credit terms. These purchases totaled $36,000.

The various expenses account included only prepaid expense-type items.

Required: From the limited information given, determine what probably occurred in each account during the fiscal year ending December 31; then complete each T account shown from the beginning through to the ending balances. Construct summary entries for each group to explain your analysis. Identify each transaction with an appropriate parenthetical notation.

3-9. **Comprehensive problem: T account format with preparation of financial statements.** The balance sheet shown below reflects the financial position of Guardian Corporation at December 31, 1979:

Guardian Corporation
Balance Sheet
December 31, 1979

Assets		Equities	
Current assets:		Current liabilities:	
Cash.........................	$ 27,000	Accounts payable.........	$119,000
Marketable securities.....	13,000	Notes payable.............	86,000
Accounts receivable.......	86,000	Total current liabilities	$205,000
Inventory...................	180,000		
Prepaid expenses.........	15,000	Long-term liabilities:	
Total current assets	$321,000	Bonds payable, due	
		1987......................	$350,000
Plant assets:			
Land........................	$ 59,000	Owners' equity:	
Buildings	198,000	Capital stock..............	$280,000
Machinery and		Retained earnings	63,000
equipment...............	320,000	Total owners' equity ...	$343,000
Total plant assets	$577,000		
Total assets...................	$898,000	Total equities	$898,000

The following events occurred during the fiscal year ended December 31, 1980:

(a) Marketable securities originally costing $8,000 were sold for $12,000.

(b) Cash payments for advertising totaled $24,200. These payments were immediately charged to expense when paid for.

(c) Office supplies totaling $16,000 and insurance premiums amounting to $24,000 were purchased on 20-day credit terms during the year. These items were capitalized as prepaid expenses at the time of purchase.

(d) Items purchased for inventory on 30-day credit terms during the year totaled $360,000.

(e) An unneeded parcel of land originally costing $18,000 was sold at a $3,000 loss.

(f) Credit sales during the year totaled $720,000.

(g) Prepaid insurance and office supplies that were charged to expense during the year totaled $27,000 and $20,000 respectively.

(h) A stockholder invested $31,000 of equipment in the corporation, for which the stockholder received 310 shares of $100 par value stock.

(i) Total cost of merchandise sold to customers during the year amounted to $450,000.

(j) Collections received from customers for merchandise previously sold on credit terms totaled $692,000.

(k) Utilities paid and charged to expense totaled $32,000.

(l) Total employee compensation paid during the year was $193,000.

(m) Cash payments made to creditors during the year totaled $444,000.

(n) Rental income earned and received in cash totaled $8,000.

Required: (1) Prepare a master T account structure, and post the beginning balance and information from each of the transactions to appropriate T accounts. Initiate new accounts as required.

(2) Determine the ending balance in each T account as of December 31, 1980.

(3) Prepare a single-step closing entry, and post this entry to appropriate T accounts.

(4) Prepare a balance sheet at December 31, 1980, and an income statement using the multiple-step format for the fiscal year ended December 31, 1980.

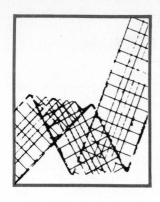

4

The Accrual Concept: Adjusting Entries

Modern accounting breaks up a continuous stream of business activity into artificial segments known as accounting periods. This creates problems. . . .

Reed K. Storey

Financial statements are normally prepared at the end of each fiscal year, but quite often they are prepared at more frequent intervals, such as semiannually, quarterly, or even monthly. Irrespective of when constructed, however, the balance sheet must reflect all of the organization's financial resources, financial obligations, and ownership equities at a particular time. Likewise, the income statement must present all revenue, expenses, other income, gains, and losses that are properly assignable to a specific period in the firm's life. This segmentation of a presumably continuous life of the business into discrete periods, each with a clear-cut start and finish, creates problems in allocating or assigning certain financial activities to one or more accounting periods. Perhaps the most critical aspect of this assignment-allocation problem centers on the relationship of cash receipts and disbursements to the timing of revenue and expense recognition.

DISTINCTION BETWEEN CASH AND ACCRUAL METHODS OF ACCOUNTING

Under the *cash basis* of accounting, all revenue, income, and gains are recognized only when cash is received; whereas expenses and losses are recognized only when cash disbursements occur. In other words, revenue and expense recognition coincides with cash flow. The cash basis of accounting is today restricted primarily to small firms which buy and sell goods and services only on cash terms. A balance sheet prepared under a strictly cash basis of accounting reflects only cash and an owners' equity section. The income statement reflects only cash inflows and outflows from normal operations that occurred during a specific period.

Under the *accrual method* of accounting, the accountant identifies revenue and expenses with specific periods of time without regard to when cash is received or paid. Revenue and expense recognition need not and usually does not coincide with cash flow. This statement can be clarified by recalling the following guidelines of accrual accounting:

(1) Revenue is normally recognized when title passes at the time of delivery of goods or performance of service, irrespective of whether or not cash has been received.

(2) Costs are matched as expenses with the revenue they helped generate irrespective of whether or not these costs have been paid for.

Because the bulk of sales, purchases, and other financial transactions are made under credit arrangements, accrual accounting is the predominant method used throughout the business community; it provides a better reflection of a firm's financial position and a more adequate measurement of net income during a particular segment of the firm's life.

The sharp distinction between accrual and cash accounting can be illustrated by focusing on several common, financial events that become particularly significant at or near the end of a financial reporting period. These examples are divided into three categories for purposes of convenience:

(1) Recognizing expenses and items of income that accrue or grow with time, but which have not yet been recorded, such as:
   (a) Wages and salaries expense.
   (b) Interest expense.
   (c) Interest income.
   (d) Rental income.
(2) Charging to expense the service benefits that are contained in various assets, such as:
   (a) Prepaid expenses.
   (b) Plant assets.
   (c) Intangible assets.

(3) Recording a valuation adjustment to accounts receivable by providing an allowance for doubtful accounts and charging the amount to uncollectible accounts expense.

UNRECORDED EXPENSES AND ITEMS OF INCOME THAT ACCRUE OR GROW WITH TIME

The first group of accruals includes employee compensation, interest charges on notes payable, interest income from notes receivable, and the recognition of rental income. These events will be analyzed within the context of Boutwell Corporation, a furniture wholesaler whose fiscal year ends on December 31.

Wages and Salaries Expense

Wages and salaries earned by the firm's employees are normally paid each Friday for services rendered during the week. Since December 31, 1979, falls on a Monday, the $700 of employee compensation earned during the last working day of 1979, will not be paid until Friday, January 4, 1980. Accrual accounting requires that a $700 liability and expense be recognized as of December 31, 1979, since this amount arose from employee services performed in 1979. The appropriate entry is shown below:

Wages and Salaries Expense (IS)   700
    Wages and Salaries Payable (CL)   700
        Recognition of a liability and an expense for employee compensation incurred during the last working day of 1979.

The wage and salary liability is removed in the 1980 fiscal year at the time cash payment is made to employees. Under cash basis accounting, there is no recognition of any liability or expense during fiscal year 1979. Instead, the $700 expense is recognized only on January 4, 1980, when cash payment is made to employees.

Interest Expense

On September 30, 1979, Boutwell Corporation borrowed $50,000 payable in six months from a local bank. Terms of the agreement were that the firm should repay the $50,000 loan on March 31, 1980, plus interest computed at an annual rate of 8 percent. The accountant recorded the transaction as shown below:

1979
Sept. 30   Cash (CA) 50,000
        Notes Payable (CL)............................   50,000
           Six-month, 8% loan obtained on September 30, 1979, due March 31, 1980.

The total amount of interest due for payment on March 31 is $2,000, derived as follows: The principal amount of the loan (P = $50,000) times the number of years outstanding (n =½ year) times the annual interest rate (i = 8%), equals the total amount of interest (I) that must be paid on the due date. The calculation is expressed as follows:

$$P \quad \times \quad n \quad \times \: i \: = \quad I$$
$$\$50,000 \times \text{½-year} \times .08 = \$2,000$$

Assuming that each month contains 30 days, the corporation incurs a liability for interest payable at the rate of approximately $11.11 per day ($2,000 ÷ 180 days). It would be impractical to record the daily interest accrual for so small an amount.

The accountant is confronted with a substantial problem at the end of the fiscal year. A balance sheet must be prepared as of December 31, 1979, which will include all liabilities that are due; and net income must be determined and reported for the fiscal year by matching appropriate expenses with recognized revenue. Assuming no prior accrual entries have been recorded in this instance, the accountant must recognize a $1,000 interest liability to the bank that accrued during the last three months of fiscal year 1979 ($2,000 × ½ of the 6-month period), even though this amount would not be paid until March 31,1980. The simultaneous recognition of interest expense is reflected in the same entry. It is presumed that this interest expense is associated with and helped generate the revenue recognized during the fiscal year ending December 31, 1979. The following entry is recorded on that date:

1979

Dec. 31 Interest Expense (IS)	1,000	
Interest Payable (CL)............................		1,000
Accrue three months interest liability, and match the interest expense with revenue recognized during the 1979 fiscal year.		

On the date of payment, March 31, 1980, an additional $1,000 interest liability and expense must be recognized, as shown below:

1980

March 31 Interest Expense (IS)..............................	1,000	
Interest Payable (CL)............................		1,000
Record interest liability and expense for the final three months of the bank loan.		

At this point, no cash has yet flowed from the firm to repay the loan or interest liability.

Assuming the loan plus interest is paid on March 31, 1980, the following entry would be made:

```
1980
March 31  Notes Payable (CL)................................  50,000
          Interest Payable (CL)............................  2,000
             Cash (CA) ........................................          52,000
             Record repayment of note and interest
             liability.
```

In the illustration, one half of the interest actually paid in 1980 was identified as an expense of 1979, and the remaining half as an expense of 1980. It is also important to note that the repayment of the $50,000 principal is not an expense of any period; merely the repayment of a loan.

Under the cash basis of accounting, the total $2,000 interest payment would be recognized as an expense of 1980, the year in which the cash outflow occurred. No expense or liability would be recognized on December 31, 1979.

The two preceding entries were made on March 31, 1980, to clearly distinguish between (1) the recognition of an expense, and (2) the repayment of a liability in that year. Normally, however, only one entry would be recorded on March 31, 1980, when the total payment of $52,000 is made. The following entry condenses and replaces both preceding entries:

```
1980
March 31  Notes Payable (CL)................................  50,000
          Interest Payable (CL)............................  1,000
          Interest Expense (IS).............................  1,000
             Cash (CA) ........................................          52,000
             Recognize $1,000 interest expense in
             1980, plus repayment of note plus ac-
             crued interest payable.
```

Under either recording procedure, the net financial impact on the status of liabilities and income determination in 1980 is identical.

Interest Income

On October 31, 1979, the corporation was notified that one of its largest customers was experiencing a temporary cash shortage. Boutwell Corporation's management agreed to loan the customer $30,000 for nine months at an annual interest rate of 12 percent. The loan plus interest is to be repaid on July 31, 1980. The October 31 transaction is recorded as follows:

```
1979
Oct. 31  Notes Receivable (CA).............................  30,000
            Cash (CA).........................................          30,000
            Loan made to customer for nine months at
            12% interest, due July 31, 1980.
```

The total amount of interest due Boutwell Corporation at July 31, 1980, can be determined as follows:

$$P \times n \times i = I$$
$$\$30,000 \times \text{¾-year} \times .12 = \$2,700$$

Again assuming each month contains 30 days, it would be impractical to make approximately 270 entries to record the $10 interest that would become a receivable each day the note is outstanding. However, the balance sheet prepared as of December 31, 1979, must reflect all receivables due Boutwell Corporation; and the income statement must reflect the revenue that pertains to the fiscal year ending December 31, 1979. Although the customer is not required to liquidate the note until July 31, 1980, Boutwell Corporation has a monetary claim against the customer as of December 31, 1979, of $30,000 plus approximately $600 of interest receivable accrued during the preceding two months ($2,700 × 2/9 of the nine-month period). The year-end entry by which to record the $600 interest receivable and interest income earned during 1979, is shown below:

```
1979
Dec. 31  Interest Receivable (CA).............................    600
             Interest Income (IS)...............................            600
             Record interest receivable and interest in-
             come for first two months of the nine-
             month note.
```

Notice that this $600 of interest income was earned during 1979, even though the comparable amount of cash will not be received until July 31, 1980. Under the cash basis of accounting, no income nor any receivable is recognized at December 31, 1979.

The condensed one-step entry shown below is recorded at July 31, 1980, to reflect the $2,100 interest earned on this particular note during 1980, along with the receipt of cash in payment of the customer's obligation:

```
Cash (CA)......................................................    32,700
    Interest Income (IS).........................................            2,100
    Interest Receivable (CA)...................................              600
    Notes Receivable (CA)......................................           30,000
        Removal of the interest that was receivable at De-
        cember 31, 1979, and recognition of interest in-
        come of $2,100 in 1980. (Total interest due on
        note of $2,700 − $600 earned in 1979 = $2,100
        earned in 1980.)
```

Under the accrual method of accounting, only $2,100 of the total $2,700 interest payment actually received in 1980 is recognized as income attributable to operations of 1980. Cash basis accounting would have treated the entire $2,700 receipt as earned in 1980.

Rental Income

On September 1, 1979, Boutwell Corporation received $6,000 for one year's rental effective as of that date on warehouse space which the corporation rented to a local firm at $500 per month. This receipt of cash is regarded as unearned income (or a performance liability), and is recorded as shown on date of receipt:

```
1979
Sept. 1   Cash (CA) ..........................................   6,000
               Unearned Rental Income (CL) ................              6,000
               Receipt of rent covering twelve months,
               effective September 1, 1979.
```

At the end of 1979, four months of this advance payment must be recognized as rental income that was earned during the year. The accountant records that income recognition as follows:

```
1979
Dec. 31  Unearned Rental Income (CL) .....................   2,000
               Rental Income (IS) ...............................              2,000
               Recognition of rental income for the last
               four months of fiscal year 1979 at $500
               per month.
```

The remaining two thirds of the advance payment, or $4,000, will be recognized as income earned during the 1980 fiscal year. Cash basis accounting would recognize the total advance payment of $6,000 as earned in 1979, with no portion of the amount being treated as earned in 1980.

EXPENSING BENEFITS CONTAINED IN VARIOUS ASSETS

Under the accrual concept, the original cost of financial resources, such as prepaid expenses, plant assets, and intangible assets, are usually capitalized as assets at the date of purchase. With the exception of land, the service benefits contained in these assets are subsequently charged to expense as they are consumed or expire in the process of generating revenue.

Prepaid Expenses

As explained in Chapter 3, prepaid expense items, such as insurance, rent, and various types of supplies, contain benefits that are expected to be matched as expenses with revenue during the normal operating cycle or the next 12 months, whichever is longer. The benefits contained in these capitalized costs may be charged to expense in one or more of the following ways:

(1) With time, in the case of prepaid rent and insurance.
(2) As supplies are physically consumed.
(3) At the direction of management.

To illustrate, on January 1, 1979, Boutwell Corporation paid $6,000 for a fire and casualty insurance policy which covered a 12-month period beginning on that date. In addition, $8,000 of office and delivery supplies were purchased under 30-day credit terms in January, 1979. The accountant recorded these two transactions in the following summary entry:

Prepaid Expenses (CA)	14,000	
Cash (CA)...		6,000
Accounts Payable (CL)......................................		8,000
Payment of insurance premiums in cash, and purchase of supplies on credit.		

The liability was subsequently liquidated in late January.

An entry could be made at the end of each month to record the expiration and expensing of $500 of insurance and the consumption of supplies as reported by various clerks. However, it is usually more expedient to prepare only one entry at the end of the fiscal year to reflect information compiled for the entire year. For example, clerks in charge of various supplies notified the accounting department on December 30, 1979, that $1,500 of the supplies purchased in January remained on hand. The supervisor inspected these unused supplies the following day and determined that various items costing $200 were so damaged as to be unusable. The following summary assists in preparing the December 31 entry:

PREPAID IITEM	BALANCE IN JANUARY, 1979	EXPIRED WITH TIME DURING 1979	PHYSICALLY CONSUMED DURING 1979	DETERMINED BY THE SUPERVISOR TO BE DAMAGED	BALANCE AT DECEMBER 31, 1979
Insurance					
premiums ...	$ 6,000	$6,000 (a)	—	—	—
Supplies	8,000	—	$6,500	$200	$1,300 (b)
Total	$14,000	$6,000	$6,500	$200	$1,300

(a) Expired insurance = $500 per month × 12 months = $6,000.
(b) As reported by clerks and supervisor.

The entry at year-end to record the expensing of various prepaid items is shown at the top of the following page.

An alternate method that is often used to handle various prepaid expenses is called *immediate expensing*. The total cost of all

1979
Dec. 31 Insurance Expense (IS)..............................   6,000
      Office and Delivery Supplies Expense (IS)   6,700
         Prepaid Expenses (CA)   12,700
         Charge to expense various prepaid items
         that expired or were consumed or dam-
         aged during 1979. (Damaged supplies
         could be treated as a miscellaneous loss.)

items acquired in January (or during the year) may be immediately charged to expense, rather than capitalized as was done in the preceding illustration. The January entry to reflect the immediate expensing appears as shown below:

Insurance Expense (IS)..   6,000
Office and Delivery Supplies Expense (IS)   8,000
    Cash (CA)...   6,000
    Accounts Payable (CL)......................................   8,000
    Charge to expense all prepaid items acquired
    under cash and credit terms.

At December 31, the accountant makes an adjusting entry to capitalize as prepaid expenses any unexpired items or usable supplies that remain on hand at year-end. This adjusting entry can be prepared from the last column of the preceding summary, as indicated below:

1979
Dec. 31 Prepaid Expenses (CA)   1,300
      Office and Delivery Supplies Expense (IS).   1,300
      Capitalize unused supplies at December
      31, 1979.

Either method provides identical financial results for fiscal year 1979. The alternate method just described, usually requires fewer adjustments at the end of the accounting period, if the service benefits contained in prepaid items are expected to expire or be entirely consumed during that accounting period. In the above example, no adjustment was required at the end of 1979 for the insurance premiums that were purchased on January 1, 1979. However, if interim financial statements were prepared during the fiscal year, an adjustment would be required to capitalize the portion of insurance (or other prepaid item such as rent) that had not yet expired.

Under the cash basis of accounting, all prepaid expense items would be charged to expense at the time of purchase. No adjustment would be made at the end of the fiscal year to capitalize any unexpired or unused prepaid items.

Plant Assets

Plant assets include buildings, machinery, equipment, and furniture and fixtures, which are capitalized as costs and subsequently matched against revenue as expenses.

Prepaid expenses and plant assets resemble each other in that both contain service benefits which are consumed or expire during normal operations. However, two fundamental differences distinguish them. First, the benefits contained in plant assets are expected to be consumed or expire over a longer period of time, usually exceeding one year. For example, the consumption or expiration of these benefits extend beyond 30 to 40 years in the case of buildings, or 5 to 10 years for machinery and equipment. Second, these plant assets are rarely recorded immediately as an expense and subsequently adjusted at year-end, as was done under the alternate arrangement previously presented for prepaid expenses. The normal procedure under accrual accounting is to capitalize the original cost of a plant asset, and then expense a portion of that cost during each year of the asset's expected useful life. This is called the *depreciation process*. That portion of the original cost which is periodically charged to expense is called *depreciation expense*. Land is never depreciated for purposes of accounting.

To illustrate, Boutwell Corporation recorded the purchase of a large piece of equipment for $80,000 on January 1, 1979, as shown below:

```
1979
Jan. 1   Equipment (NA)...................................   80,000
             Cash (CA).........................................          80,000
             Equipment capitalized at date of pur-
             chase.
```

Engineering personnel estimated that this asset's useful life would be approximately 20 years, and that its resale or salvage value at the end of that time would be zero. Management decided to recognize the annual consumption of service benefits contained in the equipment in equal increments during its useful life, by what is called the *straight-line depreciation method*. The total original cost ($80,000) less any estimated resale value (zero) divided by the estimated service life (20 years), provides the amount of depreciation expense ($4,000) that is matched with and deducted from revenue during each year of the asset's useful life:

$$\frac{\text{Annual}}{\text{depreciation}} = \frac{\text{Original cost} - \text{Salvage value}}{\text{Service life}} = \frac{\$80,000 - \$—0—}{20 \text{ years}} = \$4,000$$

However, a significant procedural problem arises which must be resolved before any depreciation expense can be recorded for 1979. The original cost of all plant assets must be reflected in the general ledger, because many users of financial statements frequently require such specific information. At the same time, that portion of the asset's original cost which has expired or been consumed must also be reflected.

This predicament is resolved by creating an account called Accumulated Depreciation, which in technical language is *contra* to the *parent* account in which the original cost of the plant asset is reflected. The contra account, Accumulated Depreciation, is linked directly to its parent account, in this instance Equipment; it contains a credit balance that is opposite to the usual debit balance in the parent account.

The entry by which to record one year of depreciation expense, using the straight-line method, at December 31, 1979, is shown below:

```
1979
Dec. 31  Depreciation Expense (IS)........................    4,000
             Accumulated     Depreciation — Equipment
             (NA)............................................              4,000
             Depreciation expense of $4,000 for 1979.
```

Depreciation Expense is an income-statement-related account which reflects the amount of the equipment's original cost that was allocated as an expense to the current fiscal year, 1979. Accumulated Depreciation — Equipment is the balance-sheet-related contra account in which is accumulated the amount of the particular plant asset's original cost that has been charged off as expense during the current and prior fiscal years. This contra account and the parent account with which it is directly linked are presented below in T account format:

PARENT ACCOUNT		CONTRA ACCOUNT	
		ACCUMULATED DEPRECIATION —	
EQUIPMENT (NA)		EQUIPMENT (NA)	
1979		1979	
Jan. 1	80,000	Dec. 31	4,000

Both of these accounts are classified as plant assets. When the balances in the two accounts are added algebraically, the $76,000 that is derived represents the undepreciated cost of the plant asset. Restated, as of December 31, 1979, $76,000 of the equipment's original cost of $80,000 remains to be written off and allocated to subsequent accounting periods as an expense of operations.

Information contained in these two T accounts could be presented on the balance sheet as of December 31, 1979, in either of the following ways:

(1) Equipment (original cost)... $80,000
　　Less accumulated depreciation — equipment........................ 4,000
　　　Undepreciated cost of equipment $76,000

(2) Equipment (net of $4,000 accumulated depreciation) $76,000

A similar entry by which to record depreciation expense will be prepared at the end of each of the next 19 fiscal years until the entire $80,000 original cost of the equipment is charged to expense and the undepreciated cost of the equipment is reduced to zero.

Several critical observations concerning the depreciation process warrant emphasis at this point:

(1) The accumulated depreciation account does not represent cash, nor does it represent a cash fund with which to replace the asset at the end of its useful life.

(2) The undepreciated cost is frequently referred to as the *book value* of the asset. However, this book value does not reflect the current market or resale value of the asset at a particular time. It merely represents the undepreciated portion of the asset's original cost. The depreciation process is not a valuation process.

(3) The depreciation process is an allocation, over several accounting periods, of the original cost of the plant asset as an expense, which is matched with and deducted from the revenue that the asset helped to generate. If the entire original cost of this equipment was immediately expensed upon purchase, expenses would be overstated in 1979 but understated in each of the 19 subsequent years. In other words, immediate expensing would result in an improper matching of revenue and expense over the life of the going concern or the asset, whichever is presumed shorter.

(4) The amount of annual depreciation expense recorded is largely determined by management's estimate of the expected time over which the benefits contained in each plant asset will be released.

Intangible Assets

Accountants apply the term *amortization* to the cost allocation process by which the original cost of an intangible asset, such as patents, copyrights, franchises, and licenses, is charged as an expense to fiscal periods.

Assume that Boutwell Corporation purchased patent rights to a special furniture finishing oil for $20,000 on July 1, 1979. Because of rapid technological development in this area, management estimated that these patent rights would be obsolete within five years. This estimate overrules the fact that a patent certificate is issued to an original inventor for 17 years. The accountant records the patent purchase of July 1, as follows:

```
1979
July 1   Patents (NA)........................................  20,000
            Cash (CA)........................................              20,000
            Capitalization of intangible asset, with
            expected service life of five years.
```

Management recommended that the original cost of this asset be charged to expense or amortized in equal increments over the next five years. However, due to the midyear purchase only one half of the yearly amount is amortized during the fiscal year ended December 31, 1979. The following entry is prepared at the end of 1979, to record patent amortization:

```
1979
Dec. 31  Amortization Expense (IS)..........................  2,000
            Patents (NA)......................................             2,000
            Amortization of patent for six months in
            1979.
```

A similar entry will be recorded at the end of 1980, except that the amount of amortization expense for a year will be $4,000.

Two explanations may be given why the contra-account format is not normally used in the case of patents and other intangible assets. First, the monetary amounts involved in intangibles are usually smaller compared to the original cost and accumulated depreciation of plant assets. Second, there is usually less necessity to refer to the original cost of intangible assets.

VALUATION ADJUSTMENT OF ACCOUNTS RECEIVABLE

Under accrual accounting, revenue is normally recognized when title and delivery of merchandise are transferred to customers, or when services have been performed irrespective of whether or not cash has been received. Most companies that sell goods and services under credit arrangements support the observation that some portion of the credit customers fail to pay their obligations. The principle of conservatism dictates that some adjustment should be made in the financial records to reflect the estimated uncollectible portion of accounts receivable outstanding. The following discussion presents a procedure whereby that valuation adjustment to accounts receivable and sales revenue can be accomplished.

Sales made by Boutwell Corporation totaling $900,000 during the 1979 fiscal year were all made under 30-day credit arrangements. The Accounts Receivable balance at December 31, 1979, was $88,000. Management expects that most of these outstanding accounts can be collected during the first part of 1980. However, it is also aware, from prior experience, that some portion of this $88,000 balance will probably never be collected. Thus, the accountant is confronted with two formidable problems:

(1) Approximately how much of the $88,000 balance in Accounts Receivable will probably never be collected?
(2) How might the Accounts Receivable balance be adjusted downward to reflect the more realistic amount which management expects to ultimately collect?

Two commonly used methods by which to resolve these problems are presented below:

(1) Percentage-of-sales.
(2) Aging-the-accounts.

Percentage-of-Sales Method

On the basis of past experience, management of Boutwell Corporation anticipates that approximately 1 percent of the $900,000 total sales made during 1979, or $9,000, will probably never be collected. However, at December 31, 1979, management finds it impossible to identify which specific customers will probably not pay their bills. Hence, the total anticipated loss of $9,000 cannot be directly subtracted from the Accounts Receivable balance of $88,000. The detailed reasoning behind this inability to adjust Accounts Receivable directly is outlined below.

The following summary entry condenses the several entries that were undoubtedly made during 1979 to record credit sales of merchandise:

Accounts Receivable — Control (CA) 900,000
    Sales (IS)... 900,000
        Summary entry to record total sales made on 30-
        day credit terms during 1979.

The "Control" notation attached to Accounts Receivable in the above entry indicates that this account reflects the aggregate of all individual customer account receivable cards or sheets maintained by the accounting department. The balance reflected in this account, Accounts Receivable — Control, at any particular time must coincide precisely with the sum-total of all balances reflected on each customer's individual account receivable record card or sheet at that same date.

For example, if City Furniture Company purchases $3,000 worth of furniture from Boutwell Corporation on credit, Accounts Receivable — Control of Boutwell Corporation is increased (debited) by $3,000. At the same time, a like amount of $3,000 is posted to City Furniture Company's individual account receivable card or sheet. When City Furniture Company pays its bill in full, Accounts Receivable — Control will be decreased (credited) by $3,000, and a similar posting made to the individual account receivable card of City Furniture Company will reduce its outstanding balance by $3,000. In short, any entry which affects Accounts Receivable — Control must be simultaneously coordinated with some individual customer's account receivable card or sheet. If the adjustment for the estimated uncollectible accounts of $9,000 (thereby decreasing the year-end balance to $79,000) is directly credited to Accounts Receivable — Control at December 31, 1979, this presumes that specific customers who will not pay their accounts are identified. But this is not the case, since specific identification was impossible at December 31, 1979.

The valuation and procedural problems in this instance are usually resolved in the following manner under accrual accounting. Although Accounts Receivable — Control cannot be credited directly, it can be credited indirectly by creating a contra account that is linked with the parent control account. A $9,000 credit to a contra current asset account called Allowance for Doubtful Accounts has the same overall impact as a direct credit of $9,000 to the control account. The offseting debit in this entry made at December 31, 1979, would be to an expense account called Uncollectible Accounts Expense, as shown below:

```
1979
Dec. 31  Uncollectible Accounts Expense (IS)..............   9,000
             Allowance for Doubtful Accounts (CA)........              9,000
             Record the estimated accounts receivable
             likely to prove uncollectible.
```

The relationship between the contra and parent account is illustrated in T account format as follows, assuming that the balance in each account at January 1, 1979, was zero, and that the collection of accounts receivable during the year totaled $812,000:

PARENT ACCOUNT		CONTRA ACCOUNT
ACCOUNTS RECEIVABLE — CONTROL (CA)		ALLOWANCE FOR DOUBTFUL ACCOUNTS (CA)

Bal. at Jan. 1, 1979 —0—		Bal. at Jan. 1, 1979 —0—
Total credit sales made during 1979 900,000	Collections during 1979 812,000	Valuation adjustment from above entry 9,000
Bal. at Dec. 31, 1979 88,000		Bal. at Dec. 31, 1979 9,000

When the $9,000 credit balance in the contra allowance account at December 31, 1979, is subtracted from the parent control account balance at the same date, the *net accounts receivable* balance of $79,000 will reflect the amount of receivables expected to be collected ultimately. This information would be presented on the firm's balance sheet at December 31, 1979, in either of the following ways:

(1) Accounts receivable — control $88,000
    Less allowance for doubtful accounts 9,000

    Net accounts receivable $79,000

(2) Accounts receivable (net of $9,000 estimated uncollectible
    accounts) $79,000

The Control notation is normally deleted from the balance sheet in actual practice, but it will be retained in this and the following chapter for pedagogic purposes.

The reasoning behind the $9,000 debit to Uncollectible Accounts Expense is as follows. Total credit sales during 1979 were $900,000. If the 1 percent estimate for doubtful accounts proves reasonably accurate, then sales revenue is overstated in 1979 by $9,000. This overstatement of revenue can be adjusted downward by debiting either Sales directly for $9,000, or some expense or loss account for the same amount. Customary accounting procedure specifies that the $9,000 debit be made to Uncollectible Accounts Expense, rather than to Sales or some loss account.

The net impact of the foregoing adjustment on income determination for the 1979 fiscal year is summarized as shown below:

Total sales $900,000
Less uncollectible accounts expense 9,000
    Net sales made in 1979 estimated to be collectible $891,000

The preceding adjusting entry provides a more realistic and accurate representation of the value of accounts receivable outstanding at the end of the particular period. In addition, it also provides a more realistic determination of income earned during that fiscal period.

Under the cash basis of accounting, $812,000 of sales would be recognized during 1979, and the uncollected balance of $88,000 of sales existed at the end of 1979 would be recognized as earned only when and if cash is collected in a subsequent accounting period.

The accrual procedure recognizes that the estimated $9,000 uncollectible accounts expense occurred during the period when the sales were made, rather than at a later date when specific customers accounts can be identified. This deduction from revenue is usually considered a normal expense of doing business even though the term "loss" might appear to be a more appropriate designation based on the definition of loss presented in an earlier chapter. The real loss in situations of this type is the cost of the "free" merchandise or services that were "given away." But practicality and materiality constrain the accountant from subdividing cost of goods sold into two portions: (1) that which is a bonafide expense resulting from collectible sales (cost of goods sold); and (2) that which is the "loss" item, (cost of goods "given away").

Aging-the-Accounts Method

An alternate method that is commonly employed to estimate the amount of uncollectibles is called *aging-the-accounts*. Under this method, the balance in Accounts Receivable — Control at a specific date is segregated and aged according to the number of days that each account has been outstanding since its date of sale. The primary rationale underlying this process is the presumption that the longer an account receivable has been outstanding, the more likely it will ultimately prove to be uncollectible.

The process is illustrated in the analysis shown below for the Boutwell Corporation at December 31, 1979. For example, $60,000 of the $88,000 balance in Accounts Receivable at December 31, 1979, (Column 1) has been outstanding for less than thirty days. Management estimates that 5 percent of this amount of $60,000 (Column 2), or $3,000, will likely prove to be uncollectible. Applying this method to other accounts, the total amount estimated to be ultimately uncollectible is $10,600, as shown at the bottom of Column 3.

Days Outstanding Since Sale Was Made	(1) Accounts Receivable Outstanding as of December 31, 1979	(2) Percentage Likely To Prove Uncollectible	(3) Estimated Amount Uncollectible (1) × (2)
0–30	$60,000	5%	$ 3,000
31–60	10,000	10	1,000
61–90	9,000	20	1,800
91–120	6,000	40	2,400
Over 120	3,000	80	2,400
Total	$88,000		$10,600

The entry that would be prepared to provide the allowance for estimated uncollectibles in this instance is shown on the following page.

1979

Dec. 31 Uncollectible Accounts Expense (IS).............. 10,600
                Allowance for Doubtful Accounts (CA)........   10,600
                Record estimated uncollectible accounts
                receivable by the aging method.

The overall impact on Boutwell Corporation's financial status caused by the aging method of estimating uncollectibles is summarized as shown below:

Balance Sheet

Accounts receivable — control...................................... $ 88,000
Less allowance for doubtful accounts.............................   10,600
     Net accounts receivable.. $77,400

Income Determination

Total sales... $900,000
Less estimated uncollectible accounts expense.................   10,600
Net sales made in 1979 estimated to be collectible.......... $889,400

The amount calculated by this method need not coincide with the amount derived under the percentage-of-sales method described previously, although it is not uncommon for the two methods to yield relatively similar results. Either method of estimating future uncollectible accounts receivable is acceptable. Each is usually based on estimates derived from past experience. Should these estimates prove to be either too high or too low in subsequent periods, the percentages can be adjusted as future year-end accruals are made.

Write-Off of Specific Accounts as Uncollectible

A question which follows logically after determining the estimated uncollectibles is: how should a specific account that is proven uncollectible be handled? Many firms do not use either of the procedures previously outlined for providing an allowance for uncollectibles and recognizing an expense. Instead, management waits until a specific account is proven uncollectible before any expense is recognized. For example, if Boutwell Corporation did not use either estimating method, no provision for doubtful accounts would be made, nor would any associated expense be recognized in 1979. Instead, sales for 1979 would be reported as $900,000 without any reduction being recorded due to anticipated uncollectible expense; and net accounts receivable would be reflected at $88,000 on the balance sheet at December 31, 1979.

Assume that a customer's $3,000 account, which arose from sales made during 1979, was determined to be uncollectible in

1980. In the absence of either estimating procedure, the following entry would be recorded in 1980:

Uncollectible Accounts Expense (IS).........................   3,000
   Accounts Receivable — Control (CA)   3,000
   Write-off of specific account proven uncollectible
   in 1980.

This method of handling proven uncollectibles results in a mismatching of revenue and expenses. An estimate of likely uncollectibles based on past experience, and the recognition of this amount as an expense of the business during the period in which the sales occurred, should be adopted as standard accounting practice. Making some estimate of uncollectibility is superior to ignoring the problem until a customer cannot or does not pay.

In instances where either estimating procedure has been implemented into the accounting process, the appropriate way to handle the specific $3,000 account receivable proven to be uncollectible in 1980, is shown below:

Allowance for Doubtful Accounts (CA)......................   3,000
   Accounts Receivable — Control (CA)   3,000
   Write-off of specific customer's account proven un-
   collectible in 1980.

It is of considerable importance to notice that Uncollectible Accounts Expense does not appear in the above entry. Assuming Boutwell Corporation adopted the percentage-of-sales method, management provided on December 31, 1979, a $9,000 allowance for doubtful accounts which was based on sales made during 1979, and charged that same amount as an uncollectible accounts expense to operations of 1979. The impact of the above entry on the income statement and net accounts receivable for 1980 is zero! Assuming there were no other intervening sales, collections of accounts receivable, or specific account write-offs, the net accounts receivable balance after this write-off would be the same as on December 31, 1979, as shown below:

	BALANCE AT DECEMBER 31, 1979 (CREDIT)	WRITE-OFF OF $3,000 ACCOUNT (CREDIT)	BALANCE IN 1980 IMMEDIATELY AFTER WRITE-OFF (CREDIT)
Accounts receivable — control...	$88,000	$(3,000)	$85,000
Less allowance for doubtful accounts.............	(9,000)	3,000	(6,000)
Net accounts receivable	$79,000	$ —0—	$79,000

SUMMARY OF ACCRUAL ACCOUNTING AND ADJUSTING ENTRIES

The financial impact of seven of the previous nine adjusting entries on the income statements for Boutwell Corporation's fiscal years ended December 31, 1979 and 1980, is summarized below. The equipment depreciation expense of $4,000 and patent amortization expense of $2,000 are not included in this summary because most firms, whether they use cash or accrual basis accounting, usually charge the service benefits contained in plant and intangible assets to expense in annual increments as previously described. Under accrual basis accounting, $700 of wages and salaries were charged to expense in 1979, even though not paid until 1980. Cash basis accounting, on the other hand, recognized the $700 as an expense in the period in which it was paid. The other financial events can be explained in a similar fashion.

Boutwell Corporation
Effect of Selected Financial Events on Income Statements
For Years Ended December 31, 1979 and 1980

	ACCRUAL ACCOUNTING (CREDIT)		CASH ACCOUNTING (CREDIT)	
	1979	1980	1979	1980
Wages and salaries expense........	$ 700	——	——	$ 700
Interest expense	1,000	$ 1,000	——	2,000
Interest income	(600)	(2,100)	——	(2,700)
Rental income..........................	(2,000)	(4,000)	$ (6,000)	——
Insurance expense	6,000	——	6,000	——
Office and delivery supplies expense...................................	6,700	1,300[1]	8,000	——
Uncollectible accounts expense ...	9,000[2]	——	——	9,000[3]
Total net effect	$20,800	$ (3,800)	$ 8,000	$ 9,000
Two-year total net effect	$17,000		$17,000	

Assuming:
[1] Supplies of $1,300 on hand at December 31, 1979, are consumed and charged to expense during 1980.
[2] The percentage-of-sales method is adopted.
[3] Specific sales totaling $9,000 made in 1979 were not collected in 1980. Under a strictly applied cash basis of accounting, accounts receivable do not exist.

Although the impact of the seven events in this instance on the two-year period resulted in an overall reduction in net income of $17,000 irrespective of the basis of accounting, notice that $12,800 ($20,800 − $8,000) of expenses-net-of-other-income were shifted from 1979 to 1980 under cash basis accounting. Restated, net income reported for 1979 under accrual basis accounting was $12,800 less than the net income that would have been reported under cash basis accounting. This situation reverses itself in the fiscal year ended December 31, 1980.

QUESTIONS

1. How often may financial statements be prepared?

2. Outline the principal difference between the recognition of revenue and expense under the accrual basis, and the cash basis of accounting.

3. What appears to be the reason why accrual basis accounting is more widely used among business organizations than the cash basis alternative?

4. Identify the major categories into which year-end adjusting entries required by accrual basis accounting may be grouped.

5. Prepare whatever entry will be required at the end of a fiscal period to record the liability for $1,500 unpaid employee compensation incurred during the final three days of that period.

6. Present the equation, and identify each term in that equation, by which the total amount of interest income or expense can be determined on a note receivable or note payable.

7. Prepare a sample journal entry (no monetary amounts need to be shown) to record the accrual of interest at the end of a fiscal period on: (a) a note payable: and (b) a note receivable.

8. Present: (a) the two-step method, and (b) the one-step condensed procedure by which to record the payment on June 30, 1980, of a $1,000 9-month note payable at 10% annual interest. Assume that an appropriate accrual entry was made at the end of the fiscal year, December 31, 1979, and that the note was originally signed on September 30, 1979.

9. A rental agency received a check for $4,800 on September 1, 1979, in payment of eight months rent, effective September 1, 1979. The agency's fiscal year ends each December 31. Prepare the entry by which to record: (a) the cash receipt in September; and (b) the accrual of income at December 31, 1979.

10. Explain in detail the main distinctions between the two methods by which prepaid expense items can be charged to expense during a fiscal period. For illustrative purposes, assume that on March 1, a firm, whose fiscal year ends each December 31, paid $3,600 for a 1-year insurance policy effective on March 1.

11. (a) In what respect is charging to expense the service benefits contained in prepaid expense items, plant assets, and intangible assets similar? (b) In what respects are they dissimilar?

12. Determine the amount of depreciation expense that would be recorded in each year of a machine's 10-year useful life under the straight-line method, assuming the machine's original cost was $50,000 with zero salvage value at the end of its life.

13. Explain what the depreciation process is.

14. (a) Define a contra account; and (b) provide two instances where it is frequently used.

15. "The current market or resale value of a plant asset can be determined by subtracting the amount of accumulated depreciation from the asset's original cost." Explain to what extent this statement is true or false.

16. What is meant by the term "book value" of equipment?

17. "When a piece of machinery wears out and is retired or sold, the amount reflected in the accumulated depreciation account can be used to replace that asset." Evaluate this conception of what the accumulated depreciation account represents.

18. (a) In what way is the amortization of intangible assets, such as patents, similar to the depreciation of plant assets? (b) In what way are they dissimilar?

19. Explain in detail what the allowance for doubtful accounts is designed to accomplish.

20. Prepare the entry to provide for $7,000 of estimated uncollectible accounts receivable at the end of a fiscal year.

21. Identify and explain two frequently used methods whereby the amount of uncollectible accounts receivable may be estimated at the end of an accounting period.

22. Explain how a specific customer's account receivable for $1,500 would be written off as uncollectible under each of the following procedures: (a) When the allowance for doubtful accounts mechanism is used. (b) When the allowance for doubtful accounts mechanism is not used.

23. Present two ways by which information contained in each of the following sections could be reflected on the balance sheet at year-end: (a) The debit balance in Accounts Receivable — Control is $63,000, and the balance in its related contra account is $2,600. (b) The debit balance in Equipment is $87,000, and the balance in its related contra account is $13,000.

EXERCISES

1. **Employee compensation.** Employees of Llamas Woolen Co. always receive their paychecks on the second and fourth Friday of each month. This being the case, employee compensation totaling $27,000 for labor services performed during the last five working days of the firm's fiscal year ending December 31, 1978, will not be paid until Friday, January 12, 1979.

Required: (a) Prepare the entry required at December 31, 1978, assuming the firm used the accrual method of accounting. (b) Prepare the entry required at January 12, 1979, assuming the firm used the cash basis of accounting. (c) Compare the difference in impact on net income and cash flow for each of the fiscal years ended December 31, 1978, and 1979, using accrual versus cash basis of accounting to handle the payroll situation described above.

2. Employee compensation probable transactions. Partial information with respect to employee compensation during the current fiscal year ended December 31 is shown below in the two T accounts and "additional data" segment:

WAGES PAYABLE (CL)		WAGES EXPENSE (IS)	
Bal. at Jan. 1	3,600	—0—	
?	?	?	
Bal. at Dec. 31	?	?	

Additional data:

(1) All wage expenses incurred during the fiscal year were recorded as a liability prior to payment.

(2) The wages payable account reflected a $1,300 net decrease during the fiscal year just ended.

(3) Total wages paid to employees during the fiscal year amounted to $89,400.

Required: Reconstruct a summary of financial events that probably occurred during the fiscal year just ended with respect to these two T accounts. Prepare entries to explain those events, and provide supporting calculations where appropriate.

3. Note payable sequence. Joanne Raphael, sole owner of the Ceramic Pottery Works, obtained an $18,000, 8-month, 12% annual interest rate bank loan on August 1, 1979, to solve a temporary cash crisis. The firm's fiscal year ends December 31.

Required: (a) Prepare an appropriate accrual entry at December 31, 1979, to recognize the firm's liability for interest on the note to the bank, assuming no prior interest accruals have been made. Show all calculations. (b) Prepare two entries at the date of payment to record: (1) interest expense for 1980; and (2) the payment of the note plus interest. (c) Ignoring item (b), prepare a single entry at the date of payment to record interest expense for 1980 and payment of the note plus interest.

4. Interest calculations. Assume that all months contain thirty days.

Required: Answer the following and show calculations: (a) Determine the total interest due at maturity on a $16,000, 10-month, 12% annual interest rate note payable. (b) What is the annual rate of interest on a $30,000, 14-month note payable if the total interest due at maturity is $2,800? (c) When must a note payable be paid, if the principal amount of the note is $62,000, its annual interest rate is 10%, the total amount of interest due at maturity is $4,650, and it was written on September 30, 1979? (d) What is the principal amount of a 4-month note whose annual interest rate is 15%, and the total interest due at maturity is $375?

5. Note receivable sequence. Lucille Dittermore purchased several items of furniture during the early summer of 1979 for $3,000 on 90-day credit terms. About two months after purchase, Dittermore notified the furniture store's credit manager that since her teaching contract for the ensuing year will not be renewed, she would be unable to pay her bill until sometime in 1980. An arrangement was worked out whereby she was permitted to convert her account receivable into a note receivable on August 31, 1979. Terms of the $3,000 note required payment of the note plus interest on April 30, 1980, at 15% annual interest. The furniture store's fiscal year ended each October 31.

Required: (a) Prepare the entry to record the financial event of August 31, 1979, in the firm's acounting records. (b) Prepare an appropriate accrual entry for the firm at the end of its 1979 fiscal year. (c) Prepare one compound entry on April 30, 1980, to record the payment of the note and interest in full by Dittermore.

6. **Prepaid expense items: immediate capitalization.** Falcon Enterprises purchased the following prepaid expense items during March on the terms indicated below:

ITEM	CASH PAYMENT	30-DAY CREDIT ARRANGEMENTS
Factory supplies	$ 3,000	$16,000
Administrative supplies	12,000	—
Rent (for one year, effective March 1)	—	18,000
Insurance (for nine months, effective April 1)	7,200	—
Total	$22,200	$34,000

The balance in Prepaid Expenses at March 1 was zero, and only those prepaid expense items shown above were purchased during the remainder of the fiscal year ended September 30. Unused factory and administrative supplies on hand at the end of the fiscal year were $3,800 and $2,400, respectively.

Required: (a)Prepare a summary entry for March to record the purchases, assuming all items were immediately capitalized. (b) Prepare any necessary accrual or adjusting entry at the fiscal year-end.

7. **Prepaid expense items: immediate expensing.** Refer to all information supplied in Exercise 6 above.

Required: (a) Prepare a summary entry for March to record the purchases, assuming all items were immediately expensed. (b) Prepare any necessary accrual or adjusting entry at the fiscal year-end.

8. **Prepaid expense items: mixed treatment.** The following cash purchases of various prepaid expense items were recorded during September, 1979.

ITEMS	IMMEDIATELY EXPENSED	IMMEDIATELY CAPITALIZED
Office supplies	$ 8,500	—
Maintenance supplies	16,000	—
Insurance (one year fire and casualty policy, effective September 1, 1979)	—	$ 6,600
Rent (nine months, effective October 1, 1979)	—	18,000
Advertising	12,000	—
Total	$36,500	$24,600

Office and maintenance supplies unused at the end of the fiscal year, December 31, totaled $4,200 and $5,000, respectively. Other than to record the cash purchases, no other entries were made during the fiscal year to the prepaid expenses account.

Required: (a) Prepare an entry at the fiscal year-end to record any necessary adjustments to the two supply expense accounts. (b) Prepare the necessary accrual entry at the fiscal year-end to record insurance and rent expense. (c) What, if any, adjustment is warranted at the fiscal year-end to handle the advertising item? Explain.

9. **The depreciation amortization process.** Suburban Foundry Corp. purchased the plant assets shown below on January 1, 1980, with the expected useful life as indicated. Salvage value of each depreciable plant asset at the time of its disposal or retirement was estimated to be zero:

PLANT ASSET	ORIGINAL COST	USEFUL LIFE
Land	$ 48,000	Infinite
Building	186,000	20 years
Machinery and equipment	310,000	5 years

In addition, a group of patents for an improved foundry process was purchased for $35,000 on July 1, 1980. The estimated useful life remaining in the patents was seven years, with no residual value anticipated at the end of that time. The company's accounting department always uses the straight-line depreciation and amortization methods to charge service benefits contained in plant and intangible assets to expense.

Required: (a) Prepare a compound entry to record the appropriate amount of depreciation expense on each plant asset shown above at December 31, 1980. (b) Prepare an appropriate entry to record patent amortization expense at December 31, 1980.

10. **Depreciation and interest accruals.** Trexler Corp. purchased a parcel of land containing a warehouse for $160,000 on July 1, 1980. Ten percent of the total cost was apportioned to the land. The estimated useful life remaining in the building was 16 years, with no resale or salvage value at the end of that time. These plant assets were purchased under a 4-year, 10% mortgage note payable arrangement, with the first interest payment of $16,000 due on July 1, 1981. The firm's fiscal year ends each December 31, and straight-line depreciation is used.

Required: (a) Prepare the entry to record the purchase of the plant assets. (b) Prepare the necessary accrual entry to record the liability for interest at December 31, 1980. (c) Prepare the December 31, 1980, entry to record depreciation expense.

11. **Estimated uncollectibles: percentage-of-sales method.** Sales generated during two fiscal years ended December 31 are shown below:

	1979	1980
Cash sales	$140,000	$180,000
Credit sales (30-day terms)	320,000	440,000
Total sales	$460,000	$620,000

The controller believes that 1½% of credit sales made during 1979 and 1% of 1980's credit sales will probably prove ultimately uncollectible. The credit balance in Allowance for Doubtful Accounts at January 1, 1980, was $5,000.

Required: (a) Prepare the valuation adjusting entry that is warranted at the end of each of the two fiscal years. (b) Assuming $4,675 of specific accounts receivable were proven uncollectible during fiscal year 1980, determine the ending balance in the allowance account at December 31, 1980.

12. Estimated uncollectibles: aging-of-accounts method. The $940,000 Accounts Receivable — Control balance of Fashion Industries at March 31, 1980, was aged and segregated into days outstanding since sales were made, as shown below. In addition, the controller's estimate of accounts likely to prove uncollectible within each age segment is indicated:

DAYS OUTSTANDING SINCE SALES WERE MADE	ACCOUNTS RECEIVABLE — CONTROL BALANCE AT MARCH 31, 1980	PERCENTAGE LIKELY TO PROVE UNCOLLECTIBLE
0– 45	$520,000	3%
46– 90	170,000	8
91–135	60,000	12
136–180	90,000	20
181–270	60,000	40
Over 270	40,000	75
Total	$940,000	

Required: Prepare the adjusting entry at March 31, 1980, to provide for estimated uncollectible accounts receivable. Show calculations.

13. Writing-off uncollectible accounts receivable. A customer of Vermillion Corporation who purchased $4,800 worth of merchandise on 60-day credit terms in September of the fiscal year ended December 31, 1979, was determined bankrupt in 1980 before the account was paid. The controller instructed the chief accountant to write off the entire amount as definitely uncollectible.

Required: (a) Assuming the corporation makes no provision for estimated uncollectibles, prepare an entry to reflect the write-off of this specific account in 1980. (b) Ignoring (a) and assuming that the corporation makes provision for estimated uncollectible accounts receivable at the end of each fiscal year, prepare the entry that would be made in 1980 to comply with the controller's directive. (c) Compare the difference in the effect on the net accounts receivable balance and income determination in the 1980 fiscal year between handling the specific account written off under assumptions (a) and (b).

PROBLEMS

4-1. Interest accruals: two perspectives. Wursted Corp. sold an assortment of fabrics to Klamath Knitwear Co. on June 1, 1979, for $9,000 under a note receivable arrangement. The note carried an annual interest rate of 12% and both interest and the note were to be repaid on March 1, 1980. The fiscal years of Wursted Corp. and Klamath Knitwear Co. end on September 30 and December 31, respectively. Assume that each month contains 30 days for purposes of this problem.

Required: (1) Prepare any entry that is required on September 30, 1979, in each firm's accounting records.

(2) Prepare any entry that is required on December 31, 1979, in each firm's accounting records.

(3) Prepare the entry in each firm's accounting records to reflect the payment of the note plus interest on its due date, using the one-step procedure.

4-2. Estimating uncollectibles. The controller of Fleet Corp. was debating the merits of various methods by which to estimate uncollectible accounts receivable and to provide an allowance for those uncollectibles at the fiscal year-end, December 31. The possibilities were narrowed down to two alternatives:

(a) Provide an allowance for uncollectibles of 1¼% of sales made during the fiscal year just ending. Sales totaled $840,000 and were made under 40-day credit terms.

(b) Detailed aging of the year-end accounts receivable balance, as summarized below:

ACCOUNTS RECEIVABLE — CONTROL BALANCE AT DECEMBER 31	DAYS SINCE SALES WERE MADE	ESTIMATED PERCENTAGE LIKELY TO BECOME UNCOLLECTIBLE
$ 68,000	0–40	3%
25,000	41–80	6
16,000	81–120	10
7,000	121–160	20
10,000	Over 160	40
$126,000		

Required: (1) Prepare the entry that would be made at December 31, using the percentage-of-sales method to estimate uncollectibles. Show calculations.

(2) Prepare the entry that would be made at December 31, using the aging-of-accounts method. Show calculations.

(3) Indicate which method the controller should adopt. Explain why.

4-3. Selected accruals. A public accounting firm was hired by Oxford Publishing Co. during the latter part of December, 1979, to assist the company's accounting staff in its year-end closing procedures. The accounting firm's review of transactions for fiscal year 1979 uncovered the following accrual omission or problems:

(a) The balance in Prepaid Expenses at December 31, 1979, was composed of the following items:

Pressroom supplies	$31,000
Insurance policy premiums	18,000
Rent	12,000
Maintenance supplies	26,000
Total	$87,000

Eighty percent of the insurance premiums and 70% of the rent expired during 1979, but were not yet charged to expense. All pressroom supplies were consumed during the year, but none was recorded as an expense item. Only $10,000 of maintenance supplies remained unused at December 31, 1979.

(b) A $120,000 bank loan was obtained on January 1, 1979, on which 8% annual interest was payable each January 1, beginning 1980.

No interest accrual was entered in the records at the end of 1979 on this specific loan.

(c) Various copyrights were obtained on July 1, 1979, from various other publishing houses at an accumulated cost of $75,000. Management's practice was to amortize copyright as an intangible asset by the straight-line method over its estimated 15-year useful life. No amortization expense was recorded on these copyrights for 1979.

(d) Two plant asset accounts reflected the following information for fiscal year 1979:

	BUILDINGS (NA)	EQUIPMENT (NA)
Bal. at Jan. 1	110,000	840,000
Purchased on Jan. 1	16,000	120,000
Bal. at Dec. 31	126,000	960,000

All buildings included in the December 31 balance were purchased since 1965, and all had a useful life of 30 years with an estimated salvage value of zero at the end of that time. All equipment included in the December 31 balance was purchased since 1975, and had a useful life of 5 years with no salvage value at the end of that time. Despite such information, no depreciation expense was recorded as of December 31, 1979.

(e) The company received $24,000 on July 1, 1979, for one year's rent, effective that date, on unused warehouse space. The accountant properly credited $24,000 to Unearned Rental Income upon receipt of cash, but made no further adjustment during the year.

Required: (1) Prepare necessary accrual entries at December 31, 1979, for each omission or discrepancy noted by the public accounting firm.

(2) Determine the total impact of all accrual entries made on 1979's net income.

4-4. Notes receivable portfolio. The credit manager of Berstroms Inc., habitually audited the portfolio of customer notes receivable shortly after the close of each fiscal year. The summary shown below for a portion of that portfolio was submitted to the credit manager by the portfolio custodian in January, 1980, to assist in the annual audit for the fiscal year ending December 31, 1979:

CUSTOMER NAME	ORIGINATION DATE	TERM OF NOTE	PRINCIPAL AMOUNT	ANNUAL INTEREST RATE
A. Baker	Sept. 30, 1978	8 months	$4,200	8%
T. Corvallis	Jan. 16, 1979	6 months	6,000	10
P. Ferrer	Jan. 31, 1979	5 months	5,200	9
G. Frost	Mar. 31, 1979	12 months	3,000	12

The following information supplemented the exhibit:

(a) Each month was presumed to contain 30 days for purposes of interest calculations.

(b) All accrual entries were properly recorded at December 31, 1978.

(c) Interest was always accrued semiannually at June 30 and December 31 in order that financial statements could be prepared at 6-month intervals.

(d) Each of the notes receivable plus interest was paid in full on its due date.

Required: (1) Prepare each entry made at each payment and accrual date with respect to the notes during the fiscal year ended December 31, 1979.

(2) Prepare a summary of the: (a) interest earned; and (b) interest received on each of the notes, and in total, during fiscal year 1979.

4-5. Depreciation, amortization, and interest accruals. Management of Honeywell Corp. invested considerable financial resources in various plant and intangible assets during the past quarter-century. A $200,000, 20-year, 6% bond issue was sold to the public in 1968 to provide sufficient funds with which to modernize the factory and purchase additional machinery. In 1976, several automated binders were purchased with the proceeds of a 10-year, 8%, $600,000 mortgage note payable. Interest on both long-term liabilities was payable at January 1 of each year.

A list of the major groups of plant and intangible assets used in operations at December 31, 1979, the end of the fiscal year, reflected the following information:

ITEM	DATE OF PURCHASE	ORIGINAL COST	ESTIMATED USEFUL LIFE FROM DATE OF PURCHASE
Land..............................	1955	$ 50,000	Infinite
Buildings:			
Main	1955	500,000	40 years
Annex and additions......	1968	250,000	25 years
Machinery:			
Binders	1976	600,000	5 years
Miscellaneous	1955–78	300,000	30 years
Patents...........................	1974	48,000	12 years

All plant and intangible assets were depreciated or amortized at the end of each fiscal year by the straight-line method. Estimated salvage value of each asset noted above (excluding land) was zero. The credit balances in the two accumulated depreciation accounts at January 1, 1979, were as follows:

Buildings.....................................	$410,000
Machinery	$480,000

The unamortized balance in Patents at January 1, 1979, was $28,000. No deletions or additions of plant or intangible assets occurred during 1979.

Required: (1) Prepare the entry at December 31, 1979, to record depreciation and amortization expense on the assets listed. Show supporting calculations.

(2) Prepare the entry to reflect the interest payment on the bond issue and mortgage note payable at January 1, 1979, assuming an appropriate interest accrual entry was recorded on December 31, 1978.

(3) Prepare the interest accrual entry at December 31, 1979.

(4) Prepare the plant and intangible asset sections of the balance sheet as they would appear at December 31, 1979.

4-6. Accounts receivable transactions and accruals. One of management's policies during the past decade of operating Shurefit Corp. was to write-off and charge to expense, specific accounts receivable in the fiscal period when they were proven uncollectible. The new controller strongly recommended that some provision for uncollectibles be implemented so that estimated uncollectible accounts would be charged against expense during the fiscal year in which the sales occurred, rather than when specific accounts are determined to be uncollectible. The information supplied below pertains to selected financial transactions that occurred in the fiscal year ending December 31, 1979:

(a) Total sales for 1979 were composed of the following:

Cash	$ 48,000
30-day credit	265,000
Sales made under notes receivable arrangement	15,000
Total	$328,000

(b) Two customers purchased the $15,000 worth of merchandise under the notes receivable arrangement: Watkins, Inc., purchased $6,000 on March 1, 1979; and McIntire Co. made a $9,000 purchase on September 1, 1979. In each instance, interest and principal were due in full 8 months from the date of sale, with interest accruing at an annual rate of 10%. Watkins, Inc., paid its note plus interest in full on its due date.

(c) Specific customer accounts totaling $4,000 were identified as uncollectible by the collections department before the controller could implement the new policy and make the 1979 year-end entry to create an allowance for estimated uncollectible accounts. The accounting clerk recorded these $4,000 uncollectibles as Uncollectible Accounts Expense, even though only $1,500 of that total was associated with sales made during the current year.

(d) The controller established the allowance for doubtful accounts at December 31, 1979, in the amount of 1% of all noncash sales (including notes) made during the current fiscal year. After making that entry, and following a review of item (c) above, the controller made an adjusting entry to reduce the balance in Uncollectible Accounts Expense to $5,300, ($2,500 representing proven uncollectibles from prior-year sales, plus $2,800 representing noncash sales made in 1979). The allowance account was debited in this adjusting entry.

(e) The Accounts Receivable — Control balance at December 31, 1978, was $31,000, and $26,000 at December 31, 1979. Only those events described above are to be considered in arriving at and recording the probable amount of receivables collected during the fiscal year.

Required: (1) Construct appropriate summary and accrual entries to record each of the events described in items (a) through (e).

(2) Determine the net accounts receivable balance at December 31, 1979.

4-7. Transaction analysis. Each T account shown below is related only to those accounts within the same group.

GROUP 1: INTEREST RECEIVABLE/INCOME

	CASH (CA)		NOTES RECEIVABLE (CA)		INTEREST RECEIVABLE (CA)		INTEREST INCOME (IS)	
Bal. at July 1	26,000		98,000		27,000			17,000
	?		?	?	?	?		?
	?							
Bal. at Dec. 31	92,000		117,000		?			33,000

Additional information:

(a) Sales of $630,000 were generated during the year, of which 10% were sold under notes receivable arrangement.

(b) No credits were made to cash during the period.

GROUP 2: ACCOUNTS RECEIVABLE

	CASH (CA)		ACCOUNTS RECEIVABLE — CONTROL (CA)		ALLOWANCE FOR DOUBTFUL ACCOUNTS (CA)		SALES (IS)	
Bal. at July 1	?		110,000			30,000		850,000
	?		?	?	?	?		?
				?				
Bal. at Dec. 31	164,000		86,000			27,000		938,000

	UNCOLLECTIBLE ACCOUNTS EXPENSE (IS)	
Bal. at July 1	13,000	
	?	
Bal. at Dec. 31	24,000	

Additional information:

(a) All sales were made on 45-day credit terms.

(b) No credits were made to Cash during the period.

Required: (1) Analyze each group separately, and reconstruct the events that probably occurred during the particular 6-month period.

(2) Prepare entries to explain those events, and provide supporting explanations where necessary.

(3) Complete each T account from its beginning to ending balance.

4-8. Transaction analysis: journal entry format, accrual entries, and income statement preparation. The three principal owner-managers of Rubrum Tire Corp. reviewed the following income statement that was prepared for the first six months of the fiscal year ended June 30, 1980.

Rubrum Tire Company
Income Statement
For Six Months Ended December 31, 1979

Sales..		$227,500
Cost of goods sold..		136,500
Gross margin		$ 91,000
Expenses:		
Wages and salaries......................................	$33,000	
Advertising	30,500	
Interest	21,000	
Insurance...	6,000	
Rent...	4,500	
Maintenance	3,500	
Office supplies...	2,400	100,900
Net loss..		$ (9,900)

The owners had projected that operations for the fiscal year ended June 30, 1980, would generate approximately $15,000 net income on budgeted sales of $600,000. The net loss for the first six months forced reconsideration of that estimate, and they launched an investigation into two major problems: (a) advertising and marketing activities were not generating the expected sales volume; and (b) cost of goods sold amounted to about 60% of sales ($136,500 ÷ $227,500), as compared to an anticipated 50%. The balances shown below were reflected in selected accounts at the midpoint (December 31, 1979) of the fiscal year ended June 30, 1980:

ACCOUNT TITLE	DEBIT (CREDIT)
Allowance for Doubtful Accounts......................................	$ (2,000)
Buildings	270,000
Interest Payable..	(42,000)
Machinery..	590,000
Mortgage Note Payable, 10-year, 8%, due December 31, 1982.	(400,000)
Notes Payable, short-term, 10%..	(100,000)
Wages and Salaries Payable...	(15,000)

The following selected events occurred during the last six months of the fiscal year ended June 30, 1980:

(a) The following prepaid expense items were immediately charged to expense upon acquisition:

ITEM	CASH PURCHASE	PURCHASED ON 30-DAY TERMS	TOTAL
Maintenance..................	$ 2,000	$ 5,000	$ 7,000
Insurance premiums	9,000	———	9,000
Manufacturing supplies...	1,600	7,000	8,600
Office supplies	500	2,800	3,300
Rent	6,000	———	6,000
Total.......................	$19,100	$14,800	$33,900

(b) Wage and salary liabilities (and the offsetting expenses) incurred during the period amounted to $91,000. Compensation actually paid during the last half of the fiscal year totaled $102,000. The Wages and Salaries Payable balance at June 30, 1980, reflected a credit of $4,000.

(c) The interest payable of $42,000 at December 31, 1979, was paid on January 1, 1980. Although interest expense was accrued semiannually at each June 30 and December 31, interest on both short- and long-term notes was payable annually on January 1.

(d) Cash expenditures of $21,600 for advertising were charged immediately to expense upon payment.

(e) Sales recognized during the final six months totaled $410,000, of which 80% were on 30-day credit terms, and the remainder under cash terms. Cost of goods associated with these sales amounted to $184,500.

(f) Allowance for Doubtful Accounts was increased at June 30, 1980, by 2% of the total sales generated during the entire fiscal year. The credit balance in the allowance account at June 30 after this accrual was $8,600.

(g) Depreciation expense to be recognized for the entire fiscal year was 2½% of the balance in the building account at December 31, 1979, and 5% of the balance in the machinery account at the same date. These two percentages yielded depreciation expense for the fiscal year that was equivalent to the amount calculated by the straight-line method.

Required: (1) Prepare appropriate entries required by each of the items (a) through (g). Support each entry with clarifying detail.

(2) Prepare an income statement for the fiscal year ending June 30, 1980.

4-9. Transactions analysis: T account format, accrual entries, and financial statement preparation. SportRec Corp. was chartered in Florida to begin operations on January 1, 1979, as a wholesaler of sporting and recreation equipment. Its five major incorporators invested a total of $300,000 cash in the firm on that date, and in return received 15,000 shares of $20 par value capital stock. The following list comprises a summary of transactions that occurred during the firm's first fiscal year of operations ending December 31, 1979:

(a) Plant assets were purchased at the beginning of January under the terms indicated below:

	CASH	LONG-TERM LIABILITIES	ISSUE OF CAPITAL STOCK	TOTAL
Land..................	$28,000	——	——	$ 28,000
Buildings	50,000	$200,000	——	250,000
Equipment	——	60,000	$50,000	110,000
Total..............	$78,000	$260,000	$50,000	$388,000

Eighty percent of the total cost of the buildings was financed by the sale of a $200,000, 10-year, 8% bond issue to a life insurance company on January 1. The $60,000 portion of the equipment was financed under a 5-year, 10% mortgage note payable arrangement with a local bank. Interest on both long-term debt instruments was payable each January 1, beginning 1980. The remaining $50,000 portion of equipment was obtained by issuing 2,500 shares of capital stock to a close business associate of the major stockholders.

(b) Various items of sporting and recreation equipment costing $380,000 were purchased on 30-day credit terms throughout the year. In addition, the following prepaid expense items were purchased under similar credit arrangements and immediately charged to expense at the time of purchase:

Insurance premiums (covering the 18-month period beginning January 1, 1979)	$ 36,000
Maintenance	22,000
Advertising supplies	45,000
Office supplies	5,000
Warehouse supplies	14,000
Total	$122,000

(c) Total wage and salary expense for the year was $68,000, of which $6,000 remained unpaid at December 31, 1979.

(d) Total sales for the year were $420,000, of which only 10% were sold on a cash-and-carry basis, the remainder under 45-day credit terms. Cost of goods associated with merchandise sold amounted to $190,000.

(e) A $12,000 payment was received from a retailing firm which desired to rent some unused warehousing space for twelve months, beginning July 1, 1979. The amount was treated by the accounting department as unearned income on July 1.

(f) Plant assets were to be depreciated by the straight-line method using the following additional information:

	Original Cost	Estimated Useful Life (With Zero Salvage Value)
Building #1	$210,000	30 years
Building #2	40,000	20 years
Equipment — Group A	60,000	6 years
Equipment — Group B	50,000	4 years

(g) The balance in Accounts Payable at the end of the year was $58,000.

(h) Office supplies totaling $1,500 and warehouse supplies amounting to $5,400 remained unused at the end of the year and were capitalized as prepaid expenses. In addition, the unexpired portion of insurance premiums was capitalized as a prepaid expense at December 31, 1979.

(i) The appropriate amount of interest expense was accrued as a liability at year-end, and one-half year of rental income was recognized on the same date, (see items (a) and (e) above).

(j) The controller recommended that an allowance for doubtful accounts be created amounting to 2% of the total credit sales made during the year. The only account proven uncollectible during the year amounted to $2,400. The Accounts Receivable — Control balance at year-end totaled $52,000.

Required: (1) Analyze each financial event from the date of incorporation to the end of the 1979 fiscal year; then post each event to appropriate T accounts. Provide supporting explanations, but journal entries need not be prepared. The chart of accounts required for this problem is shown below:

Cash	Mortgage Note Payable
Accounts Receivable — Control	Capital Stock
Allowance for Doubtful	Sales
Accounts	Cost of Goods Sold
Inventory	Insurance Expense
Prepaid Expenses	Maintenance Expense
Land	Marketing and Advertising
Buildings	Supplies Expense
Accumulated Depreciation —	Office Supplies Expense
Buildings	Warehouse Supplies Expense
Equipment	Wages and Salaries Expense
Accumulated Depreciation —	Interest Expense
Equipment	Depreciation Expense —
Accounts Payable	Buildings
Wages and Salaries Payable	Depreciation Expense —
Interest Payable	Equipment
Unearned Income	Uncollectible Accounts Expense
Bonds Payable	Rental Income

(2) Determine the balance in each T account at December 31, 1979.

(3) Prepare an income statement and balance sheet as of the end of the first fiscal year of operations. Assume that an appropriate closing entry was made on December 31, 1979.

DECISION CASE

4-1. **Adequacy of net income and cash flow to enable cash dividend.** Vibram Corp. was created on July 1, 1979, as a wholesale distributor of ethical and proprietary drugs. The small group of stockholders who began the firm strongly encouraged management personnel to operate the company so that a substantial cash dividend could be declared and paid near the end of the first fiscal year, June 30, 1980. The data summarized below and on page 154 comprised the financial events of the firm's first fiscal year of operations:

(a) The original investment by stockholders came from three items: (1) $100,000 cash; (2) a $160,000 warehouse and office building; and (3) a parcel of land valued at $30,000. A total of 29,000 shares of $10 par value capital stock was issued on July 1, 1979, in return for these financial resources. The estimated life of the building was 25 years, with no salvage value estimated at the end of its life. The straight-line method of depreciation was used.

(b) The following purchases occurred during the fiscal year on the terms indicated. All items except inventory were immediately expensed:

	CASH PURCHASE	30-DAY CREDIT PURCHASE	TOTAL
Inventory	—	$540,000	$540,000
Insurance (16-month policies, effective July 1, 1979)	$10,000	22,000	32,000
Rent (on trucking equipment, 1-year contract, effective January 1, 1980)	36,000	—	36,000
Administrative supplies	6,000	15,000	21,000
Maintenance supplies................	14,000	3,000	17,000
Total...................................	$66,000	$580,000	$646,000

(c) Total sales on 60-day terms during the year amounted to $816,000. The cost of goods associated with these sales totaled $490,000.

(d) Of the total $184,000 employee compensation expense incurred during the year, $4,000 remained unpaid at June 30, 1980.

(e) A short-term loan of $80,000 was obtained from the bank on September 1, 1979. The note plus interest, at an annual rate of 12%, was payable in full on July 1, 1980.

(f) The Accounts Payable balance at June 30, 1980, was $20,000.

(g) Administrative and maintenance supplies totaling $4,000 and $7,000, respectively, remained unused at the end of the fiscal year. In addition, the appropriate amounts of unexpired prepaid rent and insurance were capitalized at year-end.

(h) Appropriate accruals were made for interest and depreciation expenses at the year-end.

(i) A provision, amounting to 1¼% of total sales, was made at the year-end for receivables that were estimated to eventually become uncollectible. Specific accounts totaling $3,400 were written off as uncollectible during the year. The Accounts Receivable — Control balance at June 30, 1980, was $140,000.

Required:

(1) Prepare entries to record each of the events. Provide supporting detail.

(2) Determine the cash balance at the fiscal year-end, and the net income earned during the fiscal year.

(3) To what extent is it advisable to declare and pay a $25,000 cash dividend shortly after the close of the fiscal year? Explain and defend.

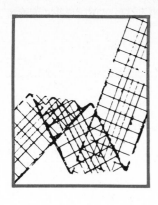

5

The Accounting Cycle

"The time has come," the Walrus said, "to talk of many things: Of shoes — and ships — and sealing-wax — of cabbages — and kings."

Address to Oysters and the Carpenter
in Through the Looking-Glass

This chapter focuses on specific adjustments and procedures that are required to prepare financial statements at the end of each fiscal year, and capsulizes the main ingredients of the accounting cycle, an overview of which is shown on page 156. The diagram highlights the sequential steps involved in the accounting process during a normal year's activity. From the analysis, journalizing, and posting of transactions, it proceeds to the preparation of financial statements, and finally to the closing and any reversing entries that are required to accumulate financial data for the ensuing fiscal period.

TRANSACTION ANALYSIS, JOURNALIZING, AND POSTING TO THE LEDGER

From the first day to the end of the fiscal year, the accounting staff assembles and analyzes source documents related to nu-

An Overview of the Accounting Cycle

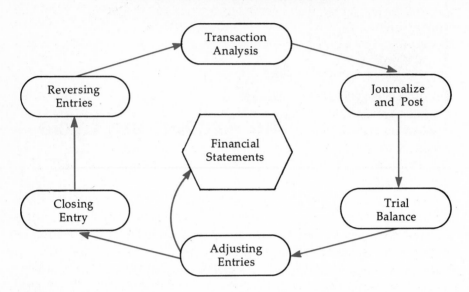

merous financial transactions. Sales slips, checks received and/or sent, purchase invoices, payroll time cards, production reports, and shipping records are but a few of the many documents which indicate that a transaction has occurred. Legal provisions which specify interest rates and payment dates, usually included in bond, mortgage, and note payable contracts, also alert the accountant to accrue at specific times interest expense or, in the case of notes receivable, interest income.

Two additional facets of the recording process warrant comment before discussing specific year-end closing procedures. These are the use of subsidiary ledger accounts and the role of special journals in journalizing transactions.

Subsidiary Ledger Accounts

Subsidiary ledger accounts are frequently maintained when further division of a particular control account is desired, such as Accounts Receivable — Control which reflects the aggregate balance of all outstanding customer accounts receivable. Each customer's account receivable card or sheet serves as a subsidiary ledger account to this control account. Postings to the control account must always be supported by postings to individual subsidiary ledger accounts so that equality is always maintained between the aggregate balance shown in the control account and the total balances reflected in the subsidiary ledger accounts. For example, assume that Hughes, Jones, and Riley purchased $100, $200, and

$400, respectively, of merchandise on credit terms. A summary journal entry to record these transactions on the seller's books is shown below:

Accounts Receivable — Control (CA) 700
    Sales (IS)..   700
      Record sale of merchandise on credit terms.

In addition to this entry, debits of $100, $200, and $400 must be posted to each of the customer's accounts. If these amounts are not posted to individual accounts, the balance shown in the control account after the entry is posted will fail to agree with the total of the balances reflected in the individual accounts receivable subsidiary ledger accounts.

Control and subsidiary ledger accounts may also be established for other accounts maintained by the firm. For example, the total original cost of all buildings may be reflected in Buildings — Control, with itemized data for each type of building shown in subsidiary ledger accounts. Inventory — Control may be subdivided into subsidiary ledger accounts for raw materials, component parts, work in process, and finished goods ready for sale. Subsidiary ledger accounts could also be originated for prepaid insurance policies, machinery and equipment, notes receivable, or notes, accounts, and bonds payable.

The "Control" notation will not be included in the account titles in the remainder of this text.

Special Journals

Up to this point in the text each transaction was recorded in the general journal in chronological order. In order to conserve time and clerical expense, many firms maintain one or more *special journals* in which are entered similar transactions that occur frequently. For example, all credit sales are recorded in a *sales journal*, rather than a multitude of daily credit sale entries being interspersed throughout the general journal. A typical format of this type of sales journal is illustrated below:

	DATE		SALE NO.	ACCOUNT DEBITED	POST. REF.	ACCTS. REC. DR. SALES CR.	
				SALES JOURNAL		PAGE	
1	1979 Jan.	2	638	John Gray	✓	4 1 0 0 00	1
2		8	639	Barb Strouse	✓	3 2 7 5 00	2
3		15	640	Rod Samuels	✓	6 2 8 0 00	3
4		22	641	Michele Kane	✓	3 4 0 0 00	4
5		27	642	Bruce Manne	✓	5 4 6 0 00	5
6						2 2 5 1 5 00	6
7						(110) (710)	7

The total amount of $22,515 is posted at the end of the month to the two ledger accounts, Accounts Receivable and Sales, after which the respective account numbers are placed below the amount posted. In this instance, 110 is the accounts receivable account number, and 710 is the sales account number. As each amount is posted to the individual customer's accounts, a check mark (√) is placed in the Posting Reference column. Each customer's account should be kept current in case information regarding a specific balance is required.

Another frequently used special journal is the *cash receipts journal*, in which all cash received by the company is recorded. A common format for the cash receipts journal is presented below:

CASH RECEIPTS JOURNAL   PAGE

	DATE		ACCOUNT CREDITED	POST. REF.	SUNDRY ACCOUNTS CR.	SALES CR.	ACCOUNTS REC. CR.	CASH DR.	
1	1979 Jan.	2	Sales			2000 00		2000 00	1
2		8	Sales			1010 00		1010 00	2
3		10	Notes Receivable	115	1500 00			1500 00	3
4			Interest Receivable	120	45 00			45 00	4
5		13	John Gray	√			2500 00	2500 00	5
6		15	Sales			3280 00		3280 00	6
7		18	Barb Strouse	√			1700 00	1700 00	7
8		21	John Gray				1600 00	1600 00	8
9		26	Rod Samuels				3000 00	3000 00	9
10		28	Sales			5460 00		5460 00	10
11					1545 00	11750 00	8800 00	22095 00	11
12					(√)	(710)	(110)	(100)	12

Before columnar totals are posted to respective accounts at periodic intervals, special journals with more than one debit and/or credit column must be cross-footed. *Cross-footing* means that the total amount shown in all debit columns must equal the total shown in all credit columns. In the above case, the total of the credit columns ($1,545, $11,750 and $8,800) must equal the total of the debit column, $22,095. After verification, the amount credited to each customer is posted to the individual account receivable record and a check mark is placed in the Posting Reference column to show that the posting was completed. The columnar totals are then posted to Cash (100), Accounts Receivable (110) and Sales (710) in the general ledger.

The $1,545 total amount shown in the Sundry Accounts column is used for purposes of cross-footing only. A check mark is placed under this amount to indicate that the amount was considered in the cross-footing process. Since this amount is composed of more than one account (Notes Receivable and Interest Receivable in this instance), each amount must be posted to the appropriate account. The account number is then placed in the Posting Reference column to show that posting was completed. This "check-marking" device, or some variant, can apply to any special journal in which separate columns are provided for individual accounts.

Three other commonly used special journals, with frequently used columnar headings, are illustrated in abbreviated form on page 160. It should be observed that the format for each special journal may vary widely among business enterprises depending upon circumstances and tradition.

All cash disbursements by the firm are entered in the *check register* or *cash payments journal*. Tight internal control dictates that all payments should be made by means of a bank check. Additional debit columns may include prepaid rent, prepaid insurance, and advertising expense.

In the *payroll journal* (payroll register), the amount shown in the Net Pay column reflects the compensation that is payable to the employee net of the amounts withheld for employees' federal income tax, the Federal Insurance Contribution Act tax (FICA) commonly referred to as the social security tax, hospital insurance, and any other deductions.

A *purchases journal* may take either of two formats. One type, used only to record the purchase of merchandise on account, consists of one amount column requiring a debit to Inventory and a credit to Accounts Payable. This type of purchases journal has a format similar to the sales journal illustrated on page 157. The other format, as illustrated on page 160 enables a wide variety of costs incurred by the firm to be recorded. Separate columns are provided to debit various asset and expense accounts, such as Inventory, Advertising, or sundry accounts. The Accounts Payable column reflects the amounts of the vouchers that must be paid as they become due. A *voucher* is a document prepared by the accounting department for each item requiring payment.

The use of special journals and subsidiary ledger accounts facilitates the recording process, but it does not alter the sequential flow of steps previously outlined in the overview of the accounting cycle. It may be helpful to point out that the general journal is, in a sense, a "special" journal. Transactions which cannot be accommodated in the special journals, such as depreciation and amortization expense, year-end accruals, and the closing entries, are entered in the general journal as "special cases."

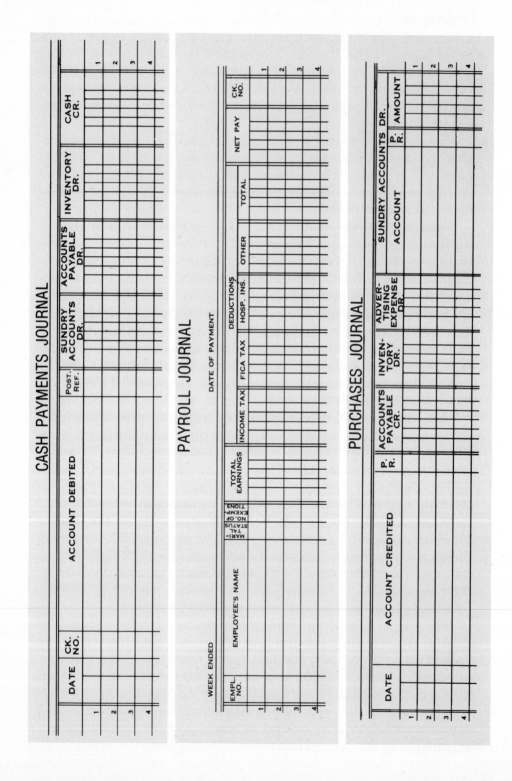

FISCAL YEAR-END PROCEDURES

Closing procedures that are normally required at the end of a fiscal year will be examined in two stages:

(1) An abbreviated illustration will introduce the technical procedures in preparing and completing a work sheet.
(2) A comprehensive problem will then draw together all elements and procedures involved in a normal, full-scale fiscal year-end closing.

The Work Sheet Illustrated

The accountant's initial task at the end of a fiscal period is to verify that all journalized transactions of that period were properly recorded and subsequently posted to the ledger. The next step is to prepare a work sheet, similar to the one shown on page 163 for the Fieldcrest Corp. at the end of its fiscal year, December 31, 1979.

The use of a work sheet greatly facilitates the gathering and organizing of essential information to determine the firm's financial position and net income for a particular period. The first work sheet procedure is to prepare a *trial balance* by listing each account title in the order that it appears in the ledger. The ending balance for each account is recorded in the appropriate debit or credit column of the trial balance section of the work sheet. The total of these two columns must be equal before proceeding further.

An overview of the sequence involved in completing the work sheet is as follows:

(1) Any adjustment that is required to an account is entered in the Adjustments columns of the work sheet.
(2) Adjustments are then added to or subtracted from the trial balance amounts for each account, and the adjusted balance is entered in the Income Statement or Balance Sheet columns, as appropriate.[1]
(3) Financial statements may then be prepared directly from the respective columns on the work sheet; the accounts and the amounts shown in the Adjustments columns are recorded in the general journal and posted to the general ledger.

Adjusting Entries. The following five adjustments will be made for Fieldcrest Corp. at the end of its fiscal year, December 31, 1979, to illustrate technical procedures involved with the work sheet. If these adjustments are not recorded, the balance sheet and income statement will contain incomplete and erroneous financial

---

[1]Some accountants prefer to insert Adjusted Trial Balance columns between the Adjustments and Income Statement columns. The format adopted in this text conserves space and lessens opportunities for error in transcribing amounts into one of the financial statement columns.

information. Each letter in parentheses identifies the entry that is shown in the Adjustments columns of the work sheet:

(a) Match inventory with recognized revenue.
(b) Recognize depreciation on equipment.
(c) Charge expired prepaid rent to expense.
(d) Recognize wages and salaries expense.
(e) Record an allowance for doubtful accounts.

(a) Match Inventory With Recognized Revenue

Although all revenue derived from sales was recorded at regular intervals during 1979, no entry was prepared to charge to expense the cost of the merchandise inventory that was transferred to customers. The chief accountant indicated that the cost of inventory associated with the $116,000 of sales made during 1979 was $75,000. The required adjusting entry is shown below:

Cost of Goods Sold (IS)....................................... 75,000
   Inventory (CA)...   75,000
     Match cost of merchandise inventory sold with revenue generated in 1979.

(b) Recognize Depreciation on Equipment

All equipment reflected in the trial balance was purchased two years earlier. The straight-line method was used to depreciate the equipment, each item of which had an expected life of five years, with no resale value expected at the end of its useful life. The depreciation expense that should be recorded for 1979 is $12,000, ($60,000 ÷ 5 years); and the adjusting entry is shown below:

Depreciation Expense — Equipment (IS) 12,000
   Accumulated Depreciation — Equipment (NA)........   12,000
     Recognition of depreciation expense for 1977.

(c) Charge Expired Prepaid Rent to Expense

The $6,000 balance in Prepaid Expenses is composed entirely of rent on a building for 1979 that was prepaid on January 1, 1979. The benefits contained in this particular asset expired during 1979 at the monthly rate of $500. The adjusting entry shown below recognizes the expiration of these benefits at December 31:

Rent Expense (IS)... 6,000
   Prepaid Expenses (CA)   6,000
     Charge prepaid rent to expense.

(d) Recognize Wages and Salaries Expense

Compensation totaling $1,500 was earned by employees during the final working days of 1979, and will not be paid until the

FIELDCREST CORP.
WORK SHEET
FOR THE YEAR ENDED DECEMBER 31, 1979

#	ACCOUNT TITLE	TRIAL BALANCE DEBIT	TRIAL BALANCE CREDIT	ADJUSTMENTS DEBIT	ADJUSTMENTS CREDIT	INCOME STATEMENT DEBIT	INCOME STATEMENT CREDIT	BALANCE SHEET DEBIT	BALANCE SHEET CREDIT
1	Cash	10 000 00						10 000 00	
2	Accounts Receivable	25 000 00						25 000 00	
3	Allowance for Doubtful Accounts		2 000 00		(e) 1 800 00				3 800 00
4	Inventory	117 000 00			(a) 75 000 00			42 000 00	
5	Prepaid Expenses	6 000 00			(c) 6 000 00				
6	Equipment	60 000 00						60 000 00	
7	Accumulated Depreciation — Equipment		24 000 00		(b) 12 000 00				36 000 00
8	Accounts Payable		30 000 00						30 000 00
9	Wages and Salaries Payable				(d) 1 500 00				1 500 00
10	Capital Stock		54 000 00						54 000 00
11	Retained Earnings		10 000 00						10 000 00
12	Sales		116 000 00				116 000 00		
13	Cost of Goods Sold			(a) 75 000 00		75 000 00			
14	Depreciation Expense — Equipment			(b) 12 000 00		12 000 00			
15	Rent Expense			(c) 6 000 00		6 000 00			
16	Uncollectible Accounts Expense			(e) 1 800 00		1 800 00			
17	Wages and Salaries Expense	18 000 00		(d) 1 500 00		19 500 00			
18		236 000 00	236 000 00	96 300 00	96 300 00	114 300 00	116 000 00	137 000 00	135 300 00
19	Net Income					1 700 00			1 700 00
20						116 000 00	116 000 00	137 000 00	137 000 00

first week in 1980. The adjustment to record this liability and recognize additional employee compensation expense for 1979 is shown below:

Wages and Salaries Expense (IS)	1,500	
Wages and Salaries Payable (CL)		1,500
Recognize wages and salaries expense.		

(e) Record an Allowance for Doubtful Accounts

The controller estimated that a provision should be made at the end of 1979 for $1,800 of credit sales made during 1979 that would probably prove uncollectible. The required adjustment is reflected in the following entry:

Uncollectible Accounts Expense (IS)........................	1,800	
Allowance for Doubtful Accounts		1,800
Record allowance for doubtful accounts.		

Completion of the Work Sheet. Each of the foregoing adjusting entries is recorded in the Adjustments columns of the work sheet. After verifying equality between these two Adjustments columns, the adjustment for each account is added to or subtracted from the amount shown in the Trial Balance columns and extended to the appropriate Income Statement or Balance Sheet columns. The Income Statement and Balance Sheet columns are then totaled. The amount necessary to make the two Income Statement columns and the two Balance Sheet columns balance, is either the net income or net loss. In this case, $1,700 is included on the "Net Income" line in the appropriate columns to complete the work sheet.

The two financial statements may be prepared directly from the work sheet, if desired, after adding the $1,700 net income to the $10,000 Retained Earnings shown in the Trial Balance. Other detailed steps involved in preparing the financial statements, and formally closing the accounting records for the fiscal year will be examined at the end of the comprehensive illustration which follows.

A Comprehensive Illustration

The following year-end adjustments will be made for Dynaflow Corporation at the end of its fiscal year, December 31, 1979. Each letter in parentheses identifies the entry that is shown in the Adjustments columns of the work sheet on pages 166 and 167:

(1) Charge various capitalized costs to expense:
    (a) Match inventory sold with recognized revenue.

      (b) Depreciate plant assets.
      (c) Amortize intangible assets.
      (d) Expense prepaid items.
  (2) Accrue income and expenses:
      (e) Interest income.
      (f) Wages and salaries expense.
      (g) Interest expense.
      (h) Rental income.
  (3) Estimate the collectibility of receivables:
      (i) Allowance for doubtful accounts.
  (4) Correct errors:
      (j) Transposition error.
      (k) Inventory error.
  (5) Distribute income:
      (l) Accrual of federal income tax expense.
      (m) Declaration of cash dividend.

Charge Various Capitalized Costs to Expense. Several costs that were originally capitalized may require adjustment at the end of the fiscal period. These include: charging inventory to expense as cost of goods sold; expensing various prepaid items; and recognizing depreciation and amortization expense on plant and intangible assets.

Match Inventory Sold with Recognized Revenue. No entry was made during 1979 to match the cost of the inventory sold with the sales generated. A convenient method which is frequently used to determine the cost of goods sold for a particular period is the following:

  (1) Determine the inventory balance at the beginning of the period.
  (2) Add the total purchases during the period.
  (3) Take a physical count of all items in inventory at the end of the period; then subtract that amount from the total of the two amounts above.

The net result of $[(1) + (2)] - (3)$ is the amount of inventory that was transferred to customers during the period, assuming there were no lost or damaged goods. This net amount is charged to expense as cost of goods sold.

The following summary illustrates the method described above to determine cost of goods sold for fiscal year 1979:

January 1, 1979, inventory balance......................................	$ 60,000
Plus purchases during 1979	260,000
Total to be accounted for (the balance shown in the inventory account at December 31, 1979, per the trial balance) ...	$320,000
Less inventory on hand per physical inventory count at December 31, 1979..	80,000
Total cost of goods transferred to customers during 1979	$240,000

The adjusting entry on page 168 reflects the charging of inventory to expense as cost of goods sold at December 31, 1979:

Dynaflow Corporation
Work Sheet
For the Year Ended December 31, 1979

Account Title	Trial Balance Debit	Trial Balance Credit	Adjustments Debit	Adjustments Credit	Income Statement Debit	Income Statement Credit	Balance Sheet Debit	Balance Sheet Credit
Cash	80,500		(j) 1,800				82,300	
Notes Receivable	10,100						10,100	
Accounts Receivable	50,000			(j) 1,800			48,200	
Allowance for Doubtful Accounts		2,000		(i) 4,500				6,500
Interest Receivable			(e) 100				100	
Inventory	320,000			(a) 240,000 (k) 2,000			78,000	
Prepaid Expenses	28,300			(d) 23,300			5,000	
Land	20,000						20,000	
Buildings	100,000						100,000	
Accumulated Depreciation — Buildings		2,500		(b) 2,500				5,000
Equipment	120,000						120,000	
Accumulated Depreciation — Equipment		12,000		(b) 12,000				24,000
Patents	15,000			(c) 1,000			14,000	
Notes Payable, 9%, short term		20,000						20,000
Accounts Payable		75,200	(k) 2,000					73,200
Wages and Salaries Payable				(f) 500				500
Interest Payable				(g) 8,100				8,100
Unearned Rental Income		5,000	(h) 4,000					1,000
Federal Income Tax Payable				(l) 37,400				37,400

Account	Trial Balance Dr	Trial Balance Cr	Adjustments Dr	Adjustments Cr	Income Statement Dr	Income Statement Cr	Balance Sheet Dr	Balance Sheet Cr
Dividends Payable				(m) 30,000				30,000
Bonds Payable, 6%, long-term		105,000						105,000
Capital Stock, $10 par		145,100						145,100
Retained Earnings		14,500	(m) 30,000					15,500
Sales		450,000				450,000		
Cost of Goods Sold			(a) 240,000		240,000			
Uncollectible Accounts Expense			(i) 4,500		4,500			
Wages and Salaries Expense	78,700		(f) 500		79,200			
Payroll Taxes Expense	5,000				5,000			
Rent Expense	3,600				3,600			
Insurance Expense	400				400			
Supplies Expense			(d) 23,300		23,300			
Interest Expense			(g) 8,100		8,100			
Amortization Expense			(c) 1,000		1,000			
Depreciation Expense			(b) 14,500		14,500			
Interest Income		300		(e) 100		400		
Rental Income				(h) 4,000		4,000		
Federal Income Tax Expense			(l) 37,400		37,400			
	831,600	831,600	367,200	367,200	417,000	454,400	455,800	493,200
Net Income					37,400			37,400
					454,400	454,400	493,200	493,200

(a)

```
Cost of Goods Sold (IS)....................................... 240,000
    Inventory (CA).............................................        240,000
        Match the cost of merchandise sold with revenue
        generated during 1979.
```

Depreciate Plant Assets. Dynaflow Corporation depreciated its plant assets that were purchased in 1978 by using the straight-line method. The expected service life of the buildings is 40 years and 10 years for the equipment, with zero resale value estimated at the end of the useful life for both types of assets. A full year of depreciation amounting to $14,500 is to be recorded, based on the following computations:

$$\begin{aligned} \text{Buildings:} \quad & 1/40 \times \$100,000 = \$\ 2,500 \\ \text{Equipment:} \quad & 1/10 \times \$120,000 = \underline{\ 12,000} \\ & \hspace{3.2cm} \underline{\$14,500} \end{aligned}$$

(b)

```
Depreciation Expense (IS) ................................... 14,500
    Accumulated Depreciation — Buildings (NA)..........        2,500
    Accumulated Depreciation — Equipment (NA) ........       12,000
        Record the consumption of benefits contained in
        plant assets during 1979.
```

Note that only one depreciation expense account is used in this illustration, although separate expense accounts could be created for each type of plant asset.

Amortize Intangible Assets. Management decided to amortize the $15,000 of patents that were acquired on January 1, 1979, in 15 equal annual amounts of $1,000:

(c)

```
Amortization Expense (IS).................................... 1,000
    Patents (NA)...............................................        1,000
        Record expensing of intangible assets per man-
        agement's policy.
```

Expense Prepaid Items. The Prepaid Expenses balance of $28,300 that was reflected on the trial balance consisted solely of office and factory supplies. A review of these supplies at the end of 1979 revealed that only $5,000 remained unused. Hence, the $23,300 difference should be charged to expense at the end of 1979, as shown below:

(d)

```
Supplies Expense (IS)........................................ 23,300
    Prepaid Expenses (CA)....................................       23,300
        Record expensing of office and factory supplies
        consumed during year.
```

Corporate policy with respect to costs incurred for rent and insurance is to charge these items to expense at the time of payment. Since the benefits contained in these items expired by the end of 1979, no year-end adjustment is necessary.

Accrue Income and Expenses. Accrual of several income and expense items required at the year-end for Dynaflow Corporation includes the recognition of interest income, wages and salaries expense, interest expense, and rent income.

Interest Income. A detailed review of the notes receivable revealed that $100 of interest should be accrued as a receivable at year-end. This amount must be recorded as earned income during 1979 even though it will not be collected until January, 1980. The adjusting entry is shown below:

(e)

Interest Receivable (CA).......................................	100	
Interest Income (IS)...		100
Record interest receivable and interest income at fiscal year-end.		

Wages and Salaries Expense. Employee compensation totaling $500 had to be accrued for the final working day in 1979, even though that amount will not be paid until January 4, 1980.

(f)

Wages and Salaries Expense (IS)	500	
Wages and Salaries Payable (CL)		500
Record the liability and expense incurred for employee compensation during the last working day of 1979.		

Interest Expense. The following schedule reflects the calculation of total interest expense for 1979:

6% annual interest on $105,000 bonds payable	$6,300
9% annual interest on $20,000 notes payable...........................	1,800
Total interest expense for 1979	$8,100

All interest for 1979 is payable during the first two days of 1980. The appropriate accrual entry at December 31, 1979, is shown below:

(g)

Interest Expense (IS)	8,100	
Interest Payable (CL)		8,100
Record interest payable and expense for 1979.		

Rental Income. Eighty percent of the $5,000 unearned rental income (see trial balance) that was received as an advance payment earlier in 1979 has been earned as of December 31, 1979. The necessary recognition of rental income is reflected in the following entry:

(h)

Unearned Rental Income (CL)	4,000	
Rental Income (IS)		4,000
Recognition of rent income for 1979, ($5,000 × .8 = $4,000).		

Estimate the Collectibility of Receivables. In instances where provision is made for estimated uncollectible accounts receivable, a valuation adjustment is normally required at the end of each fiscal year.

Allowance for Doubtful Accounts. The credit manager esti-mated that 1 percent of the total sales made during 1979 will prob-ably prove uncollectible. Since no provision for these uncollect-ibles was made during 1979, the following entry reflects the provision for doubtful accounts for the year:

(i)

Uncollectible Accounts Expense (IS)	4,500	
Allowance for Doubtful Accounts (CA)		4,500
Provision for accounts which may become delin-quent, (1% × $450,000 sales revenue = $4,500).		

Correct Errors. Two types of errors frequently arise which re-quire correction before the income statement and balance sheet are prepared and the accounting records are formally closed for the fiscal year.

Transposition Error. A *transposition error* is the misarrange-ment of some or all of the digits that appear in a correct amount. To illustrate, in mid-December a customer's $4,200 check in pay-ment on account was mistakenly journalized as $2,400. The follow-ing correction has to be recorded to adjust both the cash and ac-counts receivable accounts to the appropriate $4,200 amount involved in that transaction:

(j)

Cash (CA)	1,800	
Accounts Receivable (CA)		1,800
Correcting entry: $4,200 (correct amount) — $2,400 (incorrect entry), = $1,800 (correction).		

A credit posting to the specific customer's account must also be made. An interesting observation with respect to transposition errors is that the difference between the correct amount and the transposed amount is always evenly divisible by nine.

Inventory Error. Merchandise that had been ordered by Synaglow, Inc., a next-door business neighbor, was mistakenly received and journalized as purchased by Dynaflow Corporation during late December, 1979. In addition to the erroneous credit made to Accounts Payable for $2,000, these goods were counted in the physical inventory at the year-end. Fortunately, the account was not yet paid. The required correcting entry is shown below:

(k)

Accounts Payable (CL)..	2,000	
Inventory (CA)..		2,000
Goods erroneously received were counted in physical inventory and entered as an account payable.		

Distribute Income. The final set of adjustments that are frequently required at the end of a fiscal period pertain to the distribution of corporate income. The following adjustments illustrate the accrual of federal income tax expense and the declaration of a cash dividend to stockholders.

Accrual of Federal Income Tax Expense. The amounts shown in the Adjustments columns of the work sheet are added to or subtracted from the amounts of each income-statement-related account in the Trial Balance columns. The adjusted balance for each of these accounts is then entered in the appropriate Income Statement columns of the work sheet. Each revenue, other income, and expense item in this illustration must be considered in calculating taxable income. The calculations are shown below:

Sales..	$450,000	
Interest income	400	
Rental income	4,000	$454,400
Less expenses:		
Cost of goods sold	$240,000	
Wages and salaries...	79,200	
Supplies..	23,300	
Depreciation...	14,500	
Interest	8,100	
Payroll taxes	5,000	
Uncollectible accounts	4,500	
Rent	3,600	
Amortization	1,000	
Insurance	400	379,600
Taxable income (income before federal income tax)..		$ 74,800

The corporate federal income tax rate during 1979 is assumed, for purposes of simplicity, to be 50 percent of income before federal income tax. Hence, $74,800 times 50 percent equals $37,400 federal income tax expense. This amount is an expense chargeable to fiscal year 1979 even though it will probably not be paid until the early part of 1980. The following entry reflects the accrual of this payable and expense item:

(l)

Federal Income Tax Expense (IS)	37,400	
Federal Income Tax Payable (CL)		37,400
Record liability and expense for federal income tax on taxable income earned during 1979.		

Declaration of Cash Dividend. On December 31, 1979, the board of directors of Dynaflow Corporation declared a $30,000 cash dividend which is to be paid in cash to stockholders on January 15, 1980. The time lag between declaration and payment is necessary so as to verify stockholder records and process the dividend checks. On the date of the dividend declaration, the corporation incurred a liability to pay that dividend. The following entry is required to reflect the cash dividend declaration:

(m)

Retained Earnings (OE)	30,000	
Cash Dividends Payable (CL)...............................		30,000
Declaration of cash dividend, payable to stock-holders on January 15, 1980.		

Generally, the board is not obligated to declare a dividend on capital stock, but once the dividend is declared, it must be paid. Prior to declaring the cash dividend, board members should verify that the cash balance is sufficient to pay the dividend on the payment date. There is no necessary correlation between the $37,400 net income that was generated during the fiscal year and the $82,300 cash balance at the end of 1979.

Additional Points on Completing the Work Sheet

Before extending the remaining amounts in the Trial Balance and Adjustments columns to the Income Statement and Balance Sheet columns of the work sheet, it is important to verify that the two Adjustments columns are equal. After verification, the amount shown in the Adjustments columns for each account is added to or subtracted from its corresponding Trial Balance amount, and the result is entered in the appropriate Income Statement or Balance Sheet columns. In order to determine the federal income tax expense, each income-statement-related account should be extended to its appropriate Income Statement column. The federal income tax expense must now be extended to the Income Statement debit column.

Notice that the retained earnings account reflects a debit balance of $15,500 when extended to the Balance Sheet columns. This is because the $37,400 net income has not yet been added to the Retained Earnings adjusted balance by means of the closing entry, which will be prepared after the preparation of the financial statements.

Before the totals of the Income Statement columns and the Balance sheet columns can be verified as being equal, the balancing figure of $37,400 net income must be added to the debit column of the Income Statement and extended to the credit column of the Balance Sheet. This mechanical step is necessary because the closing entry detail is usually not included on the work sheet for purposes of clarity.

The adjusting entries can be recorded in the general journal directly from the work sheet and posted to the ledger at this point; or the accountant can record and post the adjusting and closing entries at the same time.

Preparation of Financial Statements

The income statement and balance sheet may be prepared at this point directly from the ending balances shown in their respective columns of the work sheet. This may be done before the adjusting and closing entries are journalized and posted to enable management and other interested parties to examine financial results as quickly as possible, after conclusion of the year's activities. A word of caution, however, is necessary before preparing the financial statements from the work sheet. The accountant must ensure that the following types of errors are not contained in the work sheet:

(1) Erroneous but offsetting amounts which may have been entered in the Trial Balance columns from the ledger.
(2) The omission of any necessary adjusting entries.
(3) Adjustments either made in the correct amount to the wrong accounts, or made to the correct accounts but in the wrong amount.
(4) Erroneous extensions of data into the Income Statement or Balance Sheet columns.

The balance sheet of Dynaflow Corporation is presented on page 174. The income statement, which is presented on page 175, is displayed in two acceptable formats; the multiple-step and single-step.

Dynaflow Corporation
Balance Sheet
December 31, 1979

Assets			Equities		
Current assets:			**Current liabilities:**		
Cash		$ 82,300	Notes payable		$ 20,000
Notes receivable		10,100	Accounts payable		73,200
Accounts receivable		48,200	Wages and salaries		
Allowance for doubtful			payable		500
accounts		(6,500)	Interest payable		8,100
Interest receivable		100	Unearned rental income		1,000
Inventory		78,000	Federal income tax		
Prepaid expenses			payable		37,400
(supplies)		5,000	Dividends payable		30,000
Total current assets		$217,200	Total current liabilities		$170,200
Plant assets:			**Long-term liabilities:**		
Land		$ 20,000	Bonds payable		$105,000
Buildings	$100,000				
Less accumulated			**Owners' equity:**		
depreciation —			Capital stock, $10 par		$145,100
buildings	5,000	95,000	Retained earnings		21,900*
Equipment	$120,000		Total owners' equity		$167,000
Less accumulated					
depreciation —					
equipment	24,000	96,000			
Total plant assets		$211,000			
Intangibles:					
Patents		14,000			
Total assets		$442,200	Total equities		$442,200

*$15,500 debit balance per the work sheet plus $37,400 net income.

The major distinctions between the two income statement formats are as follows: The *multiple-step* format focuses on gross margin and operating income, with other income items (and any gains or losses) segregated from the operating items. The *single-step* format, on the other hand, stresses the two major subdivisions of total income and total expenses. Other format variations are of course possible.

Dividends declared are not shown on the income statement since cash dividends are not an expense of the business, nor are they deductible from revenue in computing taxable income. Cash dividends are a distribution of net income to shareholders.

The *statement of retained earnings* is frequently prepared to summarize changes that occur in retained earnings between two dates. Dynaflow Corporation's retained earnings balance of

Dynaflow Corporation
Income Statement
For the Year Ended December 31, 1979

Multiple-Step Format			Single-Step Format	
Sales		$450,000	Sales	$450,000
Cost of goods sold		240,000	Rental income	4,000
			Interest income	400
Gross margin		$210,000	Total income	$454,400
Operating expenses:				
Wages and			Expenses:	
salaries	$79,200		Cost of goods sold	$240,000
Supplies	23,300		Wages, salaries, and	
Depreciation	14,500		payroll tax	84,200
Interest	8,100		Supplies	23,300
Payroll taxes	5,000		Amortization and	
Uncollectible			depreciation	15,500
accounts	4,500		Interest	8,100
Rent	3,600		Uncollectible accounts	4,500
Amortization	1,000		Rent and insurance	4,000
Insurance	400	139,600	Total expenses	$379,600
Operating income		$ 70,400		
Other income:			Income before federal	
Interest income	$ 400		income tax	$ 74,800
Rental income	4,000	4,400	Federal income tax expense	37,400
Income before federal			Net income	$ 37,400
income tax		$ 74,800		
Federal income tax expense		37,400		
Net income		$ 37,400		

$14,500 at January 1, 1979, was increased by the $37,400 net income of the period, and decreased by the $30,000 dividend declaration. As shown below, the ending balance in Retained Earnings is $21,900:

Dynaflow Corporation
Statement of Retained Earnings
For the Year Ended December 31, 1979

Balance, January 1, 1979	$14,500
Plus net income	37,400
Less cash dividends	(30,000)
Balance, December 31, 1979	$21,900

The Closing Entry

The year-end balance in each income-statement-related account must be zeroed out; and the net difference between these accounts must be transferred to Retained Earnings at year-end so that these accounts will be ready to receive the ensuing fiscal year's revenue and expenses without being intermingled with amounts from prior periods. The closing single-step entry shown below is journalized at December 31, 1979:

Sales (IS)	450,000	
Interest Income (IS)	400	
Rental Income (IS)	4,000	
Cost of Goods Sold (IS)		240,000
Wages and Salaries Expense (IS)		79,200
Supplies Expense (IS)		23,300
Depreciation Expense (IS)		14,500
Interest Expense (IS)		8,100
Payroll Taxes Expense (IS)		5,000
Uncollectible Accounts Expense (IS)		4,500
Rent Expense (IS)		3,600
Amortization Expense (IS)		1,000
Insurance Expense (IS)		400
Federal Income Tax Expense (IS)		37,400
Retained Earnings (OE)		37,400

　　　　Close all revenue, income, and expense accounts to Retained Earnings at the end of the fiscal year.

The alternate two-step closing procedure that was illustrated in Chapter 3 would reflect a credit to Income Summary instead of a direct credit to Retained Earnings, followed by an immediate transfer of the net amount from the income summary account to Retained Earnings.

The Independent Audit

Before releasing financial statements to the public, many companies obtain the services of public accounting firms or independent certified public accountants who examine and review the firm's records at the close of each fiscal year. Since these professionals have had exposure to many commercial and industrial problems and situations, they are in a position to provide an additional check on the accuracy and completeness of financial reports that the firm submits to the financial community. This practice is followed (in some cases it is required by law) to insure that: (1) accounting records have been properly maintained; (2) the existence of internal control and other safeguards are adequate; and (3) the financial statements properly reflect the financial condition and operations of the company.

Reversing Entries

One final step, which involves *reversing entries*, may be required. These entries are recorded after formally closing the accounting records of the fiscal year and prior to recording any financial data in the succeeding year. The reason for such entries is that routine clerical procedures or computerized programs may not coincide with the end-of-period accrual procedures. This will be made clearer in two examples presented below which explain why a recording problem is created, and how it can be resolved.

Interest Receivable and Interest Income. The established clerical procedure and computerized program within Dynaflow Corporation requires a debit to Cash and a credit to Interest Income whenever cash is received in payment of interest on outstanding notes receivable. Using this guideline, the following entry will be made in 1980 when payment is received for the $100 interest receivable that was accrued in entry (e) shown on page 169 and which appears on the balance sheet at December 31, 1979:

(A)

Cash (CA)...	100	
Interest Income (IS)..		100
Record receipt of cash and simultaneous recognition of		
interest income.		

Notice that Interest Income, not Interest Receivable, is credited in the above entry because of the standardized procedure.

If entry (A) above is not modified in some way during 1980, the receipt of $100 cash will be recognized as earned income in both fiscal years 1979 and 1980; and the $100 interest receivable that appeared on the balance sheet at December 31, 1979, will remain on the accounting records.

The following reversing entry must be made to resolve the dilemma on January 1, 1980, immediately after the records have been formally closed for the fiscal year ended December 31, 1979. This entry is made at the beginning of 1980 in anticipation that the $100 interest receivable will be collected sometime during the year:

(B)

Interest Income (IS)..	100	
Interest Receivable (CA)...		100
To reverse interest income and the interest receivable		
balance at December 31, 1979, in anticipation of interest that is expected to be collected during 1980.		

The two T accounts would appear as shown below in 1980 after entries (A) and (B) are recorded:

INTEREST RECEIVABLE (IS)			INTEREST INCOME (IS)	
100		Balance after closing entries on December 31, 1979.		—0—
	100	Reversing entry (B) made on January 1, 1980.	100	
		Entry (A) made during 1980 (the offsetting debit is to Cash).		100
—0—		Balance after entries (A) and (B) are posted.		—0—

If reversing entry (B) is not made, interest income will be overstated by $100 in 1980, and the interest receivable account will continue to be overstated by $100 until corrected.

Interest Payable and Interest Expense. A similar reversing procedure may be made with respect to interest payable and interest expense, if clerical procedures and the computer program require a debit to Interest Expense and a credit to Cash whenever cash is disbursed to pay interest, as shown below:

(C)

Interest Expense (IS)... 8,100
    Cash (CA) 8,100
        Payment of interest expense during 1980.

Assume that the preceding entry made early in 1980 represents the payment of the $8,100 interest payable that was accrued in entry (g) shown on page 169 and which appears on the balance sheet as of December 31, 1979. Again, unless entry (C) is modified, interest expense of $8,100 will be double-counted in 1979 and 1980; and the $8,100 interest payable at December 31, 1979, will remain on the accounting records.

The problem can be resolved by making the following reversing entry on January 1, 1980.

(D)

Interest Payable (CL)... 8,100
    Interest Expense (IS)... 8,100
        To reverse interest expense and the interest payable
        balance at December 31, 1979, in anticipation of interest to be paid during 1980.

The two T accounts would appear as shown below in 1980, after entries (C) and (D) are recorded:

INTEREST PAYABLE (CL)   INTEREST EXPENSE (IS)

	8,100	Balance after closing entries at December 31, 1979.	—0—	
8,100		Reversing entry (D) made on January 1, 1980.		8,100
		Entry (C) made during 1980 (the offsetting credit is to Cash).	8,100	
	—0—	Balance after entries (C) and (D) are posted.	—0—	

If this reversing entry is not made, Interest Expense will be overstated by $8,100 in 1980, and Interest Payable will continue to be overstated by the same amount until corrected.

Note that each reversing entry must be recorded immediately at the start of the ensuing fiscal year (1980), but only after the accounting records have been formally closed for the previous fiscal year (1979).

QUESTIONS

1. Using your own terminology and format, prepare a detailed diagram of specific steps involved in the accounting cycle.

2. Identify several specific source documents which the accountant might refer to in order to obtain information regarding financial transactions that occurred during a fiscal period.

3. Explain why subsidiary ledger accounts are frequently used.

4. (a) Explain the primary purpose of special journals. (b) Identify several special journals that are frequently used by the accountant.

5. Provide a format for the following special journals, including columnar headings and Dr/Cr notations: (a) cash receipts journal; (b) cash payments journal.

6. Define (a) cross-footing, and (b) a transposition error.

7. Provide a format for each of the following special journals, including columnar headings and Dr/Cr notations: (a) payroll journal; (b) purchases journal.

8. Explain in detail the format of the work sheet and how it is used to facilitate the accounting process at the end of a fiscal period.

9. Enumerate the types of adjusting entries that are frequently required at the end of an accounting period. Explain why these adjustments or corrections are essential to the accounting process.

10. Provide a sample journal entry (amounts need not be shown) to record each adjusting entry identified in Question 9 above.

11. Explain how the cost of goods sold during a period can be determined at the end of that period.

12. Assuming a time lag existed between the declaration and the payment of a cash dividend to stockholders, illustrate with sample jour-

nal entries (amounts need not be shown) how the (a) declaration, and (b) payment of the dividend would be treated in the accounting records.

13. "An accurate balance sheet and income statement may always be prepared directly from the balances shown in the last four columns of the work sheet if that work sheet crossfoots and balances." Indicate several circumstances which might make this statement less than completely accurate.

14. Identify those significant features which distinguish the single-step from the multiple-step income statement

15. Describe the statement of retained earnings.

16. Explain why the closing entry is essential. Illustrate two methods of making the closing entry.

17. To what extent is it necessary to show the (a) closing entry and (b) any reversing entries on the work sheet?

18. Identify several advantages which accrue to companies that hire the services of outside accountants to audit internal accounting records and procedures at periodic intervals.

19. Explain why reversing entries may be required at the beginning of the next fiscal period after the records of the past fiscal period have been closed. Provide an example using interest payable and interest expense accounts to explain the process.

EXERCISES

1. Sales journal. The transactions described below occurred in Calva Sporting Goods Company on the dates indicated:

January 4 — Merchandise was billed on sales slip #62 to P. Klader for $732 under 30-day credit terms.

January 7 — Merchandise was billed on sales slip #63 to N. Spurlock for $89 under 30-day credit terms.

January 7 — Cash sales for the first week totaled $1,648.

January 10 — Merchandise was billed on sales slip#64 to R. Castle for $416 under 40-day credit terms; and to H. Clauser on sales slip #65 for $68 under similar terms.

January 12 — Merchandise was billed on sales slip #66 to T. Baines for $275 under 30-day credit terms.

January 14 — Cash sales for the second week totaled $2,104.

January 14 — The accountant discovered that the billing to N. Spurlock on January 7 should have been recorded as $98.

Required: (a) Prepare a sales journal, using the format presented in this chapter. (b) Record each of the transactions described above in the sales or general journal (as appropriate), the only two journals in use in the company. (c) Describe in detail the specific steps required at the close of business on January 14, assuming postings were made to the general and subsidiary ledgers at the end of each two-week period. Account number 100 was assigned to Cash, 110 to Accounts Receivable, and 820 to Sales.

2. Cash payments journal. The following transactions occurred in Johnson's Pizzeria on the dates indicated:

June 16 — Check #87 for $327 was paid to the Mutual Insurance Company for a fire and casualty insurance premium covering the period June 16 through December 31. The amount was immediately charged to expense.

June 18 — Check #88 for $148 was paid for various food preparation items that were capitalized as inventory.

June 18 — Check #89 for $568 was paid to a vendor for various supplies that had been previously capitalized when purchased in May under 30-day credit terms.

June 21 — Check #90 for $600 was issued for six-months rent, effective July 1. The amount was immediately charged to expense.

June 25 — Check #91 for $293 was issued to a vendor for various prepaid supplies which were immediately capitalized as a prepaid expense.

June 29 — Check #92 for $87 was issued to a local garage in payment of an account payable for repairs made on a delivery truck during the last half of May.

Required: (a) Prepare a cash payments journal, using the format presented in this chapter. (b) Record each of the above transactions in the cash payments journal. (c) Place appropriate check marks and account numbers in the cash payments journal at June 30, the date at which all information in special journals for the last half of June was posted to the ledger. Assigned account numbers were:

100 Cash	520 Accounts Payable
320 Inventory	830 Insurance Expense
410 Prepaid Expenses	840 Rent Expense

3. Cost of goods sold determination. The inventory of merchandise that was on hand at January 1, 1979, in the Hawthorne Hardware Co. totaled $116,000. Purchases of goods for inventory that were made under 30-day credit terms during the fiscal year ended December 31, 1979, amounted to $839,000. A physical inspection of merchandise at the end of 1979 revealed that $74,000 of merchandise remained unsold and in saleable condition. No goods had been lost or damaged during 1979.

Required: (a) Determine the cost of goods sold for the fiscal year ended December 31, 1979. (b) Prepare the entry that should be made at the year-end to record this item of expense.

4. Depreciation and amortization expenses. A parcel of land containing a building was purchased on January 1, 1979, by the Merritt Corp. for $380,000. The controller assigned 10% of that total cost to the land. The building was estimated to have a remaining useful life of 30 years, with $21,000 salvage value estimated at the end of that time. On July 1, 1979, the firm incurred a cost of $60,000 for several patents. These patents were expected to have a useful life of 12 years, with no residual salvage value at the end of that time. Straight-line depreciation or amortization was used on all plant and intangible assets.

Required: Prepare an adjusting entry at the end of the fiscal year, December 31, 1979, to record the appropriate amount of depreciation and amortization expenses.

5. **Prepaid expense items.** The following prepaid expense items were purchased during the fiscal year ended December 31, 1979; and were either immediately capitalized or charged to expense as noted below:

	IMMEDIATELY CAPITALIZED	IMMEDIATELY EXPENSED
Rent for 16 months, effective January 1, 1979...		$16,000
Insurance for an 18-month period, effective January 1, 1979..........................		9,000
Office supplies	$14,000	
Factory supplies	36,000	
Total...	$50,000	$25,000

A physical count of the supplies at December 31, 1979, revealed that $3,000 of office supplies remained on hand at the year-end, as compared to $8,000 of factory supplies.

Required: Prepare an adjusting entry to properly reflect the four expenses associated with the above items for the 1979 fiscal year.

6. **Rental and interest income.** Selected information contained in the work sheet at December 31, 1979, for Stardust Mfg. Corp. is shown below:

ACCOUNT TITLE	TRIAL BALANCE Debit	TRIAL BALANCE Credit
Notes Receivable...	40,000	
Interest Receivable...	——	
Unearned Rental Income......................................		24,000
Interest Income		4,000
Rental Income		——

Additional data concerning these five accounts are supplied below:

(1) Interest at an annual rate of 10% was not accrued for the last six months of 1979 on the notes receivable outstanding at December 31, 1979. Interest receivable was expected to be received during the next fiscal year.

(2) The amount of unearned rental income reflected on the work sheet was received on August 1, 1979, for rent on an unused portion of an annex at the rate of $3,000 per month, effective August 1, 1979.

Required: (a) Prepare any adjusting entries that may be required at December 31, 1979, based on the information supplied above. (b) Determine the balance in each of the accounts shown above at December 31, 1979, after recording the adjusting entries.

7. **Employee compensation and interest expense.** Selected information contained in the work sheet at December 31, 1979, for Stardust Mfg. Corp., is shown below:

ACCOUNT TITLE	TRIAL BALANCE Debit	TRIAL BALANCE Credit
Notes Payable, 12%, short-term.............................		40,000
Interest Payable..		——
Wages and Salaries Payable....................................		——
Mortgage Note Payable, 10%, due March 31, 1990......		100,000

ACCOUNT TITLE	TRIAL BALANCE Debit	Credit
Bonds Payable, 8%, due December 31, 1984..............		250,000
Interest Expense...	18,600	
Wages and Salaries Expense.................................	640,000	

Additional information concerning these accounts is noted below:

(1) Interest on the short-term notes was payable at the beginning of each quarter, for example, January 1, April 1, etc.

(2) Interest on both long-term liabilities was payable semiannually at each January 1 and July 1.

(3) The liability for employee compensation incurred on the last working day of 1979 was $2,600, payable on January 4, 1980.

Required: (a) Prepare any adjusting entries that may be required at December 31, 1979, based on the information supplied. (b) Determine the balance in each of the accounts at December 31, 1979, after recording the necessary adjusting entries.

8. Provision for uncollectibles. Total sales in Parliament Corporation of $874,000 for the fiscal year ended December 31, 1979, were divided as shown below:

Cash sales	$170,000
Credit sales under 30-day credit terms	659,000
Credit sales under note receivable arrangements...................	45,000
Total sales	$874,000

During a review of these sales at the end of 1979, the controller discovered a transposition error that occurred in a customer's account. The sale to A. Pinet under 30-day credit terms for $95,000 was erroneously recorded as $59,000. In addition, the controller directed the accountant to provide for estimated uncollectibles in the amount of 1½% of the total credit sales (after corrections) for 1979. No provision had yet been made for these estimated uncollectibles.

Required: Prepare the two adjusting entries at December 31, 1979, that are required by the above information.

9. Distribution of net income. Income before federal income taxes amounted to $127,000 for the fiscal year ended June 30, 1980. However, prior to recording federal income tax expense at the rate of 50% of taxable income, the chief accountant discovered that a $14,000 tax deductible fire loss on inventory that had occurred in March, 1980, was overlooked and never recorded. The federal income tax accrued on taxable income earned during the fiscal year ended June 30, 1980, was payable during the year ended June 30, 1981. In addition, the board of directors on June 30, 1980, declared a cash dividend equivalent to 30% of corrected net income after taxes, payable to stockholders on July 10, 1980. No dividend had yet been recorded as of June 30, 1980.

Required: Prepare the three adjusting entries required by the above information assuming the formal closing entry was properly made at the end of the fiscal year.

10. Income statement preparation from adjusted trial balance. The balance for each account, after all adjusting and correcting entries were recorded at December 31, 1979, the end of the fiscal year for the Rivera Corporation, is shown below:

| | ADJUSTED TRIAL BALANCE AT DECEMBER 31, 1979 |
ACCOUNT TITLE	(CREDIT)
Accumulated Depreciation — Building and Equipment	$(216,000)
Allowance for Doubtful Accounts	(12,500)
Cost of Goods Sold	550,000
Depreciation Expense — Building and Equipment	54,000
Dividends Payable	(12,500)
Federal Income Tax Expense	28,000
Insurance Expense	8,000
Interest Expense	26,000
Interest Income	(6,000)
Interest Payable	(2,500)
Interest Receivable	1,200
Office Supplies Expense	12,000
Prepaid Expenses	17,200
Rent Expense	31,000
Rental Income	(14,000)
Sales	(916,000)
Uncollectible Accounts Expense	9,000
Wages and Salaries Expense	190,000
Wages and Salaries Payable	(8,500)

Required: Prepare an income statement for the fiscal year ended December 31, 1979, using: (a) the multiple-step format; and (b) the single-step format.

11. Closing entry and statement of retained earnings. Refer to the data provided in Exercise 10.

Required: (a) Prepare the closing entry that was probably recorded at December 31, 1979, using the single-step procedure. (b) Prepare a statement of retained earnings for the fiscal year ended December 31, 1979. The credit balance in Retained Earnings was $122,000 at January 1, 1979. The only cash dividend to stockholders during 1979 was declared on December 31, 1979, for $12,500, payable January 10, 1980.

12. Reversing entries. The procedures handbook and computerized program that was in operation in the Stone Shoe Co. contained the following directive:

Whenever interest is received or paid, the offset to the cash account must be an appropriate income-statement-related account. For example:

```
Interest Expense (IS) ..........................................  xx
    Cash (CA) ..................................................          xx
        Record interest payment.
```

The year-end adjusting entries that were recorded by the head accountant on December 31, 1979, the end of the 1979 fiscal year, affected the following accounts by the amounts indicated:

ACCOUNT TITLE	DEBIT	CREDIT
Interest Expense	$8,400	
Interest Income		$ 700
Interest Payable		8,400
Interest Receivable	700	

Required: (a) Prepare any reversing entries which the head accountant must record at the beginning of the 1980 fiscal year to conform with the standardized directive. (b) Illustrate with appropriate T accounts the problem that would be created in 1979 and in 1980, if the interest paid during fiscal year 1980 included the amount accrued at December 31, 1979, and a reversing entry was not made on January 1, 1980, for interest expense.

PROBLEMS

5-1. Sales and cash receipts journals. Bonsigli's Furniture Co. maintains three journals: general, sales, and cash receipts. All credit sales under 30-day terms are recorded in the sales journal and notes receivable are recorded in the general journal. The format for the sales and cash receipts journals are as presented previously in this chapter. The firm's fiscal year ended each September 30. Account numbers were assigned as shown below:

Cash	100	Performance Liability	370
Notes Receivable	105	Sales	600
Accounts Receivable	110	Interest Income	660
Notes Payable	340	Rental Income	670

The transactions described below and on page 186 occurred during February on the dates indicated:

February

3   Sales on 30-day credit terms to:

> D. Lipsch ....Sales slip #143 .... $1,350
> B. Mort ....Sales slip #144 .... $1,330

4   Collection of the following accounts from:

> T. Bronson $1,200
> A. Friend $2,600
> R. Knight .... $ 450
> Q. Thorn .... $ 150

6   A $3,500 sale under a 40-month note receivable arrangement to B. Shart.

7   Total cash sales of $2,620 during the first seven days of February.

9   Receipt of $1,240 from C. Culp in payment of a $1,200 note receivable plus interest income of $40. This note was originated in October of the previous year.

11   A check for $600 was received with an order for merchandise which was temporarily out of stock.

13   Collection of the following accounts:

> P. Fry .... $ 460
> A. Ashcroft $1,140

14   Sales on 30-day credit terms to:

N. Fritch ....Sales slip #145 .... $2,200
F. Frank ....Sales slip #146 .... $ 960

14   Total cash sales of $3,240 during the period February 8–14.

18   A $7,500 loan for six months was obtained from the bank.

20   P. Prince forwarded $1,620 in payment of a $1,590 note plus $30 interest. The note was originally signed the previous December.

21   Cash sales totaled $2,780 during February 15–21.

24   Sales under 30-day credit terms to:

P. George ....Sales slip #147 .... $ 320
A. Prince.................Sales slip #148 .... $1,240

25   An account receivable for $230 from X. Splane was written off as uncollectible. The firm's chart of accounts included Allowance for Doubtful Accounts.

26   Collection of accounts receivable from:

D. Lipsh... $1,250
A. Friend .... $ 300

28   Receipt of $1,000 rental payment for the 5-month period, beginning October 1 of the previous year.

28   Cash sales totaled $4,250 during the final week of February.

Required: (1) Prepare the three journals maintained by Bonsigli's Furniture Co.

(2) Enter each transaction in the appropriate journal.

(3) Place appropriate notations in the sales and cash receipts journals to indicate that specific amounts were posted to the general and subsidiary ledgers at the end of February.

5-2. Purchases and cash payments journals. Speedfast Corp. maintains three journals: purchases, cash payments, and general. The format of the first two journals is, with one exception, the same as presented previously in this chapter. The sole exception is that a Wages and Salaries Payable (Dr) column is placed between the Sundry Accounts (Dr) and Accounts Payable (Dr) columns in the cash payments journal. Account numbers were assigned as indicated below:

Cash...................................	100	Advertising Expense.............	705
Inventory	210	Insurance Expense................	708
Prepaid Expenses	320	Interest Expense..................	710
Accounts Payable	510	Rent Expense......................	725
Wages and Salaries Payable....	520		

The events described below occurred on the dates indicated. The firm's fiscal year ends each December 31. The content of each journal was posted to the general and subsidiary ledgers at the end of each month.

June

2   Merchandise costing $4,620 was purchased for inventory on 30-day credit terms from Pinehurst Corp.

3   An invoice was received for six-months' rental payment on a vacant garage for $2,600, effective June 1. The amount, which was payable by June 15, was immediately charged to expense.

6 An account payable due Foresman Corp. for $840 was paid with check #216.

7 Employee compensation totaling $5,130 was paid to employees on checks #217–229. Wages and salaries expense was previously recorded in the payroll journal.

9 Additional merchandise costing $3,790 was purchased for inventory on 30-day credit terms from Townley Co.

9 A billing for an insurance premium for $1,650 was received from State Mutual Insurance Co. and was immediately charged to expense. The bill was to be paid on or before June 15.

11 Check #230 was written to the Provident Press for $815 of advertising in the various editions of the newspaper.

12 Office supplies amounting to $720 were purchased on 30-day credit terms from Neuse Suppliers Corp. and immediately capitalized as a prepaid expense.

14 Check #231 was forwarded to Berkshire Mills for $2,880 of materials purchased for inventory under COD terms.

14 Employee compensation totaling $4,650 was paid to employees on checks #232–246. Wages and salaries expense was previously recorded in the payroll journal.

15 Check #247 was forwarded to the bank for interest amounting to $430 on a short-term bank loan. The amount was charged to interest expense.

15 Check #248 was issued to the landlord for the $2,600 rent liability recorded on June 3. In addition, check #249 was mailed to State Mutual Insurance Co. for the insurance billing received on June 9.

21 Employee compensation totaling $5,720 was paid on checks #250–263. Wages and salaries expense was previously recorded in the payroll journal.

26 A bill for $280 was received from Capital Press for advertising copy layout work. The bill was due for payment by July 15. The amount was immediately charged to expense.

28 Employee compensation totaling $6,620 was paid on checks #264–278. Wages and salaries expense was previously recorded in the payroll journal.

Required: (1) Prepare the purchases and cash payments journals maintained by Speedfast Corp.

(2) Enter each transaction in the appropriate journal.

(3) Place appropriate notations in the cash payments and purchases journals to indicate that specific amounts were posted to the general and subsidiary ledgers at the end of June.

5-3. Adjusting entries: capitalized costs. The chief accountant of Gollier Mfg. Co. noticed during the last week of December that the following items warranted adjusting entries prior to closing the accounting records for the fiscal year ended December 31, 1979:

(a) The debit balance in Inventory at December 1, 1979, reflected $96,400. Recorded purchases for inventory during December totaled $49,270, and the annual physical check of inventory on hand at December 31 disclosed that $53,410 actually remained in inventory at various plant sites. An entry to record the cost of goods sold for December was not yet recorded.

(b) The following items remained capitalized as prepaid expenses at December 31, 1979:

Insurance premiums (1 year at $600 per month, beginning October 1, 1979) .... $ 7,200
Rent (1½-years advance payment at $1,000 per month beginning June 1, 1979) 18,000
Repair and maintenance supplies 46,400
    Total $71,600

A physical count at December 31, 1979, revealed that only $13,000 of repair and maintenance supplies remained on hand.

(c) Office supplies of $37,100 and advertising costs of $31,800 had been expensed immediately at the time of purchase. However, $13,900 of office supplies remained unused in the office stockroom on December 31, 1979.

(d) The following entry was recorded on December 14, 1979.

Utilities Expense (IS).. 68,200
    Accounts Payable (CL)..................................   68,200
    Payment due January 5, 1980.

Further investigation revealed that this utility bill was actually for $28,600. The account payable was not yet paid as of December 31, 1979.

(e) The debit balance in the buildings account at December 31, 1979, was $160,000; and $360,000 in the machinery and equipment account. The estimated useful lives of these plant assets were 25 years for all buildings and 12 years for all machinery and equipment, with no residual salvage value estimated for either type asset. All plant assets were purchased during the period January 1, 1973, through December 31, 1978. No depreciation expense was yet recorded for fiscal 1979.

Required: (1) Prepare the necessary adjusting entries for each of the five items as of December 31, 1979.

(2) Determine the net effect of these adjusting entries on net income for the fiscal year ended December 31, 1979.

5-4. Adjusting entries: interest, rent, and employee compensation. The amounts shown below for the accounts indicated were reflected in the Trial Balance column on the work sheet of the Joster Corp. as of the end of the fiscal year, December 31, 1979:

	TRIAL BALANCE	
	Debit	*Credit*
Interest Receivable...............................	—	
Interest Payable..................................		—
Wages and Salaries Payable......................		—
Unearned Rental Income.........................		21,000
Interest Expense.................................	17,000	
Wages and Salaries Expense	384,000	
Interest Income		9,600
Rental Income		13,400

The information described below was made available to the supervisor of the accounting department during the process of summarizing the financial activities of the firm for the 1979 fiscal year.

(a) Two notes receivable remained outstanding at December 31, 1979, one for $12,000 and the other for $8,000, both of which originated on October 1, 1979. The $12,000, 8-month note contained an annual interest rate of 10%; whereas the other was due for payment plus interest at 11% on March 1, 1980.

(b) A $200,000, 9%, 20-year bond issue due January 1, 1990, required semiannual interest payments at each January 1 and July 1. On April 1, 1979, a $160,000, 10% loan was obtained from a local bank under a short-term note payable arrangement which required quarterly interest payments beginning July 1, 1979.

(c) A $12,200 liability was incurred for employee compensation during the final six working days of December. This amount will be paid to employees on the first Friday of January, 1980.

(d) The $21,000 balance in Unearned Rental Income was received on August 1, 1979, as an advance payment for seven-months' rent, effective that same date. None of this amount had yet been recognized as income during fiscal 1979.

Required: (1) Prepare an abbreviated work sheet containing only the account titles listed.

(2) Enter each adjustment required by the above information in the appropriate column of the work sheet. Formal journal entries need not be prepared, but supporting detail should be shown beneath the abbreviated work sheet.

(3) Extend the final balance for each account into the appropriate Income Statement or Balance Sheet column.

5-5. Interpretation of T account information. The following T accounts reflects transactions which occurred during the year ended December 31, 1979. Each of the two parts is to be considered independently.

PART 1: INTEREST INCOME

Bookkeeping procedures required a debit to Cash and a credit to Interest Income whenever cash is received in payment for interest.

INTEREST INCOME (IS)

Reversing entry at Jan. 1, 1979	400	Posting from cash receipts journal during 1979	4,600
Closing entry at Dec. 31, 1979	4,720	Adjusting entry at Dec. 31, 1979	520

Required: (1) How much interest income was reported on the 1979 income statement?

(2) How much cash was received for interest during 1979?

(3) How much cash was probably received during 1979 for interest that was earned during 1978?

(4) How much cash is expected to be received in 1980 for interest income reported in 1979?

(5) Assuming the same accounting procedures were used in 1979 and 1980, prepare the reversing entry at January 1, 1980.

PART 2: INTEREST EXPENSE

Bookkeeping procedures required a debit to Interest Expense and a credit to Cash whenever cash is paid for interest.

INTEREST EXPENSE (IS)

Posting from cash payments journal during 1979	6,300	Reversing entry at Jan. 1, 1979 250
Adjusting entry at Dec. 31, 1979	570	Closing entry at Dec. 31, 1979 6,620

Required: (1) How much interest was paid during 1979?

(2) How much interest expense appeared on the 1979 income statement?

(3) How much interest expense of 1979 is intended to be paid during 1980?

(4) How much interest expense of 1978 was probably paid during 1979?

(5) How much was paid in 1978 for interest expense of 1979?

(6) Assuming the same accounting system used during 1979 is adopted during 1980, prepare the appropriate reversing entry at January 1, 1980.

5-6. Adjusting entries and the work sheet. The trial balance shown on top of page 191 was prepared from the general ledger of the Delta Corporation at 1979's fiscal year-end.

The following items require recording prior to the preparation of financial statements for the fiscal year ended December 31, 1979:

(a) The sale of $13,000 of marketable securities on December 15, 1979, was incorrectly recorded as $31,000. The sale resulted in no gain or loss.

(b) The chief accountant estimated that uncollectible accounts would probably total 2% of total sales for 1979. No provision for this allowance was yet recorded during 1979.

(c) Two construction companies were unable to pay their accounts at the year-end. The receivables clerk recommended that the $2,900 total amount be written off as uncollectible, and that the two accounts be forwarded to the firm's lawyer for further action against the delinquent customers.

(d) The physical inventory taken on December 31, 1979, revealed that $67,000 of inventory remained on hand.

(e) The following prepaid expense items are to be charged to expense at the year-end:

Repairs and maintenance supplies	$10,500
Office supplies	4,300
Insurance premiums	4,500
Rent	6,100
Total	$25,400

(f) Administrative and office salaries totaling $5,700 for the last half of December remain to be accrued. The amount is to be paid to employees at the end of the first week in January, 1980.

Delta Corporation
Trial Balance
For the Year Ended December 31, 1979

	Debit	Credit
Cash...	24,000	
Marketable Securities	4,500	
Accounts Receivable	77,000	
Allowance for Doubtful Accounts......................		4,000
Inventory	322,000	
Prepaid Expenses	49,100	
Land...	24,000	
Buildings	132,000	
Accumulated Depreciation — Buildings............................		38,300
Machinery and Equipment..............................	232,700	
Accumulated Depreciation — Machinery and Equipment		84,000
Notes Payable — Bank, short-term...................................		50,000
Accounts Payable		37,000
Interest Payable...		——
Dividends Payable..		——
Wages and Salaries Payable.............................		——
Mortgage Note Payable, 10-year.......................		80,000
Bonds Payable, 20-year....................................		120,000
Capital Stock, $100 par		89,500
Retained Earnings		31,000
Sales...		465,000
Cost of Goods Sold	——	
Expenses:		
Administrative and Office Salaries...............................	71,800	
Advertising and Marketing	29,900	
Depreciation (total).......................................	——	
Insurance	——	
Interest	10,400	
Office Supplies..	——	
Rent	——	
Repair and Maintenance Supplies	——	
Uncollectible Accounts	——	
Utilities..	21,600	
Interest Income		200
	999,000	999,000

(g) Depreciation expense that was to be recorded on buildings for 1979 was 10% of the final balance in the buildings account; and depreciation expense on equipment and machinery was to be in an amount sufficient to reduce its book value to $125,000 at year-end.

(h) Interest expense and interest payable for the last six months of fiscal year 1979 were to be derived from the following schedule. All interest was payable semiannually at July 1 and January 1:

	DATE LOAN OBTAINED	ANNUAL INTEREST RATE
Notes payable — bank	January 1, 1979	12%
Mortgage note payable, 10-year	July 1, 1970	8
Bonds payable, 20-year................	January 1, 1968	7

(i) A $5,000 cash dividend was declared on December 31, 1979, payable on January 10, 1980, even though a net loss was expected for 1979.

Required: (1) Enter the trial balance on a work sheet.

(2) Enter the appropriate amounts for each item which requires recording in the adjustments columns of the work sheet. Formal journal entries need not be prepared, but essential supporting detail should be shown beneath the work sheet.

(3) Extend the proper amounts into the appropriate columns of the work sheet for each account at December 31, 1979.

(4) Prepare the closing entry to transfer all income statement account balances to Retained Earnings; and determine the balance in Retained Earnings at December 31, 1979, after making the closing entry.

5-7. Comprehensive end-of-year sequence: work sheet, adjusting and closing entries, and financial statement preparation. Following a careful review of the trial balance shown below, the treasurer of Wholesale Drugs, Inc., discovered several omissions and errors that required adjustment before financial statements could be prepared at the close of the fiscal year, December 31, 1979.

Wholesale Drugs, Inc.
Trial Balance
For the Year Ended December 31, 1979

	Debit	Credit
Cash	52,400	
Marketable Securities	4,250	
Notes Receivable	13,000	
Accounts Receivable	75,000	
Allowance for Doubtful Accounts		4,900
Interest Receivable	——	
Inventory	365,000	
Prepaid Expenses	2,100	
Land	30,800	
Buildings	47,000	
Accumulated Depreciation — Buildings		21,000
Furniture and Fixtures	173,500	
Accumulated Depreciation — Furniture and Fixtures		41,200
Notes Payable, 10%, short-term		23,500
Accounts Payable		115,005
Interest Payable		——
Federal Income Tax Payable		——
Performance Liability		2,400
Unearned Rental Income		8,000
Wages and Salaries Payable		——
Notes Payable, 8%, due April 1, 1985		60,000
Capital Stock, $50 par		130,000
Retained Earnings		108,350
Sales		407,000
Cost of Goods Sold	——	

	Debit	Credit
Expenses:		
Wages and Salaries	40,200	
Catalog Preparation	30,500	
Sales Commissions	27,000	
Depreciation	———	
Advertising	18,500	
Rent	12,000	
Repairs and Maintenance	9,200	
Utilities	8,705	
Office Supplies	6,200	
Interest	3,600	
Insurance	2,400	
Uncollectible Accounts		———
Federal Income Tax	———	
Interest Income		———
Rental Income		———
	921,355	921,355

The omissions and errors are described below and page 194:

(a) The balance in ending inventory was established at $139,000 following the physical count of inventory which was completed on December 31, 1979.

(b) Depreciation expense to be recorded for 1979 on buildings was 5% of the amount shown in the buildings account on the trial balance. The depreciation expense for 1979 on furniture and fixtures was 10% of its book value as reflected in the trial balance.

(c) Management's practice was to immediately charge to expense almost all prepaid items at the time of their purchase. The following prepaid items which were initially debited to expense accounts remained unexpired or were still useable at the year-end:

Insurance	$ 1,550
Office supplies	4,700
Rent on a warehouse	6,600
Repair and maintenance items	3,950
Total	$16,800

(d) Interest receivable and income of $370 were not yet accrued on outstanding notes receivable. All notes receivable that were reflected on the trial balance are due for collection during the first three months of 1980.

(e) Compensation totaling $4,700 which was earned by employees for the last week of 1979 will be paid in January, 1980. The year-end accrual entry was to be divided between Wages and Salaries Expense ($1,600), and Sales Commission Expense ($3,100).

(f) Interest on the long-term notes payable was payable semiannually at April 1 and October 1. The short-term note originated on July 1, 1979, and interest was payable at maturity, July 1, 1980.

(g) The entire amount of unearned rental income was received on July 1, 1979, in payment of one year's rent, effective the day of receipt, on some unused premises which Wholesale Drugs, Inc., had leased to a furniture store.

(h) The treasurer estimated that 1% of total sales that were made during 1979 will probably prove to be uncollectible.

(i) On December 31, 1979, the ledger clerk discovered that an entry was recorded on November 20, 1979, which erroneously charged $6,000 to Catalog Preparation Expense. The amount should have been charged to Advertising Expense.

(j) The federal income tax rate used by the firm to determine its income tax liability at the year-end was 50% of income before tax.

Required: (1) Prepare a work sheet, and enter all necessary adjustments in the appropriate adjustments columns. Although formal entries are not required, each adjustment should be adequately supported with detail, if they are not self-evident, beneath the work sheet.

(2) Extend all accounts to the appropriate work sheet columns.

(3) Prepare the closing entry at December 31, 1979.

(4) Prepare a balance sheet and a multiple-step income statement for the 1979 fiscal year.

(5) Prepare a statement of retained earnings for the year ended December 31, 1979. Assume that the balance in retained earnings at December 31, 1978, was the same as that shown on the trial balance prior to the adjustments.

5-8. Review of accounting principles. Refer to the two financial statements of Dynaflow Corporation that are shown on pages 174 and 175. Prepare a summary indicating how each of the first seven accounting principles (discussed in Chapter 1, pages 18–21) is related to specific items or segments that are reflected in those financial statements.

DECISION CASE

5-I. Work sheet and adjustments: dividend policy. Account titles with associated balances at March 31, 1980, is shown below and on page 195 for the Montclair Corporation:

Montclair Corporation
Trial Balance
For the Year Ended March 31, 1980

	Debit	Credit
Accounts Payable		109,000
Accounts Receivable	116,920	
Accumulated Depreciation — Buildings		25,000
Accumulated Depreciation — Machinery and Equipment		83,000
Allowance for Doubtful Accounts		8,000
Amortization Expense	—	
Bonds Payable, 6%, 20 years, due December 31, 1982		50,000
Buildings	46,000	
Capital Stock, $10 par		81,000
Cash	29,000	

	Debit	Credit
Cost of Goods Sold	252,000	
Depreciation Expense	27,000	
Dividends Payable		—
Machinery and Equipment	246,000	
Federal Income Tax Expense	—	
Federal Income Tax Payable		8,200
Fire Loss	—	
Insurance Expense	3,800	
Interest Expense	2,250	
Interest Income		470
Interest Payable		—
Inventory	132,000	
Land	3,000	
Maintenance Expense	2,160	
Marketable Securities	4,000	
Marketing Expense	14,000	
Mortgage Note Payable, 8%, 10 years, due April 1, 1981		48,000
Salaries Expense	19,800	
Office Supplies Expense	2,040	
Patents	18,000	
Prepaid Expenses	6,000	
Property Tax Expense	870	
Retained Earnings		25,370
Sales		473,000
Uncollectible Accounts Expense	—	
Utilities Expense	4,200	
Warranty Expense	—	
Warranty Liability		18,000
	929,040	929,040

The controller discovered several events which occurred during the final days of March, 1980, that required adjustments to the foregoing trial balance amounts:

(a) One-half year's depreciation on $10,000 of machinery which was purchased at the beginning of October 1979, was not yet charged to expense during the fiscal year just ended. The estimated life of that machinery was 5 years, and straight-line depreciation was the standard policy for depreciating all of the firm's plant assets. In addition, land for expansion purposes was purchased for $5,000 cash on March 29, but the clerk neglected to record the transaction.

(b) The balance in Patents reflected intangibles with a remaining life of 9 years at April 1, 1979. The annual amortization of $2,000 was not yet recorded for the current fiscal year.

(c) The board of directors at its meeting on March 30 recommended that the liability for warranties on products be reduced by one third of the amount reflected in the trial balance. Experience during the last few years indicated that warranty claims were running substantially below original estimates. The adjustment involved a credit to the warranty expense account.

(d) The controller estimated that 2% of total sales generated in the fiscal year just completed would probably prove to be uncollectible. In addition, a memorandum was discovered from the receivables clerk stating that a particular $1,700 account was proven to be uncollectible on March 29. The controller agreed to write off the account as delinquent.

(e) A fire destroyed some inventory in one section of a warehouse during the night of March 30. The physical inventory completed during the regular shift that day revealed $53,000 of inventory on hand. The physical count taken on the morning of March 31 disclosed available inventory of $49,000. The $132,000 amount shown on the trial balance reflected the balance in inventory prior to the physical inventory count of March 30. The difference between the $132,000 and $53,000 was determined to be the unrecorded cost of goods sold during the first quarter of 1980. The insurance company notified the controller during the evening of March 31 that none of the inventory fire loss was covered by the insurance policy that was currently in force.

(f) Interest on the bond issue was payable each July 1 and January 1. Interest on the mortgage note was payable at each April 1.

(g) Interest income totaling $400 that was earned on marketable securities for the last half of the fiscal year was received on March 31, but was not yet recorded.

(h) Federal income tax expense was calculated at 50% of total taxable income after all adjustments had been made.

(i) In view of the relatively high net income generated during the year, the board declared a $3.40 cash dividend per share of capital stock on March 30, payable April 4, 1980.

Required:
(1) Enter the trial balance for each account on a work sheet in the normal sequence, Cash through the income-statement-related accounts.

(2) Although formal adjusting journal entries need not be prepared for each event listed, each adjustment should be adequately explained, if it is not self-evident, beneath the work sheet.

(3) Extend all account balances to the appropriate income statement or balance sheet columns.

(4) Evaluate the wisdom of the board's declaration of the $3.40 per share dividend that is payable on April 4, 1980.

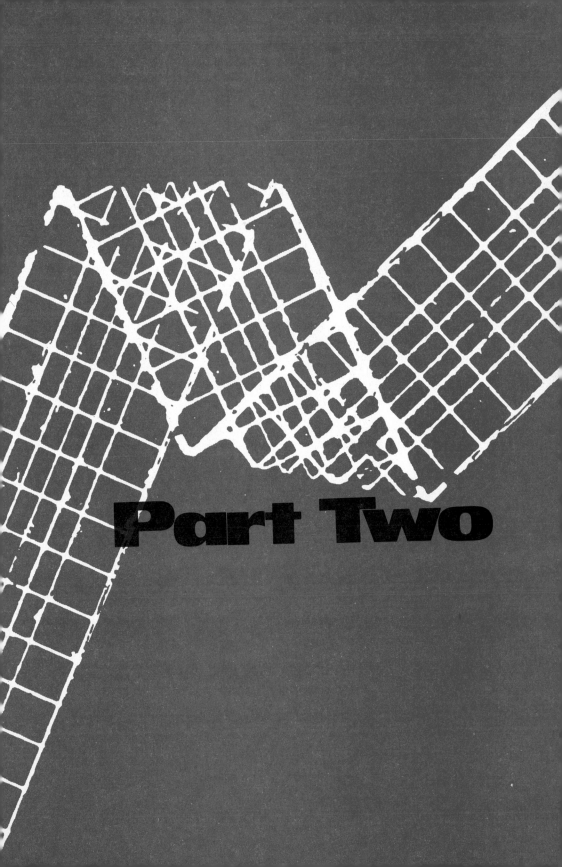

Part Two

Valuation Alternatives and Refinements

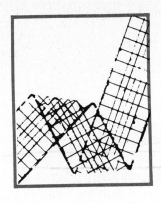

6
Alternate Measures of Value

"The question is," said Alice, "whether you can make words mean so many different things."

Discussion with Humpty Dumpty in
Through the Looking Glass.

One of accounting's four objectives as outlined in Chapter 1 is to measure the value of financial events and transactions in terms of money. The concept of value threads continuously through accounting and presents the discipline with its greatest challenge. The challenge arises because each monetary amount that is reflected in the accounting records, and subsequently on the balance sheet and income statement, is based on some concept of value measurement. Even though value is a familiar concept, it lacks uniform definition. Hence, interpretation and controversy remain endless. In short, the one true value of any particular item, be it a specific asset or an entire business enterprise, is seldom obvious to the observer.

The structural and procedural framework of accounting that has thus far been presented will be expanded in this second part of the text so as to probe more deeply into the significance of value to accounting and to users of financial information. In addition, the ensuing discussion may serve to partially dispel the frequent misconception that accounting is the only system available by which to measure "true worth" or "true value."

ALTERNATE SYSTEMS OF VALUATION

Accounting has traditionally defined the *value* of an asset as the exchange price which arises during the arms-length bargaining process between a buyer and seller. This valuation basis is referred to as the *historical cost* principle. The following illustration reveals several other measures of value that can emerge under a given set of circumstances.

A delivery truck was purchased by Volstead Supermarkets on January 1, 1980, for $8,000. The salvage value anticipated at the end of its five-year life was zero. Straight-line depreciation was used in the company for all depreciable plant assets. Management forecasted that the new truck could increase annual operating income, before depreciation and income tax, by $3,000 because of a higher sales volume and decreased repair and maintenance expenses. As an alternative to buying, a truck of the same type could have been rented from a leasing firm at an annual charge of $1,900 for five years. The leasing company would pay all normal repair and maintenance costs during the five-year period.

The list price of this model of delivery truck increased to $8,800 at the end of the fiscal year, December 31, 1980. This 10 percent increase happened to coincide with the 10 percent increase in the general price level during 1980. No significant improvements in quality or design occurred during 1980 to account for the price rise in this particular truck model. The corporation had declined an offer to sell the truck to a nearby dry-cleaning establishment for $7,000 during December. Near the end of December, the controller estimated that the truck could have been sold to a used truck dealer for $6,800, net of transfer and disposal costs. Also at year-end, several used truck dealers indicated that a one-year old truck similar to the one purchased by Volstead Supermarkets on January 1 could have been sold to the public for about $7,200.

A considerable number of options can be identified from this information by which to measure the value of this particular asset, both at the date of purchase and near the end of its first year of use. A few of these options are summarized in the table shown on the following page.

The several possible values for this particular truck vary over a considerable range: between $15,000 to $8,000 as of January 1, 1980; and from $12,000 to $6,400 as of the end of that year. An

OPTION	MONETARY VALUE		BASIS OF VALUATION
	January 1, 1980	December 31, 1980	
1	$15,000	$12,000	The $3,000 higher annual operating income before depreciation and income tax expenses that was forecast to be generated by the truck.
2	$ 9,500	$ 7,600	The total cost to rent the truck during its useful life, at $1,900 per year.
3	$ 8,000		The purchase price, or historical cost.
4		$ 7,200	The _current replacement cost_ of a similar one-year old truck at December 31, 1980.
5		$ 7,040	The assumed book value of a one-year old truck adjusted for the 10 percent increase in the general price level during 1980. $8,000 × 110% = $8,800 adjusted original cost, less one year's depreciation of $1,760, or ($8,800 ÷ 5 years).
6		$ 7,000	The offer to purchase which was subsequently declined near the end of 1980, or the _opportunity cost_ of not selling.
7		$ 6,800	The estimated selling price to a used car dealer, net of transfer and disposal costs, or _net realizable value_.
8		$ 6,400	The undepreciated original cost, or _book value_, based on the actual purchase cost at January 1, 1980, less the straight-line depreciation.

accountant would normally record the $8,000 purchase price (option 3) as the historical cost or value of the asset in the firm's accounting records on January 1, 1980. The book value of that asset at the end of its first year of life would be reflected in those records as $6,400 (option 8), which is the historical cost less $1,600 accumulated straight-line depreciation for 1980. Each of the remaining six options, however, contain some validity as a basis for measuring the value of the truck.

Option 1 suggests that the real value of the truck to Volstead Supermarkets is the future earning capacity that the equipment is expected to generate over its remaining lifetime: $15,000 as of January 1, 1980; and $12,000 as of one year later. These two amounts can be restated on what may be referred to as an _after-tax cash flow_ basis (assuming a federal income tax rate of 50 percent) as shown on page 202.

Additional annual operating income before depreciation and income tax expenses (assumed to represent net cash inflow) ...	$3,000
Less annual depreciation expense (straight-line)	1,600
Additional annual income before federal income tax expense..	$1,400
Less federal income tax expense (50%), which will ultimately result in a cash outflow when tax is paid	700
Additional annual net income..	$ 700
Add back depreciation expense (since this particular item of expense does not require any cash outflow from the firm...........	1,600
Additional annual after-tax cash flow	$2,300

Hence, the total additional after-tax cash flow that the truck is anticipated to generate as of January 1, 1980, is $11,500 ($2,300 × 5 years), and $9,200 ($11,500 − $2,300), as of December 31, 1980. Notice that each of these amounts exceed the original cost and end-of-year book value by a substantial margin.

Option 2 reflects another valuation basis for the truck: the total cost at two specified dates that would be required to obtain the service benefits contained in the truck through a rental agreement rather than a purchase. The supermarket's management may have decided that the monetary and qualitative benefits associated with complete ownership would outweigh any expenditures for repairs and maintenance that might be incurred over the service life of the truck since the leasing company agreed to pay for all normal repair and maintenance costs.

The current replacement cost of $7,200 at the end of 1980 (option 4) represents the price at which a comparable model one-year old truck could have been purchased. On the other hand, the book value of the truck at the end of 1980, when adjusted to compensate for the effects of the 10 percent inflation during the year (Option 5), approximates $7,040 ($6,400 historical cost book value × 110 percent = $7,040). A significant problem in using this latter amount as an objective basis for measurement is that the price of many assets, particularly this truck, may not be affected to the same extent or even in the same direction as the change that occurred in the general price level during the year.

Option 6 reflects an opportunity cost of $7,000 to the company in declining to sell the truck in December to the dry-cleaning establishment. Another type of opportunity cost is the net realizable value of $6,800 (Option 7) that might have been received had the truck been sold to a used truck dealer. Management may have been unwilling to dispose of the truck at either of these two possible prices, even though both exceeded the historical cost book value of $6,400 at year-end, because the same truck could not have been replaced for less than $7,200, (Option 4).

The principal reasons why most accountants believe each of the valuation bases, other than historical cost, is unsatisfactory can be briefly summarized below:

(1) Option 1 and its after-tax cash flow variation, would be discarded as a basis for value measurement because the forecasted higher annual operating income is based on conjecture and future events that may not occur.

(2) Options 2, 4, 6, and 7 would be discarded as bases for value measurement because the firm did not actually enter into any of these types of transactions. It neither rented, replaced, nor sold the truck.

(3) Option 5 would be rejected as the primary basis for value measurement by most accountants because of the previously mentioned observation that any change in the price of this particular truck during the past year may not have been attributable to changes in the general price level.

The accountant would contend that the appropriate baseline by which to measure the value of any particular asset should be the *objective* and *verifiable* amount which emerged from the arms-length bargaining between a buyer and a seller. The recommended valuation base is historical cost, in this case $8,000 as of January 1, 1980, and a book value of $6,400 at the end of its first year of life. None of the other six options would be shown in the accounting records, either because the specific transaction had not occurred or the amounts involved are too conjectural.

Nevertheless interpretations of value other than historical cost are frequently applied for a variety of purposes to situations that arise in financial and economic decision-making. The several interpretations mentioned help to widen the perspectives and understanding of the manager, analyst, or other users of accounting information so that better decisions may be made.

This chapter provides an introduction to the concept of value with respect to accounting and the related discipline of economics. A brief comparison will highlight some fundamental distinctions between the accountant's and the economist's perspective toward value, with particular attention directed at the general problem of asset valuation. The concept of present value and the discounting process will be introduced in the latter half of the chapter, together with applications of the present value concept to selected accounting and financial problems.

DISTINCTIONS BETWEEN PERSPECTIVES OF ACCOUNTING AND ECONOMICS TOWARD VALUE MEASUREMENT

The discussion which dealt with the definition of income in Chapter 3 revealed one of the fundamental distinctions between the frames of reference used by the accountant and the economist to measure value. Examination of the following topics will disclose additional points of distinction between the two disciplines:

(1) Focus and scope.
(2) Approach to quantification.
(3) Valuation of an asset.

Focus and Scope

The primary focus of accounting is the single organization unit, such as a corporation, partnership, or proprietorship. The accountant implicitly assumes that the productive resources of people, money, and materials are acquired and apportioned within a specific firm for the sole benefit of the firm and its ownership interests. Only indirectly would the accountant consider these productive resources to be administered for the benefit of society-at-large. This restricted viewpoint of accounting is a logical extension of the business entity principle, and the assumption that "under the guidance of some invisible hand," the individual, business or organizational unit usually serves society best by nurturing its own interest.

Recall that the broadest definition of income used by the accountant is revenue, other income, and gains less expenses and losses, in other words "profit". The far more inclusive definition used by the economist states that income equals the profits earned by all business establishments plus wages, rents, and interest earned by all members of society. From another perspective, the accountant normally recognizes income in the form of revenue only at the point where legal title to or physical possession of goods or services is transferred to the customer. To paraphrase the principle of conservatism, anticipated sales are not realized sales.

In addition, the accountant believes that the practical requirements of providing interested parties with periodic assessment of a firm's operations necessitate the drawing of a line at some convenient but definitive point in the production-distribution cycle of the firm, such as the end of the fiscal year. The economist, however, prefers to recognize all aspects of income within the firm and society at each stage in the production cycle. The economist would argue that small increments of income should be considered to be earned by the firm at each point where wages are paid to employees and as rent and interest costs are incurred: costs which help to move a product or service nearer the point of ultimate sale to the consumer.

Economics encompasses broader fields of inquiry than does accounting. At one moment the economist may focus on an individual firm, the supply and demand for factors of production from the firm's perspective, or on various price-cost relationships within the firm. This is the *micro* (or small) orientation of economics. At another instant, attention may switch to the aggregative impact that individual and organizational decisions with respect to resource allocation have on the total economy of a nation. This latter approach is one aspect of the *macro* (or gross) side of economics. The macroeconomist, and to some extent the microeconomist, tends to be more concerned with the impact which the allocation of resources within the firm has on society, rather than on the firm itself. In addition, the economist frequently moves into the area of political economics where attention is directed to such subjective and argumentative topics as social equilibrium, welfare economics, and the redistribution of wealth among various socioeconomic groups.

Approach to Quantification

The discipline of economics tends to stress the theoretical and conceptual aspects of value, several of which may not be easily applied to financial problems and decisions that are encountered daily within a firm. For example, students and business executives alike frequently experience difficulty in transferring such concepts as the "supply and demand curve" and "marginal utility" to the construction of detailed pricing strategies for a new product line.

Accounting emphasizes the pragmatic application of economic principles and theories to events that actually occur in the business environment. Goods and services are traded, liabilities are incurred and paid, and financial resources undergo continual transformation. Accounting attempts to trace, quantify, interpret, and communicate summaries of a multitude of transactions as concisely and clearly as possible to a wide range of interested parties.

Although each approach looks at the business environment somewhat differently, each contributes to a more complete understanding and resolution of financial problems that emerge in an organization. In this respect, economic theory and accounting practice complement and reinforce each other.

An Illustration. The following illustration will help to clarify several of the essential differences in scope, approach, and degree of quantification between the two disciplines. Assume that an individual had, as a student, spent an average of $4,000 in each of four years to attain a college degree. One fourth of the $16,000 total outlay had been borrowed under long-term arrangements from a local bank, and the remainder had been obtained from a savings account and other personal resources. An accountant could conceivably make the following entry to summarize the net result of all financial transactions during that four-year period. The account titles in the entry are more suggestive than precise:

Capitalized Cost of College Education (NA)............... 16,000
   Capital — Graduate (OE)................................. 12,000
   Long-Term Liability (LL)..................................... 4,000
     Capitalize as an intangible asset the expenditure
     of financial resources obtained from personal and
     borrowed funds during the four-year period to at-
     tain a college degree.

The capitalized cost of the graduate's education can be considered to be a noncurrent intangible asset which contains future service benefits, not the least of which may be the student's anticipated higher earning potential. The above entry reflects considerable objectivity and a relatively precise quantification in monetary terms of numerous financial events that transpired during the four-year period. Going one step further, the accountant might conceivably wish to amortize as an expense the $16,000 capitalized intangible asset in equal increments of $2,000 to each of the graduate's next eight annual income statements, in the same way that service benefits contained in a patent or depreciable asset would be handled in the accounting records.

An economist, on the other hand, might suggest that some additional information might well be included in the entry. For example, the argument could be made that the individual sacrificed an approximate $8,000 annual income during the four years of college attendance that could otherwise have been earned by entering an occupation immediately upon high school graduation. This $32,000 of lost income could be considered an additional imputed opportunity cost of the college degree. Aside from possessing more knowledge, greater analytical ability, a diploma, and perhaps a technical skill to evidence learning experience, the graduate was financially $48,000 ($16,000 + $32,000) less well off upon receipt of the college degree than had a vocation been pursued immediately after receiving the high school diploma. The following expanded entry could conceivably be constructed to reflect this additional capitalization of the economist's imputed income that was sacrificed while attending college. Again, account titles are merely suggestive and descriptive:

Capitalized Cost of College Education (NA)..............	16,000	
Capitalized Cost of Income Sacrificed from Lost Employment Opportunities (NA)................................	32,000	
Imputed Additional Investment in the College Degree (OE)		32,000
Capital — Graduate (OE)................................		12,000
Long-Term Liability (LL).....................................		4,000
Capitalize as intangible assets the actual costs incurred plus the imputed income sacrificed in attaining a college degree.		

Although neither of the two preceding entries would probably ever be recorded, they enable a deeper insight into the economic impact of the events surrounding the pursuit of the undergraduate degree during the four-year period. Whereas the accountant focused only on the monetary transactions which actually occurred, the economist ventured beyond those limits into a broader area of less certain, imputed expenditures based on conjecture. In this respect, the accountant's entry is more objective and verifiable than that of the economist's expanded but perhaps no less realistic version. This latter hypothetical entry cannot be entirely ignored in assessing the value, worth, or cost of the graduate's total educational experience.

The economist might wish to extend the illustration further. Both society and the graduate normally expect to benefit from the increased knowledge and expertise that the graduate will probably bring to the resolution of future problems encountered during a chosen career. But the present value which society or the individual might assign to these future expectations and benefits is quite difficult to quantify. Only slightly more measurable might be the graduate's hope and expectation that a higher income will be earned because of attaining the degree. How high the income will be is uncertain, but hopefully it would be sufficient to recover during the next 40 to 45 years the total $48,000 actual and imputed cost of the educational experience. This aspect of undertaking a college education will be further explored during the discussion of present value and the discounting process.

Valuation of an Asset

Both the accountant and economist view an asset as a package containing potential service benefits that will be released as the asset is utilized to generate future income. Restated, the asset represents a present expenditure of funds for future earning potential that is expected in most cases to exceed the expenditure. Few businesses would incur costs for inventory, equipment, buildings, or other assets unless this was the reasonable expectation. The accountant records the exchange price, which the two parties to the transaction agreed upon, as the cost or value of the asset actually purchased, since that amount is quantifiable, objective, and verifiable. On the other hand, there are two common methods by which an economist often determines the cost or value of an asset, as described below.

First, the economist establishes the value of a specific asset with reference to the cheapest alternative whereby a similar service could have been obtained. For example, a production manager elects to obtain a metal-shaping service by purchasing a machine press for $20,000 that is expected to last ten years, rather than rent the same service in the form of another machine at $100 per month for the same period. Assuming the two packages of service benefits would yield equal outputs, the economist could argue that the cost of the purchased press should be $12,000 ($100 per month × 12 months × 10 years), which is the cheaper alternative available. The economist considers the $8,000 differential cost of the purchased machine as a cost incurred because of a personal or company preference to own rather than to rent the service. Although this valuation basis may appear unrealistic at first glance, a decision-maker must assess all relevant alternatives before finally deciding to buy or rent, make or sell, or ultimately to continue in business or liquidate.

Second, the economist establishes the value of an asset by estimating the future incomes that the asset is expected to help generate over its useful life. These future incomes can then be reduced to a present value by a process referred to as *discounting*.

PRESENT VALUE AND THE DISCOUNTING PROCESS

The *present value concept* may be stated as follows: The dollar received today is more valuable than the dollar received one year from now, because the dollar received today can be immediately invested to earn interest during the year, and hence become more valuable than the dollar that would be received a year later. Conversely and for the same reason, the dollar spent today is more valuable (or costly) than the dollar spent in the future. Both statements reflect what is referred to as the *time value of money*, which means that the dollar has a value which varies with time.

The element in the economy that accounts for this phenome-
non is the role played by the interest rate, which in effect is the
rent paid by a borrower to the lender for the use of money during
a particular period. Interest is the price which compensates the
lender for the risk and uncertainty involved in lending money to
others. For example, $1,000 invested today at 6 percent interest
compounded annually will increase to $1,060 at the end of the first
year, and to $18,420 at the end of 50 years. By simply reversing the
time sequence and using the same interest rate, the $1,060 that
will be received at the end of the first year and the $18,420 that
will be received at the end of the fiftieth year are each worth only
$1,000 today.

It must be noted, however, that the changing time value of
money, which is attributable to the role of the interest rate, is
quite distinct from any change in the purchasing power of the
dollar that occurs during periods of inflation or deflation. Rising
prices caused by inflationary pressures, rather than a change in
the prevailing interest rate structure, is the factor which largely
accounts for any decrease in the ability of the dollar to command
goods and services in the market place. For example, if between
the time $100 is earned and spent the general price level doubles
from 100 to 200, the purchasing power of that $100 falls to $50.
This diminishing purchasing power of the dollar may have no
direct relationship to the prevailing interest rate structure that
exists in our economy.

Determining the Future Value of a Lump Sum: Compounding

The following equation is used to determine the future value
of a lump-sum of money that is invested today at a particular interest rate:

$$F_n = P(1 + i)^n \qquad\qquad [1]$$

F_n = The future value of a lump sum of money at a specific future
period (n).

P = The lump sum of money invested today or at the beginning of a
period. This is frequently called the Principal or the Present Value.

i = The interest rate, expressed as a percent.

n = Number of periods over which the original lump-sum invested (P)
plus any accrued interest remains invested.

Notice that "n" in the expression $(1 + i)^n$ possesses the attributes
of an exponent. This exponential function accounts for the enormous power that any specific interest rate has over money.

To illustrate this power, assume that $1,000 is invested at Jan-
uary 1, 1980, in a financial institution which guarantees that 6 per-

cent interest compounded annually will be earned on that deposit, payable at the end of each year. Interest will accrue throughout 1980 on the total deposit ($1,000) that exists at the beginning of that year. At the end of the first year, the $1,000 principal plus the 6 percent interest earned on that principal will have accumulated to $1,060. This amount can be determined from Equation 1 as follows:

$$F_1 = \$1,000(1 + .06)^1 = \$1,000(1.06) = \$1,060$$

If this $1,060 is left on deposit throughout the second year, the deposit will reflect a balance of $1,123.60 at December 31, 1981. This amount can be determined in either of the following two ways:

P = $1,000 AT JANUARY 1, 1980	P = $1,060 AT JANUARY 1, 1981
$F_2 = P(1 + i)^2$	$F_1 = P(1 + i)^1$
$F_2 = \$1,000(1 + .06)^2$	$F_1 = \$1,060(1 + .06)^1$
$F_2 = \$1,000(1.06)\,(1.06)$	$F_1 = \$1,060(1.06) = \$1,123.60$
$F_2 = \$1,000(1.1236) = \$1,123.60$	

Under either approach, 6 percent interest compounded annually is earned during the second year (1981) on both the original principal ($1,000) that existed at January 1, 1980, plus the interest earned ($60) during the first year. If the interest rate was specified as "6 percent interest simple, annually," interest would have been earned annually on only the original principal of $1,000.

The graph shown on page 211 reflects the growth at discrete intervals over a 50-year period of the original deposit of $1,000 which is invested at 6 percent interest compounded annually. The equation for determining the value of $1,000 at the end of the 50th year is:

$$F_{50} = \$1,000(1 + .06)^{50} = \$1,000(18.420) = \$18,420$$

The 6 percent column of Table 1 in the Appendix on page 636 contains arithmetic factors for the expression $(1 + i)^n$ by which the original amount of the principal invested (P) is multiplied to determine its value at specific future dates. For example, the future value of $1,000 invested today at 6 percent interest compounded annually for 50 years is determined merely by multiplying the $1,000 principal by the factor shown in the 6%/50-period cell of Table 1, or 18.420. Hence, $1,000 × 18.420 = $18,420.

If the $1,000 originally invested on January 1, 1980, earned 6 percent compounded semiannually (or interest accrued twice per year, for example at June 30 and December 31), the total amount invested at December 31, 1980, would be $1,061. Three percent interest (½ × 6 percent) would be earned on the balance that ex-

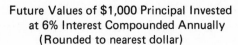

Future Values of $1,000 Principal Invested
at 6% Interest Compounded Annually
(Rounded to nearest dollar)

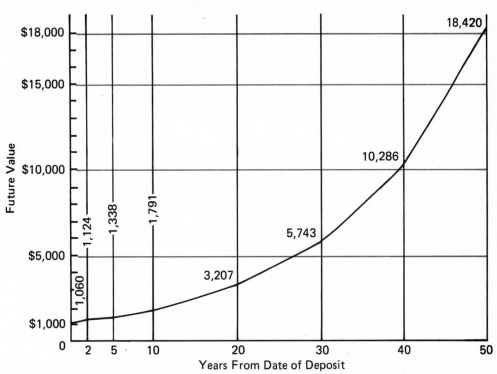

isted at the beginning of each 6 months for two 6-month periods. The amount to which the original $1,000 deposit would have grown by December 31, 1980, would be calculated as shown below:

$$F_2 = \$1,000(1 + .03)^2 = \$1,000(1.061) = \$1,061$$

The factor 1.061 is located in the 3%/2-period cell of Table 1.

The preceding discussion verifies the general statement that whenever the interest rate exceeds zero, "the dollar received today will become more valuable than the dollar received tomorrow."

The "Rule of 70". A guideline that is frequently used to determine the approximate number of years required to double an original investment at a particular interest rate is referred to as the *Rule of 70.* Seventy divided by a particular interest rate compounded annually will indicate the approximate number of years required to double an investment; for example, 70 ÷ 2% = 35 years. Reference to Table 1 in the Appendix indicates that the factor 2.000 in the 2 percent column is associated with 35 years, the time required to double the original investment. Other comparisons are shown below for various interest rates compounded annually:

INTEREST RATE COMPOUNDED ANNUALLY	YEARS TO DOUBLE THE ORIGINAL INVESTMENT	
	Using the Rule of 70	*Locating the 2.000 Factor in Table 1 of the Appendix*
2%	35 years	35 years
2½	28	slightly over 28 years
3	23.3	about 23½ years
4	17½	slightly less than 18 years
5	14	slightly over 14 years
6	11.7	slightly less than 12 years
8	8.75	slightly over 9 years
10	7	about 7½ years
12	5.8	over 6 years

Determining the Present Value of a Lump Sum: Discounting

What is the value today of $1,060 that will be received one year from now if 6 percent interest compounded annually can be earned during that year? Restated: How much money must be invested today at 6 percent interest compounded annually to equal $1,060 one year hence? A rearrangement of Equation 1 provides the solution to such problems, as shown below:

[1] $F_n = P(1 + i)^n$ ⟶ $P = \dfrac{F_n}{(1 + i)^n}$ [2]

The above rearrangement was accomplished by multiplying each side of Equation 1 by $\dfrac{1}{(1 + i)^n}$, as shown below:

$$\frac{F_n}{(1 + i)^n} = \frac{P(1 + i)^n}{(1 + i)^n}$$

Then by canceling similar terms on the right, the above equation becomes:

$$P = \frac{F_n}{(1 + i)^n}$$

The symbolic notation used in Equation [2] is the same as that used in Equation [1], with the exception that P is usually referred to in Equation [2] as the Present Value, instead of as the Principal.

The present value of $1,060 that will be received one year hence, discounted at 6 percent interest compounded annually, is determined as follows:

$$P = \$1,060 \left[\frac{1}{(1 + .06)^1}\right] = \$1,060 \left[\frac{1}{1.06}\right] = \$1,060(.943) = \$1,000*$$

*Rounded to the nearest dollar.

The present value, or the value now, of $1,060 that will be received one year from now, *discounted* at 6 percent interest compounded annually, is $1,000.

The present value of $1,124 that will be received two years hence, discounted at 6 percent interest compounded annually, is also $1,000. This can be determined as shown below:

$$P = \$1,124 \left[\frac{1}{(1.06)^2}\right] = \$1,124 \left[\frac{1}{(1.06)(1.06)}\right]$$

$$= \$1,124 \left[\frac{1}{1.124}\right] = \$1,124 \,(.890) = \$1,000 \text{ (rounded)}$$

And the present value of $18,420 that will be received 50 years hence, discounted at the same interest rate, is also $1,000:

$$P = \$18,420 \left[\frac{1}{(1.06)^{50}}\right] = \$18,420 \left[\frac{1}{18.420}\right] = \$18,420 \,(.054) = \$1,000 \text{ (rounded)}$$

Table 3 in the Appendix on page 638 provides factors for the expression $\frac{1}{(1 + i)^n}$ by which the future value (F_n) is multiplied to calculate its present value. For example, the factor shown in the 6%/50-period cell in Table 3 is .054. Notice that each present value factor shown in Table 3 is the reciprocal of its respective factor shown in Table 1. For example, the present value factor .054 that is shown in Table 3 is the reciprocal of the future value factor 18.420 which is reflected in the 6%/50-period cell of Table 1: $\frac{1}{18.420} =$ .054 when rounded to three decimal places.

The graph shown on page 211 illustrates another way of viewing the present value concept and the discounting process. Each of the eight future values identified on the curve has a present value of $1,000. Specifically, the present value of $3,207 to be received 20 years from today, discounted at 6 percent interest compounded annually is $1,000 ($3,207 × .312 = $1,000 rounded).

If the interest rate is stated as 6 percent compounded semiannually, the present value of $1,061 to be received one year hence can be determined as follows:

$$P = \$1,061 \left[\frac{1}{(1 + .03)^2}\right]$$

The 6 percent interest rate is halved because 3 percent interest is earned each 6 months, for two 6-month periods. The complete calculation is shown on page 214.

$$P = \$1,061 \left[\frac{1}{(1.03)(1.03)}\right] = \$1,061 \left[\frac{1}{1.061}\right] = \$1,061\,(.943) = \$1,000 \text{ (rounded)}$$

To summarize, the dollar that will be earned or received in the future is less valuable than the dollar earned or received today. Likewise the dollar that will be paid in the future is less costly than the dollar paid today.

Application of Present Value Concept

The present value concept can be applied to a variety of investment problems. For example, an artist is considering spending $500 at the beginning of the year for paint supplies, materials, and miscellaneous equipment that will be consumed during the year to paint a landscape. A customer has agreed to buy the picture for $600 at the end of the year. Also assume that, as an alternative, the artist could invest the $500 at 10 percent interest compounded annually. Should the artist paint the landscape, or invest the $500 at 10% interest? Ignoring the income tax and the value of the artist's labor, the problem can be approached as follows:

The value at the end of one year of $500 invested at 10% compounded annually is $550, calculated as follows:

$$F_1 = \$500\,(1 + .10)^1 = \$500\,(1.1) = \$550$$

The calculation is made easier by referring to the factor shown in Table 1 of the Appendix at the 10%/1-period cell: $500 × 1.100 = $550. Since the $600 which the artist anticipates receiving at the end of the year exceeds the future value of the $500 original investment by $50, the decision would probably be made to purchase supplies, materials, and equipment and proceed to paint the scene.

This problem can also be approached by using the reverse reasoning involved in the present value concept. The present value of $600 received one year hence, discounted at 10 percent interest compounded annually, is $545 as calculated below:

$$P = \$600 \left[\frac{1}{(1.100)^1}\right] = \$600\,(.909) = \$545 \text{ (rounded)}$$

The calculation is again simplified by locating the factor .909 in the 10%/1-period cell of Table 3. In short, the artist would have to invest $545 at the beginning of the year at 10 percent interest compounded annually to earn $600 by the end of the year. By investing only $500 in supplies and equipment, the same $600 future income can be obtained.

Based on the estimates provided, the $500 investment is expected to earn a return of 20 percent, compounded annually. This return is determined by solving the following equation:

$$P = \left[\frac{F_1}{(1 + i)^1} \right]$$

$$\$500 = \$600 \left[\frac{1}{1 + i} \right]$$

$$\frac{1}{1 + i} = \frac{\$500}{\$600} = .833$$

The present value factor .833 is shown in Table 3 of the Appendix at the 20%/1-period cell. An alternate method to determine this rate of return is to solve the above equation for the interest rate, i, as shown below:

$$\frac{\$500}{\$600} = \frac{1}{1 + i}$$

$$\$500(1 + i) = \$600$$

$$\$500 + \$500i = \$600$$

$$\$500i = \$100$$

$$i = \frac{\$100}{\$500} = .2, \text{ or } 20\%$$

A Series of Payments

Two variations of a single idea have been presented: (1) the value at a future date of a lump-sum that is invested now; and (2) the value now of a lump sum that will be received at a future date. There are many investments, however, which take forms such as the following:

(1) A series of equal amounts invested at uniform intervals which provide a certain amount of money at a future date.

(2) A lump-sum investment made now which provides a series of annual incomes over several future periods.

A life insurance annuity contract is an example of the first type. An individual may purchase an annuity contract by depositing equal annual premium payments for a designated number of years. After completing this series of annual payments, the fund that was built up with the insurance company may be returned to the annuitant in equal annual payments over a specified number of years, each annual repayment being larger than the original annual premium payments to the company. The amount returned annually to the annuitant represents a sum equal to the original annual premium plus interest which the insurance company has earned on that premium through investments of various types.

The purchase of a machine today that is expected to generate a series of annual incomes (or savings) over several future years is an example of the second type. Each of the two types of series of payments is subsequently discussed in greater detail below.

Determining the Future Value of a Series of Payments. Assume that $1,000 is invested at the end of each year for 20 years beginning December 31, 1979, and that each $1,000 installment earns 10 percent compounded annually. The value of the first deposit at the end of 1980, immediately prior to the second deposit, is $1,100 or $1,000(1 + .10)^1$. If the second installment made on December 31, 1980, remains invested throughout 1981, the accumulated value at December 31, 1981, is $2,310, or $2,100(1 + .10)^1$, immediately prior to the third deposit. If this investment pattern spans 20 years, the total amount invested after the twentieth $1,000 annual installment is made on December 31, 1998, will be $57,275.

The following equation, which is merely a variation of Equation 1, provides the solution to investment problems of this type, when the deposit is made at the end of a period for a given number of periods.

$$F = A \left[\frac{(1 + i)^n - 1}{i} \right] \qquad [3]$$

F = The future value of a series of equal payments.
A = The amount invested or paid in each period.
i = The interest rate, expressed as a percent.
n = Number of periods over which the series of payments (A) extends.

Using data from the preceding illustration, the future value at December 31, 1980, after the second $1,000 installment is made, is calculated as follows:

$$F = \$1,000 \left[\frac{(1 + .10)^2 - 1}{.10} \right] = \$1,000 \left[\frac{1.210 - 1}{.10} \right] = \$1,000 \left[\frac{.21}{.10} \right]$$
$$= \$1,000 \,(2.100) = \$2,100$$

The future value at December 31, 1981, after the third installment is made, is shown below:

$$F = \$1,000 \left[\frac{(1 + .10)^3 - 1}{.10} \right] = \$1,000 \left[\frac{1.331 - 1}{.10} \right] = \$1,000 \left[\frac{.331}{.10} \right] = \$1,000 \,(3.310)$$
$$= \$3,310$$

The future value of the series of annual $1,000 installments at December 31, 1998 (the end of the twentieth period), after the twentieth installment is made, is calculated as follows:

$$F = \$1,000 \left[\frac{(1 + .10)^{20} - 1}{.10} \right] = \$1,000 \left[\frac{6.7275 - 1}{.10} \right] = \$1,000 \left[\frac{5.7275}{.10} \right]$$
$$= \$1,000 \ (57.275) = \$57,275$$

The $57,275 amount may be obtained by referring to the factor 57.275 that is reflected in the 10%/20-period cell of Table 2 of the Appendix on page 637. Table 2 provides arithmetic factors for the expression $\frac{(1 + i)^n - 1}{i}$ that is contained in Equation 3.[1]

If the interest rate was stated at 10 percent compounded semi-annually, the 5 percent column in Table 2 can be searched to locate the factor corresponding to the number of 6-month periods involved. For example, the future value at June 30, 1989, of a series of twenty, $500 semiannual installments made each December 31 and June 30, beginning December 31, 1979, and which will earn 10 percent interest compounded semiannually is determined as shown below:

$$F = \$500(33.066) = \$16,533$$

The factor 33.066 is located in the 5%/20-period cell of Table 2 in the Appendix.

If, on the other hand, the interest rate was stated at 10% percent compounded quarterly, the 2½ percent column can be searched for the appropriate number of 3-month periods. For example, the future value at September 30, 1984, of a series of twenty, $250 quarterly installments made each December 31, March 31, and so on, beginning December 31, 1979, and which will earn 10 percent interest compounded quarterly, is determined as shown below:

$$F = \$250(25.545) = \$6,386$$

The factor 25.545 is located in the 2½%/20-period cell of Table 2.

Determining the Present Value of a Series of Payments. An example of an investment of a lump-sum that will provide a series of annual incomes over several future periods, would be the purchase of equipment which is expected to generate annual incomes for a certain number of years.

To illustrate, assume management requires that any investment undertaken must earn at least an 8 percent return on that investment. Should management invest $100,000 today in a project

---

[1]Factors provided in Table 2 are for a series of payments made at the end of a period. If the amount invested occurs at the beginning of each period, Table 2 may be converted to a series paid in advance by taking one more period and subtracting the amount of one installment. For example, if $1,000 is deposited on January 1, 1980, at 10 percent interest compounded annually, and at the beginning of each of the next nine years, the future value of this series of payments at the end of the tenth year, December 31, 1989, will equal $17,531: $1,000 (18.531 − 1.000) = $1,000 × 17.531 = $17,531.

that is expected to produce an after-tax cash flow of $24,000 at the end of each of the next 5 years? At first glance, this investment appears wise since an annual income of $24,000 over the 5-year period equals $120,000, which exceeds the investment required by $20,000. But this annual income that will be earned in the future is not worth $24,000 today, because the present value of the dollar expected to be received in the future is less than the dollar that is actually received today. Since the decision with respect to the prospective investment must be made now, it would be convenient if management could determine the present value of that series of future incomes. Once determined, this discounted amount can then be compared with the present value of the investment, in this instance $100,000, that is required to generate those incomes.

The following modification to Equation 1 is available to solve such problems:

$$P_n = A \left[\frac{1 - \dfrac{1}{(1 + i)^n}}{i} \right] \qquad [4]$$

P_n = The present value of a series of equal incomes (or payments).
A = The amount received (or paid) in each period.
i = The interest rate, expressed as a percent.
n = Number of periods over which the series of receipts (or payments), A, extends.

By applying this equation, management can quantitatively determine if the proposed investment will achieve the required 8 percent return. This can be determined as shown below:

$$P = \$24,000 \left[\frac{1 - \dfrac{1}{(1 + .08)^5}}{.08} \right] = \$24,000 \left[\frac{1 - \dfrac{1}{1.4693}}{.08} \right]$$

$$= \$24,000 \left[\frac{1 - .6806}{.08} \right] = \$24,000 \left[\frac{.3194}{.08} \right] = \$24,000 \, (3.993) = \$95,832$$

The present value of the $24,000 to be received at the end of each of the next five years, discounted at 8 percent interest compounded annually is $95,832, or $4,168 less than the present value of the investment required to generate that particular stream of incomes. Based on this quantitative analysis alone, management would be advised not to invest $100,000 in this project.

Annual after-tax cash flows (A) would have to approximate $25,044 to equal the $100,000 investment, as shown below:

$$\$100,000 = A(3.993)$$

$$A = \frac{\$100,000}{3.993}$$

$$A = \$25,044$$

However, other factors may warrant investment in the project. For example, the project might provide the pioneering firm with a long-run competitive edge in a developing market if the investment provides a new product that could be introduced and sold now.

Arithmetic factors which represent the expression $\dfrac{1 - \dfrac{1}{(1 + i)^n}}{i}$ are located in Table 4 on page 642 of the Appendix. The factor 3.993 in the preceding calculation is shown in the 8%/5-period cell of that table.[2]

Relationships Between the Tables in the Appendix

Close examination of the four tables in the Appendix will reveal certain fundamental relationships between them, an understanding of which will provide additional insight into the critical role that interest rates play in the compounding and discounting process. For example, the present value factor 3.993 that is located in the 8%/5-period cell of Table 4 equals the sum of the first five present value factors located in the 8 percent column of Table 3:

$1 Received at the End of a Period	Present Value Factor	
1	.926	
2	.857	
3	.794	Table 3
4	.735	
5	.681	
Present value factor for $1 received at the end of each period for five periods	3.993	Table 4

Each future value factor that is shown in Table 1 is directly related to its respective present value factor shown in Table 3; that is, each present value factor in Table 3 is the reciprocal of its respective future value factor shown in Table 1. This relationship is illustrated at the top of page 220, assuming a $1 lump-sum is invested now to earn 5 percent interest compounded annually for three years.

Finally, the close relationship between Tables 1 and 2 may be revealed in the following illustration. Suppose the problem is to

---

[2]To convert Table 4 so that the present value of $1 that is received (or paid) at the beginning of a period for n periods can be determined, use the factor that is shown for one less period and add 1.000. For example, the present value of $1,000 received at the beginning of each year for five years, beginning today, discounted at 8 percent interest compounded annually, is $4,312: $1,000 (3,312 + 1.000) = $1,000 × 4,312 = $4,312.

TABLE 1	TABLE 3
FUTURE VALUE OF $1 INVESTED FOR THREE YEARS	PRESENT VALUE OF $1 RECEIVED AT THE END OF THE THIRD YEAR

$$F_n = P(1 + i)^n$$

$$P = \frac{F_n}{(1 + i)^n}$$

$$= \$1(1 + .05)^3$$

$$= \frac{F_n}{(1 + i)^3}$$

$$= \$1 \times \frac{1}{(1 + .05)^3}$$

$$= \$1(1.05)(1.05)(1.05)$$

$$= \$1 \times \frac{1}{(1.05)(1.05)(1.05)}$$

◀ *The Reciprocal* ▶

$$= \$1 \times 1.158$$

$$= \$1 \times \frac{1}{1.158}$$

$$= \$1 (.864)$$

$$= \underline{\underline{\$1.158}}$$

$$= \underline{\underline{\$.864}}$$

determine the future value of a series of $1 investments at the end of the fourth year, and that each investment is made at the beginning of each year for four years and earns 6 percent interest compounded annually. The relationship between the 6 percent columns of Tables 1 and 2 is shown below:

$1 INVESTED AT THE BEGINNING OF YEAR	AMOUNT IS INVESTED FOR	FUTURE VALUE FACTOR	
1	4 years	1.262	
2	3 years	1.191	Table 1
3	2 years	1.124	
4	1 year	1.060	
Future value factor at the end of four years for $1 invested at the beginning of each year for four years...		4.637*	Table 2

*In this instance, Table 2 has been converted to a series of investments made at the beginning of the year by selecting the future value factor for one more year and subtracting 1.000; in other words, 5.637 − 1.000 = 4.637.

The fundamental reason for the close interrelationships that exist between the four tables in the Appendix is that each table is derived from the compounding Equation [1] that was originally shown on page 209, $F_n = P(1 + i)^n$. Notice that each of the four tables may be used with problems that involve either the receipt or payment of money.

Application of the Present Value Concept to Selected Financial Problems

The foregoing presentation of the present value concept and the discounting process provides a useful background by which to penetrate more deeply into several accounting and financial problems that frequently confront the accountant in the areas of valuation and decision-making. The problems selected for additional examination in the remainder of this chapter include: (1) valuation of an asset; (2) reexamination of the value of a college education illustration; and (3) valuation of a business enterprise.

Valuation of an Asset. Recall that the economist sometimes establishes the value of an asset by estimating the future incomes which the asset is expected to generate over its useful life. To illustrate in detail how this valuation process can be accomplished, assume that management purchased for $250,000 a special-purpose machine that was expected to generate an annual after-tax cash flow income of $40,000 during its 10-year expected life. The estimated total after-tax cash flow of $400,000 generated during the 10-year period exceeds the asset's original cost by $150,000. At first glance, the real value of this machine may appear to be $400,000, rather than its $250,000 purchase cost. However, the present value concept states that monies received in the future are less valuable today than those received today.

If management has established a guideline that requires all of the firm's investments to generate an annual return of 8 percent, the present value of this special-purpose machine can be approximated as follows:

$40,000 annual after-tax cash flow × 6.710 = $268,400

The present value factor for a series of annual incomes received for 10 years, discounted at 8 percent is located in Table 4 of the Appendix in the 8%/10-period cell. Using this method, an economist may quickly conclude that the present value of this machine to the company is $268,400, or $18,400 more than its original cost. The machine's discounted future earning potential can be considered by the economist to be a better reflection of the asset's "true worth" than the asset's purchase cost, irrespective of how objective and verifiable that purchase cost may be.

The accountant maintains, however, that the value established by the economist in applying the present value concept is uncertain because: (1) it is dependent on a future pattern of earnings that may either exceed or fall short of the predictions; and (2) it is subject to what may be termed a conjectural or arbitrary requirement of investment returns demanded by management. With respect to this second point, an accountant could argue that the present value of this special-purpose machine could vary considerably depending on what rate of return a particular management requires on its investments at any specific time. The accountant contends that such a basis is excessively arbitrary and capricious. In short, establishing the value of an asset by means of the present value concept contains too much uncertainty and conjecture to warrant being included in the accounting records of the company.

Nevertheless, present value analysis is an extremely helpful concept and analytic tool that can assist management in deciding whether or not a particular investment should be made. For example, if management required a 10 percent return on investment projects, purchase of the special-purpose machine previously mentioned might not be recommended because the present value under these circumstances would fall short of the purchase cost by $4,200, as shown below:

$40,000 annual after-tax cash flow × 6.145 = $245,800 present value

Another instance where the present value concept and the discounting process can be used to determine the value of an asset is when a firm purchases an asset under a deferred payment plan. To illustrate, management purchased and took possession of a piece of equipment on January 1, 1980, under a financial arrangement whereby it agreed to pay the vendor $11,198 at December 31, 1980. The equipment could have been purchased for an immediate cash payment of $10,000 on January 1, 1980. An accountant would probably record the purchase of the equipment at January 1, 1980, as shown in the entry below:

```
Equipment......................................................  11,198
    Accounts Payable ..........................................            11,198
        Purchase of equipment at January 1, 1980 under
        1-year credit terms.
```

An argument could be made, however, that a more realistic cost of the machine should be $10,000, since that was the cash outlay required for the equipment on January 1. The $1,198 additional cost incurred at year-end could be interpreted as the interest expense required from the purchaser to defer payment for one year. The *implicit interest rate* charged by the vendor in this instance is calculated as shown below:

$$P = \frac{F_n}{(1 + i)^n}$$

$$\frac{\$10,000 \text{ purchase cost}}{\text{at January 1, 1980}} = \frac{\$11,198 \text{ purchase cost at December 31, 1980}}{(1 + i)^1}$$

$$\frac{1}{(1 + i)^n} = \frac{\$10,000}{\$11,198} = .893$$

Reference to Table 3 of the Appendix reveals that the present value factor .893 for one period in the future appears in the 12 percent column. In other words, the purchaser was charged an annual interest rate of 12 percent under this particular financial arrangement. Using this interpretation, the following hypothetical entries can be conceptualized to reflect the purchase of and payment for the equipment at January 1 and December 31, 1980, respectively:

```
1980
Jan. 1   Equipment ...........................................   10,000
             Accounts Payable.................................            10,000
             Purchase  of  equipment;  payment  de-
             ferred until December 31, 1980.

1980
Dec. 31  Accounts Payable.....................................   10,000
         Interest Expense .....................................    1,198
             Cash ...............................................            11,198
             Payment  for  equipment  purchased  on
             January 1, 1980.
```

Although these last two entries would probably never be recorded, present value analysis can be an extremely effective device for examining in detail a particular transaction to appraise the wisdom of management's activities and decisions.

Reexamination of the Value of a College Education. Although most reasons for attending college are probably noneconomic, the decision whether or not to pursue a baccalaureate degree can be approached strictly from a financial viewpoint. Recall that the economist viewed the graduate as having invested the equivalent of $48,000 in obtaining a college education which was thought to be recoverable through higher potential earnings over the next 40 years. How much higher must the graduate's annual earnings be for 40 years in order to recover the $48,000 educational investment, if the graduate requires a return of 6 percent compounded annually on the investment? The question may be analyzed as follows:

P = The present value of the $48,000 investment in the college education.

n = The number of periods (40 years) over which the excess potential earnings will be generated.

i = The interest rate demanded by the graduate, in this case 6 percent compounded annually.

A = The annual excess earnings that must be generated because of the college education.

This information may be summarized in the following manner, using Equation 4:

$$P_n = A \left[\frac{1 - \frac{1}{(1+i)^n}}{i} \right]$$

$$\$48{,}000 = A \left[\frac{1 - \frac{1}{(1+.06)^{40}}}{.06} \right]$$

The present value factor that is equivalent to the information enclosed in the bracketed portion above is located in the 6%/40-period cell of Table 4, or 15.046. Therefore, $48,000 = A(15.046), and A = $3,190, rounded to the nearest dollar. Hence, if the graduate earns approximately $3,200 higher annual income for 40 years due to a college education, the $48,000 investment will be recovered.

This calculation gives the appearance of precision; however, it must be quickly emphasized that the amount is based on several critical assumptions, as outlined below:

(1) The period over which the investment will be recovered.
(2) The interest rate that the graduate may actually earn by investing financial resources in other alternatives.
(3) The future higher earning increment being generated in a uniform pattern over the 40-year period.

One or more of these estimates may prove incorrect. Nevertheless, an analysis of this type may be helpful in making decisions and narrowing future employment opportunities. In addition, the decision whether or not to pursue a college degree, if for solely economic reasons, may be made easier if the expenditures and sacrificed incomes involved in a college education can be projected at high school graduation. Finally, this type of analysis forces the decision-maker to make as explicit as possible all assumptions and information that may impinge on the problem confronted. In short, this appraisal requires as much attention to detail, disciplined thought, and sequential analysis as does the accounting process itself.

Valuation of a Business Enterprise. The value of a business can rarely be determined by simply totaling all assets that are reflected on the firm's balance sheet at a specific date. Nor does accounting make any pretense that the precise total value of a large enterprise like General Motors Corporation at June 30, 1978, equaled the $29,731,406,982.12 total assets that was reported in the corporation's detailed internal report. One of the most important reasons why the total reported assets of a business enterprise at a specific moment fails to reflect the "true worth" of that entity is because those total assets reflect historical costs that were incurred in different periods; and the purchasing power of the dollar may have changed considerably during the intervening years. In addition, several valuation adjustments are based on estimates. The following selected examples provide additional supporting evidence that the value of a company cannot be accurately derived from its assets:

(1) Receivables are often stated net of an estimated allowance for doubtful accounts.
(2) Marketable securities may be reflected at their original purchase cost or at their current market value, whichever is lower.
(3) Inventory is often stated at its purchase cost, even though the current cost to replace that inventory may substantially exceed that historical cost.
(4) The original costs of plant assets probably reflect amounts that were paid in periods when the purchasing power of the dollar differed substantially from today's dollar.
(5) The original costs of depreciable plant assets that have been charged to expense in prior years, and which are reflected in the accumulated depreciation accounts, are usually based on an estimated life and salvage value of these assets.

In addition, the depth and capacity of managerial and creative talents are never shown as an asset of the firm on the balance sheet. Furthermore, items such as unfilled back orders or plans for expansion into new product lines are rarely reflected, much less quantified. In short, the reader of financial statements is wisely advised never to view the balance sheet as reflecting the precise, accurate, or true value of a going business.

An approach that uses the present value concept to more closely approximate the value of a business is often suggested. This method presupposes that any going concern may be viewed as a large-scale asset, or a package of assorted assets, which contains potential service benefits in the form of financial resources from which a series of future net incomes is generated. A review of a firm's past profit performance can sometimes provide valuable clues to estimate its future income-generating ability.

In Chapter 5, for example, the Dynaflow Corporation earned $37,400 net income during the fiscal year ended December 31, 1979. Its balance sheet at that date reflected total assets of $442,200. The rate of return on those assets during 1979 can be approximated as shown below:

$$\frac{\text{Net income}}{\text{Total assets at year-end}} = \frac{\$\ 37,400}{\$442,200} = 8.5\%$$

Management of Dynaflow Corporation may project that the company is capable of generating an average annual net income of about $70,000 during the next 20 years, or slightly less than double the amount earned during its first full year of activity. Assuming that the Dynaflow Corporation will continue to earn, for the next 20 years, a similiar rate of return on total assets as it earned during 1979, a projection of the firm's present value may be derived as shown below:

P = The present value of the corporate entity, the unknown in this instance.

A = Estimated annual net income that the corporation is expected to generate.

n = Number of periods over which the expected net income is expected to be earned, 20 years in this instance.

i = Approximately 8 percent return on total assets.

Using Equation [4], the data can be combined in the following manner to approximate the present worth or value of the Dynaflow Corporation:

$$P = A \left[\frac{1 - \dfrac{1}{(1 + i)^n}}{i} \right]$$

$$P = \$70,000(9.818)* = \$687,260$$

*The factor 9.818 was obtained from the 8%/20-period cell in Table 4.

From the above calculation, it appears that the estimated present value of Dynaflow Corporation is approximately 50 percent more than the total assets reflected on the balance sheet at December 31, 1979. Notice that the apparent precision of this estimate suffers all of the drawbacks noted in the previous analysis of the college education; any estimate of the future may prove incorrect, plus considerable subjectivity may surround these estimates. The present value concept and the discounting process do, however, provide an alternate method by which to approximate the worth of a going concern aside from a detailed listing of its assets. But, in either case, conclusions that are drawn from such a quantitative analysis must be viewed with considerable caution.

QUESTIONS

1. Of what importance to the accounting discipline is the concept of value and its measurement?

2. What attributes of "value" make the concept particularly challenging to the accountant?

3. What principle is generally used within accounting by which to measure the value or cost of a specific asset? Why has the accountant elected to adopt this particular principle?

4. Identify and define at least four methods (other than historical cost) by which the value or cost of a depreciable asset might be measured. Explain why an accountant would probably not record any of these costs or values in the accounting records of an organization.

5. Indicate how the additional annual after-tax cash flow that a specific depreciable asset is expected to generate could be determined. Assume: that the asset's original cost was $10,000, with no salvage value estimated at the end of its 10-year life; that the asset is expected to generate an increase in annual operating income of $2,500; that the federal income tax rate is 50%; and that the straight-line method was used to depreciate this asset.

6. Identify the major distinctions between accounting and economics with respect to focus and scope.

7. Describe how the disciplines of accounting and economics differ in their approach to quantification.

8. Distinguish between how an accountant and an economist might attempt to establish the value of an asset.

9. Explain what is meant by the "time value of money."

10. Explain in what respect the time value of money concept is similar to or different from the purchasing power of the dollar concept.

11. After defining each symbol in the equation to determine the future value of a lump-sum investment, convert that equation so that the present value of a lump-sum investment may be calculated.

12. Explain the distinction between compounding (future value) and discounting (present value).

13. Determine the following values, using the appropriate tables in the Appendix: (a) The value 5 years hence of a $1,000 lump-sum investment made today and invested at 10% compounded annually; (b) The value 5 years hence of a $1,000 lump-sum investment made today and invested at 10% compounded semiannually.

14. Determine the following values, using the appropriate tables in the Appendix: (a) The future value at the end of the tenth year of a series of $1,000 investments made annually at the end of each year, beginning one year from today, invested at 10% compounded annually; (b) The future value at the end of the tenth year of a series of $500 investments made semiannually, beginning 6 months from today, invested at 10% compounded semiannually.

15. Determine the following values, using the appropriate tables in the Appendix: (a) The present value of a lump-sum investment of $1,000 to be received 5 years from today, discounted at 10% compounded annually. (b) The present value of a lump-sum investment of $1,000 to be received 5 years from today, discounted at 10% compounded semiannually.

16. Determine the following values, using the appropriate tables in the Appendix: (a) The present value of $1,000 received at the end of each year for 5 years, discounted at 10% compounded annually; (b) The present value of $500 received at the end of each 6 months for 5 years, discounted at 10% compounded semiannually.

17. In which table, column, and row in the Appendix would the factor to determine the present value of $1,000 received one year from now be located, if the interest rate was stated as 12% compounded: (a) annually; (b) semiannually; (c) quarterly; (d) monthly.

18. Using the "Rule of 70," determine the approximate number of years required for a lump-sum investment of $750 to increase to $1,500, if that money is invested at 8% interest compounded annually.

19. Would you recommend that a manager invest $32,000 now in a project which is expected to generate an annual after-tax cash flow of $10,000 at the end of each of the next 4 years if stockholders demand that any investment made by the corporation must generate a minimum return of 15% compounded annually?

20. Explain why the factor that is located in the 12%/6-period cell of Table 4 in the Appendix is almost identical to the sum of the first six factors in the 12% column of Table 3.

21. Using the factor located in the 6%/15-period cell of Table 1 in the Appendix, explain any relationship that exists between that factor and the factor shown in the same cell of Table 3.

22. Explain why the first three factors located in the 3% column of Table 1 in the Appendix would equal the factor located in the 3%/4-period cell of Table 2, if Table 2 were to be converted to the future value of $1 received (or paid) at the beginning of a period for 4 periods.

23. What aspects inherent in the present value concept make its use as a method by which to value an asset or a business enterprise less than absolutely accurate and precise?

24. The balance sheet is often cited as a valuation statement that may reflect a mixture of past, present, and estimated values. Cite at least four account titles that tend to support this statement.

25. Evaluate the following comment: "One of the best ways to determine the present value of a business enterprise, including its managerial, research, and development capabilities is: (a) to view it as a large-scale asset that contains future service benefits in the form of earning potential; and (b) to discount that stream of expected earnings over the estimated life of the business."

EXERCISES

1. After-tax cash flow. Bifurcation Laboratories, Inc., purchased one of the last available models of a laser-beam machine for $48,000 in October, 1979. The machine is estimated to have no salvage value at the end of its 8-year life and straight-line method of depreciation is used to depreciate all machinery and equipment. The treasurer forecasts that this piece of equipment would probably generate an increase in annual operating income before depreciation and tax expenses of about $8,500 over its 8-year life. The federal income tax rate of 50% was used for analytical purposes, and the corporation's fiscal year ended each September 30.

Required: Determine the after-tax cash flow that the treasurer estimates the laser-beam machine will generate over its expected life.

2. Capitalized cost of training program. Shirley Tinbergen is deciding whether to enroll in a 1-year training program that would enable her to become a data processing specialist, or to accept employment as a sales clerk in a retail chain store. The estimated cost of the training program is $4,000, including tuition, books, and miscellaneous fees. Upon completion of the program, Tinbergen plans to secure a processing specialist position for an indefinite period of time. On the other hand, the total income that can be earned in one year as a sales clerk is estimated at about $7,300.

Required: (a) Assuming that all of the estimates described are accurate, and that the $4,000 training cost is paid from Tinbergen's personal resources, prepare the entry to reflect the capitalized cost of the educational experience. (b) What additional information might an economist include in the above entry to reflect the "full cost" of this educational experience?

3. **Future value of lump-sum investments.** Determine the future value at the date indicated below for each of the following lump-sum investments made on January 1, 1980. Appropriate tables in the Appendix may be consulted, except that the calculation for requirement (d) must be obtained by actual computation.

	SUM INVESTED (P)	INTEREST RATE	DATE
(a)	$ 4,000	8% compounded annually	January 1, 1983
(b)	$ 6,000	8% compounded semiannually	July 1, 1983
(c)	$ 8,000	8% compounded quarterly	April 1, 1984
(d)	$10,000	9% compounded semiannually	January 1, 1981

4. **Lump-sum investment unknowns.** (a) At what rate of interest compounded annually must a $5,000 sum be invested to equal $8,570 at the end of 7 years from date of investment? (b) What lump-sum amount invested at 4% compounded annually will equal $11,384 at the end of 9 years from the date of investment? (c) How many years must a $7,000 lump-sum remain invested at 6% compounded annually to equal $14,084? (d) What lump-sum amount invested at 10% compounded quarterly for 4 years will equal $13,365?

5. **Future value of a series of equal investments.** Determine the future value of the following series of investments immediately after the final deposit is made. The first deposit is made on January 1, 1980, in each instance:

	SUM INVESTED AT THE BEGINNING OF EACH PERIOD	NUMBER OF DEPOSITS MADE	INTEREST RATE
(a)	$2,000 annually	6	5% compounded annually
(b)	$3,000 semiannually	6	6% compounded semiannually
(c)	$4,000 quarterly	16	10% compounded quarterly
(d)	$4,000 semiannually	14	10% compounded semiannually

6. **Series of equal investment unknowns.** (a) Determine the amount that must be invested at the beginning of each year, starting today, to equal $54,304, immediately after the 15th deposit, if the interest rate is 8% compounded annually. (b) What interest rate compounded semiannually must be earned on $2,500 invested at the beginning of each 6-month period, starting today, to equal $60,742.50 immediately after the 20th deposit is made? (c) How many investments of $3,000 must be made at the beginning of each quarter, beginning today, to grow to $49,557, if 10% compounded quarterly is earned on that series of equal investments? (d) Bob Clemens, who celebrated his 40th birthday today, desires to have a lump sum of $61,065 available when he reaches age 53. If he can invest his money at 6% interest compounded semiannually, determine the

amount he must invest at the beginning of each 6-month period starting today, assuming the last deposit will be made on his 53d birthday.

7. **Present value of lump-sum investments.** Determine the present value today, June 30, 1980, of each amount shown below that will be received on the date indicated, discounted at the interest rate indicated:

	FUTURE VALUE OF LUMP SUM	DATE	INTEREST RATE
(a)	$10,000	June 30, 1985	14% compounded annually
(b)	$12,000	December 31, 1989	12% compounded semiannually
(c)	$12,000	September 30, 1983	12% compounded quarterly
(d)	$14,000	June 30, 1982	60% compounded quarterly

8. **Present value of lump-sum investment with unknowns.** (a) What interest rate compounded annually will reduce a future value of $24,000, at March 15, 1983, to a present value of $16,200 at March 15, 1980? (b) How many years must a lump sum whose future value is $6,000 at September 30, 1988, be discounted at 16% compounded semiannually to yield a present value of $1,890? In effect, determine "today's" date. (c) Calculate the present value on September 30, 1980, of the $8,000 inheritance which Sue Jacobs will receive when she reaches her 21st birthday on December 31, 1983. Assume that Jacobs could otherwise invest her money at 6% compounded quarterly. (d) Determine the present value of $27,378 that will be received 2 years hence if the interest rate is 17% compounded annually. (Since the factor must be calculated, round the present value of the lump sum to the nearest dollar.)

9. **Present value of a series of equal amounts.** Calculate the present value of each of the following series of equal amounts received at the end of each period according to the interest rate and timing schedule shown below. (Round each answer to the nearest dollar.)

	AMOUNT OF PAYMENT RECEIVED	NUMBER OF PERIODS RECEIVED	INTEREST RATE
(a)	$ 700	4 annual periods	8% compounded annually
(b)	$2,600	7 semiannual periods	14% compounded semiannually
(c)	$8,100	27 quarterly periods	20% compounded quarterly
(d)	$ 200	24 monthly periods	24% compounded monthly

10. **Present value of a series of investments with unknowns.** (a) Determine the amount that must be received at the end of each year for 16 years at 6% interest compounded annually to equal a present value of $20,212. (b) What interest rate compounded semiannually would make a present value of $16,980 equal to a series of $3,000 equal payments received at the end of each 6 months for 6 years? (c) How many equal payments of $1,000 must be received at the end of each quarter to equal a present value of $14,992 if the interest rate is 8% compounded quarterly? (d) Determine the annual after-tax cash flow that must occur at the end of each year for 5 years to justify a $56,865 investment in a particular piece of machinery, assuming management requires a return of 10% compounded annually on any investment that is made.

11. Varied future and present value situations. (a) Carlos Bonaventura plans to invest $1,000 each 6 months, starting today, at 6% interest compounded semiannually hoping to accumulate a total amount of $11,000 immediately after the 9th deposit. Determine the amount by which his objective will exceed or fall short. (b) What must be the amount of each semiannual investment to exactly meet the objective stated in item (a)? (c) A business associate desires to withdraw $5,000 from an investment fund at the end of each year for 6 years beginning at the end of the 1st year. Determine the amount that must be invested today to enable this objective to be achieved if the fund will earn 8% compounded annually.

12. Present value of accounts receivable. The Accounts Receivable balance of the Bentsen Corporation at January 1, 1980, was $120,000. One third of this balance is expected to be collected on March 31, 1980, and the remainder on June 30, 1980. If management requires that each financial resource owned by the firm earns at least 16% compounded quarterly, determine the present value of the Accounts Receivable balance at January 1, 1980.

PROBLEMS

6-1. Ambiguity in pinpointing value. In November, 1979, the Ronsteads placed their suburban residence with a real estate agent for immediate sale. In 1957, the home had been sold to the original owner for $16,000, including the lot. The Ronsteads purchased it from that original owner in 1966 for $21,400 ($4,000 cash down payment, and the balance due under a 6% 20-year mortgage note arrangement) from a local savings and loan association. Monthly mortgage payments were $124.67.

In 1957, the county had assessed this property for tax purposes at 60% of its original sale price, or $9,600 ($16,000 × .6). Because of inflation and the need for additional county revenues, the county in 1974 reassessed all properties located in this development. The assessor placed a valuation of $20,000 on the Ronstead property; and the 1979 tax rate on residential property was 60%, or $12,000 in the case of the Ronstead property. The Ronsteads insured their home against fire, windstorm, and other natural disasters at its estimated replacement cost of $47,000. Several homes in the same development were being sold at $40,000–$45,000 each, with the real estate agent receiving a 6% commission based on the transaction price. In other words, an agent who sells a home for $40,000 will receive a $2,400 commission ($40,000 × .6), and $37,600 is given to the seller. The Ronsteads hope to sell their home for at least $44,000.

Three prospective buyers have expressed interest in buying the Ronstead residence by making tentative offers of $38,000, $41,000, and $43,500. The Ronsteads are seriously considering the purchase of a new home in another section of the city for approximately $58,000 as soon as their current property is sold.

Required: (1) Determine the value of the Ronstead property to each of the following persons or organizations under the following circumstances:

(a) The Ronsteads in 1966.
(b) The Ronsteads in 1979.
(c) The real estate agent if the property is sold in 1979.
(d) Each of the three current prospective buyers.
(e) For insurance purposes.
(f) For county property tax purposes in 1979.
(g) The savings and loan association which holds the Ronstead mortgage.
(h) The original owner in 1957.
(i) The builder of the residence in 1957.
(j) The original owner in 1966.
(2) What is the "true or real value" of the Ronstead residence?

6-2. **Alternate valuation bases.** The Yost Mfg. Corp. purchased and installed a conveyor system in one of its plants on January 1, 1980, at a cost of $420,000. The life of the system was estimated at 10 years, with a forecasted salvage value of $20,000 at the end of that time. Straight-line depreciation was used to allocate the capitalized cost of all depreciable plant assets to expense at yearly intervals.

Several other cost bases emerged during the fiscal year ended December 31, 1980, by which to value this particular conveyor system:

(a) An almost identical system could have been rented during the entire 10-year period at an annual cost of $38,000, payable at the end of each year. The rental agreement stated that all normal repair, maintenance, and insurance costs were to be paid by the user of the equipment.
(b) Management estimated that the purchased system would enable the corporation to increase its cash operating income (before depreciation and tax expenses) by $60,000 during each of the next 10 years.
(c) A competitor in another city offered to purchase the conveyor system from Yost Mfg. Corp. in September, 1980, for $400,000. Yost Mfg. Corp's management declined the offer.
(d) Management estimated that the system could have been sold to a used-machine dealer in November for $330,000, net of removal and disposal costs.
(e) The system could have been replaced at the end of 1980 with a similar model and age conveyor at a cost of $360,000.

Required: (1) Determine the cost of the conveyor system under each of the alternatives identified below:
(a) Undiscounted future earning capacity on an after-tax cash flow basis, assuming an income tax rate of 50%.
(b) Current replacement cost at the end of 1980.
(c) Least costly alternative at the date of purchase.
(d) Historical cost at the purchase date.
(e) Net realizable value in November, 1980.
(f) Book value at December 31, 1980.
(g) The value sacrificed (or opportunity cost) by declining the competitor's offer.
(2) Specify the value or cost that an accountant would attach to the conveyor system at the beginning and at the end of 1980. In addi-

tion, indicate why an accountant would probably choose to ignore five of the monetary amounts determined in part (1) for purposes of valuation and financial reporting.

6-3. Career decision-making. Wayne Morgan expects to complete the mathematics-engineering curriculum at the area community college and receive the Associate in Arts degree. He had prepared himself during the last two years for either of two careers; a commercial airline pilot or a ship captain in the merchant marines. Although his physical condition, mental aptitude, and emotional stamina equip him for either alternative, he finds it extremely difficult to decide which medium of transportation, sea or air, would bring greater satisfaction in the long-run.

One of Morgan's friends, who is an accounting-finance major at the same college, suggested that a financial approach might add a new dimension to the solution of the career dilemma. At his friend's suggestion, Morgan assembled the following information, and presented it to his "financial advisor."

Airline Pilot. Attendance at a nearby commercial airline school for 1 year will cost $11,000 payable in advance, including room, board, and miscellaneous expenses. Upon successful completion of the program, Morgan will possess commercial, instrument, and multi-engine ratings (jet and propellor). Graduates of this particular school are in such demand that several commercial airlines virtually guarantee each graduate a position as flight engineer at a starting annual salary of $12,000, and $15,000 for the second year. For the next 6 years, he will serve as a copilot at an average annual salary of $20,000 during the first 4 years, and $27,000 during the last two. After that period, he would qualify as a captain drawing an average annual salary of $40,000. Mandatory retirement age from active flight status is normally 60, and a pilot would have to pass rigorous physical, mental, and emotional evaluations each 6 months while on active flight status.

Ship Captain. The training period at a maritime academy is 2 years, at an annual cost, including room, board, and miscellaneous expenses, of $8,000 per year payable in advance at the beginning of each year. Upon successful completion of the course, any of several ship lines hire most maritime graduates as a second mate at an average annual salary of $12,000. After serving for 2 years as second mate, he may be promotable to first mate at an annual salary of $22,000 for 3 years. Thereafter, he will be eligible to assume a captaincy at a salary of $40,000 per year, depending on the type of vessel and area of operation. Mandatory retirement age from active status, and the periodic physical, mental, and emotional checkups are almost identical to airline regulations.

Morgan and his colleague decided to evaluate the two alternatives for the first 9 years, since the annual salary under either alternative after the 9th year would be identical. The following assumptions were agreed upon: the date of graduation from the community college is now; any financial resources during the next decade can earn 7% compounded annually; all payments are made and salaries earned at the beginning of the year; and taxes of all types are ignored.

Required: (1) Determine the undiscounted total cash flow for the nine-year period under each career alternative.

(2) Using 7% interest compounded annually, calculate the present value of the expenditures and incomes for each alternative. Round all computations to the nearest hundred dollars.

(3) Based on your analysis, which alternative appears to be more financially rewarding at this time? Which alternative would you suggest for Morgan to pursue?

6-4. Present value of a future amount. Angela Jabara, who is celebrating her 20th birthday today, has decided to forego some of life's pleasures during her twenties so as to enjoy some luxuries during her forties. After consulting with a financial adviser, she constructed a plan whereby she would deposit with a life insurance company 10 equal annual amounts, beginning today and ending on her 29th birthday, so that she would be able to receive 10 annual payments of $10,000 starting at age 40. The insurance company issued a contract to Jabara stating that the company would invest her deposits to earn 8% interest compounded annually on all monies accumulated in her account.

Required: Determine the amount that Jabara must deposit with the insurance company beginning today.

6-5. Determining future and present values. The parents of Pedro Gutierrez have arranged to borrow a total of $20,000 over a 4-year period to pay for his college education. Their plan is to borrow $5,000 on September 1 of each of 4 years, beginning September 1, 1979. The first repayment of the loan in 6 equal annual installments will begin on September 1, 1983. This schedule of repayments will enable the total debt to be extinguished after the 6th installment is paid on September 1, 1988. The institution which is loaning the funds to the Gutierrez family is charging 8% interest compounded annually.

Required: Determine the amount of each equal annual installment that must be made, beginning September 1, 1983. Round all calculations to the nearest dollar.

6-6. Imputed interest rate on an installment purchase. On January 1, 1980, Blenheim Publishing Co. purchased a letter press under the following terms: $300,000 due in 5 equal semiannual installments beginning July 1, 1980. The letter press could have been purchased on January 1, 1980, for $267,120 cash.

Required: Determine the implicit rate of interest compounded semiannually that the vendor appeared to be charging under this installment purchase arrangement.

6-7. Valuation of a business. Creighton Corporation earned $217,920 net income during the fiscal year just ended. The total assets reflected on the balance sheet at the end of that fiscal year amounted to $1,816,000. The firm is believed capable of generating an average net income of about $260,000 during each of the next 25 years. In addition, management expects the firm to continue to earn a similar rate of return on its total assets in each of the next 25 years.

Required: (1) Determine the rate of return earned on the total assets for the year just ended. (2) Determine an approximate present value of the firm based on the assumptions stated above.

6-8. Compounded interest. In December, the Board of Directors of Valley Savings and Loan Association was considering the merits of paying 12% interest on certain long-term certificates of deposit compounded either annually, semiannually, quarterly, or monthly. The association currently held approximately $10 million shareholder deposits in these particular long-term certificate deposit accounts.

Required: Determine how much interest would ultimately be paid on the $10-million of certificates during the next year, assuming that the principal and all accrued interest are left on deposit for the entire year and that 12% interest is compounded:

(1) Annually.
(2) Semiannually.
(3) Quarterly.
(4) Monthly.

DECISION CASES

6-I. Purchase or not to purchase. The controller of Kryster Corporation projected that a certain machine costing $283,232 today will be able to generate an annual after-tax cash flow of $32,000 over the machine's 16-year life. The machine is expected to have no salvage value at the end of that life. Management requires that all plant assets used in the firm earn at least a 12% return compounded annually.

Required:
(1) Assuming that all cash flows are generated at the end of each year, what would be your recommendation with respect to purchasing this particular machine?
(2) Determine the return that this machine is projected to earn over its useful life, expressed in terms of an interest rate compounded annually.

6-II. Cash or credit purchase. The Perkiomen Corp. intends to purchase a central air conditioning system for its manufacturing and administrative facilities on January 1, 1980. The firm has the option of paying for the system in either of the following ways:

(a) Payment of $380,200 cash on January 1, 1980.
(b) Payment of $100,000 cash on January 1, 1980, and 3 installments of $100,000 payable each 6 months beginning July 1, 1980.

The treasurer is quite certain that the firm can earn at least an 8% return, compounded semiannually on its financial resources during the next 2 years.

Required:
(1) Assuming all other conditions of the sale are identical, which option would you recommend for the purchase of the air conditioning system?
(2) Determine the approximate implicit interest rate compounded semiannually that the seller of the air conditioning system is charging under the credit purchase arrangement, (option b).

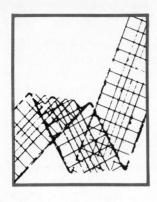

7
Aspects of Liquidity: Quick Assets and Current Liabilities

> *Some for the Glories of This World; and Some*
> *Sigh for the Prophet's Paradise to come; Ah, take*
> *the Cash, and let the Credit go.*
>
> Rubaiyat of Omar Khayyam
> Quatrain XIII, 5th version.

Managers of business enterprises are committed to two financial goals:

(1) Maintaining profitability by effectively using the financial resources at their command to generate net income;
(2) Maintaining liquidity by assuring that sufficient cash and near-cash resources are available when needed to pay financial obligations.

These two horns of a dilemma confront the financial administrator with the perennial challenge of maintaining an optimum balance between them. This chapter concentrates on selected facets and valuation problems associated with two components of liquidity: the quick assets and current liabilities.

QUICK ASSETS

The quick assets include cash, marketable securities, and receivables (net of any allowance for estimated uncollectibles) which are intended to be converted into cash within a relatively short time, although the conversion period may on occasion exceed three or four months. This conversion process includes the sale of marketable securities or the collection of accounts, notes, and interest receivable. Inventory and prepaid expenses are the principal current assets excluded from quick assets.

Cash and Cash Control

Cash is of unique importance to any organization because of its command over goods and services, and because of its easy transportability and transferability, irrespective of the bearer.

The cash account reflects the balance, at a specific time, of all cash that will be used in current operations over which the company has control. This includes: (1) cash in the bank; (2) deposits in transit to the bank; and (3) cash that is available within the company. The cash balance normally excludes cash that has been restricted for specific purposes, such as a cash fund that may be required for the retirement of bonds under provisions of a bond indenture. A cash fund of this type would normally be classified as a long-term investment on the balance sheet.

Many companies maintain multiple bank accounts, particularly if the company is geographically dispersed. In addition to providing financial flexibility, the maintenance of two or more bank affiliations enables management of the firm to have access to more lines of credit and to develop financial relationships within several communities. Particular areas of interest associated with the cash account are the treatment of bank overdrafts, the mechanics of bank reconciliations, and the need for adequate control of cash that circulates within the company.

Bank Overdrafts and the Quick Ratio. An overdrawn bank account is the equivalent of a short-term loan on which the bank may charge interest until it is fully paid. The amount of any *overdraft* that is material should be disclosed by reflecting it on the balance sheet as a current liability. To illustrate, assume that a company maintains two bank accounts, one of which is overdrawn by $8,000 and the other shows a debit balance of $20,000. The temptation arises to reflect the net cash balance of $12,000 on the balance sheet, as shown below in abbreviated form:

	NETTING TECHNIQUE	
Quick Assets		*Current Liabilities*
Cash (net)........................... $12,000		Accounts and notes payable
Marketable securities		(total)................................ $4,000
and net receivables (total).. 4,000		
Total quick assets................ $16,000		Total current liabilities $4,000

Application of the full disclosure technique dictates that the balance in each bank account should be reflected as shown below:

FULL DISCLOSURE TECHNIQUE			
Quick Assets		*Current Liabilities*	
Cash (1st National Bank)	$20,000	Overdraft (3d Union Bank) ...	$ 8,000
Marketable securities and		Accounts and notes payable	
net receivables (total)	4,000	(total)	4,000
Total quick assets	$24,000	Total current liabilities	$12,000

The net cash balance in either case is $12,000, and total quick assets exceed current liabilities by $12,000. The difference in their impact on the quick ratio, however, can be dramatic. The *quick ratio* is defined as total quick assets divided by total current liabilities. The quick ratio based upon the netting technique in this instance is 4:1 ($16,000 ÷ $4,000), whereas the full disclosure technique reveals a quick ratio of only 2:1 ($24,000 ÷ $12,000). This means that under the netting technique, four dollars of quick assets appear to be available with which to pay each dollar of current liabilities; whereas under the full disclosure technique, only two dollars of quick assets exist for each dollar of current liabilities.

Credit institutions often regard the quick ratio as a principal measure of a firm's liquidity position; the higher the ratio, the more secure is the firm's liquidity position. (However, an excessively high ratio, such as 5:1, may indicate an unprofitable use of the firm's financial resources. It is the maintenance of this delicate balance between liquidity and profitability that is the essence of the finance manager's dilemma.) The netting technique conceals the overdraft, as the quick ratio is manipulated upward, or "window dressed," to appear more favorable than it actually is. Astute financial analysts expend considerable effort to uncover this type of window dressing by looking beyond the surface of the financial statements of firms seeking loans or credit arrangements. Use of the netting technique may, however, be justified in instances when the amount of the overdraft is relatively insignificant.

Bank Reconciliation. The amount of cash under the control of a firm is of general concern to management, but the exact balance at a specific moment can be critical when a company faces a position of tight or low liquidity. The procedure which enables an analyst to determine the exact amount of cash subject to the company's withdrawal at a specific date is called reconciling the bank statement, or *bank reconciliation*. Bank reconciliations are normally prepared upon receipt of the monthly bank statement.

Balances shown on the bank statement and in the company's cash account at the date of reconciliation may not coincide for various reasons. Guidelines and the steps involved in the reconcilement process of the bank statement and cash account are illustrated below:

ADJUSTMENTS TO BANK STATEMENT	ADJUSTMENTS TO CASH ACCOUNT BALANCE
Add deposits in transit to the the bank that were omitted from the statement.	Add collections made by the bank of which the company remains unaware until notified by the bank, such as collection of notes, interest, or accounts receivable from the company's customers.
Deduct outstanding checks (checks written by the company which had not yet cleared banking channels at the date of reconciliation).	Deduct bank service costs and any interest charges which appear on the bank statement and which have not yet been recorded by the company.
Correct errors between amounts shown on canceled checks that are returned with the statement and amounts shown on the statement itself.	Correct errors between amounts shown on canceled checks and the amounts shown in the company's records.

To illustrate, the balance reflected in the cash account of Montrose Corp. at December 31, 1979, was $36,500. The bank statement dated December 31, 1979, that was received from the 1st City Bank showed that the company's cash balance at the bank on that date was $42,000. The following items were included on the bank statement but are not yet recorded in the company's books:

(1) A $300 charge for banking services rendered.
(2) One month's interest charge of $5,000 on a loan made by the bank to the corporation.
(3) Collection of $2,000 by the bank from a customer of Montrose Corp. The $2,000 included $150 interest on the note receivable which had not previously been recorded as interest income by the firm.
(4) Returned canceled check #741 had been correctly written for $56,000, but was transposed on the bank statement as $50,600.
(5) Included in the canceled checks was a check written by Montclaire Corp. for $6,200. This amount was shown on the statement as charged to Montrose Corp.'s bank account.

The bank was unaware of the following items at December 31, 1979, which were reflected in the company's accounting records:

(1) A deposit of $24,000 was in transit to the bank on December 31, 1979.
(2) Check #741 for $56,000 had been erroneously recorded in the company's cash and accounts payable accounts for $65,000 credit and debit, respectively.
(3) Checks written by the company through December 31, 1979, which were not returned with this or prior monthly bank statements totaled $24,600.

The bank reconciliation made on December 31, 1979, to determine the amount of cash subject to the company's withdrawal on that date is as follows:

Montrose Corp.
Bank Reconciliation
December 31, 1979

Adjustments to Bank Statement		Adjustments to Cash Account	
Balance per bank statement dated December 31, 1979 ..	$42,000	Cash balance per company's ledger at December 31, 1979	$36,500
Add: Deposit in transit	24,000	Add: Transposition error on transaction associated	
Montclaire Corp. check received in error	6,200	with check #741	9,000
Deduct: Transposition error on		Note and interest	
check #741	(5,400)	receivable collection .	2,000
Outstanding checks...	(24,600)	Deduct: Bank service charge ..	(300)
		Interest charge	(5,000)
Adjusted balance	$42,200	Adjusted balance	$42,200

A variety of other bank reconciliation formats are possible, such as a top-to-bottom or vertical arrangement.

Following the bank reconciliation, a journal entry is prepared by Montrose Corp. at December 31, 1979: (1) to correct the transposition error on check #741; (2) to record the bank service and interest charges; and (3) to record the collection of the $1,850 note receivable and $150 of interest income. This entry is shown below:

Cash	5,700	
Interest Expense	5,000	
Administrative Expense	300	
Accounts Payable		9,000
Notes Receivable		1,850
Interest Income		150
Corrections required for bank reconciliation.		

The bank service charge is treated as an administrative expense. In addition, the check that was drawn on Montclaire Corp. must be returned to the bank, together with a notification that Montrose Corp.'s balance as shown in the bank's records at December 31, 1979, should be increased by $800 (the $6,200 Montclaire Corp. check less the $5,400 bank's transposition error).

Although the bank reconciliation process entails considerable time and effort to inspect the journal, ledger, bank statement, individual checks, and other documents, the procedure is necessary to ensure tight control over this highly liquid and negotiable financial resource.

The Petty Cash Fund System. A cardinal principle of cash control is never to permit personnel who handle cash to also have access to: (1) cash records of the organization; (2) the general and special journals; or, (3) the general and subsidiary ledgers. Whenever this time-tested principle is violated, the possibilities for embezzlement and other fraudulent activities increase substantially. An application of this principle to the daily operations of most organizations can be illustrated with the petty cash fund system.

Petty cash funds are frequently established to maintain close control over cash used within the firm to handle small expenditures and at the same time to separate custodianship of the fund from the accounting records of the company. These funds are usually handled by designated custodians, such as cafeteria cashiers, store clerks, and secretaries in charge of travel expenses. Once the decision is made as to the purpose, size, and custodianship of the petty cash fund, the following entry is made, assuming the monetary amount of the fund is established at $500:

Petty Cash	500	
Cash		500
Transfer $500 from unrestricted cash to the petty cash fund.		

The designated custodian of the fund is thereafter responsible for maintaining detailed records, invoices, and memoranda of all cash received into and disbursed from the fund. Until the monetary amount of this fund is altered in the future, no further entry will be made which will affect the petty cash account.

Company policy normally prescribes that the fund should be replenished periodically to the amount of cash available in the fund when it was originally established. This procedure is designed to assure that: (1) the fund is properly maintained and administered; (2) the fund is audited periodically; and (3) its cash balance remains adequate to handle normal expenditures. To illustrate, if cash in the fund falls below a certain amount, for example $200, the custodian prepares a detailed report to request that the accounting office replenish the fund to its original $500 cash balance. Assume that at the end of the fund's first week of operation the following information is available:

Cash balance at beginning of the week..............................		$500
Purchase of postage stamps..	$100	
Payment to executive for reimbursement of travel expenses incurred during a business trip.......................................	200	
Office supplies received from a vendor who requested immediate cash payment for goods delivered............................	75	375
Cash balance at the end of the week		$125

Although the fund at the end of the first week contains only $125 cash, its total monetary amount remains at $500 as designated in the general ledger. The $375 disparity is supported by documentation which the custodian forwards to accounting office personnel, who in turn issues a check for $375 to replenish the cash balance. This replenishment is initiated by the following journal entry:

Prepaid Office Supplies...	175	
Travel Expense..	200	
Cash		375

      Reimbursement of petty cash fund from $125 to $500 cash balance. The prepaid account includes postage stamps and other office supplies.

Note that the petty cash account does not appear in the entry. To do so would alter the authorized monetary amount of the fund as shown in the general ledger.

Marketable Securities

Investment of excess idle cash in marketable securities transforms unproductive cash into an earning asset while retaining the advantage of high liquidity. Short-term government bonds, U.S. Treasury bills and notes, short-term commercial paper (called *marketable debt securities*) and short-term investments in securities of other companies that are listed on national stock exchanges (called *marketable equity securities*), tend to be quickly convertible into cash in the money markets should the need arise. In addition, portfolios of these types of securities usually provide income to the investing firm. For example, a large corporation lends $12 million of its excess idle cash to another enterprise over a normal two-day weekend at 6 percent interest compounded annually, thereby generating $4,000 additional income, as determined below:

$$\$12,000,000 \times .06 \times 2/360 = \$4,000 \text{ interest income}$$

This amount earned each week-end for one year would total $208,000 ($4,000 × 52 weeks).

Marketable securities are normally recorded at their original purchase cost; and any interest or dividends subsequently earned or received on these securities are recognized as interest income or dividend income. Investments in marketable debt securities are usually reflected on subsequent balance sheets at their purchase cost. Temporary investments in marketable equity securities, however, must be reflected at their cost or current market value, whichever is lower in accordance with Statement No. 12 of the Financial Accounting Standards Board. This basis of valuation is referred to as the *lower of cost or market rule*. A comprehensive illustration will examine this valuation process in greater detail.

An Illustration of Marketable Securities Valuation. Information with respect to Skowron Corporation's portfolio of short-term marketable securities that existed at the end of the fiscal year, December 31, 1979, is shown below: *income statement under loss & gains*

SECURITY	(1) PURCHASE COST (RECORDED IN LEDGER)	(2) MARKET VALUE AT DECEMBER 31, 1979	(3) UNREALIZED GAIN (LOSS)
U.S. Treasury Notes (short-term)......	$ 54,000	$ 54,000	—0—
Agrippa Corp.......	60,000	63,000	$ 3,000
Clydesdale, Inc.....	42,000	36,000	(6,000)
Easton Corp.........	28,000	24,000	(4,000)
Total...............	$184,000	$177,000	$ (7,000)

These securities were purchased during the latter part of 1979 at the cost noted in column (1) above. The current market value for each security at December 31, 1979, which appears in column (2), was obtained from the last market quotation of 1979 on one of the national stock exchanges.

Since the total market value of the portfolio is $7,000 less than its total recorded purchase cost, the portfolio must be revalued downward to the lower of cost or market.[1] This $7,000 downward revaluation of the short-term marketable securities portfolio is recorded: (1) by recognizing an unrealized loss on the income statement; and (2) by writing down the recorded cost of the portfolio by means of a revaluation allowance account, as shown:

```
1979
Dec. 31  Unrealized Loss on Marketable Securities (IS)..   7,000
             Allowance for Decline in Value of Market-
                able Securities (CA)..........................        7,000
             Revaluation of marketable securities
             portfolio to the lower of cost or market
             at fiscal year-end.
```

Note the following items from the above entry:

(1) The amount of recognized loss and downward revaluation is the lower of the portfolio's aggregate cost or market value rather than the difference between the portfolio's cost and an item-by-item valuation determination of the lower of cost or market for each marketable security.[2] The lower of

---

[1]*Statement of Financial Accounting Standards, No. 12,* "Accounting for Certain Marketable Securities" (Stamford: Financial Accounting Standards Board, December, 1975), pars. 8 and 11.

[2]*Ibid.,* pars. 8 and 31.

cost or market of this portfolio under an item-by-item valuation approach would have been $174,000 as shown below:

SECURITY	(1) PURCHASE COST (RECORDED IN LEDGER)	(2) MARKET VALUE AT DECEMBER 31, 1979	(3) LOWER OF COST OR MARKET ITEM-BY-ITEM
U.S. Treasury Notes (short-term).....	$ 54,000	$ 54,000	$ 54,000
Agrippa Corp.....	60,000	63,000	60,000
Clydesdale, Inc...	42,000	36,000	36,000
Easton Corp.......	28,000	24,000	24,000
Total..............	$184,000	$177,000	$174,000

(2) This $7,000 unrealized loss is often referred to as a *holding loss*, or a "paper loss," incurred from holding securities during a period when their market value fell below their original cost.

(3) The unrealized loss of $7,000 would appear on the income statement under the "Other gains and losses" caption.

(4) Allowance for Decline in Value of Marketable Securities is a current asset account that is directly associated with and contra to the marketable securities account.

The portfolio of marketable securities would be reflected in the current asset section of Skowron Corporation's balance sheet at December 31, 1979, as shown below:

Marketable securities (at cost)... $184,000
Less revaluation allowance to the lower of cost or market........   7,000
                                                                   $177,000

The $177,000 amount is referred to as the portfolio's *carrying value* as of December 31, 1979.

An additional piece of information, shown as a footnote to the financial statements prepared as of December 31, 1979, should include the amount of *gross unrealized gains* and the *gross unrealized losses* incurred on the portfolio. In this instance, the gross unrealized gain is $3,000 [Agrippa Corp. per column (3)], and the gross unrealized loss is $10,000 ($6,000 Clydesdale, Inc., plus $4,000 Easton Corp.); which equals the *net unrealized loss* of $7,000 that is reflected on the income statement.

Subsequent Sale of Marketable Securities. The short-term U.S. Treasury notes in the preceding illustration were redeemed by the federal government on March 15, 1980, upon payment of $54,000. On the same date, all securities held in Agrippa Corp. and Easton Corp. were sold for $65,000 and $26,000, respectively. A *net realized gain* of $3,000 was recognized at the time of sale as shown in the following entry:

1980
Mar. 15 Cash 145,000
        Marketable Securities   142,000
        Gain on Sale of Marketable Securities (IS).   3,000
        Record sale of marketable securities.

	PURCHASE COST	PROCEEDS FROM SALE	GAIN (LOSS)
U.S. Treasury Notes	$ 54,000	$ 54,000	—0—
Agrippa Corp.	60,000	65,000	$5,000
Easton Corp....................	28,000	26,000	(2,000)
Total	$142,000	$145,000	$3,000

Subsequent Revaluations. The portfolio of marketable securities must be reexamined at each financial reporting date, whether at year-end or midyear, to determine if that portfolio requires any adjustment to the revaluation allowance contra account. To illustrate, assume that: (1) interim financial statements are prepared at midyear, June 30, 1980; (2) several shares of Hawkes Corp. capital stock were purchased for $55,000 during April, 1980; and (3) the current market value of the securities in the portfolio at June 30, 1980, is as shown below:

SECURITY	(1) PURCHASE COST	(2) MARKET VALUE AT JUNE 30, 1980	(3) UNREALIZED GAIN (LOSS)
Clydesdale, Inc.........	$42,000	$38,000	$(4,000)
Hawkes Corp.	55,000	56,000	1,000
Total	$97,000	$94,000	$(3,000)

The balance in the revaluation allowance account at the last reporting date, December 31, 1979, was $7,000 credit. The ending balance in that same account at June 30, 1980, must be adjusted upward to reflect $3,000 credit, which is the total amount shown in column (3) above. Hence, a debit of $4,000 to the revaluation allowance account, and the simultaneous recognition of a $4,000 unrealized holding gain, will accomplish that objective.

The entry to adjust the revaluation allowance account upward to reflect an unrealized holding gain is shown with an accompanying explanation:

1980
June 30 Allowance for Decline in Value of Marketable
        Securities (CA) 4,000
        Unrealized Gain on Marketable Securi-
        ties (IS)   4,000
          Record unrealized gain on portfolio
          of marketable securities.

Under no circumstance may the upward adjustment of the revaluation allowance account result in a debit balance in that account. If the current market value of the portfolio rises, any prior
revaluation downward can only be reversed to the extent that the
carrying amount of the portfolio may not exceed its original purchase cost.[3] In short, the carrying value of the portfolio of marketable securities may never exceed the original cost of the securities
in that portfolio.

Notes and Interest Receivable

A *promissory note* is an unconditional promise made by the
maker of the note to pay a certain sum (principal) plus interest to
the holder of the note on or before a specified date. The three most
common uses of notes receivable in business transactions are: (1)
to sell merchandise under more stringent credit terms than contained in the account receivable arrangement; (2) to convert a customer's account receivable to the status of a note receivable and (3)
to occasionally lend funds to selected officers and employees of the
firm.

Interest on short-term notes is conventionally calculated on the
basis of a 360-day or 12-month year. For example the amount of
interest which will be earned on a $1,000, 60-day note receivable
which bears interest at 6 percent compounded annually is calculated as follows:

$$I = Pni$$
$$I = \$1,000 \times \frac{60 \text{ days}}{360 \text{ days}} \times .06$$
$$I = \$10$$

I = The amount of interest that will be earned.
P = The principal or face amount for which the note was written.
n = The fractional part of a year over which interest will be earned.
i = The interest rate, normally compounded annually.

Whenever the terms of a note are stated as 6 percent for 60
days, the total interest due at maturity can be determined by
merely shifting the decimal point in the principal amount ($1,000)
two places to the left, ($10.00).

Discounting Interest Bearing Notes Receivable. It is not uncommon for the holder of a note receivable to convert it into cash
before the note's maturity date. The process by which this is accomplished is called *discounting*. The holder of the note usually
presents it to a bank, and in return receives cash equal to the ma-

---

[3]*Ibid.*, par. 29(c).

turity value of the note less an amount which the bank charges for assuming the risk of accepting the note prior to its due date.

Assume that Helen Trembley purchased $1,200 of merchandise and signed a note dated October 31, 1979, promising to pay the Warfield Company $1,200 plus 8 percent interest compounded annually four months from the date of the note. The sale transaction is recorded by Warfield Company as follows:

```
1979
Oct. 31  Notes Receivable ....................................    1,200
              Sales..............................................            1,200
         Sale of merchandise under a note receiv-
         able arrangement. Due date of the note
         is February 28, 1980.
```

The total interest that becomes payable on the note at its due date is $32 ($1,200 × 4/12 year × .08), or about .2666 cents per day.

On November 30, 1979, the controller of the store discounted the Trembley note at its bank at 10 percent interest compounded annually in order to alleviate a sudden liquidity crisis. This transaction is divided into two entries for purposes of clarity: (1) the accrual of interest income and interest receivable at the date of discounting; and (2) the discounting of the note at the bank.

Accrual

```
       1979
(1)    Nov. 30  Interest Receivable .......................        8
                    Interest Income .........................            8
                Record  interest  receivable  and
                interest income on the Trembley
                note  at  November  30,  1979:
                $1,200 × 1/12 year × .08 =
                $8.
```

Discounting

```
       1979
(2)    Nov. 30  Cash ......................................  1,201.20
                Discount Expense (IS) ....................      6.80
                    Notes Receivable ......................            1,200.00
                    Interest Receivable ....................                8.00
                Note  receivable  discounted  at
                the bank at 10% interest.
```

Entry (2) requires additional explanation. The amount of cash that is received by the store must be determined from the reference point of the note's *maturity value*, or $1,232 (the $1,200 principal plus $32 interest due at maturity), which the bank expects to collect from Trembley on February 28, 1980. The bank discounted this maturity value at 10 percent compounded annually over the 3-month period remaining before the note matures. The interest rate at which notes are discounted by banks usually exceeds the rate shown on the note to compensate the new holder of the note for the risk of possible noncollection should the maker fail to pay the note at maturity. The bank determined the amount of discount or interest that it would charge Warfield Company in the following manner:

$$I = \$1,232.00 \times 3/12 \text{ year} \times .10 = \$30.80$$

The *cash proceeds* of $1,201.20 which appears in entry (2) was determined by subtracting the discount from the maturity value of the note ($1,232.00 − $30.80 = $1,201.20).

The total value of the note to Warfield Company at November 30, 1979, was $1,208 ($1,200 face value plus $8 interest earned to the date of discount). Since the company received only $1,201.20 for an asset worth $1,208, it sold the note, from its point of view, at a discount of $6.80 which is considered an expense of 1979.

It is interesting to observe that the bank will actually earn about 10.3 percent interest on the transaction if the maker honors the note. The bank will ultimately receive $30.80 interest income ($1,232.00 − $1,201.20) for the discounted note. The 10.3 percent interest rate is derived as follows:

$$i = \frac{I}{Pn}$$

$$i = \frac{\$30.80}{\$1,201.20 \times 1/4 \text{ year}}$$

$$i = 10.3\%$$

As illustrated in entry (2), the notes receivable and interest receivable accounts are credited, since the note and the interest are no longer receivables of the company. However, a footnote to the balance sheet dated December 31, 1979, should disclose the fact that the store remains contingently liable on the discounted note. In the event Trembley fails to pay the note and interest to the bank at maturity, Warfield Company must reimburse the bank for the maturity value of the note. This event would be recorded in the accounting records of Warfield Company as shown below:

```
1980
Feb. 28  Dishonored Notes and Interest Receivable (CA)   1,232
             Cash ................................................          1,232
             Cash forwarded to the bank and repos-
             session of the dishonored Trembley note.
```

Should Trembley neglect to pay the debt, the store would probably write the note off as a loss, and perhaps take legal action to seek reimbursement from the customer.

Discounting Non-Interest-Bearing Notes Receivable. Although less commonly seen, the non-interest-bearing note is used sufficiently to warrant a brief discussion of its principal characteristics.

Assume that Harry Herrera purchased $972.50 worth of merchandise from the Ahearn Corp. on October 31, 1979, for which he gave the company a $1,000, 3-month, non-interest-bearing note, payable January 31, 1980. The term "non-interest-bearing-note" is a misnomer, because although no interest rate is specified in the note, an *implicit interest rate* can easily be determined.

In this instance, the $972.50 debt on October 31 must be repaid with $1,000 at the end of the following January. The difference between the maturity value of the note, $1,000, and its debt value at the date of origination, $972.50, is the amount of implicit interest contained in the note. Dividing the amount of implicit interest by the maturity value of the note, times the fractional part of the year for which it will be outstanding, yields the implicit interest rate. The calculation shown below is derived using a slight modification of the general equation provided previously to determine the interest rate, i, when the other elements (P, n and I) are known:

$$\text{Implicit } i = \frac{\text{Maturity value of note less debt value of note}}{\text{Maturity value of note} \times \text{fractional part of year,}}$$
$$\text{note is outstanding}$$

$$= \frac{\$1,000.000 - \$972.50}{\$1,000.00 \times 1/4 \text{ year}} = \frac{\$27.50}{\$250.00} = 11\%$$

In short, Ahearn Corp. discounted Herrera's note at an implicit interest rate of 11 percent compounded annually.

Another way of phrasing the same idea is to recognize that $972.50 is the present value of $1,000.00 that will be received 3 months hence if that amount is discounted at 11 percent interest compounded annually. This can be closely approximated by determining that the present value factor .9725, ($972.50 ÷ $1,000) would appear in the 1-period row of Table 3 of the Appendix between the 2½% and 3% columns, or approximately 2¾%. Hence, 2¾% times 4 (12 months ÷ 3 months) equals 11 percent compounded annually.

Note that the firm will actually earn 11.3 percent interest when the *debt value* of this note, $1,000, is received on January 31, 1980. The calculation of the actual interest rate is shown below:

$$i = \frac{I}{Pn} = \frac{\$27.50}{\$972.50 \times 1/4 \text{ year}} = 11.3\%$$

To summarize, the receipt of the note by Ahearn Corp. at the time of the sale may be recorded as shown below:

```
1979
Oct. 31  Notes Receivable ................................. 1,000.00
             Sales...........................................              972.50
             Unamortized Discount (CA)..................              27.50
             Sale of $972.50 merchandise under a
             3-month non-interest-bearing note re-
             ceivable arrangement.
```

Unamortized Discount is a contra asset account that is directly associated with and subtracted from Notes Receivable on the balance sheet.[4]

At the close of the firm's 1979 fiscal year, two thirds of the discount will have been earned ($27.50 × ⅔ = $18.33), and the following entry would be recorded:

```
1979
Dec. 31  Unamortized Discount (CA)......................    18.33
             Interest Income ...............................              18.33
             Interest income earned during the fis-
             cal year ended December 31, 1979.
```

Collection of the note plus interest of $9.17 ($27.50 × ⅓) on January 31, 1980, would be reflected in the following entry:

```
1980
Jan. 31  Cash................................................. 1,000.00
             Unamortized Discount (CA).....................     9.17
             Interest Income ...............................               9.17
             Notes Receivable ............................           1,000.00
             Payment of non-interest-bearing note
             receivable plus associated interest.
```

If the note is not honored by Herrera at maturity, the same entry as shown above would be recorded, except that a debit to Dishonored Notes and Interest Receivable (CA) would replace the debit to Cash. If subsequent collection efforts prove successful, the $1,000 in this dishonored account would be eliminated with a credit, as cash is collected. If efforts prove unsuccessful, the amount in the dishonored account would be charged off as a loss on the income statement, as shown below:

```
Loss on Dishonored Notes and Interest Receivable (IS)...... 1,000
    Dishonored Notes and Interest Receivable (CA)...........            1,000
        Harry Herrera's previously dishonored note and in-
        terest receivable charged off as a nonrecoverable
        loss.
```

---

[4]*Accounting Principles Board Opinion No. 21*, "Interest on Receivables and Payables" (New York: American Institute of Certified Public Accountants, 1971), par. 16.

Accounts Receivable

The main valuation problem associated with accounts receivable is that some provision for uncollectible accounts, usually based on experience, should be recorded at each fiscal year-end to revalue the accounts receivable balance downward so as to reflect a more realistic estimate of collectibility. As previously discussed, the two ledger accounts involved in providing for these estimated uncollectible receivables are (1) Uncollectible Accounts Expense; and (2) Allowance for Doubtful Accounts, the latter being a contra asset account to Accounts Receivable. Other topics in the area of receivables that warrant brief discussion include: sales discounts; sales returns and allowances; and selected credit extension and collection policies.

Sales Discounts. The assumption has been made to this point in the text that goods and services sold under credit terms, such as 30-day credit sales, are recorded by the seller at their full retail or invoice price. In actual practice, however, the majority of credit sales are usually made under terms that provide an attractive incentive for the purchaser to pay promptly. For example, a steel manufacturer may sell most of its finished steel to various customers under the terms "2/10, net 30," which means that: a 2 percent discount from the invoice price will be deducted if the bill is paid within 10 days from the invoice date; if not paid within 10 days, the full amount is due within 30 days.

To illustrate the accounting treatment of this common credit sale arrangement, assume that Balfour Steel Corp. sold $1,000 of steel sheet to Kimberley Co. on August 1 under 2/10, net 30 terms. The sale was recorded in the books of Balfour Steel Corp. at the full invoice price less the 2 percent discount allowed for payment within 10 days, as shown below:

```
Aug. 1  Accounts Receivable.........................................  980
            Sales....................................................      980
            Sale of steel sheet to Kimberley Co. under
            2/10, net 30 terms:
            Invoice price..................................  $1,000
            Less 2% discount ($1,000 × .02) ........      20
               Price less discount .......................  $  980
```

The sale is usually recorded "net of discount" because most customers are expected to take advantage of the discount contained in such terms. In this instance, Kimberley Co. either pays $980 on or before August 11 or waits until August 31 to forward $1,000 to Balfour Steel Corp. Kimberley Co. can save $20 by paying twenty days earlier, which is equivalent to an *effective* annual interest rate of 36.73 percent, as shown below:

$$\$980 \times \frac{20 \text{ days}}{360 \text{ days}} \times i = \$20$$

$$\$54.44 \times i = \$20$$

$$i = \frac{\$20.00}{\$54.44} = 36.73\% \text{ effective annual interest}$$

If the invoice is not paid until August 31, Balfour Steel Corp. would earn $20 interest for loaning the equivalent of $980 to Kimberley Co. for 20 days.

Receipt of payment by Balfour Steel Corp. on August 11 and 31 would be recorded as shown below:

	Aug. 11	Aug. 31
Cash	980	1,000
Accounts Receivable	980	980
Interest Income	——	20

Sales Returns and Allowances. Customers receiving partially damaged or incomplete shipments are frequently granted an allowance which the customer may deduct from the invoice price at the time of payment. Sometimes, previously billed merchandise is returned to the vendor for refund or credit because of substantial damage or erroneous shipment. In both cases, a contra sales account called Sales Returns and Allowances is debited for the full price less the appropriate discount of the merchandise returned. Assume Kimberley Co.'s receiving department discovered that the previous $980 shipment contained wrong-sized steel, and that Balfour Steel Corp. authorized the customer to return it for full credit. The transaction is recorded on the vendor's books as shown below, assuming that the sale of the merchandise was recorded at $980 net of discount:

Sales Returns and Allowances (IS)	980	
Accounts Receivable		980
Return of erroneous sized steel sheet.		

The balance in Sales Returns and Allowances is deducted from Sales on the income statement, rather than treated as an expense.

The cost of goods associated with the returned merchandise is zeroed out or revised upon receipt of the steel, assuming that its cost to Balfour Steel Corp. was $560:

Inventory	560	
Cost of Goods Sold		560
Record receipt of returned merchandise as addition to inventory.		

Provision for estimated sales returns and allowances are usually not made at each fiscal year-end since the amount involved is normally not significant.

Credit Extension and Collection Policies. Extension of credit to customers usually entails risk of noncollectibility, the end-result of which may vary between the extremes of bankruptcy to considerable profit. The following situation which occurred in a large department store during the later 1970's illustrates several dilemmas that business executives face when they must decide whether or not to extend or liberalize credit terms to customers.

The newly elected president believed that the company's sales volume could be markedly increased if the surrounding community was advised that the store was liberalizing its credit policy by extending 30-day charge terms to all applicants. The credit manager, a long-time employee of the store, was apalled at such a revolutionary and financially risky suggestion, arguing that a majority of these new accounts would probably prove uncollectible, thereby resulting in a lower revenue and net income. Although most of the departmental buyers and other executives agreed with the credit manager's line of reasoning, the president's suggestion was finally implemented.

After the policy had been in effect three months, the credit manager reported to the president that sales volume had increased about 20 percent. The manager pointed out, however, that this increase was largely offset by the failure of many new charge customers to pay their accounts, plus the increased expense of bookkeeping in the credit and collections department required by the higher volume of credit sales. The president responded that these preliminary results were not a surprise and that relatively high credit losses were expected at the beginning of the plan. The credit manager was instructed to sort out the best credit risks from the new charge customers during the next six months and to deny further credit to those found unduly late or delinquent in payment of their accounts.

At the end of the plan's first year, total revenue net of uncollectible accounts expense reflected an increase of 30 percent over what had been experienced before the president's arrival; and the credit manager's total departmental expenses showed only a slight increase over what had existed prior to the new policy. Although initially risky, the experience proved quite profitable over the long run. Throughout the experiment, constant monitoring of outstanding accounts receivable enabled controlled financial planning.

Application of Present Value Analysis to Receivables. As suggested in the above illustration, failure of customers to pay their accounts under the terms specified can result in additional expenses to the seller, and possibly cause a cash shortage within the firm. The critical need to collect receivables within the terms specified by the seller can be dramatized by using present value analysis. Assume that a firm's Accounts Receivable balance net of the Allowance for Doubtful Accounts at January 1, 1980, is $400,000. If this entire amount is collected within the firm's prescribed terms of 30 days, and if the firm can normally expect to earn an average return of approximately 12 percent compounded monthly on its total financial resources, then the present value at January 1 of the $400,000 net receivables is $396,000. This amount can be determined with reference to the 1 percent column of Table 3 in the Appendix, as shown below:

$$P_1 = \frac{\$400,000}{(1 + .01)^1} = \$400,000\,(.990) = \$396,000$$

If, however, this net receivables balance will not be collected until the end of March, 1980, the discounted value at January 1, 1980, would be $388,400, as calculated below:

$$P_3 = \frac{\$400,000}{(1 + .01)^3} = \$400,000\,(.971) = \$388,400$$

Note that this latter amount is $11,600 below the net value of receivables shown on the balance sheet at January 1, 1980.

Neither of the above discounted amounts, which reflect the estimated present value of net accounts receivable, would ever appear on a balance sheet for the following reasons: (1) the exact time-span between the balance sheet date, January 1, and ultimate collectibility is difficult to predict; and (2) the return which the firm earns on each of its financial resources may be difficult to pinpoint. Despite these objections, however, management should be aware of the relevance of the present value concept to the valuation of receivables. In this illustration, the $7,600 differential ($396,000 − $388,400) represents the approximate opportunity cost to the firm of carrying customers an additional 60 days from February 1 to March 31. Any delay by credit customers to comply with preannounced credit terms can easily and quickly lead to severe liquidity problems within the firm, and may necessitate *factoring,* or selling, the accounts receivable to a financial institution.

Factoring. During a general business decline, such as when a predominant employer in a community is on strike, credit customers of various firms may take a longer time to liquidate their accounts than that specified in the credit terms. However, these firms' accounts and notes payable must be paid so as to maintain their credit rating. What may result is a "tight" cash position since collections of receivables are delayed. Should the situation become critical, a firm may be forced to factor, or sell, some or all of its accounts receivable at a substantial discount to a bank or a factoring agent to obtain needed cash.

For example, assume that $500,000 of accounts receivable, net of a $50,000 allowance for doubtful accounts, are factored to a financial institution for only $440,000 cash. The following entry is made at the date of factoring:

Cash	440,000	
Allowance For Doubtful Accounts	50,000	
Loss on Factoring Accounts Receivable (IS)	60,000	
Accounts Receivable.....................................		550,000
Record the factoring of accounts receivable to		
a financial institution.		

The loss account in the above entry is regarded as an interest charge incurred due to factoring the receivables at an amount below their book value. The financial institution purchasing these receivables normally assumes responsibility for their collection.

CURRENT LIABILITIES

Current liabilities are financial obligations which are expected to be paid with assets that are now, or will be, classified as current during the ensuing fiscal year.[5] For practical purposes, this means that current liabilities are financial obligations that are expected to be paid with cash during the next twelve months. The liabilities most frequently classified as current include:

Accounts payable	Performance liability (or unearned
Interest payable	income)
Notes payable (short term, and the	Taxes payable (federal, state, and
current portion of long-term ob-	local)
ligations that will come due	Wages and salaries payable
within the next fiscal year)	

With the exception of any currently due portion of long-term obligations, these liabilities tend to be incurred to finance current assets and current operating expenses. Long-term liabilities tend

---

[5]*Accounting Research Bulletin No. 43*, "Restatement and Revision of Accounting Research Bulleting" (New York: American Institute of Certified Public Accountants, 1953), Chapter 3A, par. 7.

to be incurred to finance noncurrent assets such as plant, equipment, and machinery.

Employee Compensation and Related Items

In addition to wages and salaries expenses, other items associated with employee compensation include taxes, contributions, and related fringe benefits:

(1) Withholdings from wages and salaries earned by employees for federal, state, and local income taxes.

(2) Payments by the employee and employer under provisions of the Federal Insurance Contributions Act, otherwise known as social security. In 1979, the tax rate is 6.13 percent on the first $22,900 of compensation earned by each employee during the 1979 calendar year, or $1,403.77. This amount is deducted from the employee's paycheck, and is matched by an equal assessment on the employer.[6]

(3) The unemployment insurance compensation tax is normally assessed only on the employer. Currently, the portion due to the state agency is 2.7 percent of the first $6,000 ($162) earned by each employee during the calendar year (subject to a merit rating allowance depending on the firm's record of steady employment), plus an additional .7 percent of the first $6,000 ($42) which is payable to the federal government.

(4) Life, medical, and accident insurance premiums plus any contributions made to pension plans, each of which may or may not be shared between the employer and employee.

The total of all of these liabilities incurred and/or paid by the employing firm, including compensation for sick days, holidays, and vacations, is commonly referred to as the "fringe benefit package." These benefits in many instances may approach 25 to 30 percent of an employee's base pay.

A brief example will illustrate some of the complexities involved in accruing several of the liabilities previously noted. Assume that the wages and salaries earned by Sylvex, Inc., employees during the first week of October totaled $160,000. The amount withheld from employees' wages for federal and state income taxes totaled $21,000. The FICA tax assessed on both the employer and on all nonexempt employees amounted to $6,700, for a total social security tax payable of $13,400 (several employees attained the exempt $22,900 earnings level earlier in the year). Unemployment insurance taxes totaled $600 (most employees exceeded the $6,000 exempt level earlier in the year), and the total medical and life insurance premiums payable of $3,800 was shared equally by the employer and employees. This information is journalized as follows:

---

[6]Current tax tables must be consulted because the tax rate and/or base are changed frequently. For example, the rate remains at 6.13% during 1980, but the base is raised in that year to $25,900.

Wages and Salaries Expense	160,000	
FICA Tax Expense................................	6,700	
Unemployment Tax Expense	600	
Insurance Expense	1,900	
Insurance Premiums Payable		3,800
Unemployment Tax Payable		600
FICA Tax Payable		13,400
Employees Income Tax Payable................		21,000
Wages and Salaries Payable		130,400

Record payroll and related items for the first week of October.

The total "take-home" pay of employees, $130,400, represented by the credit to Wages and Salaries Payable is computed below:

Wages and salaries earned by employees....................		$160,000
Less: Federal, state and local income taxes withheld	$21,000	
FICA tax assessment.......................................	6,700	
Medical and life insurance.............................	1,900	29,600
Net take-home pay		$130,400

The total compensation expense incurred by the company amounted to $169,200 represented by the total charges to the four expense accounts:

Wages and salaries...	$160,000
Employers share of FICA	6,700
Unemployment taxes..	600
Medical and life insurance	1,900
Total...	$169,200

Lines of Credit and Compensating Balances

Virtually all large and many small firms establish *lines of credit* at their local banks. This enables management to obtain funds without going through the formal procedures of initiating a note payable whenever the need for funds arises. For example, the firm may establish an open line of credit with a local bank to a limit of $500,000. Interest is normally charged only on the portion of that amount which is actually borrowed during a specific period.

Banks sometimes require that a medium- to high-risk borrower must leave on deposit with the bank a specified portion of the funds borrowed. This unused portion is called a *compensating balance* Assume that a company borrows $1,000,000 at an interest rate of 10 percent compounded annually, or $100,000 interest per year. The bank stipulates that 20 percent of the amount borrowed must always remain on deposit at the bank throughout the period of the loan. In effect, the loan is actually made for only $800,000, since only that amount is available for use by the borrowing firm. Hence, the real or effective interest rate that is charged by the bank in this instance has been increased to 12½ percent compounded annually: $100,000 interest charge ÷ $800,000 principal actually borrowed.

RELATIONSHIP BETWEEN LIQUIDITY, CASH FLOW, AND NET INCOME

There is a common but mistaken belief that cash flow and net income are synonomous terms; and that a one-to-one direct correlation exists between the cash balance and profit. The following illustration proves that this is not necessarily true. Four abbreviated situations are shown in which net income is $100 in each case, yet cash flow ranges from a positive $100 to a negative $60. The following journal entries recreate the relevant transactions.

Situation A

All sales were made on cash terms, and all expenses were paid:

Cash (CA)	100	
Sales (IS)		100
Cash sale of goods or services.		
Expenses (IS)	60	
Cash (CA)		60
Payment for expenses that were matched with recognized revenue.		

The net impact of these two events on cash flow is an increase of $40.

Situation B

All sales were made on cash terms, but none of the expenses were paid:

Cash(CA)	100	
Expenses (IS)	60	
Accounts Payable or Other Liabilities (CL)		60
Sales (IS)		100
Sale of goods or services on cash terms, and expensing of items not yet paid.		

The net impact on cash flow in this instance is an increase of $100.

Situation C

All sales were made on credit terms, and none of the accounts receivable were collected. However, all expenses were paid:

Accounts Receivable (CA)	100	
Expenses (IS)	60	
Cash (CA)...		60
Sales (IS)..		100

      Sale of goods or services on credit terms, and cash pay-
ment of all items that were expensed.

The net impact on cash flow is a decrease of $60.

Situation D

All sales were made on credit terms, and none of the accounts receivable were collected. None of the expenses were paid:

Accounts Receivable (CA)	100	
Expenses (IS)	60	
Accounts Payable (CL)		60
Sales (IS)..		100

      Sale of goods or services on credit terms, and expensing
of items not yet paid.

The net impact on cash flow is zero.

	SITUATION			
	A	*B*	*C*	*D*
Sales..	$100	$100	$100	$100
Expenses....................................	60	60	60	60
Net income.................................	$ 40	$ 40	$ 40	$ 40
Change in cash balance	+$ 40	+$100	−$ 60	$–0–

Summary

    The four situations illustrate the extremes that are possible. Had each situation been tempered with partial payments for expenses or receipts of cash for sales, the same conclusion would emerge: There is no necessary relationship between cash and net income. This conclusion arises from an application of the accrual principle which is rephrased as follows:

(1) Revenue can be recognized irrespective of the receipt of cash.
(2) Expenses can be recognized without regard to the outflow of cash.

QUESTIONS

    1. Identify and explain the twin goals between which the financial manager must maintain an optimum balance.

    2. Define the following terms and explain their relevance to liquidity: (a) the quick assets; and (b) the quick ratio.

    3. (a) Identify the components that may comprise the balance in the cash account, and (b) explain the unique importance of cash to organizations.

4. (a) What is a bank overdraft? (b) How should a bank account that is significantly overdrawn be classified on the balance sheet? Explain why.

5. Explain window dressing with respect to information contained on financial statements.

6. Identify the specific focal point toward which the periodic bank reconciliation process is directed.

7. Construct a framework outlining the general procedure by which the reconciliation process is accomplished, including the principal adjustments that may be required either to the bank statement or to the firm's cash account.

8. What is the underlying principle of cash control?

9. (a) Define a petty cash fund. (b) Distinguish between the monetary amount of the petty cash fund and the cash amount in the fund at a particular time.

10. (a) Explain in what sense cash, particularly excess idle cash, can be considered an expensive or costly asset? (b) Suggest a way whereby excess idle cash may be converted into a productive, earning asset.

11. Distinguish between the value at which a temporary investment in: (a) short-term government bonds, U.S. Treasury bills and notes, and short-term commercial paper; and (b) the capital stock of other corporations are usually reflected on the balance sheet.

12. Several shares of the capital stock of Monogram Corp. that comprise the total portfolio of marketable securities in Claudett, Inc., were purchased in June 1979 by Claudett, Inc., for $12,000. At the end of Claudett, Inc.'s fiscal year, December 31, 1979, the market value of these shares was $10,500. The shares were sold for $12,200 on March 31, 1980. Prepare the entry in the records of Claudett, Inc., to record: (a) any adjustment required at December 31, 1979; (b) the sale of the shares in 1980; and (c) any adjustment at December 31, 1980, assuming the balance in Marketable Securities at that date was zero.

13. Explain to what extent a portfolio of marketable equity securities could be revalued upwards by means of debiting the revaluation allowance account.

14. (a) Distinguish a holding loss from a realized loss, and (b) distinguish a holding gain from a realized gain. (c) Define the carrying value of a portfolio of marketable securities.

15. Determine the amount that would be received by the holder of a $4,000, 12%, 6-month note receivable dated October 1, 1979, upon discounting that note at the bank at 14% on October 1, 1979.

16. A $2,100, 10%, 4-month note receivable, which had previously been discounted at a local bank, was dishonored by the maker. (a) Prepare the entry that would be recorded by the original holder of the note at the time the note was dishonored and returned to the original holder. (b) Prepare the subsequent entry to record the unsuccessful effort by the original holder to collect this note.

17. Define and explain the unamortized discount account.

18. (a) Determine the implicit interest rate on a note receivable that contained the following phrase: "I promise to pay $2,000 to Apex Corporation on July 31, 1979." The note was signed on April 30, 1979, for the purchase of $1,950 of merchandise. (b) Calculate the actual interest rate

compounded annually on the debt value of the above note. (Round answer to two decimal places.)

19. (a) Explain the meaning of the credit terms "4/20, net 40" that appeared on an invoice which indicated a full price of $2,000. (b) Determine the effective interest rate contained in those terms. (Round answer to two decimal places.)

20. Prepare the entry to record the receipt by the vendor of undamaged merchandise which had previously been sold at a full invoice price of $1,000 under credit terms 4/10, net 30. The cost of goods sold associated with that merchandise was $730.

21. What appears to be the central question involved in determining whether or not to extend credit terms to customers with whom the firm has had no prior credit experience?

22. (a) Determine the approximate present value of $60,000 of accounts receivable which are not expected to be collected until two months from now. Assume that management can normally earn a 12% return, compounded monthly, on the firm's total financial resources. (b) Why would this aproximate value probably never appear in the accounting records?

23. What is factoring?

24. (a) Identify several deductions from an employee's paycheck that account for the difference between gross pay and "take-home" pay. (b) Identify those items which comprise the total expenditure made by an employer for employee compensation.

25. What is a line of credit?

26. A particular bank's policy requires borrowers to maintain a 15% compensating balance. Of what significance is this policy to a company which borrows $100,000 from that bank for one year at an interest rate of 10% compounded annually, or $10,000 per year?

27. Present an example illustrating how it might be possible for a firm's cash balance to reflect a $6,000 decrease during a fiscal year even though it earned $32,000 net income during that same period.

EXERCISES

1. Quick assets and quick ratio. The following accounts in Dryton Corp. reflected balances at March 31, 1980:

ACCOUNT TITLE	DEBIT (CREDIT)
Accounts Payable	$ (96,000)
Accounts Receivable	120,000
Allowance for Decline in Value of Marketable Securities	(3,000)
Allowance for Doubtful Accounts	(3,000)
Cash	63,000
Cash — Restricted for Bond Retirement in 1985	94,000
Dividends Payable	(18,000)
Interest Income	(3,000)
Interest Payable	(6,000)
Interest Receivable	2,000
Inventory	140,000
Investment in Sancraft Corp.	32,000
Marketable Securities	50,000

ACCOUNT TITLE	DEBIT (CREDIT)
Mortgage Note Payable, due July 1, 1984	(240,000)
Notes Payable, short-term	(70,000)
Notes Receivable	16,000
Performance Liability	(7,000)
Prepaid Expenses	35,000
Taxes Payable	(48,000)
Uncollectible Accounts Expense	2,000

Required: (a) Determine the total amount of quick assets at March 31, 1980. (b) Determine the quick ratio at March 31, 1980.

2. Impact of overdraft and marketable securities on the quick ratio. The information shown below was available to the chief accountant at June 30, 1979, upon completion of the bank reconciliation for each of the three bank accounts maintained by the Wifram Corp.:

BANK ACCOUNT	BALANCE AT JUNE 30, 1979 (OVERDRAFT)
Dallas National Bank	$ 80,000
Fort Worth Exchange Bank	(110,000)
Houston State Bank and Trust	45,000
Total	$ 15,000

PORTFOLIO OF MARKETABLE EQUITY SECURITIES	
Original purchase cost	$ 87,000
Lower of cost of market	57,000

The total of all balances in the notes, interest, and net accounts receivable accounts amounted to $226,000 at June 30, 1979. Total current liabilities (excluding any overdrafts) totaled $218,000 at the same date.

Required: (a) Calculate the quick ratio under each of the following circumstances. Carry all calculations to one decimal place.

(1) The overdraft is netted, and the portfolio of marketable securities is reflected at its original purchase cost.

(2) The overdraft is netted, and the portfolio is reflected at the lower of cost or market.

(3) The overdraft is fully disclosed as a liability, and the portfolio is reflected at its original purchase cost.

(4) The overdraft is fully disclosed, and the portfolio is reflected at the lower of cost or market.

(b) Indicate which of the above methods should be used to determine the quick ratio. Explain why.

3. **Bank reconciliation elements.** Listed are six items which affect the bank reconciliation:

(1) A customer's account receivable balance was paid directly to the bank during May.

(2) The company was charged for services rendered by the bank during May, as indicated on the bank statement.

(3) Several checks that had been drawn by the company remained outstanding at the time of reconciliation.

(4) A deposit was in transit to the bank on May 31.

(5) The bank had deducted an amount from the company's bank account for interest on a loan made previously by the bank to the company.

(6) A check for $30 was correctly entered in the company's records and returned with the May statement. It was reflected on the bank statement at $3.

Required: Indicate in the format shown below whether each of the six items should be added to or subtracted from: (a) the balance per the bank statement at the end of May; or (b) the balance in the company's cash account at the time of the bank reconciliation process. Place a check mark in the appropriate column.

	BALANCE PER BANK STATEMENT		BALANCE PER COMPANY'S CASH ACCOUNT	
Item	Add to	Subtract from	Add to	Subtract from
(1)	_____	_____	_____	_____
(2)	_____	_____	_____	_____

4. The petty cash fund. The Gomble Co. established a petty cash fund on January 10, of $800 under the custodianship of Liz Bledsoe. The following transactions affected the fund during the remainder of January:

(1) Postage stamps were purchased from the U.S. Postal Service for $68. The stamps were immediately used to mail an advertising brochure to various customers of the company.

(2) An out-of-town customer requested one Friday at 5:10 p.m. that Bledsoe accept payment of $145 for merchandise which was purchased on account the previous month. Since the accounting office closes sharply at 5 p.m. each Friday, Bledsoe deposited the money in the petty cash fund.

(3) The firm's general manager received $465 from the fund as a travel advance for a business trip she planned to take.

(4) Office supplies were delivered to Bledsoe. Terms of delivery were COD and Bledoe paid the delivery person $160 from the fund.

(5) Bledsoe paid $116 from the fund for pencils, stationery, and a desk lamp which were purchased at a local office supply store for the general manager's office.

All office supplies that were purchased in transaction (4) and (5) remained unused as of January 31.

Required: (a) Prepare the journal entry to establish the fund on January 10. (b) Determine the monetary amount of the fund at the end of January. (c) Determine the cash balance in the fund at January 31. (d) Prepare a journal entry at January 31 to reimburse the fund to its original balance.

5. Valuation of marketable securities. The following marketable securities were purchased by Tansim Corp. at the respective costs indicated during the last 6 months of 1979. The market value of each of these securities is also shown. These securities were the first ever purchased by the firm, and no revaluation adjustment had been made for this portfolio of securities since the dates of purchase. The firm's fiscal year ended each December 31. All shares of Xenon, Inc., were sold during February, 1980, for $41,000.

Marketable Security	Original Purchase Cost	Market Value at December 31, 1979
U.S. Treasury Notes..............	$ 18,000	$ 18,000
U.S. Government Bonds........	29,000	29,000
Pressbar Corp. (500 shares of capital stock).....................	46,000	41,000
Xenon, Inc. (760 shares of capital stock	37,000	39,000
Total..............................	$130,000	$127,000

Required: (a) Prepare any entry that may be required at December 31, 1979, to revalue this portfolio. (b) Indicate any gross unrealized gains and gross unrealized losses incurred on this portfolio since the date of purchase. (c) Prepare the entry to record the sale of the Xenon, Inc., shares of capital stock.

6. The marketable securities revaluation allowance. Some short-term U.S. Government bonds, and several shares of capital stock of Burnside, Inc., and Delta Corp. were purchased during June for $27,000, $16,000, and $31,000, respectively. At the end of the purchaser's fiscal year, December 31, the market value of each investment was $27,000, $12,000, and $37,000, respectively. No other marketable securities were purchased or sold during this fiscal period, and no marketable securities were ever held by this firm prior to the current fiscal year.

Required: Determine the carrying value at which this portfolio of securities would be reflected on the purchaser's balance sheet at December 31.

7. Notes receivable sequence involving discounting. Brainard Co. accepted on November 1, 1979, a $60,000, 8%, 6-month note receivable from a customer, in payment for merchandise purchased on the same date. The note was discounted at 10% interest by a local bank on January 1, 1980. The customer paid the note plus total interest due on April 30, 1980. Brainard Co.'s fiscal year ended each December 31, and the company never used reversing entries.

Required: (a) Prepare whatever journal entry may be required in the records of Brainard Co. at December 31, 1979. (b) Prepare whatever entry may be required in the firm's records on the date the note was discounted at the bank. (c) Prepare whatever entry may be required in the company's records when the note was paid on April 30, 1980. (d) Determine to one decimal place the actual interest rate which the bank earned on this note.

8. Notes receivable — dishonored. Oscar Moreno signed and gave a promissory note to Musicians, Inc., on July 31, 1979, for the purchase of $1,800 of musical instruments. The credit manager discounted the 10% note at the bank on September 30 at 12%. The firm's fiscal year ends each September 30. On the due date of the note, December 31, 1979, Moreno was unable to pay any of the principal or interest due on the note.

Required: Prepare a journal entry to record each of the following transactions: (a) The fiscal year-end interest accrual immediately prior to discounting the note at the bank. (b) The discounting of the note at the bank. (c) Repossession of the dishonored note by the music store on the date that Moreno was unable to honor the note.

9. Non-interest-bearing note receivable sequence. Vanin Corp. sold a parcel of land on July 1, 1979, for $18,000, and obtained a non-interest-bearing note receivable for $20,000, payable July 1, 1980. Vanin Corp.'s fiscal year ends each December 31.

Required: (a) Prepare the entry that would be recorded at the date of sale, assuming the land had originally been purchased by Vanin Corp. for $15,000. (b) Determine the implicit interest rate of the note. (c) Prepare the entry that would be recorded at December 31, 1979. (d) Prepare the entry that would be recorded at the date of the note's payment.

10. Sales discount terms. The Risston Co. sold merchandise to Fabricators, Inc., on June 29, 1979, and billed the customer the $40,000 full invoice price under the terms 3/10, net 25. The invoice was dated July 1.

Required: (a) Prepare the entry to record the sale of the merchandise in the records of Risston Co. (b) Determine the effective annual interest rate contained in these terms of sale.

11. Present value analysis of accounts receivable. The Accounts Receivable balance amounted to $400,000 on January 1, 1979. The controller anticipated that one quarter of these accounts would probably not be collected until the end of March 1979; one half at the end of June 1979; and the remainder at the end of September 1979. The firm normally required 8% return compounded quarterly on each of its noncash quick assets.

Required: Determine the present value of the Accounts Receivable balance at January 1, 1979.

12. Employee compensation. All wage and salaried employees of Hardwick Corp. were paid at semimonthly intervals. Information shown below pertained to the payroll for the period ending March 15:

(1) The gross amount of wages and salaries totaled $300,000.
(2) The amount withheld for federal and state income taxes was 16% of gross wages and salaries.
(3) The full amount specified under provisions of the Federal Insurance Contributions Act was withheld from all paychecks at this particular point in the year. (Use 6.13%). This amount was matched by the firm.
(4) The appropriate amount of unemployment insurance compensation tax was accrued on behalf of all employees at this point in the year. (Use 3.4%). Round calculation to the nearest dollar.
(5) Deductions from employee paychecks for health and life insurance premiums amounted to 2% of the gross wages and salaries. This deduction from paychecks was matched by the corporation.

Required: (a) Prepare the entry to record the payment of the payroll for the period ending March 15. Assume that amounts withheld from employee paychecks and amounts assessed against the employer were payable to various government agencies and insurance companies at the end of each month. (b) Calculate the total take-home pay of all employees and the total expense incurred by the corporation for compensation during the 15-day period.

13. Disparity between cash flow and net income. In each following situation, sales and expenses were $500,000 and $300,000, respectively:

(1) Forty percent of all sales were made on credit terms. Although none of the accounts receivable were yet collected, all expenses were paid.

(2) All sales were made for cash, but only 70% of the expenses were paid.

(3) Eighty percent of all sales were made on credit terms, although only 50% of the accounts receivable were collected. None of the expenses were paid.

(4) Thirty percent of all sales were for cash, and all credit sales were as yet uncollected. All expenses were paid.

Required: Determine the net income and the effect on cash flow resulting from each of the four situations above.

PROBLEMS

7-1) Impact of overdrafts and revalued portfolio of marketable securities on the quick ratio. Bank accounts were maintained by Orbiter Corp. in the four cities indicated below to facilitate financial transactions and flows of cash between each of the firm's major plant locations:

BANK ACCOUNT	BALANCE AT MARCH 31 (OVERDRAFT)
Citizens Bank & Trust of Topeka......................	$ (64,000)
First National Bank of Reno.............................	280,000
Portland Security Bank	(136,000)
San Francisco National Bank............................	420,000
Total..	$500,000

The firm also maintained a portfolio of marketable securities in which excess idle cash was invested. Although the original cost of securities in the portfolio totaled $114,000, the portfolio's current market value on March 31 was $90,000, with the revaluation allowance account reflecting a $5,000 credit balance on March 31.

Total quick assets (except those mentioned above) amounted to $210,000 at March 31, and total current liabilities (excluding any overdrafts) amounted to $600,000 at the same date. Included as a current liability was a $200,000 note payable at the San Franciso bank which contained the provision that in the event the quick ratio falls below 1.3:1, the $200,000 note would be immediately subject to payment.

Required: (1) Determine the quick assets and quick ratio at March 31, after appropriately revaluing the portfolio of marketable securities, using the netting technique.

(2) Determine the quick assets and the quick ratio at March 31, after appropriately revaluing the portfolio, using the full disclosure technique.

(3) Using information contained in the preceding item (2) determine the quick assets and the quick ratio at March 31 after the terms of the note payable have been complied with. Carry all calculations to two decimal places.

7-2. Bank reconciliation. The account of Stabler Company at the Salt Lake City Bank had been reconciled and appropriate adjusting entries were made on November 30. The reconciliation at that date reflected the following information:

Balance per bank statement dated November 30	$1,158	
Add deposit in transit to bank	311	$1,469
Less outstanding checks:		
#46...	$11	
#50...	23	
#51...	41	75
Balance subject to company's withdrawal at November 30.........		$1,394

The following details were extracted from company records and the bank statement at the end of the following December:

COMPANY RECORDS			BANK STATEMENT DATED DECEMBER 31	
Deposits Made	*Checks Written*		*Canceled Checks*	*Deposits*
$ 184	#52	$ 60	$ 11	$ 311
212	#53	195	18	184
484	#54	96	3 SC	CM 198
300	#55	215	60	212
$1,180	#56	18	215	484
	#57	43	195	$1,389
		$627	9*	
			$511	

SC — Service charge for December.

CM — Credit memo indicating the bank's collection of a customer's account receivable due Stabler Company.

* — This check was drawn by the Table Company.

The debit balance shown in the company's cash account at December 31 was $1,947.

Required: (1) Prepare the bank reconciliation as of December 31.

(2) Prepare any journal entries that must be made by the Stabler Company accountant at December 31. In addition, indicate what, if any, communication the accountant should make with the bank after the reconciliation is complete.

7-3. Bank reconciliation-comprehensive. Con Fruit Company's chief accountant began the monthly reconciliation of the firm's account with the First National Bank at the end of April. The firm's cash balance as shown in the general ledger at April 30 reflected $46,445, whereas the cash balance shown on the bank statement dated April 30 was $3,961. The several items shown below affected the April reconcilement.

The following checks were written and appropriately recorded in the firm's cash disbursements journal (the check register) during April:

CHECK NUMBER	AMOUNT	CHECK NUMBER	AMOUNT
2086	$ 4,827	2091	$ 28
2087	3,612	2092	3,278
2088	10,045	2093	8,620
2089	847	2094	5,412
2090	1,186	2095	45
			$37,900

Deposits forwarded to the bank were as follows:

DATE	AMOUNT	DATE	AMOUNT
April 4	$14,320	April 23	$ 2,419
April 10	8,416	April 27	6,224
April 12	3,015	April 30	3,025
April 16	9,881		$47,300

The bank statement reflected the following information:

Balance at March 31...			$42,644
Add: Deposits:	$ 7,600		
	14,320		
	1,468		
	3,015		
	9,818		
	2,419		
	6,224	$44,864	
Collections from Con Fruit Co. customers on accounts receivable:			
O. Frait	$ 231		
T. Schmit....................................	87	318	45,182
			$87,826
Deduct: Cancelled checks:			
	$7,618	$45,100	
	3,240	1,186	
	941	8,620	
	4,827	5,412	
	847	28	
	3,612	2,044	$83,475
Service charges:			
March......................................	$ 28		
April.......................................	37		65
Interest on loan for April			325
			$83,865
Balance at April 30			$ 3,961

Investigation of various journal entries, prior reconciliations, and cancelled checks revealed the following information:

(a) The first deposit shown on the bank statement ($7,600) was in transit to the bank on March 31.

(b) The third deposit shown on the bank statement ($1,468) is a transposition error. The deposit shown on the firm's record for April 10 ($8,416) is correct.

(c) The fifth deposit shown on the bank statement ($9,818) is correct; whereas the deposit as recorded by the company on April 16

($9,881) was in error, as was its credit entry offset to Accounts Receivable.

(d) Until the statement was received the company was unaware that two customers had paid their accounts receivable at the bank.

(e) The following outstanding checks, which had not yet cleared banking channels as of March 31, appeared on the March bank reconciliation:

#2082	$ 7,618
#2083	1,400
#2084	3,240
#2085	941
	$13,199

(f) Check #2088 ($10,045) was written for the proper amount, but the amount shown for this canceled check on the bank statement ($45,100) is a transposition error.

(g) The canceled check for $2,044 was drawn by the Con Truck Corp.

(h) The service and interest charges were not previously recorded by the accounting department.

Required: (1) Prepare a complete reconciliation of the cash balance subject to Con Fruit Company's withdrawal at April 30.

(2) Prepare any necessary entries that are required by the reconciliation, and specify any communication that must be made with the bank.

(3) Optional. Verify the cash balance per the company ledger at April 30 by working from the balance per the bank statement dated March 31.

7-4. Portfolio of marketable securities: comprehensive. The composition of the portfolio of marketable securities held by Tricor, Inc., at the end of its fiscal year, December 31, 1979, is reflected below:

SECURITY	PURCHASE COST	MARKET VALUE DECEMBER 31, 1979
U.S. Bonds (short-term)..........	$ 68,000	$ 68,000
U.S. Treasury Notes..............	47,000	47,000
Delmarva Corp.	113,000	125,000
Heitzer, Inc.	76,000	71,000
Total.............................	$304,000	$311,000

The credit balance that existed in the revaluation allowance account at December 31, 1979, immediately before any revaluation adjustment was made at the end of the fiscal year, was $10,000.

The following transactions occurred during the fiscal year ended December 31, 1980, with respect to this portfolio:

July 21, 1980: Redeemed U.S. bonds and Treasury notes for $68,000 and $47,000, respectively. Sold Delmarva Corp. securities for $131,000, and Heitzer, Inc., securities for $73,000.

August 18, 1980: Purchased capital stock of Fortran Corp. for $162,000.

The market value of the Fortran Corp. securities at the end of the 1980 fiscal year, was $159,000.

Required: (1) Determine the gross unrealized gains and losses on the portfolio of marketable securities at December 31, 1979.

(2) Prepare the entry to record the revaluation of the portfolio to the lower of cost or market at December 31, 1979.

(3) Prepare the entry to record the sale of the marketable securities on July 21, 1980.

(4) What entry must be prepared at the end of the 1980 fiscal year to revalue the portfolio to the lower of cost or market?

(5) Optional. Assuming the quick ratio was 1:1 on December 31, 1979, after all adjustments had been made, with current liabilities totaling $816,000 at that date; and assuming further that the total current liabilities and total quick assets (except the carrying value of the portfolio of marketable securities) were the same at December 31, 1980, as at December 31, 1979: determine the quick ratio at December 31, 1980, after all adjustments had been made. (Carry answer to two decimal places.)

7-5. Interest-bearing note receivable sequence. Julia Martinez purchased a variety of musical instruments for her 7-member dance band on April 30, 1979, from Aireol Music, Inc. The total amount of the purchase amounted to $6,600, and Martinez gave the company an 8-month note which bore interest at an annual rate of 14%. The music company's fiscal year ended each June 30.

The firm's chief accountant discounted the note at the bank on July 31, at a discount rate of 17%. When the bank discovered that Martinez was unable to pay the principal and interest due on the note at the date of payment, the bank returned the note to the music company requesting cash to be forwarded to the bank. Aireol Music, Inc.'s chief accountant wrote off the note plus accrued interest as uncollectible on May 1, 1980.

Required: (1) Prepare the entry to record the sale on May 1, 1979.

(2) Prepare whatever entry is required at June 30, 1979.

(3) Prepare two entries at the date of discounting the note at the bank: (a) to accrue any interest receivable and income; and (b) to record the discounting of the note.

(4) Determine the actual rate of interest that the bank charged at the time of discounting this note. (Carry calculation to one decimal place.)

(5) Record the entry the music store would make on the date it received the dishonored note from the bank.

(6) Record the entry that would be entered in the music store's records on May 1, 1980.

7-6. Non-interest-bearing note receivable sequence. Romero LaRocca purchased a pure-bred Arabian stallion and a complete line of equestrian gear for his horse-breeding farm from Northwood Stables on May 31, 1979. Terms of purchase were: an immediate cash payment of $1,000 and the remainder due on November 30, 1979, under a $56,000 non-interest-bearing note receivable arrangement. If LaRocca had paid cash on May 31, the total purchase price would have been $53,920.

The fiscal year of Northwood Stables ends each July 31; the firm did not use the reversing entry procedure; and LaRocca forwarded $56,000 to the Northwood Stables on the due date of the note.

Required: (1) Prepare the entry to reflect the sale of items indicated previously in the accounting records of Northwood Stables on May 31.

(2) Determine the implicit interest rate of this note.

(3) Determine the actual interest rate the firm expects to earn on the debt value of this note. (Carry calculation to two decimal places.)

(4) Prepare whatever entry may be required at the end of the fiscal year, July 31, 1979.

(5) Prepare the entry to reflect the payment of the note on November 30, 1979.

(6) Optional. Ignoring item (5), prepare the entry to record the discounting of the note at the local bank at 14% annual interest on July 31, 1979, immediately after recording entry (4).

7-7. Sales discounts, returns, and allowances. Biotronics, Inc., sold several items to Frittston Wholesalers under the credit terms 3/10, net 40. The merchandise was received by the wholesaler on April 3, 1980, and was checked against the invoice dated April 3, 1980, which reflected a full invoice price of $48,000. One batch of items in the shipment, which was billed at a full invoice price of $3,200, had to be returned to the vendor on April 8 due to an error in shipment. The vendor authorized the return and granted the wholesaler full credit on that particular portion of the order. In addition, the wholesaler's receiving clerk notified Biotronics, Inc., on April 10 that $350 of damage had been done to one of the batches shipped due to improper packing. The vendor allowed the customer to deduct $350 at the time of payment.

Required: (1) Prepare the entry to record the sale of Biotronics, Inc., assuming the cost of goods associated with this shipment was $32,000.

(2) Determine the effective annual interest rate contained in the above terms. (Carry calculation to one decimal place.)

(3) Prepare the entry to be made by Biotronics, Inc., to record the return of the undamaged merchandise that had been shipped in error. The cost of goods associated with this erroneous shipment totaled $2,100.

(4) Prepare the entry to record the allowance granted on April 10 on the vendor's books.

7-8. Cash flow and net income. Dave, Vicky, and Steve formed a temporary partnership for the purpose of selling ice cream and hamburgers at a 3-day city carnival. Each contributed $120 toward the project. They all agreed to hire a short-order cook for $120, and to pay 10% of gross sales to the city for utility usage and the exclusive right to sell ice cream and hamburgers at the affair.

At the end of festivities on June 10, the three partners accumulated all financial records and prepared the statement on page 272.

They disposed of the few scraps of food, and decided to distribute the $735 that was actually in the cash box. The $5 shortage was assumed to have arisen from making change during the weekend. Steve suggested that the $735 balance be split three ways as (as originally agreed), and close up shop. Vicky mentioned that they had yet to pay the cook and the city. Some doubt existed however on how to handle Dave's $20 withdrawal.

D.V.S. Partnership
Statement of Cash Receipts and Disbursements
For the Three-Day Period, June 8–10

Cash receipts from:		
Partners	$360	
Sales of hamburgers and ice cream	920	$1,280
Cash disbursements for:		
Meat products...	$220	
Milk, sugar, eggs, and other ice cream ingredients....................	110	
Rental of freezer, cook-top, and other equipment......................	85	
Hamburger buns	80	
Catsup, relishes, etc.	25	
Dave's personal expenses..	20	540
Cash balance supposed to be on hand at close of business activity..		$ 740

Required: (1) Prepare an income statement for the 3-day period covering the activities of the concession partnership.

(2) Determine how the $735 cash balance should be distributed
among each creditor and partner.

DECISION CASE

7-I. A liquidity crisis with respect to accounts receivable. The treasurer of the American Bridge Corp. confronted the firm's finance committee with a severe short-term liquidity problem and explained that approximately $200,000 of additional cash would be required during the
next 6 months to pay several 'existing and certain-to-be-incurred wage
and salary, tax, and interest liabilities. Three aspects of the problem were
outlined to the committee:

(a) The firm's accounts receivable totaling $220,000 will probably be
collected 6 months hence, and not before.

(b) A factoring agency had stated it would be willing to purchase
these accounts receivable at a 10% discount, and thereafter assume responsibility for collecting the accounts from the corporation's customers.

(c) A $200,000 6-month loan could be obtained from a local bank at
an annual interest rate of 16%. The relatively high rate required
by the bank was due to the imminent liquidity crisis confronting
the corporation.

Required: Indicate which of the following alternatives you would
recommend to the board's finance committee for approval:

(1) Sell the accounts receivable to the factoring agency immediately.

(2) Obtain the $200,000 loan from the bank; then repay that loan
with proceeds from the collection of accounts receivable 6 months
hence.

(3) Support your recommendation with calculations of the cashflows
over the 6-month period, plus any qualifying remarks.

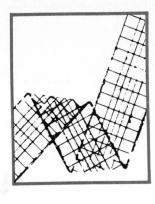

8
Inventories

But many that are first shall be last;
And the last shall be first.

Matthew 20:16

Inventories comprise a sufficiently important topic to warrant a separate chapter for the following reasons:

(1) Conversion of inventory into salable goods is the major thrust of all merchandising and manufacturing enterprises.
(2) Inventories of purchased and manufactured goods are usually large both in terms of dollar and physical volume relative to other assets.
(3) Costs which flow through the inventory account have a significant impact on income determination.
(4) Complex problems of control and supervision arise because of the volume and variety of goods that pass through the inventory account.
(5) Several cost-expense flows and at least two valuation alternatives are available by which to account for transactions involved in the inventory-cost of goods sold cycle.

This chapter will concentrate on developing an understanding of the variety of acceptable ways to determine: (1) the cost of goods sold during a period; and (2) the balance in inventory at a particular time. The relevance of these two aspects of inventory management is that both directly affect the determination of net income, income and property tax assessments, and the financial position of the company. In addition, several decisions that managers make with respect to inventory planning and control frequently influence inventory replenishment and dividend payment policies.

This chapter will examine in the following sequence:

(1) Different methods for recording inventory purchases.
(2) Two types of inventory accounting systems.
(3) Several inventory costing methods.
(4) Selected inventory valuation methods.

RECORDING INVENTORY PURCHASES

Several preliminary aspects involved in recording purchases of inventory require clarification at this point. These include: (1) deciding which items to include in inventory; (2) distinguishing between types of inventories; (3) identifying the accounts involved; and (4) determining the cost at which to record purchases.

Includable Items

All goods that are available for subsequent sale to customers and to which the firm has legal title are includable in its inventory. This constraint excludes goods held *on consignment* from other business entities. For example, television sets in the temporary possession of a retailer, the title to which is held by the manufacturer, are excluded from the retailer's inventory account as one of its financial resources. The entity holding the title, in this case the manufacturer, legitimately includes the TV sets in its inventory even though possession is temporarily held by another entity.

A technical question occasionally arises concerning the precise point at which title passes to the buyer of goods. If goods are shipped FOB (free on board) destination from a seller in Dallas to a buyer in Chicago, the seller normally pays the shipping charges from Dallas to Chicago. In this case, legal title does not pass to the buyer until the goods have reached their destination in Chicago; and technically, revenue is not recognized by the seller until the goods arrive at that point. On the other hand, if goods are shipped from the seller FOB Dallas, title is transferred to the Chicago buyer at Dallas, and the buyer is responsible for payment of freight charges to its location in Chicago. In this case, the seller would be technically correct in recognizing revenue when the goods are shipped from Dallas.

Types of Inventory

Merchandising firms include wholesalers, retailers, and jobbers who sell goods that do not substantially change from the form in which they were purchased. For example, dresses purchased by a retail department store are immediately capitalized as inventory and remain substantially in the form purchased until sold. *Manufacturing firms*, on the other hand, purchase materials and component parts which are subsequently converted or assembled during the manufacturing process into products that are eventually sold to wholesalers, retailers, and other customers. The typical manufacturer segregates the inventoriable items into categories using a three-stage classification system: (1) raw materials and component parts; (2) work in process, or products that are at some intermediate stage of being completed; and (3) finished goods that are available for sale to customers.

Specialized and complex topics and issues involving inventories of manufacturers are deferred for development in textbooks that deal with cost, managerial, and intermediate accounting. This text will focus only on inventories of merchandising firms and finished goods inventories associated with manufacturing entities.

Accounts Involved

Many merchandising and manufacturing firms record purchases of inventory by debiting Merchandise Inventory or Inventory-Raw Materials and Component Parts (CA), respectively. These capitalized costs are subsequently charged to expense as cost of goods sold during the period in which the goods are transferred to customers. Some entities use a more elaborate structure to segregate the elements of cost associated with inventoriable items among several account titles, such as: Merchandise Inventory (CA); Purchases (CA); Freight In (CA); and Purchases Returns and Allowances (CA).

To illustrate, assume that the debit balance in the merchandise inventory account of Hanison Mercantile Co. at January 1, 1979, was $4,000, and that the balance in each of the last three accounts noted above was zero at the same date. The total amounts that were reflected on all invoices for inventoriable items purchased on credit terms during 1979 totaled $15,000, including $540 freight charges. One vendor allowed Hanison Mercantile Co. to return merchandise costing $600 that had been damaged in transit, and to deduct that amount from the invoice price at the time of payment. The recording of these transactions during 1979 is summarized in the T accounts shown below. Only the inventory-related accounts are shown.

MERCHANDISE INVENTORY		PURCHASES	
Bal. at Jan. 1	4,000	(a)	14,460

FREIGHT IN		PURCHASES RETURNS AND ALLOWANCES	
(a)	540	(b)	600

(a) Invoices received totaling $15,000 = $14,460 purchases + $540 freight charges. (Accounts Payable would have been credited a total of $15,000 during the year.)

(b) Return of damaged merchandise, with Accounts Payable being debited $600 at the time the merchandise was returned.

The amount of inventory on hand at the end of the fiscal year, December 31, 1979, was $2,500. The cost of goods sold for the year is determined from the above information, as shown below:

Beginning inventory balance, January 1		$ 4,000
Plus: Purchases...	$14,460	
Freight in...	540	
Purchases returns and allowances	(600)	14,400
Total cost of goods available for sale during 1979 ..		$18,400
Less ending inventory, December 31		2,500
Cost of goods sold		$15,900

Purchases, Freight In, and Purchases Returns and Allowances are normally regarded as temporary accounts and their balances are customarily zeroed or closed out at the end of each fiscal period. This "zeroing out" process, and the recognition of cost of goods sold for the period can be recorded in one adjusting entry on December 31, as shown below:

Cost of Goods Sold	15,900	
Purchases Returns and Allowances	600	
Purchases...		14,460
Freight In..		540
Merchandise Inventory		1,500
Zero out temporary accounts associated with inventoriable items, and recognize cost of goods sold during 1979:		
Inventory balance at January 1, 1979.....................................	$4,000 debit	
Less inventory balance at December 31, 1979	2,500 debit	
Adjustment required at December 31, 1979	$1,500 credit	

The reason why several companies maintain these four inventory-related accounts is to facilitate identification and monitoring of the significant elements associated with purchases of inventoriable items. The majority of illustrations presented in this text, however, will adopt the single inventory account which will include all purchases, freight in, and purchases returns and allowances transactions. The summary entry to reflect transaction (a), using the single inventory account method, is as follows:

```
Merchandise Inventory .......................................    15,000
    Accounts Payable ...........................................              15,000
        Record purchases ($14,460), plus freight charges
        ($540).
```

The return of merchandise in transaction (b) is shown below:

```
Accounts Payable ..............................................       600
    Merchandise Inventory ......................................               600
        Return of damaged goods.
```

The entry to recognize cost of goods sold at December 31 is shown below:

```
Cost of Goods Sold ...........................................    15,900
    Merchandise Inventory ......................................            15,900
        Recognize cost of goods associated with sales dur-
        ing 1979.
```

Under either method, the year-end balance in Merchandise Inventory is $2,500; and the cost of goods sold is $15,900 for the fiscal year ending December 31, 1979.

Recorded Cost: Net or Gross

The assumption made up to this point is that purchases of inventory are recorded at cost. In actual practice, however, inventory purchased under credit arrangements may be recorded at either *net cost* or *gross cost*. The distinction between the two methods centers on the treatment of the purchase discount taken.

To illustrate, on April 10, Bonomo Corp. purchased $1,000 of merchandise with credit terms, 4/10, n/30. This means that if the invoice is paid on or before April 20, the buyer pays only $960 [$1,000 − (.04 × $1,000)]; if not, the $1,000 gross amount must be paid on or before May 10. Assuming that the firm uses the gross cost method of recording purchases, Merchandise Inventory and Accounts Payable are increased $1,000 upon receipt of merchandise without regard to the discount involved. If, on the other hand, the net cost method is used, each of those accounts are increased by $960, or net of the purchase discount. Entries to record the purchase under each method are shown below in comparative format:

	GROSS COST METHOD	NET COST METHOD
Apr. 10 Merchandise Inventory	1,000	960
Accounts Payable	1,000	960
Record purchase of merchandise on April 10, terms 4/10, net 30.		

Discount Taken. Under the net cost method, if the invoice is paid on April 20, Cash and Accounts Payable are decreased by $960. Two options exist for recording the entry at the time of payment within the discount period under the gross cost method: (1) the inventory account may be adjusted downward by $40 to reflect the discount taken; or (2) the discount taken may be reflected by crediting the income statement account, Purchases Discount (IS). These entries are presented below in comparative format:

	GROSS COST METHOD		NET COST METHOD
	(1) Adjust Inventory Downward	(2) Recognize Income	
Apr. 20 Accounts Payable	1,000	1,000	960
Merchandise Inventory	40	——	——
Purchases Discount..........	——	40	
Cash.........................	960	960	960
Record payment of invoice on April 20. Discount taken.			

If inventory is adjusted downward under option (1) of the gross cost method, the cost accumulated in Inventory will be stated at the same amount as under the net cost method, $960. However, if Purchases Discount is credited under option (2) of the gross cost method, the items purchased will continue to be costed at $1,000, and the discount will be reported on the income statement under the "Other income" caption.

Discount Lost. If the invoice is not paid within the discount period and is paid on April 30, the following entry will be recorded under each of the two methods to reflect the discount lost:

	GROSS COST METHOD	NET COST METHOD
Apr. 30 Accounts Payable.................................	1,000	960
Discounts Lost (IS)	——	40
Cash	1,000	1,000
Record payment of invoice on April 30. Discount lost.		

The lost discount under the net cost method would be reported on the income statement as an operating expense.

Although inventory purchases may be recorded by either the net cost or gross cost methods, the method adopted should be used consistently thereafter.

Accountants and managers who favor the net cost method offer two supporting arguments. First, the expense incurred by not taking cash discounts should be treated as a cost of managerial inefficiency, rather than as an additional cost of inventory. Inability or neglect to take cash discounts when offered can result in extremely high annual interest charges. Note that the effective interest rate compounded annually that is included in the terms 4/10, net 30, can be calculated as shown below:

$$i = \frac{I}{Pn} = \frac{\$40}{\$960 \times \dfrac{20 \text{ days}}{360 \text{ days}}} = \frac{\$40}{\$53.33} = 75\%$$

Since banks rarely charge business establishments interest rates exceeding 16–20 percent compounded annually on short-term loans, management should take cash discounts whenever offered, even if doing so may require obtaining a short-term loan.

A second argument for adopting the net cost method is the difficulty that arises in explaining how income can be earned under option (2) of the gross cost method by paying off a financial obligation (an account payable) within the discount period. Unless otherwise specified, the net cost method of recording inventory purchases will be used throughout the remainder of this text.

INVENTORY ACCOUNTING SYSTEMS

After journalizing the cost of merchandise and materials purchased, a *stock record card* is usually prepared for each type of item purchased. The stock record card normally reflects the date of each purchase, the number of units purchased, and the unit and/or total cost of each purchase. Comparable data for any purchases returns and allowances are also reflected on these cards.

The two principal methods that exist for accounting for inventories during the period are known as (1) the *perpetual* and (2) the *periodic* systems. The principal distinction between these two inventory accounting systems centers on the extent to which the stock record cards are used to determine: (1) the cost of goods sold for a period; and (2) the inventory balance at the end of that period.

The Perpetual System

Under the *perpetual method* of inventory accounting, a continuous detailed record of items purchased and sold from inventory is maintained on each stock record card. As goods are sold, Cost of Goods Sold is debited and the inventory account is credited. Because the balance of items in inventory at any specific time is reflected on each card, a physical count is not required to determine the cost of goods sold for a particular period. However, most firms which adopt this system do take a physical count to verify the accuracy of the stock record cards. Any discrepancy between the ending balance, as reflected on the cards, and the actual count is usually charged to expense as Cost of Goods Sold or as a loss due to pilferage or damage.

This "count" is commonly referred to as the *physical inventory*. Because of the cost, complexity, and time required, physical counts are usually made only once a year, either during a period of slack activity or when the inventory stock is relatively low and easy to assess. For example, manufacturers of automobiles normally take the physical count during the late summer immediately prior to changing production facilities over to the new models; whereas retail department store merchants usually undertake their physical inventory during January or February, following the Christmas season and January "white sales."

To illustrate the perpetual inventory method, assume that the beginning inventory of a home appliance dealer at January 1, 1979, consisted of 1,000 food waste disposers at $50 cost per unit. Purchases during the 1979 fiscal year totaled 5,025 units at $50 cost per unit, including freight charges. Twenty-five of these units were damaged in transit and returned to the manufacturer during the year for full credit. The total number of disposers sold during 1979 was 5,200. The ending inventory balance at December 31, 1979, would be determined as shown below:

		DOLLARS		UNITS
Beginning inventory balance at January 1, 1979 (1,000 units × $50 cost per unit, from record cards)		$ 50,000		1,000
Add: Purchases during the year including freight, (5,025 units × $50 cost per unit, from record cards).....................................	$251,250		5,025	
Less returns and allowances (25 units × $50 cost per unit from record cards).................	1,250	250,000	25	5,000
Total available for sale during 1979............		$300,000		6,000
Deduct cost of goods sold for 1979 (5,200 units × $50 cost per unit, from record cards).......................		260,000		5,200
Ending inventory at December 31, 1979.................		$ 40,000		800

Using the following notation, the inventory balance can be determined at the end of 1979:

$$BI + (P - RA) - CGS = EI$$

| Beginning Inventory | + | (Purchases − Returns and Allowances) | − | Cost of Goods Sold | = | Ending Inventory |

The Periodic System

Under the periodic system of inventory accounting, a continuous detailed record is made in the inventory account and on the individual stock record cards of all purchases and returns and allowances. However, as goods are sold under the periodic system of inventory accounting, no entry is made to the inventory account, nor is any entry made to individual stock record cards to indicate the sale of these goods. To determine the number and cost of specific items that were transferred to customers during the period, a physical count of the inventory at the end of the period is required. It is only after the physical count has been taken that an accurate journal entry can be prepared to reflect the cost of goods sold for the period.

To illustrate, using the previous example, the physical count at December 31, 1979, revealed that 800 disposers remained on hand. One method of determining the cost of goods sold for 1979 under the periodic system is shown below:

	DOLLARS		UNITS
Beginning inventory balance at January 1, 1979 (1,000 units × $50 cost per unit, from record cards)		$ 50,000	1,000
Add: Purchases during the year, including freight, (5,025 units × $50 cost per unit, from record cards).. $251,250			5,025
Less returns and allowances (25 units × $50 cost per unit, from record cards)................. 1,250		250,000	25 5,000
Total available for sale during 1979.............		$300,000	6,000
Deduct ending inventory at December 31, 1979 per physical count (800 units × $50 cost per unit).......		40,000	800
Cost of goods sold for 1979...................................		$260,000	5,200

The above tabulation may be summarized to determine the cost of goods sold:

$$BI + (P - RA) - EI = CGS$$

| Beginning Inventory | + | (Purchases − Returns and Allowances) | − | Ending Inventory | = | Cost of Goods Sold |

Only upon completion of the physical count and the preceding tabulation can the cost of goods sold for 1979 be determined and recorded as shown below:

Cost of Goods Sold 260,000
   Merchandise Inventory   260,000
      Charge cost of inventory sold during 1979 to
      expense.

Appropriate data are entered on the stock record cards at the end of the year to reflect the above information.

The principal advantage of the perpetual system over the periodic system is that a continuous detailed record of all flows in and out of the inventory account is maintained on stock record cards, hence, closer monitoring and control of inventory is made possible. Under the periodic system, only items flowing into inventory are recorded during the year. One disadvantage of the perpetual system is the high administrative costs required to maintain the detailed stock record cards, although this cost may be partially alleviated when computerized facilities are used. Because of this cost disadvantage, the periodic system tends to be used more often by small merchants and manufacturers who sell a variety of relatively low cost merchandise.

Gross Margin Technique of Estimating Cost of Goods Sold

An alternate method by which the cost of goods sold can be approximated under the periodic system without taking a physical inventory count is referred to as the *gross margin technique*. Its use is based on the premise that the firm tends to earn a relatively stable gross margin percentage on merchandise that is sold. The gross margin percentage is calculated using information from prior periods, as follows:

$$\frac{\text{Sales} - \text{Cost of goods sold}}{\text{Sales}} = \text{Gross margin percentage}$$

To illustrate, assume that the retailer of disposers used the periodic system of inventory accounting, and that the firm normally realized a gross margin percentage of approximately 33⅓ percent on all disposers sold. The cost of disposers sold for the current period can be approximated without taking a physical inventory, if sales for the period can be determined.

Assume that sales of disposers for 1979 totaled $390,900. The cost of goods sold for that year can be estimated at $260,600, as shown at the top of page 283.

Sales..		$390,900
Less normal gross margin ($390,900 × .333)		130,300
Estimated cost of goods sold...		$260,600

The $260,600 amount is recorded as the firm's estimated cost of goods sold for 1979 in advance, or in lieu of taking the annual physical inventory.

The approximate number of disposers that should be in inventory at the end of 1979 can also be determined under this method. Assuming that 6,000 disposers costing $300,000 were available for sale during the year, the ending inventory at December 31, 1979, should contain 788 disposers costing $39,400, as calculated below:

	DOLLARS	UNITS ($50 PER UNIT COST)
Total disposers available for sale during 1979 ...	$300,000	6,000
Less estimated cost of goods sold (using gross margin technique as determined above)	260,600	5,212
Estimated ending inventory	$ 39,400	788

This quantity can be verified by an actual physical count, and in case of a discrepancy, an adjusting entry would be made to restate the cost of goods sold.

The gross margin method of estimating the cost of goods sold and the ending inventory is frequently used to establish the amount of an insurance claim in the event of an inventory loss by fire, theft, or other calamity. These estimations can be made relatively accurately if:

(1) A relatively stable gross margin is realized on merchandise that is sold;

(2) The amount of sales and purchases during the period are known.

INVENTORY COSTING METHODS

Inventory costing pertains to the sequence in which the recorded costs of inventory items are transferred from the inventory account and charged as an expense to cost of goods sold. Accountants have developed several methods to identify which costs will be reflected as the ending inventory balance on the balance sheet. Since a direct relationship exists between inventory and cost of goods sold, the method selected has a significant impact on the amounts of federal and state income taxes, local property taxes, and net income that are reflected on the income statement.

Distinction Between Dollar Cost and Physical Flow of Inventory

It is very important to understand the critical distinction that exists between the pattern in which goods physically flow in and out of inventory, and the dollar-cost pattern associated with the movement of those goods. This distinction can be illustrated using the following products: flour and coal.

Assume that batches of flour enter the storage bin from the top and are withdrawn from the bottom as sold. The first batch placed in the bin was purchased at $4 per hundredweight (cwt.), whereas the second batch costs $5 per cwt.

Flour

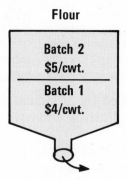

The physical flow of the flour is in a *first-in, first-out* (fifo) sequence. In effect, the flour bought first is the first to be sold. Assuming that only one batch is sold during the day, batch 2 remains in the bin at the end of the day.

Shipments of coal are stacked in a pile as they are received and are withdrawn from the top as sold. The first shipment, forming the bottom of the pile, was purchased at $14 per ton; whereas the second shipment that lies atop the pile costs $16 per ton.

Coal

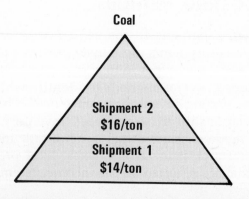

The physical flow of the coal in the pile is in a *last-in, first-out* (lifo) sequence. Those shipments purchased last are the first to be sold. Assuming that only one shipment is sold during the day, the first shipment received remains in the pile at the end of the day.

The cost that is associated with each batch of flour or shipment of coal may remain attached to that batch (as illustrated), or be separated from that batch as the respective product moves through inventory to ultimate sale. In other words, the inventory of flour that remains in the bin at the end of the day can be costed either at $5 (under the fifo method) or $4 (under the lifo method) per cwt. If the batch in ending inventory is costed at $5, then the batch that was sold would be charged to expense at $4: in which case, the fifo *dollar-cost flow* coincides with the fifo physical flow. On the other hand, if the batch remaining in inventory is costed at $4, then the batch that was sold would be charged to expense at $5: in which case, the dollar-cost flow is lifo even though the physical flow was fifo. Either treatment, if used consistently, is permissible in accounting.

Likewise, the inventory of coal remaining in the pile at the end of the day may be costed either at $14 or $16 per ton. If the ending inventory is costed at $14, the shipment that was sold would be charged to expense at $16: in which case the lifo dollar-cost flow parallels the lifo physical flow. On the other hand, if the inventory is costed at $16, the shipment that was sold is charged to expense at $14, and the dollar-cost flow is fifo even though the physical flow was lifo.

To reemphasize the point, the dollar-cost flow of goods may, but need not, coincide with the physical flow of those goods. Accounting merely insists, with occasional exceptions, that once a particular dollar-cost flow has been selected, it should be used consistently.

These observations will be integrated with an examination of the following inventory costing alternatives which are most frequently used in business:

(1) Specific identification.
(2) Fifo.
(3) Lifo.
(4) Weighted average.

The information below and on page 286 will be used to present these four costing alternatives.

The Venetian Corp. purchases window shades from various manufacturers and subsequently sells them wholesale to retailers and industrial firms. The company began operations on January 1, 1979, with no beginning inventory.

Venetian Corp.
Record of Purchases of Sales of Inventory
For the Two-Year Period January 1, 1979 Through December 31, 1980

| | PURCHASED | | | | |
	UNITS	UNIT COST	TOTAL COST	SOLD	UNITS IN INVENTORY AT END OF YEAR
1979:					
Balance at January 1					—0—
January	30	$10	$ 300		
April	50	11	550		
July	70	13	910		
October.....................	60	12	720		
Total............................	210		$2,480	130	80
1980:					
February	90	$12	$1,080		
May..........................	80	14	1,120		
August.......................	100	13	1,300		
November	120	15	1,800		
Total............................	390		$5,300	410	60*

*80 units at December 31, 1979 + 390 units purchased in 1980 − 410 units sold in 1980 = 60 units at December 31, 1980.

Specific Identification

Each item that flows through inventory may be separately identified and individually matched as an expense with the revenue that is obtained from its sale. This inventory costing procedure is referred to as *specific identification*. Its use is limited almost exclusively to sellers of low volume, sharply differentiated, and relatively expensive products, such as exquisite jewelry, furs, custom-crafted furniture, or antique classic automobiles. Multiproduct firms and those which sell high volume, standardized, and/or moderate to low-priced merchandise avoid using this method because of the time, complexity, and expense that are involved in detailed item-by-item record keeping.

This inventory costing alternative has on occasion been used to manipulate financial reports. For example, if the management of Venetian Corp. desires to reflect the highest gross margin for 1979, it could accomplish that objective by matching with revenue the costs associated with the 130 least expensive units that were purchased during 1979. These specific units would have been drawn from the following purchases:

PURCHASED IN 1979	UNITS	UNIT COST	COST OF GOODS SOLD
January	30	$10	$ 300
April	50	11	550
October	50	12	600
Total	130		$1,450

The ending inventory balance at December 31, 1979, would consequently reflect costs associated with the 80 most expensive units that were purchased during the year, as itemized below:

Purchased in 1979	Units	Unit Cost	Cost of Goods Sold
July	70	$13	$ 910
October	10	12	120
Total	80		$1,030

Adoption of the specific identification alternative for purposes of financial statement manipulation is sharply condemned and prohibited by the accounting profession.

Fifo (First In, First Out)

Perhaps the most widely adopted inventory costing alternative is fifo. Under this method, costs associated with specific purchases are matched with the revenue generated during the period on a first in, first out dollar-cost flow basis, irrespective of whether the physical flow of merchandise is fifo, lifo, or some other pattern.

Procedural details involved in this method are outlined below, using flowcharted inventory and cost of goods sold T accounts, plus information that is contained in the record of purchases and sales of inventory for Venetian Corp. shown on page 286. The focus of attention in this presentation is each fiscal year, rather than each month or quarter. The units in ending inventory at December 31 of each year were determined by physical count.

FIFO INVENTORY COSTING

	Merchandise Inventory		Cost of Goods Sold	
1979				
January — 30 × $10	$ 300		130 Units	
April — 50 × $11	550	} 1,500	Expensed	1,500
July — 50 × $13	650			
20 × $13	260			
October — 60 × $12	720			
Bal. at				
Dec. 31 — 20 × $13				
60 × $12	$ 980			

	Merchandise Inventory		Cost of Goods Sold	
1980				
Beginning				
Inventory — 20 × $13				
60 × $12	$ 980			
February — 90 × $12	1,080		410 Units	
May — 80 × $14	1,120	} 5,380	Expensed	5,380
August — 100 × $13	1,300			
November — 60 × $15	900			
60 × $15	900			
Bal. at				
Dec. 31 — 60 × $15	900			

Notice that the July, 1979 purchase of 70 units has been split into two segments; 50 units were charged to expense in 1979; and 20 units were included in 1979 ending inventory of 80 units. The other 60 units in that ending inventory were purchased in October, 1979, at the $12 unit cost. Similarly in 1980, 60 units of the November, 1980 purchases were charged to expense in 1980, with the remaining 60 units at the $15 unit cost being included in 1980's ending inventory.

Lifo (Last In, First Out)

The lifo method of inventory costing has become more widely adopted in recent years because of inflationary pressures. Under this method, costs associated with specific purchases are matched with the revenue generated during the period on a last-in, first-out dollar-cost flow basis, irrespective of whether the physical flow of merchandise is lifo, fifo, or some other pattern. Procedural details involved in lifo costing are illustrated below. Several unique features associated with this costing alternative are clarified following the exhibit.

LIFO INVENTORY COSTING

		MERCHANDISE INVENTORY			COST OF GOODS SOLD
1979					
January	— 30 × $10	300			
April	— 50 × $11	550			
July	— 70 × $13	910	} 1,630	130 Units	1,630
October	— 60 × $12	720	}	Expensed	
Bal. at					
Dec. 31	— 30 × $10				
	50 × $11	850			

		MERCHANDISE INVENTORY			COST OF GOODS SOLD
1980					
Beginning					
Inventory	— 30 × $10	300			
	50 × $11	550	}		
February	— 90 × $12	1,080	}		
May	— 80 × $14	1,120	} 5,520*	410 Units	5,520
August	— 100 × $13	1,300	}	Expensed	
November	— 120 × $15	1,800	}		
Bal. at					
Dec. 31	— 30 × $10				
	30 × $11	630			

*Includes the cost associated with 20 units of beginning inventory purchased in April, 1979: 20 units × $11 = $220.

The inventory balance of 80 units at December 31, 1979, is composed of two segments: 30 units purchased in January, 1979, at the $10 unit cost; and 50 units purchased in April, 1979, at the

$11 unit cost. The inventory balance at December 31, 1980, is composed of the following units:

PURCHASED IN 1979	UNITS	UNIT COST	INVENTORY BALANCE
January	30	$10	$300
April	30	11	330
Total	60		$630

Costs associated with 20 of the units purchased in April, 1979, were charged to expense during 1980.

The ending inventory at December 31, 1979, is referred to as the *lifo base*. Any reduction in the lifo base is obtained from the "bottom" of the base, or from the most recent *lifo layer*. In this instance, costs associated with the 20 units that were purchased at an $11 unit cost in April, 1979, are removed from that lifo base at the end of 1980.

On the other hand, assume that the inventory at the end of 1980, reflected an increase of 20 units over the ending inventory at December 31, 1979, due to the fact that 370 units were sold during 1980 of 470 units available for sale. The lifo inventory of those 100 units at December 31, 1980, would reflect a balance of $1,090, as shown below:

	PURCHASED ON	UNITS	UNIT COST	INVENTORY BALANCE
Lifo base:	January, 1979	30	$10	$ 300
	April, 1979	50	$11	550
				$ 850
1980				
Lifo layer:	February, 1980	20	$12	240
	Total	100		$1,090

Costs associated with any layer that is added to the lifo base at the end of a particular fiscal year are customarily obtained from the earliest purchases made in that year: in this instance, from the February, 1980, purchases at $12 per unit.

Weighted Average

Lifo or fifo inventory costing may be used with products which become intermingled making separate identification either impractical or impossible, such as oil, gasoline, or grain. However, the more commonly used method of inventory costing in such circumstances is the *weighted average method*. The cost associated with each unit that flows into inventory is disregarded under the weighted average method after the cost is recorded in the journal. Instead, a single weighted average cost is computed by dividing the total cost of units available for sale during the year by the total number of units available for sale during the year. The weighted average costs for 1979 and 1980 in the Venetian Corp. example are as follows, rounded to four decimal places:

$$1979: \frac{\$2{,}480 \text{ cost of purchases}}{210 \text{ units purchased}} = \$11.8095 \text{ cost per unit.}$$

$$1980: \frac{\$5{,}300 \text{ cost of purchases} + (80 \text{ units in inventory at Dec. 31, 1979} \times \$11.8095)}{390 \text{ units purchased} + 80 \text{ units in inventory at Dec. 31, 1979}}$$
$$= \$13.2867 \text{ cost per unit.}$$

The flow of costs involved in the weighted average alternative is displayed below:

WEIGHTED AVERAGE COSTING

	MERCHANDISE INVENTORY			COST OF GOODS SOLD
1979 Total purchases of 210 units	2,480	**(a)** 1,535	130 Units Expensed	1,535
Bal. at Dec. 31	**(b)** 945			

	MERCHANDISE INVENTORY			COST OF GOODS SOLD
1980 Beginning inventory, 80 units	**(b)** 945			
Total purchases of 390 units	5,300	**(c)** 5,448	410 Units Expensed	5,448
Bal. at Dec. 31	**(d)** 797			

(a) 130 units × $11.8095 = $1,535
(b) 80 units × $11.8095 = $ 945
(c) 410 units × $13.2867 = $5,448
(d) 60 units × $13.2867 = $ 797

Another format by which to summarize the essential details involved in the various inventory costing alternatives is displayed below, using the information developed for the weighted average alternative:

WEIGHTED AVERAGE COSTING

	INVENTORY BALANCE	COST OF GOODS SOLD
1979		
$\dfrac{\$2{,}480 \text{ total purchase cost}}{210 \text{ units purchases}} = \$11.8095 \text{ per unit}$		
× 80 units...	$945	
$2,480 total cost − $945 ending inventory............................		$1,535
1980		
$\dfrac{\$5{,}300 \text{ total purchase} + \$945 \text{ beginning inventory}}{390 \text{ units purchased} + 80 \text{ units in beginning inventory}}$		
= $13.2867 per unit × 60 units..	$797	
$6,245 total cost − $797 ending inventory............................		$5,448

Comparative Summary of Inventory Costing Alternatives

A comparative summary of the impact which the three major inventory costing alternatives have on the balance sheet and income statement of Venetian Corp. over the 2-year period is presented below. Results of the specific identification alternative are excluded because it is not extensively used, and because its application could reflect a wide variety of amounts for ending inventory and cost of goods sold in each year.

COMPARATIVE SUMMARY OF THREE INVENTORY COSTING ALTERNATIVES

	1979		1980	
	INVENTORY BALANCE AT DECEMBER 31	COST OF GOODS SOLD	INVENTORY BALANCE AT DECEMBER 31	COST OF GOODS SOLD
Inventory costing method	80 units	130 units	60 units	410 units
Fifo	$980	$1,500	$900	$5,380
Weighted average...........	945	1,535	797	5,448
Lifo	850	1,630	630	5,520

In this illustration the fifo method consistently reflected: (1) the highest inventory balance at each year-end; (2) the lowest cost of goods sold in each year; and consequently (3) the highest gross margin in each year. These results could have been anticipated in this instance because the unit cost increased steadily during the 2-year period. Costs associated with those units that were pur chased at higher prices near the end of each year remained in year-end inventories, leaving the lower costs associated with those units in beginning inventory and with those units that were purchased earlier in the year to be charged to expense as cost of goods sold.

At the other extreme, lifo consistently reflected: (1) the lowest inventory balance at each year-end; (2) the highest cost of goods sold in each year; and consequently, (3) the lowest gross margin in each year. Relatively lower per unit costs that were associated with the items on hand at the beginning of each period and with those items that were purchased early in the year, remained in inventory; this resulted in charging to expense the higher per-unit costs that were associated with later purchases. The weighted average cost method reflected an ending inventory balance, cost of goods sold, and gross margin that fell between the fifo and lifo extremes in each year.

Several conclusions may be derived from this analysis with respect to the fifo and lifo inventory costing methods in instances where the cost of goods purchased tends to either rise or fall.

These conclusions are summarized in the following table. The weighted average method has been omitted since it occupies a position between the fifo and lifo extremes.[1] To reiterate, once a particular inventory costing method is selected, that method should be used consistently. To do otherwise creates situations in which financial information that encompasses several years becomes incomparable. In general, the accounting profession does not encourage a change in the inventory costing method that has been used by a firm; and in most cases, the Internal Revenue Service is reluctant to allow a change.

IF THE COST OF GOODS PURCHASED DURING A PERIOD IS:	FIFO RESULTS IN A	LIFO RESULTS IN A
Rising	Higher year-end inventory balance. Lower cost of goods sold. Higher gross margin.	Lower year-end inventory balance. Higher cost of goods sold. Lower gross margin.
Falling	Lower year-end inventory balance. Higher cost of goods sold. Lower gross margin.	Higher year-end inventory balance. Lower cost of goods sold. Higher gross margin.

THE LIFO-FIFO CONTROVERSY

Considerable debate has developed among accountants, financial managers, analysts, and other executives during the past two decades with respect to which inventory costing method best reflects the ending inventory balance and cost of goods sold. Subsequent discussion examines three major issues involved in this debate:

(1) Adequacy of matching;
(2) Timeliness of the inventory balance; and
(3) Comparability of financial information.

Attention will focus on the lifo and fifo methods since the amounts shown for cost of goods sold and ending inventory under each of these two alternatives usually occupy opposite extremes.

---

[1]The presumption was made in the preceding analysis that the periodic accounting system was used in Venetian Corp. Use of this system meant that determination of the cost of goods sold for each fiscal year would have been deferred until December 31 of each year. If the accounting system used had been the perpetual method, the monetary amounts that would be reflected for the cost of goods sold and the ending inventory balance in each year would have been the same as shown previously under the specific identification and fifo costing methods. For the lifo and weighted average methods, however, amounts could have been developed under the perpetual system for the cost of goods sold and the ending inventory balance in respective years which differed somewhat from those presented above. Most accounting and financial managers recompute the cost of goods sold and the ending inventory balance at the end of each year as if the periodic accounting system were in use. Hence, the comparative summary shown on page 291 that was generated under the periodic assumption would in most cases closely approximate or be identical to what would be generated under the perpetual accounting system.

Adequacy of Matching

Inspection of the exhibits on pages 287 and 288 reveals that the lifo method tends to result in a better matching of the most currently incurred costs with current revenue than the fifo method. Under lifo, as long as the physical quantity in the ending inventory remains constant or increases, the costs associated with the units that were purchased earliest are used to cost units remaining in ending inventory. Whether the prices paid for inventory items are rising or falling, the costs associated with the most recent additions to inventory are the first to be charged to expense. Therefore, income statements that are prepared under the lifo alternative tend to more adequately reflect the impact of these price movements on cost of goods sold and net income as compared to fifo.

In contrast, the older incurred costs are the first to be charged to expense under fifo costing, followed by the expensing of more recently incurred costs in successive stages. This procedure always results in the most recently incurred costs being reflected in the fifo ending inventory balance. Hence, because the fifo method tends to match the less current costs with current revenue, the net income that is reflected on the income statement is less current than that of lifo.

Substantial differences may be reflected in financial statements that are prepared under the two methods within a time span as short as one or two years. The comparative income statement for Venetian Corp. which is presented on page 294 emphasizes the differences between fifo and lifo methods with respect to gross margin, income taxes, and net income. Information contained in these statements was derived from the comparative summary on page 291, with the addition of three simplifying assumptions: (1) each window shade was sold at $15 during 1979, and at $18 during 1980; (2) no expenses other than cost of goods sold and federal income tax incurred were considered for this illustration; and (3) the federal income tax rate is 50 percent.

Cost of goods sold reported under lifo in 1979 was $130 higher than under fifo, simply because the lifo inventory balance at December 31, 1979, was $130 lower than that reported under fifo. The lifo cost of goods sold in 1980 was $140 higher as compared to fifo, because the lifo inventory balance at December 31, 1980, was $270 less than that reported under fifo, of which $130 was carried forward from 1979 ($270 total − $130 carryover = $140).

Of perhaps greater importance is the fact that a lower gross margin was reflected in each of the two years under lifo, which

Venetian Corp.
Comparative Income Statement and Inventory Balances
For the Years Ended December 31, 1979 and 1980

	1979		
	Fifo		*Lifo*
Sales (130 units × $15)	$1,950	$130	$1,950
Cost of goods sold	1,500	Difference	1,630
Gross margin	$ 450		$ 320
Federal income tax (50%)	225		160
Net income	$ 225		$ 160
Inventory at December 31, 1979	$ 980	$130 Difference	$ 850

	1980		
	Fifo		*Lifo*
Sales (410 units × $18)	$7,380	$140	$7,380
Cost of goods sold	5,380	Difference	5,520
Gross margin	$2,000		$1,860
Federal income tax (50%)	1,000		930
Net income	$1,000		$ 930
Inventory at December 31, 1980	$ 900	$270 Difference	$ 630

resulted in $135 less federal income tax expense and net income over the 2-year period under lifo ($1,090) as compared to fifo ($1,225). The overall significance of this $135 difference in federal income tax assessment and net income between the two costing alternatives can perhaps be made more graphic merely by multiplying that amount by a thousand, or a million — multiples which are quite commonplace in modern business. Critics of lifo maintain that firms often adopt lifo merely to save on income tax assessments — a contention that may be warranted in many instances. But in view of what appears to be a continuing inflationary trend, management can partially accomplish the twin objectives of (1) conserving cash within the business in the short-run, and (2) generating higher profitability over the long-run, by adopting the lifo alternative. Current cash savings that result from lower income tax payments during earlier years may be used elsewhere in the firm to generate a higher return on total financial resources in future years. From present value analysis, the dollar earned or saved today is more valuable than the dollar earned or saved next year.

Implications that follow from this taxation issue are several. For example, if management anticipates that the cost to replenish inventory will remain high or continue an upward trend, the cash saving that results from lower income tax payments may provide funds with which to replenish inventory at the higher prices. Otherwise a loan or an additional stockholder investment might be required to finance inventory purchased. In addition, had Venetian Corp. used fifo costing, its stockholders might have insisted on higher cash dividends because of the relatively high net income reported in both years. Payment of higher cash dividends, however, would deplete cash which management needs to replenish inventory at the anticipated higher costs.

In short, one decision-making problem that confronts management with respect to which inventory costing alternative to adopt can be phrased as follows: Which is the more desirable course to pursue: (1) to reflect higher taxable income, and hence pay higher income taxes as reflected under the fifo alternative in the Venetian Corp. example; or (2) to reflect lower taxable income, but pay lower tax assessments, as reflected under lifo in this instance?

To summarize, lifo, compared to other inventory costing methods, tends to:

(1) Result in a better matching of current costs with current revenue.
(2) Recognize as cost of goods sold an amount which better reflects price level movements with respect to inventory costs, regardless of whether prices are rising or falling.
(3) Reflect lower net income when prices are rising, but higher net income when the price level is falling.
(4) Require less cash outflow for federal and state income tax payments when the price level is rising, and more cash outflow during periods of falling prices.

The last point can directly influence inventory replenishment and cash dividend policies.

Timeliness of the Inventory Balance

Fifo inventory costing reflects the most currently incurred costs in ending inventory. In the preceding illustration, the fifo inventory at December 31, 1979, reflected costs incurred late in 1979, during July and October; whereas lifo reflected costs incurred much earlier, during January and April. Again at the end of 1980, the fifo inventory balance contained costs incurred late in the year, during November. Even though the price of this inventory increased 50 percent during the 2-year period, the lifo costing alternative continued to reflect costs in ending inventory that were incurred at the relatively low prices of January and April, 1979. Had the price level declined during this same period, the lifo ending inventory would still have reflected noncurrent costs. In fact, a firm that operated for 50 years under the lifo method might reflect costs in its ending inventory that had been incurred a half century earlier: costs which might not even approximate current costs.

In short, the fifo alternative is markedly superior to lifo in reflecting the most currently incurred inventory costs on the balance sheet. Lifo's less current inventory balance, however, may offer an advantage during a period of rising prices to a firm that is located in a state or locale which levies a business property tax in direct proportion to the reported dollar value of its ending inventory.

Comparability of Financial Information

Comparative analyses between corporate financial statements, some of which reflect lifo while others reflect fifo inventory costing, often lead to confusing conclusions, particularly with respect to investment decision-making. This contention remains valid to some extent because the accounting profession and the Internal Revenue Service do not specify that any inventory costing method must be universally adopted. The accounting profession attempts to alleviate the problem of noncomparability by encouraging all companies to clearly disclose on their financial statements the inventory costing method that is used. It also requires in those instances where approval from the IRS or the accounting profession has been obtained to change inventory costing methods, that full disclosure be made of the change in the financial statements, accompanied by an explanation of how the change would have affected financial statements of recent prior periods.

To summarize the major issues involved in the controversy surrounding which inventory costing arrangement is "best" — it appears that no single inventory costing method satisfies the following two desirable objectives:

(1) Match current costs with revenue so that a more current net income amount is reflected on the income statement. Lifo costing achieves this objective better than fifo.
(2) Reflect the most recently incurred costs in the ending inventory balance that is shown on the balance sheet. Fifo costing achieves this objective better than lifo.

INVENTORY VALUATION ALTERNATIVES

It should be reemphasized that the four costing alternatives previously described are methods of accounting for the flow of dollar-costs associated with products through the inventory account. Although these methods have a direct impact on income determination, via the cost of goods sold account, technically they are not referred to as valuation alternatives. Instead, accountants have designated two alternatives by which to value the units comprising ending inventory: (1) *cost*; and (2) *the lower of cost or market*.

Valuation at Cost

The monetary amount of the ending inventory, as determined by one of the four inventory costing alternatives, could be designated as the actual cost of that inventory. The comparative summary shown below reflects the valuation at cost of the inventories presented on page 291 under each of the three principal inventory costing alternatives:

	VALUATION OF INVENTORY AT COST	
	December 31, 1979	*December 31, 1980*
Fifo	$980	$900
Weighted average	945	797
Lifo	850	630

Adoption of the cost method of valuation does not require adjusting entries at the end of respective fiscal periods.

Valuation at the Lower of Cost or Market

Inventory could also be reassessed at current market prices, which means that its value would be revised downward if the current market prices were below cost. For purposes of valuing the ending inventory at the lower of cost or market, *market* is usually defined as the cost at which individual items in the inventory could be replaced at the end of the current fiscal year. For purposes of this discussion, the market price at which Venetian Corp. could replace its ending inventory at December 31, 1979, is $12 per unit, and $15 per unit at December 31, 1980. Hence the *market value* of the ending inventory at each of these dates is as follows:

	MARKET VALUE OF ENDING INVENTORY
December 31, 1979 (80 units × $12)	$960
December 31, 1980 (60 units × $15)	900

This information may be integrated into the preceding exhibit, as shown on page 298.

VALUATION OF INVENTORY

	December 31, 1979	December 31, 1980
At cost:		
Fifo	$980	$900
Weighted Average	945	797
Lifo	850	630
At market	$960	$900

Adjustment at December 31, 1979. The above exhibit indicates that in only one instance was "market" less than "cost." The value of the ending inventory at December 31, 1979, if reflected at cost under the fifo alternative, would be $980; whereas at market, it would be $960. If fifo costing is used by Venetian Corp., adoption of the more conservative lower of cost or market rule will require that an adjusting entry be made at December 31, 1979, to revalue the ending inventory balance, as reflected in the accounting records, downward by $20. This downward revaluation is considered an *unrealized holding loss*, in the same sense as is a downward revaluation of the portfolio of marketable equity securities. The revaluation entry is shown below:

1979
Dec. 31 Unrealized Loss on Inventory (IS) 20
      Merchandise Inventory Revaluation to Lower of Cost
        or Market (CA) 20
          Record revaluation downward of inventory to
          lower of cost or market. Fifo costing used.

The unrealized holding loss is reflected on the income statement under the "Gains and losses" caption; whereas the inventory revaluation account is a contra current asset that is directly associated with its parent inventory account. The restated inventory balance can be reported on the balance sheet at December 31, 1979, in either of the following ways:

Merchandise inventory at cost	$980
Less revaluation to lower of cost or market	(20)
Merchandise inventory at lower of cost or market	$960

or

Merchandise inventory at the lower of cost ($980) or market	$960

If Venetian Corp. adopted either the weighted average or lifo costing alternative, no revaluation entry would be required at December 31, 1979, because "market" was above "cost" in each instance.

Adjustment at December 31, 1980. Since the cost basis of inventory valuation under each of the three costing alternatives is equal to or less than the market basis at December 31, 1980, no downward revaluation entry is required at that date. However, the downward revaluation that was recorded at the end of 1979, under the assumption that the firm had adopted fifo costing, must be reversed to the extent that the inventory balance net of any revaluation may not exceed the $900 cost amount at December 31, 1980. Restated, the inventory revaluation account can never reflect a debit balance; or the net carrying value of the inventory on the balance can never exceed cost. Therefore, the adjusting entry required at December 31, 1980, under the fifo alternative would be as shown below:

1980
Dec. 31 Merchandise Inventory Revaluation to Lower of Cost or
        Market (CA) 20
           Unrealized Gain on Inventory (IS) 20
           Record revaluation upward to cost by reversing
           December 31, 1979 entry. Fifo costing used.

If the above entry is not recorded, the net inventory balance shown on the balance sheet at the end of 1980 would be $880 ($900 fifo cost basis less the $20 credit balance in the inventory revaluation account).

Taxation Refinements. Unrealized holding losses on inventory that are recorded under the lower of cost or market rule are considered by the Internal Revenue Service as being deductible from revenue and other income in determining taxable income. Any subsequent reversal of an unrealized holding loss — in effect, an unrealized holding gain — is treated as taxable income. Two additional refinements due to tax regulations must be considered when applying the lower of cost or market rule to inventory valuation:

(1) The lower of cost or market rule cannot be applied if the firm has adopted lifo inventory costing. Only the cost method of inventory valuation may be applied for tax purposes under lifo costing.[2] A firm that uses lifo for tax purposes may not use an inventory method other than lifo for purposes of reports to shareholders, partners, or other proprietors.[3]

(2) The lower of cost or market rule must be consistently applied, where permitted (such as with the fifo or weighted average alternatives), to each item in inventory for tax purposes.[4] The taxpayer must use the lower of

---

[2]*Internal Revenue Code of 1954 and Regulations, Section 1.472-2(b).* Currently approved financial accounting guidelines for external reporting purposes place no such restriction on the applicability of the lower of cost or market rule. See *Accounting Research and Terminology Bulletins — Final Edition No. 43,* "Restatement and Revision of Accounting Research Bulletins" (New York: American Institute of Certified Public Accountants, 1961) Ch. 4, Statement 5.

[3]*Revenue Ruling 75-49,* Internal Revenue Service.

[4]*Internal Revenue Code of 1954 and Regulations, Section 1.471-4(c).* Currently approved financial accounting guidelines for external reporting purposes allow either the aggregate or item-by-item method to be applied in revaluing ending inventory to the lower of cost or market. See *Accounting Research and Terminology Bulletins — Final Edition, loc. cit.,* Statement 7.

cost or market, "item-by-item," and not the lower of cost or market "aggregate." This sharp distinction is clarified below.

Assume that a steel wholesaler determined the value of five grades of steel in its ending inventory, as follows:

	(1)	(2)	(3)
	AT COST (FIFO)	AT MARKET	AT LOWER OF COST OR MARKET
Grade of Steel	Purchase Cost Recorded in the Ledger	Market Value at End of Year	Item-by-Item
A	$ 5,000	$ 4,000	$ 4,000
B	6,000	6,500	6,000
C	3,000	2,500	2,500
D	7,000	8,000	7,000
E	1,000	700	700
Total	$22,000	$21,700 (aggregate)	$20,200

If the lower of cost or market rule is used, the ending inventory must be valued at $20,200 for tax purposes [the lower of columns (1) and (3)], rather than $21,700 [the lower of columns (1) and (2)].

Comparative Summary of Inventory Valuation Alternatives

The comparative summary shown below presents four bases by which the inventory balance at each year-end can be determined for Venetian Corp. The impact that each valuation method has on the income statement is also reflected in this summary.

COMPARATIVE SUMMARY OF INVENTORY VALUATION METHODS

	BALANCE SHEET			INCOME STATEMENT		
	(1) Inventory	(2) Inventory Revaluation (Credit)	(3) Net Inventory on Balance Sheet (1) + (2)	(4) Cost of Goods Sold	(5) Unrealized (Gain) or Loss	(6) Net Impact on Income Statement (4) + (5)
1979 Fiscal Year						
Cost basis:						
Fifo	$980	——	$980	$1,500	——	$1,500
Weighted average	945	——	945	1,535	——	1,535
Lifo	850	——	850	1,630	——	1,630
Lower of cost or market basis:						
Fifo	980	$(20)	960	1,500	$20	1,520
1980 Fiscal Year						
Cost basis:						
Fifo	$900	——	$900	$5,380	——	$5,380
Weighted average	797	——	797	5,448	——	5,448
Lifo	630	——	630	5,520	——	5,520
Lower of cost or market basis:						
Fifo	900	——	900	5,380	$(20)	5,360

The summary indicates four different net inventory balances (column 3) that could be reflected on the balance sheet at December 31, 1979, ranging from $850 to $980. Three could be reflected at the end of 1980, ranging from $630 to $900. What might be considered a "net cost of goods sold" amount (column 6), reflects four different amounts each for 1979 and 1980. Perhaps the most significant insight to be derived from this exhibit is that noncomparable information can be generated by the vast number of business entities throughout the country, depending on which inventory costing alternative is used and whether the ending inventory is valued at cost or the lower of cost or market. Financial analysts who are confronted by such a wide array of possibilities with respect to inventory values might easily arrive at confusing conclusions regarding the current financial position and profitability of various firms. This confusion can be lessened, though not entirely eliminated, if a firm adopts the accounting guidelines outlined previously:

(1) Clearly identify in its financial statements the method of inventory costing and valuation used.
(2) Consistently use whichever method of inventory costing and valuation basis that has been adopted.
(3) Fully disclose the effect that a change in inventory costing or valuation method has on information contained in current and recent financial statements.

The Current Replacement Cost Experimental Program

In March, 1976, the Securities and Exchange Commission issued a directive pertaining to corporations whose stock is listed on national stock exchanges and to corporations that anticipate offering their stock to the public. The firms whose inventories and gross plant assets exceed $100 million and amount to more than 10 percent of its total assets, must disclose, either in a footnote or in a separate section of the financial statements that are required to be filed with the SEC: (1) the current cost of replacing inventories and productive capacity (plant assets); and (2) the amount of cost of goods sold and depreciation expense when computed under a current replacement cost basis. This directive is part of an experimental program which became effective for periods beginning after December 25, 1975. The SEC does not yet require the publication of current replacement cost information in financial statements that are circulated to the public or to any group other than the SEC.

Considerable discussion and controversy have emerged with respect to furnishing *current replacement cost* (CRC) information, even on the limited basis prescribed by this directive. The CRC designation is not to be confused with the "current market price" that is used for purposes of valuing inventory under the lower of cost or market rule. Although the monetary amounts that might be generated under each term could on occasion coincide for specific assets, CRC is a broad costing concept which represents a complete departure from the historical cost (HC) principle. HC is based on the premise that the price actually paid for an asset is the amount reflected in the accounting records as the cost of that asset. On the other hand, the CRC concept specifies that the cost at which an asset, in its present condition, could be replaced is the monetary amount that should be reflected in the records as the cost of that asset.

Proponents of CRC maintain that this concept would give explicit recognition in accounting records to the significant impact that inflation has had on various assets during the past two decades. Many adherents claim that expenses, such as cost of goods sold and depreciation expense which are based on the HC principle, do not adequately reflect the "true" cost of doing business in today's world of constantly increasing price levels. Others assert that boards of directors may be unwisely distributing corporate earnings to stockholders in the form of cash dividends when, because of inflationary pressures, more financial resources should be retained in the firm with which to replenish inventory and other operating assets at increasing prices. Application of CRC would, it is argued, enable higher cost of goods sold and depreciation expense to be reflected on the income statement, resulting in lower income before taxes — which in turn might reduce income tax assessments and suggest to executives that the higher profits as shown under HC are deceptive and unreal.

The principal objections to adopting CRC as an alternative to HC are outlined below:

(1) The historical cost principle is a time-tested, proven method of accounting for financial resources and obligations of business organizations.

(2) Application of HC is objective, verifiable, and well understood.

(3) Adoption of current replacement cost would lead to a wide variety of subjective judgments with respect to determining the exact replacement cost of each asset in its present condition.

(4) Many firms would not replace their inventories or plant assets with exact in-kind duplicates.

(5) The burden of calculating annually the CRC of each asset would require excessive and unjustifiable costs.

As of this date, the current replacement cost program specified by the SEC directive is completely experimental, and is being applied to a relatively narrow spectrum of business enterprises in the United States. The results obtained from this project will influence whether the CRC program will be extended to other firms, result in substantial modifications, or be discontinued.

QUESTIONS

1. Identify several factors which account for the importance of inventory in business organizations.

2. Of the items in the physical possession of a firm, indicate the criteria that are used to determine which items should be included in its inventory.

3. What is meant by goods held on consignment?

4. A Boston firm purchased goods from a Detroit vendor. Explain the significance of the terms "FOB Detroit": (a) to the vendor; (b) to the purchaser.

5. Explain the major distinctions between inventories of a merchandiser and of a manufacturer.

6. (a) Identify three accounts that might be used to supplement the inventory account in recording transactions involving inventoriable items. (b) Explain how the balances in these three accounts are handled at the end of a fiscal year.

7. Present a format to determine the cost of goods sold at the end of a period, assuming that a physical inventory has been taken and four inventory-related accounts are maintained by a merchandising firm.

8. (a) Prepare an entry, using the comparative format, to record the payment on May 25 of an invoice that was received on May 1 for the purchase of $3,000 of merchandise under credit terms of 3/20, net 30, assuming the purchase was recorded using: the gross cost method; the net cost method. (b) Determine the effective interest rate compounded annually that is contained in these credit terms. Carry calculation to one decimal place.

9. Give several arguments for adopting the net cost method of recording inventory purchases.

10. What is the physical count?

11. (a) Explain the main characteristics of the perpetual method of inventory accounting. (b) Identify its major strengths and weaknesses.

12. (a) Explain the principal attributes of the periodic method of inventory accounting. (b) Identify its major advantages and disadvantages.

13. Express the principal distinction between the periodic and perpetual systems of inventory accounting by means of two mathematical equations — particularly with respect to determining the cost of goods sold for the period or the inventory balance at the end of that period.

14. Organize the following pieces of information to determine the amount of insurance claim following a fire loss, using the gross margin technique of estimating cost of goods sold under the periodic inventory accounting system: (a) total purchase cost of units available for sale during the period immediately preceding the fire; (b) total dollar sales of units during the same period; (c) the normal gross margin percentage;

and (d) the cost of undamaged units in inventory immediately following the fire per a physical inventory count. Indicate the key assumption in your analysis.

15. The dollar-cost flow and the physical flow of inventory items are so similar that the two terms, for all practical purposes, are synonomous. Comment on the validity of this statement.

16. Identify and briefly describe the four inventory costing alternatives most frequently used in business enterprises.

17. Under what conditions might each of the following inventory costing methods be used: (a) specific identification; (b) weighted average.

18. Define and explain the terms "lifo base" and "lifo layer."

19. If the price level with respect to inventory items steadily declined during the fiscal year, identify and explain which of the three major inventory costing alternatives would probably result in the highest federal income tax expense for that year.

20. Under what circumstances might a firm experience a net increase in inventory in terms of physical units during a period, yet reflect a net decrease in the dollar value of the inventory during that same period?

21. Identify and explain three principal issues that are involved in the lifo-fifo controversy.

22. Identify and briefly describe the two inventory valuation alternatives: (a) cost; and (b) the lower of cost or market.

23. To what extent may an unrealized holding gain on inventory be recognized?

24. Identify and briefly explain several taxation refinements that are relevant to inventory costing and valuation procedures.

25. Identify three recommendations which the accounting profession has proposed to minimize confusion that may result from the variety of inventory valuation alternatives available for use in business.

26. (a) Enumerate several arguments that support the current replacement cost principle as applied to inventories. (b) Identify several arguments which favor retention of the historical cost principle.

EXERCISES

1. Inventory-related accounts. The inventory account of Batswarb Corp. contained a $32,000 debit balance at January 1, 1979. Each of the other three inventory-related accounts (Purchases, Freight In, and Purchases Returns and Allowances) reflected a zero balance at the same date. Total purchases during the fiscal year ended December 31, 1979, amounted to $816,000, including $14,100 freight in charges. Of these purchases, various vendors granted Batswarb Corp. allowances totaling $800. A physical inventory taken on December 31, 1979 revealed that the ending inventory was $17,000 higher than at the beginning of the year.

Required: (a) Determine the cost of goods sold for Batswarb Corp. during the 1979 fiscal year. (b) Prepare the entry at December 31, 1979, to recognize cost of goods sold and to zero out each of the three temporary inventory-related accounts.

2. **Recording inventory purchases at gross or net cost.** Cressans Corp. purchased $200,000 (gross cost) of merchandise for its inventory on October 1 under credit terms of 2/10, net 40.

Required: (a) Prepare an entry to record the purchase of this merchandise using: the gross cost method; and the net cost method. (b) Record the payment of this invoice on October 10 using: the gross cost method, where the discount is recognized as income; and the net cost method. (c) Ignoring (b), record the payment of this invoice on October 31, using: the gross cost method; and the net cost method.

3. **Implicit interest in credit terms.** Refer to Exercise 2 above. Determine the effective interest rate compounded annually that is contained in those credit terms. Round answer to one decimal place.

4. **Perpetual accounting system.** Alumina, Inc., purchased aluminum recreational chairs from various manufacturers for subsequent resale to retail merchandisers. Selected information extracted from the stock record card for this product is displayed below:

	PURCHASES			SOLD	BALANCE	
	(1)	*(2)*	*(3)*	*(4)*	*(5)*	*(6)*
		Cost per	*Total*			*Total*
	Units	*Unit*	*Cost*	*Units*	*Units*	*Cost*
1979						
January 1					1,000	$15,000
January	3,000	$15.60	$46,800			
February				800		
March				1,400		
June	1,500	16.00	24,000			
August				1,300		
September				1,100		
October	1,000	17.00	17,000			
November	500	17.50	8,750			
December				1,400		

The company uses the perpetual accounting system and fifo inventory costing. The purchase cost per unit includes freight charges; and no purchases returns or allowances occurred during 1979 with respect to this type of chair.

Required: Using a format similar to that shown on page 280: (a) Determine the cost of the chairs sold during 1979. (b) Determine the number of chairs and their dollar value that should theoretically be in ending inventory at December 31, 1979.

5. **Periodic accounting system.** Constructo Corp. purchased window air conditioners from various wholesalers for subsequent resale to residential and commercial customers. Information with respect to the Model 64P air conditioner is displayed on page 306.

The company uses the periodic accounting system and fifo inventory costing. The purchase cost per unit includes freight charges; and no purchases returns or allowances occurred during 1979 with respect to this particular air conditioner model. The physical inventory taken at December 31 revealed 56 Model 64P air conditioners on hand.

	PURCHASES		
	(1)	(2)	(3)
	Units	Cost per Unit	Total Cost
1979			
Balance at January 1	40	$150	$ 6,000
January	60	$155	$ 9,300
March	70	155	10,850
April	90	160	14,400
May	120	165	19,800
June	130	170	22,100
July	110	175	19,250
August	80	180	14,400
November	30	185	5,550

Required: Using a format similar to that shown on page 280: (a) Determine the ending inventory dollar-balance at December 31, 1979. (b) Determine the cost of goods sold (units and dollars) for 1979.

6. **Gross margin technique.** The inventory of the Modernairre Shoppe contained 400 assorted dresses at March 31, 1979. These dresses were purchased at a unit cost of $12. An additional 300 of similar type dresses were purchased during the second quarter of 1979 at the same unit cost. The usual midyear physical count of inventory could not be made on June 30, due to a heavy work load. The manager of the store nevertheless requested the accountant to furnish a report of gross margin on sales for the second quarter of 1979, in addition to the inventory balance that should be available at June 30. The periodic inventory system is used in the store. A review of the sale slips for the period April 1 through June 30, 1979, revealed that sales totaled $9,750. The accountant was informed that the normal gross margin on sales realized by the shop was 30%.

Required: (a) Estimate the cost of goods sold for the second quarter of 1979. (b) Based on the calculation in (a), determine the approximate number and total cost of dresses that should be in inventory at June 30, 1979.

7. **Fifo inventory cost.** Balboa Corp. began operations with no inventory on January 1, 1979, and its first fiscal year ended December 31. Purchases and sales of inventory during that first fiscal year are shown below. The company uses the periodic accounting system.

	PURCHASES				SALES	
	Units	Cost per Unit	Total Cost			Units
January	20,000	$1.00	$ 20,000	February		15,000
February	40,000	1.10	44,000	March		30,000
April	10,000	1.20	12,000	June		50,000
May	40,000	1.15	46,000	July		10,000
August	50,000	1.10	55,000	September		25,000
October	50,000	1.15	57,500	December		50,000
November	20,000	1.25	25,000			
Total	230,000		$259,500			180,000

Required: Assuming fifo inventory costing was used, determine the: (a) Inventory balance that should exist at December 31, 1979 (units and dollars). (b) Cost of goods sold during the first fiscal year.

8. **Lifo inventory costing.** Refer to the preliminary information and the data displayed in Exercise 7.

Required: Assuming lifo inventory costing was used, determine the: (a) Inventory balance that should exist at December 31, 1979 (units and dollars). (b) Cost of goods sold during the first fiscal year.

9. **Weighted average costing.** Refer to the preliminary information and the data displayed in Exercise 7.

Required: Assuming weighted average costing was used, determine the: (a) Inventory balance that should exist at December 31, 1979 (units and dollars). (b) Cost of goods sold during the first fiscal year.

10. **Inventory costing alternatives during deflation.** The cost of a company's inventory purchases consistently decreased during a particular period. Assuming the number of items in inventory at the beginning and the end of that period were equal, select the correct statement(s) from those shown below:

(a) Fifo inventory costing would result in a higher cost of goods sold than would lifo.

(b) Lifo inventory costing would result in a lower gross margin than would fifo.

(c) Weighted average inventory costing would result in a higher gross margin than would fifo, but a lower gross margin than would lifo.

(d) Specific identification inventory costing could not result in an income tax liability any greater than under lifo, fifo, or weighted average inventory costing.

(e) Lifo inventory costing would result in a lower year-end inventory balance than would fifo.

(f) Weighted average inventory costing would result in a higher year-end inventory balance than would lifo, but a lower year-end balance than would fifo.

(g) Lifo inventory costing would result in a higher income tax liability compared to fifo or weighted average costing. *LIFO~tax deflation*

(h) Weighted average inventory costing would result in a higher year-end inventory balance than would fifo, but a lower year-end balance than would lifo.

11. **Valuation alternatives.** The total cost of 110,000 yards of nylon carpeting available for sale during the fiscal year ended December 31, 1979, in Carpeteria, Inc., amounted to $824,000. The cost of goods sold during the year, as determined under each of three inventory costing alternatives, is shown below:

Fifo	$718,000
Weighted average	747,500
Lifo	794,000

The current market price at which the firm could replace its 8,000 yards of carpeting in ending inventory at December 31, 1979, was $8.25 per yard.

Required: (a) Determine the value of the ending inventory at December 31, 1979, under each of the three inventory costing alternatives, using the cost valuation basis. (b) Determine the value of the ending inventory at

December 31, 1979 under each of the three inventory costing alternatives, using the lower of cost or market valuation basis. (c) Prepare any necessary adjusting entry at the end of 1979 to revalue the inventory balance from cost to the lower of cost or market under each of the three inventory costing alternatives. Assume the balance in the inventory-revaluation account immediately prior to the adjusting entry was zero.

12. **Inventory costing for income tax purposes.** A coffee merchant furnished the following data with respect to five grades of coffee in inventory at the end of a particular fiscal period:

GRADE OF COFFEE	AT COST (FIFO BASIS)	AT MARKET (AS OF THE END OF THE PERIOD)
Standard	$ 40,000	$ 44,000
Good	75,000	63,000
Better	112,000	116,000
Excellent	150,000	141,000
Superb	96,000	98,000
Total	$473,000	$462,000

Required: (a) Determine the value of the ending inventory for tax purposes, using the lower of cost or market basis. (b) Based on the information derived in part (a), prepare an entry that is required at the end of this period to revalue the coffee inventory from cost to the lower of cost or market. Assume the credit balance in the inventory-revaluation account immediately prior to this adjusting entry was $12,000.

PROBLEMS

8-1. **Inventory-related accounts.** The balances at January 1, 1979, in the four inventory-related accounts maintained by Dranby-of-Cleveland Corp. are shown below:

Merchandise Inventory.................... $85,200
Purchases.. —0—
Freight in .... —0—
Purchases Returns and Allowances...... —0—

The following transactions occurred during the fiscal year ending December 31, 1979, which affected inventoriable items:

(a) Purchases of inventory on 30–40 day credit terms amounted to $827,000, excluding transportation charges.
(b) Freight and trucking charges associated with purchases totaled $6,400.
(c) Purchases totaling $4,700 that were included in item (a) were returned to various vendors due to damage or erroneous shipment. Each vendor allowed full credit on merchandise that was returned.
(d) Goods totaling $16,900, which were received on consignment from three firms during November, remained unsold as of the end of 1979.
(e) The physical inventory taken on December 31, 1979 revealed that the merchandise actually on hand and to which the firm possessed title totaled $64,000.

(f) Two shipments were in transit to Dranby-of-Cleveland Corp. as of December 31, 1979: (1) goods totaling $26,300 that were purchased from a Denver firm under terms FOB Denver; and (2) goods totaling $19,800 that were purchased from a Chicago company under terms FOB Cleveland. Neither shipment had arrived at Cleveland as of December 31, 1979.

Required: (1) Prepare T accounts for each of the four inventory-related accounts. Post the beginning balance to each account.

(2) Enter each of the transactions, as required, in the appropriate inventory-related accounts. T accounts need not be prepared for other than the four inventory-related accounts.

(3) Determine the ending balance in each account prior to any adjustment entry that may be required by item (5) below.

(4) Determine the cost of goods sold for 1979.

(5) Prepare an adjusting entry at December 31, 1979, to recognize the cost of goods sold during the year and to close out whatever balances are reflected in the three inventory-related accounts other than Merchandise Inventory. Do not post this entry to the T accounts.

8-2. **Alternative methods of recording inventory purchases.** During the monthly meeting of division managers, the purchasing manager of Fabricators Corp. described the advantages of recording inventory purchases by the gross cost method, emphasizing the option under which income is recognized when accounts payable are paid within the discount period. The manager's presentation sharply denounced the accounting department's practice of recording purchases at net cost.

"Virtually all invoices from vendors are stated at gross, with discount and payment terms usually shown in smaller print elsewhere on the invoice. Recording at gross is far simpler and will result in fewer clerical errors when calculating purchase discounts. We purchase approximately $130 million gross cost of merchandise each year, on which we usually take advantage of at least 98% of the customary 3/20, net 40 credit terms that are offered.

"If purchases are recorded at gross cost, the company's federal income tax will be lower, because cost of goods sold will be stated at a higher amount. Should we ever enter a period when it might be desirable to reflect a lower cost of goods sold amount on the income statement, we can easily switch to the net cost method. In addition, the gross cost method informs our stockholders of the efficiency and regularity with which management takes purchase discounts by reflecting those discounts taken on the income statement.

"Finally, my department should be given more recognition than it currently receives with respect to the efficiency with which we handle the large dollar amount of purchases made by this corporation. The gross cost method will make stockholders and top management more aware of our significant contribution to this firm."

Required: (1) Prepare summary entries to record the annual credit purchases totaling $130 million mentioned above by: the net cost method; and the gross cost method. Determine the effective interest rate compounded annually (carried to one decimal place) contained in the terms mentioned.

(2) Prepare a summary entry under each method discussed by the purchasing manager to reflect payment of the liabilities, assuming 98% of the purchases discounts are taken.

(3) Using data from (1) and (2), determine the monetary amounts that would be reflected as cost of goods sold, purchases discounts taken, and purchases discounts lost on the income statement under each of the two methods of recording purchases. Assume that all inventory purchases were charged to expense as cost of goods sold during the year. In short, determine the net impact on taxable income of recording purchases by each of the two methods.

(4) Assess the validity of each argument presented by the purchasing manager.

8-3. Determining an insurance claim by the gross margin technique. The entire stock of refrigerators that were stored in the 15th Street warehouse of Thompson Wholesale Co. was completely demolished by a tornado during the twilight hours of July 15, 1979. Fortunately, all invoices for the appliances that were received during 1979; a summary of each day's sales by major category of merchandise; and all financial statements of the company for each fiscal year (ending December 31) were available in the company vault located in the administration building.

Following the disaster, the general manager was able to piece together the information shown below in order to establish a claim with the local insurance adjuster.

REFRIGERATOR TYPE	UNITS IN INVENTORY AT DECEMBER 31, 1978	UNITS PURCHASED AND RECEIVED FROM JANUARY 1 THROUGH JULY 6, 1979
Double-door	46	38
15.8 cubic foot	34	41
Economy	87	114
Total	167	193

The receiving clerk recalled that no refrigerators had been delivered to the warehouse, nor had any invoices been received during the 10-day period preceding the tornado.

The general manager was able to determine from invoices that the prices charged by various manufacturers for the following refrigerator models remained quite uniform during the past 12 months, as shown below:

Double-door	$217
15.8 cubic foot	182
Economy	163

All refrigerators were sold to retailers, on which the Thompson Wholesale Co. realized a 30% gross margin. The total refrigerator sales for the first 6½ months of 1979 were $68,130, divided as follows:

Double-door	$22,010
15.8 cubic foot	13,520
Economy	32,600

Required: Determine the amount of insurance claim (dollars and units) that the manager should file with the insurance adjuster for the loss of refrigerators.

8-4. Inventory analysis from limited information.   sells
only #2 grade fuel oil to residential and commercial customers for heat-
ing requirements. The inventory at December 31, 1978, reflected a balance of 140,000 gallons and $63,000. One year later, the inventory was
reduced to 130,000 gallons and $58,500. The total cost of oil that was
charged to expense during the fiscal year ended December 31, 1979, was
$385,680, which included 800,000 gallons sold and 3,500 gallons lost from
tank leakage. The market price per gallon at which Swann Petrol Co.
could purchase #2 grade fuel oil at December 31, 1979 was 52 cents per
gallon.

Required: (1) Determine the number of gallons of #2 grade fuel oil that
the company purchased during 1979, and the total cost of those
purchases.
(2) The average price at which the company purchased #2 fuel oil
during 1979 appears to have: decreased, increased, or remained
unchanged compared to the cost per gallon in inventory at December 31, 1978. Select the best answer and give reasons for that
selection.
(3) What inventory costing alternative was probably used by Swann
Petrol Co. during 1979?

8-5. **Inventory costing alternatives with tax implications.** The cost of
purchases for inventory steadily increased during Bannon Corp's. first
year of operations ended December 31, 1979. The schedule of bathroom
plumbing fixtures purchased during the year reflects the following information:

DATE	UNITS	COST PER UNIT	TOTAL PURCHASE COST
January	500	$40	$ 20,000
February	300	43	12,900
April	700	45	31,500
June	200	50	10,000
July	400	50	20,000
September	300	57	17,100
November	600	60	36,000
December	200	62	12,400
Total	3,200		$159,900

The inventory of these fixtures at December 31, 1979, totaled 400 units.
The other 2,800 fixtures were sold at $70 per unit during the year. The
firm uses the periodic accounting system.

Required: (1) Determine the inventory balances at December 31, 1979,
and the cost of goods sold for 1979 assuming the use of:
(a) Fifo inventory costing.
(b) Weighted average inventory costing. (Carry the weighted
average per unit cost to five decimal places, but round total
amounts to the nearest dollar.)
(c) Lifo inventory costing.
(2) Annual property tax assessments are levied by the county on the
year end inventory balance. The tax rate is 3% of that inventory
balance. Determine the 1979 property tax expense that would be
incurred by Bannon Corp. under each of the three inventory costing alternatives noted in (1).

(3) Prepare abbreviated comparative income statements for the firm's first fiscal year for each of the three costing alternatives. Assume the federal income tax rate is 50% on income before federal income tax. Ignore all expense items not included in the preceding information; and assume that the property tax expense is deductible from revenue in computing federal income tax.

8-6. Inventory costing alternatives, with dividend payment implications. Fabric Centers, Inc., began its ninth fiscal year on July 1, 1979, under new management with zero inventory. A new owner-management group had gained control of the firm late in June, 1979. Its first positive action was to liquidate the entire stock of existent inventory at the seven mideastern stores through an immediate "close-out/renewal" sale. The intent was to stock and sell a new line of high-quality retail yard goods as of July 1, 1979.

Inventory record cards maintained for each of the two lines of fabrics sold at the seven retail outlets reflected the following information with respect to purchases for the fiscal year ended June 30, 1980:

PURCHASES
(RUNNING YARDS AT $ PER RUNNING YARD)

Date	Wool	Nylon
1979		
July	6,000 @ $4.50	6,000 @ $2.00
August	8,000 @ 4.50	10,000 @ 2.10
September	7,000 @ 4.75	18,000 @ 2.20
October	12,000 @ 4.75	22,000 @ 2.30
November	16,000 @ 5.00	14,000 @ 2.40
December	8,000 @ 5.00	15,000 @ 2.60
1980		
January	9,000 @ 5.25	17,000 @ 2.80
February	12,000 @ 5.25	25,000 @ 2.90
March	6,000 @ 5.50	20,000 @ 3.00
April	18,000 @ 5.50	16,000 @ 3.10
May	15,000 @ 5.75	14,000 @ 3.30
June	14,000 @ 6.00	7,000 @ 3.40
Total	131,000 $685,750	184,000 $495,500

Each buyer of raw materials within the organization anticipates that the purchase cost of each fabric will continue to rise steadily during the next three or four years. Management still had the option at June 30, 1980, to select any type of inventory costing alternative for financial reporting and income tax purposes. The choices were narrowed down to fifo, weighted average, and lifo.

Revenue generated during the fiscal year ended June 30, 1980, at the seven stores is shown below:

	RUNNING YARDS SOLD	AVERAGE RETAIL PRICE PER RUNNING YARD
Wool	114,000	$8.00
Nylon	172,000	3.25

Total expenses (excluding cost of goods sold and federal income tax expense at 50% of income before income tax) for the entire fiscal year amounted to $200,000. At June 30, 1980, the total number of issued and outstanding shares of capital stock was 4,000.

Required: (1) Determine the inventory balance at June 30, 1980, and the cost of goods sold for the fiscal year ending June 30, 1980, by each of the three alternatives. (Carry the weighted average purchase cost per yard to four decimal places, but round total amounts to the nearest dollar.)

(2) Prepare a comparative income statement for the fiscal year ended June 30, 1980, for each alternative being considered.

(3) Which costing alternative should management select at the end of June, 1980? Explain why.

(4) Assuming that sufficient cash exists at June 30, 1980, with which to pay a $30 per share cash dividend, determine whether the directors should declare a $10, $20, or $30 per share dividend. Relate this suggestion to the recommendation in item (3).

8-7. **Inventory valuation alternatives.** The controller of Instanta Corp. was gathering information concerning inventory matters in order to explain the significance of various inventory costing and valuation alternatives to the board of directors at its next quarterly meeting. The assistant controller supplied the following information with respect to the ending inventory balance under three inventory costing alternatives:

	INVENTORY BALANCE AT DECEMBER 31, 1979	INVENTORY BALANCE AT DECEMBER 31, 1980
Fifo	$216,000	$253,000
Weighted average	198,000	227,000
Lifo	156,000	181,000

The total value of units in the ending inventory at prevailing market prices at December 31, 1979, and 1980, were $194,000 and $236,000, respectively. The inventory-revaluation account had never been used in Instanta Corp. up to December 31, 1979.

Required: (1) Assuming fifo inventory costing was adopted during this 2-year period, prepare any necessary journal entries to:
(a) Value the ending inventory at cost on: December 31, 1979; and December 31, 1980.
(b) Value the ending inventory at the lower of cost or market on: December 31, 1979; and December 31, 1980.

(2) Assuming weighted average costing was adopted during this 2-year period, prepare any necessary journal entries to:
(a) Value the ending inventory at cost on: December 31, 1979; and December 31, 1980.
(b) Value the ending inventory at the lower of cost or market on: December 31, 1979; and December 31, 1980.

(3) Assuming lifo costing was adopted during this 2-year period, prepare any necessary journal entries to:
(a) Value the ending inventory at cost on: December 31, 1979; and December 31, 1980.
(b) Value the ending inventory at the lower of cost or market on: December 31, 1979; and December 31, 1980.

(4) Explain what impact, if any, the recognition of unrealized holding losses or gains on inventory under the lower of cost or market valuation alternative would have on taxable income.

8-8. Inventory costing and valuation alternatives: comprehensive. Rug Wholesalers, Inc., makes quarterly purchases of two types of high quality wool rug stock to take advantage of the quantity discounts frequently offered by manufacturers on large orders. Its inventory of carpeting stock at December 31, 1978, the end of the fiscal year, was composed of the following amounts:

TYPE MATERIAL	SQUARE YARDS	PURCHASE COST PER SQUARE YARD	TOTAL COST
Exotic	7,000	$12	$ 84,000
Standard	12,000	10	120,000
Total	19,000		$204,000

Purchases from manufacturers during the 2-year period, January 1, 1979, through December 31, 1980, are displayed below:

	EXOTIC			STANDARD		
Date	Square Yards Purchased	Cost per Square Yard	Total Purchase Cost	Square Yards Purchased	Cost per Square Yard	Total Purchase Cost
1979						
January	10,000	$12.10	$121,000	15,000	$10.10	$151,500
April	8,000	12.20	97,600	12,000	10.20	122,400
July	13,000	12.20	158,600	16,000	10.10	161,600
October	8,000	12.30	98,400	14,000	9.90	138,600
Total	39,000		$475,600	57,000		$574,100
1980						
February	13,000	$12.30	$159,900	13,000	$10.00	$130,000
May	12,000	12.40	148,800	14,000	10.10	141,400
August	9,000	12.20	109,800	12,000	10.20	122,400
November	14,000	12.10	169,400	16,000	10.30	164,800
Total	48,000		$587,900	55,000		$558,600

The total square yards sold and the selling price per square yard to retailers during the 2-year period are shown below:

	TOTAL SQUARE YARDS SOLD		PRICE PER SQUARE YARD	
	Exotic	Standard	Exotic	Standard
1979	35,000	54,000	$14.40	$12.00
1980	53,000	60,000	14.20	12.20

Required: (1) Determine the inventory balance at each fiscal year-end, and the cost of goods sold during each fiscal year, assuming the fifo inventory costing alternative was used by Rug Wholesalers, Inc., in both years.

(2) Determine the same items as in (1), assuming the lifo method was used by the firm in both years.

(3) Determine the same items as in (1), assuming the weighted average method was used in both years. Carry weighted average cost per unit calculations to four decimal places, but round total amounts to the nearest dollar.

(4) Prepare abbreviated comparative income statements to reflect the gross margin for each of the two years ended December 31, under each of the three inventory costing alternatives.

(5) Determine the amount, if any, by which each of the ending inventory balances determined previously under each costing alternative would require adjustment at the end of each year to the lower of cost or market valuation basis. Base calculations on the income tax refinements discussed on pages 299–300. "Market" is defined in this instance as the last cost at which Rug Wholesalers, Inc., purchased rug stock during each year. The balance in the inventory revaluation account was zero at December 31, 1978.

(6) Prepare any necessary adjusting entries at the end of each fiscal year under each of the three alternatives to reflect ending inventory at the lower of cost or market.

DECISION CASES

8-I. Taking advantage of discount terms. Eezunit Corp. purchased merchandise costing $500,000 at gross invoice price on July 1. Terms of purchases were 4/15, net 30. The company maintained an open line of credit with a local bank that enabled the firm to borrow up to $1½ million at 10% annual interest. Only $300,000 had been borrowed against this credit line as of mid-July.

Required:
(1) Prepare entries to record the payment for the merchandise on July 16 by: the net cost method; and the gross cost method whereby income is recognized when accounts payable are paid within the discount period.
(2) Determine the effective annual interest rate contained in the terms of purchase.
(3) Assume that the firm's cash balance was inadequate at July 16 to take advantage of the discount terms offered. What financial arrangement is available to management whereby the cash discount can still be taken? Would you recommend that management use this arrangement if the cash balance available to the firm on July 31 was forecast to be sufficient to pay the full gross invoice price of $500,000? Support your recommendation with appropriate calculations.

8-II. Estimation of theft by gross margin technique. The president of Pacific Wholesalers suspected thievery of several items of merchandise by employees, particularly items that were easily disassembled or sufficiently small to conceal in clothing. Suspicions were aroused during April when complaints were received from several retailers who claimed that shortages were frequently found when orders of transistor radios and pocket calculators were inspected upon receipt. The president was aware that an investigation would be hampered because the periodic system of accounting was used within the company. Fifo costing was also used by the firm.

The assistant controller was asked to supply whatever information might prove helpful to pinpoint the extent of any problem that might have developed since the end of the previous fiscal year on December 31. The following report was submitted on April 14:

	TRANSISTOR RADIOS	POCKET CALCULATORS
Units in inventory on December 31 per physical count...............................	19,600	7,600
Cost per unit.....................................	$8.40	$29.25
Units purchased since January 1:		
January..	4,200	1,400
February.......................................	3,600	3,100
March..	5,100	2,700
April (to April 13)............................	2,700	1,800
Total...	15,600	9,000
Average cost per unit of purchases since January 1....................................	$8.40	$30.00
Average gross margin realized on merchandise billed to retailers	30%	25%
Sales recorded from January 1 through April 13...	$343,200	$496,400
Units physically counted in warehouse on April 13	5,100	3,500

Required:

(1) Determine the units of each type of merchandise that are unaccounted for on April 14.

(2) Establish the monetary extent of the apparent loss in terms of gross margin.

(3) Assuming that the apparent loss realized during the first 3½ months is representative of the loss that might be realized on these two items during an entire year, would you recommend that: (a) an additional inventory clerk be hired at an annual salary of $7,200 to maintain perpetual inventory records for these items of merchandise; and (b) a quarterly physical inventory count of these items be implemented at an additional cost of $400 per quarterly count? Show supporting calculations.

8-III. **Impact of deflation on financial statements.** Consolidated Industries, Inc., created a new coal division on January 1, 1979, to purchase various grades of coal from mining companies. After cleaning and processing, the firm expects to sell the coal to steel manufacturers in several middle-Atlantic states. No coal was in the division's inventory at the beginning of its fiscal year of operations on January 1, 1979. Purchases of two grades of coal during the subsequent 2-year period ending December 31, 1980 are shown at the top of the following page.

At December 31, 1979, management anticipated that the purchase cost per ton of each grade would probably stabilize near the price paid during the final quarter of 1979. At that time, management had to make a decision whether to adopt the lifo or fifo inventory costing alternative. The decision was important, since the alternative to be selected must be used consistently, and permission to change would have to be obtained from various corporate and government officials.

	GRADE A			GRADE B		
Date	*Tons*	*Cost per Ton*	*Total Cost*	*Tons*	*Cost per Ton*	*Total Cost*
1979						
January–March...........	2,400	$22	$ 52,800	3,800	$28	$106,400
April–June.................	4,600	21	96,600	6,400	29	185,600
July–September..........	5,800	18	104,400	4,700	27	126,900
October–December	1,700	17	28,900	2,300	25	57,500
Total 1979............	14,500		$282,700	17,200		$476,400
1980						
January–March...........	4,800	$16	$ 76,800	3,500	$24	$ 84,000
April–June.................	5,100	15	76,500	9,200	26	239,200
July–September..........	7,600	17	129,200	5,800	23	133,400
October–December	3,900	14	54,600	6,400	21	134,400
Total 1980............	21,400		$337,100	24,900		$591,000

Total sales during the division's first two fiscal years were as follows:

Fiscal year ended December 31	GRADE A		GRADE B	
	Tons	*Dollars*	*Tons*	*Dollars*
1979..........	12,500	$312,500	14,700	$525,500
1980..........	19,400	397,700	23,000	708,400

Required:
(1) Determine the cost of goods sold in each of the two fiscal years, and the inventory balance at December 31 of each year, under each alternative being considered.

(2) Prepare abbreviated comparative income statements for each of the two years under each costing alternative.

(3) Based on only the analysis of the first fiscal year of operations and management's forecast of stabilized prices for the future as of December 31, 1979, indicate which costing alternative should be adopted at December 31, 1979. Explain why.

8-IV. Inventory replenishment policy under lifo costing. The controller of Globe Corp. was debating on December 28, 1979, whether the merchandise inventory should be replenished before or after the close of the current fiscal year ending December 31, 1979. Globe Corp. had adopted lifo inventory costing in 1957 and had used it consistently since that time. Prior to 1979, the firm's inventory of each of its two types of merchandise had never fallen below the balance reflected in inventory at December 31, 1978, as shown below:

Item A: 200 units × $40 per unit (the prevailing cost in 1957)..... $ 8,000
Item B: 150 units × $120 per unit (the prevailing cost in 1961).... 18,000

Inventory balance at December 31, 1978 .... $26,000

Purchases of both items during fiscal year 1979 were:

Item A: 3,100 units at an average cost of $84 per unit.
Item B: 2,500 units at an average cost of $274 per unit.

All 1979 purchases of these two items had been sold as of December 28, 1979. The inventory balance at the close of business on December 28, 1979, was $26,000, composed of the items shown at December 31, 1978.

The firm's marketing vice-president held sufficient back orders to ensure that both types of merchandise could be easily sold by December 31, 1979. Total 1979 sales, including the "sure sales" for the final three days of 1979, amounted to $1,780,000. Cost of goods sold for 1979, excluding the two items A and B for the final three days, amounted to $1,300,000. Projected total other expenses, except federal income tax at 50%, for the entire fiscal year were $350,000.

The controller was most concerned about the replenishment problem of these two items, because the purchase cost per unit at December 28, 1979, of items A and B were $86 and $275, respectively. It was believed that the cost would rise to $88 and $279, respectively, during the first ten days of January, 1980.

Required: Provide a detailed analysis to assist the controller in reaching a decision on whether to replenish the inventory with 200 units of item A and 150 units of item B before or after the end of fiscal year 1979. For purposes of this analysis, assume that federal income taxes incurred on 1979 taxable income must be paid by January 10, 1980; and that terms of purchase for items A and B are cash-on-delivery. What appears to be the key consideration that emerges from the analysis? What decision do you recommend that the controller make?

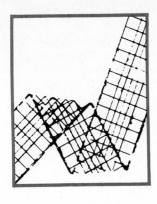

9
Plant Assets, Natural Resources, and Intangibles

Although depreciation is usually figured by some apparently exact formula, every accountant knows that the estimates are really very rough, being subject to large and unpredictable errors and involving arbitrary corrections and assumptions.

Paul A. Samuelson
Economics, 10th Edition

Plant assets, natural resources, and intangibles are assets with relatively long useful lives, and are consumed over an extended period while providing benefits for the purpose of generating revenue. The normal method by which the capitalized costs are charged to expense is shown at the top of page 320.

PLANT ASSETS

Plant assets can be classified into real property or personal property. Real property, such as land has physical substance; the same is true with personal property, such as furniture, equipment, and machinery. Because of this physical substance, they are considered *tangible assets*.

ASSET	NORMAL METHOD OF CHARGING TO EXPENSE
Plant Assets	
Land (often shown separate from plant assets)..	Rarely charged to expense
Buildings Equipment and machinery Furniture and fixtures	Depreciation
Natural Resources	
Minerals, oil, gas, timber, and other wasting assets	Depletion
Intangibles	
Patents and copyrights Franchises and licenses Organizational costs Goodwill	Amortization
Research and development costs	Charged to expense

Acquisition

The *capitalized cost* of a plant asset is the expenditure, either in cash or incurred liability, that was made to obtain the asset and enable it to render future benefits. The following items are usually included as the capitalized cost of the asset:

(1) The purchase price, net of any cash discounts.
(2) Transportation and installation expenditures.
(3) Expenditures for tools that will be used primarily with the asset, such as special jigs and fixtures.
(4) Expenditures for trial runs and employee training costs that are incurred to the point when normal operations begin.
(5) Storage costs, property taxes, insurance premiums, and interest charges on any debt that is incurred to the point when normal operations begin.

In addition, expenditures for improvements, rehabilitation, or replacement of parts which either: (1) increase the asset's productivity or capacity; (2) extend the asset's life; or (3) decrease operating costs of the asset beyond original expectations, are normally capitalized as part of the asset's depreciable cost.

Illustration of a Purchase. A unit of equipment was acquired from a dealer at a cost of $30,000 with a discount of 2 percent if payment is made within 30 days. The cost to ship the equipment to the purchaser's plant was $1,500. Additional costs of $900 were incurred to install the equipment, and the cost of a trial run before it was used for operations amounted to $200. The cost of this equipment is computed at the top of page 321.

Invoice cost		$30,000
Less cash discount (2% of $30,000)		600
		$29,400
Add: Shipping cost	$1,500	
Installation cost	900	
Trial run	200	2,600
Cost of equipment		$32,000

The cash discount should be deducted even though payment may be made after 30 days. Any discount lost is a cost of financial mismanagement and is not a proper cost of the asset.

Journal entries to record the acquisition and installation of the equipment are given below:

Equipment	29,400	
Cash		29,400
Payment to dealer for equipment.		

Equipment	2,600	
Cash		2,600
Payment of freight, installation, and trial run costs.		

Several Assets Acquired as a Unit. Sometimes several assets are purchased as a unit, rather than individually. In this case, a problem arises as to how the total purchase price should be allocated among the individual assets.

To illustrate, on May 1, 1980, Weston Corporation purchased for $1,000,000 a group of plant assets, an appraisal of which reveals the following:

	MARKET VALUE AT MAY 1, 1980	PERCENTAGE OF TOTAL MARKET VALUE
Land	$ 225,000	15%
Building No. 1	750,000	50
Building No. 2	75,000	5
Equipment	450,000	30
Total	$1,500,000	100%

An acceptable basis by which to allocate the total purchase cost of $1,000,000 is the percentage that each asset bears to the total appraised market value, as follows:

	PERCENTAGE OF TOTAL MARKET VALUE	COST APPORTIONMENT % × $1,000,000
Land	15%	$ 150,000
Building No. 1	50	500,000
Building No. 2	5	50,000
Equipment	30	300,000
Total	100%	$1,000,000

Management contracted to have Building No. 2 removed because it could not be used for management's purpose. The cost to demolish Building No. 2, less any salvage received, amounted to $11,000. As land was the desired asset, its cost is therefore adjusted to $211,000 computed as follows:

Land...	$150,000
Building No. 2	50,000
Cost of demolition	11,000
	$211,000

Apparently, in making the purchase, management considered the land to be worth enough to justify the removal of Building No. 2.

The entry to record the assets under the assumption that the purchase and demolition costs were paid in cash is given below:

Land	211,000	
Building...	500,000	
Equipment	300,000	
Cash		1,011,000
Allocation of $1,011,000 expenditure among various plant assets.		

Maintenance and Repairs

After buildings and equipment are placed in operation, costs are incurred to keep the assets in good working conditions.

Maintenance costs such as cleaning, lubricating, and painting are regular recurring costs to keep the assets in efficient operation. Some companies follow a policy of preventive maintenance to reduce the inconvenience and cost of breakdowns. The costs of maintenance normally are charged to expense when incurred.

Repair costs that keep recurring and are relatively small in amount and do not extend the life of the asset are called *ordinary repairs*. For example, ordinary repairs of an automobile would consist of the replacement of spark plugs, a fan belt, or other minor parts needed to keep the car in good working condition. These minor repair costs, although incurred at irregular intervals over the life of the asset, are generally charged to expense.

Depreciation

Eventually a plant asset loses its ability to give useful service. The reasons for this are:

(1) Physical exhaustion and technological deterioration.
(2) Economic obsolescence.
(3) Inadequacy.

Most plant assets begin the process of *physical exhaustion* and *technological deterioration* the moment they are placed in operation. Despite careful and constant maintenance and repair programs, ordinary wear tends to gradually reduce the productivity of these assets during their useful life.

Economic obsolescence refers to the deterioration in plant assets caused by design and technical improvements in more recent models of machinery, buildings, and fixtures. For example, improvements contained in the latest model punch press may place a one-year old press that is in current use at a distinct competitive disadvantage, even though it may still be in good operating condition.

Inadequacy refers to deterioration caused by plant assets becoming unsuited to satisfy the current demands placed on them by the firm's present line of products, markets, or managerial decisions. For example, the Ford Tri-Motor airplane is capable of carrying passengers over long distances, but at considerably less speed and in less comfort than demanded by the current clientele of modern jet airliners.

The Depreciation Process. Each plant asset may deteriorate at a different rate for any of the above reasons. Accountants attempt to measure and record this deterioration by the process called *depreciation*. Inasmuch as the plant asset yields benefits over the years, it would be improper to charge its entire cost to the year of its acquisition or to any particular year. As benefits are derived from the use of the asset, a portion of its cost is charged each year to depreciation expense, with a corresponding credit to accumulated depreciation. The asset is reflected in the records at its original cost; and the accumulation of depreciation expense from past years and the current year is recorded in a separate account designated as Accumulated Depreciation. The capitalized cost of the plant asset minus the accumulated depreciation is referred to as the *book value* or the *undepreciated cost* of the asset.

The depreciation process is not a valuation process. The book value of an asset does not represent the current market or replacement value of the asset at any particular time. Moreover, the amount reflected in the accumulated depreciation account does not represent a recovery of the original cost of the asset, nor does it represent a cash fund with which to replace the asset at the end of its useful life. Recovery of the original cost is normally achieved only by successful operation of the business, that is, by selling sufficient goods and services to reimburse the company for previous expenditures for plant assets as well as for the capitalized cost of inventories and other expenses.

Depreciation expense is deductible from revenue and other income in determining income before federal and most state income taxes. Assume that a firm was entitled to record $30,000 depreciation expense in a specific year. If no depreciation expense was recorded in that year, the income tax expense and consequent cash outflow to government agencies would be larger than if depreciation expense had been recorded. The following comparative summary will help to clarify this point.

	DEPRECIATION EXPENSE NOT RECORDED		DEPRECIATION EXPENSE RECORDED
Income before depreciation and income tax expense............................	$100,000		$100,000
Less depreciation expense..................	—		30,000
Income before income tax expense....	$100,000		$ 70,000
Less income tax expense (estimated 50 percent)	50,000	$15,000 difference	35,000
Net income.....................................	$ 50,000		$ 35,000

Note that cash outflow to the federal and/or state government is $15,000 less when depreciation expense is recorded. In effect, the $30,000 of recorded depreciation expense provides the firm with a $15,000 tax saving, commonly referred to as a *tax shield*. Thus, recording the appropriate and legally allowed amount of depreciation expense preserves cash in the business that would otherwise flow to government agencies. To reiterate, the depreciation process does not provide a cash fund for the replacement of plant assets.

The Major Depreciation Methods. Depreciation expense reflects the cost of the benefit that was derived from the use of the asset during the year; however, this cannot be measured precisely. The three most common methods of depreciation used to attain a practical matching of cost against revenue are:

(1) Straight-line
(2) Units-of-production
(3) Accelerated depreciation
    (a) Sum-of-the-years-digits
    (b) Double-declining balance

Straight-Line. The straight-line method charges to expense the depreciable base of a plant asset's capitalized cost in equal amounts over its useful life. The *depreciable base* under the straight-line method is the capitalized cost of the asset less its estimated residual salvage value. For example, assume that Stevens Company acquired machinery on January 1, 1979, at a cost of $220,000, and that the machinery was estimated to have a useful life of 5 years with a residual salvage value of $20,000 at the end of 5 years. The depreciable base of $200,000 ($220,000 − $20,000) is divided by the asset's estimated useful life (5 years) to determine the depreciation expense in each year of that useful life.

$$\frac{\text{Depreciable base}}{\text{Useful life}} = \frac{\text{Capitalized cost} - \text{Residual salvage value}}{\text{Useful life}}$$

$$= \frac{\$220,000 - \$20,000}{5 \text{ years}}$$

$$= \$40,000 \text{ annual depreciation expense}$$

The entry to be recorded at the end of each fiscal year, 1979 through 1983, is as follows:

Depreciation Expense — Machinery	40,000	
Accumulated Depreciation — Machinery		40,000
Annual depreciation expense for machinery.		

If the asset is used beyond 5 years, no further depreciation expense may be recorded because the asset cannot be depreciated below its residual salvage value. At the end of 5 years, the asset's book value would be reflected at $20,000, ($220,000 capitalized cost less $200,000 accumulated depreciation). In the event the machinery is sold after 1983 for $15,000, the following entry would be recorded to recognize a $5,000 loss on the sale.

Cash	15,000	
Accumulated Depreciation — Machinery	200,000	
Loss on Disposal of Plant Assets	5,000	
Machinery..		220,000
Loss on sale of machinery. Book value at time of sale was $20,000.		

The straight-line method is simple, but not entirely realistic. A plant asset may not release its benefits at a uniform rate over the year. Also, the total annual expense associated with a specific plant asset tends to increase with the years. As a general rule, maintenance and repair expenses increase as the asset ages; and if an equal amount of depreciation is charged to each year, the total annual expense for use of the asset will increase. A better alternative is to have the total annual cost of depreciation, combined with repairs and maintenance costs, made more uniform over the years.

Units-of-Production. Under the units-of-production method of depreciation, the capitalized cost of the plant asset is expensed on the basis of the number of units produced by the asset. Thus, the service life of the asset is expressed in terms of production units rather than years. The Stevens Company machinery was estimated to contain a productive capability of 400,000 units of output during its life. The depreciable base is the same as under straight-line, and the depreciation rate is determined as follows:

$$\frac{\text{Depreciable base}}{\text{Total production units}} = \frac{\text{Capitalized cost} - \text{Residual salvage value}}{\text{Total production units}}$$

$$= \frac{\$220,000 - \$20,000}{400,000 \text{ units}}$$

$$= \$.50 \text{ per unit}$$

If 100,000 units are produced during its first year of operation, the depreciation expense for 1979 would be recorded as follows, (100,000 units × $.50 per unit = $50,000):

Depreciation Expense — Machinery........................	50,000	
Accumulated Depreciation — Machinery................		50,000
Depreciation expense for 100,000 units produced during the period.		

After the asset has produced 400,000 units, no further depreciation expense may be recorded because the asset cannot be depreciated below its residual salvage value.

This depreciation method presumes that the major cause or basis for the deterioration of an asset is its productive utilization; and in this respect, the units-of-production method may more adequately reflect the actual consumption of the asset's productive capacity than the straight-line method. However, the two remaining causes of deterioration, economic obsolescence and inadequacy, are apt to be ignored. Record keeping that is required for each plant asset under the units-of-production method tends to be very detailed and expensive; and for this reason, the method is less frequently used in business than the straight-line or the two methods subsequently described.

Accelerated Depreciation Methods. Sum-of-the-years-digits and double-declining balance are referred to as methods of accelerated depreciation because larger portions of the capitalized cost are expensed during the earlier years of life than under straight-line. In general, these two accelerated methods of depreciation may be used for tax purposes only on plant assets that: (1) have an expected life of at least 3 years; and, (2) were either purchased new by the current owners after 1953, or were built or rebuilt by or for the current owner after 1953.

Sum-of-the-Years-Digits. The annual depreciation charge under the *sum-of-the-years-digits* (SYD) method is determined by applying a changing fraction to the asset's depreciable base (capitalized cost less residual salvage value). The numerator of the fraction is the number of years remaining in the asset's useful life, and the denominator is the sum of the numbers that represent the total years of useful life. When applied to the Stevens Company illustration, the depreciation expense for each year is determined as follows:

	(1)	(2)	(3)
			DEPRECIATION EXPENSE RECORDED
	FRACTION OF DEPRECIABLE		
YEAR	BASE TO BE EXPENSED	DEPRECIABLE BASE	(1) × (2)
1	5/15	$200,000	$ 66,667
2	4/15	200,000	53,333
3	3/15	200,000	40,000
4	2/15	200,000	26,667
5	1/15	200,000	13,333
15	15/15		$200,000

Double-Declining Balance. The *double-declining balance* (DDB) method provides the most accelerated rate of depreciation of the methods currently available for income tax purposes. Although residual salvage value is not considered in determining the depreciable base, the asset may not be depreciated below its residual salvage value. The depreciation expense recorded under this method in the first year is twice the straight-line rate times the capitalized cost. Thereafter, twice the straight-line rate is applied to the undepreciated cost of the asset. Calculations to determine depreciation expense under DDB are shown below for the Stevens Company.

	(1)	(2)	(3)	(4)
			DEPRECIATION EXPENSE	
	TWICE THE	UNDEPRECIATED	RECORDED	CUMULATIVE
	STRAIGHT-LINE	COST AT	(ROUNDED TO	DEPRECIATION
	RATE	BEGINNING	NEAREST DOLLAR)	EXPENSE
YEAR	(2 × 20%)	OF YEAR	(1) × (2)	RECORDED
1	40%	$220,000	$ 88,000	$ 88,000
2	40	132,000	52,800	140,800
3	40	79,200	31,680	172,480
4	40	47,520	19,008	191,488
5	40	28,512	8,512*	200,000
			$200,000	

*Only $8,512 depreciation expense may be recorded in the fifth year since the asset may not be depreciated below its residual salvage value of $20,000. In the absence of this constraint, $11,405 ($28,512 × 40%) could have been charged to expense in 1983.

A company may not convert from straight-line to an accelerated method of depreciation if straight-line had been adopted for a specific asset or group of assets. It may, however, convert from DDB or SYD to straight-line at any time. If the conversion is made, subsequent straight-line depreciation expense must be prorated over the asset's remaining life on the basis of the asset's undepreciated cost at the time of conversion less the estimated residual salvage value. A major reason why a firm may wish to convert from DDB to straight-line is because plant assets that are estimated to have no residual salvage value will never become fully depreciated under DDB.

To illustrate, assume that Steven Company's machinery was estimated at the date of purchase, January 1, 1979, to have no residual salvage value. The depreciation schedule by DDB for the first 5 years is shown below in Column 2:

	(1)	(2)	(3)
			DEPRECIATION EXPENSE RECORDED BY DDB (YEARS
	UNDEPRECIATED COST AT	DEPRECIATION EXPENSE	1–3), AND BY STRAIGHT-
YEAR	BEGINNING OF YEAR BY DDB	RECORDED BY DDB	LINE (YEARS 4–5)
1	$220,000	$ 88,000	$ 88,000
2	132,000	52,800	52,800
3	79,200	31,680	31,680
4	47,520	19,008	23,760
5	28,512	11,405	23,760
		$202,893	$220,000

At the end of the fifth year, $17,107 of the asset's capitalized cost remains to be expensed under DDB ($220,000 capitalized cost − $202,893 accumulated depreciation). The company will find it advantageous for income tax purposes to convert to straight-line during the fourth year, 1982. Assuming at January 1, 1982, that the remaining useful life of the machinery is 2 years, and the estimated residual salvage value is zero, the undepreciated capitalized cost would be $47,520 as shown in column 1 above. Conversion to straight-line at January 1, 1982, will allocate that undepreciated capitalized cost in two equal amounts of $23,760 over the remaining years, 1982 and 1983, as shown in column 3.

Comparison of Depreciation Methods. In the examples given, the same total amount of depreciation was recorded over the years regardless of the method chosen. With no change in the income tax rate or changes in revenues and expenses other than depreciation, the income tax will also be the same for all depreciation methods.

The differences in the application of depreciation methods and income taxes are differences in *timing*. When accelerated methods of depreciation are used, depreciation expense is larger in the early years than when straight-line is used, resulting in lower income taxes. The company will then have a temporary use of cash which would otherwise have been paid for income taxes. True, in later years, the depreciation deduction under an accelerated method will be less than that under the straight-line method, and therefore, income taxes will be more, assuming maintenance expenses remain constant. The significant point is that the company had the advantage of using the cash resources in the early years and investing these cash resources to earn returns. This follows the principle previously discussed that present resources can earn more than resources to be received in the future. Present resources can be put to work now to earn a return, while future resources cannot earn a return until they become available.

A comparison of straight-line depreciation with the DDB method for the first year is given below under the assumption that the income tax rate is 50 percent and that income before depreciation and income tax is $400,000.

	STRAIGHT-LINE DEPRECIATION	DOUBLE-DECLINING BALANCE DEPRECIATION
Income before depreciation and income tax expense	$400,000	$400,000
Less depreciation expense	40,000	88,000
	$360,000	$312,000
Less income tax expense (50%)	180,000	156,000
Net income	$180,000	$156,000

Assume that the tax benefit from using the accelerated depreciation of $24,000 ($180,000 − $156,000) is invested to earn 15 percent compounded annually. At the end of the second year, the company would realize a permanent gain of $1,800 (15% of $24,000 invested × 50% tax rate). Although the tax saving is only temporary, inasmuch as higher taxes must be paid in later years, the return on the assets available is permanent.

The Accelerated Depreciation Controversy. Over the years, there has been considerable disagreement between the advocates of straight-line depreciation and the advocates of accelerated depreciation. It can be argued that accelerated depreciation is computed by formula and that the results do not necessarily measure the real deterioration in plant assets for any particular year. It can also be argued that straight-line depreciation does not measure the real deterioration for any one year. Depreciation by its very nature defies precise measurement.

The opponents of accelerated depreciation also believe that these methods are often adopted by companies solely as a means of obtaining tax savings, and not from any sincere belief that depreciation is being measured more accurately. On the other hand, it may be argued that a plant asset which delivers uniform services in production plus the additional benefit of tax savings in the early years of its life, is delivering more total service in its early years. Hence, this should be recognized by larger depreciation charges in the early years and by smaller charges in the later years.

Several additional arguments support the adoption of accelerated depreciation as shown below:

(1) Tax savings in earlier years conserve more net working capital (current assets less current liabilities).

(2) The permanent gains realized from earlier tax savings enable many firms to replace plant assets at higher prices.

(3) Accelerated depreciation may help to reflect a more uniform level of total expenses associated with specific plant assets. As the asset grows older, repair and maintenance expenses tend to increase. Total expenses may in part be leveled by recording less depreciation expense under an accelerated method during the later years of the asset's life.

(4) Stockholders and directors who are aware that reported net income will be lower during the earlier years under accelerated depreciation may be less inclined to seek and declare large cash dividends which might be better used to pay for recently purchased plant assets or to replace plant assets at higher prices.

Sale or Trade-In

Plant assets may be sold with a gain or loss being recognized as the difference between the book value of the asset sold and the proceeds from sale. Or, the asset may be traded as part of a transaction to acquire a similar asset.

Sale. Assume that Lopez Corporation sold a unit of equipment for $7,000. Data with respect to the equipment are given below:

Cost of equipment	$20,000
Less accumulated depreciation	12,000
Book value of equipment	$ 8,000

Inasmuch as only $7,000 was received for equipment having a book value of $8,000, the company sustained a loss of $1,000. The transaction is recorded as follows:

Cash	7,000	
Accumulated Depreciation — Equipment	12,000	
Loss on Disposal of Plant Assets	1,000	
Equipment		20,000
Sale of equipment having a book value of $8,000.		

Had the asset been sold for $9,000, a gain of $1,000 would have been recognized.

Trade-In. Instead of selling the equipment, assume that Lopez Corporation traded it in for a new unit of similar-type equipment which carried a list price of $30,000. The dealer granted a trade-in allowance equal to the old equipment's fair market value of $7,000, and expected to receive $23,000 cash plus the old equipment. The recorded cost of the new equipment would be equal to the fair market value of the asset traded in plus the cash paid, or $30,000. The transaction would be recorded as shown below:

Equipment (new)...	30,000	
Accumulated Depreciation — Equipment..................	12,000	
Loss on Disposal of Plant Assets.............................	1,000	
Equipment (old)		20,000
Cash..		23,000
Trade-in of old equipment for new similar-type equipment, plus cash payment of $23,000.		

The $1,000 loss on the trade is the difference between the old equipment's book value of $8,000 and its fair market value of $7,000.

To illustrate another possible situation involving these same plant assets, assume that the fair market value of the old equipment was established at $8,500, but the dealer granted a $9,500 trade-in allowance on the old equipment, thereby expecting to receive cash payment of only $20,500. The same general rule is used to determine the capitalized cost of the new equipment: namely, the recorded cost of the new equipment is equal to the fair market value of the old asset ($8,500 in this instance) plus the $20,500 cash payment. This transaction, which results in the recognition of a $500 gain, is shown below:

Equipment (new)...	29,000	
Accumulated Depreciation — Equipment..................	12,000	
Gain on Disposal of Plant Assets		500
Equipment (old)		20,000
Cash..		20,500
Trade-in of old equipment for new similar-type equipment, plus cash payment of $20,500.		

The $500 gain is the difference between the old asset's book value of $8,000 and its fair market value of $8,500.

Restating the general rule for financial reporting purposes that applies to trade-in transactions involving similar-type plant assets: a gain or loss is recognized on the trade-in of a plant asset for a similar-type plant asset, and the recorded cost of the new plant asset is equal to the fair market value of the asset traded in plus the cash payment.[1]

For income tax purposes, however, neither a gain nor a loss is recognized on trade-ins of similar-type plant assets. Instead, the capitalized cost of the new asset is adjusted by any unrecognized gain or loss on the trade. A gain is deducted, and a loss is added. For example, the new equipment's recorded cost in the last journal entry above would be $28,500, ($29,000 minus the $500 unrecognized gain), and no gain would be shown. The depreciable base of this new asset for tax purposes would then be $28,500, assuming no residual salvage value.

In planning, a company can benefit by selling old equipment if a loss must be incurred. By selling the old equipment, a tax loss can be taken, whereas no loss can be deducted for tax purposes in a trade-in transaction. On the other hand, it is better to trade if a gain would result. A gain would be taxed on a sale, but would not be taxed on a trade-in transaction. A decision-making guideline for this type of situation can be summarized as "sell your losses and trade your gains."

NATURAL RESOURCES

Natural resources are noncurrent assets which include minerals, oil and gas pools, timber, and other natural deposits. Accounting refers to these resources as *wasting assets*, since the asset wastes away as the benefits that are contained in the resource are extracted. The process by which the capitalized cost of a natural resource is allocated as expense to subsequent accounting periods is called *depletion*.

Two significant aspects of natural resources that concern an accountant are: (1) determining the monetary amount at which to capitalize a natural resource; and (2) determining the amount of annual depletion expense.

Capitalization of a Natural Resource

When a natural resource is purchased, the purchase cost is normally capitalized, then prorated as depletion expense to subsequent accounting periods as its benefits are extracted. However, when a natural resource is discovered at no cost, a major question

---

[1]Treatment of the complexities involved in nonmonetary transactions is deferred to more advanced accounting texts. See *Opinions of the Accounting Principles Board, No. 29,* "Accounting for Nonmonetary Transactions" (New York: American Institute of Certified Public Accountants, May, 1973).

arises whether or not to reflect a monetary value of the discovered asset in the accounting records. Considered opinion ranges from not recording the asset at all to recording the asset at the estimated sales value of the resource after full development. The following discussion presents a position between these extremes, whereby the discovered natural resource would be capitalized at an amount representing the difference between the estimated total revenue that the resource might generate less total projected extraction, processing, and delivery costs. This differential will be referred to as the *net value* of the resource.

To illustrate, West Oil Company obtained, at a nominal cost, extraction rights to oil reserves that might lie within the boundaries of a particular section of land. Tests indicated the probable presence of a pool containing approximately 6,000,000 barrels of oil. Management estimated the total revenue that might be obtained from the pool at $90,000,000, based on a selling price of $15 per barrel of crude oil delivered to the refinery. After deducting projected extraction, processing, and delivery expenditures of $36,000,000, the net value of the pool was estimated at $54,000,000.

The following arguments may be advanced for not capitalizing $90,000,000, as the cost of the probable discovery:

(1) Substantially less than 6,000,000 barrels of crude oil may be contained in the pool.
(2) The current selling price of $15 per barrel may decrease sharply.
(3) Expenditures for extraction, processing, and delivery would be ignored.

However, to reflect no monetary value for the discovery would appear to be a significant understatement of the total financial resources of the firm. The potential net value of a discovered natural resource that is based on scientific evidence warrants consideration for its being reflected as an asset of the firm.

An entry to record the capitalization of the discovery at its estimated net value of $54,000,000 is shown below. The owners' equity account is normally shown on the balance sheet between capital stock and retained earnings.

Discovered Natural Resource (NA)	54,000,000	
Valuation of Oil Pool (OE).......................		54,000,000
Estimated net value of the discovered oil pool.		

The two accounts shown above will be decreased at the rate of $9 per barrel as oil is extracted and sold, ($54,000,000 ÷ 6,000,000 barrels). The income statement will not be affected by the above entry, nor by the subsequent $9 per barrel decrease of the two accounts. If less than 6,000,000 barrels were ultimately extracted, the amount remaining in each account when the well is exhausted would be zeroed out by means of an adjusting entry. If more than 6,000,000 barrels were sold, the amount in each account would have been previously reduced to zero.

Depletion Expense

Determination of depletion expense is complicated by federal income tax regulations that allow the taxpayer to use either the *cost* or *percentage* method to compute taxable income. Prior to 1975, the percentage method of depletion was allowed for the large oil and gas producers, but this provision was repealed for these two industries. However, this method is still used by companies engaged in coal and mineral extraction.

Assume, for example, that Fresno Company purchased mineral rights to develop a silver deposit for $5,000,000. This amount was capitalized as the cost of the natural resource in the noncurrent asset account, Silver Mineral Rights. Geologists estimated that the deposit had a value of $60 per ton with about 1,000,000 tons in the tract. During the fiscal year ended December 31, 1979, 300,000 tons were extracted, processed, and delivered at a cost of $25 per ton.

Computation of the depletion expense by each of the two methods follows.

Cost Method. The amount of depletion expense is determined by first calculating the depletion expense rate based on the capitalized cost of the asset, and then multiplying that rate by the quantity sold during the period as shown below:

$$\frac{\text{Capitalized cost of the wasting asset}}{\text{Estimated number of units in the asset}} = \text{Depletion expense rate}$$

$$\frac{\$5,000,000}{1,000,000} = \$5 \text{ per ton}$$

$$\text{Depletion expense} = 300,000 \text{ tons} \times \$5 \text{ per ton}$$
$$= \$1,500,000.$$

The depletion rate is comparable to the units-of-production depreciation method applied to plant assets. For financial reporting purposes, the entry to record depletion expense for 1979 is normally based on the cost method, as shown below.

```
Depletion Expense — Silver Mineral Rights........  1,500,000
    Accumulated   Depletion — Silver   Mineral
    Rights .............................................           1,500,000
    Depletion using the cost method.
```

Percentage Method. For income tax purposes only, depletion may be computed by applying a specific percentage to the gross revenue obtained from the sale of the natural resource. In the case of silver, gold, and copper the specific percentage is 15 percent. The taxpayer may use the larger of the two amounts determined by the cost or percentage method for tax purposes. However, the depletion deduction may not exceed 50 percent of the taxable income derived from the property calculated prior to the depletion deduction.

Determination of federal income tax expense in 1979 for Fresno Company is shown below, assuming a tax rate of 50 percent.

	(1) PERCENTAGE METHOD (TAX COMPUTATION PURPOSES ONLY)	(2) ACTUALLY RECORDED AND REFLECTED ON INCOME STATEMENT
Sales (300,000 tons × $60 per ton).................	$18,000,000	$18,000,000
Less extraction, processing, and delivery expenses (300,000 tons × $25)......................	7,500,000	7,500,000
Income before depletion and federal income tax...	$10,500,000	$10,500,000
Less depletion expense:		
(Cost method).....................................		1,500,000
(Percentage method, 15% of revenue) ...	2,700,000	
Income before federal income tax..................	$ 7,800,000	$ 9,000,000
Less federal income tax expense(50% of $7,800,000)...	3,900,000	3,900,000
Net income...		$ 5,100,000

Information shown in Column (1) is used solely to determine income tax, and the information in Column (2) is recorded for financial reporting purposes. Note that both the cost and the percentage methods result in depletion amounts lower than 50 percent of the taxable income derived from the producing property, or $5,250,000 ($10,500,000 × .50).

The $2,700,000 depletion allowance permitted by federal regulations is used only for tax computation purposes. It is not unusual for a taxpayer to expense for tax purposes over the production life of the property an amount which substantially exceeds the capitalized cost of the asset. There is no limit on the aggregate amount of depletion that may be deducted for tax purposes over the life of the property under the percentage method. The taxpayer is permitted to take a deduction by the percentage method in the year when taxable income is derived from the property.

Current Value of Plant Assets and Natural Resources

As stated earlier in the chapter, plant assets and natural resources are accounted for on an original or historical cost basis. However, a question arises as to what should be done when the costs are outdated as a result of price level changes. Different solutions have been proposed, but so far no general agreement has been reached as to how the problem should be resolved.

The Securities and Exchange Commission requires that supplemental replacement cost information be furnished by companies filing with the SEC. In addition to furnishing the current replacement cost of the inventory at the end of the year, the company is expected to give as additional information the estimated current replacement cost of the plant and equipment assets. Also, the company must reveal the depreciated cost of such assets for each year, and the approximate amount of depreciation expense for the two most recent years based on the average current replacement cost.

As an example of how the supplemental information with respect to plant assets may be reported, data from the 1977 annual report for American Telephone and Telegraph Company are presented below:

(Amounts are in millions of dollars)

YEAR 1977	HISTORICAL COST	AT REPLACEMENT COST	DIFFERENCE
Telephone plant investment:			
For which replacement costs have been determined	$ 98,038	$141,641	$43,603
Included at historic cost	3,821	3,821	—
Total	$101,859	$145,462	$43,603
Accumulated depreciation	19,461	35,162	15,701
Net telephone plant investment	$ 82,398	$110,300	$27,902
Depreciation expense	$ 5,045	$ 6,738	$ 1,693

INTANGIBLE ASSETS

Plant assets and natural resources are frequently referred to as tangible assets since they possess physical or material characteristics. *Intangible assets* include financial resources which contain no physical or material attributes but which do provide evidence of legal rights or claims to property or permit a person or a business to engage in specific activities.

Copyrights, Patents, Franchises, and Organizational Costs

A *copyright* grants authors, composers, and artists exclusive rights to make and dispose of their work during their lifetime and extends for 50 years after death. A *patent*, which is granted by the federal government, confers upon the inventor exclusive rights to make, use, and sell the invention or discovery for a period of 17 years. A *franchise* or *licensing agreement* is a contractual arrangement whereby the holder is granted exclusive geographical or jurisdictional rights to sell goods or services of a particular manufacturer, merchandiser, or distributor. This right may be for a limited time or for an indefinite period.

Intangible assets, like plant assets, are expected to yield benefits over the years. Hence, the expenditures incurred to obtain these intangible assets should be capitalized. These expenditures are subsequently *amortized* as their benefits are consumed or expire over the shorter of their legally specified or estimated useful life. These intangibles may be amortized for income tax purposes by any method other than double-declining balance or sum-of-the-years-digits. The usual entry to record amortization expense includes a debit to Amortization Expense and a credit to the specific intangible asset account, rather than a credit to an accumulated amortization account.

Expenditures that are incurred for legal and incorporation fees during the initial stages of establishing a business are called *organizational costs*. They should be capitalized as an intangible asset. Tax regulations allow such costs that are incident to the creation of business either to be amortized over a 5-year or longer period or to be expensed when the business is dissolved.

Research and Development Costs

Expenditures for research and development projects are not capitalized but are instead charged to expense when incurred.[2] In the past, a company had the option of capitalizing these expenditures and amortizing them as benefits were derived from a newly developed product line, or writing them off to expense when incurred. The justification for capitalization was that the expenditures were incurred for the purpose of obtaining future benefits from an improved process or a new product line. Often the expenditures did not result in any new development or were very difficult to identify with any particular time periods. Hence, accounting theory supports and tax regulations allow immediate expensing of such expenditures. An additional justification for immediate expensing is that these expenditures have in recent years become ordinary and necessary business expenses that are required to keep pace with competing organizations.

---

[2]*Statement of Financial Accounting Standards, No. 2,* "Accounting for Research and Development Costs" (Stamford: Financial Accounting Standards Board, 1974).

Goodwill

The normal connotation of goodwill is expanded in commerce and industry to mean good customer relations, an above-average credit rating, or a reputation for quality merchandise and service. In the context of accounting and finance, *goodwill* is defined as the present value of a firm's earnings in excess of the normal earnings of the industrial group of which it is a member. A metal fabricator that normally earns 10 percent return on its total financial resources, as opposed to the metal fabricating industrial norm of 7 percent, may be presumed to possess goodwill. Its existence may result from excellent customer relations and superior products, an outstanding managerial group, innovative research and development, or location factors.

Formal recognition of goodwill as an intangible asset and its measurement in monetary terms usually arises when a business is purchased by another enterprise. To illustrate, assume that the directors and management of Apex Corporation identified for possible purchase a small manufacturer of laser equipment. Top management believed that the purchase of Laser Research would help the anticipated expansion of Apex Corporation's product lines and fill an existing gap in its specialized laboratory equipment. More important, they felt that Apex Corporation would be strengthened by the addition of the creative competence possessed by Laser Research's group of electrical engineers.

The net assets (total assets less total liabilities) of Laser Research totaled $400,000 at the date of initial negotiations. A professional appraiser and a certified public accountant verified that the recorded cost of all Laser Research assets represented their current fair market value. Laser Research's return on net assets (net income divided by net assets) during the previous 6 years had averaged about 15 percent, whereas the industrial group of which it was a member had experienced approximately 10 percent return on the same basis during the same period. Because of this performance, Apex Corporation's management believed that Laser Research possessed an unrecorded intangible value in excess of its $400,000 net assets. Management and the stockholders of Apex Corporation were prepared to pay the owners of Laser Research some premium for this intangible value over and above its $400,000 of net assets. The value of that premium, called goodwill, may be determined in several ways:

(1) Plain bargaining.
(2) Multiple of average past earnings in excess of the industrial norm.
(3) Capitalization of the present value of excess earnings.

Plain Bargaining. Perhaps the most common approach to determine the ultimate purchase price, including goodwill, is *plain bargaining*, whereby the buyer and seller usually begin negotiations at opposite extremes and a compromise is eventually reached. In this example, an offer of $430,000 cash was accepted by the owners of Laser Research. Upon payment of $430,000 cash to the owners of Laser Research, all assets and liabilities of Laser Research were transferred to the accounting records of Apex Corporation. The entry on Apex Corporation's records is shown below:

Assets, Net of Liabilities, Received From Laser Research — (Suspense).....................................	400,000	
Goodwill	30,000	
Cash		430,000
Record the purchase of the net assets of Laser Research.		

The *suspense account* is a temporary account designation that is often used pending subsequent division of the assets and liabilities into particular account categories.

Multiple of Average Past Earnings in Excess of the Industrial Norm. Assume that Laser Research's net income in each of the past 6 years averaged approximately $60,000, and that $40,000 would have been earned by the "industrial norm" on the same $400,000 of net assets during the same period ($400,000 $\times$ 10 percent return on net assets). The $20,000 difference represents the average annual earnings that Laser Research generated in excess of the industrial norm. Both parties might agree to the purchase of a specific number of years of those excess earnings, such as 2½ years. In this case, $50,000 goodwill would be recorded on the records of Apex Corporation ($20,000 $\times$ 2½ years).

Capitalization of the Present Value of Excess Earnings. This approach most nearly coincides with the technical definition of goodwill as used within accounting and finance. The amount of goodwill may be determined by answering the following question. What is the present value of the previously determined $20,000 of excess annual earnings, if they are to be generated for an infinite period of time, discounted at the 10 percent earning rate that is experienced by the industrial norm?

Reference to the 10 percent column of Table 4 in the Appendix indicates that the present value factor for $1 that is received annually for 50 years is 9.915. At infinity, ∞ , that factor would approach 10.000 ($\frac{1}{.10}$ = 10.000). Therefore: P ∞ = $20,000 (10.000) =

$200,000. This method suggests a premium for goodwill of $200,000, a basis upon which the two companies may negotiate.

The American Institute of Certified Public Accountants recommends that goodwill be capitalized as an intangible asset, and that it should be amortized by the straight-line method over its estimated life or 40 years, whichever is shorter.[3] However, the portion of goodwill that is amortized in any fiscal year is not deductible from revenue and other income in determining federal income tax expense.

Assume that a value of $200,000 was accepted for goodwill and that this cost was recorded along with the cost of the other assets and the liabilities at the date of acquisition. In each of the next 40 years, assuming this to be the maximum period, the amount of amortization would be $5,000 as shown below:

Amortization of Goodwill......................................	5,000	
Goodwill..		5,000

Amortization of goodwill for 1 year ($200,000 ÷ 40).

QUESTIONS

1. How are noncurrent assets distinguished from other assets of the business enterprise?

2. What do the following terms have in common: (a) Depreciation; (b) Depletion; (c) Amortization. Identify the type of noncurrent assets with which each term is usually associated. Which particular noncurrent asset is rarely associated with any of these three terms?

3. Identify and explain three reasons for the deterioration that occurs in plant assets.

4. Why does the accountant reject complete expensing of the capitalized cost of plant assets at the time of purchase, or at the time of their retirement or sale?

5. The credit balance in the accumulated depreciation account reflects a reserve with which a retired or worn out plant asset can be replaced. In addition, the current value of the plant asset may be determined by subtracting that balance from the capitalized cost of the asset. Comment in detail on these two statements.

6. In what limited sense may the depreciation process be considered a means of providing cash?

7. Determine the cost of a machine purchased according to the following terms:

Invoice price of machine, $15,000.
Cash discount of 2 % allowed if payment is made in 30 days.
Shipping charges to the purchasing company, $900.
Salary for the month of an operator who will be reassigned to operate the new machine, $1,000.

[3]Opinions of the Accounting Principles Board, No. 17, "Intangible Assets" (New York: American Institute of Certified Public Accounts, Inc., 1970).

8. Should the costs to clean and lubricate machinery be capitalized or expensed? Explain.

9. Two years ago, a company purchased equipment at a cost of $28,000. Depreciation of $8,000 was deducted in the first year, and depreciation of $6,400 was deducted in the second year. Determine the book value of the equipment at the end of the second year. Can the book value be considered as being equivalent to the market value? Explain.

10. Is the tax advantage from accelerated depreciation only a temporary advantage which will become a disadvantage when the accelerated deduction is less than straight-line depreciation? Explain.

11. Accelerated depreciation is computed by a set formula, and the pattern of depreciation may bear no relationship to the deterioration of the plant asset. Can this same argument be used against straight-line depreciation? Explain.

12. When a plant asset is sold, how is the gain or loss on the sale determined?

13. What implications for decision-making are contained in the income tax treatment of trade-in transactions which involve plant assets?

14. (a) Identify one basis whereby the total cost of land and plant assets that were acquired as a unit can be prorated among the individual assets. (b) In which noncurrent asset account should the cost of a building purchased with the intention of subsequent removal be capitalized?

15. (a) How might the value of a discovered mineral deposit be reflected on the balance sheet? (b) Present a sample entry to record the extraction of benefits contained in the capitalized cost of the discovered natural resource.

16. (a) Explain how depletion expense for a wasting asset is calculated by each of the following methods: cost and percentage. (b) Which amount of depletion expense, as determined in (a) is usually recorded in the accounting records; and which amount of depletion expense is used for purposes of income tax determination?

17. A franchise is not a tangible asset, but instead, is a contractual agreement. Should the cost of the franchise be expensed at the time the franchise is granted or should the cost be capitalized? Explain.

18. If research and development costs can provide benefits for future years, why should the costs be charged to expense?

19. Explain how goodwill would be recorded if annual earnings in excess of normal annual earnings were computed at $16,000, and if the discount rate to be used in determining the present value of the excess earnings was 10%. If the goodwill is to be amortized over 40 years, how much goodwill should be charged to expense each year?

EXERCISES

1. **Acquisition of machinery.** On November 1, Hodson Supply Company purchased a machine tool from a dealer at a cost of $11,500. The dealer agreed to allow a discount of 1% if payment is made on or before December 1. Hodson Supply Company paid freight to a motor express company in the amount of $380 to have the machine delivered. In preparation for installation of the machine, wooden beams were bolted to the

concrete floor at a cost of $60. When the machine was delivered, additional costs of $160 were incurred to set the machine in place. Hodson Supply Company paid the dealer for the equipment on December 18.

Required: Determine the cost of the machine tool, showing the detailed composition of the cost.

2. Acquisition of land and buildings. A tract of land with two brick buildings and a small wooden shed on it was acquired from a realtor at a cost of $400,000. An appraisal showed that the land had a value of $60,000; one of the brick buildings (No. 1) had a value of $450,000; the other brick building (No. 2) had a value of $84,000; and the wooden shed had a value of $6,000. After the property was acquired, the wooden shed was removed at a cost of $500, and materials from the shed were sold for $200.

Required: Record, by journal entry, the acquisition of these assets showing the proper distribution of the cost to each asset. Show computations.

3. Ordinary repairs and maintenance. Last year, Bell Machine Company incurred the following costs in connection with equipment: $800 to lubricate various machines; $60 to replace a small belt on a motor; $70,000 for a new unit of equipment; $120 to replace transmission fluid in four units of equipment; $140 for a routine inspection of equipment in search for worn parts that would soon need replacement; and $50 to replace a small gear wheel that was worn.

Required: List and identify the costs that can be properly classified under Maintenance and Repairs Expense.

4. Straight-line and units-of-production depreciation. A large drill press was purchased by Conway Machine Company at a cost of $18,000. The company estimated the useful life of the press at 5 years with a residual salvage value of $3,000 at the end of 5 years. On the basis of production, the company estimates that the press has a useful life of 100,000 hours with a residual salvage value of $3,000.

Required: (a) Compute the depreciation expense each year by using the straight-line method. (b) Compute the depreciation for a year in which the press was operated for 30,000 hours, using the units-of-production method.

5. Sum-of-the-years-digits depreciation. Caldwell and Benner purchased a crane for transporting heavy materials within the plant. The installed cost of the crane amounted to $375,000. Management has estimated that the crane will probably have a useful life of 10 years, with a net salvage value of $45,000 at the end of 10 years. Depreciation is to be computed using the sum-of-the-years-digits method.

Required: Prepare a table to show the depreciation expense each year.

6. Double-declining balance depreciation. A unit of loading equipment was acquired by Ianno Builders, Inc., at a cost of $80,000. Management estimates that the loading equipment should have a useful life of 5 years with a residual salvage value of $10,000 at the end of the 5 years. Depreciation is to be computed using the double-declining balance method.

Required: Prepare a table to show the depreciation expense each year.

(7.) Comparison of major depreciaton methods. A compressor was purchased at a cost of $150,000 by Federal Gauge Company on January 1,
1979. The service life of the equipment was estimated at 4 years with a
residual salvage value of $30,000 at the end of 4 years. The engineering
department estimated that the compressor was capable of producing approximately 1,500,000 units of work during its lifetime. The output of
the compressor during the fiscal year ending December 31, 1979, was
750,000 units and 250,000 units in each of the fiscal years 1980, 1981, and
1982.

Required: (a) Determine the depreciable base that is applicable to each
of the following depreciation methods: straight-line; sum-of-the-years-
digits; double-declining balance; and units-of-production. (b) Calculate
and present in tabular form the depreciation expense to be recorded
under each of the methods in the fiscal years 1979 through 1982. In 1981,
switch from double-declining balance to straight-line.

(8.) Conversion from double-declining balance to straight-line. The
Penny Company purchased several items of machinery and equipment
during January, 1979, at a total cost of $300,000. The double-declining
balance method was selected to depreciate these plant assets. Their expected useful life was estimated at 6 years from the date of purchase,
with no residual salvage value at the end of that period. At the time the
depreciation method decision was made, the controller noticed the following directive that was contained in a reliable tax reporting service: A
taxpayer may switch to straight-line from double-declining balance, bas-
ing future depreciation expense on the asset's undepreciated cost (less
salvage, if any) and remaining life. Both salvage value and useful life
must be redetermined from circumstances existing at the time of the
switchover.

Required: (a) Calculate the depreciation expense that would be recorded
at the end of each fiscal year (December 31) for the 6-year period, beginning December 31, 1979, by using the double-declining balance and
straight-line methods. Round all calculations to the nearest dollar. (b) At
what point would it appear advisable to convert from double-declining
balance to straight-line, assuming the residual salvage value and remaining useful life at the date of conversion remained as originally estimated
at the date of purchase?

9. Sale of plant assets. During the first week of October, 1979, the Bray
Finishing Company sold a machine for $160,000. The machine had been
acquired on July 1, 1974, at a cost of $350,000. It was depreciated by the
straight-line method on the basis of an estimated useful life of 10 years
with a residual salvage value of $50,000.

Required: (a) Compute the total accumulated depreciation on the machine at date of sale. (b) Determine the book value of the machine. (c)
Prepare a journal entry to record the sale of the machine.

10.Trade-in of depreciable asset. Amwell Parts Company owns a punch
press originally costing $25,000 and having a book value of $11,000. The
fair market value of the press is $15,000. This press is being traded in on
a new punch press that has a list price of $42,000. The dealer has granted
a trade-in allowance of $16,000 on the old press in exchange for the new
one and expects to receive a cash settlement of $26,000.

Required: (a) Prepare a journal entry to record the trade-in for financial reporting purposes. (b) Record the trade as it would be recorded for income tax purposes.

11) **Depletion.** In order to encourage the development of potential energy sources, the government granted Prince Mining Company the rights to mine coal on public lands at a nominal cost. The coal company estimates coal reserves on this grant at approximately 1,000,000 tons. The current market price of coal is $80 per ton, and the cost to extract, process, and deliver the coal to the market has been estimated at $30 per ton.

Required: (a)Record by journal entry the acquisition of the coal tract. (b) In the first year of operation, the company extracted and sold 300,000 tons at the price and costs given. Prepare a journal entry or entries in connection with the depletion of the tract.

12. Goodwill. Altonah Company purchased Bliss Processing Company. The net assets of Bliss Company amounted to $850,000 at an appraised market value. A return on net assets of 10 percent is considered to be normal. Over the past several years, Bliss has reported a net income each year of $120,000. It was agreed that Altonah Company should purchase 5 years of earnings in excess of normal as the price of goodwill.

Required: (a) Determine the value to be placed on goodwill. (b) If goodwill is to be written off over its estimated useful life of 10 years, how much goodwill should be amortized each year?

PROBLEMS

9-1. Capitalization of expenditures. A tract of land with a brick building and a cement block building was acquired by Bass Chemicals, Inc., at a cost of $450,000 on May 1, 1979. Appraised market values at date of purchase were as follows: land, $100,000; brick building, $375,000; and cement block building $25,000. The cement block building was demolished as originally intended at a cost of $8,000, and $3,000 was received from the sale of salvage materials.

On June 1, 1979, the company engaged a contractor to construct a new building. The building was completed and placed in operation on November 1, 1979, and the contractor received $220,000 in full payment for the construction. Insurance premiums of $400 were paid for protection of the new building during the period of construction.

Required: Determine the cost that should be assigned to the land, the brick building, and the new building.

9-2. Acquisition of machinery and depreciation. Leder Construction Company purchased a grader at a cost of $24,000 with a discount of 2% allowed if payment is made in 30 days. Freight costs of $400 were incurred to have the grader delivered. Auxiliary parts for the grader were purchased and installed at a cost of $2,800. Before placing the grader in operation, it was tested at a cost of $200.

Based on past experience with similar units of equipment, management estimated that the grader would have a useful life of 4 years and a residual salvage value of $8,000 at the end of the 4 years. Depreciation is to be deducted by the straight-line method. Income taxes are at the rate of 50% on income before income taxes.

Required: (1) Determine the capitalized cost of the equipment.

(2) How much depreciation should be deducted each year?

(3) Determine the amount of the tax savings each year that will result from the depreciation deduction.

9-3. Depreciation. On July 1, 1979, Jefferson Patterns, Inc., acquired a building at a cost of $1,400,000. According to estimates, the building should have a useful life of 20 years with a residual salvage value of $200,000 at the end of the 20 years. Equipment, having an invoice cost of $800,000 with a cash discount of 1% if paid within 30 days, was delivered and installed at an additional cost of $2,500 on July 1, 1979. This equipment was estimated to have a useful life of 10 years with a residual salvage value of $100,000 at the end of the 10 years. A specialized cutting machine was also acquired on July 1, 1979, at a cost of $60,000. The company management could not arrive at a fair estimate of the useful life of this machine on a time basis, but did estimate that the machine should be able to deliver 200,000 machine hours of work with no residual salvage value at the end of the 200,000 hours.

Straight-line depreciation was taken on all of the assets with the exception of the specialized machine, and depreciation on the specialized machine was recorded by the units-of-production method.

Required: Record depreciation on the noncurrent assets for the year ended December 31, 1979, and for the year ended December 31, 1980. The specialized machine was operated for 30,000 machine hours in 1979, and for 80,000 machine hours in 1980.

9-4. Comparison of depreciation methods. On January 1, 1979, Montgomery Processing Company purchased equipment used to blend various ingredients at a cost of $80,000. The estimated life of the equipment was 5 years with an expected residual salvage value of $5,000 at the end of its useful service. Management had to decide which of the following methods of depreciation should be used to allocate the cost of the equipment as expense over the 5-year period.

(a) Straight-line depreciation.

(b) Sum-of-the-years-digits depreciation.

(c) Double-declining balance depreciation. Compute the depreciation in the fifth year so as to reduce the equipment's book value to its residual salvage value. Round all computations to the nearest dollar.

Each year the company is expected to earn income in excess of the depreciation expense. The income taxes are at the rate of 50% of income before income taxes.

Required: (1) Prepare a comparative summary to reflect the depreciation expense that would be recorded in each of the 5 years by each alternative described above.

(2) Assuming that management could invest funds to yield an average return of 10% compounded annually, determine the present value at December 31, 1979, (rounded to the nearest dollar) of the tax saving that would result from depreciation expense under each of the three alternatives above. Assume that the fed-

eral income tax is paid at the end of each fiscal year on taxable income for that year.

(3) Indicate which depreciation method you would recommend that management adopt. Explain.

9-5. Sell or trade. On October 1, 1975, Melendez Engineering Co. acquired a unit of excavation equipment at a cost of $135,000. Straight-line depreciation has been deducted on the basis of the equipment having a useful life of 10 years with a residual salvage value of $15,000 at the end of the ten years.

On June 30, 1980, Simon Contractors, Inc., offers to pay $70,000 for this equipment. Ramon Melendez, the president of Melendez Engineering Co., has been considering a trade of the excavation equipment on a new unit of equipment at a price quoted by the dealer at $175,000. The fair market value of the old equipment is $70,000. The dealer tells Melendez that he will allow $75,000 if the equipment is traded in on the new unit.

Required: (1) Prepare a journal entry assuming that Melendez sells the old equipment. Prepare another entry for the purchase of the new equipment, assuming a cash price of $175,000.

(2) Prepare a journal entry for the trade-in transaction, assuming that Melendez elects to trade.

(3) Give a journal entry to show how the trade-in transaction would be recorded for income tax purposes.

(4) Should Melendez sell the equipment or should he trade it in on the new equipment?

9-6. Treatment of plant assets and natural resources. The four Escabar brothers created Zincbar Corporation in January, 1979, for the purpose of exploiting a deposit of sphalerite that was expected to yield 10,000 tons of refined zinc. The corporation was chartered in Idaho under an infinite-life arrangement because the Escabars intend to diversify into other mineral exploration and mining ventures as soon as this sphalerite deposit is exhausted. At the time of incorporation, the owners decided to end each fiscal year on December 31, and to capitalize as a cost of the mineral deposit the following expenditures that had been incurred prior to 1979:

Prospecting costs	$31,000
Assay and registration of claim fees	8,000
Deeds to mineral rights	51,000
Total	$90,000

Each owner received 2,250 shares of $10 par value Zincbar Corporation capital stock at the time of incorporation.

Additional capital expenditures incurred during the first month of operations included the following items:

Plant and buildings	$ 86,000	Nonmovable from mining site once built. No residual salvage value at end of life.
Machinery and equipment	$380,000	Transportable to other locations. Estimated life, 10 years, with no residual salvage value.

These expenditures were financed by a $466,000 loan from an Idaho bank which required 8% annual interest to be paid at each December 31 on the balance outstanding at the end of each calendar year. The loan principal is to be retired in 3 equal installments beginning December 31, 1979.

In January, 1979, the four owners estimated that the ore would be extracted at a rate which would yield 2,000 tons of refined zinc in 1979 and 4,000 tons each year in 1980 and 1981. The price of partially refined zinc delivered to manufacturers and processors is expected to remain at $300 per ton through the 3-year extraction period.

The capitalized costs of the plant and buildings are to be depreciated at the rate of extraction and sale of the ore. This means that 20% of the total depreciation will be deducted in 1979, and 40% in each of the two following years. Machinery and equipment are to be depreciated by the straight-line method.

Anticipated costs of the total operations (exclusive of depreciation, depletion, and interest expense) are shown below.

Extraction......	$ 250,000
Smelt and preliminary refine	860,000
Delivery......	90,000
Administrative and miscellaneous......	140,000
	$1,340,000

During the 3-year period, the actual extraction, sales price, and expense figures closely approximated the original estimates. The net value of the sphalerite deposit (exclusive of depreciation, depletion, and interest expense) was capitalized at the beginning of 1979. The Internal Revenue Service allowed 22% of the gross revenue that was derived from the sale of sphalerite ore as the depletion expense allowance.

Required: (1) Prepare a compound entry to record the capitalization of the $90,000 discovery expenditures and the net value of the sphalerite deposit at January 1, 1979.

(2) Prepare a compound entry at the end of each fiscal year, 1979 through 1981, to record: (a) depreciation expense; (b) depletion expense by the cost method; and (c) the reduction in the net value of the sphalerite deposit. Assume that 2,000 tons of refined zinc were extracted and sold in 1979, and 4,000 tons in each of the years 1980 and 1981.

(3) Prepare comparative income statements for each of the fiscal years 1979 through 1981. Assume that the federal income tax rate on taxable income was 50% and that the anticipated $1,340,000 cost of total operations shown above were incurred and expensed in a pattern which coincided with the extraction and sale of the refined sphalerite ore. Show all necessary supporting detail.

9-7. Amortization of intangible assets. Western Sounds, Inc., was chartered in Nashville, Tennessee on January 1, 1979, to create, manufacture, and distribute long-playing stereo record albums throughout the United States. During the first fiscal year of operations ending December 31, 1979, the following cash expenditures were incurred at the dates indicated for several intangible assets and other items that appeared to closely resemble such assets:

Item of Expenditure	Date of Expenditure	Amount
Copyrights (original).....................................	January 1	$42,000
Franchise (to distribute records bearing the Auburn label)..	January 1	56,000
Incorporation/organization costs......................	January 1	15,000
Licenses (to reproduce and sell selected Midway and Highland records)..............................	January 1	39,000
Management development and training costs....	April 1–July 31	32,000
Patent (for special high fidelity recording).........	January 1	20,000
Research and development............................	May 1	56,000
Sales promotion	Continuously during the year	157,000
Total..		$417,000

The copyrights, though having a relatively long legal life, are expected to yield almost all of their benefits over a 5-year period. The franchise allows Western Sounds, Inc., to distribute Auburn records until December 31, 1983, at which time the franchise becomes subject to renegotiation. Western Sounds' controller believed it would be appropriate to expense the incorporation/organization expenditures over a 5-year period. The Midway license ($15,000) covers the 3-year period ending December 31, 1981, whereas the Highland agreement ($24,000) expires on December 31, 1984. Both licenses are subject to the same type of review procedure that applies to the franchise agreement. Because of the accelerated pace of technological developments within the industry, the patent is expected to benefit the firm for only four years.

Required: (1) Prepare one summary entry to record the above expenditures, indicating which items should be capitalized and those that should be immediately expensed in 1979.

(2) Prepare one entry at December 31, 1979, to record amortization expense with respect to the various items listed above.

(3) Which, if any, of the items expensed in (1) and (2) would not be deductible from revenue in determining the federal income tax expense for 1979?

9-8. Determination and amortization of goodwill. Linda Rosetti, a proprietor, has operated for several years in the production and sale of perfumes, lotions and soaps. A condensed statement of financial position at June 30, 1979, is given at the top of page 349.

Avery Products, Inc., entered into negotiation with Rosetti to purchase the proprietorship.

During the past six years, Rosetti generated profits averaging $140,000 per year, on which she paid personal income taxes to the federal government at a rate of 40%. The directors of Avery Products, Inc., recognize that if and when the proprietorship is merged into the corporation, the future income generated by this segment would be taxed for federal tax purposes at about 50%.

An appraiser was hired by both parties, and the following information was taken from the appraiser's report dated June 30, 1979.

Linda Rosetti
Balance Sheet
June 30, 1979

Assets

Current assets:

Cash, net accounts receivable, inventory, and prepaid expenses .. $ 346,000

Plant assets:

Land, building, and equipment, net of depreciation................. 1,254,000

Total assets $1,600,000

Equities

Current liabilities:

Accounts and notes payable, accrued liabilities...................... $ 150,000

Long-term liability:

Mortgage note payable, due December 31, 1986..................... 750,000

Owner's equity:

Capital, Linda Rosetti 700,000

Total equities $1,600,000

(a) The current market value of land is $60,000 higher than the amount reflected in the company's records.

(b) The current market value of the building is $25,000 below stated book value.

(c) The current market value of equipment is $65,000 above stated book value.

After both parties approved the appraiser's recommendations, the stockholders of Avery Products, Inc., executed a written purchase contract with Rosetti according to the following guidelines:

(a) The normal return after taxes on net assets experienced by the industry during the previous 5 years was 7%, whereas Rosetti's return (net of income taxes at the 50% rate) on the net assets as appraised on June 30, 1979, had approached 8% over the same period.

(b) The goodwill premium to be paid to Rosetti above the net assets as appraised at June 30, 1979, was to be equal to the one percentage point difference between her earning rate and the industry's earning rate on the appraised net assets. That difference, stated in dollars, was to be considered an infinite series of annual net incomes which were to be discounted to the present value at the industry's normal earning rate.

Required: (1) Prepare the entry at June 30, 1979, to record the cash purchase on the books of Avery Products, Inc., assuming the value of goodwill is determined by capitalizing the present value of the proprietorship's excess earnings. Round goodwill to the nearest thousand dollars.

(2) Assuming the corporate directors decide to amortize the goodwill over the maximum period recommended by the accounting profession, determine the amortization expense to be recorded in

each of those years. What portion of this amount would be deductible for income tax purposes?

DECISION CASE

9-1. **Trade-in versus sale-purchase.** The management of Morales Trade Company planned to replace the large steam boiler with one that possessed newer features for adaptability to air conditioning. The old boiler was purchased for $300,000 several years earlier and its book value at the planned date of disposal was $50,000. Two alternatives were under consideration for disposing of the old and acquiring the new boiler:

Alternative A. Sell the old boiler to Arroya Metals Company for $75,000 cash and immediately purchase the new boiler from Hernandez Boiler Corporation for $400,000 cash.

Alternative B. Trade in the old boiler plus $325,000 payment to Hernandez Boiler Corporation. The old boiler's fair market value on the date of trade was $75,000.

The expected life of the new boiler was ten years, with $50,000 salvage value estimated at the end of its serviceable life. Straight-line depreciation is deducted by the company.

Required:
(1) Prepare the two journal entries required by Alternative A at the date of acquisition.
(2) Prepare the journal entry required by Alternative B at the date of acquisition.
(3) Determine the depreciable base for the new boiler under each alternative; and determine the depreciation expense that income tax authorities would probably allow each year under each alternative.

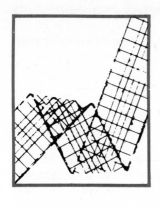

10
Long-Term Liabilities

It's almost as respectable to owe a million as to own a million.

John Maynard Keynes

The service benefits that are contained in assets can be financed in a variety of ways. Three of the most common are purchasing, renting, and leasing with options to buy. Cash payments that are required under any of these alternatives may be obtained from sources such as the sale of stock to investors, the generation of funds through normal operations, borrowing under short-term credit arrangements, obtaining funds by borrowing under long-term notes, or by selling bonds to long-term creditors. This chapter concentrates on topics pertaining to long-term creditor financing.

The extent of creditor financing depends on managerial decisions and attitudes toward its use, and on the nature of the business. Approximately 54 percent of the total equities reflected on the balance sheets of American manufacturers, merchandisers, transportation firms, and utilities are provided by creditors. The portion of total equities contributed by nonownership interests may range from 20 percent in certain manufacturers of electric lighting and wiring equipment, to 80 percent for selected general building contractors. The largest banking and diversified financial institutions in the United States are about 90 percent creditor-financed.

LIABILITY CLASSIFICATIONS

Financial obligations are normally divided into current and long-term liabilities on the balance sheet. However, some liabilities that are classified as current, such as short-term notes payable, may be continuously renewed, and hence may be viewed as the equivalent of long-term debt commitments. Current debt tends to be incurred to finance current assets, whereas long-term obligations are usually incurred to finance plant assets.

Liabilities can also be segregated into three other technical categories, although they are rarely classified as such in financial statements:

(1) Definite liabilities, the monetary amount of which is certain.
(2) Definite liabilities, the monetary amount of which can be estimated.
(3) Contingencies, the incurrence of which is probable, and for which the monetary amount is reasonably determinable.[1]

The first group includes notes, bonds, interest, accounts, and employee compensation payable for which the amount is certain.

The second group includes reliable estimates for such obligations as income taxes and employee pensions. Although income tax obligations are definite, the specific amount of federal and state income taxes payable for a period is subject to final review and verification by respective government authorities. Instead of financing employee retirement benefit plans with specified payments to an external financial institution such as a life insurance company, employee pension funds are often created and financed within the employing firm. Although the time and number of employee retirements cannot be predicted precisely, they can be estimated with sufficient accuracy to warrant recognition of ultimate liability to pensioners under provisions of a company's retirement program.

The third group, contingencies, may include reasonably determinable estimates of: (1) obligations to customers for goods that were sold under warranty; (2) pending legal litigation filed against the company for such items as personal injury caused by product defects, or for alleged violation of government regulations; and (3)

---

[1]*Statement of Financial Accounting Standards, No. 5*, "Accounting for Contingencies" (Stamford: Financial Accounting Standards Board, March, 1975), par. 3, 4, 8, and 10.

actual or possible assessments by both government and non-government institutions.

Many business enterprises estimate their liability for potentially defective goods that are sold under warranty agreements. Such estimates of liability are usually based on previous experience, and are recognized at the time of sale by crediting a warranty liability account and debiting Warranty Expense. The warranty liability account is debited when cash payments are made to honor commitments made under the various warranty agreements. If the amounts actually paid to honor warranty agreements at subsequent dates markedly differ from original estimates, appropriate adjustments may be made at periodic intervals. Reasonably determinable amounts that are involved in probable legal claims and other assessments are also subject to recognition as liabilities in regularly prepared financial statements.

If a "reasonable possibility" exists that a liability has been incurred (in other words, less than probable, but more than a remote chance), and/or the amount of that liability cannot be reasonably estimated, disclosure by means of a footnote appended to financial statements may provide sufficient notice that potential problems may require resolution in the future.

LONG-TERM DEBT TERMINOLOGY

The two most common credit arrangements by which firms obtain long-term debt capital are: (1) mortgage notes, and (2) bonds. Before proceeding into a detailed discussion of these long-term liabilities, certain terms require clarification.

In the case of a *mortgage note*, the "note" portion contains various provisions under which the loan is made, such as the interest rate, interest payment dates, and the maturity date. The "mortgage" portion evidences the borrower's pledge of specific property as collateral to secure the loan. Title to the pledged property is normally retained by the borrower unless default occurs. Funds are usually obtained under a mortgage note arrangement from a single creditor institution or from an individual.

A *bond issue* is the long-term credit device most frequently used in instances where the required funds are sufficiently large to preclude obtaining the entire amount from a single creditor. The bond issue is normally sold to the general public or to several creditor institutions by an *underwriter*, who in turn forwards the funds received from the sale of the bonds to the issuing company. The *indenture contract*, which may be held by a trustee who acts as intermediary between the issuer and the bondholders, specifies the amount and terms of the loan, the interest rate, interest payment dates, and the maturity date. Most bond certificates are issued in denominations of $1,000, with interest rates normally stated no finer than eighths of a percentage point, such as 8 ⅜%.

Interest payments are usually payable semiannually or quarterly under either type of long-term debt financing. Bonds may be issued with interest coupons attached, in which case the bondholder surrenders each coupon at the appropriate date at a bank in return for the interest installment that is currently due. If coupons are not attached, the borrower remits to bondholders-of-record, through the trustee, the required interest payments at prescribed dates.

The interest rate that is printed on the face of each bond is called the *coupon*, *stated*, or *nominal* rate of interest. For example, the issuer of a $1,000 bond which bears a coupon rate of 8 percent, interest payable semiannually, would be required to pay to the bondholder $40 interest each six months. The bond may be sold at more or less than *face value*, depending on the credit rating of the company and the general level of interest rates existent in the financial markets. For example, a $1,000 bond may be sold for $900, or in technical terms, at a $100 discount. Although the issuer receives less than the face amount of the bond, payment of $80 interest is still required each year. In effect, the issuer is paying a rate of interest in excess of 8 percent on the $900 actually borrowed. The interest rate that is computed on the basis of the market value of the bond is referred to as the *market*, *effective*, or *yield* rate of interest.

A bond issue may be secured or unsecured. A *secured* bond may be secured with real property, such as buildings or land (real estate mortgage bonds); personal property, such as machinery and equipment (chattel mortgage bonds); or intangible property, such as corporate and government securities (collateral trust mortgage bonds). An *unsecured* bond, called a *debenture* bond, is supported solely by the general credit rating and financial reputation of the borrower. Holders of mortgage notes or bonds usually have little or no controlling voice in the direction of the borrower's operations. However, if one or more interest payments or the principal is in default, lenders may be entitled to exercise control over the debtor's operations. In such instances, creditors may restrict dividends to stockholders, or in extreme circumstances may obtain complete control of company affairs.

Bonds are sometimes issued in *series*, whereby one or more portions of the total original issue are subject to retirement or redemption at specified intervals. *Income bonds* provide that the issuer must pay interest only if a specified minimum amount of net income is earned. *Participating bonds* enable bondholders to participate in the earnings of the borrower in excess of the bond's coupon rate. Some bond issues are *convertible* into capital stock of the issuer under prescribed conditions at specific dates. Subsequent discussion will stress the debenture type of bond issue, although the general principles involved apply to most long-term debt instruments.

BONDS PAYABLE

The following debenture bonds were sold to the general public by the Durango Corporation on January 1, 1979:

Principal amount:	$100,000
Denomination of each bond:	$1,000
Maturity date:	December 31, 1983
Coupon interest rate:	10 percent, payable semiannually at each June 30 and December 31

This issue of debentures will be used to illustrate the major aspects of bond issues; and the present value concept will be interwoven throughout the discussion to enable a more penetrating understanding of the principles involved.

Two Streams of Payment

A bond issue requires accounting for two streams of payment, in this case: (1) the repayment of the $100,000 principal to bondholders on December 31, 1983; and (2) the ten semiannual interest payments of $5,000 each to bondholders, beginning June 30, 1979. These two streams of payment may be visualized on the time-scale shown below:

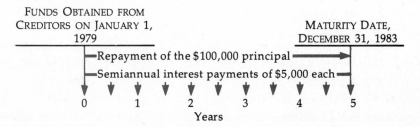

FUNDS OBTAINED FROM CREDITORS ON JANUARY 1, 1979

MATURITY DATE, DECEMBER 31, 1983

Repayment of the $100,000 principal

Semiannual interest payments of $5,000 each

0   1   2   3   4   5

Years

Restated, the corporation must repay to bondholders a total of $150,000 during the 5-year period, consisting of the $100,000 borrowed principal due December 31, 1983, plus $50,000 interest that is composed of ten equal payments of $5,000.

Present Value of Net Outstanding Debt

One of the most critical computations surrounding a bond issue is to determine its present value of net outstanding debt at a specific point in time. In this instance, the present value of the net outstanding debt of the Durango Corporation bond issue on the date it was sold, January 1, 1979, can be determined as shown below, assuming the market rate of interest equaled its 10 percent coupon rate:

Present value of the $100,000 principal that must be repaid in a lump-sum five years hence, discounted at 10% interest compounded semiannually ($100,000 × .614*) .... $ 61,400

Present value of a series of ten $5,000 semiannual interest payments, discounted at 10% interest compounded semi-annually ($5,000 × 7.722*) 38,610

Present value of net outstanding debt at date of issue, January 1, 1979.. $100,010**

*Respective present value factors were obtained from the 5%/10-period cell of Tables 3 and 4 in the Appendix on pages 638 and 641.
**The $10 rounding difference arises from carrying present value factors to only three decimal places.

Almost every subsequent monetary calculation that is related to the bonds is derived from this present value of the issue's net outstanding debt.

Issue at Par

The sale of bonds at *par* means that the debtor sold each of the $1,000 bonds at 100 percent of its face value, or $1,000. The entry to record the sale of these debentures "at 100", or par, on January 1, 1979, is shown below:

Cash... 100,000
    Bonds Payable.. 100,000
        Record sale of bonds at par, or at 100.

Note that the net outstanding debt is comprised of two present value components, rounded to the nearest hundred dollars, as shown below:

Present value of principal repayment.................................... $ 61,400
Present value of 10 semiannual interest payments................. 38,600

Present value of net outstanding debt at date of issue, January 1, 1979 .... $100,000

Although this breakdown is never shown in the accounting records, the derivation emphasizes the fact that the present value concept is implicitly and importantly reflected in the monetary amounts recorded in the bonds payable account.

The entry at the end of each subsequent 6-month interval, beginning June 30, 1979, to record the payment of $5,000 interest is shown below:

```
Interest Expense .............................................   5,000
    Cash .....................................................            5,000
        Record semiannual interest payment at each June
        30 and December 31, during the 5-year life of the
        bond issue.
```

Notice that the present value of the net outstanding debt of this bond issue after the first interest payment remains at $100,000, rounded to the nearest hundred dollars. Present value factors shown in the following calculation were obtained from the 5%/9-period cell in Tables 3 and 4:

```
Present value of principal repayment ($100,000 × .645) ........... $ 64,500
Present value of nine remaining interest payments ($5,000 ×
    7.108)................................................................   35,500
        Present value of net outstanding debt at July 1, 1979 ........  $100,000
```

The present value of the principal portion increased approximately $3,100 since January 1, 1979 (from $61,400 to $64,500), because the maturity date is six months nearer at July 1, 1979, than at the time of issue. On the other hand, the present value of the interest payments decreased approximately $3,100 since January 1, 1979 (from $38,600 to $35,500), because only nine $5,000 interest payments remain until maturity.

If the entire debenture issue remains outstanding until maturity on December 31, 1983, the following entry would be made to record the final interest payment and the repayment of the principal amount:

```
Bonds Payable............................................... 100,000
Interest Expense .............................................   5,000
    Cash .....................................................            105,000
        Record final interest payment, and repayment of
        principal at maturity, December 31, 1983.
```

Issue at a Discount

The majority of bond issues are sold either at a discount or a premium, rather than precisely at par or "100." This occurs because the coupon rate, which is printed on the face of each bond,

more risk so pay more

seldom coincides with the current market or effective rate of interest that the money markets assign to a specific bond issue. As indicated previously, financial institutions and individuals who are active in the money markets continuously reevaluate the risk characteristics of borrowing firms and of particular bond issues. These constant reappraisals result in establishing a specific market rate of interest at which each bond issue will be sold. Selling a bond issue at a *discount* means that the financial community has decided that these particular bonds should be paying a higher interest rate under prevailing market conditions than that currently provided by the coupon or stated interest rate.

The coupon rate of the Durango Corporation $100,000 debenture issue is 10 percent compounded semiannually, which means that a $5,000 interest payment must be paid by the issuer to bondholders each six months during the 5-year life of that issue. The financial community may decide, however, because of certain risk characteristics inherent in either the issue or the corporation, that this issue should sell for a price below par, thus automatically increasing the market or effective rate of interest that will be paid on this bond issue.

Assume that the market rate of interest on the Durango Corporation 10 percent debentures was established by the financial community to yield 12 percent compounded semiannually. The question immediately arises as to how much the corporation should expect to receive, or lenders should be willing to pay, for these 10 percent bonds at January 1, 1979, to yield 12 percent interest to maturity. Present value analysis again provides the answer, with the present value factors obtained from the 6%/10-period cell of Tables 3 and 4:

Present value of the $100,000 principal that must be repaid in a lump-sum five years hence, discounted at 12% compounded semiannually ($100,000 × .558) $55,800

Present value of a series of ten $5,000 semiannual interest payments, discounted at 12% compounded semiannually ($5,000 × 7.360) 36,800

Present value of net outstanding debt at date of issue, January 1, 1979 .... $92,600

In the above calculation, the principal and semiannual interest payments are discounted to their respective present values by using factors associated with the 12 percent market rate of interest, rather than the 10 percent coupon interest rate.

The corporation expects to receive (and investors are willing to pay) $92,600 on January 1, 1979; in return for which the debtor is required to pay $150,000 to bondholders over a period of five years.

in two streams: (1) the $100,000 principal repayment on December 31, 1983, plus (2) the ten $5,000 semiannual interest payments beginning June 30, 1979. If the issuer received less than $92,600, it would have to pay more than 12 percent interest to maturity; and if more than $92,600 was received, it would be paying less than 12 percent to maturity. In short, the analysis indicates that the $100,000, 10 percent Durango Corporation bond issue would be sold for $92,600, or at a $7,400 discount, in a money market which requires that this specific issue yield an interest rate of 12 percent compounded semiannually to maturity.

The entry to record the sale of this bond issue at January 1, 1979, under these circumstances is shown below:

```
Cash............................................................  92,600
Discount on Bonds Payable (LL)............................   7,400
    Bonds Payable.............................................           100,000
        Record sale of debentures at 92.6 or 92.6% of
    par.
```

Note that Discount on Bonds Payable is a long-term liability account that is contra to Bonds Payable. The net outstanding debt balance at January 1, 1979, could be shown on the balance sheet in either of the following ways:

```
Long-term liabilities:
    Bonds payable, 10%, 5 years, due December 31, 1983.......... $100,000
    Less bond discount.....................................................   7,400
        Net outstanding debt balance......................................  $ 92,600

or
Bonds payable, 10%, 5 years, due December 31, 1983, net of
    $7,400 discount .........................................................  $ 92,600
```

Amortization of Bond Discount. The $7,400 discount is periodically amortized as an expense over the 5-year life of the bond issue, rather than charging the entire amount to expense or treating it as a loss at the date of issue. The two most common methods by which this discount may be amortized are: (1) straight-line; and (2) effective interest rate.

Straight-line amortization charges an equal amount of bond discount to expense during the life of the bond issue, in the same way that straight-line depreciation is used to charge an equal amount of the original cost of depreciable plant assets to expense over their useful lives.

Calculations under the more expedient and simpler, but less theoretically correct, straight-line method are shown below:

$$\frac{\text{Original bond discount}}{\text{Number of periods}} = \frac{\$7,400}{10 \text{ periods}} = \frac{\$740 \text{ amortization at each}}{6\text{-month interval}}$$

The entry to record straight-line bond discount amortization at each interest payment date, beginning June 30, 1979, is as follows:

Interest Expense	5,740	
Discount on Bonds Payable (LL)		740
Cash		5,000
Record interest payment at each 6-month interval, and reflect amortization of bond discount by the straight-line method.		

Under the *effective interest rate* method of bond discount amortization, the market rate of interest at which the issue was sold is used to determine the total interest expense that is incurred on the net outstanding debt balance during each 6-month period. The calculation to determine bond discount amortization at June 30, 1979, is shown below:

Market rate of interest charged on the net outstanding debt at January 1, 1979, during the 6-month period ending June 30, 1979 ($92,600 × .06)	$5,556
Less actual interest payment at June 30, 1979	5,000
Bond discount amortized at June 30, 1979	$ 556

The effective interest rate method explicity recognizes that Durango Corporation actually borrowed $92,600 from bondholders during the 6-month period ending June 30, 1979, on which bondholders require a return of 12 percent interest compounded semi-annually, or $5,556. The entry to record the interest payment and bond discount amortization at June 30, 1979, under the effective interest rate method is shown below:

Interest Expense	5,556	
Discount on Bonds Payable (LL)		556
Cash		5,000
Record interest payment and amortization of bond discount by the effective interest rate method at June 30, 1979.		

A comparison of the net outstanding debt balance at June 30, 1979, after the above entries are recorded under each of the two methods of amortization, is shown below:

	STRAIGHT-LINE	EFFECTIVE INTEREST RATE
Bonds payable	$100,000	$100,000
Less bond discount:		
$7,400 − $740	6,660	
$7,400 − $556		6,844
Net outstanding debt balance	$ 93,340	$ 93,156

Under straight-line amortization, $740 of bond discount is charged to expense at the end of each six months; hence, the net outstanding debt balance of the bond issue increases by $740 each six months. The effective interest rate method, on the other hand, gives explicit recognition to the market rate of interest at which the bonds were originally sold in order to determine the amount of amortization. This more complex and theoretically more accurate calculation reflects a net outstanding debt balance that increases at the beginning of each 6-month period by unequal incremental amounts. In other words, increasing amounts of discount are charged to expense at each 6-month interval, which in turn are added to the net outstanding debt balance each six months during the life of the bond issue. For example, $589 of bond discount would be charged to expense at December 31, 1979, as determined below:

Market rate of interest charged during the six months ending December 31, 1979, on the net outstanding debt at July 1, 1979 ($93,156 × .06)...	$5,589
Less actual interest payment at December 31, 1979...................	5,000
Bond discount amortized at December 31, 1979	$ 589

The entry to record the interest payment and bond discount amortization at December 31, 1979, by each of the two methods is shown below in comparative format:

	STRAIGHT-LINE	EFFECTIVE RATE
Interest Expense.................................	5,740	5,589
Discount on Bonds Payable (LL)...........	740	589
Cash..	5,000	5,000

Record interest payment and bond discount amortization at December 31, 1979.

The complete schedule of bond discount to be amortized at the end of each 6 months over the 5 years under the effective interest rate method is shown on page 362.

To summarize, whereas straight-line amortization of the bond discount remains constant at $740 throughout the 5-year period, amortization under the effective interest rate method gradually increases from $556 at June 30, 1979, to approximately $939 at December 31, 1983. The diagram shown at the top of page 363 illustrates this comparison.

Issue at a Premium

A bond issue that is sold in the financial markets to yield a lower rate of interest to maturity than the stated coupon rate is said to be sold at a *premium*. Assume that the financial community

(1) Net Outstanding Debt ($100,000 — Unamortized Discount) at	(2) Total Interest Expense (12% Market Rate Compounded Semiannually Charged on Net Outstanding Debt Balance) (1) × .06	(3) Amortization of Bond Discount (2) — $5,000 Semiannual Interest Payment	(4) Unamortized Bond Discount at
January 1, 1979 $100,000 − $7,400 = $92,600			July 1, 1979 $7,400 − $556 = $6,844
July 1, 1979 − 93,156	$5,556	$ 556	January 1, 1980 $6,844 − $589 = 6,255
January 1, 1980 − 93,745	5,589	589	July 1, 1980 − 5,630
July 1, 1980 − 94,370	5,625	625	January 1, 1981 − 4,968
January 1, 1981 − 95,032	5,662	662	July 1, 1981 − 4,266
July 1, 1981 − 95,734	5,702	702	January 1, 1982 − 3,522
January 1, 1982 − 96,478	5,744	744	July 1, 1982 − 2,733
July 1, 1982 − 97,267	5,789	789	January 1, 1983 − 1,897
January 1, 1983 − 98,103	5,836	836	July 1, 1983 − 1,011
July 1, 1983 − 98,989	5,886	886	January 1, 1984 − 72*
	5,939	939	
Total amortized bond discount		$7,328*	

*The total amount of bond discount amortization falls short of equalling the original balance of $7,400 by $72 due to rounding.

BOND DISCOUNT AMORTIZATION

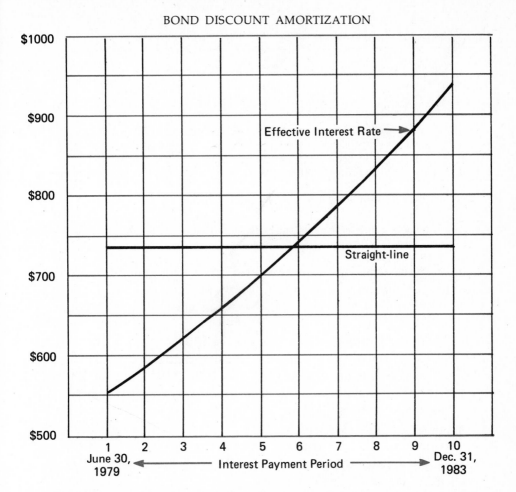

appraised the riskiness of the Durango Corporation, 10 percent debentures to be less than other comparable issues available in the money market at January 1, 1979. Specifically, the financial community decided that these bonds should be sold at a price that would yield 8 percent interest compounded semiannually to maturity. Under such circumstances, the borrower could expect to receive (and the lenders could expect to pay) more than par when these debentures are sold. The table at the top of page 364 summarizes whether bonds will be sold at par, a premium, or a discount, depending on whether the market interest rate equals, exceeds, or falls below the coupon interest rate.

The price at which these bonds, which bear a coupon rate of 10 percent, can be sold in a market that requires an 8 percent market yield to maturity is shown below the table. Present value factors were obtained from the 4%/10-period cell of Tables 3 and 4.

IF THE COUPON INTEREST RATE	THE BONDS WILL BE SOLD AT
Equals the market interest rate......	Par, or 100% of the face amount of the bonds.
Is greater than the market interest rate	A premium, or more than the face amount of the bonds.
Is less than the market interest rate	A discount, or less than the face amount of the bonds.

Present value of the $100,000 principal that must be repaid in a lump-sum of five years hence, discounted at 8% compounded semiannually ($100,000 × .676)	$ 67,600
Present value of a series of ten $5,000 semiannual interest payments, discounted at 8% compounded semiannually ($5,000 × 8.111)	40,555
Present value of net outstanding debt at date of issue, January 1, 1979	$108,155

Again, note that the principal and interest payments are discounted using the present value factors associated with the 8 percent market rate of interest, rather than the 10 percent coupon rate.

Durango Corporation would receive $108,155 from purchasers of the 10 percent bond issue that was sold to yield 8 percent to maturity. The entry to record the sale of the debentures at 108.155 percent of par is shown below. The premium of $8,155 is reflected in the bond premium account, which is associated directly with the bonds payable account.

Cash	108,155	
Bonds Payable		100,000
Premium on Bonds Payable (LL)		8,155
Record sale of debentures at 108.155% of par on January 1, 1979.		

The bonds payable section would appear in either of the ways shown below at January 1, 1979:

Long-term liabilities:

Bonds payable, 10%, 5 years, due December 31, 1983	$100,000
Plus bond premium	8,155
Net outstanding debt balance	$108,155

or

Bonds payable, 10%, 5 years, due December 31, 1983, including $8,155 bond premium	$108,155

Amortization of Bond Premium. The amount received in excess of par is amortized at each interest payment date over the 5-year life of the bond issue, using either the straight-line or effec-

tive interest rate methods. In effect, the amount of the bond premium that will be amortized is deducted from each $5,000 interest
payment to determine the net interest expense incurred at each
semiannual interest payment date. Under straight-line amortization, $816 of bond premium would be amortized each six months,
as shown below:

$$\frac{\text{Original bond premium}}{\text{Number of periods}} = \frac{\$8,155}{10 \text{ periods}} = \$816 \text{ amortization at each} \atop \text{6-month interval}$$

Determination of the premium to be amortized at June 30,
1979, using the effective interest rate alternative is shown below:

Actual interest payment at June 30, 1979.................................	$5,000
Less market rate of interest incurred during the six months end-
ing June 30, 1979, on the net outstanding debt at January 1,
1979 ($108,155 × .04)...	4,326
Bond premium amortized at June 30, 1979........................	$ 674

The entry that would be recorded at June 30, 1979, to reflect the
$5,000 payment of interest and the amortization of bond premium
under each method is shown below in comparative format:

	STRAIGHT-LINE	EFFECTIVE INTEREST RATE
Interest Expense....................................	4,184	4,326
Premium on Bonds Payable (LL)..............	816	674
Cash...	5,000	5,000

Record payment of interest and bond premium at June 30, 1979, by
straight-line and effective interest rate methods.

Note that amortization of the bond premium reduces the amount
of net interest expense. Instead of interest expense being computed at the 10 percent coupon rate for each 6-month period, it is
effectively reduced to the market rate of 8 percent.

The net outstanding debt balance at July 1, 1979, under the
effective interest rate method is $107,481 ($108,155 less the $674
premium amortized at June 30, 1979). The amortization of bond
premium at December 31, 1979, by the effective interest rate
method would be $701: $5,000 interest payment less ($107,481 net
outstanding debt balance at July 1, 1979 times .04). The entry that
would be recorded at December 31, 1979, under each method of
amortization is shown below:

	STRAIGHT-LINE	EFFECTIVE INTEREST RATE
Interest Expense...................................	4,184	4,299
Premium on Bonds Payable (LL)..............	816	701
Cash...	5,000	5,000

Record payment of interest and recognition of bond premium amortization at December 31, 1979.

The semiannual amortization of bond premium will remain constant at $816 under the straight-line method throughout the 5-year period. Amortization under the effective interest rate method, however, will gradually increase from $674 at June 30, 1979, to approximately $960 at December 31, 1983. Determination of this latter amount may be accomplished as shown below:

Present value of $100,000 at July 1, 1983, that must be repaid
    in a lump-sum on December 31, 1983, discounted at 8%
    compounded semiannually ($100,000 × .962) .... $ 96,200
Present value at July 1, 1983, of ten $5,000 interest payments
    that must be made on December 31, 1983, discounted at 8%
    compounded semiannually ($5,000 × .962) ....:...................   4,810

    Net outstanding debt at July 1, 1983............................. $101,010*

*Rounding discrepancy of $50 between $960 and $1,010.

The present value factor, .962, was obtained from the 4%/1-period cell of Table 3. The $5,000 interest payment − ($101,010 × .04) = $5,000 − $4,040 = $960 bond premium amortization at December 31, 1983.

Bond Retirement Prior to Maturity *Know*

Bonds are frequently retired prior to their stated maturity date by *redemption*, or calling them at a price above the face amount of the bonds. Provisions for calling all or some portion of a bond issue are usually stated in the indenture contract at the time the bonds are originally sold. A *call premium* is normally paid to bondholders for either of the following reasons: (1) to cushion the effect of surrendering future interest payments that bondholders would otherwise be entitled to receive if the bonds were held to maturity; and/or (2) to reimburse bondholders for the inconvenience of locating other investments in which to reinvest their financial resources earlier than anticipated.

To illustrate early bond retirement, the management of Durango Corporation decided to call the entire $100,000 bond issue for redemption on December 31, 1982, one year prior to the normal maturity date. The bonds are presumed to have been originally issued at the $7,400 discount as discussed previously on pages 359–361. The call premium was 3 percent, or $3,000 above the $100,000 face amount of the bond issue. The major complexities involved in retiring a bond issue prior to its normal maturity date include:

(1) Determining the total amount of cash to transfer to creditors for the principal, the call premium, and any accrued interest.

(2) Determining the amount of bond discount or premium that remains to be amortized at the date of retirement.
(3) Determining any loss if the bonds were issued at a discount (or gain if the bonds were issued at a premium), that must be recognized at retirement.

Under straight-line amortization, the amount of unamortized bond discount at December 31, 1982, is $2,220, or $740 times three 6-month periods. The total amount of cash that must be forwarded to bondholders is $108,000, composed of: $100,000 principal; $5,000 semiannual interest payment; and the $3,000 call premium. Total interest expense is $5,740, composed of the $5,000 interest payment plus $740 bond discount amortization for the final 6 months of 1982. The remaining $1,480 of unamortized bond discount ($2,220 − $740 amortized on December 31, 1982), plus the $3,000 call premium, must be treated as a loss on retirement of the bonds.[2] The entire entry to record the retirement of these debentures on December 31, 1982, is shown below:

Bonds Payable	100,000	
Interest Expense	5,740	
Loss on Redemption of Bonds (IS)	4,480	
Discount on Bonds Payable (LL)		2,220
Cash		108,000

      Retirement of $100,000 debentures on December 31, 1982, at 103, using straight-line amortization.

The amount of bond discount that remains to be amortized at July 1, 1982 (or just before December 31, 1982), under the effective interest rate method is $2,635, as determined below. Respective present value factors were obtained from the 6%/3-period cell of Tables 3 and 4:

Present value at July 1, 1982, of the $100,000 principal that would normally be repaid on December 31, 1983, discounted at the 12% market interest rate compounded semiannually ($100,000 × .840)...	$ 84,000
Present value of a series of three $5,000 interest payments that would be made on December 31, 1982, June 30, 1983, and December 31, 1983, discounted at 12% ($5,000 × 2.673)	13,365
Net outstanding debt at July 1, 1982..............................	$ 97,365*

    *The $98 discrepancy between this amount and the $97,267 shown in the left column of the schedule on page 362 is due to rounding.

Face amount of the bond issue...	$100,000
Less net outstanding debt at July 1, 1982	97,365
Unamortized bond discount at July 1, 1982	$ 2,635

---

[2]*Opinions of the Accounting Principles Board, No. 26,* "Early Extinguishment of Debt" (New York: American Institute of Certified Public Accountants, 1972), par. 20; and *Statement of Financial Accounting Standards, No. 4,* "Reporting Gains and Losses from Extinguishment of Debt" (Stamford: Financial Accounting Standards Board, March, 1975), par. 8 and 9.

The total interest expense for the last six months of 1982 is $5,842, as shown below:

$97,365 net outstanding debt at July 1, 1982 × .06 = $5,842

The bond discount that would be charged to expense at December 31, 1982, is $842 ($5,842 − $5,000 interest payment). The remaining $1,793 ($2,635 − $842) of unamortized bond discount at December 31, 1982, plus the $3,000 call premium paid for early redemption, would be treated as a loss incurred on bond retirement. The entire entry to record the retirement of these debentures on December 31, 1982, under the effective interest rate alternative is shown below:

Bonds Payable...	100,000	
Interest Expense	5,842	
Loss on Redemption of Bonds (IS)	4,793	
Discount on Bonds Payable (LL)		2,635
Cash		108,000

> Retirement of $100,000 debentures on December 31, 1982, at 103, using the effective interest rate method of amortization.

SPECIAL TOPICS

Financing a business enterprise through long-term debt encompasses a broad spectrum of topics, complexities, and controversies, such as detailed taxation technicalities and the extent to which a firm may or should be financed. Subsequent discussion will be narrowed down to the following three topics that are of sufficient importance to warrant examination in this introductory exposure of financial accounting:

(1) Direct reduction loans.
(2) Long-term leases.
(3) Deferred income taxes.

Direct Reduction Loans

Many businesses regarded as poor financial risks, and most individuals, who desire to purchase items that require substantial outlays of capital over relatively long periods of time, such as a home or an automobile, are usually able to obtain long-term financing only through what is called a *direct reduction loan*. As previously discussed, bond issues and long-term notes payable usually require that the borrower make regular interest payments to the lender at specific periods throughout the life of the loan, and then repay the principal in a lump-sum at maturity. *Direct reduction loans*, on the other hand, require that the borrower

repay the principal and interest in uniform installments throughout the life of the loan, so that the principal amount borrowed
during the financing period is constantly decreasing. This type of
long-term financing is sometimes called a *self-amortizing loan*.

To illustrate this financing arrangement, assume that management of Tristan Corporation required $100,000 with which to ex-
pand its manufacturing operations. A bank was located on January 1, 1979, that was willing to loan the firm the necessary
capital. The bank specified that the loan was to be secured by the
manufacturing equipment that would be purchased with the proceeds from the loan, and that the loan be repaid in eight equal
installments of $16,103, payable at each June 30 and December 31,
beginning June 30, 1979. In effect, the firm was required to pay a
total of $128,824 ($16,103 × 8 payments) over the 4-year period for
the $100,000 loan.

Although the interest rate contained in this loan is not explicitly stated, nor intuitively obvious, it can be determined as
shown below:

$$\frac{\text{Principal amount of loan}}{\text{Amount of each installment}} = \frac{\$100,000}{\$16,103} = 6.210$$

Examination of the 8-period row in Table 4 of the Appendix,
where the factor closest to 6.210 is located, reveals that the implicit
interest rate of this loan is 12 percent compounded semiannually.
Restated, the present value at January 1, 1979, of a future series of
eight equal payments of $16,103 made at the end of each six
months, discounted at 12 percent interest compounded semiannually, is $100,000 ($16,203 × 6.210). The entry to record the loan at
January 1, 1979, is as follows:

```
Cash ..........................................................  100,000
    Notes Payable (LL) ......................................          100,000
        Record loan obtained at an implicit interest
        rate of 12% compounded semiannually.
```

The schedule of the loan repayment shown on page 370 discloses how each payment of $16,103 is divided between the princi-
pal and interest components. All amounts have been rounded to
the nearest dollar.

Entries to record the first two and the last two installment payments are shown below to illustrate the recording procedure:

	1979 June 30	1979 December 31	1982 June 30	1982 December 31
Interest Expense	6,000	5,394	1,772	912
Notes Payable (LL)	10,103	10,709	14,331	15,197
Cash	16,103	16,103	16,103	16,109

Record interest and principal repayments at four selected dates.

(1) Principal Balance AT	(2) 12% Semiannual Interest Charge (1) × .06	(3) Portion of Principal Retired $16,103 − (2)	(4) Principal Balance AT (1) − (3)
January 1, 1979 — $100,000	$ 6,000	$ 10,103	June 30, 1979 — $89,897
July 1, 1979 — 89,897	5,394	10,709	December 31, 1979 — 79,188
January 1, 1980 — 79,188	4,751	11,352	June 30, 1980 — 67,836
July 1, 1980 — 67,836	4,070	12,033	December 31, 1980 — 55,803
January 1, 1981 — 55,803	3,348	12,755	June 30, 1981 — 43,048
July 1, 1981 — 43,048	2,583	13,520	December 31, 1981 — 29,528
January 1, 1982 — 29,528	1,772	14,331	June 30, 1982 — 15,197
July 1, 1982 — 15,197	912	15,197*	December 31, 1982 — —0—
Total............	$28,830	$100,000	

*Due to rounding, the principal portion of the final installment was increased by $6 to reduce the principal balance at December 31, 1982, to zero.

This type of financing arrangement tends to decrease the riskiness of the loan to the lender because some portion of the principal is being repaid at regular intervals throughout the life of the loan, rather than in one lump sum at maturity as with most bond issues. From the borrower's standpoint, however, the entire $100,000 principal is not available for use throughout the term of the loan. For example, the amount that is actually being used by Tristan Corporation is constantly decreasing every six months as shown in column (1) of the preceding schedule. In fact, the amount of principal borrowed during the final 6-month period of the loan is only $15,197.

Long-Term Leases

Rental and lease agreements enable an organization to obtain the use of land, buildings, and equipment, usually for a stated period of time. Agreements by which to secure the service benefits contained in plant assets without actually purchasing those financial resources has markedly increased during the past 25 years, particularly since the 1960's. The following introductory discussion will be restricted to the treatment of rental and leasing agreements from the standpoint of the *lessee*, or tenant, who rents or leases the plant assets from the *lessor*, the owner of the property.

Distinction Between Capital Leases and Operating Leases.
Rental and lease agreements can be divided into two categories: (1) capital leases; and (2) operating leases.

Capital leases are those which meet at least one of the following four criteria[3]:

(1) The lease transfers title of the property to the lessee by the end of the lease term.
(2) The lease contains a bargain purchase option, which allows the lessee to purchase, at its option, the leased property for a price which is sufficiently lower than the expected fair rental value of the property at the date the option becomes exercisable.[4]
(3) The lease term equals 75 percent or more of the estimated economic life of the leased property, so long as the beginning of the lease term does not fall within the last 25% of the total estimated economic life of that property.
(4) The present value of the minimum lease payments (excluding all executory costs such as insurance, maintenance, and taxes to be paid by the

---

[3]*Statement of Financial Accounting Standards, No. 13,* "Accounting for Leases" (Stamford: Financial Accounting Standards Board, November, 1976), par. 7.
[4]*Ibid.,* par, 5c. The fair value is defined as the price for which the property could be sold in an arms-length transaction between unrelated parties.

lessor) . . . . . equals or exceeds 90 percent of the fair value of the leased property after an adjustment for any related investment tax credit retained by the lessor, so long as the beginning of the lease term does not fall within the last 25 percent of the total estimated economic life of the property. The lessee shall compute this present value using the lower of the lessee's incremental borrowing rate (the interest rate at the inception of the lease that would have been incurred to borrow over a similar term the funds needed to purchase the leased asset), or the implicit rate of interest (if determinable) computed by the lessor.[5]

Operating leases are defined by FASB Statement No. 13 as all other leases that fail to meet at least one of the previously mentioned criteria. The customary accounting treatment of operating leases is to charge to expense all rental payments that have been incurred and expired during a specific period of time. The only significant information, other than the amount of rent expense which appears on the income statements, which FASB Statement No. 13 requires to be disclosed in the lessee's financial statements is that the future minimum rental payments which are required as of the latest balance sheet date should be clearly identified in the aggregate and for each of the five succeeding fiscal years.[6]

Capital Leases. In general, FASB Statement No. 13 requires that any capital lease agreement, as defined previously, that is entered into after 1976 must be reported on the balance sheet of the lessee at the present value of all future lease payments, both as a plant asset and as a long-term liability. Prior to the issuance of this statement, many firms that obtained the use of plant assets under capital leasing arrangements did not reveal that fact in their published financial statements. In many cases, failure to disclose such financial arrangements substantially understated both plant assets and financial obligations of specific business entities. The asset is depreciated over its useful life as though it were purchased and owned by the lessee, and the liability is handled in a manner similar to a direct reduction loan financing arrangement. The following example will illustrate the entire procedure.

Copperweld Corp. obtained the use of several items of new equipment from the National Leasing Company under the following capital leasing agreement:

Period of Lease: Three years, beginning January 1, 1980, with title to the property being transferred to the lessee on December 31, 1982.
Lease Payment: Three annual payments of $50,000, beginning January 1, 1980. No executory costs are involved in these payments.
Lessee's Incremental Borrowing Rate: 12 percent compounded annually.
The equipment could have been purchased on January 1, 1980, from the National Leasing Company for a cash payment of $131,300.

---

[5]*Ibid.*, par. 7d.
[6]*Ibid.*, par. 16b.

<u>Estimated Life of Equipment:</u> Three years, with zero salvage value estimated at the end of that life.
The fiscal year of the lessee ends each December 31.

The present value of this capital lease is $134,500, based on Copperweld Corp.'s incremental borrowing rate of 12 percent, as shown below:

$$\$50,000 \text{ annual payment} \times 2.690 = \$134,500$$

The factor 2.690 is derived from Table 4 of the Appendix at the 12%/2-period cell after adding 1.000 to the factor 1.690. The first of the three payments required under the lease is to be made on January 1, 1980, the beginning of the lease. The present value at January 1, 1980, of $1 is $1 (or $1 × 1.000); whereas the present value factor for $1 that is spent one year later on January 1, 1981, is .893; and .797 for $1 that is paid on January 1, 1982, (see Table 3). The sum of these three factors is 2.690 (1.000 + .893 + .797). The implicit interest rate charged on this leasing agreement is 15 percent compounded annually, as determined below:

$$\frac{\text{Purchase price of equipment if paid for in total on January 1, 1980}}{\text{Annual payment for three years, beginning January 1, 1980}} = \frac{\$131,300}{\$50,000} = 2.626$$

The factor 2.626 is derived from Table 4 at the 15%/2-period cell after adding 1.000 to the 1.626 factor. The lessee's incremental borrowing rate of 12 percent should be used in this instance to determine the present value of the lease agreement since it is less than the lessor's implicit rate of 15 percent. (See the fourth criterion outlined on page 371.)

The entry to record the capitalization of this lease agreement on January 1, 1980, on the books of the lessee is shown below:

```
Lease Equipment Under Capital Leases (NA) ............. 134,500
   Obligations Under Capital Leases (LL) ..................       134,500
      Record capitalization of leased equipment on
      January 1, 1980.
```

Although the lease liability could technically be divided into a current and a long-term segment because a $50,000 payment is due for payment on January 1, 1980, such refinement will be ignored for purposes of this introductory exposure to capital leases. The initial $50,000 payment under terms of the lease is reflected below:

```
Obligations Under Capital Leases (LL) .................... 50,000
   Cash ......................................................       50,000
      Payment of initial installment of January 1, 1980,
      under lease.
```

The following schedule presents the separation of each $50,000 lease payment between its interest and principal components during the period of the lease:

(1) BALANCE OF LEASE OBLIGATION AT	(2) 12% ANNUAL INTEREST CHARGE (1) × .12, EXCEPT AT JANUARY 1, 1980	(3) PORTION OF LEASE OBLIGATION PAID $50,000 − (2)	BALANCE OF LEASE OBLIGATION REMAINING (1) − (3)
January 1, 1980 − $134,500	—0—	$ 50,000	January 2, 1980 − $84,500
January 2, 1980 − 84,500	$10,140	39,860	January 2, 1981 − 44,640
January 2, 1981 − 44,640	5,357	44,640*	January 2, 1982 − —0—
Total..........................	$15,497	$134,500	

*This last payment was decreased by $3, due to rounding, to reduce the lease obligation balance to zero.

The entire sequence of entries that would be recorded during the term of the lease with respect to the lease obligation, following the two entries shown previously, is displayed as shown below in comparative format. The data is extracted from the foregoing schedule:

	1980 December 31	1981 January 1	1981 December 31	1982 January 1
Obligations Under Capital Leases (LL).		39,860		44,640
Interest Expense	10,140		5,357	
Interest Payable.......		10,140		5,357
Interest Payable....	10,140		5,357	
Cash..................		50,000		49,997
	Interest accrual.	Cash payment.	Interest accrual.	Cash payment.

The lessee would charge the capitalized costs of these leased plant assets to expense over their expected useful lives by whichever depreciation method is used by the firm. It should be emphasized at this point, however, that the life of the leased assets need not coincide with the term of the lease. For example, the expected life of the assets may exceed (or in unusual cases, fall short of) the length of the lease. Cooperweld Corp. uses straight-line depreciation; hence, the annual depreciation expense during the equipment's estimated 3-year life is approximately $44,833 ($134,500 ÷ 3 years). The entry to be recorded at each fiscal year-end of 1980, 1981, and 1982, is shown below:

Depreciation Expense — Leased Equipment................ 44,833
    Accumulated Depreciation — Leased Equipment (NA).   44,833
        Record annual depreciation expense on leased
        equipment during its 3-year life.

FASB Statement No. 13 stipulates that all assets obtained under capital leasing arrangements, the associated accumulated depreciation, and the related lease obligations shall be separately identified on the lessee's balance sheet. The depreciation expense recognized on such assets should also be separately disclosed on the income statement. In addition, the future lease payments as of the balance sheet date must be disclosed in the aggregate and for each of the five succeeding fiscal years.[7] These requirements could be presented on the balance sheet for Copperweld Corp. as of December 31, 1980:

Assets		Equities	
Plant assets:		Long-term liabilities:	
Leased equipment	$134,500	Obligations under capital leases	$84,500*
Less accumulated depreciation on leased equipment	44,833	*Total lease payments required over the next two years amount to $100,000, payable in $50,000 installments on January 1, 1981 and 1982.	
Net leased equipment	$ 89,667		

The $44,833 depreciation expense on the leased equipment would be disclosed as a separate item on the income statement for each of the fiscal years ended December 31, 1980 through 1982.

Deferred Income Taxes ~~know~~

Companies often depreciate their plant assets by using one method for purposes of reporting to its owners and the financial community, but adopting another method for income tax determination purposes. This practice does not violate generally accepted accounting principles. Subsequent discussion will concentrate on the depreciation of plant assets and the effect it has on deferred income tax.

The principal reasons why depreciation is frequently calculated by different methods for different purposes can be explained as follows. Management may feel that straight-line depreciation best reflects the actual consumption of service benefits contained in its depreciable plant assets; hence, this method should be used for financial reporting purposes. On the other hand, management may wish to take advantage of the tax savings that are provided by one of the accelerated methods of depreciation during the early years of a plant asset's life, such as sum-of-the-years-digits or double-declining-balance. An accounting procedure which results

---

[7]*Ibid.*, par. 13 and 16a.

in the recognition of deferred income taxes has been developed that enables both objectives to be accomplished.

Assume that Delray Corp. purchased machinery on January 1, 1979, for $400,000. Expected life of the machinery is four years, with no salvage value at the end of that useful life. The company uses straight-line depreciation for financial reporting purposes, but sum-of-the-years-digits for income tax determination purposes. The firm's fiscal year ends each December 31.

Determination of the depreciation expense for each year under each of these depreciation methods during the 4-year period ending December 31, 1982, is shown below:

	STRAIGHT-LINE ($400,000 ÷ 4 YEARS)	SUM-OF-THE-YEARS-DIGITS ($400,000 × 4/10, 3/10, 2/10, AND 1/10, RESPECTIVELY)
1979	$100,000	$160,000
1980	100,000	120,000
1981	100,000	80,000
1982	100,000	40,000
Total	$400,000	$400,000

The depreciation expense actually recorded at the end of each of the four years is $100,000, as shown below:

```
Depreciation Expense — Machinery........................ 100,000
    Accumulated Depreciation — Machinery...............        100,000
        Record straight-line depreciation expense at each
        December 31, 1979 through 1982.
```

Assume that Delray Corp. generated $300,000 income before depreciation and federal income tax expense in each of the four years, 1979 through 1982. The lower portion of the income statement for each of those four fiscal years using the straight-line method of depreciation would appear as shown below:

Income before depreciation and income tax expense...............	$300,000
Depreciation (straight-line) expense	100,000
Income before income tax	$200,000
Federal income tax (50%)	100,000
Net income...	$100,000

However the federal income tax that would be currently payable at the end of each of these four fiscal years using the sum-of-the-years-digits would be as shown below:

	1979	1980	1981	1982
Income before depreciation and federal income tax.....................	$300,000	$300,000	$300,000	$300,000
Depreciation (sum-of-the-years-digits) expense	160,000	120,000	80,000	40,000
Income before federal income tax....	$140,000	$180,000	$220,000	$260,000
Federal income tax (50%)...............	70,000	90,000	110,000	130,000

In other words, the income tax expense recorded for each of the four years remains constant at $100,000 in this instance; but the income tax that actually becomes payable at the end of each year increased from $70,000 as of December 31, 1979, by $20,000 increments to $130,000 as of December 31, 1982. This distinction between income tax expense recorded and the income tax which becomes payable can be displayed, as shown below for the fiscal year ending December 31, 1979:

	TAX DETERMINATION PURPOSES — NOT RECORDED (SUM-OF-THE-YEARS DIGITS)	FINANCIAL REPORTING PURPOSES — RECORDED (STRAIGHT-LINE)
Income before depreciation and federal income tax expenses	$300,000	$300,000
Less depreciation expense	160,000	100,000
Income before federal income tax	$140,000	$200,000
Federal income tax expense (50%)	70,000	100,000*
Net income		$100,000

*Only $70,000 is payable as of December 31, 1979. The remaining $30,000 becomes payable in subsequent years.

The entry to reflect: (1) the federal income tax expense; (2) the income tax that is currently payable; and (3) the deferred income tax at December 31, 1979, is shown below:

```
1979
Dec. 31  Federal Income Tax Expense...................  100,000
              Federal Income Tax Payable (CL)..........            70,000
              Deferred Income Tax (LL) ...................            30,000
                 To record current income tax payable
                 and deferred income tax at 1979 fiscal
                 year-end.
```

Although the $30,000 balance in Deferred Income Tax could be reflected on the balance sheet between the long-term liabilities and owners' equity sections, Opinion No. 11 issued by the Accounting Principles Board recommends that it be classified as a long-term liability.[8] Although the portion of deferred income tax that is currently due (if determinable) could be classified as a current liability, this technical refinement will be ignored to simplify discussion.

The entry that would be recorded at the end of each of the remaining fiscal years, 1980 through 1982, is shown on page 378 in comparative format:

---

[8]*Opinions of the Accounting Principles Board, No. 11,* "Accounting for Income Taxes" (New York: American Institute of Certified Public Accountants, 1967), par. 59.

	1980 December 31	1981 December 31	1982 December 31
Federal Income Tax Expense	100,000	100,000	100,000
Deferred Income Tax (LL).................		10,000	30,000
Deferred Income Tax (LL)..............	10,000		
Federal Income Tax Payable (LL)	90,000	110,000	130,000

Record income tax expense, income tax payable, and deferred income tax at fiscal year-end.

Note that the balance in the deferred income tax account has been reduced to zero at the end of 1982.

As stated previously, this procedure, which recognizes deferred income taxes, enables the firm to legitimately use one method of depreciation for financial reporting purposes while simultaneously adopting another method of depreciation for tax determination purposes.

A controversy surrounds deferred income taxes which can be summarized as follows. Many accountants feel that the deferred income tax which becomes payable in subsequent periods should be reflected as a liability on the balance sheet, even though the balance will gradually be reduced to zero as depreciable plant assets reach the end of their useful lives. This is the approach that was presented in the preceding discussion, and it is the viewpoint favored by the Financial Accounting Standards Board, the successor to the Accounting Principles Board. Nonetheless, a substantial number of accountants believe that in instances where depreciable plant assets are replaced at a uniform or increasing rate, the balance in the deferred income tax account may never decrease, much less be reduced to zero. Hence, deferred income taxes should never be recognized. This latter group would instead record as federal income tax expense only that amount which actually becomes payable at the end of each fiscal year. Their approach, using data generated in the illustration on page 376, is shown below in comparative format for years 1979 through 1982:

	1979	1980	1981	1982
Federal Income Tax Expense.....................	70,000	90,000	110,000	130,000
Federal Income Tax Payable..............	70,000	90,000	110,000	130,000

Record income tax expense at each fiscal year-end. No recognition of deferred income tax.

QUESTIONS

1. Identify three categories into which liabilities may be classified other than the two which are customarily shown on the balance sheet.

2. Indicate the appropriate accounting treatment in instances where a reasonable possibility exists that a liability has been incurred, and/or the amount of that liability cannot be reasonably estimated.

3. Indicate the principal differences between obtaining long-term debt capital by issuing: (a) mortgage notes payable; (b) bonds payable.

4. Distinguish between: (a) the coupon, stated, or nominal interest rate; and (b) the market, effective, or yield rate of interest.

5. (a) Identify three types of secured bonds and the collateral associated with each. (b) Indicate what an unsecured bond is normally called.

6. Illustrate what is meant by the phrase, "a bond is composed of two streams of payment," using a debenture issue consisting of $100,000, 10-year, 8% interest payable semiannually. Assume that the coupon and market rates of interest at the date of issue are identical.

7. Explain under what circumstances a bond issue might be sold at a discount or at a premium.

8. Determine the present value of the net outstanding debt at the date of issue of the following bond issue: $100,000, 10-year, 8% interest payable semiannually. The bond issue was sold to yield 10% to maturity.

9. Determine the present value of the net outstanding debt at the date of issue of the following bond issue: $100,000, 10-year, 8% interest payable quarterly. The bond issue was sold to yield 6% to maturity.

10. Explain two common methods by which bond discount or bond premium may be amortized at periodic interest payment dates throughout the life of the bond issue. Indicate the principal advantage and disadvantage of each method.

11. Which of the two methods of amortization would reduce income taxes to a minimum during the early life of the bond issue that was originally sold at: (a) a discount; (b) a premium?

12. Explain: (a) the nature of a call premium; and (b) why the debtor often pays such a premium to bondholders when a bond issue is retired prior to its regularly scheduled maturity date.

13. Explain the accounting treatment of the call premium and any unamortized bond discount (or bond premium) that remains when a bond issue is retired prior to its regularly scheduled maturity date.

14. In what respects does a direct reduction loan differ from a normal bond issue?

15. Determine the implicit interest rate included in a $100,000, 4-year direct reduction loan that requires a payment of $7,961 at the end of each quarter.

16. Identify the main characteristics that distinguish a capital lease from an operating lease.

17. Determine the present value of a capital lease which requires 20 annual payments of $60,000 beginning today. The lessee's incremental borrowing rate is 10% compounded annually.

18. Determine the implicit interest rate compounded annually that is charged by a lessor on a capital lease agreement on a building which specifies that a payment of $47,931 is required at the end of each year for 20 years, beginning one year from today. The building could have been purchased today with a cash payment of $300,000.

19. Identify what disclosures with respect to capital leases should be made on financial statements of the lessee, according to the provisions of FASB Statement No. 13.

20. Explain specific accounting procedures that could give rise to the recognition of deferred income taxes.

21. Explain the controversy surrounding deferred income taxes.

EXERCISES

1. Liability classification. The account balances shown below were located in the general ledger of the Satex Corporation on December 31, 1979. A lawsuit was filed by the state on November 30, 1978, against the corporation for alleged violations of the state's Air and Water Pollution Act. Monetary damages, in the event of conviction, were estimated to range between $150,000 to $800,000.

	BALANCE AT DECEMBER 31, 1979 (DEBIT)
Accounts Payable	$142,800
Bonds Payable, 8%, 19-year, due December 31, 1986	200,000
Deferred Income Tax	32,000
Discount on Bonds Payable	(12,000)
Federal and State Income Tax Payable	198,700
Interest Payable	12,000
Mortgage Note Payable, 9%, due June 30, 1980	60,000
Notes Payable (short-term)	75,000
Obligations Under Capital Leases, final payment due June 30, 1984	84,000
Unearned Rental Income	2,400
Wages and Salaries Payable	7,000
Warranty Liability	18,800
Total Liabilities	$820,700

Required: (a) Prepare a partial balance sheet, classifying the above financial obligations as they would normally appear on the balance sheet at December 31, 1979. In addition, indicate any supplementary remarks that would be appropriate to reflect on the balance sheet. (b) Segregate the above financial obligations into the following categories:

(1) Definite liabilities, certainty of amount.
(2) Definite liabilities, estimated amount.
(3) Contingencies, probable incurrence and reasonably determinable amount.
(4) Other items not classified above.

2. Long-term debt terminology. On June 30, 1979, the directors of Yandell Corp. approved the sale of $250,000 of unsecured bonds to the public at 100. Interest amounting to $5,000 is payable at the end of each quarter, beginning September 30, 1979, for forty quarters. The firm's fiscal year ended each December 31.

Required: (a) What is the technical name of the type of bonds issued by the corporation? (b) Determine the coupon or stated interest rate, and the market or effective rates of interest of this bond issue at the date of sale. (c) Calculate the present value of the net outstanding debt at June 30, 1979. (d) Prepare the entry to be recorded on September 30, 1979.

3. **Bonds issued at a discount: straight-line amortization.** By the time the two hundred $1,000 debentures were received by the Turex Corporation from the engraver on January 1, 1980, the financial community had decided that this bond issue, which bore a coupon rate of 7%, should sell at a price that would yield 8% to maturity. The debentures have a maturity date of December 31, 1992, with interest payable semiannually at each June 30 and December 31. The entire debenture issue was sold on January 1, 1980, to yield 8% to maturity.

Required: (a) Determine the proceeds that the Turex Corporation received from bond purchasers on the date of issue. (b) Determine at what percent of par the issue was sold, rounded to two decimal places. (c) Prepare the entry that would be recorded at the date of issue. (d) Prepare the entry that would be recorded on the first interest payment date, assuming the use of straight-line amortization of bond discount. Round computations to the nearest dollar.

4. **Bonds issued at a premium: effective interest method of amortization.** The management of Zealand Enterprises sold an $800,000, 9%, 7-year bond issue to the public on April 1, 1980, to finance its regional expansion program. Interest is payable semiannually on September 30 and March 31, beginning September 30, 1980. The financial community decided on the date of issue that this particular bond issue should sell at a price which would yield an interest rate of 8% to maturity. Zealand Enterprises used the effective interest method to amortize bond discount and bond premium.

Required: (a) Prepare the entry to record the sale of this bond issue. Show all calculations. (b) Prepare whatever entry is required at the first interest payment date. Round all calculations to the nearest dollar. (c) Prepare the entry that would probably be recorded at the time the entire bond issue is retired on the final interest payment date, March 31, 1987. Round calculations to the nearest dollar.

5. **Early retirement of bonds originally issued at par.** The Ribrun Corp. issued its $200,000, 8%, 6-year bond issue on July 1, 1975, at par. Interest was payable quarterly, beginning September 30, 1975. Proceeds from the bonds were used to purchase a modernized plant facility. The directors decided that sufficient cash was being generated to retire the entire issue one year early on June 30, 1980. A call premium of 4½% was paid to bondholders to induce early retirement.

Required: (a) Prepare the entry to record the early retirement of the bond issue on June 30, 1980. (b) Determine the amount of interest that was saved, net of the call premium, by retiring the bonds early.

6. **Early retirement of bonds originally issued at a premium: straight-line amortization.** A $400,000, 9%, 7-year bond issue was sold by Cognoleum, Inc., to the public on January 1, 1975, to yield 8% interest compounded semiannually to maturity. Interest was payable at each June 30 and December 31; and the firm used the straight-line method to amortize bond discount and bond premium. The entire bond issue was called for early retirement on December 31, 1980, with a 3% call premium being offered to bondholders.

Required: (a) Determine the total proceeds received by Cognoleum, Inc., at the date of issue. Show all calculations. (b) Prepare the entry to retire the bonds on the interest payment date, December 31, 1980. Round all calculations to the nearest dollar.

7. **Early retirement of bonds originally sold at a discount: effective interest method of amortization.** The Zotwin Corporation sold its $600,000, 9%, 12-year bond issue to the public on January 1, 1969, to yield 10% to maturity. Interest was payable semiannually at each June 30, and December 31; and the effective interest method was used to amortize bond discount and bond premium. The cash flow generated by the firm was sufficient to allow management to retire the entire issue one year early on December 31, 1979, by offering a call premium of 4% to bondholders.

Required: Prepare the entry to retire the entire bond issue, showing all calculations. Carry all calculations to the nearest dollar.

8. **Cost of a direct reduction loan.** On July 1, 1979, Marina Santos, the sole proprietor of the Santos Company, obtained a $100,000, 5-year bank loan with which to expand the firm's operations. Terms of the loan required a payment of $12,329 at the end of each six months, beginning December 31, 1979, and ending June 30, 1984. Santos determined that the interest rate implied in the terms of the loan was about 4.66% compounded semiannually, as determined below:

Ten equal payments of $12,329..	$123,290
Less principal amount of the loan.....................................	100,000
Total payments for interest...	$ 23,290

$23,290 ÷ 10 payments = $2,329 interest payment each six months on the $100,000 loan.

$2,329 ÷ $100,000 = 2.33% interest each six months × 2 periods
= 4.66% interest compounded semiannually.

Santos was extremely pleased to have obtained such a low-cost loan, since many well-seasoned and financially solid companies in the area were reported to be currently paying in excess of 6% interest on bank loans.

Required: (a) Determine the implicit interest rate of the loan which Santos obtained. (b) Illustrate Santos' failure to understand the terms of the loan by calculating the first two semiannual interest payments that would be made on the loan. Round calculations to the nearest dollar.

9. **Capital lease of machinery.** Due to a poor cash position, management of the Formalloy Corp. decided on January 1, 1980, to sign a 5-year capital lease for several pieces of expensive machinery, rather than purchase the items for $250,000. Terms of the lease required five equal payments of $67,000, beginning December 31, 1980; and title to the machinery would be transferred to the Formalloy Corp. at the termination of the lease upon payment of the final $67,000 installment. Estimated service life of these plant assets was 10 years, with no salvage value at the end of that life. The corporation depreciates all of its plant assets by the double-declining-balance method. The interest rate that Formalloy Corp. would have had to pay to borrow funds with which to purchase this machinery on January 1, 1980, was 10% compounded annually.

Required: (a) Prepare the entry that would be recorded by Formalloy Corp. on January 1, 1980. (b) Prepare the entry at the end of the fiscal year, December 31, 1980, to reflect the lease payment and any depreciation expense on this machinery. Round calculations to the nearest dollar.

10. Incremental borrowing and implicit rates of interest in leases. A newly hired accountant in the Kitset Corp. received a copy of a capital lease from the firm's controller on January 1, 1980, along with the request that relevant features of the lease be journalized at the earliest opportunity. The 6-year lease, effective January 1, 1980, dealt with several pieces of equipment that had been acquired from the Longmont Co. Terms of the lease required that twelve equal semiannual payments of $23,000 be forwarded to Longmont Co., beginning January 1, 1980. The accountant learned from the controller that Longmont Co.'s incremental borrowing rate was 12% compounded semiannually, and that the equipment could have been purchased outright from Longmont Co. on January 1, 1980, for $195,477 cash.

Required: (a) Calculate the lessor's implicit rate of interest compounded semiannually that could be derived under terms of this lease agreement. (b) Prepare the entry that should be recorded as of January 1, 1980, to reflect the capitalization of this lease agreement. (c) Prepare the entry as of January 1, 1980, to record the initial lease payment of $23,000.

11. Deferred income tax. One of the principal tasks accomplished by the Swifttach Corporation when it began operations on January 1, 1977, was to purchase machinery and equipment costing $660,000. These plant assets were expected to have a salvage value of $60,000 at the end of their 3-year life. The firm uses straight-line depreciation for financial reporting purposes and sum-of-the-years-digits for income tax determination purposes. The federal income tax rate is 50%; income before depreciation and federal income tax was $450,000 in each of the three fiscal years ended December 31, 1977, 1978, and 1979.

Required: (a) Prepare a schedule to reflect the depreciation expense that would be calculated under each of the two methods described above for each of the three fiscal years 1977 through 1979. (b) Prepare a schedule to determine the federal income tax expense and the federal income tax payable for each of the three fiscal years. (c) Prepare the entries, in comparative format, to record federal income tax expense, federal income tax payable, and any deferred income tax at the end of each of the three fiscal periods.

PROBLEMS

10-1. Issue bonds at a discount. The Biorhythm Corp. sold its $600,000, 9%, 8-year bond issue to the public on January 1, 1979, to yield 10% interest compounded semiannually to maturity. The firm's fiscal year ended each December 31, and interest was payable at each June 30 and December 31.

Required: (1) Prepare the entry to record the issuance of these bonds on January 1, 1979.

    (2) Prepare the entry to record the first interest payment on June 30, 1979, assuming the use of: (a) straight-line amortization; (b) the effective interest rate method. Carry calculations to the nearest dollar.

    (3) Prepare the entry to record the second interest payment at the end of fiscal year 1979, assuming the use of: (a) straight-line amortization; (b) the effective interest rate method. Carry calculations to the nearest dollar.

    (4) Determine the net cash received and retained by the corporation during the entire first year that these bonds were outstanding, assuming the use of: (a) straight-line amortization; (b) the effective interest rate method. Ignore income tax implications.

10-2. Sale of bonds at a premium. An $800,000, 7%, 7-year issue of debentures was sold by the Frankel Company to several financial institutions on January 1,1979. This issue sold at a price to yield a market rate of 6% compounded quarterly. Interest is payable at the end of each quarter, beginning March 31, 1979. The entire bond issue will be retired on its scheduled maturity date of December 31, 1985.

Required: (1) Determine the amount of cash which the Frankel Company received from the sale of these debentures on January 1, 1979.

    (2) Indicate how this debenture issue might appear on the Frankel Company's balance sheet immediately after the sale.

    (3) Prepare the entry to record the payment of interest on the second interest payment date, June 30, 1979, assuming the use of: (a) straight-line amortization; (b) the effective interest rate method. Round calculations to the nearest dollar.

    (4) Prepare the entry to record retirement of the debentures on December 31, 1985, assuming the use of: (a) straight line-amortization; (b) the effective interest rate method. Carry calculations to the nearest dollar.

10-3. Early retirement of bonds originally issued at a discount. Montmoy Corp., whose fiscal year ends each December 31, sold a $300,000 issue of 10-year, 7% debentures on January 1, 1971, at 93.165% of par. Interest was payable semiannually on each June 30 and December 31. The entire bond issue was retired at the time of interest payment on December 31, 1978, by offering bondholders a call premium of 4½%.

Required: (1) Prepare the entry that was recorded by Montmoy Corp. on January 1, 1971.

    (2) Determine whether the bond issue was sold on January 1, 1971, to yield 10% or 8% interest compounded semiannually to maturity.

    (3) Prepare the entry recorded by the corporation at the first interest payment date if straight-line amortization of bond discount was used. Carry calculations to the nearest dollar.

    (4) Prepare the entry to record the early retirement of the bonds, assuming that the effective interest rate method of bond discount amortization was used throughout the life of the bond issue. Carry calculations to the nearest dollar.

10-4. Early retirement of bonds originally sold at a premium. Farsite, Inc., sold its $500,000, 9%, 20-year bond issue on April 1, 1962, for the purpose of financing an expansion of operations. The money market in the region where the firm was located decided that this bond issue should be sold at an 8% market rate of interest compounded semiannually. Interest was payable at each September 30 and March 31. The entire issue was called for redemption on September 30, 1979, by offering bondholders a call premium inducement of 4¾%.

Required: (1) Determine the cash proceeds received by Farsite, Inc., at the time the bonds were issued. Round calculations to the nearest dollar.
   (2) Prepare the entry that would have been recorded on the first interest payment date, September 30, 1962, assuming the firm used the effective interest rate method of bond premium amortization. Carry calculations to the nearest dollar.
   (3) Prepare the entry to record the retirement of the bond issue on the interest payment date, September 30, 1979, assuming the firm used the straight-line method of bond premium amortization. Carry calculations to the nearest dollar.
   (4) Determine the cash saved, net of the call premium, by retiring the bonds early. Ignore income tax implications.

10-5. Partial early retirement of debentures. Nustream, Inc., sold an $800,000, 10%, 10-year bond issue at 104% of par on January 1, 1972. Bond discount and bond premium were amortized by the straight-line method, with interest payable quarterly beginning March 31, 1972. Sufficient cash had been generated during the latter 1970's that management decided to retire $600,000 of the bond issue on the interest payment date, December 31, 1979, by offering a call premium of 5% on the portion retired. The remaining $200,000 portion was to be retired at the regularly scheduled maturity date.

Required: (1) Prepare the entry to record the sale of the bonds on January 1, 1972.
   (2) Prepare the entry to record the redemption of the portion retired early on December 31, 1979, plus all interest due.
   (3) Determine the amount of interest, net of the call premium, that was saved by the early retirement. Ignore income tax implications.
   (4) Prepare the entry to retire the remaining portion on the regularly scheduled maturity date, plus all interest due.

10-6. Comparative analysis: mortgage note payable and direct reduction loan. Management of the Geoff Corp. was investigating the following two financial arrangements whereby $360,000 might be obtained on January 1, 1980, to expand manufacturing facilities:
   Alternative A: Obtain funds under a $360,000, 8%, 4-year mortgage note payable arrangement from a local bank. Interest is payable semiannually, beginning June 30, 1980.
   Alternative B: Obtain a $360,000, 4-year direct reduction loan from another local bank, the terms of which require repayment in eight equal installments of $52,371, beginning June 30, 1980.

Required: (1) Prepare the entries to be recorded on the first two interest payment dates under Alternative A.

(2) Determine the implicit interest rate contained in the terms of Alternative B.

(3) Prepare the entries to be recorded on the first two installment payment dates under Alternative B. Round calculations to the nearest dollar.

(4) Optional. Assuming that Geoff Corp. can earn 12% interest compounded semiannually on its financial resources, determine which financing arrangement appears more attractive from a present value standpoint at January 1, 1980. Round calculations to the nearest dollar.

10-7. Capital lease of a harbor tugboat. Harborways, Inc., of New York City, obtained the use of an in-harbor tugboat under the terms of a capital lease that was signed on January 1, 1979. The 7-year lease required the lessee to make an $87,000 payment every six months, beginning January 1, 1979, with the final payment due on June 30, 1985. Title to the tugboat would be transferred to the lessee on the final payment date. The estimated life of the boat is 10 years, with an estimated salvage value of $70,000 at the end of that life. The firm uses the double-declining balance method of depreciation on all depreciable plant assets; and its incremental borrowing rate is 10% compounded semiannually.

The tugboat could have been purchased on January 1, 1979, from the lessor, Mid-Atlantic Shipyards Corp., for $857,211.

Required: (1) Determine whether the lessor's implicit interest rate is higher or lower than the lessee's incremental borrowing rate.

(2) Prepare the entry to record capitalization of the lease on January 1, 1979.

(3) Prepare the entry to record the initial lease payment.

(4) Prepare the entry on June 30, 1979, to record the second lease payment and the appropriate amount of depreciation expense. Round calculations to the nearest dollar.

(5) Prepare that portion of the balance sheet that reflects information relevant to the above capital lease at the end of Harborways, Inc.'s fiscal year, June 30, 1979.

10-8. Deferred income tax. The sum-of-the-years-digits method of depreciating plant assets is used for income tax purposes by the Pilpul Corp. Straight-line depreciation, however, is used for recording and financial reporting purposes. The firm began operations on January 1, 1976, and the income earned before depreciation and federal income tax (50% rate) is shown below for each of the years indicated:

FISCAL YEAR ENDED DECEMBER 31	INCOME BEFORE DEPRECIATION AND FEDERAL INCOME TAX
1976	$360,000
1977	400,000
1978	450,000
1979	500,000
1980 (Projected)	540,000

All depreciable plant assets owned by the firm were purchased for $900,000 on January 1, 1976, each of which had an expected life of 5 years with no salvage value at the end of that time. Management's intent was to replace all depreciable plant assets with new and improved models at the beginning of 1981.

Required: (1) Prepare a schedule to indicate the depreciation expense for the plant assets in each of the five years, using the straight-line and sum-of-the-years-digits (SYD) methods.

   (2) Determine the income tax expense and the income tax payable at the end of each of the five years, 1976 through 1980 projected.

   (3) Prepare the entries in comparative format to record the income tax expense, income tax payable, and any deferred income tax at the end of each of the five fiscal years. Indicate the balance that remains in the deferred income tax account after the December 31, 1980, entry.

DECISION CASES

10-I. **Amortization of bond discount and bond premium for tax purposes.** One of America's largest business enterprises sold a $200-million, 7%, 20-year bond issue to the public on January 1, 1979, interest payable semiannually on each June 30 and December 31. The debentures were sold to yield 8% interest compounded semiannually to maturity.

Required:
   (1) After determining the cash proceeds received by the firm from the sale of these debentures, prepare the entry to record the semiannual payment of interest and amortization of bond discount, using the straight-line method of amortization.
   (2) Prepare the entries to record the first two semiannual interest payments, including amortization of bond discount, using the effective interest rate method of amortization. Round all calculations to the nearest dollar.
   (3) Based upon calculations in (1) and (2), which of the two methods of bond discount amortization would you recommend that the debtor adopt over the life of these debentures to minimize federal income tax expense during the early years of the life of the issue?
   (4) Expanding your recommendation in (3), which method of bond premium amortization would you recommend for adoption to minimize federal income tax expense during the early years of the bond issue had the debentures been issued at a premium?

10-II. **Borrowing under two financing alternatives.** At the end of 1979, management of the DeAngelis Co. was considering which of two arrangements to select on January 1, 1980, by which to finance the purchase of a building and equipment for $400,000. Each of the following two options specified an interest rate of 12% compounded quarterly:

Option A. The mortgage note payable requires that the plant assets to be purchased with the $400,000 proceeds from the loan will serve as collateral for the loan. The entire principal is to be repaid on December 31, 1986, with interest payable quarterly, beginning March 31, 1980.

Option B. The $400,000 direct reduction loan also requires that the plant assets serve as collateral for the loan. Equal quarterly installments, beginning March 31, 1980, would include interest payments and the gradual retirement of the principal over the life of the loan. The final installment is to be paid on December 31, 1986.

Required:
(1) Determine the uniform quarterly payment required under Option B. Round all calculations to the nearest dollar.
(2) Assuming the firm could earn 16% interest compounded quarterly on its financial resources, determine the present value "cost" of each option to the company at January 1, 1980.
(3) Identify which of the financing options you would recommend that management adopt.

10-III. The deferred income tax controversy. Triumph, Inc., began operations on January 1, 1976. All of the firm's automated conveyor assembly lines were depreciated by straight-line for financial reporting purposes, and sum-of-the-years-digits for tax purposes. Management felt that straight-line was the most appropriate depreciation method for financial reporting purposes, because the assembly line's benefits would be consumed in approximately equal amounts throughout its life. However, management wished to take advantage of any tax saving that might be available from accelerated depreciation.

Triumph, Inc., maintained one assembly line for each of the products manufactured in each of the fiscal years ended December 31, as shown below:

PRODUCT LINES MANUFACTURED

1976..............	A
1977..............	A and B.
1978..............	A, B, and C.
1979..............	A, B, C, and D.
1980..............	A, B, C, and D.

One complete assembly line was (and would continue to be) purchased new for $160,000 at the beginning of each fiscal year, and was used thereafter during its expected 4-year useful life on only one product line. The assembly line is then removed from service at the end of its 4th year of use and replaced by a new assembly line. In other words, one assembly line was purchased on January 1, 1976, and used only on Product A until December 31, 1979. A second assembly line was purchased on January 1, 1977, and used only on Product B until December 31, 1980. A new assembly line for use on Product A would be purchased on January 1, 1980, for $160,000 to replace the unit that was discarded on December 31, 1979. This pattern would be continued into the foreseeable future, with four being the number of assembly lines in operation at any one time from January 1, 1979, onward.

The corporation earned $400,000 income before depreciation and federal income tax in each of the fiscal years ended December 31, 1976 through 1980.

Required:
(1) Prepare a schedule to reflect the depreciation expense to be recorded under the straight-line and the sum-of-the-years digits depreciation methods in each of the five years.

(2) Determine the federal income tax that would be payable at the end of each of the five fiscal years by each of these depreciation methods. The federal income tax rate is 50% of taxable income.

(3) Prepare the entry to record appropriate amounts of income tax expense, federal income tax payable, and deferred income tax at the end of each of the five fiscal years, 1976 through 1980. A comparative entry format may be used.

(4) Explain why the income tax that has been deferred may never become payable if management of Triumph, Inc., continues the purchase and replacement policy that was instituted on January 1, 1976.

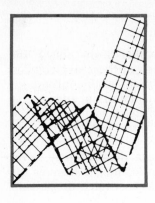

11
Stockholders' Equity

*Don't gamble! Take all savings and buy some
good stock and hold it till it goes up, then sell it.
If it don't go up, don't buy it.*

Will Rogers

The financial rights or claims by owners of a business in the total assets of the business are called the *owners' equity*. Stated another way, the owners' equity is the balance that remains after deducting the obligations to the creditors from total assets.

The three basic forms of business ownership were introduced and discussed in Chapter 1:

(1) Proprietorship
(2) Partnership
(3) Corporation

Because the corporate form of organization is predominant in our society, the owner's equity of the corporation will be stressed in this chapter.

THE CORPORATION

The owners' equity of a corporation is ordinarily designated as *stockholders' equity* or as *shareholders' equity*.

In exchange for the privilege of limited liability, the corporate owners may not withdraw their investment under normal conditions. Inasmuch as the creditors cannot attach the personal assets of the individual stockholders for satisfaction of their claims against the corporation, they must be given some protection. This protection is the assurance that the owners will not withdraw the capital that they have invested.

TWO DIVISIONS OF STOCKHOLDERS' EQUITY

A distinction is normally made between the portion of the owners' equity that may be withdrawn and the portion that may not be withdrawn. This distinction is made by dividing the stockholders' equity into two segments:

(1) *Paid-in capital* represents the total amount invested by the stockholders. The paid-in capital may in turn be divided into two parts:
   (a) An amount designated as *capital stock*, or more specifically as the par value or stated value of *common stock* or *preferred stock*, depending upon the type of stock.
   (b) Any amount invested in excess of the amount credited to a capital stock account. This amount may be designated either as a *premium on stock* or as *paid-in capital in excess of stated value*, depending upon the terms under which the stock is issued.
(2) *Accumulated earnings* represent the net earnings accumulated by the corporation. The accumulated earnings are generally designated as *retained earnings*, and represent the algebraic sum of net incomes, net losses, and dividend distributions over the life of the corporation.

VALUE OF STOCK

Various definitions of value are used in connection with capital stock. Each one serves a different purpose by relating to a specific aspect of stock. Four of the most useful are:

(1) Par or stated value.
(2) Market value.
(3) Liquidation value.
(4) Book value.

Par or No-Par Stock

Capital stock may be issued either with a par value or with no par value. If there is only one class of stock, it is usually designated on the balance sheet as capital stock or common stock. If the corporate organizers decide to issue par value stock, a value is assigned to each share. The *par value* is the amount printed on the stock certificate and is set according to the convenience of the company. For example, if only a few shares are needed to represent the total stockholders' investment, the par value may be relatively high. A total investment of $100,000 can be adequately represented by 1,000 shares, each having a par value of $100. On the other hand, an investment of $100,000 may be shared by many individuals who prefer small units, in which case 100,000 shares, each having a par value of $1 may be issued. This is similar to splitting currency into various denominations. An individual sometimes prefers to have $100 in the form of five $20 bills or ten $10 bills.

Since limited liability is a privilege extended to stockholders, they are expected to invest a minimum amount of cash or other property equal to the par value of the shares of stock issued. Par value is thus a legalistic term defining the minimum investment a stockholder is required to make when the shares are initially issued. If stock has a par value of $100, a stockholder is expected to invest assets having a value of $100 before receiving the share of stock.

Stock may also be issued with no par value being assigned to the shares. Prior to 1912 all stock was par value stock. In that year, New York passed a law permitting stock to be issued with no par value, and since then other states have passed similar laws. This law was passed to protect individuals from zealous promoters who often tried to convince investors that the par value printed on the stock certificate was the true value of the stock. The par value is seldom the "true value" of the stock. *True value* is an elusive term, but in general, it is understood to mean the going market price of the stock at any given time. Par value has no relationship to market value. The value of a stock depends upon the value of the assets of the corporation, which in turn depends upon future earning ability. Both the value of assets and future earning ability partially determine the market price of the stock. True value is not the amount printed on the stock certificate.

In some states, *no-par stock* may be issued. However, the shares may have a *stated value* which represents the minimum amount to be credited to capital stock. For all practical purposes, the stated value of no-par stock is virtually equivalent to a par value. For each share issued, the corporation must receive the stated value per share with any excess being credited to Paid-In Capital in Excess of Stated Value.

Shares issued with no stated value per share are true no-par-value shares. The total amount received from the sale of true no-par stock must be credited to Capital Stock.

Investment in Excess of Par or Stated Value. Frequently the amount invested by the stockholders is in excess of the par or stated value assigned to the shares. The amount in excess of the par value is credited to Premium on Stock or to Paid-In Capital in Excess of Par. If the stock has no par value but has been assigned a stated value per share, the excess is credited to Paid-In Capital in Excess of Stated Value.

A journal entry is given below to record the investment of $600,000 for 10,000 shares of common stock, each having a par value of $10.

Cash..	600,000	
Common Stock		100,000
Premium on Stock..		500,000
Issued 10,000 shares of stock.		

The stockholders' equity section of the balance sheet, assuming no other stock transactions, would appear as follows:

Stockholders' equity:		
Common stock, $10 par value, 10,000 shares authorized and outstanding..............................	$100,000	
Premium on stock...	500,000	
Total stockholders' equity		$600,000

If the 10,000 shares were issued with no par value but with a stated value of $10 per share, the stockholders' equity would appear as shown above, except that the caption "Paid-in capital in excess of stated value" would be used instead of "Premium on stock." If there were neither a par value nor a stated value per share, the entire amount invested, $600,000, would be credited to Capital Stock.

Market, Liquidation, and Book Value of Stock

The *market value* is the price at which a share of stock can be bought or sold, and is a measurement of the worth of the stock at the time of the market quotation. For example, the par value of Schering-Plough Corporation is $1 a share but on December 31, 1976, the market value of each share was quoted by the New York Stock Exchange at $44.75. On this date, a share of the stock could be purchased or sold for $44.75, which is considerably more than the value printed on the stock certificate. Market value is determined by many forces, including the general economic outlook, the estimated future profits of the company, and various other factors that influence buyers and sellers in the market.

The liquidation value per share has significance only when the corporation is either dissolved or considered for dissolution. The *liquidation value* per share is the amount received from the sale of assets, less deductions for payments to creditors, divided by the number of outstanding shares. The amount realized from the sale of the assets may be considerably different from the amount shown for these assets in the accounting records because the records are seldom revised to restate the assets at their current values.

Book value per share is based solely on the stockholders' equity, as shown on the corporate balance sheet, divided by the number of shares outstanding. The stock may or may not be worth this amount either on a going-concern basis or in liquidation. For example, the 1976 annual report of Schering-Plough Corporation shows a total common stockholders' equity of $707,109,000, with 54,083,867 shares of stock outstanding.

$$\frac{\text{Total stockholders' equity}}{\text{Number of shares outstanding}} = \frac{\$707,109,000}{54,083,867} = \$13.08 \text{ book value per share}$$

The market value of Schering-Plough Corporation stock at $44.75 is considerably higher than the book value of the stock, because investors are apparently willing to pay a premium due to the expected growth and future earnings of the company. Thus, there may be a wide discrepancy between book value and market value.

CLASSES OF STOCK

Provision may be made in the corporate charter for more than one class of stock. If there are two types, they may be designated as *preferred stock* and *common stock*.

Preferred Stock

Preferred stock, as the term implies, has certain privileges not granted to common stock. In exchange for these privileges, however, the preferred stock may be denied full voting rights and full participation in sharing the corporate earnings.

Preference Dividend Rate. Preferred stock agreements generally specify that dividends of a specified dollar amount per share or a certain percentage of par or stated value per share be paid on the preferred stock before any dividends may be paid on the common stock.

Cumulative Right to Dividends. Before any dividend can be paid on the common stock, dividends not paid in past years on preferred stock must be paid along with the current dividend.

Dividends that have not been declared for the past years are called *dividends in arrears*.

Participation. After the preferred stock has received the stated preferential dividend, and after the common stock has received the specified percentage or designated amount per share, the preferred and common stock may share dividends on a pro rata basis with or without a limit to the participation.

For example, assume that there are 10,000 shares of $50 par value preferred stock ($500,000) with a 5 percent preferred dividend rate and a participation privilege of dividends up to 10 percent of the par value of the outstanding stock. Assume further that there are 10,000 shares of $100 par value common stock ($1,000,000). Preferred stockholders will receive the 5 percent dividend based on the par value of the outstanding preferred stock before any dividend can be declared on the common stock, after which the common stockholders will receive a 5 percent dividend based on its outstanding par value. The balance of the dividends will then be shared on the basis of one third to preferred and two thirds to common, which is the ratio of the par value of the two classes of stock, until each class has received a total of 10 percent of the par value of their respective outstanding stock. Beyond this point, the remaining balance of dividends, if any, will go to common stock.

To illustrate, a firm declared a total of $90,000 in dividends to be distributed to both classes of stock mentioned above.

	PREFERRED STOCK	COMMON STOCK	DIVIDENDS
Par value, outstanding............................	$500,000	$1,000,000	
Preference of 5% to preferred ($500,000 × .05)..	$ 25,000		$25,000
Equalize common at 5% rate ($1,000,000 × .05)..		$ 50,000	50,000
			$75,000
Participation share pro rata (⅓: ⅔) of $15,000 balance ($90,000 − $75,000)........	5,000	10,000	15,000
Total dividends................................	$ 30,000	$ 60,000	$90,000

Note that the $90,000 amount available for participation is under the 10 percent limit of the total par value of outstanding stock: $1,500,000 × .10 = $150,000.

Assume, on the other hand, that total dividends of $180,000 are to be distributed. The dividends would be distributed as shown on the following page.

	PREFERRED STOCK	COMMON STOCK	DIVIDENDS
Par value, outstanding............................	$500,000	$1,000,000	
Preference of 5 percent to preferred..........	$ 25,000		$ 25,000
Equalize common at 5 percent rate...........		$ 50,000	50,000
Participation share pro rata until total limit of 10 percent is reached................	25,000	50,000	75,000
			$150,000
Balance of dividends to common stock ($180,000 − $150,000).........................	——	30,000	30,000
Total dividends.............................	$ 50,000	$ 130,000	$180,000

In this example, the preferred stock received the limit in participation: $500,000 outstanding par value $\times$ .10 = $50,000. Any additional dividends beyond the $150,000 go to the common shareholders.

Liquidation. If the preferred stock is to be retired, it may be retired at a premium; or in the event of dissolution, the preferred stock may have preference over the common stock in the distribution of net assets.

Convertible. The preferred stock may be exchanged for common stock under certain specified terms.

Common Stock

The common stockholders have the final residual equity in the corporation. Their claims to corporate assets are satisfied only after all claims to creditors and preferred stockholders have been satisfied. The ultimate responsibility for managing the affairs of the corporation, however, rests upon the common stockholders who usually elect the board of directors, who in turn hire the executive officers. Generally the common stockholders have full voting powers and enjoy a larger share of the earnings if the corporation is successful but suffer larger losses if the corporation is unsuccessful. However, with the limited liability feature of the corporation, the losses of stockholders are limited to the amount invested.

STOCK ISSUED FOR PROPERTIES OR SERVICES

Stock may be issued in exchange for properties other than cash or for services received. It is sometimes difficult to place a value on the properties and services received. If the shares of stock issued in exchange for properties and services have an established market value, the value of the stock may be assigned to the properties or services received. If no value can be established for the shares of stock, the properties or services may be assigned a value by appraisal or by reference to an outside market price.

Assume that a piece of equipment with an appraised value of $30,000 is transferred to a corporation in exchange for 2,000 shares of common stock, each with a par value of $1 but with no available market value quoted per share. The value of the stock issued would then normally be established by reference to the appraised value of the equipment. This is illustrated in the journal entry below:

```
Equipment.....................................................   30,000
     Common Stock ............................................            2,000
     Premium on Stock.........................................           28,000
     Issued 2,000 shares of stock for equipment.
```

TREASURY STOCK

Capital stock issued by the corporation and reacquired either by purchase or donation is designated as *treasury stock*. A corporation may buy its own stock (1) for permanent retirement, (2) to make the reacquired shares available to employees under a stock option plan, or (3) for reissuance of the stock to employees as a bonus. Treasury stock is ordinarily recorded in the account records at cost, with the cost shown as a separate deduction from the total stockholders' equity on the balance sheet.

To illustrate, assume that a corporation has two classes of stock outstanding: preferred and common. There are 5,000 shares of preferred stock outstanding, each share having a par value of $100. The stock was issued at $110 a share and has a preferred dividend rate of 7 percent on the par value. There are 1,000,000 shares of no-par common stock authorized with a stated value of $5 per share. The corporation issued 800,000 shares for $12,000,000. There are 50,000 shares of common stock in the treasury which were acquired at a unit cost of $25, or a total cost of $1,250,000. Hence, 750,000 shares of common stock are issued and outstanding. The undistributed net earnings that have accumulated since the corporation was formed amount to $7,500,000. The stockholders' equity section of the balance sheet appears as shown at the top of page 398.

The following journal entry reflects the purchase of the treasury stock:

```
Treasury Stock ..........................................   1,250,000
     Cash................................................              1,250,000
     Acquisition of 50,000 shares of treasury
     stock at a cost of $1,250,000.
```

Stockholders' equity:

7% preferred stock, $100 par value, 5,000 shares authorized and outstanding............	$ 500,000	
Premium on preferred stock	50,000	$ 550,000
No-par common stock, $5 stated value, 1,000,000 shares authorized, 800,000 shares issued; treasury stock, 50,000 shares (deducted below).....................................	$4,000,000	
Paid-in capital in excess of stated value.........	8,000,000	12,000,000
Retained earnings......................................		7,500,000
Total..		$20,050,000
Less common treasury stock, 50,000 shares, at cost...		1,250,000
Total stockholders' equity		$18,800,000

Assume at a later date that 10,000 of the treasury shares are sold for $30 a share. The journal entry to record the transaction is:

Cash..	300,000	
Treasury Stock		250,000
Paid-In Capital from Sale of Treasury Stock		50,000
Sale of 10,000 shares of treasury stock at $5 a share in excess of acquisition cost.		

The increase in the stockholders' equity from the sale of treasury stock is not earned through the normal business operations, hence, it must not appear on the income statement and must not be credited to Retained Earnings. A corporation does not realize income by dealing in its own stock. The treasury stock is not an asset of the corporation. The difference between the acquisition cost and the amount realized from selling the stock is treated as an adjustment to stockholders' equity. In the above example, the cost of the treasury stock was reduced to $1,000,000 after the sale of 10,000 shares, and the total paid-in capital identified with the common stock increased to $8,050,000.

DIVIDENDS AND RETAINED EARNINGS

A corporation may declare dividends periodically, often on a quarterly or annual basis. *Dividends* are a distribution of the earnings of a firm to the stockholders, usually in the form of cash. If assets other than cash are distributed, such as part of the merchandise inventory, the dividend is said to be a *property dividend*. Dividends are declared only on the outstanding shares of stock.

Cash Dividends

A dividend is not an expense of doing business and should not, under any circumstances, be shown on the income statement as an expense. Instead, a dividend is the portion of net income distributed to the owners in the form of an asset, usually in cash.

The equity of the stockholders in retained earnings is reduced by the amount of the cash dividend. When the board of directors declares the dividend, a liability arises for the payment of that dividend. A journal entry is given below for the declaration of a $10,000 dividend.

Retained Earnings	10,000	
Cash Dividends Payable		10,000
Dividend declared on stock.		

Sometimes, instead of charging Retained Earnings directly, the charge will be made to an account entitled Cash Dividends. At the end of the fiscal year, the cash dividends account would be closed to Retained Earnings.

When the dividend is paid, usually within a few weeks after it is declared, the liability will be eliminated, and the asset distributed to the stockholders will be reduced. The journal entry for the payment is:

Cash Dividends Payable	10,000	
Cash		10,000
Payment of dividend.		

Stock Dividends

A company may also issue shares of its own stock as a dividend. By means of the *stock dividend*, the company shifts retained earnings available for dividends to the common stock and paid-in capital accounts. To the extent of the dividend, earnings are capitalized and become a part of the legally stated capital. Under normal conditions, common stock and paid-in capital may not be withdrawn but are a part of the permanent capital structure. Hence, the declaration of a stock dividend, rather than a cash dividend, transfers retained earnings to permanent capital, thus retaining asset value within the firm to the extent of the stock dividend. The stockholder continues to have the same proportionate interest in the firm, but the market value of each share may tend to be somewhat lower because of the increased number of shares outstanding.

With a stock dividend, the stockholder does not possess anything that was not owned before. If this is true, then what is the purpose of a stock dividend? The corporation may have been successful in earning profits, but top management may desire to hold within the firm assets that were realized in the earning process and put those assets to use in earning even larger profits in future years. By means of the stock dividend, there is a formal commitment of earnings to the permanent capital structure. Even the companies that pay generous dividends reinvest a portion of their profits. The stock dividend generally attracts favorable attention because, in effect, the directors are telling the investment community that the company has been successful and has plans for future growth.

Many investors prefer to have their earnings reinvested. The prospect of future growth in earnings tends to increase the market value of the stock, and the stockholder who does not need current income may not want cash or property dividends that are subject to income taxes. At a later date, the investor hopes to realize a gain from the sale of the stock because of the increased market value.

It is not always easy to determine what effect a stock dividend will have on the market value of the shares; however, market value must be taken into consideration when the company issues a stock dividend. In a case where a stock dividend has little effect on the market value of the outstanding shares, retained earnings is reduced by an amount equal to the market value of the shares issued as a stock dividend, and the common stock and paid-in capital in excess of par (or stated value) accounts are increased by a corresponding amount.

For example, in 1977 Dart Industries, Inc., distributed a 3 percent stock dividend of 673,500 shares (par value $1.25) at a market value of $31.50 per share. A dividend of 3 percent is usually considered to be a small dividend that will have little effect on the market value of the outstanding shares. This dividend is recorded as follows (rounded to nearest thousand dollars):

Retained Earnings....................................	21,215,000	
Common Stock......................................		842,000
Paid-In Capital in Excess of Par		20,373,000
Issuance of 673,500 shares having a par value of $1.25 per share as a stock dividend.		

Note that Dart Industries, Inc., reduced the retained earnings by the market value of the shares issued as a stock dividend (673,500 shares × $31.50 market value = $21,215,000, rounded to nearest thousand dollars). A total corresponding increase was made to Common Stock and Paid-In Capital in Excess of Par. Common stock has been increased by the par value of each share multiplied by the number of shares (673,500 × $1.25 par value = $842,000), and the excess of $20,373,000 has been credited to the account, Paid-In Capital in Excess of Par.

In some cases, the number of additional shares to be issued as a stock dividend may have a material effect upon the market value of the outstanding shares. In this case, retained earnings should be reduced by only the par value of the shares issued with a corresponding credit to the common stock account. For example, assume that Helena Company had 500,000 shares of common stock outstanding, each share having a par value of $5. A stock dividend of 20 percent was declared. At the time the dividend was declared, the stockholders' equity appeared as follows:

Common stock, $5 par; 800,000 shares authorized, 500,000
    shares issued and outstanding...................................... $2,500,000
Premium on stock..   500,000
Retained earnings..   3,200,000
      Total stockholders' equity $6,200,000

If a dividend of 20 percent of the outstanding stock influences the market value of the stock, it would be appropriate to transfer an amount from retained earnings to common stock equal to the par value of the additional shares issued as shown below:

Retained Earnings 500,000
    Common Stock   500,000
      To record 20 percent stock dividend: 20% of
      500,000 shares = 100,000 shares; 100,000 shares
      × $5 par = $500,000.

If there is to be a substantial increase in the number of shares, it may be more appropriate to consider the distribution as a stock split, not as a stock dividend.

Stock Splits

A *stock split* is not a dividend nor does it affect retained earnings. Nevertheless, it is discussed at this point because of the difficulty in distinguishing a stock dividend from a stock split.

Assume that a stockholder owns 100 shares with a market value of $60 per share. The board of directors decides on a 2 for 1 stock split, in which case each stockholder would be given an additional share of stock for each share held. After the split, the stockholder owns 200 shares and with no other factors operating in the market, the stock should sell for approximately $30 per share ($6,000 ÷ 200 shares). If the stock is split 3 for 2, the stockholder will own 150 shares, which is an increase equal to 50 percent of the shares held; and the market price of each share would probably be reduced to $40 ($6,000 ÷ 150 shares). Provision is usually made for the purchase or sale of any fractional shares.

The line of distinction between a stock dividend and a stock split is based upon magnitude. The American Institute of Certified Public Accountants recommends that if the number of additional shares issued is less than 20 or 25 percent of the outstanding shares, the transaction should be recorded as a stock dividend rather than as a stock split.[1] One purpose of a stock split is to reduce the market price of each share to a level where it will attract the attention of small investors. If relatively few additional shares are issued, the market price may not be affected to any great extent, and the transaction may be more properly treated as a stock dividend.

No formal journal entry is required for the stock split. The transaction is much the same as splitting currency into lower denominations, such as converting a $10 bill into ten $1 bills. There is no transfer within the stockholders' equity section nor is there any outflow of assets accompanied by a reduction in retained earnings, as in the case of a cash or stock dividend. Two notations are made on the appropriate financial statements: (1) the par or stated value of each share of stock is reduced by the split; (2) the number of outstanding shares is increased. Aside from this memorandum entry, no entries are made in the accounting records.

EARNINGS PER SHARE

Often the earnings per share of common stock are computed to give additional information to the shareholders. If there is only one class of stock outstanding and earnings are entirely from normal operating activity, the computation can be made quite easily by dividing the net income for the year by the number of outstanding shares. With more than one class of stock outstanding, the earnings must be reduced by the amount of obligation to the holders of preferred stock before computing the earnings per share of common stock.

If a company has realized a gain or loss from a transaction that can be described as an extraordinary item, the earnings per share should be computed to show the earnings per share from normal

---

[1]*Accounting Research and Terminology Bulletins — Final Edition*, No. 43, "Restatement and Revision of Accounting Research Bulletins" (New York: American Institute of Certified Public Accountants, 1961) p. 53.

activity, and the earnings per share from the extraordinary item.[2] Gains or losses from the sale of plant assets and similar transactions that may be expected to recur from time to time are not considered to be extraordinary items. Also, adjustments to correct prior period earnings are not considered to be extraordinary. The adjustments to correct prior period earnings should be shown as corrections of the beginning balance of retained earnings. To qualify as an *extraordinary item*, the item must: (1) be unusual in nature; (2) occur infrequently; and (3) be material in amount.[3]

Assume that a company with 2,000,000 shares of common stock outstanding reports a net income on regular operating activity of $6,000,000, and a loss of $2,000,000 from an earthquake after an adjustment for income taxes. When the net income and loss are combined, the result would be $4,000,000, and the earnings per share would be reported at $2 ($4,000,000 ÷ 2,000,000 shares). With this amount given as earnings per share, the public would be misled into believing that the $2 per share was the normal earnings per share, when in fact, the normal earnings per share amounts to $3 ($6,000,000 ÷ 2,000,000 shares). A more complete reporting of the earnings per share should be made as follows:

Earnings from normal operations after income taxes ($6,000,000 ÷ 2,000,000)	$3.00
Loss from earthquake after income taxes ($2,000,000 ÷ 2,000,000)	1.00
Total net earnings per share	$2.00

Dilution of Earnings per Share

Sometimes securities are issued with a provision that they may be converted to common stock. *Options* or *warrants* may also be granted which give the holder of certain securities the right to acquire shares of common stock at a specified price. The option or warrant will be attractive to the holder only if and when the market price of the stock exceeds the *exercise price*. Such a provision means that additional shares of common stock may be issued when the securities are exchanged for common stock or when the options or warrants are exercised. With a given amount of net income and a larger number of common shares outstanding, the earnings per share will be lower. This constitutes a *dilution of earnings*. Stockholders and other interested persons may overlook the fact that additional shares may be issued and may be inclined

[2]*Opinions of the Accounting Principles Board, No. 15*, "Earnings per Share" (New York: American Institute of Certified Public Accountants, 1969).

[3]*Opinions of the Accounting Principles Board, No. 30*, "Reporting the Results of Operations" (New York: American Institute of Certified Public Accountants, 1973).

to believe that the present earnings per share will continue into the future. Information should be provided to show how earnings per share will be affected if additional shares are issued by either a conversion of securities or by exercise of options or warrants.[4]

Using the data from the previous example, assume that the company had a debt outstanding in the amount of $15,000,000 with an interest rate of 8 percent. The debt agreement specifies that the debt may be converted to 1,000,000 shares of common stock at the option of the holder.

With the debt conversion, the company will no longer have to pay an annual interest expense of $1,200,000 ($15,000,000 × .08); but instead, there will be a total of 3,000,000 (2,000,000 + 1,000,000) shares outstanding. The interest of $1,200,000 is deductible in the computation of income taxes, and assuming a tax rate of 50 percent, the interest expense after taxes would be $600,000. Assuming there is a debt conversion, the adjusted net income is computed as follows:

Earnings from normal operations after income taxes..............	$6,000,000
Add interest expense if debt is converted ($1,200,000 × 50%)	600,000
Adjusted earnings from normal operations after income taxes	$6,600,000
Less loss from earthquake after income taxes.......................	2,000,000
Net income for the year (adjusted)....................................	$4,600,000

The earnings per share computation follows:

	WITHOUT CONVERSION	WITH CONVERSION
Net income from normal operations:		
$6,000,000 ÷ 2,000,000..........................	$3.00	
$6,600,000 ÷ 3,000,000..........................		$2.20
Loss from earthquake after income taxes:		
$2,000,000 ÷ 2,000,000..........................	(1.00)	
$2,000,000 ÷ 3,000,000..........................		(.67)
Total earnings per share..........................	$2.00	$1.53

APPROPRIATIONS OF RETAINED EARNINGS

The retained earnings account measures the stockholders' interest in accumulated earnings, but does not necessarily measure the amount that may be distributed in dividends. Certain restrictions may be imposed, stating that a given portion of the retained earnings must be retained within the corporation while the specific restriction is in force. This does not mean that the retained earnings are reduced. Instead, they are appropriated for a given purpose.

---

[4]Ibid.

A restriction against retained earnings should not be interpreted to mean that a fund has been set aside for a designated purpose. Neither cash nor any other asset has been placed in a special fund by the appropriation. The appropriation of retained earnings means that dividends may not be declared to the extent of the restriction. This limitation operates to hold assets within the firm, but the assets are free to circulate in any form and are not set apart in any fund for a special purpose. A special cash or investment fund may be provided in addition to the appropriation.

Restrictions upon retained earnings may be classified by type, as follows:

(1) Legal restrictions.
(2) Restrictions by contract or agreement.
(3) Voluntary restrictions imposed by the board of directors.

Legal Restrictions

The law may impose limitations to protect society from wrongful acts of the stockholders. For example, a corporation may not buy treasury stock at a cost higher than the amount available for dividends shown in retained earnings. Without this restriction, the stockholders could vote to have the corporation purchase all of their shares, and leave the creditors with assets of perhaps dubious value or, at the very least, with assets that are barely equivalent to the creditors' equity. To permit the corporation to purchase its own stock without limit would defeat the purpose of the law prohibiting stockholders from withdrawing the amount invested as stated capital of the firm.

Assume that the board of directors of a corporation with no retained earnings authorizes the corporation to acquire its own stock. The principal stockholders can sell their shares of stock to the corporation if there are no legal restrictions, and the creditors and other stockholders would be placed at an unfair advantage when the company is in a precarious condition.

In still another situation, assume that a corporation has retained earnings of $5,000,000, with no restriction upon the distribution of dividends. The corporation then purchases treasury stock at a cost of $1,500,000. This transaction restricts the amount of retained earnings available for dividends by $1,500,000, and the retained earnings available for dividends becomes $3,500,000 ($5,000,000 − $1,500,000). Sometimes the restriction will be merely noted on the financial statements, and no formal entry will be made. However, if a formal entry to show the classification is desired, it would be made as follows:

Retained Earnings	1,500,000	
Appropriation for Treasury Stock.................		1,500,000

Appropriation for the purchase of treasury
stock.

When the treasury stock is reissued, the restriction is removed, and the entry may be reversed. For example, assume that all of the treasury stock purchased above is sold for $1,800,000. The entries to record the sale of the treasury stock and to remove the restriction on retained earnings are:

Cash..	1,800,000	
Treasury Stock		1,500,000
Paid-In Capital from Sale of Treasury Stock		300,000

Sale of treasury stock.

Appropriation for Treasury Stock....................	1,500,000	
Retained Earnings		1,500,000

Restriction on retained earnings removed by
sale of treasury stock.

Restrictions by Contract or Agreement

A contract or agreement may impose a limit upon retained earnings. For example, a bond agreement may state that while the debt is outstanding, earnings of a certain amount may not be withdrawn. An obligation to make periodic payments on a debt may impose enough strain on the resources without incurring further risk by too generous a distribution of assets to stockholders as dividends.

Voluntary Restrictions

The board of directors may voluntarily decide that retained earnings should be appropriated, thereby retaining asset value for future growth and expansion. There may be other reasons, for example, the board may authorize a restriction to guard against unforeseen contingencies.

Appropriations on the Balance Sheet

The retained earnings section of a balance sheet is shown at the top of page 407, showing appropriations resulting from requirements of the law, debt agreements, and from voluntary action of the board.

When the restrictions no longer apply, they should be removed. If for example, plant expansion involves the construction

Retained earnings:
Appropriated:
 For treasury stock $2,150,000
 Required by bond agreement 1,400,000
 For plant expansion 2,000,000 $5,550,000
 Unappropriated...   2,300,000
  Total retained earnings........................... $7,850,000

of a building at a cost of $1,200,000 and the acquisition of equipment at $600,000, the following entry will be made to record the construction and acquisition:

Building 1,200,000
Equipment.. 600,000
Cash..   1,800,000
 Acquisition of plant assets for cash.

Since there is no longer any reason for the $2,000,000 restriction upon retained earnings for future plant expansion, the following journal entry should be made to remove the restriction.

Appropriation for Plant Expansion 2,000,000
Retained Earnings   2,000,000
 Removal of restriction on retained earnings.

This portion of the retained earnings is now available for dividends. As a matter of policy, however, it may be wise to wait until the new plant assets demonstrate earning power before declaring dividends.

QUESTIONS

1. Name the three basic forms of business ownership.
2. How is the owners' equity of a corporation designated?
3. Creditors may look to the personal assets of stockholders to collect their claims against the corporation. Comment on this statement.
4. What are the two basic divisions of stockholders' equity on the balance sheet and what do they represent?
5. Explain why the market value of a stock may or may not agree with the liquidation value, the book value, or the par or stated value.
6. If stock is issued in exchange for property, how can a value be determined for the property?
7. What special privileges may be granted to preferred stockholders?
8. What advantages do the common stockholders have that are usually not available to the preferred stockholders?
9. What is treasury stock? When treasury stock is acquired, how is it recorded in the accounting records?
10. How is a "gain" from the sale of treasury stock treated?
11. How is a stock dividend recorded in the accounting records?

12. Why might some investors prefer stock dividends to cash dividends?

13. How does a stock dividend differ from a stock split?

14. Are the retained earnings of a corporation reduced when the retained earnings are appropriated?

15. What is the purpose of a law that prohibits a corporation from buying treasury stock at a cost in excess of the amount of retained earnings available for dividends?

16. Aside from restrictions imposed by law, what other types of restrictions may require the appropriation of retained earnings?

17. The stockholders' equity section of a balance sheet for Allen Products, Inc., at December 31, 1980, is given below:

Common stock, $5 par value, 5,000,000 shares authorized, issued and outstanding..................................	$ 25,000,000
Premium on stock...	50,000,000
Retained earnings...	136,500,000
Total stockholders' equity	$211,500,000

(a) If it is assumed that all of the shares were issued at one time at a given amount, how much was received for each share? (b) The company plans for a 3 for 2 stock split and after the split hopes to continue its policy of distributing cash dividends of $1 per share with the distribution to be covered by current income. What is the minimum amount that must be earned each year if this policy is to be continued? (c) From the information given, determine how much a stockholder will receive if (1) he or she sells a share of stock; or (2) the company is liquidated.

18. Selected data from the stockholders' equity section of a balance sheet for Cumberland Mills, Inc., at June 30, 1980, is given below. The treasury stock cost $750,000.

Common stock, $10 par value, 500,000 shares authorized, 380,000 shares issued, 50,000 shares — treasury stock........	$3,800,000
Total retained earnings...	4,560,000

(a) How many shares are eligible to receive dividends? (b) How many additional shares can be issued without amending the charter? (c) What is the maximum amount that can be distributed as dividends? (d) If the treasury stock is resold, what effect would this have on retained earnings?

19. Descriptions abstracted from the stockholders' equity section of a balance sheet are given below:

(1) Preferred 8% stock, $10 par value, cumulative and participating to 10%, 600,000 shares authorized, 520,000 shares issued and outstanding.

(2) No-par common stock, $1 stated value, 8,000,000 shares authorized, 7,200,000 shares issued; treasury stock — 300,000 shares.

(a) In connection with the preferred stock, what is meant by cumulative and participating to 10%? (b) If a stockholder owns 100 shares of preferred stock, what is the minimum amount the stockholder expects to receive each year in dividends? the maximum amount? (c) Common stock has been assigned a stated value of $1 per share. Does this mean that it cannot be traded on the market for less than $1 per share?

EXERCISES

1. Corporate balance sheet. A charter was granted to Eicher Patterns, Inc., that permits the issuance of 100,000 shares of capital stock with a par value of $10 each. Eicher transferred assets from a proprietorship to the newly formed corporation. These assets were appraised at the following values:

Cash...	$171,800
Accounts receivable	164,300
Inventory	142,800
Machinery and equipment.............	217,400
Total assets..............................	$696,300

Accounts payable of the proprietorship in the amount of $46,300 are to be assumed by the corporation. Eicher received 25,000 shares of stock for the net investment.

Other investors received 8,000 shares of stock upon the investment of $208,000 in cash.

Required: Prepare a balance sheet for Eicher Patterns, Inc., at the date of formation.

2. Corporate balance sheet. Fern Valley Processors, Inc., was authorized to issue 250,000 shares of no-par stock with each share being assigned a stated value of $5. One stockholder received 20,000 shares of stock upon the investment of $240,000 in cash. On the same date, another stockholder received 8,000 shares for an inventory of merchandise. At a later date, another stockholder received 70,000 shares for a factory building appraised at $1,050,000. Equipment costing $185,000 was purchased for cash.

Required: Prepare a balance sheet for Fern Valley Processors, Inc., at the completion of the transactions listed.

3. Stockholders' equity with preferred stock. Cordova Products, Inc. was authorized to issue 5,000,000 shares of common stock with no par value but with a stated value of $5 per share. On June 30, 1979, there were 3,400,000 shares issued and outstanding for which the company received $25,500,000.

At June 30, 1979, the company was authorized to issue 250,000 shares of 8%, cumulative, preferred stock with each share having a par value of $10. All authorized shares were issued at a price of $25 per share.

The retained earnings on June 30, 1979, amounted to $2,820,000.

Required: (a) Prepare the stockholders' equity section of the balance sheet on June 30, 1979. (b) Explain what privileges have been granted to the preferred stockholders.

4. Cash dividends with preferred stock. Dahlman Industries, Inc., has both preferred and common stock outstanding. On September 30, 1979, there were 80,000 shares of 8% preferred stock outstanding, each share having a par value of $100. A provision enables the preferred stock to participate with common stock in dividends up to 4% above the stated preference rate. On the same date, there were 2,500,000 shares of common stock outstanding with a par value of $1 per share. The board of directors voted to distribute a total of $1,385,000 in dividends to both classes of stock.

Required: Determine the dividends that should be paid to the preferred shares and to the common shares. Show how much the preferred shares are to receive based on preference and based on participation.

5. Cash dividends with preferred stock. Alison Suppliers, Inc., had 200,000 shares of $1 par value common stock outstanding as of April 30, 1979. The stock was originally issued at an average price of $5 per share. The company also had 10,000 shares of 6% preferred stock outstanding. Each share of preferred stock has a par value of $100. The board of directors voted to declare a total of $120,000 in dividends on both classes of stock for the year ended April 30, 1979.

Required: Determine the dividends that should be paid to the preferred shares and to the common shares.

6. Cash dividends with preferred stock. As of June 30, 1979, Everett Products Company had 7% cumulative preferred stock outstanding. No dividends were paid on the preferred stock during the fiscal year ended June 30, 1978. There were 50,000 shares of $100 par value preferred stock outstanding on June 30, 1979. On the same date, there were 3,000,000 shares of $1 par value common stock outstanding. The board of directors declared a total of $800,000 in dividends on both classes of stock during the fiscal year ended June 30, 1979.

Required: Determine the dividends to be paid to preferred stockholders to comply with the cumulative dividend provision. How much should be paid to preferred stockholders for the current dividend due? How much dividend should the common shareholders receive?

7. Stock dividends. On September 30, 1979, the stockholders' equity of Quigney Patterns, Inc., was as follows:

Common stock, $5 par value, 8,000,000 shares authorized, 6,400,000 shares issued and outstanding......................	$ 32,000,000
Premium on stock..	9,600,000
Retained earnings..	63,200,000
Total stockholders' equity	$104,800,000

The company earned substantial profits, but the board of directors has plans for expansion and desires to conserve cash that would otherwise be distributed as dividends. A stock dividend of 6% was declared and distributed at a time when the market value of each share of stock was $30.

Required: Give the journal entry to record the distribution of the 6% stock dividend.

8. Treasury stock. Roeder Processing Co. had 4,300,000 shares of common stock outstanding as of April 30, 1979. The stock had a par value of $10 per share but was issued at a price of $16 per share. The company was authorized to issue 5,600,000 shares of stock.

During the month of May, the company purchased 120,000 shares of its own stock at a total cost of $2,520,000.

Total retained earnings at May 31, 1979, amounted to $16,340,000.

Required: Prepare the stockholders' equity section of the balance sheet at May 31, 1979. Show the restriction on retained earnings resulting from the treasury stock acquisition.

9. Balance sheet for a new corporation. A charter of incorporation was issued to Katz Patterns, Inc., giving them authority to issue 500,000 shares of stock, each having a par value of $10. On June 30, 1980, the company issued 160,000 shares upon receipt of $15 per share. On the same date, a stockholder transferred assets to the corporation in exchange for stock. These assets were appraised at the following values:

Inventories	$ 163,000
Land	27,000
Building	1,840,000
Equipment	670,000
Total assets	$2,700,000

Required: Prepare a balance sheet for the newly-formed corporation.

10. Book value of common stock. The stockholders' equity section of the balance sheet for GCA Corporation at December 31, 1976, is given below.

Stockholders' equity:
Common stock, $.60 par value; 7,000,000 shares authorized; 1,812,783 shares outstanding after deducting 86,898 shares held in the treasury	$ 1,087,000
Paid-in capital in excess of par	9,269,000
Retained earnings	13,124,000
Total stockholders' equity	$23,480,000

Required: (a) Determine the book value per share of common stock. (b) If the board of directors declared 10% cash dividend, how much would be paid in total dividends? (c) From the information given, is it possible to determine the market value or the liquidation value?

11. Cash and stock dividends. Werley and Amey, Inc., declared a 10% cash dividend on common stock. After the cash dividend was declared, the company declared a 5% stock dividend when the market value of each share was $40. Both dividends were distributed. Prior to the cash dividend declaration, the stockholders' equity section of the balance sheet appeared as follows:

Common stock, $10 par value; 5,000,000 shares authorized; 2,400,000 issued and outstanding	$24,000,000
Premium on stock	8,000,000
Retained earnings	53,000,000
Total stockholders' equity	$85,000,000

Required: (a) Determine the total amount of the cash dividend and the stock dividend. (b) Prepare the stockholders' equity section of the balance sheet after both dividends were declared and issued.

12. Stock split. The board of directors of Mesquite Products, Inc., would like to increase the interest of small investors in its stock. At the present time, the stock is selling for $180 per share. Plans are being made for a 5 for 1 stock split. The charter has been amended to reduce the par value of the stock and to increase the number of authorized shares. The stock-holders' equity section of the balance sheet before the stock split appears below.

Common stock, $50 par value; 1,000,000 shares authorized; 800,000 shares issued and outstanding	$ 40,000,000
Premium on stock..	10,000,000
Retained earnings..	87,600,000
Total stockholders' equity	$137,600,000

Required: Prepare the stockholders' equity section of the balance sheet after the stock split.

13. Treasury stock. Garcia Mines, Inc., had 2,800,000 shares of common stock outstanding as of March 31, 1979. The company was given authorization in the charter to issue 5,000,000 shares of common stock, each share having a par value of $5. The 2,800,000 shares were issued at an average price of $7 per share. During the month of April, the company acquired 300,000 shares of its stock on the market at a price of $12 per share. At the end of April, the company had a balance in retained earnings of $15,850,000. During the month of May, the board of directors declared a cash dividend of $1 on each outstanding share of common stock.

Required: (a) Prepare the stockholders' equity section of the balance sheet at April 30, 1979. (b) Determine the total amount of the dividends declared in May, 1979.

PROBLEMS

11-1. Transactions for a corporation. Selma Supply Company, Inc., was given a charter allowing it to issue 500,000 shares of no-par common stock with a stated value of $10 per share.

(a) Upon receipt of the charter, the corporation issued 300,000 shares of common stock in exchange for $4,500,000 cash.

(b) Cash of $980,000 was paid for an inventory of merchandise and $740,000 was paid for equipment. A building costing $2,800,000 was acquired upon the payment of $800,000 in cash with the balance financed by a 10-year mortgage note.

(c) Additional capital was raised by the authorization and issuance of 6% preferred stock that may be converted to common stock under specified conditions. The preferred stock had a par value of $100 per share. The company issued all of the authorized 10,000 shares for $1,200,000.

(d) During the first year of operation, the company sold merchandise costing $820,000 for $2,300,000 cash.

(e) Cash of $340,000 was paid for various other expenses of operation, and $160,000 was paid for interest on the mortgage note for the year. Aside from the long-term note, there were no liabilities at the end of the year.

(f) Depreciation of $60,000 was taken on the equipment, and depreciation of $100,000 was taken on the building.

(g) Dividends were paid on the preferred stock, and a dividend of $1 a share was paid on the common stock.

Required: (1) Prepare journal entries for the transactions. Omit closing entries.

(2) Prepare a balance sheet at the end of the first year of operation.

11-2. Corporate formation and subsequent operations. Sarah Schwartz has been in business for many years as a dealer in precious stones and jewelry. On April 30, 1979, she planned to reorganize her business as a corporation, Quality Gems, Inc., which was formed by a group of local business persons. The balance sheet for Schwartz is given at April 30, 1979:

Sarah Schwartz
Balance Sheet
April 30, 1979

Assets

Cash	$ 33,450
Accounts receivable	42,180
Inventory	87,740
Equipment, net of accumulated depreciation of $18,600	58,300
Total assets	$221,670

Equities

Notes payable to banks	$ 15,000
Accounts payable	53,230
Interest payable on notes and loans	4,200
Loans payable	50,000
Capital, Sarah Schwartz	99,240
Total equities	$221,670

A charter was obtained for the corporation authorizing it to issue 250,000 shares of common stock with each share having a par value of $10. The corporation was also authorized to issue 1,000 shares of $100 par value preferred stock. The preferred stock has an 8% preference rate and a right to participate in earnings with the common stock for an additional 4% above the preference rate.

The following information is given:

(a) On May 1, 1979, 40,000 shares of common stock were sold for $640,000. All of the authorized preferred stock was sold for $110 per share.

(b) The assets of Schwartz were appraised on May 1, 1979. The inventories were valued at $128,800, and the equipment was valued at $42,000. Cash and accounts receivable were accepted at book value, and no adjustments were made to the liabilities. Goodwill was valued at $20,000.

(c) The assets and liabilities were transferred to the corporation on May 1, and shares of common stock were issued to Schwartz on the basis of the appraisal.

(d) In August 1979, Modern Fashions, Inc., transferred to the corporation a building that was appraised at $840,000. Cash of $300,000 was paid, and 30,000 shares of common stock were issued in the exchange.

(e) On October 1, 1979, the company purchased 2,000 shares of its common stock for $40,000.

(f) Net income for the fiscal year ended April 30, 1980, was reported at $218,600. Total dividends of $119,800 were declared and paid on both classes of stock at the end of the fiscal year.

Required: (1) Prepare a balance sheet for the corporation on May 1, 1979.

(2) Prepare a stockholders' equity section of the balance sheet at April 30, 1980.

(3) Determine the amount of dividends paid on the preferred stock and on the common stock.

(4) What is the book value per share of common stock on April 30, 1980? Can the stock be sold for this amount on April 30, 1980?

11-3. Balance sheet and initial transactions for a new corporation. Spokane Building Supplies, Inc., has been formed to manufacture and distribute insulation material, wood paneling, and various materials to be used in home construction. The charter permits the corporation to issue 1,000,000 shares of common stock, each share having a par value of $1.

Melvin Keyes transferred assets of his own business to the corporation, and the corporation assumed the liabilities of the business. The assets as revalued at current market values, the goodwill of the business as negotiated by Keys and the corporation, and the liabilities are listed below:

Assets

Cash	$114,670
Accounts and notes receivable	113,860
Inventory	187,420
Land	22,000
Building	281,000
Machinery and equipment	176,400
Goodwill	55,000
Total assets	$950,350

Liabilities

Notes payable	$ 60,000
Accounts payable	104,300
Accrued operating expenses	15,200
Total liabilities	$179,500

Supplemental information:

(a) The corporation issued 77,085 shares of stock to Keyes in exchange for the assets, net of liabilities.

(b) Various shareholders invested cash of $3,280,000 for 328,000 shares. The corporation purchased a building, paying $1,840,000 cash. Also, machinery and equipment costing $465,000 were purchased for cash.

(c) During the first fiscal year of operation, the company reported a net income of $810,170 and paid total dividends of $243,051 to the stockholders.

Required: (1) Prepare a balance sheet at the time of incorporation, assuming that the common stock was issued before the commencement of operations.

(2) Prepare the stockholders' equity section of the balance sheet at the end of the first fiscal year of operations after declaration of the dividends.

(3) Determine the book value per share of common stock.

11-4. Treasury stock and dividends. The stockholders' equity section of the balance sheet for Rockport Manufacturing Company, Inc., at October 31, 1979, is given below:

Stockholders' equity:

7% preferred stock, $50 par value, cumulative; 400,000 shares authorized, issued and outstanding	$20,000,000
Premium on preferred stock	2,000,000
Common stock, $5 par value; 1,000,000 shares authorized; 780,000 shares issued; 720,000 shares outstanding	3,900,000
Premium on common stock	7,800,000
Retained earnings (Note A)	7,680,000
	$41,380,000
Less common treasury stock, at cost..........................	1,800,000
Total stockholders' equity	$39,580,000

Note A: Retained earnings must not be reduced below $1,800,000 by dividend payments while the 60,000 shares are in the treasury.

Supplemental information:

(a) During the fiscal years ended October 31, 1978 and 1979, no dividends were declared.

(b) The company declared total dividends of $3,980,000 on November 1, 1979.

Required: (1) Determine the amount of dividends to be distributed to the preferred stock and the amount of dividends to be distributed to the common stock.

(2) How much more dividends can be distributed without violating the restriction imposed by acquisition of the treasury stock?

11-5. Dividends and retained earnings. The stockholders' equity section of the balance sheet for Fort Worth Products, Inc., at March 31, 1978, is given at the top of page 416.

Supplemental information:

(a) Dividends were not paid on the preferred stock in the fiscal year ended March 31, 1978.

(b) During the fiscal year ended March 31, 1979, the company reported a net income of $1,572,000 and declared total dividends of

Stockholders' equity:

6% preferred stock, $100 par value, cumulative; 30,000 shares authorized, issued, and outstanding		$ 3,000,000
Premium on preferred stock		150,000
Common stock, $10 par value; 500,000 shares authorized; 380,000 shares issued and outstanding		3,800,000
Premium on common stock		1,520,000
Retained earnings:		
Appropriated for outstanding bonded indebtedness	$4,200,000	
Unappropriated....................................	730,000	4,930,000
Total stockholders' equity		$13,400,000

$580,000. The bonded indebtedness was retired during the fiscal year ended March 31, 1979, but the board of directors decided to conserve net working capital by declaring dividends of only $580,000 for the fiscal year.

Required: (1) Determine the amount of dividends to be paid on the preferred stock and on the common stock.

(2) Give the composition of the retained earnings at March 31, 1979.

11-6. Stock dividends and cash dividends. Brunswick Chemicals, Inc., has been expanding its operations over the past few years and has had increasing profits. The board of directors, following past practice, declared a cash dividend of $3 per share on the outstanding shares. In addition, a 6% stock dividend was declared after declaration of the cash dividend. The market value of each share at the time of the dividend declaration was $50.

The stockholders' equity section of the balance sheet prior to the actions of the board is given below:

Stockholders' equity:

Common stock, $10 par value; 800,000 shares authorized; 650,000 shares issued and outstanding	$ 6,500,000
Premium on stock..	2,600,000
Retained earnings..	9,430,000
Total stockholders' equity	$18,530,000

Required: (1) Prepare journal entries to record both the cash dividend and the stock dividend. Assume that distribution of the dividends was made at the time of their declaration.

(2) Prepare the stockholders' equity section of the balance sheet after distribution of the dividends.

11-7. Stock split and cash dividends. The board of directors of Gainesville Industries, Inc., authorized a 2 for 1 split of the common stock. The par value of the stock is to be revised to reflect the split, and the number of authorized shares is also to be increased accordingly.

After the split, the company declared and paid a dividend of $1.50 per share on the outstanding shares. The capital stock sold at a price of $40 before the stock split.

The stockholders' equity section of the balance sheet prior to the actions of the board is given below at the top of the following page.

Stockholders' equity:
Common stock, $10 par value; 100,000 shares authorized;
   84,000 shares issued and outstanding.......................... $ 840,000
Premium on stock.. 336,000
Retained earnings... 6,341,000
     Total stockholders' equity $7,517,000

Required: (1) Prepare journal entries to record both the stock split and the cash dividend. Assume that distribution of the dividend was made at the time of declaration.

(2) Prepare the stockholders' equity section of the balance sheet after the stock split and the dividends.

(3) With no other factors present, what should each share of stock sell for after the split?

11-8. Earnings per share with dilution effect. Allman Tool Company, Inc., reported income of $54,000,000 before a fire loss of $8,000,000 and before income taxes. Income taxes are at the rate of 40%.

Debenture notes were outstanding at December 31, 1979. Provisions with respect to the notes are summarized below:

(a) These are 8% debenture notes in $1,000 denominations amounting to $40,000,000.

(b) The notes become due on June 30, 1995.

(c) The holder of the notes may convert the notes to common stock, receiving 50 shares of stock for each $1,000 note.

A portion of the stockholders' equity section of the balance sheet at December 31, 1979, appears below:

Common stock, $5 par value; 20,000,000 shares authorized;
   12,000,000 shares issued and outstanding...................... $60,000,000
Premium on common stock 24,000,000

At December 31, 1979, the common stock had a market value of $18 per share.

Required: (1) Compute the earnings per share without considering the dilution effect of the convertible notes.

(2) Compute the earnings per share after taking into account the dilution effect of the convertible debenture notes.

DECISION CASE

11-I. Dividend policy. During the past two years, Craig Building Supply, Inc., has been expanding its facilities. While the expansion was in progress, the board of directors appropriated retained earnings to restrict the payment of dividends during the period when resources were needed for building and growth. Pertinent information concerning the company follows:

(a) There are 150,000 shares of 8% preferred stock authorized and outstanding. The stock has a par value of $100 per share and has a cumulative right to dividends.

(b) The company has also issued 780,000 shares of $5 par value common stock out of 1,000,000 shares authorized.

(c) The retained earnings section of the stockholders' equity on the balance sheet at December 31, 1979, before considering action of the board of directors at their December meeting, is given below:

Retained earnings:

Appropriated for plant expansion...........................	$18,500,000
Unappropriated...	3,420,000
Total retained earnings.......................................	$21,920,000

(d) During the year ended December 31, 1979, the expansion program was completed, and the new facilities were placed in operation late in the month of November, 1979.

(e) The board of directors voted at the December meeting to release the restriction upon retained earnings, and to reclassify the appropriation for plant expansion as unappropriated retained earnings.

(f) Dividends have not been paid for two years, 1978 and 1979.

(g) The board of directors declared dividends on the preferred stock for the years 1978 and 1979.

There was some difference of opinion among the board members with respect to dividend policy on the common stock. Some board members would like the common stock to receive dividends on the same percentage basis as the preferred stock to compensate for the two years that the common shareholders were denied dividends. Another segment of the board of directors prefer to be more cautious and wait for the expanded operation to show results. Hence, they recommend only an 8% dividend on common stock for the current year since there is no existing policy to give common shareholders dividends that were unpaid in past years.

Required: Which dividend policy do you favor? Explain with supporting computations.

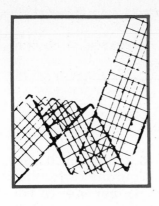

12
Corporate Combinations

Union gives strength.

Aesop

A corporation may acquire some or all of the voting common stock of another corporation. If a corporation acquires a relatively small percentage of the total stock of another corporation, there is virtually no control; and the acquisition may be treated as an ordinary investment. On the other hand, if the percentage of stock acquired is substantial, there will be some degree of control, or even complete control, if all of the stock is owned. In some cases, the stock of one corporation may be issued in exchange for the stock of another corporation.

TYPES OF BUSINESS COMBINATIONS

Three basic types of business combinations are as follows:

(1) Merger.
(2) Consolidation.
(3) Acquisition.

In a *merger*, one of the corporations continues and the other corporation loses its identity in an enlarged entity. In a *consolidation*, a new corporation is formed to take over the properties and assume the liabilities of the combining corporations. When one company acquires a controlling interest in the stock of another company, and both companies retain their separate corporate identities, the combination may be called an *acquisition*.

DEGREE OF OWNERSHIP

It is difficult to make an exact judgment as to how much stock of a corporation must be held to enable the acquiring corporation to exercise a significant degree of control. In general, certain guidelines have been established for the following percentages of ownership:[1]

  (1) Less than 20 percent ownership.
  (2) Between 20 and 50 percent ownership.
  (3) Over 50 percent ownership.

Less Than 20 Percent Ownership

With less than 20 percent ownership, the acquiring corporation is unlikely to have any significant degree of control. The investment is maintained in the records at cost, and any dividends received on the investment are reported as income.

Between 20 and 50 Percent Ownership

If the acquiring corporation owns between 20 and 50 percent of the stock, it exercises some degree of control, but not enough to warrant combining the financial statements to show the related companies as a single economic entity. The investment, however, should be accounted for by the equity method. Under the *equity method*, the investment is increased by the share of net income identified with the number of shares owned, and is reduced by net losses and dividend distributions.

For example, assume that Company A acquired 3,000 shares of the common stock of Company B at a cost of $18,000. Company B had a total of 10,000 shares of common stock outstanding. One year after date of acquisition, Company B reported a net income of $15,000, and distributed dividends to the common stockholders amounting to $6,000.

Company A would record its share of Company B's net income as follows:

---

[1]*Opinions of the Accounting Principles Board, No. 18*, "Equity Method for Investments in Common Stock" (New York: American Institute of Certified Public Accountants, 1971.)

Investment in Co. B (NA)... 4,500
   Income from Co. B (IS)   4,500
     To record 30 percent of the net income of Co. B
     (3,000 shares ÷ 10,000 shares), and to adjust the
     investment to an equity basis.

The dividends would be recorded as follows:

Dividends Receivable (or Cash)................................. 1,800
   Investment in Co. B   1,800
     To reduce investment by amount of dividends re-
     ceived (30% × $6,000). The equity is reduced by
     realization of a part of the investment.

On an equity basis, the investment would be shown at
$20,700, after recording Company A's share of the net income and
the dividend ($18,000 + $4,500 − $1,800).

Over 50 Percent Ownership

When the acquiring corporation owns more than 50 percent of
the stock, it has a voting control. The investment is accounted for
by the equity method, and under appropriate circumstances, consolidated financial statements may be prepared for the related
companies.

REASONS FOR COMBINATIONS

Corporations have sought the advantages of business combination for many years, and this interest has been stimulated in
recent years by the rapid development of new product lines and
the desire for diversification. Even a large established company
may find it difficult and time-consuming to enter a new line of
business. As an alternative, it may seek out a smaller company
that has developed a promising concept in a specialized area. The
small company and the large company can help each other as follows:

(1) The small company may have technical competence, but may lack the
necessary capital to develop its product lines adequately.
(2) The large company may possess the required capital for development,
but may require additional expertise in developing new product lines.

With increased emphasis being placed on growth of earnings,
management may seek rapid growth through combination. Sometimes, the earnings for a combined operation will be larger than
the sum of the earnings that could be obtained if the corporations
operated alone. This apparent contradiction of the law of arithme-

tic arises, in part, because of the increased efficiency of operating on a large scale.

Business combinations may even be necessary for survival. In a competitive environment, business may virtually be forced to grow. If a small company lacks sufficient capital for expansion, it may have to combine with another company or fall behind its competitors.

The government is also interested in business combinations, and may prohibit some combinations on the grounds that they will weaken competition in a given field. Without this regulation, control could be so concentrated that a few companies might dominate an entire industry.

To summarize, some of the important advantages of business combinations are:

(1) Improved competitive position.
(2) Increased efficiency from large scale operation.
(3) Increased technical and financial strength.
(4) Integrated operations extending, perhaps, from the source of raw materials to the ultimate consumer.
(5) Diversified product lines through a combination of companies with different product lines.
(6) Better opportunity to obtain funds at a reasonable cost.
(7) Superior ability to attract high caliber managerial talent.

METHODS OF COMBINATION

As stated earlier. a business combination may be classified by type, as a merger, consolidation, or acquisition; individual corporations may lose their identities as corporations, or may continue as separate entities. The combination may be formed either by *purchase* or *pooling of interests*. The principal distinction between the two methods is whether or not a change in ownership has occurred.

A *purchase* is a buy and sell situation. The purchasing corporation buys the stock of the selling corporation. The stockholders of the purchased corporation sell their interests, and after the transaction, they are no longer owners. On the other hand, in a *pooling of interests* there is usually an exchange of stock rather than a purchase and sale. The stockholders of the companies involved in the combination are not eliminated. The pooling of interests arrangement assumes that all stockholders join together and share interest in a combined entity. Instead of owning an interest in a relatively small entity, the stockholders of each company in the group now own an interest in a larger entity. Each of the two methods of combination will be examined separately.

Purchase

In a purchase situation, the buyer does not necessarily pay a price equal to the cost of the assets as shown on the seller's accounting records. From the buyer's point of view, the seller's recorded cost is irrelevant. For example, a buyer may pay $12 for an asset that is shown on the seller's records at $10. The accountant views the value of an item in a sales-purchase transaction as the negotiated price after arms-length bargaining between the two parties. The cost recorded in the records of the buyer is the price paid for the item, which in this case is $12.

Similarly, a business is sold on the basis of its value at the time of the transaction rather than on the basis of the cost figures that are shown on the records of the seller. Furthermore, a going business often has a value in addition to the value assigned to the net assets (total tangible assets less liabilities). If a business produces above-average earnings, it possesses some degree of goodwill which the buyer may pay for.

Consolidated Statements. A company which purchases a controlling interest in another company is called the *parent company*. The company that is purchased is called the *subsidiary company*. In addition to the financial statements that are prepared for each separate company, consolidated statements may be prepared for the combined companies.

Under certain circumstances, *effective control* may be achieved with less than 50 percent ownership. It is also possible that effective control cannot be exercised even with over 50 percent ownership when large holdings of shares are concentrated in the hands of relatively few shareholders. Assuming the acquiring company can exercise actual control, consolidated statements may be prepared when the degree of control is over 50 percent.

In some cases, it may not be appropriate to combine statements even though the parent has 100 percent control. For example, a manufacturing company may own a finance company. The two companies are so dissimilar with respect to the assets employed and methods of operation that consolidated statements would be of little value. Under these circumstances, separate financial statements for each individual company should be published.

Purchase: 100 Percent Control. Assume that Company P purchased 100 percent of Company S by buying all of the latter's stock for $420,000. Company S is to be continued as a separate corporation, and a consolidated balance sheet is to be prepared at the date of acquisition. Assume also that Company P purchased 20 percent of the stock of Company T for $50,000. Company P does not have a controlling interest in Company T, and the investment in Company T will be shown on both the balance sheet of Company P and the consolidated balance sheet as an investment in an unconsolidated company.

Assume that the assets and equities of Company S have been appraised. All of the assets have a value of $340,000 which is approximately equal to their book value.[2] The goodwill has been determined by negotiation at a value of $80,000.

Net book value of Company S (capital stock and retained earnings)	$340,000
Value of goodwill	80,000
Value of the firm	$420,000

The balance sheets for the two companies, Company P and Company S, immediately after acquisition are shown on a consolidated work sheet as shown below. Columns are given for elim-

Company P and Company S
Work Sheet for Consolidated Balance Sheet
Date of Acquisition

	Trial Balance		Eliminations		Consolidated Balance Sheet
	Company P	Company S	Debit	Credit	
Assets					
Cash	510,000	70,000			580,000
Accounts Receivable	335,000	80,000			415,000
Inventory	365,000	240,000			605,000
Investment in Company S	420,000			(a) 420,000	
Goodwill			(a) 80,000		80,000
Investment in Company T	50,000				50,000
Total assets	1,680,000	390,000			1,730,000
Equities					
Accounts Payable	150,000	50,000			200,000
Capital Stock — Company P	670,000				670,000
Capital Stock — Company S		30,000	(a) 30,000		
Retained Earnings — Company P	860,000				860,000
Retained Earnings — Company S		310,000	(a) 310,000		
Total equities	1,680,000	390,000	420,000	420,000	1,730,000

---

[2]As a practical matter, tangible assets are usually worth more or less than book value. For purposes of simplicity, however, it will be assumed that the values are the same in this text.

inations and/or adjustments, and a consolidated balance sheet is given in the right-hand column. To simplify the illustration, all paid-in capital is combined and labeled as capital stock. This will not affect the essential mechanics of consolidation; and when statements are published, separate captions can be shown for Premium on Stock, Paid-In Capital in Excess of Par or Stated Value, or other segments. Goodwill is recorded as part of the entry to eliminate the investment account and the stockholders' equity of the subsidiary company.

The following work sheet entry illustrates the procedure of elimination:

(a) Capital Stock — Company S.........................	30,000	
Retained Earnings — Company S..................	310,000	
Goodwill..	80,000	
Investment in Company S		420,000
To eliminate the stockholders' equity of Company S against investment in Company S, and to recognize goodwill.		

This entry does not appear in the accounting records of either company. It is only a work sheet entry which is used in the consolidation process.

The assets and the equities of the two companies, after making any adjustments or eliminations, are combined on the consolidated balance sheet. The capital stock and the retained earnings of the parent company become the stockholders' equity of the combined companies.

Purchase: 90 Percent Control. Assume that Company P purchased only 90 percent of the stock of Company S for $369,000. The book value of 90 percent of Company S is $306,000 [90% of ($30,000 capital stock + $310,000 retained earnings)]. Hence, with no additional value attributed to the tangible assets, the goodwill is $63,000 ($369,000 − $306,000). The remaining 10 percent of the stock of Company S is held by other stockholders who are designated as the *minority interest*. A consolidated work sheet is shown at the top of page 426.

In consolidation, the stockholders' equity of the subsidiary company is eliminated. The goodwill is identified, and the minority interest is shown at 10 percent of the stockholders' equity of Company S, $34,000 (10% of $340,000).[3]

---

[3]Some accountants take the position that the total goodwill for the firm should be recognized, imputing a value of goodwill for the minority interest from the parent's share of goodwill. Using this approach, the goodwill would be valued at $70,000 ($63,000 parent goodwill ÷ .9). As a practical matter, the goodwill, as determined by negotiation with the parent company is not necessarily related to total goodwill for the firm.

Company P and Company S
Work Sheet for Consolidated Balance Sheet
Date of Acquisition

	Trial Balance		Eliminations		Consolidated Balance Sheet
	Company P	Company S	Debit	Credit	
Assets					
Cash	561,000	70,000			631,000
Accounts receivable	335,000	80,000			415,000
Inventory	365,000	240,000			605,000
Investment in Company S.......	369,000			(a) 369,000	
Goodwill.........................			(a) 63,000		63,000
Investment in Company T	50,000				50,000
Total assets	1,680,000	390,000			1,764,000
Equities					
Accounts payable................	150,000	50,000			200,000
Capital stock — Company P...	670,000				670,000
Capital stock — Company S...		30,000	(a) 30,000		
Retained earnings — Company P	860,000				860,000
Retained earnings — Company S		310,000	(a) 310,000		
Minority interest				(a) 34,000	34,000
Total equities..............	1,680,000	390,000	403,000	403,000	1,764,000

A consolidating work sheet entry is given below:

```
(a)  Capital Stock — Company S........................     30,000
     Retained Earnings — Company S..................    310,000
     Goodwill..............................................     63,000
          Investment in Company S .........................              369,000
          Minority Interest in Company S .................               34,000
          To eliminate the stockholders' equity of
          Company S, and to recognize goodwill
          and the minority interest.
```

The minority interest in a subsidiary company is sometimes shown on a consolidated balance sheet as a liability of the consolidated entity. In showing the minority interest as a liability, it is assumed that the consolidated statements are prepared from the point of view of the parent company. Hence, the minority shareholders are outsiders, and the obligation of the parent to these shareholders should be depicted as a liability. Strictly speaking, it is not a liability in the sense that there is an outstanding claim to be paid. Some accountants view the consolidation as an entity that should include the minority shareholders. In this case, the minority interest would be appropriately labeled and shown as a part of the stockholders' equity. As a compromise, the minority interest is shown on the balance sheet as a separate item between the liabilities and the stockholders equity, since it is considered a hybrid item that is neither a liability nor a part of consolidated stockholders' equity.

A consolidated balance sheet prepared from the work sheet is given below:

Company P and Consolidated Subsidiary
Consolidated Balance Sheet
Date of Acquisition
(90% Ownership of Co. S)

Assets

Current assets:		
Cash..........	$631,000	
Accounts receivable.........................	415,000	
Inventory.............	605,000	$1,651,000
Investment in Company T.......................		50,000
Goodwill.........................		63,000
Total assets...............		$1,764,000

Equities

Current liabilities:		
Accounts payable		$ 200,000
Minority interest.............		34,000
Stockholders' equity:		
Capital stock.............	$670,000	
Retained earnings	860,000	1,530,000
Total equities.............		$1,764,000

Consolidation — Years Following Acquisition. In the years following acquisition, the parent company records its share of the net income earned by the subsidiary company by a debit to its investment account and a credit to Income from Subsidiary Company. This income is reported as other income on the income statement of the parent company. If the subsidiary company reports a net loss, the parent debits Loss from Subsidiary Company and credits the investment account. The parent company's share of dividends declared by a subsidiary company is recorded by debiting Dividends Receivable and by crediting the investment account. The dividend to the parent is a realization, in part at least, of its share of the net income of the subsidiary. When the dividend is collected, Cash is debited and Dividends Receivable is credited. The investment account, as a result of these recorded transactions, reflects the equity of the parent company in the subsidiary company.

Note that the net income earned and retained by the subsidiary company at the date of acquisition is eliminated in the consolidation process when the retained earnings of the subsidiary company is eliminated. The retained earnings of the subsidiary does not become a part of consolidated retained earnings.

Company P has a 90 percent interest in subsequent net incomes and net losses of Company S, and the minority stockholders retain a 10 percent interest. Company P also has a 20 percent interest in subsequent net incomes and net losses of Company T. In the years following acquisition, a consolidated income statement, as well as a consolidated balance sheet, will be prepared for Company P and Company S. Inasmuch as Company P does not own a controlling interest in Company T, Company T cannot be included in the consolidation process. Instead, the investment in Company T is shown as an investment on both the balance sheet for Company P and on the consolidated balance sheet.

Company P will record its share of the net incomes of Company T as increases to the investment account, and will reduce the investment by its share of net losses and dividends distributed. This method of maintaining the investment account in Company T is called the *equity method* and is in accordance with Accounting Principles Board Opinion No. 18, which states that investments in unconsolidated subsidiary companies (companies in which less than controlling interest is held) be shown on an equity basis on a consolidated balance sheet when the interest is 20% or more.[4]

First Year After Acquisition. In the first year after acquisition, Company S reported a net income of $120,000. Company P decided to amortize the goodwill of $63,000 over 10 years, writing off $6,300 each year ($63,000 ÷ 10) on the income statement. The amortization is to be included as a part of the consolidated operating and other expenses. The amortization of goodwill follows the practice recommended by the Accounting Principles Board that goodwill may be amortized over a period not to exceed forty years.[5]

Company P recorded 90 percent of the reported net income of Company S ($120,000 × .90), or $108,000 as shown in the following entry:

---

[4]*Opinions of the Accounting Principles Board, No. 18*, "The Equity Method of Accounting for Investments in Common Stock" (New York: American Institute of Certified Public Accountants, 1971).

[5]*Opinions of the Accounting Principles Board, No. 17*, "Intangible Assets" (New York: American Institute of Certified Public Accountants, 1970).

```
Investment in Company S ..................................... 108,000
  Income from Company S ....................................           108,000
     90% of the net earnings of Company S that ac-
     crue to Company P.
```

Company T reported a net income of $40,000, and Company P recorded its share of this net income as follows:

```
Investment in Company T...................................    8,000
  Income from Company T.....................................            8,000
     Share of earnings of Company T ($40,000 × .20).
```

Elimination entries to consolidate Company P and Company S are given below:

```
(a)  Capital Stock — Company S........................    30,000
     Retained Earnings — Company S..................   310,000
     Income from Company S ............................   108,000
     Goodwill..............................................    56,700
     Amortization of Goodwill...........................     6,300
       Investment in Company S .........................              477,000
       Minority Interest in Company S ..................               34,000
          Elimination of stockholders' equity of Com-
          pany S at the beginning of the year, and
          the parent's share of net income for the
          year from Company S. Recognition of
          goodwill and amortization of goodwill for
          the year. Elimination of investment and a
          recognition of minority interest at the be-
          ginning of the year.

(b)  Minority Interest in Net Income of Company S ...    12,000
     Minority Interest in Company S ..................                12,000
          To recognize minority share of net income
          for the year, 10% of $120,000.
```

Elimination entry (a) accomplishes the following purposes:

(1) It eliminates the stockholders' equity of Company S at the beginning of the year.
(2) It eliminates the parent company's share of the net income from Company S for the year.
(3) The unamortized goodwill is recognized.
(4) The portion of goodwill amortized during the year is recognized.
(5) The investment in Company S is eliminated.
(6) The minority interest in Company S at the beginning of the year is recognized.

Elimination entry (b) identifies the minority stockholders' share of the net income of Company S, and adds it to the total minority interest in Company S.

Consolidated work sheets for the income statement and balance sheet are given at the top of pages 430 and 431.

Company P and Company S
Work Sheet for Consolidated Income Statement
For the First Year After Acquisition

	Trial Balance		*Eliminations		Consolidated Income Statement
	Company P	Company S	Debit	Credit	
Sales.............................	1,500,000	600,000			2,100,000
Cost of goods sold..............	820,000	380,000			1,200,000
Operating and other expenses	360,000	100,000	(a) 6,300		466,300
Total expenses.............	1,180,000	480,000			1,666,300
Operating income	320,000	120,000			433,700
Income from Company S........	108,000		(a) 108,000		
Income from Company T........	8,000				8,000
Net income, combined..........	436,000	120,000			441,700
Less minority interest in net income of Company S........			(b) 12,000		12,000
Consolidated net income.......					429,700

*Elimination entries are carried forward to the retained earnings section of the consolidated balance sheet work sheet.

The retained earnings of Company P after the amortization of the goodwill for the year becomes the consolidated retained earnings. Note that the consolidation entries have eliminated all of the retained earnings of Company S as follows:

(a) Elimination of retained earnings of Company S at the beginning of the year $310,000

(a) Elimination of the parent's share of the net income of Company S for the year.. 108,000

(b) Elimination of the minority's share of the net income of Company S for the year. (Shown as part of the total minority interest) 12,000

    Total retained earnings — Company S $430,000

Second Year After Acquisition. Additional aspects of consolidation are illustrated for the second year after acquisition by assuming that Company S sells merchandise to Company P. Intercompany sales must be eliminated, otherwise sales would be counted twice: once when recorded as an intercompany sale, and again when the merchandise is sold to outsiders. If any intercompany merchandise remains in the inventory of a member of the consolidated group at the end of the year, the intercompany profit must be removed so that the inventory will be properly stated on a cost basis.

Company P and Company S
Work Sheet for Consolidated Balance Sheet
End of First Year After Acquisition

	Trial Balance		Eliminations		Consolidated Balance Sheet
	Company P	Company S	Debit	Credit	
Assets					
Cash	651,000	110,000			761,000
Accounts receivable.............	455,000	140,000			595,000
Inventory.........................	485,000	280,000			765,000
Investment in Company S.......	477,000			(a) 477,000	
Investment in Company T.......	58,000				58,000
Goodwill.........................			(a) 56,700		56,700
Total assets	2,126,000	530,000			2,235,700
Equities					
Accounts payable...............	160,000	70,000			230,000
Capital stock — Company P...	670,000				670,000
Capital stock — Company S...		30,000	(a) 30,000		
Retained earnings — Company P	1,296,000		(a) 6,300*		1,289,700
Retained earnings — Company S		430,000	(a) 310,000 (a) 108,000* (b) 12,000*		
Minority interest in Company S				(a) 34,000 (b) 12,000	46,000
Total equities..............	2,126,000	530,000	523,000	523,000	2,235,700

*Brought forward from income statement work sheet.

This can be illustrated by the following situation. Assume that a child buys an article for $10 and sells it to the parent for $15. The child has made a $5 profit, and the cost to the parent is $15. From the family point of view, however, the article costs $10, and no profit has been made.

In the second year after Company P acquired Company S, Company S sold merchandise costing $200,000 to Company P for $300,000. All of this merchandise was subsequently sold to outsiders by the end of the year.

An entry for consolidating purposes to eliminate the intercompany sales and cost of goods sold follows:

(a) Sales   300,000
     Cost of Goods Sold   300,000
       Elimination of intercompany sales and cost
       of goods sold.

The intercompany sales of $300,000, as entered by Company S, are eliminated. Also, the cost of goods sold of $300,000 recorded by Company P when the goods were sold to outsiders is eliminated. The consolidated income statement will properly show cost of goods sold at $200,000, which was the cost of the goods when originally purchased from outsiders. Sales will be correctly shown at the amount they were billed when Company P sold the merchandise to outsiders.

Assume also that Company P owes Company S $80,000 at the end of the second year for the merchandise purchased during the year. The intercompany receivable and payable would be eliminated as follows:

(b) Accounts Payable — Company P.....................	80,000	
Accounts Receivable — Company S.............		80,000
To eliminate intercompany receivable and payable.		

Company S reported a net income of $160,000. Company P would record its share of the net income as follows:

Investment in Company S..................................	144,000	
Income from Company S.................................		144,000
90% share of net income of $160,000 ($160,000 × .90).		

Company T reported a net income of $75,000, and Company P would record its 20 percent share as follows:

Investment in Company T..................................	15,000	
Income from Company T................................		15,000
20% share of net income of $75,000 reported by Company T.		

The following elimination entries follow the same pattern that was illustrated for the first year following acquisition. The stockholders' equity of Company S at the beginning of the year and the parent company's share of the net income of Company S are eliminated. The remaining goodwill of $50,400 ($56,700 − $6,300) and the amortization of goodwill are also recognized. The goodwill amortized in past years must be entered as a debit to the retained earnings of Company P, because no entry was ever made in the parent's records for this amortization. The investment in Company S is eliminated, and the minority interest at the beginning of the year is established. In the other elimination entry, the minority share of net income in the amount of $16,000 is transferred to the total minority interest.

(c) Capital Stock — Company S........................   30,000
     Retained Earnings — Company S..................   430,000
     Income from Company S   144,000
     Goodwill..   50,400
     Amortization of Goodwill...........................   6,300
     Retained Earnings — Company P..................   6,300
        Investment in Company S   621,000
        Minority Interest in Company S   46,000
        Elimination of stockholders' equity of Com-
        pany S at beginning of year, parent's
        share of income of Company S, and invest-
        ment in Company S. Goodwill recognized
        along with current amortization and amor-
        tization from past years. Minority interest
        at the beginning of the year recognized
        ($34,000 + $12,000 = $46,000).

(d) Minority Interest in Net Income of Company S...   16,000
     Minority Interest in Company S   16,000
        To recognize minority share of net income
        for the year (10% of $160,000).

Consolidated work sheets for the income statement and balance sheet are shown below and at the top of page 434.

Company P and Company S
Work Sheet for Consolidated Income Statement
For the Second Year After Acquisition

	Trial Balance		Eliminations		Consolidated Income Statement
	Company P	Company S	Debit	Credit	
Sales..........................	2,000,000	800,000	(a) 300,000		2,500,000
Cost of goods sold..............	950,000	430,000		(a) 300,000	1,080,000
Operating and other expenses	380,000	210,000	(c) 6,300*		596,300
Total expenses	1,330,000	640,000			1,676,300
Operating income	670,000	160,000			823,700
Income from Company S........	144,000		(c) 144,000*		
Income from Company T........	15,000				15,000
Net income (combined).........	829,000	160,000			838,700
Less minority interest in net income of Company S........			(d) 16,000*		16,000
Consolidated net income.......					822,700

*Carried to retained earnings on consolidated balance sheet work sheet.

In the consolidation process, the retained earnings of the parent company, including the share of the net earnings, losses, and dividends of the subsidiaries, become the consolidated re-

Company P and Company S
Work Sheet for Consolidated Balance Sheet
For the Second Year After Acquisition

	Trial Balance		Eliminations		Consolidated Balance Sheet
	Company P	Company S	Debit	Credit	
Assets					
Cash	956,000	180,000			1,136,000
Accounts receivable.............	430,000	150,000			580,000
Accounts receivable —					
Company P		80,000		(b) 80,000	
Inventory	925,000	270,000			1,195,000
Investment in Company S.......	621,000			(c) 621,000	
Investment in Company T.......	73,000				73,000
Goodwill			(c) 50,400		50,400
Total assets	3,005,000	680,000			3,034,400
Equities					
Accounts payable...............	130,000	60,000			190,000
Accounts payable —					
Company S	80,000		(b) 80,000		
Capital stock — Company P...	670,000				670,000
Capital stock — Company S...		30,000	(c) 30,000		
Retained earnings —					
Company P	2,125,000		(c) 6,300*		
			(c) 6,300		2,112,400
Retained earnings —					
Company S		590,000	(c) 430,000		
			(c) 144,000*		
			(d) 16,000*		
Minority interest in Company S				(c) 46,000	
				(d) 16,000	62,000
Total equities...............	3,005,000	680,000	763,000	763,000	3,034,400

*Brought forward from income statement work sheet.

tained earnings. Also note that the amortization, past and present, that has never been recorded on any set of records must be considered during the consolidation process.

Pooling of Interests

With a *pooling of interests*, there is no change in ownership, thus there is no buy or sell transaction. Instead, the stockholders of the pooling companies have the same relative interests as they had before, except that they are all part of a larger combined entity. Similarly, assets and equities are not restated at fair market values. With no change in ownership, there is no reason to restate the values of assets and equities as would be the case if the stockholders of one company sold their shares to a purchasing company. The assets and equities, including the retained earnings, are combined as stated on the records of the separate companies.

Assume, for example, that Company A and Company B plan to pool their interests. The pooling will be accomplished by the issuance of shares of Company A to the shareholders of Company B in exchange for their shares in Company B. The former shareholders of Company B are now shareholders of an enlarged Company A, and continue as proportionate owners along with the original owners of Company A stock.

A balance sheet for the pooling of interests appears below:

Companies A and B
Balance Sheet
Date of Pooling of Interests

	Immediately Before Pooling		Immediately After Pooling
	Company A	Company B	Combined
Assets			
Cash....................................	$ 85,000	$ 30,000	$115,000
Accounts receivable.................	110,000	45,000	155,000
Inventory..............................	175,000	65,000	240,000
Total assets........................	$370,000	$140,000	$510,000
Equities			
Accounts payable	$ 20,000	$ 10,000	$ 30,000
Capital stock.........................	300,000	100,000	400,000
Retained earnings	50,000	30,000	80,000
Total equities......................	$370,000	$140,000	$510,000

The stock of Company B, $100,000, is transferred from the shareholders of Company B to Company A, and the shareholders of Company B receive the stock of Company A in the exchange. Company B may or may not continue as a separate corporate entity.

Pooling of Interests vs. Purchase

The difficulty in distinguishing between a purchase and a pooling of interests has been a source of controversy in accounting and business circles. In general, a pooling of interests is possible when each company in the arrangement is of approximately the same size. Under these circumstances, the stockholders of the individual companies may be represented proportionately and may have a true voice in management.

The validity of a pooling arrangement can seriously be questioned, however, when a large company combines with a relatively small company. For example, the Smith family owns a small corporation which produces auto parts. Can they pool their interests with General Motors? Even if the family receives shares of General Motors stock, it is unlikely that it will have any real voice in the management of General Motors. The business, for all intents and purposes has been sold, and the family has received General Motors stock in payment.

Accountants and financial analysts feel that the pooling of interests arrangement, in many cases, has been abused. For example, in pooling, an acquiring company may record the assets of the merged companies at original cost and issue stock for considerably more than the original cost of the assets. The assets may be subsequently sold with a profit being recognized on the transaction. The Accounting Principles Board has published a guideline that permits a pooling type of merger but only under certain limited conditions.[6] Considerable controversy still surrounds the problem of how business combinations should be handled.

Management may tend to favor the pooling of interests method partly because the assets and equities are combined without adjustment. In a purchase transaction, the assets are adjusted to fair market values at the date of purchase. Due to increasing prices and other factors, these values are generally higher than the recorded book values. Furthermore, with no transfer of ownership under the pooling arrangement, goodwill is not recorded. Hence, in a pooling of interests, the asset base will generally be lower.

An advantage of having a lower asset base is that a given amount of net income will reflect a higher rate of return. Management is not particularly interested in showing assets at higher amounts; but it often prefers to reflect a higher rate of return, since this rate is one means used by investors and others to evaluate the success of the firm.

The following example compares the rates of return, assuming a purchase in one case and a pooling of interests in the other, with a difference of $400,000 in the basis of the assets.

---

[6]*Opinions of the Accounting Principles Board, No. 16,* "Business Combinations" (New York: American Institute of Certified Public Accounts, 1970).

$$\text{Purchase: } \frac{\$250,000 \text{ net income}}{\$1,600,000 \text{ asset base}} = 15.6 \text{ percent return}$$

$$\text{Pooling: } \frac{\$250,000 \text{ net income}}{\$1,200,000 \text{ asset base}} = 20.8 \text{ percent return}$$

Note that the rate of return is higher with the pooling of interests treatment because the asset base has not been adjusted upward as would generally be the case when the combination arises from a purchase transaction.

The distinction between a pooling of interests and a purchase is not easy to make. However, the problem must eventually be resolved if financial statements are to reflect the true nature of the combination.

QUESTIONS

1. Explain how an investment is increased or decreased by the equity method of accounting.

2. What are some of the most important advantages to be derived from business combinations?

3. How does a purchase differ from a pooling of interests?

4. What is a parent company, and what is a subsidiary company?

5. What basic accounts are involved when eliminations are made in the consolidation procedure?

6. What is meant by a minority interest, and why is it sometimes shown as a liability on the consolidated balance sheet?

7. How is the minority interest determined for a consolidated balance sheet?

8. What is the maximum period of time over which goodwill may be amortized?

9. How does a parent company account for the profits earned by subsidiary companies in the year subsequent to acquisition?

10. Are the adjustments and eliminations for consolidating purposes recorded in the accounts of the respective companies? Explain.

11. Why would the asset base tend to be lower in a pooling of interests than in a purchase transaction?

12. Why must intercompany transactions be eliminated in the consolidation procedure?

13. Why might management tend to prefer a pooling of interests to a purchase in a business combination?

14. What portion of the net income of the parent company and of the subsidiary is included in consolidated net income?

15. Company A purchased 40% of the outstanding stock of Company B at a cost of $630,000. Company B reported a net income of $150,000 for the year following acquisition of the stock by Company A, and no dividends were declared during the year. What amount should be shown for

the investment at the end of the year following acquisition? Should consolidated statements be prepared for Company A and Company B? Explain.

16. Company P purchased all of the outstanding stock of Company S at a cost of $840,000. At the time of acquisition, capital stock of Company S was $500,000 and its retained earnings were $270,000. The excess of the cost of the stock over the book value was attributed to goodwill. Give the elimination entry for consolidation.

17. Company R purchased 80% of the outstanding stock of Company S at a cost of $390,000. At the time of acquisition, capital stock of Company S was $300,000 and retained earnings were $120,000. Determine the total minority interest at date of acquisition.

18. Company M acquired 70% of the outstanding stock of Company N at a cost of $680,000. The excess of the cost of the stock over the book value was assigned to goodwill. At date of acquisition, Company N had capital stock of $750,000 and retained earnings of $150,000. During the first year after acquisition, Company N reported a net income of $200,000. Goodwill is to be amortized over 10 years. What amount should be shown in the records of Company M as investment in Company N at the end of the first year after acquisition? How much would be shown as goodwill on the consolidated balance sheet at the end of the first year after acquisition? Determine the minority interest at the end of the first year after acquisition.

19. Company A owns 90% of the outstanding stock of Company B. Company A reported a net income for the first year after acquisition from its own operations of $260,000. Company B reported a net income of $120,000 for the same year. Goodwill arising from the acquisition of Company B's stock amounted to $40,000 and is to be amortized over 20 years. Determine the consolidated net income for the first year after acquisition of Company B's stock.

EXERCISES

1. Investments in other companies. On July 1, 1979, Company W purchased 10% of the capital stock of Company X at a cost of $65,000. On the same date, Company W purchased 30% of the stock of Company Y at a cost of $330,000 and 80% of the stock of Company Z at a cost of $480,000. At the end of the fiscal year, June 30, 1980, Company X reported a net income of $40,000; Company Y reported a net income of $160,000; and Company Z reported a net income of $210,000. Company Z paid dividends of $120,000 in the year ended June 30, 1980.

Required: (a) Determine the amount to be shown as the investment in Company X, Company Y, and Company Z on the records of Company W at June 30, 1980. (b) Which of the three companies, X, Y, or Z, may be consolidated with Company W in the preparation of financial statements?

2. **Consolidated balance sheet — 100% purchase.** Boston Company purchased all of the outstanding stock of Dugan Equipment, Inc., for
$380,000 on September 1, 1979. Balance sheets for the two companies
immediately following the purchase transaction are given below:

	Boston Company	Dugan Equipment, Inc.
Assets		
Cash...	$184,000	$153,000
Accounts receivable.........................	168,000	186,000
Merchandise inventory	245,000	121,000
Investment in Dugan Equipment, Inc......	380,000	
Total assets..................................	$977,000	$460,000
Equities		
Accounts payable	$167,000	$ 80,000
Capital stock.................................	600,000	250,000
Retained earnings	210,000	130,000
Total equities...............................	$977,000	$460,000

Required: Prepare a consolidated balance sheet for the two companies at
September 1, 1979, using a work sheet to make the eliminations.

3. **Consolidated balance sheet — 90% purchase.** Fresco Company purchased 90% of the outstanding stock of Rome Products, Inc., on May 1,
1979, at a cost of $640,000. The excess of the cost of the investment over
book value was attributed to goodwill. Balance sheets for the two companies at the date of acquisition are given below:

	Fresco Company	Rome Products, Inc.
Assets		
Cash...	$ 314,000	$169,000
Accounts receivable.........................	721,000	272,000
Merchandise inventory	893,000	314,000
Investment in Rome Products, Inc.	640,000	
Total assets..................................	$2,568,000	$755,000
Equities		
Accounts payable	$ 226,000	$ 55,000
Capital stock.................................	800,000	480,000
Retained earnings	1,542,000	220,000
Total equities...............................	$2,568,000	$755,000

Required: Prepare a consolidated balance sheet for the two companies,
using a work sheet to make the eliminations.

4. Consolidated balance sheet — 80% purchase. Parsons Glass Company paid $640,000 for 80% of the capital stock of Flint Optical Company on July 1, 1979. Balance sheets for the two companies immediately following the purchase transaction are given below:

	Parsons Glass Company	Flint Optical Company
Assets		
Cash...	$ 485,000	$363,000
Accounts receivable..........................	315,000	318,000
Merchandise inventory	475,000	231,000
Investment in Flint Optical Company......	640,000	
Total assets..................................	$1,915,000	$912,000
Equities		
Accounts payable	$ 165,000	$112,000
Capital stock.................................	900,000	350,000
Retained earnings	850,000	450,000
Total equities...............................	$1,915,000	$912,000

Required: Prepare a consolidated balance sheet for the two companies at July 1, 1979, using a work sheet to make the eliminations.

5. Consolidated balance sheet — after acquisition. On September 1, 1978, McNair Products Company acquired all of the outstanding stock of Bewley Tube Company at a cost of $840,000. Bewley Tube Company did not issue or retire capital stock during the fiscal year ended August 31, 1979, and no dividends were paid during the fiscal year. The net income for the fiscal year ended August 31, 1979, was reported by Bewley Tube Company at $420,000. Balance sheets for the two companies are given below at August 31, 1979. Goodwill, if any, is to be amortized over 10 years.

	McNair Products Company	Bewley Tube Company
Assets		
Cash...	$ 527,000	$ 278,000
Accounts receivable..........................	426,000	314,000
Merchandise inventory	645,000	688,000
Investment in Bewley Tube Company	1,260,000	
Total assets..................................	$2,858,000	$1,280,000
Equities		
Accounts payable	$ 130,000	$ 50,000
Capital stock.................................	600,000	400,000
Retained earnings	2,128,000	830,000
Total equities...............................	$2,858,000	$1,280,000

Required: Prepare a consolidated balance sheet for the two companies, using a work sheet to make the eliminations. Any excess of cost of investment over book value of the stock is to be assigned to goodwill.

6. Consolidated balance sheet — after acquisition, minority. Laacke Drilling Company purchased 80% of the capital stock of Dollinger Tool Company on June 30, 1978, at a cost of $480,000. Any excess of the cost of the stock over its book value is to be goodwill. During the fiscal year ended June 30, 1979, Dollinger Tool Company reported a net income of $150,000 and declared and paid dividends of $80,000.

Balance sheets for the two companies are given at June 30, 1979.

	Laacke Drilling Company	Dollinger Tool Company
Assets		
Cash...	$ 741,000	$174,000
Accounts receivable..........................	148,000	126,000
Merchandise inventory	87,000	184,000
Investment in Dollinger Tool Company ...	536,000	
Equipment, net of accumulated depreciation.....................................	933,000	312,000
Total assets....................................	$2,445,000	$796,000
Equities		
Accounts payable	$ 477,000	$126,000
Capital stock..................................	1,000,000	240,000
Retained earnings	968,000	430,000
Total equities.................................	$2,445,000	$796,000

Required: Prepare a consolidated balance sheet for the two companies, using a work sheet to make the eliminations.

7. Consolidated income statement — minority. Fishman Produce Company owned 70% of the capital stock of Sylvester Farms, Inc., for a number of years. During the year ended June 30, 1979, the two companies reported a net income as shown on the income statements given below. There were no transactions between the two companies for the fiscal year ended June 30, 1979, nor was there any consolidated goodwill.

	Fishman Produce Company	Sylvester Farms, Inc.
Sales	$8,340,000	$2,600,000
Income from Sylvester Farms, Inc.	350,000	
Total revenue	$8,690,000	$2,600,000
Cost of goods sold	$6,820,000	$1,250,000
Operating expenses	630,000	850,000
Total expenses.............................	$7,450,000	$2,100,000
Net income....................................	$1,240,000	$ 500,000

Required: Prepare a consolidated income statement for the two companies for the fiscal year ended June 30, 1979. Use a work sheet.

8. **Consolidated balance sheet — after acquisition.** Leith Metal Company acquired all of the outstanding stock of Marianna Parts, Inc., at a cost of $480,000 on July 1, 1979. At that time, Marianna Parts, Inc., had capital stock of $250,000 and retained earnings of $230,000. During the fiscal year ended June 30, 1980, the subsidiary company reported a net income of $105,000 and paid dividends of $30,000. Balance sheets for the two companies are given below at June 30, 1980. Leith Metal Company recorded the dividend from the subsidiary as income.

	Leith Metal Company	Marianna Parts, Inc.
Assets		
Cash...	$ 122,000	$124,000
Accounts receivable.........................	216,000	210,000
Merchandise inventory	272,000	336,000
Investment in Marianna Parts, Inc.	480,000	
Total assets...................................	$1,090,000	$670,000
Equities		
Accounts payable	$ 202,000	$115,000
Capital stock.................................	120,000	250,000
Retained earnings	768,000	305,000
Total equities	$1,090,000	$670,000

Required: Prepare a consolidated balance sheet for the two companies, using a work sheet to make the eliminations.

9. **Consolidated balance sheet — after acquisition, minority.** Achorn Products Company purchased 80% of the capital stock of Castle Fabrics, Inc., on July 1, 1979, at a cost of $720,000. On that date, Castle Fabrics, Inc., had capital stock of $460,000 and retained earnings of $440,000. During the fiscal year ended June 30, 1980, the subsidiary company reported a net income of $100,000. Balance sheets for the two companies are given below at June 30, 1980.

	Achorn Products Company	Castle Fabrics, Inc.
Assets		
Cash...	$ 147,000	$ 229,000
Accounts receivable.........................	713,000	476,000
Merchandise inventory	871,000	575,000
Investment in Castle Fabrics, Inc...........	720,000	
Total assets...................................	$2,451,000	$1,280,000
Equities		
Accounts payable	$ 386,000	$ 280,000
Capital stock.................................	850,000	460,000
Retained earnings	1,215,000	540,000
Total equities	$2,451,000	$1,280,000

Required: Prepare a consolidated balance sheet for the two companies, using a work sheet to make the eliminations.

10. **Consolidated income statement — intercompany sale.** Ohio Company owns 70% of the outstanding stock of Toledo Company. During the fiscal year ended June 30, 1979, Ohio Company sold merchandise costing $450,000 to Toledo Company for $740,000. All of this merchandise was subsequently sold during the fiscal year to outside customers. Income statements for the two companies for the fiscal year ended June 30, 1979, are given below:

	Ohio Company	Toledo Company
Sales	$2,320,000	$1,740,000
Cost of goods sold	$1,570,000	$1,170,000
Operating expenses	320,000	270,000
Total expenses	$1,890,000	$1,440,000
Net income	$ 430,000	$ 300,000

Required: Prepare a consolidated income statement for the two companies for the fiscal year ended June 30, 1979. Use a work sheet.

11. **Consolidated balance sheet.** Kugler Company owns 90% of the stock of Riverdale Patterns, Inc., and 30% of the stock of Sylvan Lakes, Inc. Kugler Company has already recorded its share of the net income of the subsidiary companies for the year as increases to the respective investment accounts and as increases to its retained earnings.

Balance sheets at the end of the fiscal year for Kugler Company and Riverdale Patterns, Inc., are given below:

	Kugler Company	Riverdale Patterns, Inc.
Assets		
Cash	$ 542,000	$146,000
Accounts receivable — Riverdale Patterns, Inc.	68,000	
Accounts receivable (other)	327,000	206,000
Merchandise inventory	215,000	127,000
Investment in Riverdale Patterns, Inc.	504,000	
Investment in Sylvan Lakes, Inc.	76,000	
Plant and equipment, net of accumulated depreciation	363,000	347,000
Total assets	$2,095,000	$826,000
Equities		
Accounts payable — Kugler Company		$ 68,000
Accounts payable (other)	$ 251,000	198,000
Capital stock	650,000	100,000
Retained earnings	1,194,000	460,000
Total equities	$2,095,000	$826,000

Required: Prepare a consolidated balance sheet at the end of the fiscal year. Use a work sheet for adjustments and eliminations.

12. Investments on an equity basis. Montana Mills, Inc., has investments in four companies, with the investments stated on an equity basis at December 31, 1978. Data with respect to the four companies appear below:

	INVESTMENT AS STATED AT DECEMBER 31, 1978	PERCENTAGE OF STOCK HELD BY MONTANA MILLS, INC.	NET INCOME 1979
Brooks Company......	$315,000	70%	$160,000
Fielding Parts, Inc.....	412,000	30	120,000
Nopak Lenses, Inc. ...	210,000	10	150,000
Taveras, Inc.	478,000	100	175,000

Required: (a) State the investments on an equity or cost basis as they should appear on the parent company's balance sheet at December 31, 1979. (b) Show how the investments would appear on the consolidated balance sheet. Assume there is no goodwill.

PROBLEMS

12-1. Consolidation by purchase — 100% control. On September 1, 1979, Lasorda Tool Company purchased all of the outstanding stock of Melendez Mills, Inc., for $225,000. The difference between the cost of the investment and the book value of the stock of Melendez Mills, Inc., is considered to be goodwill. Balance sheets for the two companies at September 1, 1979, are given below:

Assets	Lasorda Tool Company	Melendez Mills, Inc.
Cash...	$ 86,000	$ 41,000
Accounts receivable..........................	110,000	58,000
Merchandise inventory	132,000	63,000
Prepaid expenses...........................	7,000	4,000
Investment in Melendez Mills, Inc.	225,000	
Plant and equipment, net of accumulated depreciation......................	138,000	87,000
Total assets..................................	$698,000	$253,000

Equities		
Accounts payable	$128,000	$ 43,000
Notes Payable...............................	70,000	10,000
Capital stock.................................	200,000	60,000
Retained earnings	300,000	140,000
Total equities...............................	$698,000	$253,000

Required: Prepare a consolidated balance sheet at September 1, 1979, using a work sheet.

12-2. Consolidation by purchase — 80% control. On April 30, 1979, Friedman Patterns, Inc., paid $300,000 cash and issued bonds in the amount of $750,000 for 80% of the outstanding stock of Schwartz Mills, Inc. The following are balance sheets of the two companies at April 30, 1979.

Assets	Friedman Patterns, Inc.	Schwartz Mills, Inc.
Cash	$ 185,000	$ 94,000
Accounts receivable — Schwartz Mills, Inc.	48,000	
Accounts receivable (other)	281,000	215,000
Merchandise inventory	543,000	392,000
Investment in Schwartz Mills, Inc.	1,050,000	
Plant and equipment, net of accumulated depreciation	846,000	516,000
Total assets	$2,953,000	$1,217,000

Equities		
Accounts payable — Friedman Patterns, Inc.		$ 48,000
Accounts payable (other)	$ 256,000	133,000
Accrued expenses payable	23,000	36,000
Bonds payable	750,000	
Capital stock	300,000	280,000
Retained earnings	1,624,000	720,000
Total equities	$2,953,000	$1,217,000

Required: Prepare a consolidated balance sheet at April 30, 1979, using a work sheet. Consider the excess of cost of investment over book value of the subsidiary's stock as goodwill.

12-3. Consolidated income statement. Several years ago, Campetti Fashions, Inc., purchased 80% of the outstanding capital stock of Ott Fabrics, Inc. During the fiscal year ended April 30, 1979, Ott Fabrics, Inc., sold merchandise costing $131,000 to Campetti Fashions, Inc., for $215,000. All of this merchandise was subsequently sold to outside customers before the end of the fiscal year.

Income statements for the fiscal year ended April 30, 1979, are given below for the two companies.

	Campetti Fashions, Inc.	Ott Fabrics, Inc.
Sales	$1,015,000	$963,000
Cost of goods sold	$ 584,000	$511,000
Wages and salaries expense	113,000	86,000
Supplies expense	37,000	21,000
Repairs and maintenance expense	31,000	23,000
Depreciation expense	28,000	16,000
Taxes and insurance expense	26,000	18,000
Utilities expense	22,000	16,000
Income tax expense	86,000	130,000
Total expenses	$ 927,000	$821,000
Net income	$ 88,000	$142,000

Required: Prepare a consolidated income statement by using a work sheet. There is no goodwill to be amortized.

12-4. Consolidated income statement. Howell Chemicals, Inc., purchased 90% of the outstanding capital stock of Wallace Suppliers, Inc., on July 1, 1978. Goodwill of $40,000 was recognized upon acquisition. The goodwill is to be amortized over 20 years. During the fiscal year ended June 30, 1979, Wallace Suppliers, Inc., sold merchandise costing $115,000 to Howell Chemicals, Inc., for $220,000. Howell Chemicals, Inc., sold all of this merchandise to outside customers during the fiscal year.

Summarized income statements for the two companies for the fiscal year ended June 30, 1979, are given below:

	Howell Chemicals, Inc.	Wallace Suppliers, Inc.
Sales......................................	$956,000	$718,000
Cost of goods sold........................	$613,000	$402,000
Operating expenses.....................	138,000	166,000
Total expenses	$751,000	$568,000
Operating income...............	$205,000	$150,000
Income from Wallace Suppliers, Inc...	135,000	
Net income	$340,000	$150,000

Required: Prepare consolidated income statements using a work sheet.

12-5. Consolidated financial statements — 100% control. Aldrich Company purchased all of the outstanding stock of Hamilton Company on April 30, 1978, at a cost of $200,000. The cost was equal to the book value at that date. During the year, Hamilton Company sold merchandise costing $40,000 to Aldrich Company for $60,000. All of this merchandise was sold during the fiscal year to outside customers. Summarized income statements for the year ended April 30, 1979, and balance sheets as of that date, are given below and at the top of page 447.

	Income Statements	
	Aldrich Company	Hamilton Company
Sales	$207,000	$148,000
Cost of goods sold	$102,000	$ 71,000
Operating expenses	45,000	33,000
Total expenses............................	$147,000	$104,000
Operating income....................	$ 60,000	$ 44,000
Income from Hamilton Company...........	44,000	
Net income	$104,000	$ 44,000

Required: Prepare consolidated financial statements. Use work sheets.

12-6. Consolidated financial statements — 80% control. Smith Parts Company acquired 80% of the outstanding stock of Waller Company on June 30, 1978, at a cost of $232,000. Goodwill of $40,000 was recognized. The goodwill is to be written off over 10 years. Summarized income statements for the year ended June 30, 1979, and balance sheets as of June 30, 1979, are given on the following page:

Balance Sheets

Assets	Aldrich Company	Hamilton Company
Cash..	$121,000	$ 79,000
Accounts receivable.........................	83,000	43,000
Merchandise inventory	152,000	138,000
Investment in Hamilton Company..........	244,000	
Total assets...................................	$600,000	$260,000

Equities		
Accounts payable	$ 97,000	$ 16,000
Capital stock.................................	150,000	50,000
Retained earnings	353,000	194,000
Total equities	$600,000	$260,000

Income Statements

	Smith Parts Company	Waller Company
Sales	$1,012,000	$319,000
Cost of goods sold	$ 604,000	$183,000
Operating expenses	118,000	36,000
Total expenses.............................	$ 722,000	$219,000
Operating income...................	$ 290,000	$100,000
Income from Waller Company	80,000	
Net income	$ 370,000	$100,000

Balance Sheets

Assets	Smith Parts Company	Waller Company
Cash...	$ 204,000	$128,000
Accounts receivable, Waller Company...	10,000	
Accounts receivable (other)................	211,000	108,000
Merchandise inventory	517,000	231,000
Investment in Waller Company	312,000	
Total assets...................................	$1,254,000	$467,000

Equities		
Accounts Payable, Smith Parts Company.		$ 10,000
Accounts payable (other)	$ 216,000	117,000
Capital stock.................................	175,000	100,000
Retained earnings	863,000	240,000
Total equities	$1,254,000	$467,000

Required: Use work sheets to prepare consolidated financial statemen.

12-7. Consolidated financial statements and unconsolidated subsidiary. Amity Products, Inc., purchased 25% of the outstanding stock of Billings Company at a cost of $40,000 on December 31, 1977. On the same date, Amity Products, Inc., purchased 80% of Condor Laboratories, Inc., at a cost of $280,000. At the date of acquisition, Condor Laboratories, Inc., had capital stock of $60,000 and retained earnings of $240,000. The excess of the cost of the investment over the book value of the stock of the subsidiary company is considered to be goodwill.

The parent company has maintained the investment accounts at original cost. Goodwill of $40,000 is to be written off in equal annual installments, and $4,000 was amortized during the year 1978.

Net income for the three companies are reported as follows in 1978:

Amity Products, Inc.	$246,000
Billings Company	20,000
Condor Laboratories, Inc.	100,000

Billings Company reported a net income of $40,000 for the year 1979.

Summarized income statements for the year ended December 31, 1979, and balance sheets as of December 31, 1979, are given below:

	Income Statements	
	Amity Products, Inc.	Condor Laboratories, Inc.
Sales	$2,300,000	$1,260,000
Cost of goods sold and operating expenses	2,050,000	1,110,000
Net income	$ 250,000	$ 150,000

	Balance Sheets	
	Amity Products, Inc.	Condor Laboratories, Inc.
Assets		
Various assets	$1,330,000	$635,000
Investment in Billings Company	40,000	
Investment in Condor Laboratories, Inc.	280,000	
Total assets	$1,650,000	$635,000
Equities		
Various liabilities	$ 110,000	$ 85,000
Capital stock	600,000	60,000
Retained earnings	940,000	490,000
Total equities	$1,650,000	$635,000

Required: Use work sheets to prepare consolidated financial statements. Enter on the work sheet the adjustments to place the investment accounts on an equity basis.

12-8. Combination by pooling of interests. The top managements of Carbon Plastics, Inc., and Wyoming Films, Inc., agreed to a pooling of interests on November 30, 1979. Carbon Plastics, Inc., issued capital stock in exchange for the capital stock of Wyoming Films, Inc. All of the capital stock in the transaction has voting rights, and management will be shared in proportion to the stock holdings represented.

Balance sheets at November 30, 1979, are given below:

	Carbon Plastics, Inc.	Wyoming Films, Inc.
Assets		
Cash...	$204,000	$156,000
Accounts receivable — Wyoming Films, Inc.	18,000	
Accounts receivable (other).................	142,000	93,000
Merchandise inventory	186,000	122,000
Plant and equipment, net of accumulated depreciation........................	217,000	173,000
Total assets.................................	$767,000	$544,000
Equities		
Accounts payable — Carbon Plastics, Inc.		$ 18,000
Accounts payable (other)	$134,000	61,000
Capital stock.................................	200,000	150,000
Retained earnings	433,000	315,000
Total equities...............................	$767,000	$544,000

Required: Using a work sheet, prepare a consolidated balance sheet.

DECISION CASE

12-I. Purchase vs. pooling of interests. The chairman of the board of directors of Midland Bearings, Inc., is examining a proposal to acquire all of the outstanding stock of Quinn and Harper, Inc. The purchase is to be financed by the issuance of additional capital stock. At June 30, 1979, Quinn and Harper, Inc., reported capital stock at $40,000 and retained earnings at $180,000. Preliminary negotiations reveal that the board of directors of Quinn and Harper, Inc., has placed a value of $100,000 on goodwill and is willing to sell all of the stock for $320,000. The goodwill is to be amortized over 10 years.

The chairman and the other board members of Midland Bearings, Inc., believe that it would be better to issue shares of stock to the shareholders of Quinn and Harper, Inc., in exchange for their stock. The transaction would then be handled as a pooling of interests instead of a purchase.

Financial statements, as presented in the financial reports for the fiscal year ended June 30, 1979, are given at the top of page 450 in summary form.

	Income Statements	
	Midland Bearings, Inc.	Quinn and Harper, Inc.
Sales	$850,000	$380,000
Cost of goods sold	$640,000	$280,000
Operating expenses	130,000	70,000
Total expenses.............................	$770,000	$350,000
Net income	$ 80,000	$ 30,000

	Balance Sheets	
	Midland Bearings, Inc.	Quinn and Harper, Inc.
Assets		
Cash	$ 77,000	$ 17,000
Accounts receivable.........................	126,000	93,000
Merchandise inventory	142,000	140,000
Plant and equipment, net of accumu- lated depreciation........................	585,000	
Total assets..................................	$930,000	$250,000
Equities		
Accounts payable	$130,000	$ 30,000
Capital stock.................................	260,000	40,000
Retained earnings	540,000	180,000
Total equities	$930,000	$250,000

The net income for each company has been estimated for the next fiscal year as follows:

> Midland Bearings, Inc................... $100,000
> Quinn and Harper, Inc.................   50,000

In projecting balance sheet data ahead to June 30, 1980, it is assumed that the inventory of each company will be increased by exactly the amount of the estimated net income for the fiscal year.

Required:
(1) Prepare an estimated consolidated balance sheet at June 30, 1980, based on the assumption that the transaction was handled as a purchase.
(2) Prepare an estimated consolidated balance sheet at June 30, 1980, based on the assumption that the transaction was handled as a pooling of interests.
(3) Compute the rate of return on total assets of the consolidated balance sheet at June 30, 1980, under both the purchase alternative and the pooling of interests alternative. Which alternative yields the higher rate of return? Why?

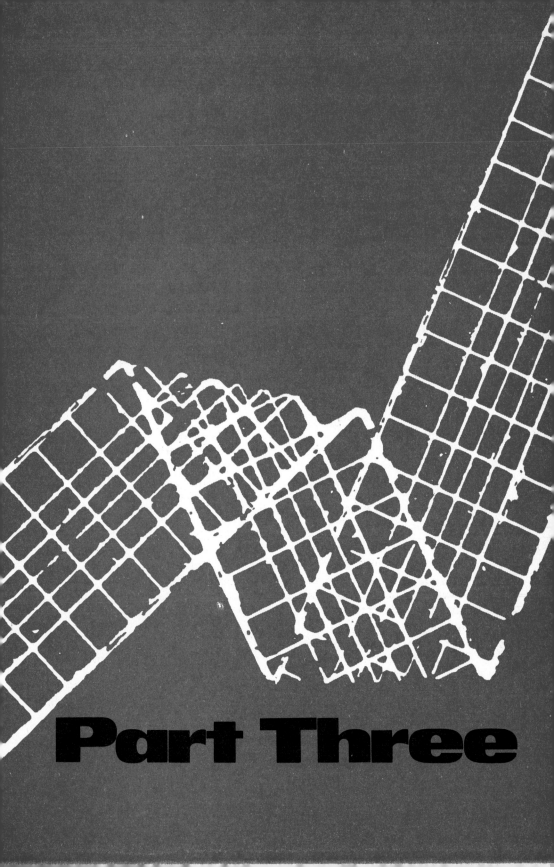

Part Three

Analysis
and
Interpretation

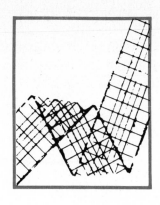

13
Analysis of Changes in Net Working Capital and Financial Position

An elephant can only be eaten in pieces.
Ancient Cambodian proverb

One of the objectives of accounting is to analyze, interpret, and communicate financial information to a broad range of persons and groups, both within and outside the organization. This chapter, in addition to reviewing procedures and concepts that are involved in organizing financial information, stresses the analysis of changes in net working capital and financial position during an accounting period. Examinations of these two areas of financial operations will: (1) bring into sharper focus significant relationships that exist between the balance sheet and income statement; and (2) illustrate a common method of recombining financial data in order to gain additional insight into the firm's financial position. Analysis of this type enables better informed managers, creditors, and investors to make more intelligent decisions.

FINANCIAL EVALUATION OF A BUSINESS ENTERPRISE

Any company may be partially evaluated by analyzing either the balance sheet or the income statement separately. For example, inspection of one or more balance sheets would reveal the specific types of debt and equity capital that have been obtained to finance the firm, as well as the apportionment of these sources among the various assets. In addition, answers to the following questions may be obtained from analyzing the balance sheet alone:

(1) Does excess idle cash exist which could be better utilized to generate higher earnings; or is the balance of cash insufficient to meet current obligations?
(2) Does the amount of receivables appear excessive; or would management be well advised to tighten up its collection policies?
(3) Is the inventory balance adequate to meet the anticipated volume of operations; or does it appear unnecessarily high?
(4) Are plant assets being overutilized, or does idle capacity exist? Has the undepreciated cost of plant assets remained relatively stable (indicating a continuous replacement of those assets as they are retired); increased (signalling an expansion of operations); or decreased (suggesting plant facilities may be nearing the point of physical exhaustion or obsolescence)?

Other significant questions can be answered by carefully examining one or more income statements apart from the balance sheet:

(1) Is the sales trend upward, stable, or downward?
(2) What is the pattern of the gross margin percentage?
(3) Are certain expenses beginning to move upward and out of control, while still others appear to be decreasing relative to sales volume?
(4) How efficient is the firm in operating at a particular volume of business, for example, as measured by its return on sales (net income divided by sales)?

However, the following types of critical questions can only be adequately addressed by examining the income statement and the balance sheet simultaneously:

(1) What is the relationship between the amount of debt and equity capital and the current level of earnings?
(2) How rapidly is inventory being converted into sold goods?
(3) What percentage of sales remains uncollected?
(4) What percentage of the capitalized cost of plant assets was expensed during the current fiscal period?

A comprehensive financial evaluation of the firm requires an approach that scrutinizes both financial statements together.

One approach which accomplishes this deals with changes in the net working capital and the financial position of the firm — changes which are examined in considerable detail in this chapter.

THE SIGNIFICANCE OF NET WORKING CAPITAL ANALYSIS

The concept of *working capital* may be defined in one of four ways:

(1) The quick assets, or current assets less inventory and prepaid expenses.
(2) The current assets.
(3) The excess of quick assets over current liabilities.
(4) The excess of current assets over current liabilities.

Net working capital, however, has a more limited connotation, and is usually defined as either the excess of quick assets over current liabilities, or the excess of current assets over current liabilities. For purposes of subsequent discussion, net working capital will be defined as the excess of current assets over current liabilities, or:

$$\text{NET WC} = \text{CA} - \text{CL}$$

The focus of net working capital analysis is the examination of the liquidity position of an organization during a specific period of time. The never-ending challenge for a financial manager is to maintain an optimum balance between short-term liquidity and overall profitability. For example, an over-allocation of a firm's financial resources among the noncurrent assets, such as plant and equipment, may help to generate excellent earnings; but to continue such a policy indefinitely could place the company in a position where creditors cannot be paid due to insufficient cash or quick assets that can be quickly converted into cash. On the other hand, excessive liquidity, such as when too large a portion of financial resources has been allocated among the current assets, may strangle the long-run profit-generating ability of the enterprise. Frequent examination of the size, composition, and any significant changes in net working capital assists financial managers to achieve a more optimum balance between these ofttimes competing horns of a dilemma. In addition, the statement of changes in financial position that appears in most annual stockholder reports allows others to monitor and evaluate management's success in maintaining this balance.

Net working capital analysis usually focuses on the liquidity position of the firm for a period of approximately six to twelve months. In brief, the analysis is concerned with determining specific changes and the reasons for these changes in each of the current accounts during a period of time. The change in net working capital can be examined historically with respect to: (1) the extent of the changes that occurred; (2) the transactions that caused the changes; and (3) the impact that those changes had on company operations. By projecting this type of analysis into the future, potential plans for operations may be translated into their impact on the expected net working capital position of the firm before plans are finalized and resources are committed to various projects. Specific danger signals may be detected and, if necessary, appropriate adjustments can be implemented and financing arranged during the planning stage before critical emergencies arise.

Subsequent discussion will concentrate on developing a methodology for net working capital analysis, which will then be extended to include analysis of changes in the firm's overall financial position.

APPROACHES TO NET WORKING CAPITAL ANALYSIS

The monetary amount of net working capital can readily be determined at any point in time merely by subtracting total current liabilities from total current assets. The primary purpose of analyzing net working capital, however, is to determine what factors caused net working capital to change during a given interval of time. The determination and analysis of specific reasons for this change may be approached using either of the following perspectives:

(1) Algebraic logic.
(2) Transaction reconstruction and analysis.

Algebraic Logic

Recall that the balance sheet equation is: assets equal liabilities plus owners' equity. Expanded into its major components, the equation becomes current assets plus noncurrent assets equal current liabilities and long-term liabilities plus owners' equity. Symbolically, this expanded equation may be expressed as:

$$CA + NA = CL + LL + OE$$

Because of the duality inherent in double-entry accounting, net working capital may be expressed in terms of either the current or noncurrent accounts. This can be accomplished merely by transferring all current liabilities (CL) to the left, and all noncurrent assets (NA) to the right of the equals sign in the above equation, as shown below:

$$\text{NET WC} = \underbrace{CA - CL}_{\text{Current accounts}} = \underbrace{LL + OE - NA}_{\text{Noncurrent accounts}} \qquad [1]$$

Note that net working capital in the one instance encompasses all the current accounts, not merely cash; and that noncurrent assets include plant assets, natural resources, intangible assets, and investments. Since net income (the difference between revenue, other income, and gains less expenses and losses) is closed to Retained Earnings (OE) at the end of each accounting period, all income-statement-related accounts are considered part of owners' equity for purposes of net working capital analysis.

Adding the Δ notation, meaning "change in", to each element in Equation [1] transforms it into a symbolic expression which accounts for the change in net working capital, as displayed below in the "net working capital" equation:

$$\underbrace{\Delta NET\ WC}_{\substack{A \\ \text{Total change}}} = \underbrace{\Delta CA\ -\ \Delta CL}_{\substack{B \\ \text{Changes in} \\ \text{current accounts}}} = \underbrace{\Delta LL\ +\ \Delta OE\ -\ \Delta NA}_{\substack{C \\ \text{Changes in} \\ \text{noncurrent accounts}}} \qquad [2]$$

In short, the total change in net working capital during a particular period of time can be analyzed by considering all changes which occurred in the current accounts or all of the changes which occurred in the noncurrent accounts.

(1) Segment A reflects the aggregate change in net working capital during a period of time; but no detail is furnished with respect to what caused that aggregate change.

(2) Segment B reflects the change that occurred during the period in the current assets and current liabilities. Further division of Segment B would provide the schedule of changes in net working capital, an example of which is shown on page 465.

(3) Segment C reflects the change that occurred during the period in each of the three major noncurrent categories. Further division of this segment would provide the statement of changes in financial position, an example of which is shown on page 477.

Transaction Reconstruction and Analysis

Net working capital analysis can also be approached by dissecting each type of financial transaction that occurred during the period under investigation. Net working capital is changed only when the transaction being examined causes a change in at least one current and at least one noncurrent account. This can be illustrated diagrammatically as shown below:

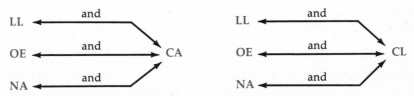

On the other hand, net working capital is never affected if the entry being examined contains only current accounts or only noncurrent accounts.

All transactions which involve noncurrent accounts and at least one current account can be segregated into two categories. One category of transactions increases net working capital, and is considered a *source* of funds; whereas the other category decreases net working capital, and is considered a *use* or *application* of funds. This can be displayed in tabular form as shown below:

SOURCES (INCREASES) OF NET WORKING CAPITAL	EACH TRANSACTION MUST INCLUDE AT LEAST ONE CURRENT ACCOUNT	USES (DECREASES) OF NET WORKING CAPITAL
Decrease in noncurrent assets.		Increase in noncurrent assets.
Increase in long-term liabilities.		Decrease in long-term liabilities.
Increase in owners' equity.		Decrease in owners' equity.

Integrative Illustrations

Each of these approaches to net working capital analysis can be illustrated and integrated by considering the following common transactions:

(1) Investment by owners.
(2) Purchase of plant assets.
(3) Purchase of inventory.
(4) Sale of merchandise.
(5) Recognition of cost of goods sold.
(6) Recognition of depreciation.

Transaction (1)

Additional Investment by Owners

A corporation sold 4,000 shares of $10 par value common stock to existing stockholders for $40,000 cash. The entry is recorded below:

```
Cash ........................................... 40,000
    Common Stock.............................          40,000
        Sale of 4,000 shares at $10 per share.
```

Since a current account and an owners' equity account are involved in this entry, both of which increased, net working capital was increased by $40,000, as reflected below:

$$\Delta NET\ WC = \Delta CA - \Delta CL = \Delta LL + \Delta OE - \Delta NA$$
$$(+\$40,000) = (+\$40,000) \qquad = \qquad (+\$40,000)$$

In short, this sale of common stock was a $40,000 source of net working capital.

Transaction (2)

Purchase of Plant Assets

Several pieces of equipment costing $120,000 were purchased under a financing arrangement whereby one third of the cost was paid in cash on delivery, with the balance due two years hence on a mortgage note payable. The entry to record this purchase is as follows:

Equipment	120,000	
Cash		40,000
Mortgage Note Payable		80,000
Purchase of equipment with $40,000 paid at delivery (⅓ × $120,000).		

Analysis of this transaction, using the algebraic approach, verifies that net working capital decreased by $40,000, as shown below:

$$\Delta \text{NET WC} = \quad \Delta \text{CA} \quad - \quad \Delta \text{CL} \quad = \quad \Delta \text{LL} \quad + \quad \Delta \text{OE} \quad - \quad \Delta \text{NA}$$
$$(-\$40{,}000) = (-\$40{,}000) \qquad\qquad = (+\$80{,}000) \qquad\qquad - (+\$120{,}000)$$

Another way of viewing the transaction is to consider that the $80,000 portion of the noncurrent asset which was offset by the long-term note had no impact on net working capital. The remaining $40,000 cash disbursement was a use of net working capital.

Transaction (3)

Purchase of Inventory

Inventory costing $75,000 was purchased on 30-day credit terms, as reflected in the following entry:

Inventory	75,000	
Accounts Payable.......................................		75,000
Purchase of inventory on 30-day credit terms.		

Net working capital was not affected by this transaction because the two accounts involved in the transaction are both current accounts. The algebraic approach substantiates this conclusion, as shown below:

$$\Delta \text{NET WC} = \quad \Delta \text{CA} \quad - \quad \Delta \text{CL} \quad = \quad \Delta \text{LL} + \Delta \text{OE} - \Delta \text{NA}$$
$$-0- \quad = (+\$75{,}000) - (+\$75{,}000) = \quad\quad -0-$$

Transaction (4)

Sale of Merchandise

Sale of merchandise under cash and 40-day credit terms during the period were $6,000 and $54,000, respectively, as shown in the following summary entry:

Cash	6,000	
Accounts Receivable....................................	54,000	
Sales..		60,000
Record sales on cash and credit terms.		

The effect of this entry on net working capital is an increase of $60,000. For purposes of net working capital analysis, all items on the income statement are considered a part of owners' equity. Sales are a source of net working capital, which can be verified by inserting appropriate data from the preceding entry into Equation [2], as shown below:

$$\Delta\text{NET WC} = \quad \Delta\text{CA} \quad - \quad \Delta\text{CL} \quad = \quad \Delta\text{LL} \quad + \quad \Delta\text{OE} \quad - \quad \Delta\text{NA}$$

$$(+\$60,000) = \begin{array}{l} +\$\ 6,000 \\ +\$54,000 \end{array} \qquad = \qquad\qquad (+\$60,000)$$

Transaction (5)

Recognition of Cost of Goods Sold

The cost of the inventory associated with the merchandise sold in Transaction (4) totaled $47,000, and is charged to expense as cost of goods sold in the following entry:

```
Cost of Goods Sold .......................................    47,000
     Inventory ................................................              47,000
          Recognition of cost of goods sold.
```

Since a current and a noncurrent account are shown in the above entry, net working capital is decreased by $47,000, as displayed below:

$$\Delta\text{NET WC} = \quad \Delta\text{CA} \quad - \quad \Delta\text{CL} \quad = \quad \Delta\text{LL} \quad + \quad \Delta\text{OE} \quad - \quad \Delta\text{NA}$$

$$(-\$47,000) = (-\$47,000) \qquad\qquad = \qquad\qquad + (-\$47,000)$$

Restated, this transaction resulted in a use of net working capital.

Transaction (6)

Recognition of Depreciation

Depreciation recorded on various plant assets for the period totaled $8,000 and is reflected in the following entry:

```
Depreciation Expense — Equipment.....................    8,000
     Accumulated Depreciation — Equipment ...........              8,000
          Record depreciation expense.
```

Since each of the accounts shown in the above entry is noncurrent, net working capital is not affected, as verified below:

$$\Delta\text{NET WC} = \Delta\text{CA} - \Delta\text{CL} = \quad \Delta\text{LL} \quad + \quad \Delta\text{OE} \quad - \quad \Delta\text{NA}$$

$$\text{—0—} \quad = \quad \text{—0—} \quad = \qquad + (-\$8,000) - (-\$8,000)$$

The impact which the preceding six transactions had on net working capital can be summarized as shown at the top of page 461. Each number in parentheses refers to the transaction.

SUMMARY OF NET WORKING CAPITAL ANALYSIS

Sources		Uses	
(1) Sale of common stock.................	$ 40,000	(2) Purchase of equipment...........	$40,000
(4) Sale of merchandise .	60,000	(5) Recognition of cost of goods sold	47,000
Total sources........	$100,000	Total uses............	$87,000

Net working capital increased by $13,000 ($100,000 − $87,000) because sources exceeded uses by that amount.

An alternate way of arriving at the same conclusion can be achieved by summarizing each of the six transactions in the format of Equation [2], as shown on page 462.

Each method used stresses one critical characteristic of net working capital analysis: net working capital is affected only when the financial transaction under investigation involves both current and noncurrent accounts. A step-by-step sequence may now be developed by which to analyze the change in net working capital that occurs under more complex circumstances in a business enterprise during an entire fiscal period.

PROCEDURE FOR ANALYSIS

The following steps are normally required to provide a systematic approach to net working capital analysis:

(1) Obtain the necessary financial statements including:
   (a) Two balance sheets, one dated at the beginning and the other dated at the end of the specified period.
   (b) An income statement for the period between these two balance sheets.
   (c) Any supplemental financial information that may be relevant to the analysis.
(2) Determine the aggregate change in net working capital during the period, by constructing a schedule of changes in net working capital.
(3) Reconcile each noncurrent account in the order shown on the balance sheet.

Obtaining the Necessary Financial Data

Financial transactions that occurred in the Jorgenson Corp. during the fiscal year ended December 31, 1979, will be used to illustrate the details involved in net working capital analysis. The initial step is to assemble the essential financial statements and information. The comparative balance sheet at the end of 1978 and 1979, the income statement for 1979, and several items of supplemental financial information are shown on pages 463 and 464. Be-

Transaction	ΔNET WC	=	ΔCA	-	ΔCL	=	ΔLL	+	ΔOE	-	ΔNA
(1) Sale of common stock	+$40,000	=	+$40,000 Cash			=			+$40,000 Capital Stock		
(2) Purchase of plant asset	-$40,000	=	-$40,000 Cash			=	+$80,000 Mortgage Note Payable			-	(+$120,000) Equipment
(3) Purchase of inventory	-0-	=	+$75,000 Inventory	-	(+$75,000) Accounts Payable	=					
(4) Sale of merchandise	+$60,000	=	+$ 6,000 Cash +$54,000 Accounts Receivable			=			+$60,000 Sales		
(5) Recognition of cost of goods sold	-$47,000	=	-$47,000 Inventory			=			-$47,000 Cost of Goods Sold		
(6) Recognition of depreciation		=				=			-$ 8,000 Depreciation Expense — Equipment	-	(-$ 8,000) Accumulated Depreciation
Total	+$13,000	=	+$88,000	-	$75,000	=	+$80,000	+	+$45,000	-	$112,000

fore beginning the analysis, however, all financial statements should be carefully inspected to insure that totals and subtotals are internally consistent, and that all account titles have been properly classified within major categories on both financial statements.

Jorgenson Corp.
Comparative Balance Sheet
December 31, 1979 and 1978

Assets	1979	1978
Current assets:		
Cash	$ 18,000	$ 12,000
Marketable securities.......................................	3,000	2,000
Accounts receivable (net of allowance for doubtful accounts)..	45,000	37,000
Inventory..	72,000	69,000
Prepaid expenses	7,000	8,000
Total current assets.....................................	$145,000	$128,000
Plant assets:		
Land	$ 8,000	$ 6,000
Buildings and equipment....................................	251,000	244,000
Less accumulated depreciation	(43,000)	(37,000)
Total plant assets.......................................	$216,000	$213,000
Total assets..	$361,000	$341,000
Equities		
Current liabilities:		
Notes payable..	$ 30,000	$ 50,000
Accounts payable	44,500	39,000
Income tax payable...	6,000	5,000
Dividends payable..	1,500	—
Total current liabilities...............................	$ 82,000	$ 94,000
Long-term liabilities:		
Bonds payable, 8%, 10 years, due December 31, 1987...	$ 80,000	$ 80,000
Discount on bonds payable.................................	(6,400)	(7,200)
Mortgage note payable, 7%, due December 31, 1982...	4,000	—
Total long-term liabilities.............................	$ 77,600	$ 72,800
Owners' equity:		
Capital stock, $10 par	$110,000	$ 90,000
Premium on stock...	8,000	6,000
Retained earnings:		
Appropriation for expansion..............................	3,000	2,000
Unappropriated...	80,400	76,200
Total owners' equity	$201,400	$174,200
Total equities	$361,000	$341,000

Jorgenson Corp.
Income Statement
For the Year Ended December 31, 1979

Sales		$200,000
Cost of goods sold		112,000
Gross margin..		$ 88,000
Expenses:		
Administrative, selling, and marketing..................	$49,600	
Depreciation	10,000	
Interest (including bond discount amortization)........	9,000	
Uncollectible accounts......................................	300	68,900
Operating income......................................		$ 19,100
Gains and losses:		
Gain on sale of marketable securities...................	$ 600	
Loss on sale of building	(500)	100
Income before federal income tax		$ 19,200
Federal income tax expense....................................		9,000
Net income		$ 10,200

Supplemental financial information associated with operations for the year ended December 31, 1979, is shown below:

(a) Land was purchased for $2,000 cash. No other transactions affected land.
(b) Machinery costing $4,000 was purchased on December 31, 1979, under a 3-year mortgage note payable arrangement.
(c) A small building was sold for $1,500 cash. The original cost of the structure was $6,000, and accumulated depreciation at the time of sale was $4,000.
(d) Additional equipment was purchased for $9,000 cash during 1979.
(e) Bond discount was amortized by the straight-line method.
(f) Two thousand shares of capital stock were sold at $11 per share.
(g) Cash dividends of $5,000 were declared during 1979.
(h) Marketable securities originally costing $1,500 were sold for $2,100.

Determining the Aggregate Change in Net Working Capital

The second step involves determining the aggregate change in net working capital during the year by identifying the change that occurred in each current account during that year. The results of this analysis for 1979 are displayed in the schedule of changes in net working capital at the top of the following page.

The $29,000 increase in net working capital during 1979 will serve as an important reference point during the subsequent analy-

Jorgenson Corp.
Schedule of Changes in Net Working Capital
For the Year Ended December 31, 1979

	BALANCE AT DECEMBER 31,		EFFECT OF CHANGE ON NET WORKING CAPITAL (DECREASE)
	1979	1978	
Current assets:			
Cash..........................	$ 18,000	$ 12,000	$ 6,000
Marketable securites...........	3,000	2,000	1,000
Accounts receivable (net)......	45,000	37,000	8,000
Inventory.......................	72,000	69,000	3,000
Prepaid expenses	7,000	8,000	(1,000)
Total current assets..........	$145,000	$128,000	$17,000
Current liabilities:			
Notes payable..................	$ 30,000	$ 50,000	$20,000
Accounts payable	44,500	39,000	(5,500)
Income tax payable............	6,000	5,000	(1,000)
Dividends payable.............	1,500	—	(1,500)
Total current liabilities.....	$ 82,000	$ 94,000	$12,000
Net working capital (CA − CL) .	$ 63,000	$ 34,000	$29,000

sis. Although the schedule clearly shows the changes that occurred in each of the current accounts during the period, it does not disclose the effect each noncurrent account had on net working capital. The next step in the analysis will attempt to identify and analyze this noncurrent aspect of net working capital.

Reconciling Each Noncurrent Account

The purpose of reconciling or determining what changes occurred in each noncurrent account in the order listed on the balance sheet, is twofold:

(1) To identify as completely as possible the transactions which caused the change in each noncurrent account during the period so as to determine what effect each of these transactions had on net working capital.
(2) To provide a systematic and thorough approach to a complex area of accounting and financial analysis. A logical, step-by-step, sequential approach to complexity can often convert what appears at first glance to be utter confusion into some semblance of coherence.

Land. Land is the first noncurrent account listed on the balance sheet presented on page 463. The $2,000 net increase in land during 1979 (from $6,000 to $8,000) is explained by referring to the first piece of supplemental information, item (a) on page 464. The following entry reflects the purchase of land for $2,000 cash:

(a)

```
Land ........................................................  2,000
    Cash ...................................................        2,000
        Record cash purchase of land.
```

Since a noncurrent and a current account appear in the above entry, net working capital was affected; it decreased because a current asset was transformed into a noncurrent asset. This transaction can be restated symbolically in the format of Equation [2], as shown below:

$$\Delta CA \quad - \quad \Delta CL \quad = \quad \Delta LL \quad + \quad \Delta OE \quad - \quad \Delta NA \quad = \Delta NET \ WC$$
$$(-\$2,000) \qquad\qquad = \qquad\qquad\qquad\qquad\qquad - \ (+\$2,000) \ = \ (-\$2,000)$$

In short, this transaction resulted in a use or application of net working capital.

Since no other transaction affected the land account during the year, and the $2,000 purchase explained the $2,000 net increase in that account, the analysis may proceed to the next noncurrent account shown on the balance sheet.

Buildings and Equipment. Since this noncurrent account is so closely linked to its contra account, Accumulated Depreciation, analysis will be expedited by considering both assets simultaneously, using the T account format shown below:

	BUILDINGS AND EQUIPMENT		ACCUMULATED DEPRECIATION	
Bal. at Dec. 31, 1978	244,000			37,000
	?	?	?	?
Bal. at Dec. 31, 1979	251,000			43,000

The critical questions that must be addressed in analyzing these two accounts are: what transactions explain the $7,000 net increase in the building and equipment account, and the $6,000 net increase in the contra account balances; and what impact did each transaction have on net working capital? A thorough analysis of these questions requires the use of the following pieces of information:

(1) Item (b) of the supplemental information, which deals with a $4,000 machinery purchase.
(2) Item (c) of the supplemental information, which deals with the sale of a building.
(3) The $500 loss on the sale of the building that is reported on the income statement.
(4) Item (d), which indicates an additional purchase of equipment for $9,000 cash.
(5) Depreciation expense totaling $10,000 which also appears on the income statement.

The following entry records the purchase of machinery:

(b)

Buildings and Equipment..	4,000	
Mortgage Note Payable		4,000
Purchase of machinery under a 3-year mortgage note payable arrangement.		

This transaction had no effect on net working capital because both accounts involved in the entry are noncurrent, as displayed below in the format of Equation [2]:

$$\Delta CA - \Delta CL = \quad \Delta LL \quad + \quad \Delta OE \quad - \quad \Delta NA \quad = \Delta NET\ WC$$
$$-0- \quad = \ (+\$4,000) \qquad\qquad\quad -\ (+\$4,000) = \quad -0-$$

The probable entry to record the sale of the building for $1,500, as described in item (c) is shown below:

(c)

Cash...	1,500	
Accumulated Depreciation....................................	4,000	
Loss on Sale of Building	500	
Buildings and Equipment..................................		6,000
Sale of building at $500 loss. Book value at time of sale ($6,000 − $4,000) = $2,000 − $1,500 (cash proceeds from sale) = $500 loss.		

The loss is reflected on the income statement under the caption: Gains and losses. The mixture of current and noncurrent accounts in this transaction resulted in a source or increase of net working capital totaling $1,500, as displayed below:

$$\Delta CA \quad - \quad \Delta CL \quad = \quad \Delta LL \quad + \quad \Delta OE \quad - \quad \Delta NA \quad = \Delta NET\ WC$$
$$(+\$1,500) \qquad\qquad = \qquad\qquad + \ (-\$500) \ - \ (-\$6,000) = \ (+\$1,500)$$
$$- \ (+\$4,000)$$

The entry that was probably entered in the journal to record the cash purchase of additional equipment that was mentioned in item (d) of the supplemental information is shown below:

(d)

Buildings and Equipment.....................................	9,000	
Cash...		9,000
Purchase of additional equipment.		

The impact of this transaction on net working capital is a $9,000 use of funds, as shown below:

$$\Delta CA \quad - \quad \Delta CL \quad = \quad \Delta LL \quad + \quad \Delta OE \quad - \quad \Delta NA \quad = \Delta NET\ WC$$
$$(-\$9,000) \qquad\qquad = \qquad\qquad\qquad\qquad\quad - \ (+\$9,000) = \ (-\$9,000)$$

Posting each of the above transactions to the two related noncurrent accounts, as shown on page 468, reveals that a discrepancy of $10,000 in the contra account requires further exploration.

	BUILDINGS AND EQUIPMENT				ACCUMULATED DEPRECIATION		
Bal. at Dec. 31, 1978	244,000						37,000
	(b)	4,000	(c)	6,000	(c)	4,000 (?)	10,000
	(d)	9,000					
Bal. at Dec. 31, 1979	251,000						43,000

The $10,000 credit needed to complete the reconciliation of the contra account is probably related to the item of depreciation expense reflected on the income statement. The entry to record this depreciation was probably as shown below:

Depreciation Expense 10,000
   Accumulated Depreciation................................. 10,000
     Record depreciation for 1979.

The impact of this transaction on net working capital is zero, as verified below:

$$\Delta CA - \Delta CL = \quad \Delta LL \quad + \quad \Delta OE \quad - \quad \Delta NA \quad = \Delta NET\ WC$$
$$\text{—0—} \quad = \quad \quad\quad + (-\$10,000) - (-\$10,000) = \quad \text{—0—}$$

Two general observations may be made at this point in the analysis. First, notice that complete reconcilement of each noncurrent account thus far examined is critical to the analysis, irrespective of whether each transaction did or did not affect net working capital. Only by considering all transactions that occurred can the analyst be assured that a complete and thorough investigation has been achieved. Second, some of the financial events may require the analyst to reconstruct entries based on what probably or most likely occurred because specific or explicit information is not provided. For example, the accumulated depreciation account was probably credited $10,000 during the year for the depreciation expense of $10,000 to have appeared on the income statement.

The first three noncurrent accounts listed on the balance sheet have now been reconciled by recreating the transactions that affected each of those accounts, thus determining their effect on net working capital for 1979. The results of that analysis may be summarized as shown below:

SOURCES	USES
Increase in Net Working Capital	*Decreases in Net Working Capital*
Sale of building.............. $1,500	Purchase of land............. $ 2,000
	Purchase of equipment.... 9,000
	$11,000

Depreciation expense on the plant assets of $10,000 had no impact on net working capital; nor did the purchase of machinery for

$4,000 under the mortgage note payable arrangement. The next group of noncurrent accounts that requires examination and reconciliation is the long-term liabilities.

Bonds Payable. The bonds payable account and its contra account, Discount on Bonds Payable, should be analyzed together since they are so closely linked. The most probable reason for the contra account's debit balance decrease of $800 (from $7,200 to $6,400) during the year is because $800 of bond discount was amortized and charged to interest expense. This amount was most likely included in interest expense of $9,000 reflected on the income statement. A partial reconstructed entry appears as follows:

(e)

Interest Expense	800	
Discount on Bonds Payable.................................		800
Record bond discount amortization for 1979.		

Net working capital was not affected by the amortization of bond discount because both accounts involved in the entry are noncurrent.

Mortgage Note Payable. The $4,000 increase that occurred in this account during 1979 was associated with purchase of machinery at the end of 1979, according to item (b) of the supplemental information. This transaction was identified previously as not affecting net working capital because both accounts involved in the entry are noncurrent.

Capital Stock and Premium on Stock. These two related accounts, plus item (f) in the supplemental information may be analyzed together. The entry that reflected the sale of the $10 par value capital stock at $11 per share is shown below:

(f)

Cash...	22,000	
Capital Stock		20,000
Premium on Stock...		2,000
Issue of 2,000 shares of $10 par stock at $11 per share: 2,000 shares × ($11 − $10) = $2,000 premium.		

Net working capital was increased $22,000 by this transaction, because one current and two noncurrent accounts increased, as shown below:

ΔCA	−	ΔCL	=	ΔLL	+	ΔOE	−	ΔNA	= ΔNET WC
(+$22,000)			=		+	$\begin{pmatrix} +\$20,000 \\ +\$\ 2,000 \end{pmatrix}$			= (+$22,000)

Retained Earnings — Appropriation for Expansion. The $1,000 net increase in this account during 1979, was probably offset by a decrease of $1,000 in the retained earnings — unappropriated account. In other words, $1,000 was transferred from unappropriated retained earnings to the appropriated portion of retained earnings for expansion purposes sometime during 1979, as shown below:

Retained Earnings	1,000	
Retained Earnings — Appropriation for Plant Expansion		1,000
Record appropriation of retained earnings for purposes of expansion.		

Since both accounts are noncurrent, net working capital was not affected.

An updated summary of the analysis reflects the following:

SOURCES		USES	
Increases in Net Working Capital		*Decreases in Net Working Capital*	
Sale of building..............	$ 1,500	Purchase of land.............	$ 2,000
Sale of capital stock.........	22,000	Purchase of equipment....	9,000
Total increases	$23,500	Total decreases............	$11,000

Retained Earnings — Unappropriated. The $4,200 net increase in unappropriated retained earnings during 1979 may be explained as follows:

Unappropriated retained earnings at December 31, 1978...		$76,200
Plus net income...		10,200
Less: Dividend declaration (item (g) of supplemental information)............................	$(5,000)	
Appropriation for plant expansion............	(1,000)	(6,000)
Unappropriated retained earnings at December 31, 1979...		$80,400

It has already been determined that the appropriation of retained earnings for plant expansion had no effect on net working capital. The entry that would have been recorded at the time the $5,000 cash dividend was declared during 1979 is shown below:

(g)

Retained Earnings	5,000	
Cash Dividends Payable....................................		5,000
Record declaration of cash dividend on capital stock.		

Net working capital was affected because a current and a noncurrent account were affected. In this instance, net working capital decreased by $5,000, as verified using symbolic notation:

$$\Delta CA \quad - \quad \Delta CL \quad = \quad \Delta LL \quad + \quad \Delta OE \quad - \quad \Delta NA \quad = \Delta NET\ WC$$
$$- (+\$5,000) = \qquad\qquad + (-\$5,000) \qquad\qquad = (-\$5,000)$$

In short, the declaration of the cash dividend was a $5,000 use of net working capital.

Additional analysis of dividends payable account reveals that $3,500 of this declared cash dividend was paid during 1979, as shown below:

Cash Dividends Payable:

Balance at December 31, 1978...	—0—
Add dividends declared during 1979.................................	$5,000
Less balance at December 31, 1979.....................................	(1,500)
Portion of cash dividends presumably paid during 1979 ...	$3,500

It is important to observe that whereas the declaration of a cash dividend does affect net working capital, the payment of a previously declared cash dividend has no effect on net working capital. The following entry would have been recorded to reflect the $3,500 payment of the previously declared cash dividend:

Cash Dividends Payable.......................................	3,500	
Cash...		3,500
Payment of previously declared cash dividend.		

Since both accounts in this entry are current, net working capital is not affected. This conclusion can be substantiated by inserting the above financial data into Equation [2], as shown below:

$$\Delta CA \quad - \quad \Delta CL \quad = \quad \Delta LL + \Delta OE - \Delta NA \quad = \Delta NET\ WC$$
$$(-\$3,500) - (-\$3,500) = \qquad\qquad —0— \qquad\qquad = \quad —0—$$

The final item which affected unappropriated retained earnings is the net income of $10,200 earned during 1979. Recall that all items which appear on the income statement may be considered part of the owners' equity because the balance in each income-statement-related account is ultimately closed to Retained Earnings at the end of each fiscal year.

A thorough, step-by-step examination of each item on the income statement to determine its impact on net working capital is vital at this point in the analysis. Each income-statement-related account can be efficiently analyzed by placing it in the context of a slightly rearranged equation, as displayed below and shown in the table on page 473:

$$\Delta OE + \Delta LL - \Delta NA = \Delta CA - \Delta CL = \Delta NET\ WC$$

For example, a credit to the sales account is normally offset by a debit to one or more of the following current accounts: Cash, Accounts Receivable, or Notes Receivable. Hence, the $200,000 sales generated by the Jorgenson Corp. during 1979 (see the income statement on page 464) increased net working capital by $200,000, because a current and a noncurrent account were involved in the transaction. By the same token, a debit to Cost of Goods Sold usually arises from an offset credit to Inventory, which is a current account. Hence, the $112,000 increase in Cost of Goods Sold during 1979 was offset by an equivalent credit to Inventory, thereby decreasing net working capital by $112,000. These two events and the remaining seven items that are reflected on the Jorgenson Corp.'s income statement are presented and analyzed in the table shown on page 473, in the order in which each appears on that statement.

Administrative, Selling, and Marketing Expense would most likely have been offset by Credits to Cash, Prepaid Expenses, and/or Accounts Payable, thereby decreasing net working capital, because a noncurrent and some current accounts were involved in the transaction. The recognition of depreciation expense during 1979 did not affect net working capital, because both accounts involved in the entry were noncurrent. (Recall the depreciation entry on page 460.)

A summary entry that was probably prepared to recognize interest expense during 1979 is reconstructed below:

Interest Expense	9,000	
Discount on Bonds Payable		800
Cash and/or Interest Payable		8,200
Summary entry to reflect recognition of interest expense during 1979.		

The appropriate amount to credit Discount on Bonds Payable in the above entry was obtained from entry (e) on page 469. The $9,000 debit to Interest Expense was inferred from the income statement; and the $8,200 credit to Cash and/or Interest Payable was the residual amount required to balance the entry. Net working capital was reduced to the extent of the decrease in the current accounts, in this instance $8,200.

Uncollectible Accounts Expense of $300 undoubtedly arose when the adjustment was made in 1979 to provide an allowance for doubtful accounts as shown below:

Uncollectible Accounts Expense	300	
Allowance for Doubtful Accounts		300
Provision for doubtful accounts receivable.		

Net working capital decreased by $300 because of this financial event.

Income-statement-related-account	ΔOE + ΔLL	=	ΔNA	=	ΔCA	−	ΔCL	=	ΔNET WC
Sales	+200,000	=		=	+200,000 {Cash, Accounts Receivable, Notes Receivable}			=	+200,000
Cost of Goods Sold	−112,000	=		=	−112,000 Inventory			=	−112,000
Administrative, Selling, and Marketing Expense	− 49,600	=		=	− 49,600 {Cash, Prepaid Expenses} or	−	(+49,600) Accounts Payable	=	− 49,600
Depreciation Expense	− 10,000	=	− (−10,000) Accumulated Depreciation	=				=	−0−
Interest Expense	− 9,000 + 800 Discount on Bonds Payable	=		=	− 8,200 Cash	or	− (+ 8,200) Interest Payable	=	− 8,200
Uncollectible Accounts Expense	− 300	=		=	− 300 Allowance for Doubtful Accounts			=	− 300
Gain on Sale of Marketable Securities	+ 600	=		=	+ 2,100 Cash − 1,500 Marketable Securities			=	+ 600
Loss on Sale of Building	− 500	=	− (−6,000) Building and Equipment − (+4,000) Accumulated Depreciation	=	+ 1,500 Cash			=	+ 1,500
Federal Income Tax Expense	− 9,000	=		=	− 9,000 Cash	or	− (+ 9,000) Taxes Payable	=	− 9,000
Total	+ 10,200 + 800	=	− (−12,000)	=	+ 23,000			=	+ 23,000

The entry that reflected the sale at a $600 gain of the marketable securities which originally cost $1,500 (see item (h) of the supplemental information), is shown below:

Cash..........	2,100	
Gain on Sale of Marketable Securities.........		600
Marketable Securities		1,500
Record sale of marketable securities.		

The mixture of current and noncurrent accounts in the above entry resulted in an increase in net working capital of $600, as substantiated below:

$$\Delta OE \quad + \quad \Delta LL \quad - \quad \Delta NA \quad = \quad \Delta CA \quad - \quad \Delta CL \quad = \Delta NET\ WC$$

$$(+\$600) \qquad\qquad\qquad = \left\{ \begin{array}{c} +\$2,100 \\ -\$1,500 \end{array} \right\} \qquad = \quad (+\$600)$$

The journal entry associated with the sale of the building at a loss was presented as entry (c) on page 467. The only impact which that transaction had on net working capital was a $1,500 increase, in other words the cash received from the sale as indicated in the table on page 473 and reported in the summary on page 481. The final item on the income statement, federal income tax expense, decreased net working capital by $9,000. The current account, Cash, or Income Tax Payable would have been involved in the entry which gave rise to the recognition of this expense item.

To summarize: all income-statement-related items increased net working capital during 1979 by $23,000, the total amount shown in the extreme right column under the caption, Δ NET WC on page 473. However, $1,500 of this amount has already been reflected as a source of net working capital on the updated summary shown on page 481. Hence, the net amount of net working capital provided by current operations is $21,500 ($23,000 − $1,500). The calculation of funds provided by current operations may be displayed on the statement of changes in financial position as shown below:

Current operations:		
Revenue, other income, and gains:		
Sales.........		$200,000
Gain on sale of marketable securities		600
		$200,600
Less expenses and losses:		
Cost of goods sold	$112,000	
Administrative, selling, and marketing.........	49,600	
Interest (excluding bond discount amortization)...	8,200	
Uncollectible accounts	300	
Federal income tax.........	9,000	179,100
Total.........		$ 21,500

The preceding method of calculating funds provided by current operations is referred to as "beginning with sales."

An alternative way of displaying income statement data to arrive at the $21,500 net working capital provided by current operations is designated as "starting from net income." Under this method, various adjustments are made to net income which either did not affect net working capital, or are shown elsewhere on the statement of changes in financial positon. The "starting from net income" format is displayed below:

Current operations:
Net income...	$10,200
Add back:	
Depreciation expense (since this transaction did not affect net working capital)...	10,000
Amortization of bond discount (since this specific event did not affect net working capital).......................................	800
Loss on sale of building (since the loss is considered at another point in the statement)	500
Total...	$21,500

Additional Clarifications

Before presenting the formal statement of changes in financial position, two aspects of this analysis warrant clarification. First: the $500 loss incurred on the sale of the building. Had this $500 loss not been added back to net income under the "starting from net income" method (or deleted from the income statement under the "beginning with sales" method) of determining net working capital provided by current operations, the loss would have been double-counted. In other words, the $1,500 cash that was received from the sale of the building, and which will be reported as a $1,500 source of net working capital on the statement of changes in financial position shown on page 477, implicitly includes the loss incurred on the sale. The entry to record the sale of the building was as follows:

Cash..	1,500	
Accumulated Depreciation.....................................	4,000	
Loss on Sale of Building	500	
Buildings and Equipment.....................................		6,000

Had the building been sold for its book value of $2,000 (original cost of $6,000 less $4,000 accumulated depreciation), the $2,000 cash received would have been reported on the statement as a source of net working capital, with no gain or loss being reflected on the income statement. Restating the clarification, any loss that is realized on the sale or disposal of a noncurrent asset must be added back to net income under the "starting from net income" format, or excluded under the "beginning with sales" format, to determine the net income provided by current operations. Likewise, any gain realized on the sale or disposal of noncurrent assets must be subtracted from net income under the "starting from net income" or excluded under the "beginning with sales" formats. Otherwise, a loss or gain that arises under such circumstances would be double-counted.

The second clarification concerns nomenclature used on the statement of changes in financial position. Most corporations publish the statement in one form or another in their annual stockholder reports, together with the balance sheet and income statement. Of interest is the fact that practically all firms which use the "starting from net income" format to determine the funds provided by current operations, indicate or suggest that depreciation and amortization expenses are sources of net working capital. The sole reason why depreciation and amortization expenses are shown as sources of net working capital is that they, unlike most other expenses, are never a use of net working capital. In only one sense may depreciation and amortization expenses be considered a "source" of anything. These expenses are deductible in determining taxable income. Hence, cash is retained or conserved that would otherwise flow out of the firm to tax authorities had depreciation and amortization expenses not been recorded.

STATEMENT OF CHANGES IN FINANCIAL POSITION — WORKING CAPITAL BASIS

Each noncurrent account that appeared on the balance sheet of the Jorgenson Corp. has been thoroughly analyzed and reconciled; and the statement of changes in financial position for 1979 may now be prepared.[1] The completed analysis is displayed below, using the "starting from net income" method of determining funds provided by current operations. Additional data shown in the upper two-thirds portion of this statement were obtained from the updated summary shown on page 470, plus the declaration of cash dividends shown in entry (g) on page 470. The third portion deals with the changes in financial position that did not affect net working capital, and is explained in greater detail in the following discussion.

---

[1]The Financial Accounting Standards Board requires that the statement of changes in financial position be presented, together with the balance sheet and income statement, when reporting financial results to the public. See *Opinions of the Accounting Principles Board, No. 19,* "Reporting Changes in Financial Position" (New York: American Institute of Certified Public Accountants, 1971).

Jorgenson Corp.
Statement of Changes in Financial Position — Working Capital Basis
For the Year Ended December 31, 1979

Sources of net working capital

Current operations:

Net income	$10,200	
Add:		
Depreciation	10,000	
Amortization of bond discount	800	
Loss on building	500	$21,500
Sale of building		1,500
Sale of capital stock		22,000
Total sources of net working capital...........		$45,000

Uses of net working capital

Purchase of land..	$ 2,000
Purchase of equipment	9,000
Declaration of cash dividends.........................	5,000
Total uses of net working capital	$16,000
Increase in net working capital	$29,000

Changes in financial position which did not affect

net working capital

Purchase of machinery through issuance of mortgage note payable	$ 4,000	
Issuance of mortgage note payable..................	(4,000)	—
Net change in financial position........................		$29,000

The $29,000 increase in net working capital during 1979 that is reflected in the above statement coincides with the amount by which net working capital increased, as reported earlier on the schedule of changes in net working capital on page 465:

Increase in total current assets	$17,000
Plus decrease in total current liabilities	12,000
Increase in net working capital...	$29,000

The cautious analyst should, however observe that agreement between the statement and the schedule does not automatically guarantee that the analysis is correct. Agreement between the two documents merely suggests that the analysis may be correct as the analyst may have included offsetting errors during the analysis.

A clearer picture of what occurred in the firm with respect to its net working capital position during the period may emerge if certain details on the above statement are combined and rearranged. For example, current operations that were retained in the firm totaled $16,500 ($21,500 funds provided by current operations, less the $5,000 cash dividends declared). Also, the net addition of plant assets during 1979 used $9,500 of net working capital, as shown below:

Purchase of land	$2,000	
Purchase of equipment	9,000	$11,000
Sale of building		(1,500)
Net use of net working capital		$ 9,500

A condensed and slightly rearranged version of the upper two-thirds of the statement might appear as displayed below:

SOURCES OF NET WORKING CAPITAL		USES OF NET WORKING CAPITAL	
Current operations retained in the firm	$16,500	Net addition to plant assets	$9,500
Sale of capital stock	22,000		
Total sources	$38,500	Total uses	$9,500

⌐Increase in net working capital = $29,000⌐

In short, management increased the firm's net working capital and expanded its plant assets during 1979, by means of current operations retained in the firm and the sale of capital stock.

Inclusion of Other Changes in Financial Position Which Did Not Affect Net Working Capital

The lower portion of the statement of changes in financial position reflects those transactions which occurred during the year that involved only the noncurrent accounts, and hence affected the firm's financial position, but which had no effect on net working capital. These type transactions are displayed below in diagrammatic form:

$$NA \xleftarrow{\text{and}} LL$$
$$NA \xleftarrow{\text{and}} OE$$
$$LL \xleftarrow{\text{and}} OE$$

The most common transactions that affect only noncurrent accounts, and consequently affect the firm's financial position, include the following:

(1) Obtaining noncurrent assets, such as plant or intangible assets and investments, through the issuance of corporate stock or the incurrence of long-term debt.
(2) Converting long-term debt into corporate stock of the firm.

The sole transaction that involved only noncurrent accounts in the Jorgenson Corp. illustration concerned the financing of the

$4,000 purchase of machinery with the 3-year mortgage note payable. The entry to record the event described by item (b) of the supplemental information is repeated below:

Buildings and Equipment.....................................	4,000	
Mortgage Note Payable......................................		4,000
Machinery financed under a 3-year note payable arrangement.		

Although net working capital was not affected by this transaction, the firm's financial position was altered. Hence, the event must be reported on the statement of changes in financial position. Notice that the two noncurrent accounts that were affected by the $4,000 machinery purchase merely offset each other.

Concluding Remarks

Thorough and correct analysis of the changes in net working capital and financial position requires:

(1) The development of an orderly, systematic procedure to attack the analysis.
(2) A comprehensive understanding of the interaction between current and noncurrent accounts and the impact on net working capital.
(3) The ability to reconstruct, from financial information that is usually available, what probably occurred in the firm during a specified period of time.

No additional financial information other than what is provided in the accounting records of the firm is required to undertake a comprehensive analysis of its net working capital or financial position. The analysis merely recombines existing financial data in a form which focuses on the intermediate liquidity position of the firm.

A comprehensive overview of the content of the statement of changes in financial position — working capital basis is shown at the top of page 480, starting from net income to determine funds provided by current operations.

Perhaps the most important detail to observe with respect to the analysis of net working capital is that the two segments of the net working capital Equation [2], $\Delta CA - \Delta CL$ and $\Delta LL + \Delta OE - \Delta NA$ represent two sides of the same coin, both of which are equal in size, and differing only in content. The net difference in the changes among the current accounts as reflected in the schedule of changes of net working capital on page 465 ($29,000 increase), precisely equals the net difference in the changes among the noncurrent assets as reflected in the statement of changes in

OVERVIEW OF THE STATEMENT OF CHANGES IN FINANCIAL POSITION—
WORKING CAPITAL BASIS

Sources of net working capital

Current operations:
Net income.
Add back income statement items that did not affect net working capital:
Depreciation, depletion, and amortization of noncurrent assets.
Amortization of bond discount.
Losses on sale of noncurrent assets and retirement of long-term liabilities.
Increase in deferred income tax.
Deduct income statement items that did not affect net working capital:
Amortization of bond premium.
Gains on sale of noncurrent assets and retirement of long-term liabilities.
Decrease in deferred income tax.
Other sources:
Proceeds from sale of noncurrent assets.
Proceeds from sale of common, preferred, and treasury stock.
Proceeds from incurring long-term debt.

Uses of net working capital

Purchase of noncurrent assets.
Retirement of noncurrent debt.
Purchase of treasury stock.
Declaration of cash dividends.

Append the following type transactions, which affect only noncurrent accounts:

(1) Increase (or decrease) in noncurrent assets, offset by an increase (or decrease) in owners' equities. For example, obtaining plant assets by issuing shares of stock.
(2) Increase (or decrease) in noncurrent assets, offset by an increase (or decrease) in long-term liabilities. For example, obtaining plant assets under long-term financing arrangements.
(3) Increase (or decrease) in owners' equities, offset by a decrease (or increase) in long-term liabilities. For example, converting long-term debt into shares of stock.

financial position on page 477 ($29,000 increase). In fact, the two segments must be equal because of the double-entry accounting system. This observation may be more clearly perceived in the summary shown on page 481.

QUESTIONS

1. Identify several questions that might be answered by examining only: (a) the balance sheet; (b) the income statement.

2. (a) Identify several questions that might be answered only by examining the balance sheet and the income statement together. (b) Briefly explain how net working capital analysis involves the examination of both financial statements.

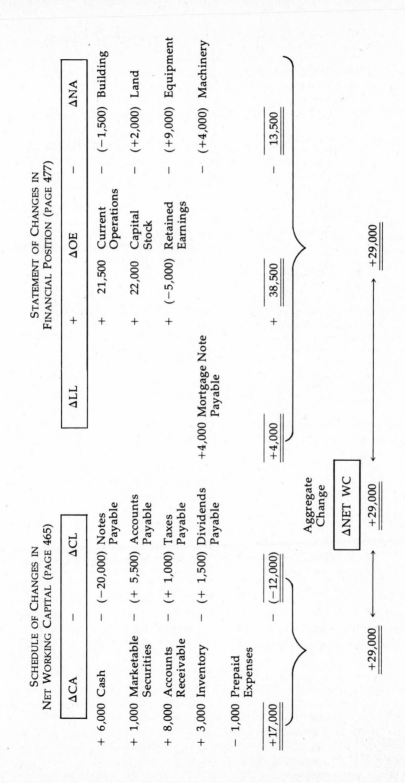

3. (a) Identify four definitions of working capital. (b) Present two commonly used definitions of net working capital, and indicate which of those definitions is emphasized in this text.

4. (a) What is the primary financial focal point of net working capital analysis? (b) How might management use the results of net working capital analysis to evaluate the financial position of the firm historically, currently, and for the future?

5. (a) Express the change in net working capital during a period, using symbolic notation that appears in the expanded balance sheet equation. Define each term in the equation. (b) Explain how the income-statement-related accounts are included in the expanded equation presented in (a).

6. Explain how the dual nature of net working capital is reflected in the equation that was derived in Question 5(a) above.

7. (a) Identify the type of accounts which must be involved in a financial transaction for net working capital to be affected. (b) Identify the combination of accounts involved in a journal entry which would have no impact on net working capital.

8. Prepare a tabular summary to indicate whether each type of non-current account (NA, LL, and OE) must increase or decrease for a financial transaction to be considered a source or a use of net working capital.

9. Explain what (a) transaction analysis, and (b) the reconciliation of noncurrent accounts mean with respect to net working capital analysis.

10. Explain the impact that each of the following transactions would have on net working capital, using the format of the net working capital Equation [2] and/or journal entry reconstruction: (a) payment of various accounts payable totaling $6,000; (b) recognition of $14,000 depreciation on machinery and equipment; (c) record sales totaling $100,000, 70% of which were sold on 30-day credit terms, and the remainder for cash; (d) conversion of a $30,000 long-term note payable into 300 shares of the firm's $100 par value common stock.

11. Identify which of the four transactions presented in Question 10 affected the financial position of the firm without having any impact on the firm's net working capital position.

12. Identify and briefly explain each of the three steps involved in net working capital analysis.

13. (a) What purpose does the schedule of changes in net working capital achieve? (b) What important aspect of net working capital analysis does this schedule not reflect?

14. (a) Using the format of the net working capital Equation [2], explain the effect on net working capital of a sale of a building for $26,600 whose book value at the time of sale was $30,000. The building's original cost was $180,000. (b) Explain how the analyst would treat any gain or loss on the sale of this building when determining the amount of net working capital that was provided by current operations, using: (1) the "beginning with sales" format; and (2) the "starting from net income" format.

15. (a) Journalize each of the following transactions and explain what effect, if any, each would have on net working capital: (1) purchase equipment costing $20,000 for cash; (2) purchase the same equipment under a long-term mortgage note payable arrangement; and (3) obtain the same equipment by issuing 200 shares of the corporation's $100 par

value common stock to the vendor. (b) Which of these transactions would cause a change in the firm's financial position without affecting its net working capital?

16. Explain the extent to which net working capital would be affected by: (a) the amortization of bond discount; (b) the amortization of bond premium; (c) the amortization of copyrights; and (d) the depreciation of plant assets.

17. Refer to Question 16 above. Using the "starting from net income" format for determining the net working capital provided by current operations, what adjustment, if any, would be required to handle each of the items that would appear on the income statement because of the four entries.

18. Prepare a sample journal entry to record each of the following financial events, and indicate its impact on net working capital: (a) a $4,000 gain was realized on the sale of marketable securities for $14,000; (b) the provision for doubtful accounts receivable totaled $22,000; (c) specific accounts receivable totaling $18,000 were written off as uncollectible.

19. Indicate which of the following transactions affected both the firm's net working capital and its financial position, after journalizing each entry: (a) purchase of treasury stock for $80,000; (b) conversion of $100,000 long-term bonds into $100,000 of the firm's capital stock; and (c) payment of accounts payable totaling $68,000.

20. Indicate the balance-sheet-related accounts that are usually associated with each of the following income-statement-related accounts: (a) Sales; (b) Cost of Goods Sold; (c) Depreciation Expense; (d) Insurance and Rent Expense; and (d) Loss on Sale of Marketable Securities.

21. Explain the essential difference between the two methods of determining the amount of net working capital provided by current operations; (a) "beginning with sales"; and (b) "starting from net income."

22. Identify the principal types of transactions that affect the firm's financial position, but which have no effect on net working capital.

EXERCISES

1. Transaction analysis. Prepare a journal entry for each of the following transactions, and indicate the amount by which net working capital was affected in the appropriate column of the format shown on page 484. If there is no effect, place a check in the "None" column. Transaction X, is given as an example. Transaction X: Machinery costing $80,000 was purchased on 30-day credit terms.

(1) Total sales amounted to $400,000, 70% of which were on 30-day credit terms and the remainder for cash.

(2) Depreciation expense totaling $72,000 was recorded on machinery.

(3) A $280,000 cash dividend was declared.

(4) The cash dividend declared in (3) was paid at the beginning of the following fiscal year. Determine the effect of this payment on net working capital during the year in which the dividend was paid.

(5) Materials costing $60,000 were purchased for inventory on credit.

(6) The cost of merchandise that was sold by a retail dress shop totaled $117,000.

EFFECT ON NET WORKING CAPITAL

JOURNAL ENTRY	Increase	Decrease	None
X: Machinery...................... 80,000			
Accounts Payable	80,000	$80,000	

2. **Transaction analysis.** Indicate in the format shown below the amount that each of the following financial transactions affected net working capital and net income. If the transaction had no effect on net working capital and/or net income, place a check in the appropriate "None" column. Provide journal entries or any clarifying comments in the "Remarks" column. Transaction X is given as an example. Transaction X: A $60,000 short-term loan was obtained from a local bank.

(1) Merchandise costing $80,000 was purchased, 75% on 30-day credit terms and the balance for cash.
(2) Merchandise costing $60,000 was sold for $96,000 on 30-day credit terms.
(3) Depreciation on the building totaling $16,000 was recognized during the year.
(4) Merchandise that was carried in inventory at $780 was damaged and written of as a total loss.
(5) All but 10% of the sales that were made in (2) above were collected during the fiscal year in which sold.
(6) Accounts payable that were associated with entry (1) above were paid off during the year.
(7) A $26,000 long-term note payable was paid off at the bank.

	EFFECT ON NET WORKING CAPITAL			EFFECT ON NET INCOME		
REMARKS	Increase	Decrease	None	Increase	Decrease	None
X: Cash (CA) 60,000						
Notes Payable (CL). 60,000			X			X

3. **Reconciliation of receivables.** The two receivables-related accounts shown below for the Fosgene Corp. reflected their normal debit or credit balances at the end of the fiscal years indicated:

	DECEMBER 31, 1980	DECEMBER 31, 1979
Accounts Receivable	$81,600	$74,200
Allowance for Doubtful Accounts...........................	7,900	7,100

Specific customer accounts written off as uncollectible during 1980 totaled $2,800. Provision for doubtful accounts during the same period amounted to $3,600. Total credit sales during the year were $900,000.

Required: (a) Reconcile the two accounts shown above, using a T account format, and prepare summary journal entries that were probably recorded during the fiscal year ended December 31, 1980, which affected these two accounts. (b) Indicate the effect of each summary transaction recorded in (a) above on net working capital during 1980, using the format of the net working capital equation: $\Delta CA - \Delta CL = \Delta LL + \Delta OE - \Delta NA = \Delta NET\ WC$.

4. Reconciliation of inventory and accounts payable. The two accounts shown below for the Fosgene Corp. reflected the normal debit and credit balances at the end of the fiscal years indicated:

	DECEMBER 31, 1980	DECEMBER 31, 1979
Inventory	$276,000	$292,000
Accounts Payable	88,000	103,000

All purchases of inventory were made under 30-day credit terms, and the only transactions that affected Accounts Payable were related to inventory purchases. Cost of goods sold during 1980 amounted to $624,000.

Required: (a) Reconcile the two accounts shown above, using a T account format, and prepare summary journal entries that were probably recorded during the fiscal year ended December 31, 1980, which affected these two accounts. (b) Indicate the effect of each summary transaction recorded in (a) above on net working capital during 1980, using the format of the net working capital equation: $\Delta CA - \Delta CL = \Delta LL + \Delta OE - \Delta NA = \Delta NET\ WC$.

5. Reconciliation of plant assets. The information shown below was extracted from the respective balance sheets at the dates indicated for the Doughty Corp.:

	DECEMBER 31, 1980	DECEMBER 31, 1979
Equipment	$160,000	$120,000
Accumulated depreciation	(72,000)	(55,000)
Net plant assets	$ 88,000	$ 65,000

A piece of equipment which originally cost $50,000 was sold during 1980 at a $3,000 gain. Depreciation recognized during 1980 amounted to $39,000. Additional equipment was purchased under a 3-year mortgage note arrangement.

Required: (a) Reconcile both noncurrent asset accounts using a T account format, and prepare journal entries that were probably recorded during the fiscal year ended December 31, 1980, which affected these accounts. (b) Indicate the impact that each transaction in (a) had on net working capital during 1980, using the format of the net working capital equation: $\Delta CA - \Delta CL = \Delta LL + \Delta OE - \Delta NA = \Delta NET\ WC$.

6. Reconciliation of long-term liabilities. Information extracted from the balance sheets of the Twistkor Corp. on the dates indicated for three long-term liability accounts is displayed below:

	DECEMBER 31, 1980	DECEMBER 31, 1979
Long-term liabilities:		
Bonds payable 9%, 5-year, issued at 94% of par	$200,000	—
Less discount on bonds payable	(9,600)	—
Net outstanding bonds payable	$190,400	—
Mortgage note payable, 7%	—	$60,000
Total long-term liabilities	$190,400	$60,000

The bond issue was sold to the public on January 1, 1980. Straight-line amortization of bond discount was used in the corporation. The mortgage note payable was converted into 3,000 shares of the firm's $20 par value common stock on July 1, 1980.

Required: (a) Prepare entries to reflect the financial transactions that affected each of the three accounts during 1980. (b) Determine the impact of each transaction in (a) above on net working capital for the fiscal year ended December 31, 1980, using the format of the net working capital equation: $\Delta CA - \Delta CL = \Delta LL + \Delta OE - \Delta NA = \Delta NET\ WC$. (c) Assuming interest was payable on each long-term liability at June 30 and December 31 of each year, determine the amount of interest expense that would be reflected on the income statement for the fiscal year ended December 31, 1980. Determine the impact of these interest transactions on net working capital for 1980.

7. **Capital stock transactions.** The transactions described below affected the capital stock account of the Joslyn Corp. during the fiscal year ended December 31, 1979. The number of shares of capital stock issued and outstanding at January 1, 1979, totaled 76,000.

(1) Four hundred shares of the firm's $10 par value capital stock was purchased for the treasury for $4,800 on May 15, 1979.
(2) A building appraised at $84,000 was obtained on June 13, 1979, from a financier who was given 7,000 previously unissued shares of the firm's capital stock.
(3) Three hundred shares of treasury stock that were purchased in (1) above were sold to investors at $13 per share on November 22, 1979.
(4) A 5% stock dividend was declared and paid to stockholders on December 15, 1979. The market price of the firm's stock was $13 on the date of declaration.

Required: (a) Prepare entries to record each of the above transactions. (b) Prepare a summary to reflect the effect of each transaction on net working capital for the fiscal year ended December 31, 1979, using the following format:

EFFECT ON NET WORKING CAPITAL

TRANSACTION	Increase	Decrease	None

8. **Schedule of changes in net working capital.** Each account listed below and at the top of page 487 for Krustwitz, Inc., reflected its normal debit or credit balance at the end of each fiscal year:

ACCOUNT TITLE	SEPTEMBER 30, 1980	SEPTEMBER 30, 1979
Accounts Payable	$110,400	$ 93,700
Accounts Receivable	91,200	86,400
Accumulated Depreciation — Buildings	92,000	82,200
Accumulated Depreciation — Equipment and Fixtures	45,800	36,200
Allowance for Doubtful Accounts	6,000	4,800
Bonds Payable, 20-year, due September 30, 1985	200,000	200,000

ACCOUNT TITLE	SEPTEMBER 30, 1980	SEPTEMBER 30, 1979
Buildings	143,300	143,300
Cash...	7,100	8,400
Capital Stock.................................	20,000	20,000
Dividends Payable..........................	3,400	2,700
Equipment and Fixtures	279,000	268,800
Interest Payable.............................	1,400	1,800
Interest Receivable.........................	1,000	900
Inventory	147,000	133,700
Investments...................................	14,000	14,000
Land...	22,600	20,600
Marketable Securities	14,400	12,700
Mortgage Note Payable, long-term	175,000	150,000
Notes Payable, short-term................	36,100	42,400
Notes Receivable	8,000	6,700
Performance Liability, short-term......	4,000	3,100
Premium on Bonds Payable..............	1,600	2,000
Prepaid Rent and Insurance..............	1,000	2,400
Retained Earnings	14,800	44,600
State and Federal Income Taxes Payable..	26,300	21,400
Treasury Stock	9,200	8,600
Wages and Salaries Payable..............	1,000	1,600

Required: Prepare a schedule of changes in net working capital for the fiscal year ended September 30, 1980.

9. Net working capital provided by current operations: "beginning with sales" format. The income statement for the Cascades Corporation is shown on page 488.

Required: Prepare a summary to reflect the net working capital provided by current operations during the fiscal year ended March 31, 1980, using the "beginning with sales" format.

10. Net working capital provided by current operations: "starting from net income" format. Refer to the income statement of Cascades Corporation presented in Exercise 9.

Required: Prepare a summary to reflect the net working capital provided by current operations during the fiscal year ended March 31, 1980, using the "starting from net income" format.

11. Statement of changes in financial position. The upper portion of the statement of changes in financial position working capital basis for the fiscal year ended June 30, 1980, in the Kurtosis Corp. is shown on page 489.

The following transactions also occurred during the fiscal year ended June 30, 1980:

(1) A $120,000 long-term mortgage note payable was converted into 12,000 shares of the firm's $10 par value common stock.
(2) A building was obtained for use as a warehouse by issuing 4,000 shares of common stock to the owner of the company from which the building was purchased. The facility was appraised at $40,000.

Cascades Corporation
Income Statement
For the Year Ended March 31, 1980

Sales...		$6,200,000
Cost of goods sold		4,030,000
Gross margin..		$2,170,000
Expenses:		
Wages and salaries......................................	$841,400	
Depreciation — equipment..............................	430,000	
Marketing and sales promotion...........................	308,900	
Depreciation — buildings	85,000	
Administrative	32,400	
Uncollectible accounts	27,700	
Interest (including $3,200 bond discount amortization)	22,400	
Property tax...	15,500	
Rent	12,000	
Insurance..	8,700	
Office supplies..	8,400	1,792,400
Operating income......................................		$ 377,600
Other income:		
Rent income...		5,300
Gains and losses:		
Gain on sale of equipment................................	$ 3,900	
Loss on sale of marketable securities	(1,800)	2,100
Income before income tax		$ 385,000
Income tax expense..		191,525
Net income...		$ 193,475

(3) A 4% common stock dividend was declared and distributed to stockholders on June 15, 1980. The total number of shares of common stock that were issued at the time of the dividend declaration was 160,000, of which 4,000 were in the treasury. The market price of the stock on the date of declaration was $12 per share.

Required: Prepare a completed statement of changes in financial position — working capital basis for the fiscal year ended June 30, 1980. Feel free to rearrange or combine the data that is reflected on the partial statement.

PROBLEMS

13-1. Transaction analysis. Unless otherwise specified, each transaction that is described or which can be inferred from the following information, occurred during the fiscal year ended December 31, 1980, in the Comstock Corp.:

Kurtosis Corp.
Statement of Changes in Financial Position — Working Capital Basis
For the Year Ended June 30, 1980

Sources

Current operations:

Net income..		$ 86,000	
Add:			
Depreciation expense — buildings.....	$ 16,000		
Loss on sale of land........................	3,000		
Depreciation expense — machinery			
and equipment	122,000		
Amortization of patents	12,000		
Amortization of bond discount	2,500	155,500	
		$241,500	
Deduct:			
Gain on sale of equipment	$ 19,000		
Amortization of bond premium...........	2,300	21,300	$220,200
Sale of land			54,000
Sale of machinery and equipment...........................			36,000
Sale of 7% debentures...			130,000
Total sources of net working capital......................			$440,200

Uses

Purchase of building	$ 72,000
Purchase of patents...	12,000
Purchase of treasury stock.....................................	8,000
Declaration of cash dividends................................	35,000
Total uses of net working capital.........................	$127,000
Increase in net working capital..............................	$313,200

(a) Marketable securities originally costing $26,000 were sold for $30,000.
(b) The $67,000 cash dividend that was declared on December 21, 1979 was paid to stockholders on January 7, 1980.
(c) Retained earnings totaling $160,000 was appropriated for plant expansion.
(d) Depreciation expense on plant assets was $84,000.
(e) Equipment originally costing $97,000 reflected a book value of $20,000 at the time of sale for $26,000.
(f) Four thousand shares of the firm's $10 par value common stock were purchased for the treasury at $13 per share in March.
(g) All of the shares purchased in (f) above were sold at an average price of $14 per share in June.
(h) A $43,000 cash dividend was declared on December 15, 1980, of which $16,000 remained unpaid as of December 31, 1980.
(i) A fire completely destroyed four delivery trucks, each costing $7,500, three days following their purchase. The insurance recovery on each truck amounted to 90% of its original cost.

(j) A $15,000 common stock dividend was declared and forwarded to stockholders in November. The market price of the stock was $15 per share at the time of the stock dividend declaration.

Required: Using the format shown below, prepare a journal entry for each of the transactions, and determine the effect each transaction had on net working capital and net income for the fiscal year ended December 31, 1980:

	EFFECT ON NET WORKING CAPITAL			EFFECT ON NET INCOME		
JOURNAL ENTRY	*Increase*	*Decrease*	*None*	*Increase*	*Decrease*	*None*

13-2. Transaction analysis. Using the format of the net working capital equation, $\Delta CA - \Delta CL = \Delta LL + \Delta OE - \Delta NA = \Delta NET\ WC$, determine the effect that each of the following transactions had on net working capital for the fiscal year ended December 31, 1980, in the Sandbury Corp. Indicate the accounts involved in each transaction, as shown in the tabular presentation on page 462; and provide supporting detail beneath the summary:

(a) Two thousand shares of $20 par value common stock that had been purchased for the treasury at $22 per share were sold to various investors at an average price of $24 per share.

(b) A building costing $350,000 was purchased by transferring 14,000 shares of previously unissued common stock to the seller.

(c) A $600,000 bond issue was converted into 6,000 shares of $100 par value preferred stock. The bond issue had originally been sold at par.

(d) A large piece of machinery, with a book value of $43,000 at the time of sale, was sold at a $4,000 loss. The original cost of the machinery was $150,000.

(e) The machine sold in (d) was replaced with one costing $175,000 under a 4-year, $150,000 mortgage note payable arrangement. A $25,000 cash down payment was made to the vendor.

(f) Flood destroyed $40,000 worth of materials in inventory. All but 10% of the loss was recovered from the insurance company under terms of the fire and casualty policy currently in force.

(g) A 3% stock dividend on common stock was declared and forwarded to stockholders in December, 1980. The total shares of issued common stock immediately prior to the stock dividend was 200,000 of which 4,000 were in the treasury. The market price of the stock on the date of declaration was $23 per share. The stock dividend was declared from previously unissued shares.

13-3. Reconciliation of receivable and long-term liability accounts. The selected financial information shown at the top of page 491 was extracted from the balance sheets of the Jonquil Corp. at the end of 1978 and 1979:

Additional information is given:

(a) Three customer accounts totaling $3,800 were written off as uncollectible during 1979. All sales were made on 30-day credit terms, and total sales for 1979 were $500,000.

	DECEMBER 31,	
	1979	1978
Current assets:		
Accounts receivable	$ 42,000	$ 39,000
Less allowance for doubtful accounts	1,150	850
Net accounts receivable	$ 40,850	$ 38,150
Long-term liabilities:		
Bonds payable, 7%, 10-year, due December 31, 1985...	$200,000	$200,000
Less discount on bonds payable........................	7,200	8,400
Net outstanding bonds.................................	$192,800	$191,600
Mortgage note payable, 8%, due December 31, 1983...	—	100,000
Total long-term liabilities.............................	$192,800	$291,600

(b) Bond discount was amortized by the straight-line method. Interest was payable on all long-term debt semiannually at each June 30 and December 31.

(c) The mortgage note payable was converted into 10,000 shares of $10 par value capital stock on July 1, 1979.

Required: (1) Reconcile accounts receivable and its contra account. Use a T account format, and prepare entries that affected each of those accounts.

(2) Prepare entries that affected each long-term liability account during 1979.

(3) Using the format shown below, prepare a summary to reflect the effect that each entry identified above had on net working capital in 1979:

EFFECT ON NET WORKING CAPITAL

TRANSACTION	Increase	Decrease	None

(4) Assuming the corporation had no liabilities other than those identified above, what amount of interest expense would have appeared on the 1979 income statement?

13-4. Reconciliation of plant assets and long-term liabilities. The balances in selected noncurrent accounts at the end of each of the two years indicated are shown below for Cartwright, Inc.:

Account Title	DECEMBER 31,	
	1979	1978
Buildings and Equipment	$930,000	$800,000
Accumulated Depreciation	(530,000)	(440,000)
Bonds Payable, 6%, 20-year, due June 30, 1999....	(100,000)	—
Premium on Bonds Payable..............................	(12,322)	—
Bonds Payable, 7%, 10-year, due June 30, 1981....	—	(200,000)

The following information relates to the firm's operations during 1979:

(a) A building was purchased on July 1, 1979. The entire cost of the building was financed solely by the issuance of the 6% bonds on that date at a market rate of interest of 5% compounded semiannually.

(b) Equipment costing $80,000 was purchased on 30-day credit terms.

(c) Two condemned buildings, on which the accumulated depreciation at the date of sale was $60,000, were sold for $7,000.

(d) The only remaining transaction that affected Buildings and Equipment and its contra account was the depreciation expense recorded for 1979.

(e) Bond premium was amortized by the effective interest rate method.

(f) The 7% bond issue was converted into 20,000 shares of $10 par value common stock of the corporation on July 1, 1979.

(g) Interest was payable on both long-term debt instruments at each June 30 and December 31.

Required: (1) Explain the net change that occurred during 1979 in each of the five accounts shown above by preparing an entry for each transaction that affected these accounts. Use the T account format to reconcile each plant asset account.

(2) Prepare a summary indicating the effect of each transaction identified in (1) on net working capital during 1979, using the format shown below:

EFFECT ON NET WORKING CAPITAL

TRANSACTION	Increase	Decrease	None

13-5. Reconciliation of inventory, prepaid expenses, and accounts payable. The balances at June 30, 1979 and 1980, in the three current accounts shown below were extracted from balance sheet information in the Dartwell Corp.:

	JUNE 30,	
	1980	1979
Inventory	$96,000	$87,000
Prepaid Insurance	9,000	14,000
Accounts Payable	(55,000)	(68,000)

The following additional information was obtained after inspecting various financial records:

(a) Cost of goods sold for the fiscal year ended June 30, 1980, was $973,000.

(b) All merchandise obtained for inventory was purchased under 30-day credit terms. No inventory losses occurred during the fiscal year.

(c) The only items that affected the credit side of the accounts payable account were the purchases of inventory, and $37,000 credit purchases of several insurance policies. All purchases of insurance policies were purchased under 25-day credit terms and were immediately capitalized.

(d) Rental charges paid and immediately charged to expense totaled $31,000 during the fiscal year ended June 30, 1980.

Required: (1) Reconcile each of the three accounts reflected above, using appropriate T accounts.

(2) Determine the impact of each transaction on net working capital and net income for the fiscal year ended June 30, 1980, using the following format:

	EFFECT ON NET WORKING CAPITAL			EFFECT ON NET INCOME		
TRANSACTION	Increase	Decrease	None	Increase	Decrease	None

13-6. Stock transactions. The transactions described below occurred during the fiscal year ended December 31, 1980, in the Yorkshem Corp. The number of shares of $100 par, 6%, noncumulative preferred stock, and $20 par common stock that were issued and outstanding at January 1, 1980, were 15,000 and 320,000, respectively. No shares of either class of stock were in the treasury at the beginning of 1980.

(a) Four thousand shares of common stock were issued in March in payment for a building appraised at $85,000.

(b) Eight thousand shares of common stock were purchased for the treasury at $21 per share during April.

(c) The co-holders of a $100,000, 5-year mortgage note payable agreed to convert that note into 1,000 shares of preferred stock during May.

(d) A 2% common stock dividend was declared and distributed to common stockholders in June. The market price per share of the stock on the date of declaration was $22. The stock was distributed from the shares in the treasury.

(e) Cash dividends totaling $157,000 were declared on common and preferred stock on December 21, 1980.

(f) The entire cash dividend due preferred stockholders had been paid by December 31, 1980; but one half of the cash dividend due common stockholders remained an outstanding liability at the year-end.

Required: (1) Determine the effect of each of the above transactions on net working capital for the fiscal year 1980, using the following format:

$$\Delta CA - \Delta CL = \Delta LL + \Delta OE - \Delta NA = \Delta NET \ WC.$$

Provide supporting detail beneath this summary.

(2) Identify the above transactions which affect the financial position of the firm during 1980, but which had no effect on net working capital during that period.

13-7. Association between balance-sheet-related and income-statement-related accounts. The income statement for the fiscal year ended December 31, 1979, of the Beowulf Corp. is shown at the top of page 494.

All except 10% of the sales made during 1979 were on 30-day credit terms. No financial liabilities for employee compensation or interest payments existed at December 31, 1979. Payments for insurance and rent were immediately capitalized as prepaid expenses. The original cost of the marketable securities sold during 1979 was $22,000.

Required: Identify the balance-sheet-related accounts and the amount that was probably associated with each income-statement-related ac-

Beowulf Corp.
Income Statement
For the Year Ended December 31, 1979

Sales...		$700,000
Cost of goods sold..		460,000
Gross margin		$240,000
Expenses:		
Wages and salaries...	$58,000	
Depreciation	16,000	
Interest (including $2,000 bond premium amortization)...	14,000	
Insurance and rent	12,000	
Uncollectible accounts.......................................	6,000	106,000
Operating income		$134,000
Gains and losses:		
Gain on sale of marketable securities		4,000
Income before income tax....................................		$138,000
Income tax expense		70,000
Net income		$ 68,000

count reflected on the above income statement. Use the format shown below.

Income-Statement-Related	
Account	$\Delta OE + \Delta LL - \Delta NA = \Delta CA - \Delta CL = \Delta NET\ WC$

13-8. Statement of changes in financial position — working capital basis. A comparative balance sheet, an income statement, and additional financial information are shown below and on page 495 for the fiscal year ended June 30, 1980, in the Rohrchem Corp.:

Rohrchem Corp.
Comparative Balance Sheet
June 30, 1980 and 1979

	1980	1979
Current assets:		
Cash..	$ 95,000	$ 80,000
Marketable securities..	29,000	32,000
Accounts receivable (net of allowance for doubtful accounts)...	61,000	58,000
Inventory...	71,000	67,000
Total current assets....................................	$256,000	$237,000
Plant assets:		
Building and equipment......................................	$681,000	$616,000
Less accumulated depreciation	(300,000)	(270,000)
Total plant assets......................................	$381,000	$346,000
Intangibles:		
Goodwill..	$ 30,000	$ 40,000
Total assets..	$667,000	$623,000

Current liabilities:

Notes payable..	$ 20,000	$ 20,000
Accounts payable	44,000	45,000
Income tax payable.......................................	45,000	38,000
Total current liabilities...............................	$109,000	$103,000

Long-term liabilities:

Notes payable...	$120,000	$150,000

Owners' equity:

Capital stock, $10 par	$250,000	$250,000
Retained earnings	188,000	120,000
Total owners' equity	$438,000	$370,000
Total equities	$667,000	$623,000

Rohrchem Corp.
Income Statement
For the Year Ended June 30, 1980

Sales...		$590,000
Cost of goods sold..		280,000
Gross margin		$310,000
Expenses:		
Wages and salaries...	$96,000	
Depreciation	38,000	
Advertising and marketing......................................	17,000	
Supplies, heat, and light	12,700	
Amortization of goodwill.......................................	10,000	
Repair and maintenance..	5,600	
Insurance and property tax	3,800	183,100
Operating income		$126,900
Gains and losses:		
Gain on sale of buildings.......................................		7,600
Income before income tax......................................		$134,500
Income tax expense		45,000
Net income		$ 89,500

Supplemental information:

(a) Additional equipment costing $100,000 was purchased on 30-day credit terms.

(b) Two buildings, having a book value of $27,000, were sold.

(c) A $30,000 portion of the long-term notes payable was paid off.

(d) Cash dividends totaling $21,500 were declared and paid in May, 1980.

Required: Prepare a statement of changes in financial position — working capital basis for the fiscal year ended June 30, 1980, using the "beginning with sales" format to determine net working capital provided by current operations.

13-9. Schedule of changes in net working capital and statement of changes in financial position — working capital basis. Several key executives of the Bitronics Corp., after seeing the financial reports for the year ended December 31, 1979, were unable to understand how $97,000 of net income could have been generated during the year, whereas net working capital decreased by a substantial amount during the same period. Amounts reflected in the various balance-sheet-related accounts as of the fiscal years ended December 31, 1978 and 1979, plus supplemental information are given below:

	DECEMBER 31,	
Accounts with Debit Balances	1979	1978
Cash	$ 72,000	$ 93,000
Accounts Receivable	122,000	136,000
Inventory	201,000	269,000
Land	44,000	44,000
Machinery and Equipment	462,000	322,000
Patents	14,000	15,000
Securities Held for Long-Term Plant Expansion	75,000	—
Treasury Stock (preferred)	5,000	—
Total	$995,000	$879,000
Accounts with Credit Balances		
Allowance for Doubtful Accounts	$ 7,000	$ 8,000
Accumulated Depreciation	191,000	166,000
Accounts Payable	166,000	146,000
Dividends Payable	20,000	—
Mortgage Notes Payable, current portion	25,000	25,000
Mortgage Notes Payable, long-term portion	125,000	150,000
Preferred Stock	50,000	50,000
Common Stock	200,000	200,000
Retained Earnings	211,000	134,000
Total	$995,000	$879,000

(a) No transactions affected the land or common stock accounts during the year.

(b) New machinery costing $186,000 was purchased on 30-day credit terms.

(c) Depreciation expense totaled $63,000 and $1,000 of patent amortization expense was recorded during 1979.

(d) Equipment with a book value of $8,000 was sold for $11,000.

(e) The $75,000 of securities were purchased during the year to be held in a separate fund for the next three to five years, pending specific plant expansion decisions to be made by the board of directors.

(f) A $25,000 portion of the mortgage notes payable came due for payment during each year.

(g) Fifty shares of preferred stock were purchased for the treasury at an average cost per share of $100.

(h) A cash dividend of $20,000 was declared on December 28, 1979, payable January 14, 1980.

Required: (1) Prepare a schedule of changes in net working capital for the fiscal year ended December 31, 1979.

(2) Prepare a statement of changes in financial position — working capital basis covering the same period.

13-10. Statement of changes in financial position — working capital basis. The comparative balance sheet for the years ended December 31, 1979 and 1980, are shown below for Twinbridge, Inc.:

Twinbridge, Inc.
Comparative Balance Sheet
December 31, 1980 and 1979

Assets	1980	1979
Current assets:		
Cash	$ 60,000	$ 50,000
Marketable securities	25,000	30,000
Accounts receivable	85,000	70,000
Allowance for doubtful accounts	(10,000)	(5,000)
Inventory	125,000	110,000
Total current assets	$285,000	$255,000
Plant:		
Land	$ 45,000	$ 40,000
Plant and equipment	280,000	260,000
Less accumulated depreciation	(30,000)	(20,000)
Total plant assets	$295,000	$280,000
Intangibles:		
Patents and copyrights	$ 40,000	$ 35,000
Total assets	$620,000	$570,000
Equities		
Current liabilities:		
Notes payable	$ 60,000	$ 40,000
Accounts payable	110,000	120,000
Income tax payable	30,000	20,000
Total current liabilities	$200,000	$180,000
Long-term liabilities:		
Bonds payable	$100,000	$100,000
Premium on bonds payable	5,000	6,000
Total long-term liabilities	$105,000	$106,000
Owners' equity:		
Capital stock, $100 par	$150,000	$100,000
Premium on capital stock	15,000	10,000
Retained earnings:		
Appropriated for contingencies	25,000	20,000
Unappropriated	125,000	154,000
Total owners' equity	$315,000	$284,000
Total equities	$620,000	$570,000

Supplemental information with respect to financial operations of Twin-bridge, Inc., during 1980 is shown below:

(a) Net income was $35,000, including cash sales of $125,000.

(b) Customer accounts totaling $3,000 were written off as uncollect-ible.

(c) Marketable securities purchased at $5,000 were sold for $7,000.

(d) Equipment originally purchased for $30,000 was sold at a $4,000 loss for $15,000 cash.

(e) As a result of a product line becoming obsolete, $6,000 of patents were charged to expense. A cash purchase of additional copy-rights was the only other transaction that affected the noncurrent assets.

(f) A $30,000 stock dividend was declared by the board of directors. Three hundred shares of stock were distributed to stockholders. The market price of the stock at the date of declaration was $100.

(g) Some additional shares of capital stock were sold to several inves-tors at a price in excess of par.

(h) The directors increased the appropriated retained earnings in an-ticipation of further expansion plans.

(i) Cash dividends of $29,000 were declared and paid in 1980.

Required: Prepare a statement of changes in financial position — work-ing capital basis for the year ended December 31, 1980. The analysis should be supported with account reconciliations and journals when ap-propriate. Do *not* prepare a schedule of changes in net working capital.

13-11. Statement of changes in financial position. Financial statements for the Mulvane Corp. are shown on pages 499 and 450.

Supplemental information:

(a) The land account was unaffected during 1979.

(b) A building costing $40,000 was obtained in September and fi-nanced under a short-term note payable arrangement.

(c) Several pieces of equipment originally costing $87,000 were sold during October. The book value of the equipment sold totaled $20,000.

(d) Additional equipment was purchased during December for cash.

(e) No patents or copyrights were purchased during 1979.

(f) The entire mortgage note payable was converted into 8,000 shares of common stock.

(g) The bonds were sold to several local financiers on January 1, 1979. Bond premium was amortized by the straight-line method.

(h) Several shares of treasury stock were sold for $14,000; and the appropriation for treasury stock and plant expansion was de-creased $11,000 at the time of the sale. No shares were purchased for the treasury during 1979.

(i) Cash dividends declared during 1979 totaled $41,000, of which $26,000 remained payable on January 16, 1980.

Mulvane Corp.
Comparative Balance Sheet
December 31, 1979 and 1978

Assets	1979	1978
Current assets:		
Cash..........	$ 37,000	$ 57,000
Marketable securities........................	18,000	28,000
Accounts receivable........................	70,000	117,000
Allowance for doubtful accounts	(35,000)	(23,000)
Inventory..............	326,000	186,000
Prepaid expenses (rent and insurance)................	12,000	8,000
Total current assets........................	$428,000	$373,000
Plant assets:		
Land..........	$ 80,000	$ 80,000
Buildings	220,000	180,000
Accumulated depreciation — building	(84,000)	(60,000)
Equipment..............	310,000	270,000
Accumulated depreciation — equipment..............	(69,000)	(90,000)
Total plant assets........................	$457,000	$380,000
Intangible:		
Patents and copyrights........................	$ 4,000	$ 8,000
Total assets........................	$889,000	$761,000

Equities

	1979	1978
Current liabilities:		
Notes payable..........	$ 90,000	$ 50,000
Accounts payable	38,000	90,000
Income tax payable........................	42,000	47,000
Interest payable........................	3,000	6,000
Dividends payable........................	26,000	27,000
Total current liabilities........................	$199,000	$220,000
Long-term liabilities:		
Mortgage note payable, due 1982	——	$ 80,000
Bonds payable, 8%, 10 years, due December 31, 1988........................	$100,000	——
Premium on bonds payable	9,000	——
Deferred income tax........................	31,000	27,000
Total long-term liabilities........................	$140,000	$107,000
Owners' equity:		
Common stock, $10 par value........................	$330,000	$250,000
Premium on stock........................	33,000	30,000
Appropriation for treasury stock and plant expansion	23,000	34,000
Unappropriated retained earnings........................	180,000	147,000
Treasury stock........................	(16,000)	(27,000)
Total owners' equity	$550,000	$434,000
Total equities........................	$889,000	$761,000

Mulvane Corp.
Income Statement
For the Year Ended December 31, 1979

Sales		$960,000
Cost of goods sold		470,000
Gross margin...		$490,000
Expenses:		
Wages and salaries	$117,000	
Depreciation — equipment	46,000	
Administrative	42,000	
Marketing and sales promotion.........................	32,000	
Depreciation — buildings..............................	24,000	
Utilities	23,000	
Rent and insurance	21,000	
Interest...	18,000	
Uncollectible accounts...................................	16,000	
Maintenance and repairs................................	6,000	
Amortization of patents and copyrights................	4,000	349,000
Operating income.......................................		$141,000
Gains and losses:		
Gain on sale of marketable securities..................	$ 3,000	
Loss on sale of equipment	(16,000)	(13,000)
Income before federal income tax		$128,000
Federal income tax expense...............................		65,000
Net income		$ 63,000

Required: (1) Determine the change in net working capital during 1979 by inspecting the current accounts. Do *not* prepare a schedule of changes in net working capital for the period.

(2) Prepare a statement of changes in financial position for 1979.

DECISION CASE

13-I. **Net working capital and future planning.** Top management of the Urwick Corp. met immediately following the close of the firm's fiscal year on December 31, 1979, to examine the balance sheet and the projected income statement for the first six months of 1980, both shown at the top of pages 501 and 502. Aside from hoping to earn a fairly sizeable net income for the first half of 1980, management intended to increase net working capital $450,000 above the level it was at on December 31, 1979.

Any increase in net working capital above $450,000 would be used to repay some or all of the short-term notes payable that were outstanding at the end of 1979. However, in the event that net working capital increased less than that amount, sufficient shares of capital stock would be sold during the first half of 1980 at an expected market price of $20 per share to assure attainment of the $450,000 objective.

Urwick Corp.
Balance Sheet
December 31, 1979

Assets		Equities	
Current assets:		**Current liabilities:**	
Cash........................	$ 270,000	Notes payable...........	$ 860,000
Marketable securities...	80,000	Accounts payable	940,000
Accounts receivable		Income tax payable.....	320,000
(net of allowance)....	760,000	Total current liabili-	
Inventory..................	1,200,000	ties..................	$2,120,000
Prepaid expenses	160,000		
Total current assets...	$2,470,000		
		Long-term liabilities:	
		Bonds payable, 6%,	
Plant assets:		10 years, due De-	
Land....................	$ 220,000	cember 31, 1986	$1,000,000
Plant and equipment		Discount on bonds pay-	
(net of $1,800,000		able	(21,000)
accumulated de-		Mortgage note pay-	
preciation).........	3,200,000	able, due June 30,	
Total plant assets.....	$3,420,000	1983....................	500,000
		Total long-term lia-	
		bilities..............	$1,479,000
Intangibles:			
Patents.................	$ 260,000		
		Owners' equity:	
		Capital stock, $10 par .	$1,600,000
		Premium on capital	
		stock	240,000
		Retained earnings	711,000
		Total owners' equity .	$2,551,000
Total assets..................	$6,150,000	Total equities	$6,150,000

Management anticipated that the only transaction which would affect the noncurrent accounts during the first six months of 1980, other than those identified on the projected income statement, would be a cash purchase of additional equipment in March for $400,000.

Required:
(1) Prepare a statement of changes in financial position — working capital basis for the six-month period ending June 30, 1980, using the "starting from net income" format to determine net working capital provided by current operations.
(2) If the increase in net working capital exceeds $450,000, prepare the entry to reflect the appropriate repayment of the short-term notes payable. On the other hand, if the net working capital objective does not appear attainable, prepare the entry to record the sale of sufficient shares of capital stock to achieve that goal.

Urwick Corp.
Projected Income Statement
For Six Months Ending June 30, 1980

Sales (all on 30-day credit terms)		$5,000,000
Cost of goods sold...		3,250,000
Gross margin		$1,750,000
Expenses:		
Wages and salaries......................................	$400,000	
Depreciation	250,000	
Administrative and marketing...........................	220,000	
Interest	80,000*	
Rent and insurance......................................	40,000	
Office supplies...	20,000	
Patents	10,000	$1,020,000
Operating income......................................		$ 730,000
Gains and losses:		
Loss on sale of equipment...............................		(50,000)**
Income before federal income tax...................		$ 680,000
Federal income tax expense...............................		340,000
Net income		$ 340,000

*Bond discount was amortized by the straight-line method at each interest payment date: June 30 and December 31.

**Original cost of the equipment was $200,000, on which $120,000 depreciation would have accumulated at the time of the anticipated sale in February, 1980.

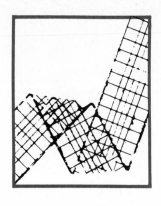

14
Analysis and Control of Cash Flow

. . . And a bigger elephant requires more bites.

Last line of ancient Cambodian proverb.

Two inherent characteristics of cash make its control and supervision of significant concern to management. First, cash is the most negotiable of financial resources possessed by any organization. A loss of cash, whether through negligence or theft, must usually be recognized and written off as an irreversible economic misfortune. Second, the *cash cycle*, which involves the conversion of financial resources, such as inventory, into cash and recycling that cash into other assets, is critical to the maintenance of liquidity and to the ultimate survival of the business.

MANAGERIAL VIEW OF CASH

The implementation of appropriate measures to constantly control and monitor the firm's cash position is of paramount concern to management. Several aspects of cash control will be highlighted prior to probing more deeply into the analysis of cash flow.

Internal Control of Cash

Extensive research, encompassing many decades and a wide variety of organizations and situations, indicates that the following are essential ingredients in the successful control of cash:

(1) Separation of responsibility among personnel, particularly with respect to those who handle cash. For example, persons in charge of maintaining individual accounts receivable records should never be allowed access to the company's cash or to other accounting records. Embezzlement, theft, and the manipulation of customer accounts are more easily accomplished if an individual has free access to cash, receivables, and other accounting records.

(2) Good communication among accounting and financial personnel. The adoption of this practice helps insure that the purpose of procedures and policies with respect to cash control is thoroughly understood and appreciated.

(3) Daily deposit in the bank of all cash and checks in excess of the immediate needs of the organization. This policy, coupled with the requirement that all cash disbursements be made by check, can be coordinated with timely bank reconciliations to pinpoint any cash discrepancies and flaws in control procedures.

(4) Competent personnel.

Detection of all irregularities and complete elimination of cash losses are rarely achieved in actual practice. First, the ingenuity of some human minds is constantly involved in attempting to circumvent and violate even the best designed system of cash control. Second, the possibility of unethical collusion between two or more persons cannot be ignored. Finally, the complexity of, and the rapid change in modern business practices and data processing techniques make procedures that seemed adequate yesterday inadequate tomorrow. Constant surveillance and continuous updatings of control procedures are essential for effective cash control.

Overcontrol of Cash

Cash can be overcontrolled. This observation is illustrated by a common trade-off situation that frequently arises in many firms. For example, should management spend $750 per month for supervisory salaries to insure that cash losses during the month do not exceed $50? Or would management be wiser to spend only $150 per month to safeguard cash, while allowing losses through pilferage or theft to approach $200 over the same period? The tighter control alternative would result in a total monthly cash outflow of $800, whereas the less stringent method of control might cost no more than $350.

In short, adequate control and supervision of cash flow necessitates retaining a sufficient, but not excessive amount of monitoring. Achieving the optimum balance between adequate control and appropriate cost requires implementation of techniques through trial and error and familiarization with approaches that have been used successfully in other organizations.

Monitoring Cash Flow

Another important aspect of cash management is the need to closely monitor cash flow. A sufficient cash balance must be available to meet financial obligations as they mature, but it must not be allowed to become so excessive that profitable opportunities are sacrificed. Large companies employ specialists who control and supervise cash that may exceed $5 billion in widely dispersed organizations. These groups have responsibility for channeling excess funds into temporary investments such as marketable securities, short-term loans to other businesses, and one- to two-week loans to commercial banks needing cash to comply with reserve requirements of the Federal Reserve System. Interest earned from these types of short-term investments usually far exceeds the funds expended to hire these specialists.

The following example illustrates the magnitude of cash balances that are maintained by some American firms and the degree of sophisticated techniques that have been developed by specialists to administer these funds. At the end of 1977, IBM maintained a cash plus short-term marketable securities balance approximating $5.4 billion. To optimize the return on this amount, specialists placed these funds in investments for as short a time period as one to three hours. For example, if cash was received after the money markets closed in New York City, specialists located in New York would immediately teletype those investible funds westward to money centers in Chicago, Los Angeles, Tokyo, and London for investment. This practice, called "following the sun" enables specialists to earn as much as $5,708 each hour per $1 billion invested, assuming an annual interest rate of 5 percent, determined as shown below:

$$\$1,000,000,000 \times .05 \times \frac{1 \text{ hour}}{365 \text{ days} \times 24 \text{ hours per day}} = \$5,708$$

Perfect timing in investing $5.4 billion every hour throughout the year will generate about $270,000,000 interest income per year, ($5,708 × 5.4 × 8,760 hours).

Relationship Between Cash Flow and Net Income

Many firms in the stage of rapid expansion generate excellent earnings, yet are unable to meet current financial obligations because cash is being converted too quickly into other types of assets that are expected to generate still higher earnings in the future. The following example illustrates how one company, Hygrade,

Inc., encountered cash flow difficulties during a recent five-month period:

Going Broke While Making a Profit[1]

As the year started, Abner Jones, the president of Hygrade, Inc., felt that the firm was in fine shape. The company made widgets — just what the consumer wanted. The company made them for 75¢ each and sold them for $1. A 30-day inventory supply was maintained, inventory was purchased under COD terms, and customers were billed on 30-day credit terms. Sales were right on target, with the sales manager predicting a steady increase. The year began this way:

January 1: Cash $1,000   Receivables $1,000   Inventory $750

During January: 1,000 widgets were sold, inventory was replenished at a cost of $750, and the receivables outstanding at January 1 were collected. By month's end, $250 net income had been earned, and the books showed:

January 31: Cash $1,250   Receivables $1,000   Inventory $750

February's sales increased, as predicted, to 1,500 units. With the corresponding step-up in sales, 2,000 units were made at a cost of $1,500 in order to maintain the 30-day inventory policy. All receivables from January sales were collected. Now the books reflected:

February 28: Cash $750   Receivables $1,500   Inventory $1,125

March sales were even better: 2,000 units. Collections: on time. Production based on the marketing forecast: 2,500 units. Operating results for the month: $500 net income. Net income to date: $1,125. The books showed:

March 31: Cash $375   Receivables $2,000   Inventory $1,500

In April, sales increased by another 500 units to 2,500. Customers were paying right on time. Production was pushed to 3,000 widgets. And the month's business netted $625 for a net income to date of $1,750. The accountant's report reflected:

April 30: Cash $125   Receivables $2,500   Inventory $1,875

May saw Hygrade really hitting stride: sales of 3,000 widgets; collections on time; production of 3,500; and a 5-month net income of $2,500. But early on the morning of June 1 the treasurer requested an emergency conference with Jones:

May 31: Cash ZERO   Receivables $3,000   Inventory $2,250

A summary of the firm's operations for the 5-month period highlights the paradoxical relationship which frequently exists between net income and cash flow:

---

[1]Adapted from *Business Week*, April 28, 1956, pp. 46–47.

Sales (10,000 units × $1) ...	$10,000	Cash balance at January 1..	$ 1,000
Cost of goods sold (10,000		Cash balance at May 31.....	—0—
units × 75¢).................	7,500		
Net income....................	$ 2,500	Decrease in cash.............	$(1,000)

How could a firm generate such a sizeable profit, yet simultaneously reflect a deficit cash position? Detailed examination of the reasons for the $3,500 disparity between net income and cash flow in this instance will be presented after the following brief introduction to cash flow analysis.

APPROACHES TO CASH FLOW

The approaches that were developed to analyze net working capital in Chapter 13 are adaptable, with only slight modification, to the analysis of cash flow. The amount by which a cash balance changes during a particular period of time can be determined simply by noting the difference between the beginning and ending cash balance for that period. The primary aim of cash flow analysis, however, is to determine what transactions caused the cash balance to change during a given time interval. Determination and analysis of these reasons can be approached from either of the following viewpoints:

(1) Algebraic logic.
(2) Transaction reconstruction and analysis.

Algebraic Logic

An expanded version of the balance sheet equation can be stated as follows with respect to cash flow: Cash plus current assets other than cash plus noncurrent assets equals current liabilities plus long-term liabilities plus owners' equity. By adding the Δ ("change in") notation before each category, and rearranging the equation, the symbolic expression for determining cash flow during a period becomes:

$$\Delta Cash = \Delta CL + \Delta LL + \Delta OE - (\Delta CA \text{ other than cash} + \Delta NA).$$

This cash flow equation can be abbreviated even further, as shown below:

$$\Delta Cash = \Delta \text{ in all equities} - (\Delta \text{ in all noncash assets}).$$

In short, the change in cash can be explained by analyzing changes that occurred in all noncash accounts. For purposes of subsequent cash flow analysis, all income-statement-related accounts will be considered a portion of owners' equity.

Transaction Reconstruction and Analysis

Cash is affected only if the cash account appears in the journal entry to record the transaction. Entries or transactions can be segregated into two categories: (1) those which increase cash; and (2) those which decrease cash. This statement is displayed in tabular format, shown on page 509.

SOURCES (INCREASES) OF CASH		USES (DECREASES) OF CASH
Decrease in current assets other than cash.	EACH TRANSACTION MUST HAVE CASH IN THE ENTRY	Increase in current assets other than cash.
Decrease in noncurrent assets.		Increase in noncurrent assets.
Increase in current liabilities.		Decrease in current liabilities.
Increase in long-term liabilities.		Decrease in long-term liabilities.
Increase in owners' equity.		Decrease in owners' equity.

Integrative Illustrations

These two approaches can be illustrated and integrated by analyzing several transactions which occur frequently in business establishments, as shown below:

(1) Sale of merchandise on credit terms.
(2) Collection of accounts receivable.
(3) Sale of a plant asset.
(4) Repayment of a short-term loan.
(5) Sale of a bond issue.
(6) Declaration of a cash dividend.

Systematic Analysis

Again, as with net working capital analysis, an orderly systematic approach is essential to analyze the change in cash which occurred during a particular period. The analysis involves the following steps:

(1) Obtain the necessary financial statements (or their equivalent) including:
   (a) Two balance sheets, one dated at the beginning of the period, and the other dated at the end of the period.
   (b) An income statement covering the period between the two balance sheet dates.
   (c) Any supplemental financial information.
(2) Determine the change in cash that occurred during the period.
(3) Reconcile each noncash account in the order shown on the balance sheet.

The Hygrade, Inc., illustration will be reexamined within this framework to introduce the general procedures involved in cash flow analysis before progressing to a more complex, comprehensive case. The financial statements for Hygrade, Inc., on page 510 were constructed from information provided in the preceding discussion.

Event	Transaction and Entry	Cash	=	ΔCL	+	ΔLL	+	ΔOE	−	(ΔCA* + ΔNA)
(1)	Merchandise was sold for $2,000 on 30-day credit terms: Accounts Receivable.... 2,000 Sales.... 2,000 Since no cash is involved in the entry, cash flow is not affected.	−0−	=					2,000	−	(+2,000)
(2)	Accounts receivable totaling $1,500 were collected: Cash.... 1,500 Accounts Receivable.... 1,500 Cash increased by $1,500.	+ 1,500	=						−	(−1,500)
(3)	Land originally costing $7,000 was sold at a gain of $2,000. Cash.... 9,000 Land.... 7,000 Gain on Sale of Land (IS).... 2,000 Cash increased by $9,000.	+ 9,000	=					2,000	− [	+ (−7,000)]
(4)	A 6-month, $4,000 note payable was repaid. Notes Payable.... 4,000 Cash.... 4,000 Cash decreased by $4,000.	− 4,000	=	−4,000						
(5)	A $60,000, 10-year bond issue was sold at par: Cash.... 60,000 Bonds Payable.... 60,000 Cash increased by $60,000.	+60,000	=			+ 60,000				
(6)	An $8,000 cash dividend was declared. Retained Earnings.... 8,000 Cash Dividends Payable.... 8,000 No cash is involved in this transaction hence, cash flow is not affected.	−0−	=	+8,000				+ (−8,000)		
	Total....	66,500	=	+4,000	+	60,000	+	(−4,000)	− [+	500 + (−7,000)]

*Current assets other than cash.

Hygrade, Inc.

COMPARATIVE BALANCE SHEET AT			INCOME STATEMENT FOR THE FIVE-MONTH PERIOD ENDED MAY 31	
	MAY 31	DEC. 31		
Cash....................	—0—	$1,000	Sales (10,000 units × $1)......	$10,000
Receivables	$3,000	1,000	Cost of goods sold (10,000	
Inventory..............	2,250	750	units × 75¢)..................	7,500
Total assets........	$5,250	$2,750	Net income	$ 2,500
Capital stock.........	$2,750	$2,750*		
Retained earnings ..	2,500	—0— *		
Total equities........	$5,250	$2,750		

*Beginning balances are inferred.

Accounts Receivable. The accounts receivable account, which is normally affected by credit sales and the collection of receivables, can be analyzed by using the T account format shown below:

ACCOUNTS RECEIVABLE

Bal. at Jan. 1	1,000		
(1)	10,000	(2)	8,000
Bal. at May 31	3,000		

The following summary entry records all sales made during the five-month period on 30-day credit terms:

(1)

Accounts Receivable	10,000	
Sales		10,000
Record credit sales.		

Cash was not affected by this summary transaction, because no cash was involved in the entry.

Since the accounts receivable account reflected a $3,000 debit balance at the end of the period, that account must have been credited a total of $8,000 during the period. The transaction that caused this decrease was probably the collection of accounts, as shown below in summary form:

(2)

Cash	8,000	
Accounts Receivable		8,000
Record collection of accounts receivable.		

This transaction provided $8,000 of cash as receivables were converted into that financial resource.

Inventory. The inventory account is normally affected by transactions that involve cash or credit purchases of inventory and the sale of inventory to customers. That account is shown below in T account format:

INVENTORY

Bal. at Jan. 1	750		
(4)	9,000	(3)	7,500
Bal. at May 31	2,250		

The entry shown below reflects the recognition of the cost of goods sold during the five-month period:

(3)

Cost of Goods Sold 7,500
    Inventory.. 7,500
        Record cost of goods sold.

Cash flow was not affected by this summary transaction.

Since the ending inventory balance is $2,250, inventory must have been replenished by the amount of $7,500 cost of goods sold plus the $1,500 inventory buildup during the five-month period, or $9,000 in total. All purchases of inventory were made under COD terms, and the summary entry to reflect total purchases during the period is shown below:

(4)

Inventory.. 9,000
    Cash... 9,000
        Purchase of inventory on COD terms.

Cash was decreased $9,000 by this transaction.

Equities. No change is assumed to have occurred in the capital stock account during the period. The $2,500 increase in Retained Earnings is ultimately explained by the $10,000 credit to Sales from entry (1) above, and the $7,500 debit to Cost of Goods Sold in entry (3). Notice that neither of these summary entries affected Cash, even though net income totaled $2,500.

At this point, all noncash accounts have been reconciled to determine: (1) what transactions affected these accounts, and (2) the effect each event had on cash flow. A statement of changes in financial position — cash basis may now be prepared, as shown at the top of page 512.

In short, the decrease in the cash balance was caused by the conversion of the cash received from the collection of receivables into inventory to satisfy the expansion in sales. It appears that an adequate profit is being earned. But, unless the cash balance is

Hygrade, Inc.
Statement of Changes in Financial Position — Cash Basis
For the Five-Month Period Ended May 31

Sources of cash	
Collection of receivables	$ 8,000
Uses of cash	
Purchases of inventory..	9,000
Decrease in cash balance	$ (1,000)

quickly replenished with a loan, accelerated collection of receivables, or the investment of additional cash by owners, the firm's cash position will further deteriorate into insolvency as sales continue to grow and additional net income is generated.

COMPREHENSIVE CASH FLOW ANALYSIS

Marinca, Inc., is a wholesale distributor of watercraft and related sporting gear. The following analysis of cash flow encompasses the fiscal year ended December 31, 1979, although an analysis for a shorter time frame can be made if interim financial statements are available. The analysis will proceed in the three-stage sequence shown on page 508: (1) obtain the necessary data; (2) determine the change in cash; and (3) reconcile each noncash account in the order shown on the balance sheet.

Obtain Necessary Financial Data

Supplemental financial information for the fiscal year ended December 31, 1979, together with the comparative balance sheet as of December 31, 1978 and 1979, are given below and on the following page. The income statement for 1979 is shown on page 514. As mentioned in Chapter 13, all totals and subtotals should be verified to ensure that they are internally consistent and that all account titles have been properly classified prior to beginning the analysis.

    (a) No marketable securities or land were purchased during 1979.
    (b) All purchases of inventory were made under 30-day credit terms and only inventory purchases flowed through Accounts Payable.
    (c) Payments for rent and insurance were immediately capitalized and subsequently charged to expense at appropriate intervals during the year.
    (d) An additional warehouse was purchased for $40,000 cash.
    (e) Equipment originally costing $30,000 was sold for $2,000. Additional machinery was purchased for cash.

Marinca, Inc.
Comparative Balance Sheet
December 31, 1979 and 1978

Assets	1979	1978
Current assets:		
Cash	$ 70,000	$ 40,000
Marketable securities.....................................	4,000	6,000
Accounts receivable......................................	180,000	160,000
Allowance for doubtful accounts........................	(13,000)	(8,000)
Inventory..	326,000	292,000
Prepaid rent and insurance	18,000	12,000
Total current assets.....................................	$585,000	$502,000
Plant assets:		
Land	$ 30,000	$ 30,000
Buildings and equipment	253,000	227,000
Less accumulated depreciation..........................	(64,000)	(51,000)
Total plant assets.......................................	$219,000	$206,000
Total assets	$804,000	$708,000

Equities	1979	1978
Current liabilities:		
Notes payable..	$ 66,000	$ 15,000
Accounts payable	184,000	178,000
Income tax payable.......................................	39,000	33,000
Cash dividends payable	16,000	10,000
Total current liabilities.................................	$305,000	$236,000
Long-term liabilities:		
Bonds payable, 8%, 10 years, due December 31, 1986	$200,000	$200,000
Premium on bonds payable..............................	7,000	8,000
Total long-term liabilities...............................	$207,000	$208,000
Owners' equity:		
Capital stock, $10 par value	$210,000	$200,000
Premium on capital stock................................	34,000	30,000
Appropriation for plant expansion......................	10,000	15,000
Retained earnings..	41,000	27,000
Treasury stock, 300 shares at December 31, 1979 ...	(3,000)	(8,000)
Total owners' equity.....................................	$292,000	$264,000
Total equities	$804,000	$708,000

(f) Cash dividends of $30,000 were declared during 1979, of which only $14,000 had been paid as of the end of 1979.

(g) One thousand shares of previously unissued capital stock were sold at an average price of $13 per share.

(h) Some treasury stock originally purchased for $5,000 was sold for $6,000.

(i) The board of directors cut back expansion plans and transferred $5,000 into Retained Earnings during December.

Marinca, Inc.
Income Statement
For the Year Ended December 31, 1979

Sales (all on 30-day credit terms)		$760,000
Cost of goods sold..		454,000
Gross margin...		$306,000
Expenses:		
Wages and salaries......................................	$70,000	
Promotion and selling	47,000	
Depreciation	33,000	
Utilities..	28,000	
Interest (including bond premium amortization)	20,000	
Rent and insurance.......................................	14,000	
Uncollectible accounts..................................	9,000	221,000
Operating income.......................................		$ 85,000
Gains and losses:		
Gain on sale of marketable securities.................	$ 3,000	
Loss on sale of equipment..............................	(8,000)	(5,000)
Income before income tax.............................		$ 80,000
Income tax expense		41,000
Net income		$ 39,000

Change in Cash and Accounts Reconciliation

The cash balance increased $30,000, ($70,000 − $40,000) between the beginning and end of 1979. The next step will be to determine in detail what caused this increase beginning with the first noncash account shown on the balance sheet.

Marketable Securities. Item (a) of the supplemental information states that no securities were purchased; and the comparative balance sheet indicates that this account decreased $2,000 during the year, from $6,000 to $4,000. The $3,000 gain on the sale of marketable securities, as reported on the income statement, suggests that the entry to record the sale of these securities was as shown below:

Cash...	5,000	
Marketable Securities...		2,000
Gain on Sale of Marketable Securities		3,000
Record sale of securities at $3,000 gain.		

Although the sale of these securities provided only $3,000 net working capital, the cash balance was increased by $5,000.

Accounts Receivable. Cash flow is frequently affected by a network of accounts which, at first glance, appear to have no direct relationship with cash. Normally, for example, the following four accounts must be analyzed simultaneously before the impact that the change in Accounts Receivable had on cash flow can be determined: Accounts Receivable; Allowance for Doubtful Accounts; Sales; and Uncollectible Accounts Expense. Construction of T accounts will simplify the reconciliation process:

ACCOUNTS RECEIVABLE

Bal. at			
Dec. 31, 1978	160,000		
(1)	760,000	(3)	4,000
		(4)	736,000
Bal. at			
Dec. 31, 1979	180,000		

SALES

	(1)	760,000

ALLOWANCE FOR DOUBTFUL ACCOUNTS

		Bal. at	
		Dec. 31, 1978	8,000
(3)	4,000	(2)	9,000
		Bal. at	
		Dec. 31, 1979	13,000

UNCOLLECTIBLE ACCOUNTS EXPENSE

(2)	9,000

Since the entire sales of $760,000 for 1979 were made on credit terms, Accounts Receivable increased a total of $760,000 as shown above in the summary (1) posting to the Accounts Receivable T account; Sales were credited with a similar amount during 1979. The entry to provide for sales is shown below:

(1)

Accounts Receivable	760,000	
Sales		760,000
Record sales for 1979.		

Uncollectible Accounts Expense reflected a $9,000 charge during 1979 (also shown on the income statement), which suggests that a provision of $9,000 was made during 1979 for accounts that were expected to eventually become uncollectible. The entry to provide for doubtful accounts is shown below:

(2)

Uncollectible Accounts Expense	9,000	
Allowance for Doubtful Accounts		9,000
Recognize provision for estimated uncollectible accounts.		

Neither credit sales nor provision for uncollectibles had any effect on cash flow. However, these two summary transactions have to be identified and analyzed to determine the ultimate effect that all transactions which directly and indirectly affect Accounts Receivable have on cash.

For the Allowance for Doubtful Accounts to balance, debits totaling $4,000 must have been made to that account during the year. The transaction that usually gives rise to a debit to this account is the write-off of specific accounts that were proven to be uncollectible during the year, as shown in the entry below:

(3)

Allowance for Doubtful Accounts............................ 4,000
    Accounts Receivable 4,000
        **Record the write-off of specific customer accounts
        proven uncollectible in 1979.**

Again, this entry had no direct effect on cash flow, because the cash account was not involved.

The final step in reconciling the beginning and ending balances of Accounts Receivable is determining that credits totaling $736,000 must have been posted to this account during the year in addition to the postings from entries (1) and (3). The summary transaction that normally explains this substantial decrease in Accounts Receivable is the collection of customer accounts, as shown below:

(4)

Cash.. 736,000
    Accounts Receivable 736,000
        Record collection of accounts receivable.

Hence, the net effect of entries (1) through (4) on cash flow is an increase of $736,000, as reflected in entry (4) above. Notice, however, that only after proceeding through four interrelated accounts in four distinct steps was this fact determinable with any degree of certainty.

Inventories. The analyst may infer from item (b) of the supplemental information that the following three accounts are interlinked and should be analyzed simultaneously to determine the impact that the following inventory-related transactions have on cash flow: Inventory; Accounts Payable; and Cost of Goods Sold. Reconciliation of the accounts, using the T account format shown at the top of page 517, will facilitate the analysis at this point.

The amount of cost of goods sold that is reflected on the income statement indicates that Inventory must have been credited

INVENTORY

Bal. at Dec. 31, 1978	292,000		
(2)	488,000	(1)	454,000
Bal. at Dec. 31, 1979	326,000		

COST OF GOODS SOLD

(1)	454,000

ACCOUNTS PAYABLE

		Bal. at Dec. 31, 1978	178,000
(3)	482,000	(2)	488,000
		Bal. at Dec. 31, 1979	184,000

a total of $454,000 during 1979 to reflect the cost of merchandise that was transferred to customers. This amount is shown above as the (1) credit posting to the inventories account. The summary entry is shown below:

(1)

Cost of Goods Sold 454,000
   Inventory... 454,000
     Charge to inventory cost of merchandise sold.

For the inventory account to reflect a balance of $326,000 at December 31, 1979, $488,000 of merchandise must have been purchased on account during the year, (see item (b) of the supplemental information). The summary entry which reflects these credit purchases totaling $488,000 is shown below:

(2)

Inventory... 488,000
   Accounts Payable 488,000
     Record credit purchases of inventory.

Neither of these two entries (1) and (2) affected cash flow directly in 1979. Nonetheless, they must be identified and analyzed to determine the ultimate effect on cash flow of all inventory-related transactions.

A $482,000 debit to Accounts Payable is necessary to complete the analysis of inventory-related transactions. Debits to this account normally arise when payables are paid, as shown below:

(3)

Accounts Payable 482,000
   Cash... **482,000**
     Record payment of accounts payable.

Analysis of these three interconnected summary entries suggests that $482,000 of cash was probably used during 1979 to pay for inventory purchases.

Prepaid Expense Items. The analyst may conclude from item (c) of the supplemental information that all purchases of prepaid rent and insurance were made with cash and immediately capitalized. Analysis of the prepaid rent and insurance account is shown below:

PREPAID RENT AND INSURANCE

Bal. at Dec. 31, 1978	12,000		
(2)	20,000	(1)	14,000
Bal. at Dec. 31, 1979	18,000		

Rent and insurance expense that is reflected on the income statement for 1979 totaled $14,000. The summary entry to charge these two prepaid items to expense is shown below:

(1)

Rent and Insurance Expense....................................14,000
   Prepaid Rent and Insurance...............................   14,000
     Record charging to expense prepaid items during 1979.

Cash flow was unaffected by the above entry.

For the prepaid account to balance, $20,000 of rent and insurance must have been purchased and prepaid with cash during 1979, as shown below:

(2)

Prepaid Rent and Insurance................................. 20,000
   Cash...   **20,000**
     Record prepayments for rent and insurance.

The effect of entry (2) on cash flow in 1979 was the use of $20,000 cash.

All current asset accounts have now been analyzed, and the results of the cash analysis thus far may be summarized below:

SOURCES OF CASH		USES OF CASH	
Sale of marketable securities...	$ 5,000	Purchases of inventory	$482,000
Collection of accounts		Prepayments of rent and	
receivable........................	736,000	insurance	20,000
Total sources..................	$741,000	Total uses.................	$502,000

Land. According to item (a) of the supplemental information, no transactions affected the land account during 1979.

Buildings and Equipment. To reconcile Buildings and Equipment and its related contra account, items (d) and (e) of the supplemental information must be analyzed, together with the depreciation expense and the loss on the sale of equipment that are reported on the income statement. These interrelated accounts are displayed below to facilitate the reconciliation process:

BUILDINGS AND EQUIPMENT

Bal. at			
Dec. 31, 1978	227,000		
(2)	40,000	(3)	30,000
(4)	16,000		
Bal. at			
Dec. 31, 1979	253,000		

DEPRECIATION EXPENSE

(1)	33,000	

ACCUMULATED DEPRECIATION —
BUILDINGS AND EQUIPMENT

		Bal. at	
		Dec. 31, 1978	51,000
(3)	20,000	(1)	33,000
		Bal. at	
		Dec. 31, 1979	64,000

The $33,000 depreciation expense reflected on the income statement had no effect on either net working capital or cash flow. This transaction must, however, be identified and analyzed to determine the impact that all transactions which affected the two noncurrent asset accounts had on cash flow. The summary entry is shown below:

(1)

Depreciation Expense	33,000	
Accumulated Depreciation — Buildings and Equipment		33,000
Record depreciation expense for 1979.		

The $33,000 credit posting that is identified as (1) in the above contra account was offset by a debit to Depreciation Expense — Buildings and Equipment.

The entry to record the cash purchase of the warehouse for $40,000 [item (d) of the supplemental information], is reflected below. This transaction used $40,000 cash.

(2)

Buildings and Equipment	40,000	
Cash		40,000
Purchase of warehouse.		

For the contra account to balance, a $20,000 debit must have been made to that account during 1979. This amount was probably associated with the transaction that involved the sale for $2,000 of equipment which originally cost $30,000, [item (e) of the supplemental information]. The entry that reflected the sale of the equipment is shown below:

(3)

Cash...	2,000	
Accumulated Depreciation — Buildings and Equipment	20,000	
Loss on Sale of Equipment....................................	8,000	
Buildings and Equipment..................................		30,000

Record sale of equipment at $8,000 loss.

The impact of the above transaction on the analysis was the generation of $2,000 cash inflow.

The cost of additional machinery purchased for cash during 1979, as stated in item (e) of the supplemental information, must have been $16,000 in order for the parent account to balance. The entry, which used $16,000 of cash, is shown below:

(4)

Buildings and Equipment.....................................	16,000	
Cash..		**16,000**

Cash purchase of machinery.

A condensation of the analysis discloses that three sources and five uses of cash have thus far been identified, as indicated below:

SOURCES OF CASH		USES OF CASH	
Sale of marketable		Purchases of inventory	$482,000
securities........................	$ 5,000	Prepayments of rent and	
Collection of accounts		insurance	20,000
receivable.......................	736,000	Purchase of warehouse........	40,000
Sale of equipment...............	2,000	Purchase of machinery	16,000
Total sources................	$743,000	Total uses....................	$558,000

Notes Payable and Accounts Payable. In the absence of other information, the analyst may assume that a net of $51,000 of short-term notes was issued during 1979, thereby causing cash to increase by $51,000. Notice, however, that a higher or lower amount of short-term loans could have been outstanding at a specific time during 1979. The net increase of $51,000 in the notes payable account merely indicates the difference between the amounts at January 1 and at December 31, 1979. Accounts Payable was previously reconciled in conjunction with analysis of the inventory account.

Income Tax Payable. The impact that income tax had on cash flow can be analyzed by reconstructing the income tax payable account, as shown below:

INCOME TAX PAYABLE

		Bal. at Dec. 31, 1978	33,000
(2)	35,000	(1)	41,000
		Bal. at Dec. 31, 1979	39,000

Income tax expense for 1979 totaled $41,000 and was probably recorded as follows:

(1)

Income Tax Expense	41,000	
Income Tax Payable		41,000
Record income tax expense for 1979.		

The entry did not affect cash flow.

For the above T account to balance, $35,000 of income tax must have been paid during 1979 as shown below:

(2)

Income Tax Payable	35,000	
Cash		35,000
Record payment of income taxes during 1979.		

Payment of income tax used $35,000 of cash in this instance.

Cash Dividends Payable. The dividends payable account is displayed below:

CASH DIVIDENDS PAYABLE

		Bal. at Dec. 31, 1978	10,000
(2)	24,000	(1)	30,000
		Bal. at Dec. 31, 1979	16,000

Item (f) of the supplemental information states that a $30,000 cash dividend was declared during 1979. The entry to record this dividend declaration is shown below:

(1)

Retained Earnings	30,000	
Cash Dividends Payable....................................		30,000
Record declaration of cash dividends during 1979.		

Although this transaction decreased net working capital by $30,000, it had no impact on cash flow.

Item (f) also states that $14,000 of the dividends declared in 1979 were paid in that year. In addition, the $10,000 balance in Cash Dividends Payable at December 31, 1978, was probably paid during 1979 in order for that account to balance. Hence, total cash dividends paid in 1979 were $24,000, as shown below:

(2)

Cash Dividends Payable	24,000	
Cash		24,000
Payment of cash dividends during 1979.		

This summary transaction decreased cash by $24,000.

Bonds Payable and Premium on Bonds Payable. Although the bonds payable account reflects no change during 1979, $1,000 of bond premium was probably amortized and reflected in the $20,000 interest expense that is shown on the income statement. Since the amortization of $1,000 of bond premium has no effect on cash flow, that amount must be added back to interest expense of $20,000 to determine the total amount of interest that was actually paid during 1979, as calculated below:

Interest expense reported on income statement........................	$20,000
Bond premium amortization which did not affect cash flow.......	+1,000
Total interest payments	$21,000

In short, the cash balance was decreased $21,000 by the payment of interest to various creditors during the year.

A summary of the impact that all transactions thus far analyzed had on cash flow is displayed below:

SOURCES OF CASH		USES OF CASH	
Sale of marketable securities........................	$ 5,000	Purchases of inventory	$482,000
Collection of accounts receivable.......................	736,000	Prepayments of rent and insurance	20,000
Sale of equipment...............	2,000	Purchase of warehouse........	40,000
Obtained short-term loans ...	51,000	Purchase of machinery	16,000
		Payment of income tax	35,000
		Payments of cash dividends .	24,000
		Interest payments	21,000
Total sources................	$794,000	Total uses....................	$638,000

Capital Stock, Premium on Capital Stock, and Treasury Stock. These three stock accounts may be analyzed together in this instance. The sale of the 1,000 shares of previously unissued capital stock at an average price of $13 per share, as reported in item (g) of the supplemental information, is reflected in the following entry:

```
Cash.............................................................    13,000
   Capital Stock ...............................................             10,000
   Premium on Capital Stock .................................              3,000
      Record sale of capital stock. Capital stock: 1,000
      shares × $10 par value per share = $10,000.
      Premium: 1,000 shares × ($13 price − $10 par) =
      $3,000.
```

This transaction increased cash by $13,000, and accounted for $3,000 of the $4,000 net increase in the premium on capital stock account during 1979.

The remaining $1,000 credit to Premium on Capital Stock probably arose in the transaction that involved the sale for $6,000 of treasury stock which was originally obtained at a cost of $5,000, as reported in item (h). That entry is recorded below:

```
Cash.............................................................     6,000
   Treasury Stock ..............................................              5,000
   Premium on Capital Stock .................................              1,000
      Sale of treasury stock at $1,000 above its acquisi-
      tion cost.
```

The cash balance was increased $6,000 because of this transaction.

Appropriation for Plant Expansion. The transfer of $5,000 from the appropriation for plant expansion account to Retained Earnings had no impact on cash flow.

Retained Earnings. The final balance sheet account to be reconciled is shown below:

RETAINED EARNINGS

		Bal. at Dec. 31, 1979	27,000
		Net income	39,000
Declaration of cash dividends	30,000	Transfer from appropriation	5,000
		Bal. at Dec. 31, 1979	41,000

The zero impact that the dividend declaration and the transfer from the appropriation account had on cash flow was previously explained. In addition, each item that appears on the income statement was considered previously, except for the following three expense items:

Wages and salaries	$ 70,000
Promotion and selling	47,000
Utilities	28,000
Total	$145,000

The analyst may safely conclude, based on supplemental information item (b), that each of these expenses was probably fully paid with cash during 1979. A summary entry to record these payments is shown below, the net result of which decreased cash by $145,000:

Wages and Salaries Expense	70,000	
Promotion and Selling Expense	47,000	
Utilities Expense	28,000	
Cash		145,000

THE STATEMENT OF CHANGES IN FINANCIAL POSITION — CASH BASIS, AND ITS INTERPRETATION

Results of the preceding analysis may now be summarized in the statement of changes in financial position — cash basis that is shown below:

Marinca, Inc.
Statement of Changes in Financial Position — Cash Basis
For the Year Ended December 31, 1979

Sources of cash

Collection of accounts receivable	$736,000
Sale of equipment	2,000
Sale of marketable securities	5,000
Obtained short-term loans	51,000
Sale of capital stock	13,000
Sale of treasury stock	6,000
Total sources of cash	$813,000

Uses of cash

Purchases of inventory	$482,000
Payment of wages and salaries, promotion and selling, and utilities expenses	145,000
Payment of income tax	35,000
Prepayments of rent and insurance	20,000
Interest payments	21,000
Purchase of warehouse	40,000
Purchase of machinery	16,000
Payment of cash dividends	24,000
Total uses of cash	$783,000

Had the Marinca, Inc., illustration involved any of the following type transactions, appropriate notations would have been included at the bottom portion of the above statement, similar to the presentation shown on page 477.

(1) Increase in noncurrent assets by means of issuing short-term debt, long-term debt, previously unissued corporate stock, or treasury stock.

(2) Conversion of short-term notes payable into long-term debt or corporate stock.

(3) Conversion of long-term debt into short-term debt or corporate stock.

The preceding statement contains considerable detail which may warrant condensation in order to more easily focus on how cash flow was affected by principal activities undertaken by the firm. For example, the following items may be grouped together and netted to determine the cash generated by normal operations:

Collection of accounts receivable...........................		$736,000
Less payments for:		
Inventory	$482,000	
Wages, salaries, promotion, selling, and utilities expenses	145,000	
Income tax..	35,000	
Rent and insurance	20,000	
Interest	21,000	703,000
Cash generated by normal operations		$33,000

The transactions that involved plant assets may also be regrouped to indicate their impact on cash flow, as shown below:

Purchase of warehouse...	$40,000
Purchase of machinery	16,000
Loss on sale of equipment...	(2,000)
Cash outflow for net additions to plant assets....................	$54,000

The two transactions that involved the firm's stock increased cash a total of $19,000: $13,000 sale of capital stock plus $6,000 sale of treasury stock. These regrouped pieces of information may be displayed in a more manageable statement to reflect cash flow for the year, as shown below:

Sources of cash

Normal operations...	$ 33,000
Sale of capital and treasury stock.....................................	19,000
Sale of marketable securities...	5,000
Obtained short-term loans	51,000
Total sources...	$108,000

Uses of cash

Net purchases of plant assets..	$ 54,000
Payment of cash dividends..	24,000
Total uses...	$ 78,000
Increase in cash balance...	$ 30,000

The statement of changes in financial position, based on either the working capital concept or the cash concept, is required by the Financial Accounting Standards Board to be submitted with the financial statements for external reporting purposes. The statement using the cash concept is particularly useful to managerial personnel who are charged with responsibility for controlling and planning the firm's cash flow position.

A comprehensive overview of the content of the statement of changes in financial position — cash basis, is provided below:

OVERVIEW OF THE
STATEMENT OF CHANGES IN FINANCIAL POSITION — CASH BASIS

Sources of Cash

Sale of marketable securities, including any gain or loss.
Receipt of interest and dividends.
Collection of accounts and notes receivable.
Sale of noncurrent assets, including any gain or loss.
Obtaining short-term or long-term loans.
Sale of stock or additional investment by owners.

Uses of cash

Purchase of marketable securities.
Payment for inventory and prepaid expense items.
Purchase of noncurrent assets.
Repayment of short-term or long-term loans.
Payment of taxes and interest.
Payment of cash dividends.
Purchases of treasury stock.
Withdrawals by owners.
Payment of operating expenses, such as employee compensation, maintenance, utilities, marketing, promotion, and administrative.

Append the following type noncash transactions:

(1) Increase in noncurrent assets by means of issuing short-term debt, long-term debt, previously unissued corporate stock, or treasury stock.
(2) Conversion of short-term notes payable into long-term debt or corporate stock.
(3) Conversion of long-term debt into short-term debt or corporate stock.

A deeper appreciation of cash flow analysis may emerge by: (1) comparing it with the analysis of net working capital; (2) examining some popularized misconceptions and misuses of cash flow; and (3) providing a brief introduction to the relationship between cash flow analysis and cash budgeting.

Comparison with Net Working Capital Analysis

Cash flow and net working capital analyses are similar in two respects. First, a certain amount of inferential reasoning is required to complete both analyses. Although the analyst may not be in a position to say with absolute certainty that a specific transaction did occur during the period, a proficiency can be developed through experience in narrowing down the possibilities that might have occurred and finally identifying from those alternatives the transaction that most likely occurred. The relationships that exist between four accounts in the preceding illustration — Accounts Receivable, Allowance for Doubtful Accounts, Sales, and Uncollectible Accounts Expense — provide an excellent example of how the analyst may proceed to recreate events that probably occurred from incomplete information.

Second, a similar three-stage approach was used in both cash flow and net working capital analyses:

(1) Obtaining necessary financial statements and supplemental financial information.
(2) Determining the change that occurred during the period in either cash or net working capital.
(3) Reconciling each account title in the order of appearance on the balance sheet by identifying transactions that affected each account, and determining their ultimate effect either on cash flow or net working capital.

Perhaps the principal dissimilarity between the analysis of cash flow and net working capital is the treatment of information contained on the income statement. The procedure that was developed in net working capital analysis is to start with either net income or with sales to determine the net working capital provided by current operations. Adjustments to income statement data were then made for transactions which had no impact on net working capital. In cash flow analysis, on the other hand, various items on the income statement are integrated into the analysis at various points based on their relevance to the particular balance-sheet-related account under review. In either event, it is important to note that both analyses ultimately consider every item that is reflected on the income statement. The principal distinction between the two analyses is the sequence in which details of the income statement are integrated into each analysis.

Misconceptions and Misuses of the Cash Flow Concept

Three common or popularized misunderstandings of cash flow warrant attention at this point. First, there is no necessary relationship between cash flow, net working capital, and net income. In the preceding Marinca, Inc., illustration, the following amounts were associated with each of these measures during the fiscal year ended December 31, 1979:

Net working capital.............	$14,000 increase
Cash flow...........................	$30,000 increase
Net income	$39,000

Only in the rarest of circumstances, or in instances where the organization is operating under a purely cash basis of accounting, will the three amounts coincide.

Second, a popularized version of cash flow that frequently appears in news articles and business publications defines the concept as net income plus depreciation (and depletion) expense. This definition of cash flow, if applied to the Marinca, Inc., example would have yielded a cash increase of $72,000 during 1979, as shown below:

Net income	$39,000
Plus depreciation expense	33,000
Cash flow......................................	$72,000

This definition of cash flow is a nondescript hybrid that approximates the amount of net working capital provided by current operations, using the "starting from net income" format.

Cash flow encompasses far more than this simplistic notion of "profit plus depreciation add back," as a quick review of the statement of changes in financial position — cash basis on page 524 will reveal. About the only attribute of this misconception, aside from its widespread misusage, is that it does recognize that depreciation expense does not affect or involve any cash flow, whereas many items on the income statement may ultimately involve or affect cash flow directly or indirectly.

Finally, some financial analysts have developed and widely publicized the concept of "cash flow per share of common stock," using the net income plus depreciation expense definition cited above as the numerator. The calculation can be expressed as shown below:

$$\frac{\text{Net income plus depreciation expense}}{\substack{\text{Number of shares of common stock} \\ \text{issued and outstanding}}} = \substack{\text{Cash flow per share} \\ \text{of common stock}}$$

If applied to the Marinca, Inc., illustration, where capital stock replaces the common stock designation, the calculation based on the number of shares existing at the end of 1979 would appear as follows:

$$\frac{\$39,000 + \$33,000}{(\$210,000 \div \$10 \text{ par}) - 300 \text{ shares in treasury}} = \$3.48$$

Aside from the criticism made above concerning the validity of measuring cash flow in this fashion, there exists a serious question with respect to the relevance of cash flow per share calculation.

Relationship Between Cash Flow Analysis and Cash Budgeting

Although cash flow analysis of the Hygrade Corp. and Marinca, Inc., examined what occurred during a previous period, perhaps a more important contribution of cash flow analysis is with respect to future operations. By projecting all revenue, expenses, and major changes that are expected to occur in the non-cash asset and equity accounts during a forthcoming period, management can become more aware of the impact that future decisions and operations will have on cash flow.

An analysis of future cash flow is executed in the same manner as outlined previously. The sole differences are that the balance sheet for the end of the projected period, the income statement for the forthcoming period, and any supplemental financial information will consist of forecasted data. Armed with a projection of cash flow, management is in a better position to understand the implications of future plans and to anticipate and counteract emergencies before they arise.

For example, arrangements to obtain loans may be made in advance of their need; or short- or long-term debt may be reduced if excess cash appears likely to be generated during the upcoming period. If inadequate cash flow appears imminent, the analyst may suggest that collection of receivables be accelerated, or that an inventory buildup be restricted or postponed. If plans call for a substantial expansion of plant facilities: an additional sale of capital stock or bond issues may be recommended; cash dividends may be curtailed; or a stock dividend may be used to replace cash dividends.

In short, cash flow analysis forces management to consider the impact that each aspect of operations had or will have on the total enterprise. Even though the specific focus of cash flow analysis is on cash, preceding analyses demonstrate that virtually every financial facet of the firm must be examined during the process of analysis. A deeper understanding of the total enterprise and of each of its elements usually leads to more informed and better decisions.

QUESTIONS

1. Identify two characteristics of cash which make its control and supervision particularly important to management.

2. Identify at least three essential ingredients of adequate internal cash control.

3. Can cash ever be considered to be overcontrolled or controlled at an excessive cost?

4. How may close monitoring and supervision of the cash balance that is maintained by a firm enable that firm to generate substantial income?

5. Under what conditions could a firm be earning net income, yet be unable to meet current financial obligations to creditors?

6. Express in symbolic terms, using an expanded version of the balance sheet equation, the change in cash flow that occurred during a particular period. Define each symbol in the equation.

7. Insert either "cash" or "noncash" in each of the blanks shown in the following sentences: The change in _____ that occurred dur-
(a)
ing a period can be analyzed by examining changes that occurred in all
_____ accounts during the period. Restated, _____ is af-
(b)   (c)
fected by a transaction only if the _____ account appears in the
(d)
journal entry that recorded that transaction.

8. Identify two transactions for each of the situations that involves the account category indicated in (1)–(5) below: (a) one which affects cash flow; and (b) one which does not affect cash flow.

	(a)	(b)
ACCOUNT CATEGORY	CASH FLOW AFFECTED	CASH FLOW NOT AFFECTED
(1) CA other than Cash		
(2) NA		
(3) CL		
(4) LL		
(5) OE		

9. Identify and briefly explain three steps that are required in order to analyze the change that occurred in cash during a specific period.

10. (a) Identify the accounts that normally must be considered in order to determine the impact that credit sales have on cash flow during a period. (b) Using T accounts, illustrate the linkage between each of the accounts identified in (a) with respect to cash flow analysis.

11. (a) Identify the accounts that normally must be considered in order to determine the impact that credit purchases of inventory items have on cash flow during a period. (b) Using T accounts, illustrate the linkage between each of the accounts identified in (a) with respect to cash flow analysis.

12. Prepare a sample journal entry for each of the following types of transactions that involve Marketable Securities: (a) cash flow is affected, but net working capital is not affected; (b) both cash flow and net working capital are affected.

13. Prepare a sample journal entry for each of the following types of transactions that involve inventory: (a) cash flow is affected, but net working capital is not affected; (b) net working capital is affected, but cash flow is not affected; (b) net working capital is affected, but cash flow is not affected; (c) neither cash flow nor net working capital is affected.

14. Prepare a sample journal entry for each of the following types of transactions that involve Equipment or its contra account: (a) net working capital is affected, but cash flow is not affected; (b) both cash flow and net working capital are affected; (c) neither cash flow nor net working capital is affected.

15. Prepare a sample journal entry that involves Income Tax Payable or Income Tax Expense which affects: (a) cash flow but not net working capital ; (b) net working capital but not cash flow.

16. Prepare a sample entry that involves Retained Earnings which affects: (a) net working capital but not cash flow; (b) both cash flow and net working capital; (c) neither cash flow nor net working capital.

17. Equipment originally costing $250,000 and having a book value of $40,000 at the time of sale, was sold at a $5,000 loss. (a) Journalize the transaction. (b) Using the net working capital equation, indicate the effect of this transaction on net working capital. (c) Using the cash flow equation, determine the effect of this transaction on cash flow.

18. Marketable securities originally costing $30,000 were sold at a $7,000 gain. (a) Journalize the transaction. (b) Using the net working capital equation, indicate the effect of this transaction on net working capital. (c) Using the cash flow equation, determine the effect of this transaction on cash flow.

19. Identify the items that may be grouped under the designation "normal current operations," in preparing the statement of changes in financial position — cash basis.

20. In what two respects are net working capital analysis and cash flow analysis similar?

21. In what respect are net working capital analysis and cash flow analysis different?

22. Explain how cash flow analysis may be used to facilitate future planning and budgeting efforts.

23. Identify at least five sources, and at least seven uses of cash.

EXERCISES

1. Cash control alternatives. The daily cash balance of the Trapps Corp. varied between $300,000 and $2,000,000, averaging $1,000,000 during each of the previous two years. During the current year, the treasurer detected losses of cash which approximated $3,000 per month. This continual loss appeared to result from obsolete or inadequate cash control procedures. To remedy the situation the treasurer is in the process of deciding which of the following three alternative control procedures would be most cost effective and practical to implement:

Alternative A. Hire three additional people at an annual salary of $15,000 each. The responsibility of this small staff would include close monitoring of the cash balance, maintenance of improved control procedures, and the investment throughout the year of excess cash in short-term investments. It is believed that these short-term investments will generate approximately $50,000 additional annual income for the firm. A one-time charge of $10,000 will be required to hire a consulting firm to design and implement the intricate system of cash control. Losses are expected to be reduced to $500 per year under this alternative.

Alternative B. Lease electronic data processing equipment at $1,000 per month. The treasurer's staff believes such equipment operated by present personnel will provide closer control and supervision of the cash balance and reduce cash losses to $3,000 per year.

Alternative C. Maintain the present system of control, with losses expected to continue averaging $3,000 per month, and with little likelihood of earning additional income from short-term investments.

Required: Prepare a comparative analysis of the three alternatives using the format shown below, and indicate with supporting comments the alternative that appears most economically advantageous to the firm to implement. Ignore income tax considerations.

ALTERNATIVE A (3-Person Staff)	ALTERNATIVE B (Electronic Data Processing Equipment)	ALTERNATIVE C (Continuation of Present System)

2. Effect of transactions on cash flow. Each of the following transactions occurred during the fiscal year ended December 31, 1980, in the Evans Corp.:

(1) Sales totaled $400,000, of which 80% were sold on 30-day credit terms, the balance being for cash.
(2) Marketable securities originally costing $18,000 were sold at a $3,000 loss.
(3) Capitalized prepaid rent and insurance totaling $16,000 were charged to expense.
(4) Land appraised at $40,000 was obtained by issuing 4,000 shares of the firm's $10 par value capital stock.
(5) Machinery originally costing $110,000, on which $95,000 depreciation had been recorded at the time of sale, was sold at a $4,000 gain.
(6) Cash dividends totaling $43,000 that were declared on December 23, 1979, were paid on January 7, 1980.

Required: Using the format shown below, determine the effect of each of the above transactions on cash flow during 1980:

EFFECT ON CASH FLOW IN 1980

TRANSACTION	Increase	Decrease	None

3. Effect of transactions on cash flow and net working capital. Each transaction described below occurred during the fiscal year ended September 30, 1980, in Kloister, Inc.:

(1) Provision for estimated uncollectible accounts amounted to $42,000.
(2) Specific customer accounts totaling $8,000 were written off as uncollectible.
(3) A building originally costing $140,000 was sold for $20,000 cash at a $14,000 loss.
(4) A $300,000, 5-year, 9% bond issue was sold at 102 on November 1, 1979.
(5) A $72,000 cash dividend on common stock was declared on September 28, 1980, payable October 10, 1981.

Required: Using the the format shown below, journalize each transaction, and determine its effect on cash flow and net working capital during the 1980 fiscal year:

JOURNAL ENTRY	EFFECT ON CASH FLOW			EFFECT ON NET WORKING CAPITAL		
	Increase	Decrease	None	Increase	Decrease	None

4. Effect of transactions on cash flow and net income. The transactions noted below occurred during the fiscal year ended June 30, 1980, in the Feldnap Corporation:

(1) A $400,000, 8-year, 10% issue of debentures was sold at 96 on July 1, 1979.

(2) Interest on the debentures described in (1) above was payable semiannually each December 31 and June 30. Straight-line amortization of bond premium and bond discount was used in the firm.

(3) Marketable securities originally costing $17,000 were sold at a $3,000 gain.

(4) Income tax payable of $43,000 at July 1, 1979, was paid during the last half of 1979; but $32,000 of the $54,000 income tax expense that was incurred during the fiscal year ended June 30, 1980, remained unpaid as of that date.

(5) A $40,000 short-term note payable was repaid at the bank.

Required: Using the format shown below, prepare the entry to record each transaction described above, and indicate the impact of each entry on cash flow and net income during the fiscal year ended June 30, 1980:

	EFFECT ON CASH FLOW			EFFECT ON NET INCOME		
JOURNAL ENTRY	*Increase*	*Decrease*	*None*	*Increase*	*Decrease*	*None*

5. Analysis of financial transactions: cash flow equation format. Using the cash flow equation, $\Delta Cash = \Delta CL + \Delta LL + \Delta OE - (\Delta CA$ other than Cash $+ \Delta NA)$, determine the impact of each of the following financial transactions that occurred in the Quissant Corp. during the fiscal year ended December 31, 1980:

(1) Machinery costing $240,000 was purchased under the following terms: 20% cash down payment and balance due in 120 days.

(2) Sales totaled $900,000, of which 10% were sold for cash, the balance being on 30-day credit terms.

(3) Total purchases of inventory during the year on 60-day credit terms was $640,000, of which $86,000 remained unpaid at December 31, 1980. The inventory balance at January 1, 1980, was zero.

(4) Of the total inventory purchases stated in (3) above, 80% were charged to expense as cost of goods sold during 1980.

(5) A theft that was detected in September, 1980, involved the loss of $16,000 inventory, $44,000 cash, and $8,000 of negotiable marketable securities.

6. Reconciliation of accounts receivable. Each of the following accounts in the Mars Corp. reflected the balance on the dates indicated below. The firm's fiscal year ended each December 31, and all sales were made on 30-day credit terms:

	DECEMBER 31	
	1980	**1979**
Accounts Receivable	$ 30,000	$ 26,000
Allowance for Doubtful Accounts	(7,300)	(6,900)
Sales	(340,000)	(316,000)
Uncollectible Accounts Expense	3,400	4,800

Required: (a) Prepare journal entries to record each transaction that occurred during the year ended December 31, 1980, with respect to the accounts. Post these transactions to Accounts Receivable and its contra account. (b) Summarize the impact that each transaction had on cash flow and net working capital during 1980.

7. **Analysis of inventory-related transactions.** The Dansk Corporation made all purchases for its inventory under 3/10, net 30 credit terms, and recorded all purchases by the net cost method. The total gross cost of merchandise purchased during the fiscal year ended December 31, 1980, amounted to $900,000. Only inventory purchases were credited to Accounts Payable, and the balance in Accounts Payable reflected an increase of $20,000 between December 31, 1979, and December 31, 1980. Although no cash discounts were lost during 1980, $17,000 of inventory was stolen during the year. The Merchandise Inventory balance was $70,000 and $64,000 at December 31, 1979 and 1980, respectively.

Required: (a) Prepare an entry to record each transaction that affected the merchandise inventory and accounts payable accounts during 1980. Post each entry to these two accounts. (b) Prepare a summary to reflect the impact of each transaction on cash flow and net income during 1980.

8. **Reconciliation of plant assets.** The account titles shown below reflect the balances indicated at the end of each fiscal year in the Austin-Healy Corporation:

	DECEMBER 31	
	1980	1979
Land	$ 83,000	$ 95,000
Buildings and Equipment	359,000	349,000
Accumulated Depreciation	(160,000)	(140,000)

Additional information with respect to all transactions that affected the above accounts during 1980 is shown below:

(1) The sole transaction affecting Land involved an $11,000 gain.
(2) New equipment costing $110,000 was obtained under a 4-year mortgage note payable arrangement.
(3) A building was sold for cash at an $8,000 loss. Depreciation recorded on the building at the time of sale was $30,000.
(4) Depreciation expense was recorded during 1980.

Required: (a) Prepare an entry to record each transaction that occurred during the year ended December 31, 1980. T accounts should be used in reconciling Buildings and Equipment and its contra accounts. (b) Summarize the effect of each transaction on cash flow and net income for 1980.

9. **Analysis of income tax transactions.** The federal income tax payable account reflected a credit balance of $47,000 and $73,000 at December 31, 1979 and 1980, respectively. Income tax expense that was recognized during the fiscal year ended December 31, 1980, totaled $106,000, of which $27,000 was deferred to future years. New plant assets were purchased within the last two years, and an accelerated depreciation method was used for tax purposes. Straight-line depreciation was used for financial reporting purposes.

Required: Prepare an entry to reflect each transaction that affected the accounts mentioned; and summarize their impact on cash flow, net working capital, and net income during 1980.

10. Analysis of bond-related transactions. A $700,000, 5-year, 10% bond issue was sold to the public on July 1, 1980, at a $15,000 premium. Interest was payable semiannually at each June 30 and December 31, and the issuer's fiscal year ended each December 31. Straight-line amortization was used in the firm. Another 7-year bond issue totaling $360,000 which had been issued at par on October 31, 1973, was converted into 3,600 shares of the firm's $100 par value preferred stock on January 1, 1980.

Required: Prepare an entry to record each transaction described above, and summarize the impact of the transactions on cash flow and net working capital for the fiscal year ended December 31, 1980.

11. Analysis of capital stock transactions. The transactions described below occurred in Kentax, Inc., during the fiscal year ended December 31, 1980. Seventy thousand shares of $10 par value Kentax, Inc., capital stock were issued and outstanding on January 1, 1980. No shares were in the treasury on that date; and the credit balance in the premium on capital stock account at the beginning of 1980 was $42,000.

  (1) Six thousand shares of capital stock were issued to the owner of a building, who in turn transferred title to that building to Kentax, Inc., during February. The building was appraised at $63,000.
  (2) One thousand shares of capital stock were purchased for the treasury at $11 per share in April.
  (3) A 2% stock dividend was distributed to stockholders from previously unissued stock during September. The market price per share of the stock was $11.50 at the date of declaration and distribution.
  (4) A cash dividend of $1 per share of capital stock was declared on December 23, 1980, of which $16,000 remained unpaid on December 31, 1980.

Required: (a) Prepare an entry to record each of the transactions described above. (b) Prepare a summary to indicate the effect of each transaction on cash flow and net working capital during 1980.

12. Rearrangement of statement of changes in financial position — cash basis. The statement of changes in financial position — cash basis shown on page 536 was prepared for the Phoenix Corp. at the end of the 1979 fiscal year. The corporation's vice president of finance felt that the statement, although accurate, contained excessive detail for presentation to the finance committee of the board of directors during its monthly meeting in January, 1980. The vice president suggested that the chief accountant rearrange and/or condense the statement in such a way that members of the committee may be better able to understand the essential reasons why the cash balance decreased during 1979.

Required: Prepare a rearranged and/or shortened version of the statement for presentation to the finance committee to highlight the main reasons for the decrease in the cash balance during 1979.

Phoenix Corp.
Statement of Changes in Financial Position — Cash Basis
For the Year Ended December 31, 1979

Sources of cash		
Collection of accounts receivable		$642,480
Collection of notes receivable		16,200
Sale of land		2,870
Sale of treasury stock		37,520
Sale of marketable securities................................		4,190
Sale of buildings		6,350
Sale of 15-year bond issue...................................		92,700
Sale of equipment and machinery.............................		7,610
Sale of previously unissued shares of common stock		48,370
Interest earned on short-term investments and notes receivable		460
Total sources of cash		$858,750
Uses of cash		
Purchase of land for expansion purposes....................		$ 3,200
Repayment of short-term notes payable		6,170
Purchase of three warehouse sheds..........................		2,390
Loss of cash through embezzlement..........................		170
Payments for expenses:		
Advertising and sales promotion	$ 58,420	
Administrative wages and salaries.........................	263,140	
Factory wages and salaries	124,210	
Federal and state income taxes	15,160	
Insurance..	890	
Interest...	1,140	
Office salaries and wages.................................	14,210	
Office supplies	760	
Property tax...	240	
Rent...	3,780	
Repairs and maintenance	1,160	
Warranty liabilities	2,430	485,540
Payments for inventory.......................................		431,780
Purchase of equipment and machinery......................		10,290
Purchase of patents..		870
Payment of cash dividends on common stock		1,610
Purchase of treasury stock		28,750
Purchase of marketable securities...........................		5,270
Total uses of cash		$976,040
Decrease in cash balance		$117,290

PROBLEMS

14-1. Analysis of transactions affecting cash flow. Each of the following transactions occurred in the Wolfram Company during the fiscal year ended December 31, 1980.

(a) A $400,000, 20-year, 9% bond issue was sold to the public on January 1, 1980 at 106. Interest on the bonds was payable semiannually at June 30 and December 31. The straight-line method was used to amortize bond discount and bond premium.

(b) Marketable securities originally costing $100,000 were sold at a $15,000 gain in June. Proceeds from the sale were immediately used to repay a $110,000 short-term note payable at the bank.

(c) Total sales in 1980 were $900,000, of which 30% were for cash and the remainder under 30-day credit terms. Ten percent of 1980 credit sales remained uncollected at December 31, 1980. The 1980 provision for estimated uncollectibles amounted to 1% of that year's total credit sales. Allowance for Doubtful Accounts reflected a credit balance of $16,000 and $17,000 at December 31, 1979 and 1980, respectively. The $80,000 of outstanding accounts receivable at December 31, 1979, were collected during 1980. Use T accounts for calculations.

(d) A piece of equipment originally costing $200,000, and having a book value of $160,000 on the date of sale, was sold at a $7,000 loss in July.

(e) All inventory was purchased on 30-day credit terms, and only inventory purchase transactions affected Accounts Payable. Cost of goods sold for 1980 totaled $650,000. Merchandise Inventory and Accounts Payable reflected the following balances at the dates indicated:

	DECEMBER 31	
	1980	*1979*
Inventory	$102,000	$85,000
Accounts Payable	(93,000)	(76,000)

Required: Using the format shown below, determine the impact that each of the above transactions had on cash flow during the fiscal year ended December 31, 1980. Support answers with calculations in the transaction analysis column.

	EFFECT ON CASH FLOW		
TRANSACTION ANALYSIS	*Increase*	*Decrease*	*None*

14-2. Analysis of transactions affecting cash flow and net working capital. Transactions described below, occurred in the Germanco Corp. during the fiscal year ended December 31, 1979.

(a) A $46,000 cash dividend was declared on December 28, 1978, but was not paid until January 6, 1979. Cash dividends declared during the 1979 fiscal year totaled $58,000, of which $7,000 remained unpaid at the end of that year.

(b) An $800,000 10-year, 7% bond issue originally sold at par and due for retirement on March 1, 1981, was converted into 160,000 shares of the firm's $5 par value common stock.

(c) A $500,000, 4-year, 6% bond issue was sold to the public at 96 on July 1, 1979. Interest was payable semiannually on June 30 and December 31. Bond discount and premium were amortized by the effective interest rate method.

(d) Total sales in 1979 amounted to $1,800,000, all of which were made under 30-day credit terms. Provision for estimated uncollectible accounts receivable during 1979 totaled ½% of that year's sales. The net decrease in the allowance account between the beginning and end of 1979 was $3,500. Accounts Receivable reflected a balance of $150,000 and $195,000 on December 31, 1978 and 1979, respectively.

(e) Total purchases of inventory were $2,000,000, 90% of which were made on 30-day credit terms, the remainder being made on cash terms. Only credit purchases of inventory flowed through Accounts Payable. The balance in Accounts Payable reflected an $80,000 net increase between December 31, 1978 and 1979; whereas the inventory account reflected an $80,000 net decrease during the same period.

(f) Prepaid Insurance and Rent reflected a balance of $34,000 and $56,000 at December 31, 1978 and 1979, respectively. Insurance and rent expense in 1979 amounted to $87,000. All prepayments of rent and insurance were made on cash terms and were immediately capitalized.

(g) Several 6% short-term notes payable amounting to $130,000 were converted into 6% notes payable, due December 31, 1982.

(h) Five thousand shares of common stock were purchased for the treasury at $6.50 per share. Patents appraised at $34,500 were subsequently obtained upon reissuance of these 5,000 shares of treasury stock.

Required: Using the format shown below, determine the impact of each item, (a) through (h), on cash flow and net working capital during the fiscal year ended December 31, 1979. Each item should be treated as one unit, even though several steps may be required to determine the net effect of that item on cash flow and net working capital. Support answers with calculations in the transaction analysis column.

	EFFECT ON CASH FLOW			EFFECT ON NET WORKING CAPITAL		
TRANSACTION ANALYSIS	Increase	Decrease	None	Increase	Decrease	None

14-3. Effect of transactions on cash flow and net income. The following transactions occurred in the Throckster Corporation during the fiscal year ended June 30, 1980:

(a) Temporary investments costing $33,000 were sold at a $5,000 gain. Interest earned during the last three months of the fiscal year on the portfolio of marketable securities totaled $4,200, none of which had been received by June 30, 1980.

(b) A building originally costing $114,000 was sold at a $21,000 gain. The accumulated depreciation on the building at the time of the sale was $67,000.

(c) A piece of machinery, originally costing $150,000 and having a book value of $40,000 at the time of disposal, was traded in on a similar machine having a list price of $183,000. The fair market value of the old machine was $36,000; and $142,000 cash was paid to the vendor of the new machine.

(d) The balances shown below were reflected in the respective accounts on the dates indicated:

	JUNE 30	
	1980	*1979*
Accounts Receivable	$79,000	$87,000
Allowance for Doubtful Accounts................	(7,000)	(9,000)

Total sales during the fiscal year ended June 30, 1980, were $883,000, 10% of which were on a cash-and-carry basis; the balance of sales was on 30-day credit terms. Specific accounts receivable written off as uncollectible amounted to $12,000.

(e) A $700,000, 7-year, 10% bond issue was sold on July 1, 1979, at 103. Interest was payable semiannually at June 30 and December 31. Straight-line amortization of bond discount and bond premium was used in the firm.

(f) Depreciation and patent amortization expenses for the entire fiscal year totaled $227,000.

(g) The balances shown below were reflected in the respective accounts on the dates indicated:

	JUNE 30	
	1980	*1979*
Inventory	$120,000	$101,000
Accounts Payable	(123,000)	(134,000)

All items purchased for inventory were obtained under 30-day credit terms, and total purchases amounted to $773,000. Only inventory purchases flowed through the accounts payable account.

Required: Using the format shown below, determine the impact of each item described on cash flow and net income during the fiscal year ended June 30, 1980. Treat each of the items (a) through (g) independently of each other in the analysis. Furnish supporting calculations in the transaction analysis column. Comment on the extent to which any gain or loss that is recognized on this trade-in transaction affects federal income tax determination for the fiscal year ended June 30, 1980.

	EFFECT ON CASH FLOW			EFFECT ON NET INCOME		
RANSACTION ANALYSIS	*Increase*	*Decrease*	*None*	*Increase*	*Decrease*	*None*

14-4. **Impact on cash flow, net working capital, and net income.** Each of the following transactions (a) through (g), occurred in the Ariston Corp. during the fiscal year 1979.

(a) The $57,000 cash dividend that was declared in December, 1978, was paid to stockholders on January 5, 1979. All except $14,000 of the $62,000 cash dividends declared in 1979 were paid to stockholders by the end of 1979.

(b) A piece of equipment originally costing $37,000 was completely destroyed by fire. Its book value was $21,000 at the time of the fire; and $17,000 cash was recovered from the insurance company following a report of the loss.

(c) Eight hundred shares of the firm's $40 par value common stock, purchased for the treasury at an average cost of $42 per share in 1975, was reissued to the owner of a building, in return for title to the building. The structure had an appraised value of $38,000 at the time of transfer.

(d) An $85,000 short-term note payable was converted into a note payable that was due for repayment on July 1, 1982.

(e) Rights to three patents, reflected in the records at $24,000, were written off as of no value due to obsolescence.

(f) Inventory valued at $16,000 was found missing and unaccounted for at the time of the annual physical count in December.

(g) Total sales during 1979 amounted to $416,000, of which $20,000 were for cash and the remainder under 45-day credit terms.

Required: Using the format shown below, determine the impact of each item on cash flow, net working capital, and net income during the fiscal year ended December 31, 1979. Treat each segment independently of each other in the analysis. Furnish supporting calculations in the transaction analysis column.

TRANSACTION ANALYSIS	EFFECT ON CASH FLOW			EFFECT ON NET WORKING CAPITAL			EFFECT ON NET INCOME		
	Increase	Decrease	None	Increase	Decrease	None	Increase	Decrease	None

14-5. **The apparent paradox of generating net income as the cash balance decreases.** After examining the following financial statements for Draper, Inc., the president of the firm found it difficult to understand how the cash balance could have decreased by $135,000 during 1979 while the firm earned a net income of $295,000 in that same year.

Draper, Inc.
Income Statement
For the Year Ended December 31, 1979

Sales (all on 60-day credit terms)		$4,000,000
Cost of goods sold		2,800,000
Gross margin		$1,200,000
Expenses:		
Wages and salaries	$305,000	
Advertising and marketing	150,000	
Insurance, rent, and office supplies	100,000	
Depreciation	50,000	
Interest	5,000	610,000
Income before income tax		$ 590,000
Income tax expense		295,000
Net income		$ 295,000

The following additional information pertained to 1979 operations:

(a) No plant assets were sold during the year.

(b) Only credit purchases of inventory (all made on 60-day terms) were reflected in Accounts Payable.

Draper, Inc.
Comparative Balance Sheet
December 31, 1979 and 1978

	1979	1978
Current assets:		
Cash..	$ 5,000	$140,000
Accounts receivable..	600,000	300,000
Inventory..	500,000	200,000
Total current assets......................................	$1,105,000	$640,000
Plant assets:		
Buildings and equipment..................................	$ 650,000	$440,000
Less accumulated depreciation	(170,000)	(120,000)
Total plant assets..	$ 480,000	$320,000
Total assets..	$1,585,000	$960,000
Current liabilities:		
Accounts payable	$ 255,000	$100,000
Income tax payable.......................................	295,000	120,000
Total current liabilities...................................	$ 550,000	$220,000
Owners' Equity:		
Capital stock, $10 par	$ 500,000	$500,000
Retained earnings	535,000	240,000
Total owners' equity	$1,035,000	$740,000
Total equities..	$1,585,000	$960,000

Required: (1) Prepare a statement of changes in financial position — cash basis for the fiscal year ended December 31, 1979.

(2) Comment on the adequacy of defining cash flow as net income plus an add-back of depreciation expense, using the Draper, Inc., illustration as background material.

(3) Drawing on information contained in the statement prepared in (1) above, explain why it might not be unusual for cash flow and net income to move in different directions or to not coincide.

14-6. Statement of changes in financial position — cash basis. The financial position of the Bodden Corp. at December 31, 1978 and 1979, is summarized in the comparative balance sheet shown on page 542, along with the income statement for the firm's fiscal year ended December 31, 1979 on page 543.

Additional information with respect to 1979 operations is provided:

(a) Marketable securities costing $47,000 were purchased and subsequently sold during the year.

(b) A provision for doubtful accounts, amounting to 1.2% of total sales, was recorded at the end of 1979.

(c) All inventory was purchased on 90-day credit terms, and only purchases of inventory flowed through Accounts Payable.

Bodden Corp.
Comparative Balance Sheet
December 31, 1979 and 1978

Assets	1979	1978
Current assets:		
Cash..	$105,000	$ 5,000
Accounts receivable, net of $16,000 allowance for		
doubtful accounts as of December 31, 1979...........	156,000	118,000
Inventory..	280,000	240,000
Prepaid rent, insurance, and office and maintenance		
supplies...	38,000	29,000
Total current assets	$579,000	$392,000
Plant assets:		
Buildings, equipment, and fixtures	$584,000	$644,000
Less accumulated depreciation	(170,000)	(130,000)
Total plant assets	$414,000	$514,000
Total assets...	$993,000	$906,000
Equities		
Current liabilities:		
Accounts payable..	$340,000	$300,000
Cash dividends payable....................................	———	40,000
Income tax payable	60,000	80,000
Total current liabilities..................................	$400,000	$420,000
Long-term liabilities:		
Bonds payable, 6½%, due December 31, 1983........	$100,000	$100,000
Premium on bonds payable	8,000	10,000
Total long-term liabilities	$108,000	$110,000
Owners' equity:		
Capital stock, $10 par	$330,000	$300,000
Retained earnings	155,000	76,000
Total owners' equity	$485,000	$376,000
Total equities...	$993,000	$906,000

(d) All prepaid items were purchased for cash and immediately capitalized at the time of payment.

(e) Fixtures originally costing $50,000, having a book value of $32,000 at the time of sale, were sold during 1979.

(f) Fully depreciated equipment originally costing $40,000 was retired from service and junked. There was no salvage value.

(g) A business associate transferred $30,000 of new equipment to the firm in return for 3,000 shares of capital stock.

Required: Prepare a statement of changes in financial position — cash basis to explain the $100,000 increase in the cash balance during the fiscal year ended December 31, 1979. Support your analysis with calculations, entries, comments, or T account reconciliations.

Bodden Corp.
Income Statement
For the Year Ended December 31, 1979

Sales (all on 30-day credit terms)........................		$2,000,000
Cost of goods sold...		1,400,000
Gross margin..		$ 600,000
Expenses:		
Salaries and wages......................................	$221,000	
Depreciation	98,000	
Insurance, rent, and office and maintenance supplies	69,000	
Uncollectible accounts..................................	24,000	
Interest	6,000	418,000
Operating income		$ 182,000
Gains and losses:		
Gain on sale of marketable securities	$ 3,000	
Loss on sale of fixtures.................................	(27,000)	(24,000)
Income before income tax..........................		$ 158,000
Federal income tax expense............................		79,000
Net income		$ 79,000

14-7. Statement of changes in financial position — cash basis. A comparative balance sheet and an income statement for the Cresswich Corp. are provided on pages 544 and 545 respectively. Additional information with respect to transactions that occurred during the year ended December 31, 1980, is as follows:

(a) No marketable securities or patents were purchased during 1980.

(b) All sales were made on 30-day credit terms, and the 1980 provision for estimated uncollectible accounts was ½ of 1% of total sales.

(c) All inventory items were purchased on credit terms, and credit purchases of inventory were the only transactions that flowed through Accounts Payable.

(d) All prepaid items were purchased on cash terms, and all purchases made in 1980 were immediately charged to expense at the time of payment.

(e) A small building was purchased for $6,000. Equipment originally costing $22,000 was sold for $4,900 cash. In addition, several pieces of equipment were purchased for $50,700 cash.

(f) Short-term notes payable totaling $14,000 were paid off.

(g) Total cash dividends of $14,300 were declared during 1980, of which $4,400 remained unpaid on December 31, 1980.

(h) The mortgage note payable was converted into 1,500 shares of the firm's capital stock.

(i) Shares of capital stock held in the treasury that were purchased in 1972 for $10,000 were sold for $10,700 cash.

(j) An appropriation of $40,000 was made for plant expansion and contingencies from retained earnings.

Cresswich Corp.
Comparative Balance Sheet
December 31, 1980 and 1979

Assets	1980	1979
Current assets:		
Cash........	$ 53,100	$ 12,700
Marketable securities........	——	1,600
Accounts receivable........	99,300	87,200
Allowance for doubtful accounts	(4,600)	(5,400)
Inventory........	90,000	120,000
Prepaid expenses (insurance and rent)........	1,400	3,200
Total current assets........	$239,200	$219,300
Plant assets:		
Land........	$ 8,600	$ 8,600
Buildings and equipment........	472,400	437,700
Less accumulated depreciation	(171,600)	(121,400)
Total plant assets........	$309,400	$324,900
Intangibles:		
Patents........	$ 4,200	$ 4,900
Total assets........	$552,800	$549,100

Equities

	1980	1979
Current liabilities:		
Notes payable........	$ 20,000	$ 34,000
Accounts payable	42,000	60,000
Income tax payable........	29,000	32,000
Cash dividends payable	4,400	8,700
Total current liabilities........	$ 95,400	$134,700
Long-term liabilities:		
Mortgage note payable........	——	$ 30,000
Bonds payable	$240,000	240,000
Discount on bonds payable........	(7,200)	(7,800)
Total long-term liabilities........	$232,800	$262,200
Owners' equity:		
Capital stock, $20 par	$124,700	$ 94,700
Premium on capital stock........	700	——
Appropriation for plant expansion and contingencies	50,000	10,000
Retained earnings	49,200	57,500
Treasury stock........	——	(10,000)
Total owners' equity	$224,600	$152,200
Total equities	$552,800	$549,100

Cresswich Corp.
Income Statement
For the Year Ended December 31, 1980

Sales		$1,180,000
Cost of goods sold		540,000
Gross margin...		$ 640,000
Expenses:		
Administrative and factory salaries and wages........	$332,700	
Advertising and marketing	92,100	
Depreciation	70,000	
Interest...	26,000	
Repairs and maintenance.................................	18,500	
Uncollectible accounts....................................	5,900	
Insurance and rent...	4,600	
Patent amortization..	700	550,500
Operating income..		$ 89,500
Other income:		
Interest earned		200
Gains and losses:		
Gain on sale of equipment...............................	$ 2,700	
Loss on sale of marketable securities	(400)	2,300
Income before income tax		$ 92,000
Income tax expense...		46,000
Net income		$ 46,000

Required: Prepare a statement of changes in financial position — cash basis for the year ended December 31, 1980. Support your analysis with explanations, such as journal entries, T account analyses, or other clarifying comments.

14-8. Statement of changes in financial position — cash basis. Financial statements of the Charger Corp. for the fiscal year ended December 31, 1979, are shown on pages 546 and 547.

Supplemental information for the fiscal year ended December 31, 1979:

(a) No marketable securities, land, patents, or copyrights were purchased during 1979.

(b) The only credits that were made to Accounts Payable during the year were associated with inventory purchases. All inventory items were purchased under 40-day credit arrangements.

(c) A building costing $40,000 was obtained in September and financed under a short-term note payable arrangement.

(d) Several pieces of equipment originally costing $87,000 were sold during October. The book value of the equipment sold totaled $20,000.

(e) Additional equipment was purchased during December for cash.

(f) Cash dividends declared during 1979 totaled $41,000, of which $26,000 were payable on January 6, 1980.

Charger Corp.
Comparative Balance sheet
December 31, 1979 and 1978

	1979	1978
Assets		
Current assets:		
Cash..	$ 37,000	$ 57,000
Marketable securities.......................	18,000	28,000
Accounts receivable.........................	70,000	117,000
Allowance for doubtful accounts	(35,000)	(23,000)
Inventory.....................................	326,000	186,000
Prepaid rent and insurance	12,000	8,000
Total current assets.....................	$428,000	$373,000
Plant assets:		
Land..	$ 80,000	$ 80,000
Buildings and equipment...................	530,000	450,000
Less accumulated depreciation	(153,000)	(150,000)
Total plant assets.......................	$457,000	$380,000
Intangibles:		
Patents and copyrights.....................	$ 4,000	$ 8,000
Total assets....................................	$889,000	$761,000
Equities		
Current liabilities:		
Notes payable...............................	$ 90,000	$ 50,000
Accounts payable	38,000	90,000
Income tax payable..........................	42,000	47,000
Interest payable.............................	3,000	6,000
Dividends payable...........................	26,000	27,000
Total current liabilities..................	$199,000	$220,000
Long-term liabilities:		
Mortgage note payable.....................	——	$ 80,000
Bonds payable, 8%, 10 years, due December 31, 1988...	$100,000	——
Premium on bonds payable	9,000	——
Deferred income tax.........................	31,000	27,000
Total long-term liabilities...............	$140,000	$107,000
Owners' equity:		
Common stock, $10 par value...............	$330,000	$250,000
Premium on stock............................	33,000	30,000
Appropriation for plant expansion	30,000	34,000
Retained earnings	173,000	147,000
Treasury stock...............................	(16,000)	(27,000)
Total owners' equity	$550,000	$434,000
Total equities..................................	$889,000	$761,000

Charger Corp.
Income Statement
For the Year Ended December 31, 1979

Sales (all on 30-day credit terms)		$960,000
Cost of goods sold		470,000
Gross margin..		$490,000
Expenses:		
Wages and salaries	$117,000	
Administrative, marketing, and sales promotion.......	74,000	
Depreciation	70,000	
Maintenance, repairs, and utilities......................	29,000	
Rent and insurance	21,000	
Interest..	18,000	
Uncollectible accounts.....................................	16,000	
Amortization of patents and copyrights.................	4,000	349,000
Operating income..		$141,000
Gains and losses:		
Gain on sale of marketable securities...................	$ 3,000	
Loss on sale of equipment	(16,000)	(13,000)
Income before income tax		$128,000
Income tax expense...		65,000
Net income		$ 63,000

(g) The entire mortgage note payable was converted into 8,000 shares of common stock.

(h) Bond premium was amortized by the straight-line method. The bonds were sold to several local financiers on January 1, 1979.

(i) Several shares of treasury stock were sold for $14,000. No shares were purchased for the treasury during 1979.

Required: Prepare a statement of changes in financial position — cash basis for the fiscal year ended December 31, 1979. Furnish supporting calculations and comments beneath that statement.

14-9. Statement of changes in financial position — cash basis and statement of changes in financial position — net working capital. The following supplemental financial information pertains to operations of the Doublay Corp. during the fiscal year ended December 31, 1979. Financial statements are shown on pages 548 and 549.

(a) No marketable securities were purchased during 1979.

(b) All materials included in inventory were purchased on credit, and only credit purchases of inventory flowed through Accounts Payable.

(c) Prepaid expenses included office supplies, insurance, and rent. These items were always purchased COD, and immediately capitalized at the time of payment.

(d) A warehouse costing $6,000 was purchased under a short-term note payable arrangement.

Doublay Corp.
Comparative Balance Sheet
December 31, 1979 and 1978

Assets	1979	1978
Current assets:		
Cash...	$ 20,000	$ 53,000
Marketable securities..	3,000	18,000
Accounts receivable...	160,000	120,000
Allowance for doubtful accounts	(18,000)	(15,000)
Inventory..	184,000	130,000
Prepaid expenses	6,000	9,000
Total current assets.....................................	$355,000	$315,000
Plant assets:		
Buildings and machinery	$612,000	$576,000
Less accumulated depreciation	(222,000)	(170,000)
Total plant assets.......................................	$390,000	$406,000
Intangibles:		
Franchises	$ 14,000	$ 16,000
Total assets..	$759,000	$737,000
Equities		
Current liabilities:		
Notes payable...	$ 90,000	$ 84,000
Accounts payable	190,000	160,000
Income tax payable..	45,000	30,000
Cash dividends payable	4,000	8,000
Total current liabilities.................................	$329,000	$282,000
Long-term liabilities:		
Mortgage note payable, due 1981	——	$180,000
Bonds payable 7%, 4 years, due December 31, 1982, issued at 96% of par...........................	$100,000	——
Discount on bonds payable................................	(3,000)	——
Total long-term liabilities...............................	$ 97,000	$180,000
Owners' equity:		
Common stock, $20 par	$190,000	$160,000
Premium on common stock..................................	11,000	11,000
Appropriation for contingencies..........................	40,000	——
Retained earnings	92,000	104,000
Total owners' equity	$333,000	$275,000
Total equities	$759,000	$737,000

(e) A machine originally costing $90,000, with a book value of $40,000 was traded for a new version of the same machine. The list price of the new machine was $120,000. Cash payment of $80,000 was made to the vendor. The fair market value of the old

Doublay Corp.
Income Statement
For the Year Ended December 31, 1979

Sales (all on 30-day credit terms).........................		$2,000,000
Cost of goods sold...		1,450,000
Gross margin		$ 550,000
Expenses:		
Salaries and wages......................................	$164,500	
Depreciation	102,000	
Sales promotion...	68,600	
Utilities, repairs, and maintenance	58,000	
Interest	15,000	
Office supplies..	12,000	
Insurance and rent	10,900	
Uncollectible accounts..................................	5,000	
Amortization of franchise agreements	2,000	438,000
Operating income		$ 112,000
Other income:		
Interest earned..		3,700
Gains and losses:		
Loss on sale of marketable securities.................		(1,700)
Income before income tax...........................		$ 114,000
Income tax expense		50,000
Net income		$ 64,000

machine coincided with its book value. No other transactions affected Buildings and Machinery.

(f) Cash dividends declared during 1979 totaled $36,000, of which $4,000 remained unpaid at the end of 1979.

(g) A $30,000 portion of the mortgage note payable was converted into 1,500 shares of the firm's common stock near the beginning of 1979. The remaining $150,000 of the note was paid off.

Required: (1) Determine the change in cash and in net working capital during the fiscal year ended December 31, 1979.

(2) Prepare a statement of changes in financial position — net working capital for the fiscal year ended December 31, 1979.

(3) Prepare a statement of changes in financial position — cash basis covering the same period.

DECISION CASE

14-I. **Cash flow analysis as a planning device.** In early January, 1980, the treasurer of the Krowder Corporation requested the financial analyst to determine whether or not the firm would be able to generate a $180,000 increase in the cash balance by the end of the firm's fiscal year, December 31, 1980. The analyst had on hand the following balance sheet dated December 31, 1979, the projected income statement for 1980, and supplementary information that related to projected 1980 operations.

Krowder Corporation
Balance Sheet
December 31, 1979

Assets		Equities	
Current assets:		Current liabilities:	
Cash...................... $	83,200	Notes payable........... $	80,000
Marketable securities...	10,800	Accounts payable	184,000
Accounts receivable.....	180,000	Income tax payable.....	16,000
Allowance for doubtful		Total current	
accounts................	(9,400)	liabilities........... $	280,000
Inventory..................	240,000	Long-term liabilities:	
Prepaid expenses	8,400	Mortgage note	
Total current assets...	$513,000	payable, due 1984 .. $	240,000
Plant assets:		Bonds payable, 6%,	
Land...................... $	24,000	10 years, due	
Equipment and fixtures.	888,600	December 31, 1987,	
Less accumulated		including bond	
depreciation	(374,000)	premium of $3,200...	203,200
Total plant assets..... $	538,600	Total long-term	
Intangibles:		liabilities...........	$443,200
Patents.................... $	8,400	Owners' equity:	
		Capital stock, $10 par . $	200,000
		Premium on capital	
		stock....................	17,200
		Appropriation for plant	
		expansion	72,000
		Retained earnings	88,400
		Treasury stock............	(40,800)
		Total owners' equity . $	336,800
Total assets..................	$1,060,000	Total equities	$1,060,000

Additional forecasted information for 1980 is shown below:

(a) The entire portfolio of marketable securities will be sold in 1980 at its book value, and will not be replaced.

(b) The balance in Accounts Receivable at December 31, 1980, is projected at $220,000. Specific customer accounts totaling $8,000 are expected to be written off as uncollectible in 1980.

(c) All purchases of inventory are made on 60-day credit terms. Only inventory purchase transactions flow through Accounts Payable. The balances of Merchandise Inventory and Accounts Payable at the 1980 year-end are projected at $280,000 and $240,000, respectively.

(d) Prepaid items include insurance, rent, and office supplies. These items are purchased only on COD terms, and are immediately

Krowder Corporation
Projected Income Statement
For the Year Ending December 31, 1980

Sales (all on 30-day credit terms)		$2,200,000
Cost of goods sold		1,340,000
Gross margin..		$ 860,000
Expenses:		
Wages and salaries	$563,000	
Depreciation	124,000	
Insurance, rent, and office supplies......................	53,600	
Advertising and sales promotion	20,000	
Interest..	19,600	
Utilities	18,800	
Uncollectible accounts......................................	12,000	
Patent amortization...	1,000	812,000
Income before income tax		$ 48,000
Income tax expense..		24,000
Net income		$ 24,000

capitalized at the time of purchase. The projected balance in Prepaid Expenses at December 31, 1980, is $6,200.

(e) A fully depreciated building costing $22,000 is to be demolished in 1980, and will not be replaced. No salvage value is anticipated on the building.

(f) Additional equipment will be purchased for $72,000 cash to complete a 2-year expansion project. No equipment would be sold.

(g) No land or patents will be bought or sold during 1980.

(h) Short-term notes payable are expected to remain unchanged throughout 1980.

(i) Bond premium totaling $400 will be amortized in 1980.

(j) The anticipated income tax expense of $24,000 for 1980 will be paid in 1981. All of the tax payable as of December 31, 1979, is to be paid during 1980.

(k) Management intends to sell all of the treasury stock at its purchase cost. In addition, 1,000 shares of unissued capital stock will be sold at $13 per share.

(l) The appropriation for plant expansion is to be reduced to zero and returned to retained earnings in December 1980.

(m) No dividends of any type are expected to be declared during 1980, nor will any long-term liabilities be retired during 1980.

Required: Prepare a projected statement of changes in financial position — cash basis for the year ended December 31, 1980. To what extent does it appear that the desired $180,000 increase in the cash balance will be achieved by December 31, 1980?

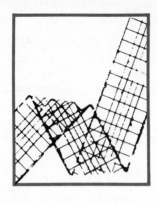

15

Financial Statement Analysis: Liquidity– Profitability–Leverage

O wad some Pow'r the giftie gie us to see oursels
as ithers see us! It wad frae monie a blunder free
us, an' foolish notion.
　　　　　　　Robert Burns, To a Louse

Financial statement analysis, like net working capital and cash flow analysis, refers to the evaluation of information presented in the balance sheet and income statement. Whereas net working capital and cash flow analyses emphasize the liquidity position of the firm, financial statement analysis encompasses a broader investigation into the following aspects of a firm's operations:

(1) *Liquidity* — the capacity of the firm to repay financial obligations within contractual time constraints.
(2) *Profitability* — the profit-generating ability of the firm.
(3) *Leverage* — the extent to which the firm is financed with current and/or long-term debt capital.

The continuing problem that confronts management is maintaining a satisfactory balance between these three financial aspects.

Comprehensive examination of quantitative measures of liquidity, profitability, and leverage helps management pinpoint specific areas that reflect improvement or deterioration, as well as detect any trouble spots that may prevent the attainment of objectives. Investors and creditors undertake frequent examination of these three areas to evaluate management's ability to maintain a satisfactory balance among them, and to appraise the efficiency and effectiveness with which management directs the firm's operations. Conclusions derived from such analyses assist both investors and creditors in deciding whether to increase or reduce their financial commitments to the firm.

Two precautions, however, should be stressed before examining financial statement analysis in greater detail. First, financial statement analysis is probably more of an art based on experienced judgment, than a mechanical procedure or scientific process based on rigid rules. Although analysts often derive a similar set of financial ratios during their investigation, it is not uncommon for two competent financial analysts to stress or perceive different attributes and to derive somewhat varied conclusions after analyzing the same financial information of a particular business enterprise.

Second, an important prerequisite to financial statement analysis is the development of an awareness of the past-present-future sequence. Analysis of accurate historical evidence can provide valuable information about what has occurred; and current financial information may often provide useful data with which to monitor and correct present and near-future operations. But a purely mechanistic extension of past and current experience into the future can only be suggestive at best, and perhaps disastrous at worst, because conditions may change significantly. Even though events in the future may be influenced by past and present activities, the certainties of tomorrow are change, risk, and uncertainty. In short, the relevance of and the momentum generated by past and present financial performance may be valid for only a short time into the future.

AN ANALYTICAL FRAMEWORK

One of the most difficult problems confronting the analyst is the almost infinite variety of financial ratios and statistical relationships that can be calculated from the quantitative information contained in financial statements. Any two or more numbers may be combined and manipulated arithmetically with or without some sense of purpose. Confusion usually results unless a selected number of significant relationships are organized around some relevant focal point. The arrangement shown on page 554, in which the focus is *return on total investment*, has proven to be a particularly useful analytical framework for financial statement analysis. Notice the following features of this framework:

(1) Each major income statement and balance sheet category is identified and then regrouped in such a way as to ultimately reflect perhaps the most significant quantitative measure of financial performance: *return on total investment* which is net income divided by total investment. Additional detail may be provided within this framework merely by expanding each major category into its specific account titles: for example, Current assets = Cash + Marketable securities + Net receivables + Inventory + Prepaid expenses.

(2) *Total investment* may be defined as either total assets or total equities, depending on whether the analyst desires to concentrate on the relationship of net income to the firm's financial resources or its financial equities.

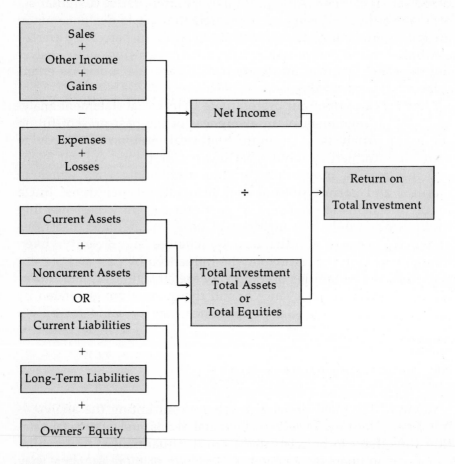

FINANCIAL RATIO ANALYSIS

Examination of the three financial aspects — liquidity, profitability, and leverage — will be integrated within the preceding analytical framework to examine and evaluate the financial condition and performance of the Chinook Corporation during the two-year period ended December 31, 1979. The comparative income statement for 1978 and 1979, and comparative balance sheet as of December 31, 1977, 1978, and 1979 are shown below and on page 556.

Chinook Corporation
Comparative Income Statement
For the Years Ended December 31, 1979 and 1978

	1979		1978	
	Amount	Percent	Amount	Percent
Sales (60-day credit terms)	$2,500,000	100.0%	$2,200,000	100.0%
Cost of goods sold.................	1,540,000	61.6	1,320,000	60.0
Gross margin.....................	$ 960,000	38.4%	$ 880,000	40.0%
Expenses:				
Depreciation	$ 165,000	6.6%	$ 162,000	7.4%
General and administrative ..	135,000	5.4	110,000	5.0
Selling and promotion.........	100,000	4.0	91,000	4.1
Interest (including discount amortization).................	90,000	3.6	101,000	4.6
Total expenses............	$ 490,000	19.6%	$ 464,000	21.1%
Operating income.....	$ 470,000	18.8%	$ 416,000	18.9%
Gains and losses:				
Gain (loss) on sale of equipment..........................	$ 30,000	1.2%	$ (4,000)	(0.2)%
Fire loss	—		(12,000)	(0.5)
Net gain.....................	$ 30,000	1.2%	$ (16,000)	(0.7)%
Income before income tax.......................	$ 500,000	20.0%	$ 400,000	18.2%
Income tax expense	250,000	10.0	200,000	9.1
Net income	$ 250,000	10.0%	$ 200,000	9.1%
6% cash dividend declared on preferred stock.................	$ 9,300		$ 9,000	
Cash dividend declared on common stock...................	$ 66,000		$ 41,000	

Notice that each balance sheet item is expressed in dollars and as a percent of total investment, and that each income statement item is expressed in dollars and as a percent of sales. Expressing each monetary amount on the balance sheet and income statement as a percent of total investment or sales, respectively, transforms the financial statements into what is referred to as *common-size statements*. The relationship of each balance sheet or income statement item to total investment or sales in one or more years becomes more readily apparent from common-size statements than from those that are expressed solely in terms of monetary amounts. For example, although long-term notes payable remained constant at $291,000 at the end of each of the three years,

Chinook Corporation
Comparative Balance Sheet
December 31, 1979, 1978, and 1977

Assets	1979 Amount	1979 Percent	1978 Amount	1978 Percent	1977 Amount	1977 Percent
Current assets:						
Cash.............................	$ 126,000	3.9%	$ 117,000	3.8%	$ 62,000	2.2%
Marketable securities........	52,000	1.6	35,000	1.1	40,000	1.5
Accounts receivable.........	670,000	20.7	606,000	19.8	508,000	18.5
Allowance for doubtful accounts	(50,000)	(1.5)	(41,000)	(1.3)	(28,000)	(1.0)
Inventory......................	671,000	20.7	495,000	16.2	403,000	14.7
Prepaid expenses............	30,000	.9	24,000	.8	12,000	0.4
Total current assets........	$1,499,000	46.3%	$1,236,000	40.4%	$ 997,000	36.3%
Investments in other corporations.	$ 70,000	2.2%	$ 70,000	2.3%	—	—
Plant assets:						
Land...........................	$ 225,000	6.9%	$ 227,000	7.4%	$ 215,000	7.8%
Buildings and equipment.....	2,359,000	72.8	2,289,000	74.8	2,134,000	77.6
Less accumulated depreciation	(913,000)	(28.2)	(762,000)	(24.9)	(596,000)	(21.7)
Total plant assets..........	$1,671,000	51.5%	$1,754,000	57.3%	$1,753,000	63.7%
Total assets...................	$3,240,000	100.0%	$3,060,000	100.0%	$2,750,000	100.0%

Equities

Current liabilities:						
Notes payable	$ 338,000	10.4%	$ 352,000	11.5%	$ 250,000	9.0%
Accounts payable	271,000	8.4	300,000	9.8	274,000	10.0
Income tax payable	195,000	6.0	156,000	5.1	134,000	4.9
Total current liabilities	$ 804,000	24.8%	$ 808,000	26.4%	$ 658,000	23.9%
Long-term liabilities:						
Notes payable	$ 291,000	9.0%	$ 291,000	9.5%	$ 291,000	10.6%
Bonds payable, 8%, 20-year, due December 31, 1984; convertible into common stock after June 30, 1979	200,000*	6.2	500,000	16.3	500,000	18.2
Discount on bonds payable	(2,000)	(0.1)	(6,000)	(0.2)	(7,000)	(0.3)
Total long-term liabilities	$ 489,000	15.1%	$ 785,000	25.6%	$ 784,000	28.5%
Owners' equities:						
Preferred stock, 6%, $100 par	$ 155,000	4.8%	$ 150,000	5.0%	$ 150,000	5.4%
Common stock, $10 par	745,000	23.0	445,000	14.5	436,000	15.9
Retained earnings	1,047,000	32.3	872,000	28.5	722,000	26.3
Total owners' equities	$1,947,000	60.1%	$1,467,000	48.0%	$1,308,000	47.6%
Total equities	$3,240,000	100.0%	$3,060,000	100.0%	$2,750,000	100.0%

*$300,000 bonds were converted into 30,000 shares of common stock on July 1, 1979.

this item decreased from 10.6 percent of total equities as of December 31, 1977, to 9.0 percent as of December 31, 1979.

Subsequent analysis will proceed as follows: (1) preliminary investigation of both financial statements; (2) intensive examination of specific liquidity, profitability, and leverage ratios; and (3) summary of highlights and conclusions of the analysis.

Preliminary Investigation

Preliminary investigation of the balance sheet reveals that the monetary balance in each account remained constant or increased between the end of 1977 and 1979, with the exception of bonds payable and discount on bonds payable. The trend of each major subcategory, expressed as a percent of total investment at each year-end, is summarized below:

BALANCE SHEET SUBCATEGORY   TREND

Assets
- Current assets .... Steady increase (from 36.3% to 46.3%).
- Investments .... Increase (from zero to 2.2%).
- Plant assets .... Steady decrease (from 63.7% to 51.5%).

Equities
- Current liabilities ..... Overall increase (from 23.9% to 24.8%).
- Long-term liabilities . Overall decrease (from 28.5% to 15.1%).
- Owners' equities ...... Steady increase (from 47.6% to 60.1%).

Some significant changes appear to have occurred in specific balance sheet accounts during the two-year period:

(1) Cash more than doubled, from $62,000 to $126,000.
(2) Accounts receivable, net of the allowance, reflected an increase of $140,000, with the allowance almost doubling from $28,000 to $50,000.
(3) Inventory reflected a $268,000 increase, and a 6.0 percentage point increase (from 14.7% to 20.7%).
(4) Buildings and equipment, net of depreciation, decreased $92,000; and reflected an 11.3 percentage point decrease during the period, (from 55.9% to 44.6%).
(5) Short-term notes payable increased $88,000.
(6) Bonds payable decreased $300,000, and reflected a 12.0 percentage point decrease.
(7) Common stock increased $309,000, and reflected a 7.1 percentage point increase.
(8) Retained earnings increased $325,000, and reflected a 6.0 percentage point increase.

Cursory inspection of the income statement indicates the following:

(1) Sales during 1979 increased $300,000, or 13.6 percent above 1978 sales.
(2) Gross margin increased $80,000; but the gross margin percentage declined 1.6 percentage points (from 40.0% to 38.4%).
(3) Although operating income increased $54,000, it remained almost constant at approximately 19 percent of sales.
(4) The $46,000 difference between gains and losses in 1978 and 1979 accounted for 46 percent of the $100,000 increase during 1979 in income before income tax expense.

Tentative insights from this introductory phase of the analysis indicate the following:

(1) Several current assets increased, suggesting that the firm may be tending toward overliquidity.
(2) The firm is becoming more heavily financed with equity capital, rather than debt capital; in other words, it is becoming more highly leveraged.
(3) Although net income increased, the increase in cost of goods sold and general and administrative expense as a percent of sales may warrant more intensive investigation and closer monitoring.

A further examination of these financial statements by means of ratio analysis may reveal other strengths or additional potential problems.

Liquidity

Liquidity, or the capacity of the firm to repay its financial obligations as they come due, was discussed in Chapters 13 and 14 with respect to net working capital and cash flow analyses. This chapter will discuss other measures of liquidity and how they may be interpreted to evaluate a firm's performance.

Measures of Liquidity. The seven measurement devices shown below provide a reasonable basis for evaluating the extent of the firm's liquidity position in 1979 and the degree of change that occurred during the two-year period. Reference to the analytical framework provided on page 554 may prove helpful in visualizing how each item that is involved in a particular ratio is related to the principal focal point — return on total investment.

MEASURES OF LIQUIDITY	
Measurement Device	*Calculation*
(1) Quick assets	Cash plus marketable securities plus net receivables.
(2) Quick ratio	Quick assets divided by current liabilities.
(3) Current ratio	Current assets divided by current liabilities.
(4) Net working capital	Current assets less current liabilities.
(5) Net working capital turnover	Sales divided by average* net working capital.
(6) Accounts receivable turnover	Credit sales divided by average* net receivables from customers.
(7) Inventory turnover	Cost of goods sold divided by average* inventory.

*The average is determined by adding the beginning and ending balances of the respective amounts and dividing by two.

Quick Assets. Assuming that the securities are quickly convertible into cash at no loss and that the net receivables are collectible, the amounts shown below indicate the cash and near-cash position of the firm at three points during the two-year period:

	1979	1978	1977	TREND
Cash............................	$126,000	$117,000	$ 62,000	Steady
Marketable securities	52,000	35,000	40,000	increase, with
Accounts receivable net ...	620,000	565,000	480,000	the larger
Total quick assets........	$798,000	$717,000	$582,000	increase in 1978

An extremely small amount of quick assets indicates that if the firm is hard-pressed to pay a liability as it comes due, management may be forced to obtain a short-term loan plus interest charges, or implement some other measure to obtain the required cash. On the other hand, an excessive amount of quick assets could indicate that these assets should be put to more productive or profitable use elsewhere in the enterprise.

Quick Ratio. The quick ratio is calculated as shown below:

$$\frac{\text{Quick assets}}{\text{Current liabilities}}$$

	1979	1978	1977	TREND
Quick assets	$798,000	$717,000	$582,000	
Current liabilities	$804,000	$808,000	$658,000	
Quick ratio..............	1:1	0.9:1	0.9:1	Slight increase

Dividing quick assets by current liabilities provides the 1979 quick ratio of 99 percent ($798,000 ÷ $804,000), which is usually rounded to and stated as 1:1, or simply as 1. Assuming that most receivables will be collected within the next quarter, the quick ratio indicates the extent to which total current liabilities can be repaid on short notice. An often used rule-of-thumb for the quick ratio is 1:1. Too high a ratio such as 5:1 suggests excess liquidity; whereas one that is too low, such as 0.3:1, may indicate inadequate liquidity in the event of a short-term liquidity crisis.

All rules-of-thumb, however, should be regarded as something less than absolute guidelines for three reasons. First, each monetary amount on the balance sheet is reported as of one date only. The week prior to or following each balance sheet date might reflect markedly different amounts. Second, circumstances that are unique to particular industries, either because of risk characteristics or traditional practices, may warrant further investigation to determine what is an appropriate amount or ratio. For example, high-risk industries or firms that are heavily financed with current liabilities may warrant higher quick ratios than such firms as regulated public utilities. Finally, what may appear today as an adequate balance or ratio may be excessive or inadequate should conditions radically change.

These three precautions must temper interpretation of all financial ratios. Perhaps the most useful guideline for trend analysis is to: (1) determine the historical pattern of specific ratios recently experienced by the company; then (2) compare the company's experience to the industry of which it is a member, if representative ratios for specific industrial categories are available.[1]

Current Ratio. The current ratio is calculated as shown below:

$$\frac{\text{Current assets}}{\text{Current liabilities}}$$

	1979	1978	1977	TREND
Total current assets........	$1,499,000	$1,236,000	$ 997,000	
Total current liabilities.	$ 804,000	$ 808,000	$ 658,000	Slight
Current ratio	1.9:1	1.5:1	1.5:1	increase

The current ratio as of the 1979 year-end is determined by dividing total current assets of $1,499,000 by total current liabilities of $804,000. This ratio indicates the firm's ability to pay all liabilities that are due within one year through the conversion of current assets into cash during normal operations. Notice that inventory and prepaid expenses are included in calculating the current ratio. These two nonquick asset items are normally charged to expense, and their costs are recovered through sales within one year from the date of the balance sheet. A frequently used guideline to evaluate the adequacy of the current ratio is 2:1, or 2. Although the current ratio in the Chinook Corporation was below 2 in each of the three years, it reflected improvement as of the end of 1979.

Net Working Capital. Net working capital is merely a rearrangement and restatement of the current ratio as current assets less current liabilities.

Net working capital = Current assets − Current liabilities

	1979	1978	1977	TREND
Current assets	$1,499,000	$1,236,000	$ 997,000	Steady increase,
Current liabilities	804,000	808,000	658,000	more than doubling
Net working capital.	$ 695,000	$ 428,000	$ 339,000	between 1977 and 1979

This calculation enables the analyst to assess the monetary amount by which current assets exceed or fall short of being able to repay

---

[1]Considerable perspective for the range of 14 different ratios experienced in 125 lines of retailing, wholesaling, and manufacturing-construction may be obtained from an annually revised publication of Dun and Bradstreet Inc., 99 Church Street, New York, New York 10007: "Key Business Ratios in 125 Lines."

current liabilities. Although there is no general rule-of-thumb to determine excessive or inadequate net working capital, an indication of the adequacy of net working capital can be obtained by relating the amount to the volume of business transacted, as measured by sales.

Net Working Capital Turnover. The turnover of net working capital is derived as shown below:

$$\frac{\text{Sales}}{\text{Average net working capital}}$$

	1979	1978	TREND
Sales..	$2,500,000	$2,200,000	
1977 net working capital		$ 339,000	
1978 net working capital	$ 428,000	428,000	
1979 net working capital	695,000		
Total.......................................	$1,123,000	$ 767,000	
Average net working capital (total ÷ 2)...........................	$ 562,000	$ 384,000	
Net working capital turnover	4.5	5.7	Decrease

The net working capital turnover as of the 1979 year-end is determined by dividing Sales of $2,500,000 by average net working capital of $562,000, [($695,000 + $428,000) ÷ 2]. Too high a turnover, such as 10 times, might indicate that the firm is financing and supporting its current level of operations with inadequate net working capital. On the other hand, an extremely low turnover, such as 2 times, would suggest that net working capital was either excessive or could support a larger volume of business. Chinook Corporation's net working capital turnover decreased 1.2 times during 1979, which means that net working capital was being used less intensively in 1979 as sales volume increased. The decrease in turnover can be explained from another perspective by noting that net working capital increased by $356,000 during the two-year period, whereas sales volume increased only $300,000.

Accounts Receivable Turnover. The receivables turnover is calculated as shown at the top of page 563.

The accounts receivable turnover as of the 1979 year-end is determined by dividing credit sales of $2,500,000 by average net receivables of $593,000, [($565,000 + $620,000) ÷ 2]. This ratio indicates the number of times that the average outstanding net receivables was turned over, or converted into cash through collections during each year. It is important when calculating the receivables turnover that only credit sales (if determinable) be used

$$\frac{\text{Credit sales}}{\text{Average net receivables}}$$

	1979	1978	TREND
Credit sales.................................	$2,500,000	$2,200,000	
1977 Accounts receivable, net		$ 480,000	
1978 Accounts receivable, net	$ 565,000	565,000	
1979 Accounts receivable, net	620,000		
Total.......................................	$1,185,000	$1,045,000	
Average receivables, (total ÷ 2)...	$ 593,000	$ 523,000	
Accounts receivable turnover	4.2	4.2	Steady

as the numerator. Using total sales which includes both cash and credit sales distorts the resulting calculation. The distortion is magnified where the percentage of total sales made on credit terms varies substantially from period to period.

Dividing the receivables turnover by 365 days reflects the average collection period of receivables, which in this case is about 87 days (365 ÷ 4.2) for each of 1978 and 1979. It appears that management allowed its customers during both years to exceed the 60-day credit terms (see the income statement) by almost one month. Reasons for this relaxation from the stated terms should be investigated. The firm's experience should be compared with other firms in the same industry or region to determine whether or not this relaxation of credit terms is warranted.

Inventory Turnover. The inventory turnover is calculated as shown below:

$$\frac{\text{Cost of goods sold}}{\text{Average inventory}}$$

	1979	1978	TREND
Cost of goods sold	$1,540,000	$1,320,000	
1977 ending inventory.........		$ 403,000	
1978 ending inventory.........	$ 495,000	495,000	
1979 ending inventory.........	671,000		
Total.............................	$1,166,000	$ 898,000	
Average inventory (total ÷ 2)........................	$ 583,000	$ 449,000	
Inventory turnover	2.6	2.9	Slight decrease

The inventory turnover as of the 1979 year-end is determined by dividing Cost of Goods Sold of $1,540,000 by Average Inventory of $583,000, [($495,000 + $671,000) ÷ 2]. The inventory turnover reflects the number of times per year that total inventory is converted into cost of goods sold. It is usually desirable to compare a firm's inventory turnover with the turnovers experienced by comparable companies. For example, it is not unusual for fresh fruit and vegetable retailers to experience an inventory turnover exceeding 120 times per year, or about once every three days (365 ÷ 120). At the other extreme, retailers of jewelry frequently reflect yearly inventory turnovers of less than three, or once every four months. Of greater importance, however, is the need to evaluate the trend in the firm under review. The slight decrease of 0.3 times from 1978 to 1979 in the Chinook Corporation indicates that inventory was converted into sold merchandise more slowly in 1979 than in 1978. Whether this trend is desirable would require detailed investigation into such aspects as changes in manufacturing techniques, labor slowdowns, or inventory stockpiling in anticipation of price increases.

Notice that each turnover ratio is calculated by dividing sales, or a major component of sales, by the item whose turnover is being determined. In the case of the inventory turnover ratio, the cost of goods sold is directly related to sales, and is the largest expense that is matched with sales.

Overall Appraisal of the Liquidity Position. Significant insights disclosed by the preceding analysis are shown below:

(1) The amount of quick assets, the quick ratio, and the current ratio increased during the two-year period. However, none of these amounts or ratios appears excessively high.

(2) Net working capital more than doubled during the two years, and net working capital turnover reflected a substantial decrease.

(3) Although the receivables turnover remained constant, management is allowing customers to exceed its 60-day credit policy by about one month. If this situation continues or becomes worse, a "cash-bind" may develop, which may force management to secure additional cash by obtaining short-term loans at substantial interest charges.

(4) The slight decrease in inventory turnover and the $268,000 increase in inventory during the two-year period may warrant further investigation.

In short, although the firm's liquidity position appears to be relatively solid, management should identify and remedy reasons for the 27-day gap between the stated and actual credit terms granted and for the decrease in the inventory turnover.

Profitability

The principal objective of a business enterprise is to operate in such a way as to generate a profit. Note that either net income or a major component of net income, such as gross margin or operating income, is included in each of the seven ratios that are used to measure a firm's profitability.

Measures of Profitability. Each of the four "return on" ratios listed below involves net income divided by the item on which the return is calculated. Again, reference may be made to the foregoing framework of financial analysis to visualize how the components in each of the following ratios relate to the major focal point — return on total investment.

MEASURES OF PROFITABILITY

Measurement Device	*Calculation*
(1) Return on average total investment.........	Net income divided by average* total assets (or total equities).
(2) Return on average owners' equity	Net income divided by average* owners' equity.
(3) Return on average common stock equity .	Net income after preferred dividend requirements divided by average* common stock equity.
(4) Earnings per share of common stock.......	Net income after preferred dividend requirements divided by average* outstanding shares of common stock.
(5) Return on sales....................................	Net income divided by total sales.
(6) Gross margin percent.............................	Gross margin divided by total sales.
(7) Operating income percent.....................	Operating income divided by total sales.

*The average is determined by adding the beginning and ending balances of the respective amounts and dividing by two.

Return on Average Total Investment. The return on average total investment is determined as follows:

$$\frac{\text{Net income}}{\text{Average total assets (or equities)}}$$

	1979	1978	TREND
Net income.................................	$ 250,000	$ 200,000	
Total assets (equities):			
1977...		$2,750,000	
1978...	$3,060,000	3,060,000	
1979...	3,240,000		
Total.....................................	$6,300,000	$5,810,000	
Average total assets..............	$3,150,000	$2,905,000	
Return on average total investment .	7.9%	6.9%	Increase

The firm's overall profitablity improved one percentage point in terms of the effectiveness with which total resources committed to the business were used. This comprehensive measure of business success can be compared to returns experienced by other firms in the same industry to determine whether or not the Chinook Corporation's profitability was above or below average in each fiscal year.

Return on Average Owners' Equity. Owners also consider the firm's ability to generate an adequate return on their investment. The return on average owners' equity is calculated as follows:

$$\frac{\text{Net income}}{\text{Average owners' equity}}$$

	1979	1978	TREND
Net income...........................	$ 250,000	$ 200,000	
Owners' equity:			
1977..................................		$1,308,000	
1978..................................	$1,467,000	1,467,000	
1979..................................	1,947,000		
Total............................	$3,414,000	$2,775,000	
Average owners' equity..	$1,707,000	$1,388,000	
Return on average owners' equity.....................................	14.6%	14.4%	Slight increase

The return on average owners' equity increased only 0.2 percentage points during the two-year period, whereas the return on average total investment increased 1 percentage point from 6.9% to 7.9%. The reason for this apparent inconsistency is that total owners' equity increased $639,000 (about 49 percent) during the two-year period, whereas total investment increased only $490,000 (about 17 percent). A large portion of the $639,000 owners' equity increase was due to the $309,000 increase in outstanding common stock during 1979. A further insight into the impact of this increase in common stock on the return to ownership interests is examined below.

Return on Average Common Stock Equity. The calculation indicates the return to common stockholders after any declaration of dividends to preferred stockholders. The ratio is derived as shown at the top of the following page.

Despite the $50,000 larger after-tax profit earned in 1979, the primary reason for the slight increase in return to common stockholders was that their total investment increased $475,000 during 1979, of which $300,000 was due to the conversion of a portion of the bond issue into 30,000 shares of common stock on July 1, 1979. In other words, 30,000 additional shares of common stock were outstanding at the end of 1979 to share in the $50,000 higher net income for 1979. In effect, common shareholders as of the end of 1978 suffered some dilution in their earnings per share during 1979 because of the additional shares of outstanding stock.

$$\frac{\text{Net income after preferred dividend requirements}}{\text{Average common stockholders' equity}}$$

	1979	1978	TREND
Net income.............................	$ 250,000	$ 200,000	
Preferred dividends:			
1978...................................		9,000	
1979....................................	9,300		
Net income after preferred dividend requirements...	$ 240,700	$ 191,000	
Common stockholders' equity:			
1977...................................		$1,158,000	
1978...................................	$1,317,000	1,317,000	
1979...................................	1,792,000		
Total.............................	$3,109,000	$2,475,000	
Average common stockholders' equity...........	$1,555,000	$1,238,000	
Return on average common stockholders' equity.............	15.5%	15.4%	Slight increase

Earnings per Share of Common Stock. The earnings per share of common stock is determined as shown below:

$$\frac{\text{Net income after preferred dividend requirements}}{\text{Average outstanding shares of common stock}}$$

	1979	1978	TREND
Net income after preferred dividend requirements.......................................	$240,700	$191,000	
Outstanding shares of common stock:			
1977...		43,600	
1978...	44,500	44,500	
1979...	74,500		
Total..	119,000	88,100	
Average shares............................	59,500	44,050	
Earnings per share of common stock........	$4.05	$4.34	Decrease

Any subsequent conversion of the remaining portion of the bond issue into common stock will further dilute the common shareholders' equity in the firm, and will reduce their earnings per share.

Many financial analysts stress through their various reporting services the importance of the earnings per share figure for corporations whose stocks are publicly traded in the national money markets. The viewpoint widely held by these experts is that the market price of a firm's stock tends to move in the same direction as its reported earnings per share. Although this observation tends to be confirmed in numerous cases, other factors also arise which affect the market price of a particular stock at a particular time, such as the general competitive and economic climate, marketing developments, and technological innovations. In addition, the earnings per share figure may be of limited significance, because it can be altered from period to period by increasing or decreasing the number of shares of stock outstanding. However, a thorough comprehensive appraisal of a firm's financial performance and position can be better achieved if based on a broad spectrum of financial ratios and sectors, rather than an analysis that is restricted to only one financial segment, such as earnings per share.

In addition to determining a firm's earnings per share, corporate owners also are interested in the percentage of earnings paid out each year in the form of cash dividends. This is commonly referred to as the *payout ratio*. The payout ratio is determined as shown below:

$$\frac{\text{Cash dividends declared to common stockholders}}{\text{Net income after preferred dividends}}$$

	1979	1978	TREND
Cash dividends declared to common........	$ 66,000	$ 41,000	
Net income after preferred dividends.......	$240,000	$191,000	
Payout ratio......................................	27.4%	21.5%	Increase

Intra-Income Statement Ratios. Examination of the comparative income statements reveals the following three financial ratios and trends:

	1979	1978	TREND
Net income......................	$ 250,000	$ 200,000	
Total sales	$2,500,000	$2,200,000	
Return on sales	10%	9.1%	Increase
Gross margin	$ 960,000	$ 880,000	
Total sales	$2,500,000	$2,200,000	
Gross margin percent........	38.4%	40%	Decrease
Operating income.............	$ 470,000	$ 416,000	
Total sales	$2,500,000	$2,200,000	
Operating income percent..	18.8%	18.9%	Relatively stable

Return on sales (net income ÷ total sales) measures the efficiency with which a particular sales volume of business was undertaken. The average return on sales experienced by all American businesses varies between 3 and 5 percent. The *gross margin percent* (gross margin ÷ total sales) reflects how well cost of goods sold, a major expense item, is being controlled. In this instance, the gross margin percent declined 1.6 percentage points from 1978 to 1979.

The *percent of operating income* (operating income ÷ total sales) provides a relatively clear picture of how efficiently the firm maintained control over its total expenses. In addition, the analyst may wish to calculate the relationship between each expense item and sales to determine the degree to which specific expenses are under control or are tending to move out of control. These percentages are reflected on the common-size comparative income statement shown previously on pages 556 and 557.

Significance of Profitability Performance. The most significant development in the profitability performance of the Chinook Corporation between 1978 and 1979 was the very slight increase in the return on average common stockholders' equity and the decrease in the earnings per share of common stock, despite a $50,000 increase in net income earned during 1979. Both of these profitability measures were affected by the partial, but substantial, conversion of the bond issue into common stock on July 1, 1979. Except for the slight decrease in the gross margin percentage, the corporation's profitability showed improvement between 1978 and 1979.

Leverage

Almost every company is financed by a combination of capital that is obtained from owner-investors (*equity capital*) and from creditors (*debt capital*). The extent to which debt capital is used to finance a business is usually referred to as *leverage* or *trading on the equity*. The fundamental economic principle underlying leverage is that whenever funds are borrowed at a lower rate of interest than the borrower can earn on those funds, the rate of return on owners' equity is increased over what it otherwise would have been had the borrowed funds been provided by the owners. A prudent level of leverage also provides the following advantages to owners of the firm:

(1) Voting control of the corporation is not diluted, nor are dividends shared with additional owners who would otherwise have furnished the funds provided by creditors.
(2) Interest expense incurred on the borrowed capital is deductible in determining taxable income, whereas dividends paid to owners are not tax-deductible expenses of the firm.
(3) During an inflationary period, the borrower benefits and the lender suffers with respect to purchasing power, because the borrowed capital is repaid in the future with dollars of less purchasing power than those originally obtained.

Borrowing too heavily, however, can invite financial difficulty primarily because interest payments and principal repayments are contractual obligations that must be honored. No contractual obligation exists for the board of directors to declare dividends, although once declared they must be paid. In addition, the return to owners of their invested capital is seldom required except in the event of the firm's liquidation. However, if sufficient earnings are not generated to cover contractual interest and principal payments, one or more of the following disadvantages from leverage may occur: (1) net income and the rate of return on owners' equity will be less than had the funds been obtained from owners; (2) creditors may be entitled to acquire partial to complete control of the firm's operations; (3) if a deflationary period occurs after funds are borrowed, the principal repayment must be made with dollars that are more valuable in terms of purchasing power than those originally borrowed; and (4) future access to money markets may be severely damaged due to a tarnished credit rating.

Measures of Leverage. The following four measures have been developed to indicate the extent to which management has financed operations with leverage, or debt capital:

MEASURES OF LEVERAGE	
Measurement Device	*Calculation*
(1) Degree of overall leverage	Total liabilities divided by total equities.
(2) Degree of long-term leverage	Long-term liabilities divided by long-term equities*.
(3) Times interest earned	Income before income tax and interest expense, divided by interest expense.
(4) Times fixed charges earned	Income before income tax and interest expense, divided by interest expense plus preferred dividend requirements.
*Long-term equities are long-term liabilities plus owners' equity.	

Degree of Overall Leverage. The degree of overall leverage (trading on the equity) is calculated as follows:

$$\frac{\text{Total liabilities}}{\text{Total equities}}$$

	1979	1978	1977	TREND
Total liabilities	$1,293,000	$1,593,000	$1,442,000	Steady decline
Total equities	$3,240,000	$3,060,000	$2,750,000	with
Degree of overall leverage	39.9%	52.1%	52.4%	substantial decrease in 1979

The degree of overall leverage at the 1979 year-end is noticeably less due to the $300,000 bond conversion into common stock. Had the remaining $200,000 of bonds been converted during 1979, overall leverage at December 31, 1979, might have declined to about 33.8% ($1,095,000 ÷ $3,240,000).

Companies that reflect relatively stable earnings and those in relatively low-risk industries, such as public utilities and railroads, tend to reflect a high degree of overall leverage.

Degree of Long-Term Leverage. This ratio reflects the percentage of long-term financing obtained from long-term debt capital. The ratio is derived as shown below:

$$\frac{\text{Long-term liabilities}}{\text{Long-term liabilities plus owners' equity}}$$

	1979	1978	1977	TREND
Long-term liabilities .	$ 489,000	$ 785,000	$ 784,000	Steady decline
Long-term equities ...	$2,436,000	$2,252,000	$2,092,000	with
Degree of long-term leverage	20.1%	34.9%	37.5%	substantial decrease in 1979

As this ratio increases, the possibility of a greater return on owners' equity also rises. However, the higher the ratio, the greater is the risk that the return on owners' equity might decline or become negative if the firm fails to generate sufficient income to cover the interest expense on the borrowed funds. The following two calculations provide an indication of whether the firm is adequately covering its interest and other fixed charges.

Times Interest Earned. The calculation is derived as follows:

$$\frac{\text{Income before income tax plus interest expenses}}{\text{Interest expense}}$$

	1979	1978	TREND
Income before income tax	$500,000	$400,000	
Interest expense	90,000	101,000	
Income before income tax and interest expense..	$590,000	$501,000	
Times interest earned...........................	6.6	5.0	Increase

Times Fixed Charges Earned. The calculation is obtained as shown at the top of page 572. Preferred dividends are fixed charges on net income, particularly if the preferred stock is cumulative. Other fixed charges that may be included in this calculation are contractual payments under operating leases.

These last two ratios indicate that the Chinook Corporation substantially covered its interest and fixed charges during the two-

$$\frac{\text{Income before income tax plus interest expense}}{\text{Interest expense plus preferred dividend requirements}}$$

	1979	1978	Trend
Income before income tax and interest expense..	$590,000	$501,000	
Interest expense	$ 90,000	$101,000	
Preferred dividends	9,300	9,000	
	$ 99,300	$110,000	
Times fixed charges earned	5.9	4.6	Increase

year period. Low or decreasing coverage indicates that the firm may be approaching the point where it will be unable to meet liability payments, and that the return being earned on debt capital is becoming less than interest charges incurred on borrowed funds.

Appraisal of the Leverage Position. The degree to which the Chinook Corporation employed leverage decreased markedly during the two-year period. Coverage of interest expense and other fixed charges appears adequate, reflecting an increase during that period. However, management might consider additional financing through debt capital to further increase the return on common stock equity and the earnings per share of common stock. A possibility exists that bondholders will convert their holdings into common stock, thereby further diluting the return to common shareholders.

Highlights and Conclusions of the Analysis

The overall financial position of the Chinook Corporation appears to have improved during the two-year period ended December 31, 1979. Liquidity appears sound, the several measures of profitability suggest an improving trend, and the exposure to risk from leverage does not appear excessive. Management should, however, direct attention to the following areas:

(1) Identify and correct causes for the month's disparity between the stated and actual credit terms.
(2) Determine whether or not the trend to build up inventory is necessary or desirable, and investigate the decrease in the gross margin percent.
(3) Consider using leverage to a greater extent if additional funds are required for expansion or operations.

Current and prospective common shareholders should, in addition to seeking answers in the foregoing areas, focus on one potential problem. Although returns on total investment and on owners' equity increased during the two-year period, further dilution of the common shareholder segment due to subsequent bond conversions may deteriorate the return to common shareholders and the earnings per share of common stock.

Review of Procedural Steps in the Analysis

A variety of methods may be used in financial analysis. The particular method used to analyze the Chinook Corporation may be summarized as follows:

    (1) Financial statements, both conventional and common-size, were examined for accuracy and to gain familiarity with the company's financial condition.
    (2) Preliminary examination of these statements revealed general trends in the major subcategories of balance sheet and income-statement-related accounts.
    (3) Tentative insights in specific areas were obtained that suggested where further investigation might be warranted.
    (4) The three critical aspects of the firm's financial condition — liquidity, profitability, and leverage — were investigated by means of ratio analyses to detect signs of strength and weakness.
    (5) Review of the preceding steps suggested tentative conclusions and potential problems that might warrant further investigation and correction.

There is, however, no prescribed pattern by which to undertake financial analysis. Each analyst develops a particular technique and style through experience. Perhaps the most important characteristics possessed by the successful analyst are flexibility, inventiveness, curiosity, and an ability to detect significant signals from large amounts of financial data.

PRECAUTIONS DURING FINANCIAL ANALYSIS

In addition to developing an awareness that financial statement analysis is more of an art than a science, the analyst should also be reminded of several other precautions during an intensive financial analysis of any business enterprise. These include:

    (1) Limitations of trend indications.
    (2) Abridgment of financial statements.
    (3) Accounting procedures.
    (4) Window dressing.
    (5) Location and type of company.
    (6) Omission of items on the financial statements.
    (7) The price-level problem and inflation.

Limitations of Trend Indications

As previously indicated, a strong temptation exists to extrapolate recent historical experience into the future. In some cases,

ns based on observed trends and tendencies are justified.
the seasoned analyst uses extreme caution in projecting
…torical data. For example, the fact that the current ratio decreased during each of the past three years is no assurance that the
downward trend will continue. In fact, by the time the analysis is
complete and the trend detected, management may have implemented policies to reverse that trend.

Abridgment of Financial Statements

Published financial statements often reflect severe abridgment
of the total number of account titles and categories actually used in
the firm by the accounting staff. For example, the 28 account titles
reflected in the Chinook Corporation's financial statements may
represent an abbreviation of 300 or more actual operating accounts
that are maintained in the ledger. More specifically, the three plant
asset account titles shown on the balance sheet may represent a
condensation of thirty or more individual plant asset accounts.
The income statement may also reflect only a small fraction of the
account titles into which the accounting department regularly cat-
egorizes revenue and expense items. In short, a financial analyst
who is not employed by the organization that is being analyzed,
usually has access to less than a complete detailed record of the
firm's financial history on which to base conclusions and make
recommendations.

Accounting Procedures

Unless footnotes or clarifying remarks are attached to the financial statements, the analyst is often uncertain or unaware of
which depreciation or inventory costing procedures are used in
the firm. For example, an unannounced conversion from fifo to lifo
costing could markedly affect income determination and valuation
of the ending inventory. Likewise, the analyst might be able to
make a more penetrating investigation if the depreciation
methods used by the firm on specific plant assets are known. Current accounting guidelines require that footnotes be included with
financial statements in corporate annual reports to signal significant changes in accounting procedures.

Window Dressing

The extent to which various managements use window dressing to make certain aspects of the business appear better than they

are is difficult to assess. However, the astute analyst and investor is aware that such practices exist. The following example illustrates an attempt to artificially improve the liquidity position of a particular corporation. One column reflects the liquidity position of the firm at December 30, 1979, whereas the other reflects liquidity immediately after management negotiated a $250,000 long-term bank loan on December 31 of the same year:

	DECEMBER 30, 1979 PRIOR TO LOAN	DECEMBER 31, 1979 AFTER LOAN
Cash and marketable securities..............................	$ 50,000	$300,000
Other current assets............	200,000	200,000
Total current assets..........	$250,000	$500,000
Total current liabilities	$200,000	$200,000
Current ratio......................	1.25:1	2.5:1
Net working capital	$ 50,000	$300,000

The balance sheet prepared as of December 31, 1979, would reflect a current ratio twice as large as that which existed the previous day, and the net working capital would be reflected at an amount six times greater than that of the previous day. An unsophisticated analyst who is unaware of the window dressing might conclude that the liquidity position of the corporation was stronger throughout the entire year than would actually have been the case.

Location and Type of Company

Specific financial ratios may span a wide range of acceptability, depending on such features as the geographic location or the type of industry in which the firm is located. The analyst must be aware of the effect of location and nature of the industry in evaluating performance. For example, labor-intensive firms in low wage rate sections of the country often reflect higher labor expense and lower plant asset depreciation, than that of equipment-intensive firms that employ relatively few but highly skilled personnel. New firms in industries that traditionally undertake high-risk projects might be financed almost entirely with owner capital because of a reluctance by creditors to loan funds to the business until financial success has been established. Companies contemplating extensive expansion in facilities and operations frequently declare very meager, if any, cash dividends even though earnings may be relatively high. Finally, companies that operate facilities in certain foreign countries often appropriate a significant portion of retained earnings to provide for the possibility that foreign governments may expropriate assets of the firm.

A recent ruling by the Financial Accounting Standards Board[2] may enable financial analysts to gain better insights into a firm's total operations. In general, Statement No. 14 requires that businesses which operate in more than one industrial sector should furnish certain financial information when the enterprise issues its financial statements. Specifically, the firm is required to identify each "significant" industry segment in which it operates, and to report particular financial information with respect to each industry segment identified. An industry segment is significant to the firm if any of the following three conditions exist:

(1) The revenue generated by the industry segment represents at least 10 percent of the combined revenue of the total enterprise.
(2) The operating income or loss earned by the segment is at least 10 percent of the combined operating income or loss of the firm.
(3) The assets attributed to the segment are at least 10 percent of the combined assets of the firm.

In general, the following financial information must be reported for each industry segment so identified:

(1) Total sales to customers and transfers to other industry segments of the enterprise.
(2) The operating income or loss that is associated with those sales and transfers.
(3) The total book value of assets that are identified and associated with that industry segment.

Foreign operations may be identifiable as a separate industry segment.

The Brunswick Corporation, for example, regularly furnishes the net sales, operating earnings, and assets for each of the four industrial segments in which it currently operates: marine power, recreation, medical, and technical.

Omission of Items on Financial Statements

Perhaps most importantly, financial statements usually exclude several critical aspects of a firm's operations, such as:

(1) The caliber, reputation, and creativity of the managerial group.
(2) Plans for new products and expansion.
(3) Merger, acquisition, and diversification plans.
(4) Status of research and development projects.
(5) Relations with suppliers, creditors, and customers.
(6) Lines of credit available to management.
(7) Union-management relations.
(8) Pending lawsuits and status of tax controversies.

---

[2]*Statement of Financial Accounting Standards, No. 14,* "Financial Reporting of Segments of a Business Enterprise" (Financial Accounting Standards Board: Stamford: 1976).

Management might be reluctant to disclose any of this information in annual reports because of its value to competitive firms. Also, some of these items are nonquantifiable in terms of dollars.

The Price-Level Problem and Inflation

Inflation and the eroding value of the dollar has had an enormous, almost incalculable, impact on the reported financial information of most American companies during the past quarter-century. Specific issues and problems surrounding appropriate methods of accounting for inflationary pressures is the subject of Chapter 16.

In short, a thorough and informed analysis of financial statements is but a first look into the complexity of the modern business enterprise. Complete understanding involves judgment and perspective, attributes which usually come with experience. Although problem areas and strong points can often be identified during a comprehensive financial analysis, identification of the reasons and persons responsible for problems and outstanding performances must be searched out by communicating with personnel within the organization.

QUESTIONS

1. (a) In what respect is financial statement analysis different from either the analysis of net working capital or cash flow? (b) In what respect are these three types of analysis similar?

2. Define each of the three financial aspects of a firm emphasized in this chapter.

3. Explain in what ways financial statement analysis may benefit both managerial personnel, owners, and creditors.

4. Explain why financial statement analysis can be viewed as more of an art than a mechanical or scientific process.

5. Why might it be unwise to predict a firm's financial future based on trends derived from historical financial information?

6. (a) Construct a diagram in which each major asset, equity, and income statement category can be related to a firm's return on total investment as the focal point of financial statement analysis. (b) Identify two alternate but equally valid definitions of total investment.

7. Define common-size financial statements, and explain their usefulness during financial statement analysis.

8. (a) Identify the seven liquidity measures, and explain how each is calculated. (b) Describe the general significance of each measure.

9. Is the increase in the quick and current ratios necessarily indicative of an improved liquidity position and general financial performance?

10. In what respect is the current ratio similar to, yet different from net working capital?

11. Why is it important to use only credit sales, if determinable, as the numerator in determining the average receivables turnover?

12. How can the average collection period of receivables be determined?

13. What financial problem may develop when: the average inventory turnover is 8 times; the average turnover of receivables is 4 times; and all purchases of inventory are made under 30-day credit terms?

14. Indicate several reasons why the analyst should be cautious in applying "rules-of-thumb" to a particular company's financial structure.

15. (a) What do all turnover ratios have in common? (b) What do all "return on" ratios have in common?

16. (a) Identify the seven profitability measures, and explain how each is calculated. (b) Describe the general significance of each measure.

17. (a) Explain how the earnings per share of common stock might reflect a decrease from the previous year even though net income remained stable during the two-year period. (b) What might a decrease in the gross margin percent indicate?

18. Define leverage or trading on the equity.

19. What fundamental principle of economics underlies leverage?

20. Sharply distinguish between the contractual obligations of debt capital versus equity capital.

21. Identify several advantages, other than a possibly increased rate of return on owners' equity, that may accrue to owners of a firm that uses a prudent amount of leverage to finance its operations.

22. Point out several dangers that could occur in a heavily levered company if sufficient earnings are not generated to cover contractual interest and principal repayments.

23. (a) Identify the four measures of leverage, and explain how each is calculated. (b) Describe the general significance of each measure.

24. How can a firm's degree of long-term leverage decrease even though its degree of overall leverage remains the same?

25. Briefly explain the five procedural steps that were developed in the chapter for financial statement analysis.

26. How might financial statement abridgment hinder the analyst in making a thorough investigation of a firm's financial condition?

27. Of what value to the financial analyst would be the complete disclosure of the accounting procedures used within the firm?

28. Illustrate how a firm's liquidity position might be window dressed to reflect a stronger financial position than that which actually existed during most of the fiscal year.

29. How might geographic location or type of company have an important bearing on the analysis and interpretation of a particular company's financial statements?

30. (a) List several relevant aspects of a firm's operation that are normally excluded from published financial statements. (b) Provide at least one reason why such information is usually excluded from financial statements or annual stockholder reports.

EXERCISES

1. Preparation of common-size statements. The balance sheet and income statement are shown on page 579 for the Parker Corp.:

Parker Corp.
Balance Sheet
December 31, 1979

Assets		Equities	
Current assets:		**Current liabilities:**	
Cash............................	$ 20,000	Notes payable	$ 50,000
Marketable securities	5,000	Accounts payable...........	60,000
Accounts receivable, net		Income tax payable	30,000
of $4,000 allowance	26,000	Total current liabilities..	$140,000
Inventory	45,000		
Prepaid expenses...........	6,000	**Long-term liabilities:**	
Total current assets	$102,000	Bonds payable, net of	
		$5,000 bond discount ...	$135,000
Investments:		Mortgage note payable ...	72,000
Windecker, Inc.	$ 36,000	Total long-term	
		liabilities..............	$207,000
Plant assets:			
Land...........................	$ 14,000	**Owners' equity:**	
Machinery and equipment	400,000	Preferred stock	$ 20,000
Less accumulated		Common stock...............	70,000
depreciation..............	(52,000)	Premium on common stock .	3,000
Total plant assets	$362,000	Retained earnings..........	60,000
		Total owners' equity.....	$153,000
Total assets.....................	$500,000	Total equities..................	$500,000

Parker Corp.
Income Statement
For the Year Ended December 31, 1979

Sales...		$300,000
Cost of good sold...................................		180,000
Gross margin......................................		$120,000
Expenses:		
Wages and salaries............................	$7,500	
Administrative and general.....................	7,000	
Depreciation	7,000	
Interest..	6,000	
Rent, insurance, utilities, and maintenance	5,000	
Advertising and sales promotion............................	3,000	
Uncollectible accounts..	2,500	
Office and clerical supplies......................................	1,000	39,000
Operating income		$ 81,000
Gains and losses:		
Gain on sale of marketable securities	$2,000	
Loss on sale of equipment.....................................	(3,000)	(1,000)
Income before income tax.................................		$ 80,000
Income tax expense		40,000
Net income		$ 40,000

Required: Convert each financial statement into a common-size statement to reflect both monetary and percentage amounts. Round all percentages to one decimal place.

2. Financial analytic framework. Refer to Exercise 1.

Required: (a) Insert the financial information presented in Exercise 1 into the framework for financial analysis shown on page 554. (b) Compute the return on total investment as of December 31, 1979. (c) Calculate the quick and current ratios at December 31, 1979. Round each calculation to one decimal place. (d) Calculate the degree of overall leverage at December 31, 1979, and the number of times interest was earned in 1979.

3. Accounts receivable turnover. Total sales in the Zwitzer Corp. during the fiscal years ended December 31, 1979 and 1980, were $600,000 and $800,000, respectively. The percent of sales made under 30-day credit terms increased from 60% in 1979 to 80% in 1980. The remaining sales in both years were made under cash-and-carry arrangements. Balances at December 31 were reflected in the following accounts:

	1980	1979	1978
Accounts Receivable	$66,000	$49,000	$38,000
Allowance for Doubtful Accounts......	(5,000)	(4,000)	(3,000)

Required: (a) Calculate the average net receivables turnover during each of 1979 and 1980, based on total sales realized in each year. Round calculations to one decimal place. (b) Calculate the average net receivables turnover during each of 1979 and 1980, based on credit sales realized in each year. Round calculations to one decimal place. (c) Evaluate which pair of computations furnishes the more reliable indication of the trend in net receivables turnover over the two-year period.

4. Window dressing of financial ratios. The information displayed below was extracted from the financial statements of the Purdy Corporation which were prepared as of the dates indicated below. However, only the financial statement dated June 30, 1980, was publicly circulated.

	JUNE 30, 1980	JUNE 27, 1980
Quick assets	$200,000	$200,000
Other current assets	200,000	200,000
Noncurrent assets..............................	500,000	500,000
Total assets.....................................	$900,000	$900,000
Current liabilities	$ 50,000	$150,000
Long-term liabilities	300,000	400,000
Owners' equity	550,000	350,000
Total equities...................................	$900,000	$900,000

The entire issue of $200,000, 10-year convertible debentures due June 30, 1983, was converted into 2,000 shares of the Purdy Corporation $100 par value common stock on June 28, 1980. In addition, a $100,000 short-term note payable was transformed into a 3-year mortgage note payable on the same date. The net income earned during the fiscal year ended June 30, 1980, was $50,000.

Required: (a) Calculate the financial relationships shown at the top of page 581 as of June 27, 1980, and June 30, 1980. Round all ratios to one decimal place, and do not calculate an average for item (4).

(1) Quick ratio.   (4) Return on owner's equity.
(2) Current ratio.   (5) Degree of overall leverage.
(3) Net working capital.

(b) Comment on the results of the above comparative analysis.

5. Evaluation of changes in earnings per share. The owners' equity section in the Kinnelworth Corp. appeared as shown below:

Owners' equity:	DECEMBER 31, 1979	DECEMBER 31, 1978
Preferred stock, $100 par, 6% cumulative.............	$120,000	$120,000
Common stock, $20 par	540,000	540,000
Retained earnings............	340,000	260,000
Treasury stock, 4,400 shares of common stock.	(96,000)	—
Total owners' equity	$904,000	$920,000

Net income earned during each of the fiscal years ended December 31, 1978 and 1979, was $87,200. Although no dividends were declared on common stock during either year, a $7,200 dividend was declared on preferred stock on December 28, 1978, and a partial $3,600 dividend on preferred stock was declared on December 27, 1979.

Required: (a) Calculate the earnings per share of common stock as of December 31, 1978 and 1979. Round each calculation to the nearest cent, but do not compute the average earnings per share at either date. (b) Comment on the apparent improved profitability performance of the Kinnelworth Corp. during 1979 based on the above analysis.

6. Identification of financial ratios. Financial statements for the Browder Corporation are shown below and at the top of page 582, with alphabetical notations replacing specific dollar amounts.

Browder Corporation
Income Statement
For the Year Ended December 31, 1979

Sales:		
Cash sales	A	
Credit sales..	B	C
Cost of goods sold...		D
Gross margin		E
Expenses:		
Advertising and promotion...	F	
General administrative...	G	
Depreciation	H	
Interest	I	
Insurance and rent	J	
Wages and salaries...	K	L
Income from income tax		M
Income tax expense		N
Net income		O
Cash dividend declared on preferred stock...............................		P
Cash dividend declared on common stock................................		Q

Browder Corporation
Balance Sheet
December 31, 1979

Assets		Equities	
Current assets:		**Current liabilities:**	
Cash....................................	a	Notes payable	m
Marketable securities	b	Accounts payable....................	n
Accounts receivable, net of allow-		Income tax payable	o
ance..................................	c	Cash dividends payable...........	p
Inventory	d	Total current liabilities..........	q
Prepaid expenses....................	e		
Total current assets	f	**Long-term liabilities:**	
		Mortgage note payable	r
Plant assets:		Bonds payable, net of bond dis-	
Land....................................	g	count	s
Buildings, net of accumulated de-		Total long-term liabilities	t
preciation	h		
Equipment and machinery, net of		**Owners' equity:**	
accumulated depreciation.......	i	Preferred stock	u
Total plant assets	j	Common stock, $10 par	v
		Premium on common stock	w
Intangibles:		Retained earnings	x
Patents................................	k	Total owners' equity	y
Total assets...........................	l	Total equities.........................	z

Required: In Column (1) of the schedule shown below, indicate the most concise method to calculate each financial relationship requested. Use appropriate capital or lower case letters. In Column (2), indicate whether the primary focus of the relationship is liquidity, profitability, or leverage. The current ratio provides a guideline.

Financial Relationship	(1) Calculation	(2) Primary Focus
(0) Current ratio	$\dfrac{f}{q}$	Liquidity
(1) Inventory turnover (at year-end only)...............		
(2) Operating income percent		
(3) Quick ratio..		
(4) Times interest earned		
(5) Degree of overall leverage............................		
(6) Gross margin percent...................................		
(7) Net working capital....................................		
(8) Return on common stock equity (at year-end only)...		
(9) Return on sales		
(10) Quick assets...		
(11) Return on total investment (at year-end only)....		
(12) Accounts receivable turnover (at year-end only).		
(13) Degree of long-term leverage		
(14) Earnings per share of common stock		
(15) Net working capital turnover		
(16) Return on owners' equity (at year-end only)......		

7. **Identification of financial relationships.** Fourteen commonly used financial relations are described below in arithmetic terms:

  (a) Current assets ÷ Current liabilities
  (b) Cost of goods sold ÷ Average inventory
  (c) Operating income ÷ Total sales
  (d) Long-term liabilities ÷ Long-term equities
  (e) Net income ÷ Total sales
  (f) Current assets − Current liabilities
  (g) Net income ÷ Average total assets or equities
  (h) (Sales − Cost of goods sold) ÷ Sales
  (i) Total liabilities ÷ Total equities
  (j) Credit sales ÷ Average net receivables
  (k) Net income after preferred dividends ÷ Average common stock equity
  (l) Income before income tax and interest expense ÷ Interest expense

$$\text{(m) Sales} \div \frac{\text{Current assets} - \text{Current liabilities at the beginning and end of the fiscal year}}{2}$$

  (n) Current assets − (Inventory + Prepaid expenses) ÷ Current liabilities

Required: Using the format shown below, place the identifying letter of each item beneath one of the three financial aspects of the firm that best describes the principal focus of that financial relationship. In addition, provide the usual name for each financial relationship. Item (a) furnishes a guideline:

<u>Leverage</u>   <u>Liquidity</u>   <u>Profitability</u>
            (a) Current ratio

PROBLEMS

15-1. Common-size statements and identification of significant shifts in liquidity and leverage. The comparative balance sheet as of December 31, 1979 and 1980, and the income statement for the fiscal year ended December 31, 1980, are displayed at the top of pages 584 and 585, respectively for the Bainbridge Corp.

Required: (1) Convert the financial statements into common-size statements, on which are reflected both dollar and percentage amounts. Round all percentages to one decimal place.
    (2) Identify significant shifts in the monetary and/or percentage amounts of specific balance sheet items between December 31, 1979 and 1980.
    (3) Identify the following relationships as of December 31, 1979 and 1980, and indicate any apparent trend. Round each relationship to one decimal place where appropriate.
      (a) Quick ratio.   (d) Degree of overall leverage
      (b) Current ratio.   (e) Degree of long-term lever-
      (c) Net working capital.   age.
    (4) Summarize significant observations from the above analyses.

Bainbridge Corp.
Comparative Balance Sheet
December 31, 1980 and 1979

Assets	1980	1979
Current assets:		
Cash	$ 37,000	$ 57,000
Marketable securities	18,000	28,000
Accounts receivable, net of allowance	35,000	94,000
Inventory	326,000	186,000
Prepaid expenses	12,000	8,000
Total current assets	$428,000	$373,000
Plant assets:		
Land	$ 84,000	$ 88,000
Buildings and equipment	530,000	450,000
Less accumulated depreciation	(153,000)	(150,000)
Total plant assets	$461,000	$388,000
Total assets	$889,000	$761,000
Equities		
Current liabilities:		
Notes payable	$ 93,000	$123,000
Accounts payable	64,000	117,000
Income tax payable	42,000	47,000
Total current liabilities	$199,000	$287,000
Long-term liabilities:		
Mortgage note payable	—	$ 40,000
Bonds payable, 8%, 10-year, due December 31, 1989	$140,000	—
Total long-term liabilities	$140,000	$ 40,000
Owners' equity:		
Common stock, $10 par value	$330,000	$250,000
Premium on stock	33,000	10,000
Retained earnings	203,000	201,000
Treasury stock	(16,000)	(27,000)
Total owners' equity	$550,000	$434,000
Total equities	$889,000	$761,000

15-2. Pros and cons of leverage. The Consuego Corporation began its first year of operations on January 1, 1979, with the sale of 40,000 shares of $10 par value capital stock to the public at $10 per share, and the issuance of $600,000, 7%, 10-year bonds at par. Interest on the bonds was payable at the end of each fiscal year, December 31. The corporation generated $62,000 income before interest and income tax expenses during 1979, and increased that amount by $60,000 during 1980. No additional stock was sold, nor were additional long-term liabilities incurred during the two-year period ending December 31, 1980. The income tax

Bainbridge Corp.
Income Statement
For the Year Ended December 31, 1980

Sales (on 30-day credit terms)		$960,000
Cost of goods sold		470,000
Gross margin		$490,000
Expenses:		
Wages and salaries	$130,000	
Depreciation	74,000	
Administrative and general	58,000	
Marketing and sales promotion	32,000	
Utilities and maintenance	29,000	
Rent and insurance	21,000	
Interest	18,000	362,000
Income before income tax		$128,000
Income tax expense		65,000
Net income		$ 63,000

rate was 50% of taxable income in both years; and no dividends were declared in either year.

Required: (1) Calculate the return on total owners' equity as of the end of each year, and the net income earned per share of capital stock in each year. Round percentages to one decimal place, and the per share earnings to the nearest cent.

(2) Calculate each of the amounts required in (1) above for each year, assuming that all long-term capital had been obtained from the sale of 100,000 shares of its capital stock at $10 per share on January 1, 1979. Use identical rounding procedures as noted in (1) above.

(3) Does it appear that stockholders benefited over the two-year period from the sale of the bond issue instead of financing the firm entirely with common stock?

15-3. Comprehensive financial statement analysis: one year. Top management of the Marvello Corporation met during the first week of January, 1980, to evaluate the financial statements shown on pages 586 and 587, and to examine the firm's 1979 financial performance.

Required: (1) Calculate each of the seven liquidity measures for 1979 and 1980, rounding each relationship to one decimal place.

(2) Determine the profitability performance by calculating each of the seven measures of profitability for 1980, rounding all ratios and percentages to one decimal place.

(3) Calculate each leverage measure, except times fixed charges earned, for 1979 and/or 1980, rounding each measure to one decimal place.

(4) Present a summary of significant conclusions and recommendations to management with respect to the liquidity, profitability, and leverage positions of the firm.

Marvello Corporation
Income Statement
For the Year Ended December 31, 1979

Sales (on 60-day credit terms)		$800,000
Cost of goods sold		560,000
Gross margin		$240,000
Expenses:		
Depreciation	$52,000	
Administrative and office	51,000	
Salaries and wages	49,400	
Advertising and marketing	38,000	
Interest	29,000	
Repairs and supplies	4,000	223,400
Operating income		$ 16,600
Other income:		
Rent and interest income		500
Gains and losses:		
Gain on sale of marketable securities	$ 700	
Loss on sale of building	(1,800)	(1,100)
Income before income tax		$ 16,000
Income tax expense		8,000
Net income		$ 8,000

Marvello Corporation
Comparative Balance Sheet
December 31, 1980 and 1979

	1980	1979
Assets		
Current assets:		
Cash and marketable securities	$ 25,000	$ 120,000
Receivables, net of allowance	290,000	250,000
Inventory	305,000	255,000
Prepaid expenses	8,000	6,000
Total current assets	$ 628,000	$ 631,000
Plant assets:		
Land	$ 8,000	$ 8,000
Buildings	47,000	42,000
Equipment	740,000	721,000
Less accumulated depreciation — buildings and equipment	(254,000)	(204,000)
Total plant assets	$ 541,000	$ 567,000
Total assets	$1,169,000	$1,198,000
Equities		
Current liabilities:		
Notes payable	$ 270,000	$ 250,000
Accounts payable	214,500	143,500
Income tax payable	6,000	5,000
Total current liabilities	$ 490,500	$ 398,500

Long-term liabilities:		
Mortgage note payable, due 1984...............................	$ 200,000	$ 200,000
Owners' equity:		
Common stock, $100 par..	$ 304,000	$ 304,000
Retained earnings..	228,500	295,500
Treasury stock..	(54,000)	—
Total owners' equity	$ 478,500	$ 599,500
Total equities..	$1,169,000	$1,198,000

15-4. Comprehensive financial statement analysis: two years. The president of the Thornberg Corp. requested the treasurer's office to prepare comparative financial statements for the previous two years for presentation at the monthly meeting of the board of directors in January, 1980. The president felt that the board should be aware of the financial performance of the firm after the authorization of a $300,000 investment in plant and equipment during 1978 and 1979. Financial statements prepared by the treasurer's office are shown below and on page 588.

Thornberg Corp.
Comparative Income Statement
For the Years Ended December 31, 1979 and 1978

	1979	1978
Sales (80% sold on 30-day credit terms in each year, the remainder on cash terms)...................	$1,800,000	$1,600,000
Cost of goods sold...	1,000,000	800,000
Gross margin	$ 800,000	$ 800,000
Expenses:		
Administrative and general............................	$ 154,000	$ 160,000
Marketing and promotion..............................	80,000	120,000
Salaries and wages.....................................	80,000	180,000
Depreciation	70,000	60,000
Interest..	34,000	33,000
Rent, insurance, utilities, supplies....................	15,000	23,000
Property tax	9,000	7,000
Total expenses.......................................	$ 442,000	$ 583,000
Operating income	$ 358,000	$ 217,000
Other income:		
Rent and interest income..............................	19,000	15,000
Gains and losses:		
Gain on sale of marketable securities	3,000	—
Loss on sale of equipment.............................	(20,000)	(40,000)
Income before income tax........................	$ 360,000	$ 192,000
Income tax expense	180,000	96,000
Net income	$ 180,000	$ 96,000
Cash dividend declared on common stock..............	$ 75,000	$ 40,000
Cash dividend declared on preferred stock............	$ 2,500	$ 2,500

Thornberg Corp.
Comparative Balance Sheet
December 31, 1979, 1978 and 1977

Assets	1979	1978	1977
Current assets:			
Cash	$ 140,000	$ 100,000	$ 80,000
Marketable securities	30,000	30,000	12,000
Accounts receivable	240,000	148,000	130,000
Allowance for doubtful accounts	(16,000)	(12,000)	(10,000)
Inventory	360,000	140,000	130,000
Prepaid expenses	2,000	4,000	8,000
Total current assets	$ 756,000	$ 410,000	$ 350,000
Investments:			
Goodsall, Inc.	$ 70,000	$ 60,000	$ 60,000
Plant assets:			
Land	$ 25,000	$ 25,000	$ 20,000
Plant and equipment	910,000	760,000	640,000
Less accumulated depreciation	(350,000)	(300,000)	(380,000)
Total plant assets	$ 585,000	$ 485,000	$ 280,000
Intangibles:			
Patents	$ 17,000	$ 13,000	$ 15,000
Goodwill	16,000	18,000	20,000
Total intangible assets	$ 33,000	$ 31,000	$ 35,000
Total assets	$1,444,000	$ 986,000	$ 725,000
Equities			
Current liabilities:			
Notes payable	$ 85,000	$ 71,000	$ 57,000
Accounts payable	205,000	104,000	83,000
Income tax payable	110,000	45,000	30,000
Total current liabilities	$ 400,000	$ 220,000	$ 170,000
Long-term liabilities:			
Mortgage note payable, due 1981*	$ 60,000	$ 200,000	$ 200,000
Bonds payable, 8%	314,000	138,000	—
Deferred income tax	14,000	12,000	14,000
Total long-term liabilities	$ 388,000	$ 350,000	$ 214,000
Owners' equity:			
Preferred stock, $100 par, 5%, cumulative	$ 50,000	$ 50,000	$ 50,000
Common stock, $20 par	310,000	170,000	150,000
Premium on common stock	8,000	8,000	4,000
Retained earnings	288,000	188,000	137,000
Total owners' equity	$ 656,000	$ 416,000	$ 341,000
Total equities	$1,444,000	$ 986,000	$ 725,000

*$140,000 of the mortgage note payable was converted into 7,000 shares of common stock at the beginning of 1979. The remaining portion of the mortgage note is expected to be converted into 3,000 shares of common stock at the beginning of 1980.

Required: (1) Calculate each of the seven measures of liquidity for the two-year period, December 31, 1977, through December 31, 1979. The three turnover ratios should be based on the average of the beginning and end of each year. Round each measure to one decimal place.

    (2) Calculate each of the seven measures of profitability for the two-year period. Where appropriate, the calculation should be based on the average of the beginning and end of each year. Round each measure to one decimal place.

    (3) Calculate each of the four measures of leverage for the two-year period, rounding each measure to one decimal place.

    (4) Present a summary of significant conclusions based on the preceding analyses.

15-5. Analysis of multi-product line firm. Outfitters, Inc., was composed of the following three product lines: athletic gear, camping equipment, and motorboats. An income statement for the fiscal year ended June 30, 1980, which displays the performance of each product line and the total company, is shown below:

Outfitters, Inc.
Income Statement
For the Year Ended June 30, 1980

	Athletic Gear	Camping Equipment	Motorboats	Total
Sales (on 45-day credit terms).	$350,000	$400,000	$150,000	$900,000
Cost of goods sold..............	150,000	200,000	70,000	420,000
Gross margin	$200,000	$200,000	$ 80,000	$480,000
Expenses:				
Wages and salaries..........	$ 99,000	$ 55,000	$ 11,000	$165,000
General and administrative	50,000	20,000	10,000	80,000
Marketing and promotion...	45,000	8,000	12,000	65,000
Depreciation	10,000	20,000	10,000	40,000
Insurance, rent, and maintenance.....................	9,000	6,000	3,000	18,000
Interest	4,000	5,000	3,000	12,000
Utilities........................	3,000	6,000	1,000	10,000
Total expenses	$220,000	$120,000	$ 50,000	$390,000
Operating income (loss) ..	$ (20,000)	$ 80,000	$ 30,000	$ 90,000
Income tax expense	10,000	40,000	10,000	40,000
Net income (loss).................	$ (10,000)	$ 40,000	$ 20,000	$ 50,000

Selected information extracted from the comparative balance sheet dated June 30, 1979 and 1980, is shown below:

	1980	1979
Receivables, net of allowance...........................	$ 190,000	$ 150,000
Merchandise inventory.....................................	70,000	50,000
Net working capital	250,000	190,000
Total assets..	1,400,000	1,260,000

Required: (1) Compute the following ratios for each product line and the entire firm for the fiscal year ended June 30, 1980, rounding each percentage to one decimal place:
  (a) Gross margin percent.
  (b) Operating income percent.
  (c) Return on sales.
(2) Calculate the following ratios for the entire firm based on appropriate average amounts during the fiscal year ended June 30, 1980. Round each calculation to one decimal place.
  (a) Accounts receivable turnover.
  (b) Inventory turnover.
  (c) Net working capital turnover.
  (d) Return on average total investment.
(3) What significant observations can be made with respect to operations of the firm during the year ended June 30, 1980?

DECISION CASE

15-I. **Setting financial performance objectives.** Management of the Rohrbach Corporation met during the first week of January, 1980, and decided to pursue the following financial objectives in 1980. The balance sheet as of December 31, 1979, is shown on page 591.

  (a) Management expects to increase 1980 sales 25% above the 1979 sales volume of $768,000. Merchandise is sold on 60-day credit terms.
  (b) Accounts receivable turnover should be six times, based on the average net receivables at the beginning and end of 1980.
  (c) The gross margin percentage objective is 37½%.
  (d) Inventory turnover, based on the average inventory at the beginning and end of 1980, is expected to be one half of the receivables turnover.
  (e) A large piece of machinery is to be purchased in January, 1980, for $30,000. A machine originally costing $20,000, on which $15,000 of depreciation has been accumulated, is to be sold for $3,000 during January. No other transactions are expected to affect plant assets during 1980.
  (f) Depreciation expense of 1980 will be 10% of the balances in the buildings and equipment and machinery accounts at December 31, 1980.
  (g) Rent and interest income is anticipated to be $6,800 for 1980. No additional income is expected during 1980. The operating income percent is projected at 19½%. The income tax rate is expected to remain at 50% of taxable income. One half of the 1980 income tax expense is expected to remain unpaid at the end of 1980.
  (h) Cash dividends declared and paid in 1980 will equal the amount by which net income exceeds $80,000. If net income falls below $80,000, no cash dividends will be declared. No other transactions are expected to affect retained earnings during 1980.
  (i) At the 1980 year-end: cash is expected to be $100,000; marketable securities are expected to increase $5,000; and the balance in pre-

Rohrbach Corporation
Balance Sheet
December 31, 1979

Assets			Equities		
Current assets:			Current liabilities:		
Cash	$	85,000	Notes payable, 8%	$	40,000
Marketable securities		10,000	Accounts payable		170,000
Accounts receivable,			Income tax payable,		
net		140,000	due by June 30,		
Inventory		240,000	1980		30,000
Prepaid expenses		5,000	Total current		
Total current assets		$480,000	liabilities	$	240,000
Plant assets:			Long-term liabilities:		
Land	$	20,000	Mortgage note		
Buildings		160,000	payable, 6%, due		
Equipment and			1985	$	130,000
machinery		590,000	Bonds payable,		
Less accumulated			10-year, 7%, due		
depreciation		(120,000)	December 31, 1982		300,000
Total plant assets	$	650,000	Total long-term		
			liabilities	$	430,000
			Owners' equity:		
			Common stock, $10 par	$	200,000
			Premium on common		
			stock		10,000
			Retained earnings		250,000
			Total owners' equity	$	460,000
Total assets		$1,130,000	Total equities		$1,130,000

paid expenses is expected to remain the same as on December 31, 1979.

(j) The long-term liabilities and current notes payable at December 31, 1979, are expected to remain constant throughout 1980. Interest is payable on all of these obligations semiannually on June 30 and December 31. The remaining expenses during 1980 include general administrative, wages and salaries, and selling.

(k) Management hopes to reflect a current ratio of 3.067 to 1 on December 31, 1980.

(l) No additional shares of stock are planned to be sold during 1980. Instead, management hopes to purchase some outstanding shares of common stock for the treasury at $20 per share.

Required:

(1) Prepare, as detailed as possible, a projected balance sheet as of December 31, 1980, and a projected income statement for 1980. Support the detail shown in each financial statement with calculations or other explanations.

(2) How many shares of common stock does it appear that management will be able to purchase during 1980 at $20 per share?

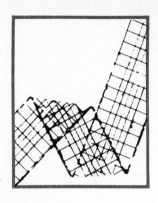

16
Analyzing the Impact of Changing Prices on Financial Statements

Inflation is like a country where nobody speaks the truth — not even an accountant.

Henry C. Wallich

Probably the most significant, challenging, and controversial issue that currently surrounds accounting is devising and implementing appropriate methods to analyze and interpret the effect inflation has on information contained in financial statements. This chapter identifies certain characteristics of accounting that tend to distort the reporting of financial results during periods of rapidly changing prices, then examines various approaches that have been suggested to provide more informative and useful financial data during such periods, and finally investigates two methods which appear to offer some promise of gaining acceptance by accounting practitioners and users of financial information.

THE ESSENCE OF THE PROBLEM

Three generally accepted accounting principles or concepts may be pinpointed which tend to create the greatest distortions in financial statements prepared during periods of significant price changes. They are:

(1) The historical cost principle.
(2) The principle of monetary measurement.
(3) The concept of realization.

Historical Cost

The purchase price associated with each financial transaction is the cost or value that is recorded in the financial records of the organization. This historical cost continues to be reflected in the accounting records until the item is sold or disposed of. To this point in the text, this foundation block of modern accounting has been accepted and applied without being seriously questioned as to its validity or relevance even during periods approaching double-digit inflation.

Money Measurement

Each recorded financial transaction is stated in terms of some monetary measure of value: the dollar in the United States, the deutschemark in West Germany, and the yen in Japan. Yet, scarcely a single currency can be identified which has provided a constant standard of measurement during the last quarter-century. For example, the value of the dollar, as measured by its purchasing power to command goods and services, has steadily diminished since the Second World War. True, a dollar is a dollar, but its purchasing power varies considerably. For example, a residence which cost $20,000 in 1966 dollars might cost approximately $55,000 or more in current dollars.

Realization

Any change that occurs in the market value of a particular asset or equity held by a business is realized or recognized only at the time of that item's disposal. For example, a parcel of land purchased in 1955 for $70,000 may today have a market value of $250,000. But instead of periodically recognizing the increasing value of the land in increments over the period it was held, accounting procedures dictate that only when the land is sold would any of the increase in its current market value be recognized in the accounting records. In this instance, assuming the land is sold for $250,000, the entire gain of $180,000 would be recognized as a lump sum in the year of sale, as shown in the following entry:

```
Cash ........................................................ 250,000
    Land ....................................................         70,000
    Gain on Sale of Land ...................................        180,000
```

The distortion caused by reflecting the entire gain in the year of sale would be similar, only in the reverse, to charging to expense the entire cost of a depreciable plant asset in the year of acquisition, rather than to properly prorate that cost to expense in smaller increments over the asset's useful life.

Only two major exceptions to the accounting rule of realization have thus far been adopted by the accounting profession: (1) marketable equity securities are required to be reflected on the balance sheet at the lower of their original cost or current market value, as discussed in Chapter 7; and (2) the value of a firm's inventory may be reflected at the lower of cost or market, as pointed out in Chapter 8. Note that in each instance, however, the principle of conservatism governs; the value of each of these items is reflected at the lower of its cost or market, not at the higher of cost or market. In short, rarely if ever does accounting permit recognition in the financial records of any upward movement in the market value of any asset or equity prior to its disposal.

Implications of the Problem

During periods in which prices are relatively stable, consistent application of these three accounting principles — historical cost, monetary measurement, and realization — helps provide relevant, informative, and useful financial information to a wide variety of constituencies. But as price levels undergo significant change, these three practices reinforce each other in ways which result in substantial distortions being reflected in financial statements.

The most pronounced distortions arising from significant changes in prices are reflected in inventory and plant assets on the balance sheet and in the cost of goods sold and depreciation expenses shown on the income statement. Assume for example that simplified and abbreviated financial statements, shown at the top of page 595 in Column (1), were prepared as of the end of a particular fiscal year, using conventional accounting principles and concepts. Note that the returns on sales and on total investment for the year were 20 percent and 5 percent, respectively.

Assume further that the current market value or cost required to replace the ending inventory balance and the merchandise sold during the year increased 10 percent above the price at which these items were purchased, and that the current market value or replacement cost of the plant assets in their condition at the end of the year increased 30 percent above their value or cost in comparable condition several years ago. Both financial statements are presented above in Column (2) after adjusting the respective amounts

	(1) CONVENTIONAL	ADJUSTMENT FACTOR	(2) ADJUSTED TO CURRENT MARKET VALUE OR REPLACEMENT COST
Balance sheet (assets only)			
Quick assets.....................	$100,000		$100,000
Inventory........................	100,000	× 110%	110,000
Net plant assets	200,000	× 130%	260,000
Total assets	$400,000		$470,000
Income statement			
Sales	$100,000		$100,000
Less: Cost of goods sold....	$ 60,000	× 110%	$ 66,000
Depreciation	20,000	× 130%	26,000
	$ 80,000		$ 92,000
Net income	$ 20,000		$ 8,000
Return on sales	20%		8%
Return on total investment (assets).........................	5%		1.7%

to their current market value or replacement cost. Inventory and cost of goods sold were revalued upward by 10 percent, and the net plant assets and depreciation expense were increased by 30 percent.

In this instance, the conventional statements reveal that both nonquick assets are understated relative to their current market or replacement value counterparts, which in turn results in related expenses being understated. This ultimately results in an overstatement of reported net income compared to the adjusted net income shown in Column (2). Based on the foregoing information, management could make a serious error in judgment if it were to believe that the firm earned a real profit of $20,000 during the year.

An astute analyst would observe that the $60,000 cost of inventory which was sold would cost approximately $66,000 to replace at prices existing at year-end; and the $20,000 depreciation expense reflected in Column (1) might be increased by 30 percent to reflect a more appropriate prorata allocation of the current market or replacement value of plant assets. Under these assumptions, real net income generated by the firm is reduced to $8,000, and the returns on sales and on total investment are lowered to 8 percent and 1.7 percent, respectively. These revaluation adjustments might enable management to gain a sharper perception of how much net earnings would be available for distribution as dividends or bonus payments without endangering the financial position of the firm during an inflationary period when assets must be replenished at higher prices to maintain productivity and capacity.

Several implications could result from failing to periodically recognize: the increasing market values or replacement costs of specific assets, and the fluctuating value of the dollar during periods of substantial inflation. Some of these are itemized below:

(1) Financial information in the same firm may become noncomparable over a period of years as the gap widens between the historical costs of various assets and their current market values or replacement costs.
(2) Reliable comparisons of the financial position and performance between various firms can become blurred, if not almost impossible.
(3) Overstated net earnings may induce union negotiating committees to press for, and management negotiators to accept higher wage, salary, and fringe benefit settlements than would otherwise be economically justified.
(4) Managers may be granted higher bonuses, governments may assess higher taxes on overstated taxable income, and stockholders may petition for larger cash dividend payouts on the basis of overstated earnings. In short, funds may be withdrawn from the firm for a variety of purposes, which in effect could represent a distribution of capital that is needed to replenish the various assets required to maintain competitive position and productive capacity. At the extreme, management could be accused of dissipating the company's capital.

DEALING WITH THE ISSUE

A variety of approaches have been suggested on how to deal with the effects of price changes on financial data. These range from the inadequate to a more promising few which evidence greater potential to resolve some, though not all inflation-induced distortions. Three inadequate approaches are dealt with first, followed by more intensive examination of those offering greater promise.

Inadequate Approaches

The inadequate approaches are:

(1) Ingore the problem.
(2) Convert to lifo inventory costing.
(3) Adopt accelerated depreciation.

Ignore the Problem. To ignore the problems induced by inflationary pressures could be interpreted to mean that financial information would continue to be assembled and published using generally accepted accounting principles without modification. Users of accounting information would be left to draw their own conclusions from traditionally prepared, unadjusted statements that are "verifiable and objectively determined." In opposition to this approach is the awareness of many persons that inflation and the diminishing purchasing power of the dollar are sufficiently critical to warrant serious attention.

The graph shown below reflects the increase that has occurred since 1959 in one of the most widely used indicators of price movements in the United States, the *Gross National Product Implicit Price Deflator*, often referred to as the GNP Deflator. Briefly, this index is constructed by first determining the total cost of a specific quantity of certain goods and services in the United States in a base year, in this case 1972. The prices during the base year are given a value of 100; the prices of all other years are expressed as a percentage of this amount.

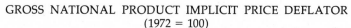

GROSS NATIONAL PRODUCT IMPLICIT PRICE DEFLATOR
(1972 = 100)

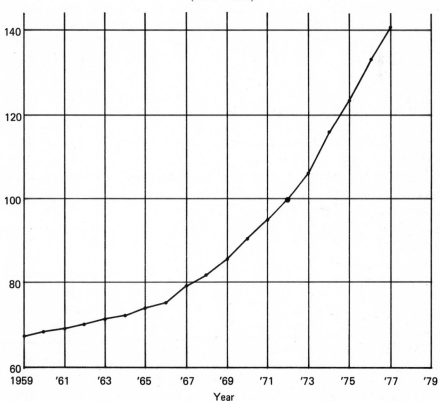

Year

Source: U.S. Department of Commerce, Bureau of Economic Analysis, *Survey of Current Business*

The next step is to determine the total cost of that same group of commodities in various other years. By dividing the total cost of these particular commodities during, for example, 1973 by the total amount they would have cost in the base year (1972), yields the implicit price deflator for 1973. For example, the actual value in 1973 of the total goods and services produced in the U.S. was $1,306.6 billion. That same GNP stated in terms of 1972 prices (the base year) was $1,235.0 billion. Hence the price level during 1973 may be said to be 1.058 ($1,306.6 billion ÷ $1,235.0 billion), an increase of 5.8 percent. The preceding graph, which displays an index of recent price level movements in the U.S., reveals that, in general, the same bundle of goods and services which cost $67.52 in 1959, cost $100.00 in 1972 and $141.29 in 1977. In other words, the price level in the U.S. more than doubled in less than 18 years.

Convert to Lifo Inventory Costing. As mentioned in Chapter 8, lifo inventory costing provides a better matching of the more current inventory costs with current revenue than that of either fifo or weighted average costing alternatives. As long as the quantity of inventory purchased equals or exceeds the quantity sold, lifo costing will provide better matching with or without inflation. Only if the inventory level decreases will costs associated with inventory items purchased in earlier periods be charged to expense; in which case lifo costing would result in mismatching current costs with current revenue. But whether the inventory level increases, remains constant, or decreases, the amount reflected on the balance sheet under lifo costing would contain costs associated with goods purchased at prices that could vary significantly from current prices. Hence, while the income statement might reflect less inflation-distorted financial information, the balance sheet could continue to reflect marked distortions.

Adopt Accelerated Depreciation. Another method recommended by some to reduce distortions in financial data is to adopt an accelerated method of depreciation, either double-declining balance or sum-of-the-years-digits. An accelerated method of depreciation allows a greater portion of the original cost of depreciable plant assets to be charged to expense during their early life. In short, an accelerated method of depreciation might enable a better or faster matching of current costs with current revenue, especially during an asset's early life, than that provided by straight-line depreciation. But in any event, the original cost of these plant assets would continue to be reflected on the balance sheet at their historical cost rather than at their current market value or replacement cost.

Both the lifo inventory valuation and accelerated depreciation suggestions suffer from two weaknesses. First, these approaches deal with only two asset categories, Inventory and Plant Assets, and with only two of numerous items normally reflected on the income statement, Cost of Goods Sold and Depreciation Expense. Changes in price levels affect almost every item on both financial statements in one way or another. Second, both approaches represent at best a partial and superficial attempt at resolving price changes on financial data, because they fail to attack and adequately deal with the heart of the inflation issue. Neither method completely resolves the problem for income-statement-related data, and the balance sheet continues to reflect costs for various items in a mixture of noncurrent and nonuniform dollars.

Approaches Offering Greater Promise

Three approaches can be identified which may provide a more adequate resolution of issues surrounding the impact of inflationary pressures on financial data:

(1) Current replacement costing (CRC).
(2) Net realizable valuation (NRV).
(3) Indexing.

Current Replacement Costing. *Current replacement costing,* (CRC), often referred to as *current value accounting*, has received considerable attention during the past two decades as an approach that may provide a direct attack on resolving financial reporting problems that arise during periods of rapidly changing prices. Several accounting bodies, respected practitioners, and recognized faculty members in the British Commonwealth (most notably England, Australia, New Zealand, and Canada), some Scandinavian countries (particularly Sweden), the Netherlands, and the United States have advocated this approach. As mentioned briefly in Chapter 8, in 1976 the Securities and Exchange Commission issued an experimental directive requiring certain U.S. corporations to disclose in financial statements filed with the SEC, the current cost of replacing inventories and plant assets and the amount of the cost of goods sold and depreciation expense that would be reflected using CRC-based data.

The distinguishing attribute of CRC is determining the current market price at which various assets, most notably inventory and plant assets, could be replaced in their present condition. This approach represents a complete departure from the historical cost (HC) basis of accounting. In order to generate CRC data for each asset, management may use any of the following sources of information: (1) bonafide estimates of current market values made by professional appraisers; (2) updated market prices from vendors for items that are purchased as inventory and plant assets; (3) specific prices reflected in publications issued by second-hand equipment and machinery dealers; and (4) informed estimates.

The following illustration provides an introductory exposure to some of the mechanics involved in constructing financial statements using CRC data, along with a comparison between HC and CRC-prepared financial statements. Financial statements for the Seaplains Corp. as of the end of its first fiscal year of operations are displayed; historical cost (HC) data are shown in Column (1), and current replacement cost (CRC) data are reflected in Column (2). Explanations supporting the CRC statements are furnished beneath the statements. The balance in Inventory and the two plant asset accounts on January 1, 1979, was zero, and the income tax rate in 1979 was 50 percent of taxable income.

Seaplains Corp.
Balance Sheet
December 31, 1979

	(1) Historical Cost (HC)	(2) Current Replacement Cost (CRC)
Assets		
Cash and receivables	$100,000	$100,000
Inventory	150,000	180,000
Plant assets	400,000	500,000
Less accumulated depreciation	(80,000)	(100,000)
Total assets	$570,000	$680,000
Equities		
Total liabilities	$320,000	$320,000
Common stock	200,000	200,000
Retained earnings	50,000	160,000
Total equities	$570,000	$680,000

Inventory, plant assets, cost of goods sold, and depreciation expense data reflected in the CRC statements are based on the following assumptions and calculations:

(1) The total inventory purchases made during 1979, costing $470,000, could have been replaced for $580,000 on December 31, 1979. The $110,000 difference between CRC and HC data would be reported as a holding gain in 1979, and could be divided between inventory and cost of goods sold as shown in the following revaluation entry:

Inventory	30,000	
Cost of Goods Sold	80,000	
Holding Gain on Inventory		110,000

Record holding gain resulting from restatement of inventory and cost of goods sold to a CRC basis.

Seaplains Corp.
Income Statement
For the Year Ended December 31, 1979

	(1) Historical Cost (HC)		(2) Current Replacement Cost (CRC)	
Sales		$700,000		$700,000
Less: Cost of goods sold..............	$320,000		$400,000	
Depreciation expense..........	80,000		100,000	
All other operating expenses.	200,000	600,000	200,000	700,000
Operating income..................		$100,000		—0—
Holding gains and losses:				
Holding gain on inventory			$110,000	
Holding gain on plant assets		——	100,000	$210,000
Income before income tax		$100,000		$210,000
Income tax expense..................		50,000		50,000
Net income...........................		$ 50,000		$160,000

(2) The plant assets that were purchased at the beginning of 1979 for $400,000 had an expected life of 5 years with zero salvage value. Straight-line depreciation was used. These assets could have been replaced with new counterparts near the end of 1979 for $500,000. The $100,000 difference between the CRC and HC data would be reported as a holding gain in 1979, as shown in the revaluation entry:

```
Plant Assets......................................... 100,000
     Holding Gain on Plant Assets.................         100,000
     Record holding gain resulting from re-
     statement of plant assets to a CRC basis.
```

(3) The depreciation expense could be increased to $100,000 (20% × $500,000 original cost under CRC), or by $20,000 as reflected in the following adjusting entry:

```
Depreciation Expense ............................ 20,000
     Accumulated Depreciation......................         20,000
     Record additional prorata depreciation
     expense based on CRC data for original
     cost of plant assets.
```

Incorporating the preceding assumptions, revaluations, and adjustments into the CRC-based financial statements results in reflecting a total investment at December 31, 1979, that is $110,000 higher than the report using HC-based information. This differential is composed of a $30,000 upward revaluation of inventory and an $80,000 upward restatement of the book value of plant assets in their estimated condition at the year-end.

Perhaps more important, however, is the observation that CRC-based data produced zero operating income, as opposed to $100,000 under the HC accounting framework. This $100,000 gap is composed of the $80,000 upward revaluation in cost of goods sold and the $20,000 additional depreciation expense that was reported under CRC. The $210,000 of unrealized holding gains helped to offset the failure to generate any operating income, as reported under the CRC framework, which ultimately resulted in an after-tax profit of $160,000. Also note that the $160,000 balance in Retained Earnings at the end of 1979, as reported under CRC, is composed of the following elements:

After-tax operating (loss)	$ (50,000)
Holding gain on inventory	110,000
Holding gain on plant assets	100,000
Retained earnings	$160,000

The comparison between HC and CRC-derived financial information suggests that if management paid the entire $50,000 net income, as reported under HC, in the form of a cash dividend to stockholders, a significant amount of the firm's resources in the form of cash would have been distributed at a time when management might be wiser to retain those funds to replenish its productive capacity at generally higher price levels. To distribute unrealized holding gains to shareholders in the form of real cash dividends may not be the most prudent policy to pursue during inflationary periods.

Another interesting observation is that the $50,000 income tax expense actually incurred in 1979, based on the $100,000 taxable income reported under conventional HC procedures, represents a tax of $50,000 on an operating taxable income of zero that would be reported under CRC accounting. Unrealized holding gains on inventory and plant assets are currently nontaxable, and CRC-determined cost of goods sold and depreciation expenses are not tax deductible.

Net Realizable Value. An approach occasionally mentioned as an alternative to the historical cost framework is *net realizable value* (NRV). The distinguishing characteristic of this approach is that the net realizable value of an asset at a particular time is the amount that could be realized from its sale net of any disposal or selling costs. For example, the NRV of a machine originally costing $50,000, that could be disposed of for $74,000 less $4,000 disposal costs, would be $70,000. An NRV-prepared balance sheet would reflect the machine at $70,000 and report an unrealized holding gain of $20,000 on the income statement to reflect the revaluation upward. In most other respects, the mechanics involved in preparing financial statements using the NRV concept closely parallel those developed for the CRC alternative.

As this text is being prepared, the FASB has distributed a draft proposing that the CRC (and to some extent, the NRV) approach be considered for adoption by large publicly owned corporations to provide supplementary financial information to financial statements prepared under traditional historical cost guidelines. Several advantages of the CRC and NRV approaches are reflected in the preceding discussion; and some of the principal objections to these two approaches are summarized below:

(1) Current replacement costs and net realizable values that might be determined for the broad spectrum of assets used in American business would tend to be far more subjective, and less verifiable and objective, than historical cost-based data. Verification of CRC and NRV for each asset would be extremely difficult if not almost impossible to audit.

(2) Although the CRC and NRV techniques address specific values for specific assets, these revised values may not adequately reflect improvements in quality or technology.

(3) Companies do not usually replace a particular asset, especially plant assets, with exactly the same type or model, new or used; and seldom does a firm replace or sell a plant asset prior to mid stream in its expected life. Replacement and disposal of most assets usually occur nearer the end of their useful lives. Derivation of CRC and NRV for a plant asset prior to actual replacement or sale may be an exercise in fiction.

(4) A current replacement cost or market value may be almost impossible to derive for those assets which are specially designed and adapted solely for use in a particular enterprise. The value of a special-purpose machine, new or used, to the user might be infinite, but to an outsider, zero.

(5) Firms in industries that experience rapidly developing technology, such as electronics and chemicals, might be less affected by conversion to CRC or NRV bases, than would companies in less technologically advancing industries, such as farm machinery, automobiles, or steel. The historical cost of the more recently acquired assets in the rapidly developing segments of the economy would tend to approximate more closely their current replacement or net realizable values.

(6) Annual administrative, clerical, and research costs required to generate and interpret CRC and NRV financial data could prove prohibitive.

(7) Conversion from the historical cost basis of accounting to either a CRC or NRV framework could be expected to generate widespread confusion within various sectors of the economy and financial community for several years following the shift.

INDEXING

Indexing is a procedure whereby all dollar amounts reflected on conventionally prepared financial statements are converted into dollars of uniform value or purchasing power by applying a general price index. The major strengths and weaknesses of this approach are discussed below, followed by a detailed examination of the indexing process and an interpretation of the results.

Major Strengths and Weaknesses

Indexing offers several advantages compared to the previously discussed approaches.

Strengths and Advantages. First, this procedure enables the adjustment of all items on financial statements, rather than being limited to inventory and depreciable plant assets as under the lifo costing and accelerated depreciation approaches. Although the CRC and NRV approaches could be applied to all financial statement items, those methods often stress the restatement of inventories and plant assets to their current replacement costs or net realizable values.

Second, the historical cost framework is retained intact. Whereas the CRC and NRV approaches would replace the historical cost premise, indexing merely applies a general price index to each piece of financial information contained in accounting records and statements that have been prepared using the historical cost basis.

Third, the mechanical details required to index financial data are well developed, and can be applied by most individuals in a relatively straightforward manner. This feature makes the results of indexing comparatively easy to verify and audit; in other words, the indexing process is "objective."

Fourth, the two general price indexes to restate financial information are the *GNP Deflator* and the *Consumer Price Index* (CPI), both of which are published monthly, quarterly, and annually, The CPI, published by the Department of Labor's Bureau of Labor Statistics is an index constructed in much the same manner as the GNP Deflator, being distinguished from the deflator by its inclusion of a narrower mix of goods and services. A plot of the CPI using a common base year of 1972, however, would reveal an almost identical curve to that shown on page 597 for the GNP Deflator. Other regional and specific industrial sector indexes are also published by government and business groups, but none of these are as well understood or widely available as the GNP Deflator and the CPI.

Finally, the index approach enables the analyst to identify purchasing power gains and losses from holding monetary items, a detailed discussion of which immediately follows the brief examination of the significant weaknesses of indexing.

Weaknesses and Shortcomings. The principal weakness and criticism of indexing is that no general price index is applicable nor relevant for all individuals, business enterprises, and financial items in an economy as widely dispersed and diversified as the United States. The specific bundle of goods and services contained in an index to adequately measure the impact of inflation on a young, single clerk, is probably quite different from one that is relevant for measuring the impact of price level changes on a middle-aged professional with two children in college. Individual assets such as machinery, equipment, parcels of land, inventory items, and rent or insurance expenditures may be affected quite differently by price movements at different times or in different locales. In fact, the current market value, replacement cost, or net realizable value of any asset may significantly deviate from movements in the general price level at a particular time. In short, no general price index has yet been developed that is relevant to all circumstances.

Second, both the CPI and GNP Deflator usually fail to reflect or explicitly identify improvements in quality or advances in technology evidenced by the variety of goods and services available in our economy. A modern sports car is a markedly different vehicle from the model T Ford, aside from the significant price differential. Although periodic updating of an index, by changing its base-year and by varying the mix of goods and services included, can resolve some of the problems surrounding shifts in quality and technology, this procedure is neither completely satisfactory nor undertaken frequently.

Finally, many analysts and managers believe that the majority of consumers of accounting information would be unable to fully comprehend the significance of indexed financial data.

Monetary and Nonmonetary Items

The indexing approach segregates all assets and equities into two categories:

(1) Monetary items.
(2) Nonmonetary items.

Movements in the general price level affect each category differently, a fact that is essentially ignored in both the CRC and NRV approaches.

Monetary Items. The *monetary items* include all assets and equities that are stated in terms of a fixed number of dollars at all times, and which do not fluctuate with changes in the general price level. In other words, monetary assets are claims to a fixed number of dollars, whereas monetary equities represent claims by others on a business or an individual to a fixed number of dollars, irrespective of changes in the price level. For example, cash is a monetary asset that is stated in terms of a specific quantity of dollars which remains constant as long as the cash is held, whether or not price changes have occurred in the economy. On the other hand, a $1,000 note payable is a monetary equity, because that amount of dollars must be repaid at some future date, whether or not the purchasing power of that $1,000 increased or decreased during the borrowing period. The more familiar monetary assets and equities are listed below:

MONETARY ASSETS	MONETARY EQUITIES
Cash	Notes payable
Marketable and long-term debt securities, such as bonds and government securities	Accounts payable
	Bonds payable
	Other payables, such as interest, taxes, employee compensation, and dividends
Notes and accounts receivable (less any allowance for doubtful accounts)	Preferred stock
Prepaid rent and insurance	

Preferred stock is usually classified as a monetary equity because it can be viewed as a claim by the preferred shareholders to a fixed number of dollars in the event the firm is liquidated, irrespective of whether the general price level increased or decreased since the stock was issued.

Nonmonetary Items. The *nonmonetary items* include all other assets and equities whose value tends to fluctuate with price level changes, rather than remain constant in terms of a fixed number of dollars. For example, prices of inventory items tend to move up or down, even though these changes may not exactly coincide with movements in the general price level. Likewise, the value of plant assets and owners' equities tend to change over periods of time. Typical nonmonetary items are identified below:

NONMONETARY ASSETS	NONMONETARY EQUITIES
Inventory	Common stock
Prepaid supplies	Premium on stock
Plant assets (less accumulated depreciation)	Retained earnings, including all income-statement-related items
Intangible assets	
Short and long-term investments in the capital stock of other corporations	

Unlike the value of monetary items, which is always stated in terms of a fixed number of dollars, the value of nonmonetary items tends to move in the same direction as the general price. It should be reemphasized, however, that movements in the value of specific nonmonetary items at any particular time or place may or may not parallel movements in the general price level.

The relationship between monetary and nonmonetary items may be regrouped, and may be expressed symbolically in a version of the expanded balance sheet equation, as shown below:

Let: QA = Quick assets. For purposes of convenience and accuracy in this instance, the designation includes cash, marketable debt securities, and all receivables net of any allowance for doubtful accounts; but it excludes marketable equity securities, which are included in the noncurrent asset (NA) classification shown below.
PI&R = Prepaid insurance and rent.
   L = All liabilities, plus preferred stock.
  OE = Owners' equities, including all income-statement-related items, but excluding preferred stock.
 Inv = Inventories.
  PS = Prepaid supplies.
  NA = Noncurrent assets, plus marketable equity securities.

$$\text{Then:}\quad \underbrace{(QA + PI\&R) - L}_{\text{Net monetary items}} = \underbrace{OE - (Inv + PS + NA)}_{\text{Net nonmonetary items}} \qquad [1]$$

Overview of the Mechanics of Indexing

A short example will be used to introduce several basic features involved in indexing before proceeding to a more comprehensive illustration. Assume that the financial position and composition of a particular firm remained unchanged during the fiscal year ended December 31, 1979, as shown below in the unadjusted comparative balance sheet. Assume also that the price level on and prior to January 1, 1979, remained constant at 100, and that it increased to 120 on December 31, 1979.

Comparative Balance Sheet
(Unadjusted)

	JANUARY 1, 1979	DECEMBER 31, 1979
Assets		
Cash	$ 40,000	$ 40,000
Land	100,000	100,000
Total assets	$140,000	$140,000
Equities		
Capital stock	$140,000	$140,000

The price index information can be used to transform conventionally prepared financial statements into statements that accomplish the following two objectives:

(1) Each amount on the financial statements can be restated in terms of dollars of uniform purchasing power, thereby enabling a comparison of dollar amounts within a statement and also with amounts shown on financial statements for different years. In other words, dollars of mixed value that are reflected on conventionally prepared statements, are translated into dollars of uniform value or purchasing power.

(2) The gains and losses which result from holding net monetary items during a period of price changes can be identified and measured.

To illustrate, each item of financial information shown on the balance sheet dated January 1, 1979, can be expressed in terms of dollars having a purchasing power that was 20 percent higher at the end of 1979, using the fraction $\dfrac{120, \text{ the price index on December 31, 1979}}{100, \text{ the price index on January 1, 1979}}$ to multiply each amount.

	JANUARY 1, 1979 (UNADJUSTED)	PRICE LEVEL ADJUSTMENT	JANUARY 1, 1979 (ADJUSTED TO UNIFORM DECEMBER 31, 1979 DOLLARS)
Assets			
Cash	$ 40,000	× 120/100	$ 48,000
Land	100,000	× 120/100	120,000
Total assets	$140,000		$168,000
Equities			
Capital stock	$140,000	× 120/100	$168,000

Restated, the purchasing power in terms of December 31, 1979 dollars of the cash and land that were held on January 1, 1979, amount to $48,000 and $120,000, respectively. Likewise, the capital stock is restated upward by $28,000 to absorb the restatement upward in these two assets and to reflect the presumed increase in the purchasing power of the capital stock in terms of December 31, 1979 dollars. The following entry, although never recorded, may clarify this restatement process for the three accounts involved:

```
Cash ................................................................  8,000
Land ................................................................ 20,000
    Capital Stock .................................................          28,000
    Adjusting entry to restate each account as of Jan-
    uary 1, 1979, to its respective purchasing power in
    terms of December 31, 1979 dollars.
```

The company appears at first glance to be in the same cash position at the end as at the beginning of the year, since a cash balance of $40,000 is reflected on the unadjusted balance sheet at both dates. However, the $40,000 cash had a purchasing power of $48,000 on January 1, 1979, in terms of the general price level existing on December 31, 1979. But because cash is a monetary asset, the $40,000 cash balance held on December 31, 1979, had a purchasing power of only $40,000 in terms of December 31, 1979 dollars. In other words, the firm lost $8,000 of purchasing power by holding the $40,000 cash balance throughout a period in which the price level rose 20 percent. This phenomenon may be clearly shown in the following calculation:

Cash balance on January 1, 1979, in terms of its purchasing
 power as of December 31, 1979, ($40,000 × 120/100) $48,000
Cash balance on December 31, 1979, in terms of its purchasing
 power as of December 31, 1979, ($40,000 × 120/120)   40,000
Purchasing power loss from holding cash during 1979 .... $ (8,000)

This type of financial misfortune is analogous to the situation in which cash savings are removed from a mattress where they had remained during a period of considerable inflation. In the above example, an additional $8,000 cash would have been required on December 31, 1979, to maintain the $48,000 purchasing power possessed by the $40,000 cash held on January 1, 1979.

The above information can now be used to construct a balance sheet for December 31, 1979, that is stated in terms of December 31, 1979 dollars, as shown below in the right-hand column:

	DECEMBER 31, 1979 (UNADJUSTED)	PRICE LEVEL ADJUSTMENT	DECEMBER 31, 1979 (ADJUSTED TO UNIFORM DECEMBER 31, 1979 DOLLARS)
Assets			
Cash.............................	$ 40,000	× 120/120	$ 40,000
Land.............................	100,000	× 120/100	120,000
Total assets	$140,000		$160,000
Equities			
Capital stock	$140,000	× 120/100	$168,000
Purchasing power (loss).....	——		(8,000)*
Total equities	$140,000		$160,000

*See preceding computation.

The $40,000 cash balance as reported on the unadjusted balance sheet at December 31, 1979, remains at $40,000 on the adjusted statement because cash, being a monetary asset, represents a claim to a fixed number of dollars. This "restatement" to $40,000 on the adjusted balance sheet may be accomplished by multiplying $40,000 by 120/120, or 1. Because land and capital stock are nonmonetary items, they are presumed to possess the same purchasing power in terms of December 31, 1979 dollars at year-end as they possessed at the beginning of the year. Whether or not the land and stock are actually worth $120,000 and $168,000, respectively, at the end of 1979 could only be verified if the land is sold and the capital stock traded in the money markets on that date. The $8,000 purchasing power loss reported on the adjusted year-end statement could technically be reported on the adjusted income statement for 1979 and subsequently closed to retained earning at year-end.

The preceding computations and reasoning may be summarized in the exhibit below to more clearly compare the conventional, unadjusted balance sheet with the adjusted statement at the beginning and end of 1979:

	UNADJUSTED		ADJUSTED TO UNIFORM DOLLARS AS OF DECEMBER 31, 1979	
	JANUARY 1, 1979	DECEMBER 31, 1979	JANUARY 1, 1979	DECEMBER 31, 1979
Assets				
Cash......................................	$ 40,000	$ 40,000	$ 48,000	$ 40,000
Land......................................	100,000	100,000	120,000	120,000
Total assets..........................	$140,000	$140,000	$168,000	$160,000
Equities				
Capital stock............................	$140,000	$140,000	$168,000	$168,000
Purchasing power loss..............	—	—	—	(8,000)
Total equities.......................	$140,000	$140,000	$168,000	$160,000

Note that the total investment, as shown in the adjusted data above, declined from $168,000 at the beginning of 1979 to $160,000 at year-end, because of the purchasing power loss incurred from holding the same cash balance at the beginning as at the end of 1979.

Comprehensive Indexing Illustration

A more comprehensive illustration of the price level adjusting process will be developed around the conventionally prepared and unadjusted financial statements displayed below and at the top of page 611 for the Tannbark Corp. These consist of a comparative balance sheet as of the beginning and end of 1979 and an income statement for the fiscal year ended December 31, 1979. Additional items of financial information are shown beneath these financial statements.

Tannbark Corp.
Income Statement
(Unadjusted)
For the Year Ended December 31, 1979

Sales (all under 30-day credit terms)..........................		$550,000
Cost of goods sold		300,000
Gross margin		$250,000
Expenses:		
Depreciation...	$ 40,000	
Other operating expenses, including income tax expense of $55,000	155,000	195,000
Net income..		$ 55,000

Tannbark Corp.
Comparative Balance Sheet
(Unadjusted)
January 1, 1979 and December 31, 1979

	DECEMBER 31, 1979	JANUARY 1, 1979
Assets		
Current assets:		
Cash...	$ 50,000	$ 40,000
Accounts receivable........................	75,000	70,000
Inventory......................................	100,000	60,000
Total current assets	$225,000	$170,000
Plant assets:		
Buildings and equipment..................	$220,000	$200,000
Less accumulated depreciation	(120,000)	(80,000)
Total plant assets	$100,000	$120,000
Total assets....................................	$325,000	$290,000
Equities		
Current liabilities:		
Accounts payable, and other current debts	$ 45,000	$ 65,000
Long-term liabilities:		
Mortgage note payable, 5-year, 8% ...	$ 35,000	$ 35,000
Owners' equity:		
Capital stock.................................	$130,000	$130,000
Retained earnings	115,000	60,000
Total owners' equity	$245,000	$190,000
Total equities..................................	$325,000	$290,000

Additional financial information:

(a) The general price level index on and prior to January 1, 1979, was 100. The price level had risen to 150 on December 31, 1979.

(b) For purposes of simplification, all sales during 1979 and other operating expenses, excluding depreciation, are assumed to have occurred at an average price index of 120.

(c) All purchases of inventory during 1979, totaling $340,000, were made under 30-day credit terms at an average price index of 120. Fifo inventory costing was used in the corporation.

(d) Equipment costing $20,000 was purchased for cash when the general price index was 120. The equipment's expected life was 4 years with zero salvage value, and a full year's depreciation was recorded on this new equipment in 1979. Straight-line depreciation was used on all plant assets.

The objective throughout this indexing illustration is to adjust all financial data to reflect dollars of uniform purchasing power as of December 31, 1979.

Determining Purchasing Power Gains and Losses on Monetary Items. The initial step in adjusting the financial data will focus on calculating any purchasing power gains and losses from holding monetary items during the year. Recall from Equation [1] on page 607, that the net monetary items (NMI) may be expressed symbolically as follows, where QA represents the quick assets as defined on page 607, PI&R is prepaid insurance and rent, and L represents all liabilities plus preferred stock:

$$NMI = (QA + PI\&R) - L$$

By adding the notation Δ ("change in") to each element in the above expression, the equation reflects the change in net monetary items during a specific period, as shown below:

$$\Delta NMI = (\Delta QA + \Delta PI\&R) - \Delta L \qquad [2]$$

Since no prepaid insurance or rent appears in this particular example, Equation [2] can be abbreviated to read: $\Delta NMI = \Delta QA - \Delta L$.

A summary, stated in unadjusted dollars, of the presumed transactions that occurred during 1979 and their impact on net monetary items is shown on the following page.

Those transactions shown in the summary which affected net monetary items during 1979 may now be analyzed and adjusted to the price level existing at December 31, 1979, in order to identify any purchasing power gain or loss on net monetary items during the year. This procedure is shown at the top of page 614, resulting in the recognition of a purchasing power loss of $13,750. Note that the $10,000 of net monetary items on January 1, 1979, possessed a purchasing power of $15,000, or an increase of 50 percent, in terms of year-end dollars. The remaining four transactions possessed a purchasing power equivalent to 25 percent more, $\left(\frac{150}{120} - 1\right)$, in terms of December 31, 1979 dollars than when the transactions are assumed to have actually occurred. This purchasing power loss of $13,750 will appear as an item on the adjusted income statement that will be prepared in the next step.

Adjusting the Income Statement. The next phase in the adjusting process is to restate the income statement in terms of year-end dollars as shown at the top of page 615.

Recall that fifo inventory costing is used in the firm. Hence, the $300,000 unadjusted cost of goods sold consisted of two segments: **(1)** the $60,000 portion in inventory on January 1, 1979, which was obtained when the price level was 100; and **(2)** the $240,000 bal-

PRESUMED TRANSACTION			*Increase*	*Decrease*	*None*
(1) Credit sales:					
Accounts Receivable..............................	550,000				
Sales...		550,000			
$\Delta QA - \Delta L = +\$550,000 - 0$..........			\$550,000		
(2) Credit purchase of inventory:					
Inventory	340,000				
Accounts Payable		340,000			
$\Delta QA - \Delta L = 0 - (+\$340,000)$........				\$340,000	
(3) Cash purchase of equipment:					
Buildings and Equipment.........................	20,000				
Cash..		20,000			
$\Delta QA - \Delta L = -\$20,000 - 0$				20,000	
(4) Payment of liabilities, or liabilities incurred for operating expenses, excluding depreciation:					
Operating Expenses (excluding depreciation)	155,000				
Cash and/or Accounts Payable...............		155,000			
$\Delta QA - \Delta L = -\$155,000$ or					
$-(+\$155,000)$				155,000	
(5) Recognition of cost of goods sold:					
Cost of Goods Sold	300,000				
Inventory		300,000			x
No monetary items involved.					
(6) Recognition of depreciation expense:					
Depreciation Expense............................	40,000				
Accumulated Depreciation		40,000			x
No monetary items involved.					
(7) Collection of accounts receivable:					
Cash...	545,000				
Accounts Receivable...........................		545,000			
Accounts receivable balance on January 1, 1979... \$ 70,000					
Plus credit sales............... 550,000					
\$620,000					
Less accounts receivable balance on December 31, 1979........................... 75,000					
Presumed collections... \$545,000					
$\Delta QA - \Delta L = (-\$545,000) +$					
$(+\$545,000) = 0$.........					x
(8) Payments for inventory purchases:					
Accounts Payable	360,000				
Cash...		360,000			
Accounts payable balance on January 1, 1979.......... \$ 65,000					
Plus credit inventory purchases......................... 340,000					
\$405,000					
Less accounts payable balance on December 31, 1979........................... 45,000					
Presumed payments.... \$360,000					
$\Delta QA - \Delta L = -\$360,000 -$					
$(-\$360,000) = $ —0—					x
Total.................................			\$550,000	\$515,000	

Tannbark Corp.
Purchasing Power Gains and Losses on Net Monetary Items
For the Year Ended December 31, 1979

	UNADJUSTED	ADJUSTING MULTIPLIER	ADJUSTED TO PRICE LEVEL AT DECEMBER 31, 1979
Net monetary items on January 1, 1979 ($110,000 QA − $100,000 L)......................................	$ 10,000	150/100	$ 15,000
Add increase in accounts receivable due to credit sales	550,000	150/120	687,500
	$560,000		$702,500
Deduct:			
Inventory purchases.................	$340,000	150/120	$425,000
Equipment purchase................	20,000	150/120	25,000
Other operating expenses, excluding depreciation	155,000	150/120	193,750
	$515,000		$643,750
Net monetary items on December 31, 1979:			
Adjusted (amount of NMI required to be held at year-end to maintain purchasing power)			$ 58,750
Unadjusted (amount of NMI actually possessed at year-end)	$ 45,000		45,000
Purchasing power loss on net monetary items			$ (13,750)

ance that was purchased during 1979 at an average price level of 120. Likewise, the $40,000 unadjusted depreciation expense consisted of two segments: (1) the $5,000 portion, representing ¼ of the $20,000 original cost of the equipment purchased in 1979 when the price level was 120; and (2) the $35,000 balance recorded on buildings and equipment that were purchased prior to 1979 when the price level was 100.

The $13,750 purchasing power loss on net monetary items is considered by many accountants to be properly disclosed on the adjusted income statement as a "special" item, rather than be reflected as a separate item in the owners' equity section on the adjusted balance sheet, although either method of presentation is permissable.[1] Note that the net income of $31,250 reflected on the adjusted income statement is $23,750 less than the unadjusted amount of $55,000.

[1]*Accounting Research Study No. 6*, "Reporting the Financial Effects of Price-Level Changes" (New York: American Institute of Certified Public Accountants, 1963), pp. 128, 131, 149–152, and 250–251.

Tannbark Corp.
Income Statement
For the Year Ended December 31, 1979

	UNADJUSTED		ADJUSTING MULTIPLIER	ADJUSTED TO PRICE LEVEL AT DECEMBER 31, 1979	
Sales............................		$550,000	150/120		$687,500
Cost of goods sold:					
Inventory at January 1, 1979, sold.................	$ 60,000		150/100	$ 90,000	
Purchases during 1979 sold........................	240,000	300,000	150/120	300,000	390,000
Gross margin		$250,000			$297,500
Expenses:					
Depreciation on equipment purchased in 1979.	$ 5,000		150/120	$ 6,250	
Other plant assets	35,000	$ 40,000	150/100	52,500	$ 58,750
Other operating expenses, including income tax expense....................		155,000	150/120		193,750
Total expenses............		$195,000			$252,500
Net income before purchasing power gain (or loss) on net monetary items...............		$ 55,000			$ 45,000
Purchasing power loss on net monetary items		———			(13,750)
Net income......................		$ 55,000			$ 31,250

Preparing Adjusted Balance Sheets. The final step in the process is to prepare adjusted comparative balance sheets that are stated in terms of December 31, 1979 dollars, as illustrated on page 617.

Each item reflected on the unadjusted balance sheet at January 1, 1979, is restated in terms of year-end uniform dollars by applying the fraction 150/100, or 3/2. On the other hand, the four monetary items shown on the unadjusted balance sheet at December 31, 1979, must be multiplied by 150/150, or 1, because those items are already stated in terms of a fixed number of year-end dollars.

The inventory balance of $100,000 was purchased when the price level was 120, hence the fraction 150/120 is applied to restate that amount in terms of uniform year-end dollars. The two plant asset accounts in this instance must be segregated into two portions: (1) the original cost, and its related accumulated depreciation, pertaining to the $200,000 of plant assets obtained when the price level was 100; and (2) the original cost, and its related accumulated depreciation, pertaining to the $20,000 of equipment purchased when the price level was 120.

The capital stock, being a nonmonetary item is presumed to have moved in the same direction as the general price. Hence its value, in terms of year-end dollars, remains the same at the end as at the beginning of the year. The adjusted retained earnings of $121,250 at December 31, 1979, is composed of the $90,000 adjusted balance at the beginning of the year, plus the $31,250 net income reflected on the adjusted income statement shown previously.

Interpreting Indexed Financial Information

A comparative analysis of financial statements that are adjusted to uniform dollars of purchasing power, with their unadjusted conventional counterparts will draw upon material presented in Chapter 13, which deals with net working capital analysis and Chapter 15, which examines financial ratio analysis.

Analysis of Net Working Capital. A comparative statement of changes in financial position for 1979 can be prepared from information reflected in the three previously presented financial statements.

(1) The statement of purchasing power gains and losses on net monetary items (page 614).
(2) The income statement (page 615).
(3) The comparative balance sheet (page 617).

The unadjusted and adjusted change in net working capital during 1979 can be determined as shown below:

	UNADJUSTED		ADJUSTED	
	December 31, 1979	January 1, 1979	December 31, 1979	January 1, 1979
Current assets	$225,000	$170,000	$250,000	$255,000
Less current liabilities	45,000	65,000	45,000	97,500
Net working capital	$180,000	$105,000	$205,000	$157,500
Increase in net working capital ..	$75,000		$47,500	

The comparative statement of changes in financial position shown at the top of page 618 identifies those transactions that occurred during 1979 which caused net working capital to change by the amounts shown above.

Tannbark Corp.
Comparative Balance Sheet
January 1, 1979 and December 31, 1979

	JANUARY 1, 1979			DECEMBER 31, 1979		
Assets	Unadjusted	Adjusting Multiplier	Adjusted to Price Level at December 31, 1979	Unadjusted	Adjusting Multiplier	Adjusted to Price Level at December 31, 1979
Current assets:						
Cash..............	$ 40,000	150/100	$ 60,000	$ 50,000	150/150	$ 50,000
Accounts receivable	70,000	150/100	105,000	75,000	150/150	75,000
Inventory	60,000	150/100	90,000	100,000	150/120	125,000
Total current assets	$170,000		$255,000	$225,000		$250,000
Plant assets:						
Buildings and equipment..	$200,000	150/100	$300,000	$220,000	200,000 × 150/100 / 20,000 × 150/120	$325,000
Accumulated depreciation	(80,000)	150/100	(120,000)	(120,000)	115,000 × 150/100 / 5,000 × 150/120	(178,750)
Total plant assets	$120,000		$180,000	$100,000		$146,250
Total assets...........	$290,000		$435,000	$325,000		$396,250
Equities						
Current liabilities:						
Accounts payable, and other current debts	$ 65,000	150/100	$ 97,500	$ 45,000	150/150	$ 45,000
Long-term liabilities:						
Mortgage note payable ...	$ 35,000	150/100	$ 52,500	$ 35,000	150/150	$ 35,000
Owners' equity:						
Capital stock......	$130,000	150/100	$195,000	$130,000	150/100	$195,000
Retained earnings...........	60,000	150/100	90,000	115,000	60,000 × 150/100 + $31,250 from the income statement	121,250
Total owners' equity	$190,000		$285,000	$245,000		$316,250
Total equities.............	$290,000		$435,000	$325,000		$396,250

Tannbark Corp.
Comparative Statement of Changes in Financial Position —
Working Capital Basis
For the Year Ended December 31, 1979

	UNADJUSTED	ADJUSTED
Sources of net working capital		
Current operations:		
Net income (from income statement)	$55,000	$31,250
Add depreciation expense (from income statement)	40,000	58,750
Deduct purchasing power gain from holding long-term mortgage note payable during 1979 (from statement of purchasing power gains and losses on net monetary items)	———	(17,500)
Total sources of net working capital	$95,000	$72,500
Uses of net working capital		
Purchase of equipment.....................................	20,000	25,000
Increase in net working capital.....................	$75,000	$47,500

With respect to the unadjusted analysis, the only transaction involving plant assets which affected net working capital was the cash purchase of equipment for $20,000. The $40,000 depreciation expense recognized during the year must be added back to the unadjusted net income of $55,000 because the recognition of depreciation has no effect on net working capital.

The same reasoning used in constructing the unadjusted statement is also applicable to the adjusted statement. The $20,000 unadjusted purchase of equipment, restated in terms of dollars of uniform purchasing power at December 31, 1979, is $25,000. The depreciation expense, restated in terms of uniform year-end dollars, is increased to $58,750, and the adjusted net income, including the purchasing power loss on holding net monetary items during 1979 is $31,250.

The unique feature of the adjusted portion of the statement is the deduction of the $17,500 purchasing power gain from holding the long-term note payable through 1979. The following rationale explains why this adjustment is necessary to determine net working capital provided by current operations.

The unadjusted $35,000 long-term mortgage note payable remained unchanged throughout 1979. Hence, it had no effect on unadjusted net working capital during 1979. That same liability, however, is a monetary item that was reported on the statement of purchasing power gains and losses on net monetary items on page 614. The $35,000 amount is included in the first line of that statement, which reads:

	UNADJUSTED	MULTIPLIER	ADJUSTED
Net monetary items on January 1, 1979 ($110,000 QA − $100,000 L)...............	$10,000	150/100	$15,000

The "$100,000 L" designation is composed of the $65,000 accounts payable and other current debts, plus the $35,000 long-term note payable. Had this long-term liability not existed during 1979, that statement of purchasing power gains and losses would have appeared with some abbreviation as shown below:

	UNADJUSTED	MULTIPLIER	ADJUSTED
Net monetary items on January 1, 1979 ($110,000 QA − $65,000 L)..................	$ 45,000	150/100	$ 67,500
Add increase in accounts receivable due to credit sales.......................................	550,000	150/120	687,500
	$595,000		$755,000
Deduct these three items that would remain the same.................................	515,000	150/120	643,750
Net monetary items on December 31, 1979:			
Adjusted......................................			$111,250
Unadjusted	$80,000		80,000
Purchasing power loss from holding net monetary items.............................			$ (31,250)

The $31,250 loss shown above in the absence of the long-term debt, mortgage note payable, is $17,500 larger than that reflected when the long-term monetary item was held by the firm during 1979. Hence, the existence of the long-term note during 1979, as adjusted to uniform year-end dollars, decreased the purchasing power loss that was reflected on the income statement by $17,500, to $13,750. Since the note is long-term, the $17,500 difference must be added back to net income to determine the net working capital provided by current operations. On the other hand, any loss in purchasing power on long-term liabilities or preferred stock would be added back to net income.

Perhaps the most significant observation that can be gleaned from this part of the analysis is that a purchasing power gain accrued to the Tannbark Corp. from holding this liability through 1979. The purchasing power of that financial obligation on January 1, 1979, stated in terms of year-end dollars, was $52,500, as reported on the adjusted balance sheet at January 1, 1979, shown on page 617. Whenever this obligation becomes due for repayment, it must be paid with only $35,000, irrespective of the purchasing power of those dollars at the time of repayment. Hence, in terms of year-end purchasing power, that financial obligation on December 31, 1979, still remains at $35,000, having declined $17,500 from its purchasing power equivalent of $52,500 on January 1, 1979. A corporate treasurer recently commented on this type of financial reality with the following remark: "Go into debt, and let inflation bail you out."

Financial Ratio Analysis. The comparative financial ratios shown on page 621 are derived from the information provided on the income statement and comparative balance sheets presented previously. Only those ratios discussed in Chapter 15 have been calculated for which information is readily available in these two Tannbark Corp. financial documents.

Differences between the unadjusted and adjusted liquidity measures are almost negligible, primarily because the principal impact of inflation is on the noncurrent nomonetary items, such as inventories and plant assets, rather than the current monetary items. The most significant differences that usually arise in this type of comparative financial analysis is in the area of profitability measures. The marked differences reflected in each of the three "return on" ratios result from the effects of inflation on the non-monetary items, particularly plant assets and inventories, elements of which are included in both the numerator and denominator of these particular ratios. Generally, the leverage measures do not reflect large differences between unadjusted and adjusted financial information, except in cases where a firm is very highly leveraged, such as public utilities and commercial banks.

Additional Comments

In short, financial statements that are adjusted to a uniform dollar basis can serve a useful function for both management and other consumers of financial information. Despite weaknesses in the indexing process, the types of statements and analyses previously discussed help focus attention on the impact that movements in the general price level have on the financial position and performance of business organizations. Management should not ignore projected price instability and recent significant changes in the price level during their decision-making activities.

For example, management might well consider increasing the level of debt used by the firm during inflation, in anticipation of repaying that debt with cheaper dollars in the future. This financial strategy is not without its dangers, however, in the event that deflation occurs or a poor financial performance is experienced. On the other hand, investments in buildings, equipment, land, and inventories might be increased, with the hope that increases in the prices of these nonmonetary assets will roughly correspond to increases in the general price level.

	DECEMBER 31, 1979	
	Unadjusted	*Adjusted*
Liquidity measures		
Quick assets	$125,000	$125,000
Quick ratio: $125,000 ÷ $45,000............	2.8	2.8
Current ratio:		
$225,000 ÷ $45,000.........................	5.0	——
$250,000 ÷ $45,000.........................	——	5.6
Net working capital	$180,000	$205,000
Net working capital turnover:		
$\dfrac{\$550,000}{.5(\$105,000 + \$180,000)}$	3.9 times	——
$\dfrac{\$687,500}{.5(\$157,500 + \$205,000)}$	——	3.8 times
Accounts receivable turnover:		
$\dfrac{\$550,000}{.5(\$70,000 + \$75,000)}$	7.6 times	——
$\dfrac{\$687,500}{.5(\$105,000 + \$75,000)}$	——	7.6 times
Inventory turnover:		
$\dfrac{\$300,000}{.5(\$60,000 + \$100,000)}$	3.8 times	——
$\dfrac{\$390,000}{.5(\$90,000 + \$125,000)}$	——	3.6 times
Profitability measures		
Return on average total investment:		
$\dfrac{\$55,000}{.5(\$290,000 + \$325,000)}$	17.9%	——
$\dfrac{\$31,250}{.5(\$435,000 + \$396,250)}$	——	7.5%
Return on average owners' equity:		
$\dfrac{\$55,000}{.5(\$190,000 + \$245,000)}$	25.3%	——
$\dfrac{\$31,250}{.5(\$285,000 + \$316,250)}$	——	10.4%
Return on sales:		
$55,000 ÷ $550,000.........................	10.0%	——
$31,250 ÷ $687,500.........................	——	4.5%
Gross margin percent:		
$250,000 ÷ $550,000	45.5%	——
$297,500 ÷ $687,500	——	43.3%
Leverage measures		
Degree of overall leverage:		
$80,000 ÷ $325,000.........................	24.6%	——
$80,000 ÷ $396,250.........................	——	20.2%
Degree of long-term leverage:		
$35,000 ÷ $280,000.........................	12.5%	——
$35,000 ÷ $351,250.........................	——	10.0%

Management should also direct attention to the firm's dividend policy during inflationary periods. For example, had management of the Tannbark Corp. been furnished only the unadjusted income statement for 1979, a distribution of the entire $55,000 reported net income in the form of cash dividends to stockholders may have been contemplated. But after viewing the adjusted income statement, it would appear that any cash dividend exceeding $31,250 might constitute a distribution of earnings accumulated in prior years, or perhaps even some of the capital originally contributed by the shareholders.

It is difficult to predict which one or combination of approaches presented previously will be adopted ultimately by the accounting profession and the financial community to deal with the effects that inflation is having on financial information. Shortcomings can be identified in any method of adjustment. But it also appears evident that the impact of inflation within the foreseeable future will not slacken.

QUESTIONS

1. Identify, then briefly explain how a relatively few generally accepted accounting principles or concepts reinforce each other to produce distortions in financial statements during periods of substantial price-level changes.

2. "A kilometer is always composed of a thousand meters, and an hour always contains sixty minutes, each of which is sixty seconds long. But the dollar is a constantly changing gauge by which to measure financial and economic value." Explain.

3. Under what conditions would a particular unit of monetary measurement provide undistorted financial information?

4. Identify any exceptions to the concept of realization that have been approved by the accounting profession.

5. Indicate the probable effect on net income, return on sales, and return on total investment from adjusting financial statements to reflect increases in the costs required to replace or replenish inventories that have been sold and plant assets that are being depreciated.

6. In what ways might the failure to recognize the increasing costs required to replace inventories and plant assets mislead management in making decisions and setting policy?

7. Briefly explain how the GNP Implicit Price Deflator or the Consumers Price Index is constructed.

8. Identify the principal strength of lifo inventory costing, and the significant reasons why it is an inadequate method by which to eliminate distortions in financial data caused by changing price levels.

9. Summarize the main advantage and the principal shortcomings in adopting one of the accelerated methods of depreciation as a device to eliminate distortions in financial information caused by inflationary pressures.

10. Identify: (a) the primary characteristic of current replacement costing (CRC); and (b) sources that might provide CRC information on specific assets held by the firm.

11. (a) Explain how restatement could be accomplished in the accounting records in instances where the current replacement cost or market value of inventory and specific plant assets have increased above

their respective historical costs. (b) What impact would such restatements have on the income statement?

12. What is the primary distinction between the current replacement costing (CRC) and net realizable valuation (NRV) approaches to valuing assets?

13. Identify at least four criticisms of the CRC and NRV approaches to dealing with distortions in financial information caused by price-level changes.

14. Point out four attributes of the indexing procedure that could be considered comparative advantages over the CRC and NRV approaches.

15. Identify the outstanding shortcoming of the indexing method of dealing with distortions in financial statements caused by price-level movements.

16. Sharply distinguish between monetary and nonmonetary items, and give examples of each type.

17. What are purchasing power gains and losses?

18. Explain how an individual or a company can experience a loss in purchasing power when its cash balance remains constant over a period of several years.

19. What is meant by the phrase, "The borrower benefits but the lender suffers during inflation."

20. Explain how index numbers can be used to convert a past dollar amount of $1,000 into current dollars, under the following circumstances: (a) the past price level was 100, and the current price level is 120: (b) the past price level was 80, and the current price level is 100.

21. Indicate the effect that each of the following transactions would have on net monetary items — increase, decrease, or no effect:

(a) Sale of merchandise on 60-day credit terms.
(b) Purchase of inventory on 30-day credit terms.
(c) Purchase of a building under a long-term note payable arrangement.
(d) Sale of common stock for cash.
(e) Collection of accounts receivable.
(f) Payment of accounts payable.

22. Indicate how purchasing power gains and losses from holding net monetary items may be reflected in financial statements.

23. How might an analyst verify whether or not the value of a particular nonmonetary item, such as a plot of land, has paralleled the movement in the general price level, as implied on a balance sheet that has been adjusted to uniform dollars of purchasing power?

24. A statement of changes in financial position adjusted to uniform dollars of purchasing power is being prepared. Indicate any adjustment that would be required with respect to a purchasing power loss or gain on bonds payable in order to determine the net working capital provided by current operations. Assume that the purchasing power loss or gain on net monetary items was reflected on the income statement.

25. Given a complete set of unadjusted and adjusted liquidity, profitability, and leverage measures, which type of measures could be expected to reflect the greatest difference between unadjusted and adjusted counterparts? Explain why.

EXERCISES

1. Conventional and "real" profitability. The Whittier Co. purchased merchandise for inventory several months ago at a cost of $70,000. The replacement cost of that inventory at the time of its sale for $110,000 had risen to $85,000.

Required: (a) Determine the net income earned by the firm and the return on sales (rounded to one decimal place) using: (1) conventional accounting procedures; and (2) the current replacement cost framework. Ignore all other expenses. (b) What appears to be the maximum amount of net income that could be distributed in the form of a cash dividend which would permit the firm to maintain a comparable level of productivity and competitiveness in the future?

2. Gross margin measurement: Fifo, Lifo, CRC. The inventories on December 31, 1979 and 1980 consisted of 20,000 units and 25,000 units, respectively. Total purchases during the fiscal year ended December 31, 1980, amount to 405,000 units costing $810,000, or $2 per unit. The cost of the inventory at the end of 1979 would have been $1.80 per unit using fifo inventory costing, and $1.20 using lifo costing. The per unit cost at which the inventory items could have been replaced on December 31, 1980, was $2.30. All units sold during 1980 were at an average unit price of $3.

Required: Calculate the gross margin and gross margin percent for 1980, and the inventory at the end of 1980 that would be reported under the following assumptions: (a) Fifo inventory costing; (b) Lifo inventory costing; and (c) The current replacement costing framework.

3. Methods of depreciation. Machinery and equipment costing $1,500,000 were purchased new at the beginning of 1977. These assets had an expected life of 5 years, with zero salvage value estimated. The cost of comparable new plant assets had risen to $2,000,000 by the end of 1979. Straight-line depreciation was used throughout the firm but management was beginning to wonder if it would have been wiser to have converted to an accelerated depreciation method several years ago.

Required: (a) Compute the depreciation expense that would be recorded in each of the 5 fiscal years ended December 31, 1977 through 1981 for these plant assets, using straight-line and sum-of-the-years-digits methods of depreciation under the conventional accounting framework. (b) Assuming that the current replacement cost of these plant assets would not increase further in the near future, calculate the depreciation expense that would be recorded in each of the years 1979, 1980, and 1981, using straight-line depreciation under the current replacement costing framework of accounting. (c) What might the above comparative analysis suggest to management with respect to establishing prices at which it sells its merchandise?

4. Impact of inflation on monetary items. Agnes Thornton purchased an annuity from an insurance company several years ago which pays a fixed sum of $9,000 annually. At the same time, an additional investment of $160,000 in railroad and utility bonds from funds remaining in her husband's estate provided her an additional constant annual income of

$12,800. The annuity and bonds were obtained when the general price level was 110. The current price index is 160.

Required: (a) How much income must Thornton receive annually from her investments to equal the purchasing power of the income received when the annuity and bonds were purchased? Round answer to the nearest dollar. (b) Determine the purchasing power loss incurred by Thornton from holding the corporate bonds. Round answer to the nearest dollar, and ignore the effect of annual interest income.

5. Portfolio containing monetary and nonmonetary investments. The Scranton family established a fund, the income from which was to be used for philanthropic purposes, when the general price level was at 80. The fund consisted of the following investments at the time it was created:

Common stock, 10,000 shares	$ 680,000
Corporate bonds	250,000
Real estate holdings	420,000
Total	$1,350,000

The common stock is currently trading at $96 per share, and the real estate has recently been appraised at $830,000. The bonds have not changed in value since the date of purchase. The current general price-level index is 140.

Required: (a) Compute the purchasing power of the fund at the time of its creation expressed in terms of the current general price index. (b) Compute the current market value of the fund. (c) How much purchasing power appears to have been lost since the fund was created?

6. Effect of transactions on net monetary items. Several transactions that occurred in the Eberle Corp. during a recent year are described below:

(1) Total sales for the year amounted to $800,000, of which 90% were under 30-day credit terms, and the remainder on cash-and-carry terms.

(2) Cost of goods sold for the year totaled $540,000.

(3) Credit sales totaling $640,000 were collected during the year.

(4) Inventory purchased for cash during the year totaled $465,000.

(5) A large piece of equipment costing $200,000 was purchased under the following terms: a 20% cash down payment; a $100,000 short-term note payable; and the balance due under a 3-year mortgage note payable.

(6) Rent totaling $16,000 for the ensuing year was paid in advance and immediately capitalized.

(7) A $40,000 short-term note was paid off at the bank.

Required: Indicate the effect of each transaction on net monetary items during the year using the following format:

	EFFECT ON NET MONETARY ITEMS		
TRANSACTION	*Increase*	*Decrease*	*None*

7. Purchasing power gains and losses on net monetary items. The Quonset Corp. was created on January 1, 1979, with the issuance of 20,000 shares of $10 par value common stock for $200,000 cash. Equipment and machinery costing $160,000 were purchased with a $40,000 cash down payment with the balance due in three years under a mortgage-note payable arrangement. These two transactions occurred when the price-level index was 100.

The company purchased $240,000 of merchandise under 30-day credit terms during 1979 when the price index was 120. Eighty percent of this merchandise was sold under 45-day credit terms for $300,000 when the price-level index was 120. Operating expenses, other than depreciation, totaling $80,000 were incurred and paid when the price index was 125. The unpaid accounts payable on December 31, 1979, that were associated with credit purchases of inventory totaled $60,000. The price index at the end of 1979 was 140.

Required: Prepare a statement of purchasing power gains and losses on net monetary items for the fiscal year ended December 31, 1979.

8. Conversion of ending balance sheet. The unadjusted balance sheet shown below was prepared using conventional accounting principles and concepts.

Milgram Enterprises, Inc.
Balance Sheet
December 31, 1980

Assets		Equities	
Current assets:		**Current liabilities:**	
Cash............................	$ 40,000	Notes payable	$ 30,000
Marketable debt securities	12,000	Accounts payable...........	60,000
Accounts receivable	120,000	Income tax payable	20,000
Inventory	80,000	Total current liabilities..	$110,000
Total current assets	$252,000	**Long-term liabilities:**	
Plant assets:		Mortgage note payable ...	$120,000
Buildings.....................	$ 90,000	**Owners' equity:**	
Less accumulated		Common stock................	$140,000
depreciation —		Premium on common stock .	12,000
buildings..................	(30,000)	Retained earnings..........	40,000
Equipment....................	220,000	Total owners' equity	$192,000
Less accumulated			
depreciation —			
equipment.................	(110,000)		
Total plant assets	$170,000		
Total assets......................	$422,000	Total equities..................	$422,000

The costs associated with the fifo inventory balance were incurred when the general price index was 148. All buildings were purchased when the price-level index was 110; and the equipment was obtained at a price level of 114. The mortgage note payable was incurred to help finance the equipment. All common stock was sold for $162,000 when the general price index was 100. The retained earnings of $40,000 was composed of two segments: (1) $30,000 was attributable to earnings when the average price index was 120; and (2) the $10,000 net income earned during the fiscal year ended December 31, 1980, when adjusted to the price level of 160 that existed at the end of 1980 (including the purchasing power loss on net monetary items), reflected a net loss of $13,055.

Required: Prepare an adjusted balance sheet to reflect uniform dollars of purchasing power as of December 31, 1980. Round all computations to the nearest dollar.

9. Net working capital analysis. Unadjusted and adjusted income statements for the fiscal year ended December 31, 1981, are shown below for the Kennamart Corp.

Kennamart Corp.
Comparative Income Statement
For the Year Ended December 31, 1981

	Unadjusted		Adjusted to the Price Level at December 31, 1981	
Sales		$980,000		$980,000
Cost of goods sold		620,000		635,000
Gross margin....................		$360,000		$345,000
Expenses:				
Administrative and marketing ...	$180,000		$190,000	
Income tax..........................	60,000		60,000	
Depreciation.......................	40,000	280,000	90,000	340,000
Net income before purchasing power (loss) on net monetary items.....................		$ 80,000		$ 5,000
Purchasing power (loss) on net monetary items		——		(12,000)
Net income (loss).....................		$ 80,000		$ (7,000)

A purchasing power gain of $5,000 on a long-term mortgage note payable was included in the purchasing power loss of $12,000 reported above. No transactions occurred during the year which affected net working capital other than those shown on the statement.

Required: Prepare a comparative statement of changes in financial position (unadjusted and adjusted) — net working capital basis for the fiscal year ended December 31, 1981.

PROBLEMS

16-1. Determination of purchasing power gains and losses. Net monetary items in the Farnsworth Corp. on July 1, 1979, totaled $240,000; and the general price-level index on that same date was 100. A summary description of transactions that occurred during the fiscal year ended June 30, 1980, is presented below and on the following page:

   (a) Credit purchases of inventory amounted to $800,000, 60% of which were made at an average price index of 120, and the remainder at an index of 125.

(b) Total credit sales amounted to $1,640,000, of which $800,000 were made at an average index of 120, and the remainder at 140. Cost of goods sold consistently amounted to 70% of sales.

(c) Three thousand shares of $10 par value common stock were purchased for the treasury at $33,000 when the price index was 110.

(d) Accounts receivable totaling $1,400,000 were collected at an average price index of 125.

(e) Invoices for credit purchases of inventory totaling $650,000 were paid at an average price index of 125.

(f) A $60,000 short-term note payable was repaid when the price index was 110.

(g) A 4-year mortgage note payable financed the purchase of $140,000 of equipment when the price index was 140.

(h) Various operating expenses totaling $375,000 were paid at an average price index of 125.

(i) Depreciation expense recognized during the year totaled $60,000 on plant assets that had been purchased when the price index was 80.

(j) Income tax expense totaled $25,000, of which none had been paid by June 30, 1980. The tax was accrued on June 30, 1980, when the price level was 150.

(k) Cash dividends declared on June 30, 1980, but which remained unpaid at year-end, totaled $20,000.

Required: (1) Prepare a summary indicating the effect on net monetary items of each transaction. Use the following format:

	EFFECT ON NET MONETARY ITEMS		
TRANSACTION	*Increase*	*Decrease*	*None*

(2) Prepare a schedule to reflect the purchasing power gain or loss incurred on net monetary items for the fiscal year ended June 30, 1980.

16-2. Comparative income statement. The Magnum Corp. income statement that was prepared using conventional accounting principles and concepts for the fiscal year ended September 30, 1980, is shown at the top of page 629.

Equipment costing $75,000 was acquired at the beginning of the fiscal year when the price index was 100. The equipment had an expected life of 5 years, with zero salvage value estimated. An itemization of the merchandise available for sale during the year is shown below:

	AMOUNT	PRICE INDEX
Inventory on September 30, 1979	$ 56,000	100
Purchases	144,000	120
Purchases	180,000	150

Fifo inventory costing was used in the company. Had lifo inventory costing been used, the cost of goods sold would have totaled $342,000. Wages and salaries of $30,000 were incurred when the price index was at 120, and an additional $52,000 of employee compensation was incurred at a price index of 150.

All items on the income statement (with the exception of cost of goods sold, wages and salaries, and depreciation) were recorded when

Magnum Corp.
Income Statement
For the Year Ended September 30, 1980

Sales..		$580,000
Cost of goods sold.................................		317,000
Gross margin................................		$263,000
Expenses:		
Wages and salaries...........................	$82,000	
Depreciation	15,000	
Advertising	7,000	
Utilities...	6,000	
Rent..	3,000	113,000
Income before income tax....................		$150,000
Income tax expense		70,000
Net income		$ 80,000

the price index was 150, the same index which existed during the last half of the fiscal year and on September 30, 1980.

Required: (1) Prepare a revised income statement using lifo inventory costing and sum-of-the-years-digits depreciation.

(2) Prepare an income statement in uniform dollars of purchasing power at a price index of 150. Assume fifo inventory costing and straight-line depreciation.

16-3. Price-level adjusted income statements and dividend policy. A conventionally prepared income statement for the past three years is shown below in summary form for Hinchcliffe, Inc.:

Hinchcliffe, Inc.
Comparative Income Statement
For the Years Ended December 31, 1980, 1979, and 1978

	1980	1979	1978
Sales	$450,000	$320,000	$240,000
Cost of goods sold	$270,000	$180,000	$130,000
Other expenses......................	75,000	60,000	54,000
Depreciation expense	30,000	30,000	20,000
Total expenses..............................	$375,000	$270,000	$204,000
Net income......................................	$ 75,000	$ 50,000	$ 36,000
Dividends..	$ 45,000	$ 30,000	$ 20,000

All amounts shown on the 1978 income statement are stated in dollars at a price index of 100.

On the 1979 income statement, $20,000 of depreciation expense is in dollars at the price index of 100, and the cost of goods sold includes $120,000 of merchandise acquired when the price index was 100. All other amounts on the 1979 statement are in dollars at the price index of 120.

On the 1980 income statement, depreciation expense is on the same price index basis as stated for 1979. Cost of goods sold in 1980 includes $180,000 of merchandise acquired when the price index was 120. All other amounts on the 1980 statement are in dollars at a price index of 150.

Dividends declared and paid in 1978 are on a price index basis of 100; in 1979, they are on an index basis of 120; and 150 in 1980. The price index is 150 on December 31, 1980.

Required: (1) Prepare comparative income statements for 1978, 1979, and 1980 stated in purchasing power dollars at a price index of 150.

(2) A Board of Directors' policy required that no more than 60% of the net income each year could be distributed in the form of cash dividends. Based on dollars having a uniform purchasing power of 150, to what extent was this policy adhered to in each of the three years? Show calculations.

16-4. Preparation of financial statements for a new business. The Cranbrook Corp. was created on January 1, 1979, when the price index was 100, upon the sale of its common stock for $900,000 cash. Additional transactions that occurred during the first year of operations ended December 31, 1979, are summarized below:

(a) Equipment costing $850,000 was purchased and financed under a 5-year mortgage note payable arrangement when the price index was 100.

(b) Merchandise costing $420,000 was purchased for inventory on 30-day credit terms at an average price index of 120.

(c) Sales of $910,000 were made on 40-day credit terms at an average price index of 130. Merchandise costing $360,000 was matched against these sales as cost of goods sold.

(d) Various operating expenses totaling $270,000 were incurred and paid for when the price index was 135.

(e) Depreciation expense of $85,000 was recognized.

(f) Cash of $570,000 was collected on accounts receivable, and cash payments of $400,000 were made on the $420,000 accounts payable.

(g) Income tax expense of $90,000 was recognized and accrued as a liability on December 31, 1979.

The price index at the end of the year was 140.

Required: (1) Determine the purchasing power gains or losses for the first year of operations.

(2) Prepare a comparative income statement, similar to that on page 615, for the initial year of operations, using unadjusted amounts and amounts adjusted to the price index of 140.

(3) Prepare a comparative balance sheet at December 31, 1979, showing unadjusted amounts and amounts adjusted to an index of 140.

16-5. Preparation of adjusted financial statements. A conventionally prepared comparative balance sheet at December 31, 1979 and 1980, and an income statement for 1980 are shown on page 631. All items reflected on

Baumbecker Corp.
Comparative Balance Sheet
December 31, 1980 and 1979

Assets	1980	1979
Cash	$ 357,500	$300,000
Accounts receivable	327,500	150,000
Inventories (fifo costing)	120,000	180,000
Equipment	405,000	360,000
Accumulated depreciation	(94,500)	(60,000)
Total assets	$1,115,500	$930,000
Equities		
Accounts payable	$ 40,000	$ 60,000
Bonds payable	120,000	120,000
Common stock	50,000	50,000
Retained earnings	905,500	700,000
Total equities	$1,115,500	$930,000

Baumbecker Corp.
Income Statement
For the Year Ended December 31, 1980

Sales (all on 30-day credit terms)		$1,030,000
Cost of goods sold	$630,000	
Operating expenses including income tax	160,000	
Depreciation expense	34,500	824,500
Net income		$ 205,500

the balance sheet at December 31, 1979, are stated at a general price index of 120, the price level that existed on that date. The index on December 31, 1980, was 180.

Depreciation expense of $30,000 was recognized during 1980 on equipment shown on the balance sheet at December 31, 1979. The remaining depreciation expense was recorded on equipment purchased in 1980. Other data relevant to 1980 operations are shown below:

	PRICE INDEX	AMOUNT
Sales	150	$190,000
Sales	180	840,000
Purchases	150	450,000
Purchases	180	120,000
Equipment	150	45,000
Operating expenses	180	160,000

All inventory items were purchased under 30-day credit arrangements.

Required: (1) Compute the gain or loss in purchasing power for 1980.
(2) Prepare a comparative income statement (unadjusted and adjusted) for 1980.
(3) Prepare a comparative balance sheet (unadjusted and adjusted) at December 31, 1979 and 1980.

16-6. Financial statement analysis. Unadjusted and adjusted financial statements pertaining to the fiscal year ended December 31, 1980, for the Elmira Utilities Company are shown below and on page 633. All adjusted data are expressed in uniform dollars of purchasing power that existed on December 31, 1980.

Elmira Utilities Company
Comparative Income Statement
For the Year Ended December 31, 1980

	UNADJUSTED		ADJUSTED	
Sales (on 30-day credit terms)		$1,090,100		$1,098,600
Expenses:				
Operating expenses	$283,200		$286,400	
Depreciation	194,300		249,700	
Advertising and marketing	122,700		123,700	
General and administrative.............	105,500		106,900	
Interest.....................................	58,700	764,400	59,200	825,900
Income before income tax		$ 325,700		$ 272,700
Income tax expense.........................		145,800		146,300
Net income before purchasing power loss on net monetary items.		$ 179,900		$ 126,400
Purchasing power (loss on net monetary items...		—		(1,300)
Net income		$ 179,900		$ 125,100
Cash dividend declared and paid on preferred stock		$ 18,300		$ 18,500
Cash dividend declared and paid on common stock..............................		$ 7,200		$ 7,500

Required: (1) Using the following format, calculate the financial measures at December 31, 1980. Round all ratios and percentages to one decimal place.

	UNADJUSTED	ADJUSTED
Liquidity measures		
(a) Quick assets		
(b) Quick ratio		
(c) Current ratio....................................		
(d) Net working capital		
(e) Net working capital turnover (at year-end only).....................................		
(f) Accounts receivable turnover (at year-end only).....................................		
Profitability measures		
(g) Return on total investment (at year-end only)...		
(h) Return on owners' equity (at year-end only)...		
(i) Return on common stock equity (at year-end only).................................		
(j) Return on sales.................................		

Leverage measures

    (k) Degree of overall leverage ....

    (l) Degree of long-term leverage..............

    (m) Times interest earned........................

    (n) Times fixed charges earned................

(2) Summarize your conclusions with respect to the analysis.

Elmira Utilities Company
Comparative Balance Sheet
December 31, 1980

	UNADJUSTED	ADJUSTED
Assets		
Current assets:		
Cash and marketable debt securities...............	$ 375,300	$ 375,300
Accounts receivable (less allowance)	122,000	122,000
Inventories	65,200	66,700
Total current assets	$ 562,500	$ 564,000
Plant assets:		
Buildings and equipment.............................	$3,425,000	$4,337,200
Less accumulated depreciation	(1,059,900)	(1,435,400)
Total plant assets	$2,365,100	$2,901,800
Total assets...	$2,927,600	$3,465,800
Equities		
Current liabilities:		
Notes Payable..	$ 89,900	$ 89,900
Accounts payable......................................	95,100	95,100
Taxes payable..	84,200	84,200
Total current liabilities...............................	$ 269,200	$ 269,200
Long-term liabilities:		
Notes payable	$ 186,300	$ 186,300
Bonds payable (issued at par).......................	1,271,600	1,271,600
Total long-term liabilities	$1,457,900	$1,457,900
Owners' equity:		
Preferred stock, $100 par, cumulative	$ 173,900	$ 173,900
Common stock, no par, no stated value............	416,900	634,600
Retained earnings......................................	609,700	930,200
Total owners' equity	$1,200,500	$1,738,700
Total equities..	$2,927,600	$3,465,800

DECISION CASE

16-I. **Inflation's impact on taxation, dividend, and pricing policies.**
The Menomic Corp. was created on January 1, 1979 as a wholesale dis-

tributorship. Transactions that occurred during its first fiscal year of operations ended December 31, 1979, are summarized below:

(a) Twenty thousand shares of $10 par value common stock were sold at par to several close business associates on January 1, 1979, when the general price index was 100.

(b) Various items of warehousing, delivery, and office equipment were purchased for $150,000 under a 3-year mortgage note payable arrangement, also at a price index of 100. No salvage value was estimated on these pieces of equipment at the end of their 5-year useful lives.

(c) Data with respect to credit purchases and credit sales of merchandise, and payments for other operating expenses are furnished below:

	TOTAL AMOUNT	PRICE INDEX
Purchases (5,000 units at $16 per unit)........	$ 80,000	110
Purchases (25,000 units at $20 per unit)	500,000	120
Sales (10,000 units at $30 per unit).............	300,000	120
Sales (15,000 units at $31 per unit).............	465,000	130
Operating expenses (excluding depreciation and income tax)	165,000	120

All purchases of inventory items were made prior to any sales being generated.

(d) The income tax rate was 50% on taxable income as derived using conventional accounting principles and concepts, without adjustments for price-level movements. The tax accrual was recorded when the price-level index was 130; and this accrual was not due for payment until the first half of 1980.

The top managers of Menomic Corp. were deliberating at the end of 1979 which method of inventory costing and depreciation to adopt. Also under consideration were two additional items: (i) the firm's future pricing policy for merchandise; and (ii) the size of the cash dividend to declare.

Required:

(1) Prepare an unadjusted income statement for the fiscal year ended December 31, 1979 under each of the following two alternatives: (A) using fifo inventory costing and straight-line depreciation; and (B) using lifo costing and sum-of-the-years-digit depreciation.

(2) Determine the purchasing power gain or loss on net monetary items in 1979 for each of alternatives A and B outlined in item (1) above. Round all calculations to the nearest dollar.

(3) Prepare an income statement for 1979 expressed in dollars of uniform purchasing power at the 130 price index for each of alternatives A and B. Round all calculations to the nearest dollar.

(4) Based on the foregoing analyses, indicate the recommendations you would make to the firm's top management with respect to:
  (a) The adoption of alternative A (fifo, straight-line), or B (lifo, SYD).
  (b) The amount of cash dividends to distribute.
  (c) The firm's future pricing policy.

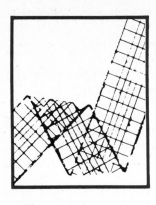

Appendix
Future Value and Present Value Tables

Table 1

FUTURE VALUE OF $1

$$F_n = P(1 + i)^n$$

Periods (n)	2%	2½%	3%	4%	5%	6%	8%	10%	12%	Periods (n)
1	1.020	1.025	1.030	1.040	1.050	1.060	1.080	1.100	1.120	1
2	1.040	1.051	1.061	1.082	1.103	1.124	1.166	1.210	1.254	2
3	1.061	1.077	1.093	1.125	1.158	1.191	1.260	1.331	1.405	3
4	1.082	1.104	1.126	1.170	1.216	1.262	1.360	1.464	1.574	4
5	1.104	1.131	1.159	1.217	1.276	1.338	1.469	1.611	1.762	5
6	1.126	1.160	1.194	1.265	1.340	1.419	1.587	1.772	1.974	6
7	1.149	1.189	1.230	1.316	1.407	1.504	1.714	1.949	2.211	7
8	1.172	1.218	1.267	1.369	1.477	1.594	1.851	2.144	2.476	8
9	1.195	1.249	1.305	1.423	1.551	1.689	1.999	2.358	2.773	9
10	1.219	1.280	1.344	1.480	1.629	1.791	2.159	2.594	3.106	10
11	1.243	1.312	1.384	1.539	1.710	1.898	2.332	2.853	3.479	11
12	1.268	1.345	1.426	1.601	1.796	2.012	2.518	3.138	3.896	12
13	1.294	1.379	1.469	1.665	1.886	2.133	2.720	3.452	4.364	13
14	1.319	1.413	1.513	1.732	1.980	2.261	2.937	3.797	4.887	14
15	1.346	1.448	1.558	1.801	2.079	2.397	3.172	4.177	5.474	15
16	1.373	1.485	1.605	1.873	2.183	2.540	3.426	4.595	6.130	16
17	1.400	1.522	1.653	1.948	2.292	2.693	3.700	5.054	6.866	17
18	1.428	1.560	1.702	2.026	2.407	2.854	3.996	5.560	7.690	18
19	1.457	1.599	1.754	2.107	2.527	3.026	4.316	6.116	8.613	19
20	1.486	1.639	1.806	2.191	2.653	3.207	4.661	6.727	9.646	20
21	1.516	1.680	1.860	2.279	2.786	3.400	5.034	7.400	10.804	21
22	1.546	1.722	1.916	2.370	2.925	3.604	5.437	8.140	12.100	22
23	1.577	1.765	1.974	2.465	3.072	3.820	5.871	8.954	13.552	23
24	1.608	1.809	2.033	2.563	3.225	4.049	6.341	9.850	15.179	24
25	1.641	1.854	2.094	2.666	3.386	4.292	6.848	10.835	17.000	25
26	1.673	1.900	2.157	2.772	3.556	4.549	7.396	11.918	19.040	26
27	1.707	1.948	2.221	2.883	3.733	4.822	7.988	13.110	21.325	27
28	1.741	1.996	2.288	2.999	3.920	5.112	8.627	14.421	23.884	28
29	1.776	2.046	2.357	3.119	4.116	5.418	9.317	15.863	26.750	29
30	1.811	2.098	2.427	3.243	4.322	5.743	10.063	17.449	29.960	30
35	2.000	2.373	2.814	3.946	5.516	7.686	14.785	28.102	52.800	35
40	2.208	2.685	3.262	4.801	7.040	10.286	21.725	45.259	93.051	40
45	2.438	3.038	3.782	5.841	8.985	13.765	31.920	72.890	163.988	45
50	2.692	3.437	4.384	7.107	11.467	18.420	46.902	117.391	289.002	50

ANNUITY

Table 2

FUTURE VALUE OF $1 RECEIVED (OR PAID) AT THE END OF A PERIOD FOR n PERIODS*

$$F = A\left[\frac{(1 + i)^n - 1}{i}\right]$$

sum of table 1

*To determine the future value of $1 received (or paid) at the beginning of a period for n periods, use the factor shown for one *more* period and *subtract* 1.000.

Periods (n)	2%	2½%	3%	4%	5%	6%	8%	10%	12%	Periods (n)
1	1.000	1.000	1.000	1.000	1.000	1.000	1.000	1.000	1.000	1
2	2.020	2.025	2.030	2.040	2.050	2.060	2.080	2.100	2.120	2
3	3.060	3.076	3.091	3.122	3.153	3.184	3.246	3.310	3.374	3
4	4.122	4.153	4.184	4.246	4.310	4.375	4.506	4.641	4.779	4
5	5.204	5.256	5.309	5.416	5.526	5.637	5.867	6.105	6.353	5
6	6.308	6.388	6.468	6.633	6.802	6.975	7.336	7.716	8.115	6
7	7.434	7.547	7.662	7.898	8.142	8.394	8.923	9.487	10.089	7
8	8.583	8.736	8.892	9.214	9.549	9.897	10.637	11.436	12.300	8
9	9.755	9.955	10.159	10.583	11.027	11.491	12.488	13.579	14.776	9
10	10.950	11.203	11.464	12.006	12.578	13.181	14.487	15.937	17.549	10
11	12.169	12.483	12.808	13.486	14.207	14.972	16.645	18.531	20.655	11
12	13.412	13.796	14.192	15.026	15.917	16.870	18.977	21.384	24.133	12
13	14.680	15.140	15.618	16.627	17.713	18.882	21.495	24.523	28.029	13
14	15.974	16.519	17.086	18.292	19.599	21.015	24.215	27.975	32.393	14
15	17.293	17.932	18.599	20.024	21.579	23.276	27.152	31.772	37.280	15
16	18.639	19.380	20.157	21.825	23.657	25.673	30.324	35.950	42.753	16
17	20.012	20.865	21.762	23.698	25.840	28.213	33.750	40.545	48.884	17
18	21.412	22.386	23.414	25.645	28.132	30.906	37.450	45.599	55.750	18
19	22.841	23.946	25.117	27.671	30.539	33.760	41.446	51.159	63.440	19
20	24.297	25.545	26.870	29.778	33.066	36.786	45.762	57.275	72.052	20
21	25.783	27.183	28.676	31.969	35.719	39.993	50.423	64.002	81.699	21
22	27.299	28.863	30.537	34.248	38.505	43.392	55.457	71.403	92.503	22
23	28.845	30.584	32.453	36.618	41.430	46.996	60.893	79.543	104.603	23
24	30.422	32.349	34.426	39.083	44.502	50.816	66.765	88.498	118.155	24
25	32.030	34.158	36.459	41.646	47.727	54.865	73.106	98.347	133.339	25
26	33.671	36.012	38.553	44.312	51.113	59.156	79.954	109.182	150.334	26
27	35.344	37.912	40.710	47.084	54.669	63.706	87.351	121.100	169.374	27
28	37.051	39.860	42.931	49.968	58.403	68.528	95.339	134.210	190.699	28
29	38.792	41.856	45.219	52.966	62.323	73.640	103.966	148.631	214.583	29
30	40.568	43.903	47.575	56.085	66.439	79.058	113.283	164.494	241.333	30
35	49.994	54.928	60.462	73.652	90.320	111.435	172.317	271.024	431.663	35
40	60.402	67.403	75.401	95.026	120.800	154.762	259.057	442.593	767.091	40
45	71.893	81.516	92.720	121.029	159.700	212.744	386.506	718.905	1358.230	45
50	84.579	97.484	112.797	152.667	209.348	290.336	573.770	1163.909	2400.018	50

(Annually)

Table 3

PRESENT VALUE OF $1

$$P = \frac{F_n}{(1 + i)^n}$$

lump
sum

Periods (n)	1%	1½%	2%	2½%	3%	3½%	4%	5%	6%	Periods (n)
1	0.990	0.985	0.980	0.976	0.971	0.966	0.962	0.952	0.943	1
2	0.980	0.971	0.961	0.952	0.943	0.934	0.925	0.907	0.890	2
3	0.971	0.956	0.942	0.929	0.915	0.902	0.889	0.864	0.840	3
4	0.961	0.942	0.924	0.906	0.888	0.871	0.855	0.823	0.792	4
5	0.951	0.928	0.906	0.884	0.863	0.842	0.822	0.784	0.747	5
6	0.942	0.915	0.888	0.862	0.837	0.814	0.790	0.746	0.705	6
7	0.933	0.901	0.871	0.841	0.813	0.786	0.760	0.711	0.665	7
8	0.923	0.888	0.853	0.821	0.789	0.759	0.731	0.677	0.627	8
9	0.914	0.875	0.837	0.801	0.766	0.734	0.703	0.645	0.592	9
10	0.905	0.862	0.820	0.781	0.744	0.709	0.676	0.614	0.558	10
11	0.896	0.849	0.804	0.762	0.722	0.685	0.650	0.585	0.527	11
12	0.887	0.836	0.788	0.744	0.701	0.662	0.625	0.557	0.497	12
13	0.879	0.824	0.773	0.725	0.681	0.639	0.601	0.530	0.469	13
14	0.870	0.812	0.758	0.708	0.661	0.618	0.577	0.505	0.442	14
15	0.861	0.800	0.743	0.690	0.642	0.597	0.555	0.481	0.417	15
16	0.853	0.788	0.728	0.674	0.623	0.577	0.534	0.458	0.394	16
17	0.844	0.776	0.714	0.657	0.605	0.557	0.513	0.436	0.371	17
18	0.836	0.765	0.700	0.641	0.587	0.538	0.494	0.416	0.350	18
19	0.828	0.754	0.686	0.626	0.570	0.520	0.475	0.396	0.331	19
20	0.820	0.742	0.673	0.610	0.554	0.503	0.456	0.377	0.312	20
21	0.811	0.731	0.660	0.595	0.538	0.486	0.439	0.359	0.294	21
22	0.803	0.721	0.647	0.581	0.522	0.469	0.422	0.342	0.278	22
23	0.795	0.710	0.634	0.566	0.507	0.453	0.406	0.326	0.262	23
24	0.788	0.700	0.622	0.553	0.492	0.438	0.390	0.310	0.247	24
25	0.780	0.689	0.610	0.539	0.478	0.423	0.375	0.295	0.233	25
26	0.772	0.679	0.598	0.526	0.464	0.409	0.361	0.281	0.220	26
27	0.764	0.669	0.586	0.513	0.450	0.395	0.347	0.268	0.207	27
28	0.757	0.659	0.574	0.501	0.437	0.382	0.333	0.255	0.196	28
29	0.749	0.649	0.563	0.489	0.424	0.369	0.321	0.243	0.185	29
30	0.742	0.640	0.552	0.477	0.412	0.356	0.308	0.231	0.174	30
35	0.706	0.594	0.500	0.421	0.355	0.300	0.253	0.181	0.130	35
40	0.672	0.551	0.453	0.372	0.307	0.253	0.208	0.142	0.097	40
45	0.639	0.512	0.410	0.329	0.264	0.213	0.171	0.111	0.073	45
50	0.608	0.475	0.372	0.291	0.228	0.179	0.141	0.087	0.054	50

Table 3 (Continued)

PRESENT VALUE OF $1

$$P = \frac{F_n}{(1 + i)^n}$$

Periods (n)	7%	8%	10%	12%	14%	15%	16%	18%	20%	Periods (n)
1	0.935	0.926	0.909	0.893	0.877	0.870	0.862	0.847	0.833	1
2	0.873	0.857	0.826	0.797	0.769	0.756	0.743	0.718	0.694	2
3	0.816	0.794	0.751	0.712	0.675	0.658	0.641	0.609	0.579	3
4	0.763	0.735	0.683	0.636	0.592	0.572	0.552	0.516	0.482	4
5	0.713	0.681	0.621	0.567	0.519	0.497	0.476	0.437	0.402	5
6	0.666	0.630	0.564	0.507	0.456	0.432	0.410	0.370	0.335	6
7	0.623	0.583	0.513	0.452	0.400	0.376	0.354	0.314	0.279	7
8	0.582	0.540	0.467	0.404	0.351	0.327	0.305	0.266	0.233	8
9	0.544	0.500	0.424	0.361	0.308	0.284	0.263	0.225	0.194	9
10	0.508	0.463	0.386	0.322	0.270	0.247	0.227	0.191	0.162	10
11	0.475	0.429	0.350	0.287	0.237	0.215	0.195	0.162	0.135	11
12	0.444	0.397	0.319	0.257	0.208	0.187	0.168	0.137	0.112	12
13	0.415	0.368	0.290	0.229	0.182	0.163	0.145	0.116	0.093	13
14	0.388	0.340	0.263	0.205	0.160	0.141	0.125	0.099	0.078	14
15	0.362	0.315	0.239	0.183	0.140	0.123	0.108	0.084	0.065	15
16	0.339	0.292	0.218	0.163	0.123	0.107	0.093	0.071	0.054	16
17	0.317	0.270	0.198	0.146	0.108	0.093	0.080	0.060	0.045	17
18	0.296	0.250	0.180	0.130	0.095	0.081	0.069	0.051	0.038	18
19	0.277	0.232	0.164	0.116	0.083	0.070	0.060	0.043	0.031	19
20	0.258	0.215	0.149	0.104	0.073	0.061	0.051	0.037	0.026	20
21	0.242	0.199	0.135	0.093	0.064	0.053	0.044	0.031	0.022	21
22	0.226	0.184	0.123	0.083	0.056	0.046	0.038	0.026	0.018	22
23	0.211	0.170	0.112	0.074	0.049	0.040	0.033	0.022	0.015	23
24	0.197	0.158	0.102	0.066	0.043	0.035	0.028	0.019	0.013	24
25	0.184	0.146	0.092	0.059	0.038	0.030	0.024	0.016	0.010	25
26	0.172	0.135	0.084	0.053	0.033	0.026	0.021	0.014	0.009	26
27	0.161	0.125	0.076	0.047	0.029	0.023	0.018	0.011	0.007	27
28	0.150	0.116	0.069	0.042	0.026	0.020	0.016	0.010	0.006	28
29	0.141	0.107	0.063	0.037	0.022	0.017	0.014	0.008	0.005	29
30	0.131	0.099	0.057	0.033	0.020	0.015	0.012	0.007	0.004	30
35	0.094	0.068	0.036	0.019	0.010	0.008	0.006	0.003	0.002	35
40	0.067	0.046	0.022	0.011	0.005	0.004	0.003	0.001	0.001	40
45	0.048	0.031	0.014	0.006	0.003	0.002	0.001	0.001	——	45
50	0.034	0.021	0.009	0.003	0.001	0.001	0.001	——	——	50

Table 3 (Concluded)

PRESENT VALUE OF $1

$$P = \frac{F_n}{(1 + i)^n}$$

Periods (n)	22%	24%	25%	26%	28%	30%	35%	40%	45%	50%	Periods (n)
1	0.820	0.806	0.800	0.794	0.781	0.769	0.741	0.714	0.690	0.667	1
2	0.672	0.650	0.640	0.630	0.610	0.592	0.549	0.510	0.476	0.444	2
3	0.551	0.524	0.512	0.500	0.477	0.455	0.406	0.364	0.328	0.296	3
4	0.451	0.423	0.410	0.397	0.373	0.350	0.301	0.260	0.226	0.198	4
5	0.370	0.341	0.328	0.315	0.291	0.269	0.223	0.186	0.156	0.132	5
6	0.303	0.275	0.262	0.250	0.227	0.207	0.165	0.133	0.108	0.088	6
7	0.249	0.222	0.210	0.198	0.178	0.159	0.122	0.095	0.074	0.059	7
8	0.204	0.179	0.168	0.157	0.139	0.123	0.091	0.068	0.051	0.039	8
9	0.167	0.144	0.134	0.125	0.108	0.094	0.067	0.048	0.035	0.026	9
10	0.137	0.116	0.107	0.099	0.085	0.073	0.050	0.035	0.024	0.017	10
11	0.112	0.094	0.086	0.079	0.066	0.056	0.037	0.025	0.017	0.012	11
12	0.092	0.076	0.069	0.062	0.052	0.043	0.027	0.018	0.012	0.008	12
13	0.075	0.061	0.055	0.050	0.040	0.033	0.020	0.013	0.008	0.005	13
14	0.062	0.049	0.044	0.039	0.032	0.025	0.015	0.009	0.006	0.003	14
15	0.051	0.040	0.035	0.031	0.025	0.020	0.011	0.006	0.004	0.002	15
16	0.042	0.032	0.028	0.025	0.019	0.015	0.008	0.005	0.003	0.002	16
17	0.034	0.026	0.023	0.020	0.015	0.012	0.006	0.003	0.002	0.001	17
18	0.028	0.021	0.018	0.016	0.012	0.009	0.005	0.002	0.001	0.001	18
19	0.023	0.017	0.014	0.012	0.009	0.007	0.003	0.002	0.001		19
20	0.019	0.014	0.012	0.010	0.007	0.005	0.002	0.001	0.001		20
21	0.015	0.011	0.009	0.008	0.006	0.004	0.002	0.001			21
22	0.013	0.009	0.007	0.006	0.004	0.003	0.001	0.001			22
23	0.010	0.007	0.006	0.005	0.003	0.002	0.001				23
24	0.008	0.006	0.005	0.004	0.003	0.002	0.001				24
25	0.007	0.005	0.004	0.003	0.002	0.001	0.001				25
26	0.006	0.004	0.003	0.002	0.002	0.001					26
27	0.005	0.003	0.002	0.002	0.001	0.001					27
28	0.004	0.002	0.002	0.002	0.001	0.001					28
29	0.003	0.002	0.002	0.001	0.001						29
30	0.003	0.002	0.001	0.001	0.001						30
35	0.001	0.001									35
40											40
45											45
50											50

series

Table 4
PRESENT VALUE OF $1 RECEIVED (OR PAID)
AT THE END OF A PERIOD FOR n PERIODS*

adding table 1

$$P_n = A\left[\frac{1 - \dfrac{1}{(1+i)^n}}{i}\right]$$

*To determine the present value of $1 received (or paid) at the beginning of a period for n periods, use the factor shown for one *less* period and *add* 1.000.

Periods (n)	1%	1½%	2%	2½%	3%	3½%	4%	5%	6%	Periods (n)
1	0.990	0.985	0.980	0.976	0.971	0.966	0.962	0.952	0.943	1
2	1.970	1.956	1.942	1.927	1.913	1.900	1.886	1.859	1.833	2
3	2.941	2.912	2.884	2.856	2.829	2.802	2.775	2.723	2.673	3
4	3.902	3.854	3.808	3.762	3.717	3.673	3.630	3.546	3.465	4
5	4.853	4.783	4.713	4.646	4.580	4.515	4.452	4.329	4.212	5
6	5.795	5.697	5.601	5.508	5.417	5.329	5.242	5.076	4.917	6
7	6.728	6.598	6.472	6.349	6.230	6.115	6.002	5.786	5.582	7
8	7.652	7.486	7.325	7.170	7.020	6.874	6.733	6.463	6.210	8
9	8.566	8.361	8.162	7.971	7.786	7.608	7.435	7.108	6.802	9
10	9.471	9.222	8.983	8.752	8.530	8.317	8.111	7.722	7.360	10
11	10.368	10.071	9.787	9.514	9.253	9.002	8.760	8.306	7.887	11
12	11.255	10.908	10.575	10.258	9.954	9.663	9.385	8.863	8.384	12
13	12.134	11.732	11.348	10.983	10.635	10.303	9.986	9.394	8.853	13
14	13.004	12.543	12.106	11.691	11.296	10.921	10.563	9.899	9.295	14
15	13.865	13.343	12.849	12.381	11.938	11.517	11.118	10.380	9.712	15
16	14.718	14.131	13.578	13.055	12.561	12.094	11.652	10.838	10.106	16
17	15.562	14.908	14.292	13.712	13.166	12.651	12.166	11.274	10.477	17
18	16.398	15.673	14.992	14.353	13.754	13.190	12.659	11.690	10.828	18
19	17.226	16.426	15.678	14.979	14.324	13.710	13.134	12.085	11.158	19
20	18.046	17.169	16.351	15.589	14.877	14.212	13.590	12.462	11.470	20
21	18.857	17.900	17.011	16.185	15.415	14.698	14.029	12.821	11.764	21
22	19.660	18.621	17.658	16.765	15.937	15.167	14.451	13.163	12.042	22
23	20.456	19.331	18.292	17.332	16.444	15.620	14.857	13.489	12.303	23
24	21.243	20.030	18.914	17.885	16.936	16.058	15.247	13.799	12.550	24
25	22.023	20.720	19.523	18.424	17.413	16.482	15.622	14.094	12.783	25
26	22.795	21.399	20.121	18.951	17.877	16.890	15.983	14.375	13.003	26
27	23.560	22.068	20.707	19.464	18.327	17.285	16.330	14.643	13.211	27
28	24.316	22.727	21.281	19.965	18.764	17.667	16.663	14.898	13.406	28
29	25.066	23.376	21.844	20.454	19.189	18.036	16.984	15.141	13.591	29
30	25.808	24.016	22.396	20.930	19.600	18.392	17.292	15.372	13.765	30
35	29.409	27.076	24.999	23.145	21.487	20.001	18.665	16.374	14.498	35
40	32.835	29.916	27.355	25.103	23.115	21.355	19.793	17.159	15.046	40
45	36.095	32.552	29.490	26.833	24.519	22.495	20.720	17.774	15.456	45
50	39.196	35.000	31.424	28.362	25.730	23.456	21.482	18.256	15.762	50
∞	100.000	66.667	50.000	40.000	33.333	28.571	25.000	20.000	16.667	∞

Table 4 (Continued)
PRESENT VALUE OF $1 RECEIVED (OR PAID)
AT THE END OF A PERIOD FOR n PERIODS*

$$P_n = A\left[\frac{1 - \dfrac{1}{(1 + i)^n}}{i}\right]$$

*To determine the present value of $1 received (or paid) at the beginning of a period for n periods, use the factor shown for one *less* period and *add* 1.000.

Periods (n)	7%	8%	10%	12%	14%	15%	16%	18%	20%	Periods (n)
1	0.935	0.926	0.909	0.893	0.877	0.870	0.862	0.847	0.833	1
2	1.808	1.783	1.736	1.690	1.647	1.626	1.605	1.566	1.528	2
3	2.624	2.577	2.487	2.402	2.322	2.283	2.246	2.174	2.106	3
4	3.387	3.312	3.170	3.037	2.914	2.855	2.798	2.690	2.589	4
5	4.100	3.993	3.791	3.605	3.433	3.352	3.274	3.127	2.991	5
6	4.767	4.623	4.355	4.111	3.889	3.784	3.685	3.498	3.326	6
7	5.389	5.206	4.868	4.564	4.288	4.160	4.039	3.812	3.605	7
8	5.971	5.747	5.335	4.968	4.639	4.487	4.344	4.078	3.837	8
9	6.515	6.247	5.759	5.328	4.946	4.772	4.607	4.303	4.031	9
10	7.024	6.710	6.145	5.650	5.216	5.019	4.833	4.494	4.192	10
11	7.499	7.139	6.495	5.938	5.453	5.234	5.029	4.656	4.327	11
12	7.943	7.536	6.814	6.194	5.660	5.421	5.197	4.793	4.439	12
13	8.358	7.904	7.103	6.424	5.842	5.583	5.342	4.910	4.533	13
14	8.745	8.244	7.367	6.628	6.002	5.724	5.468	5.008	4.611	14
15	9.108	8.559	7.606	6.811	6.142	5.847	5.575	5.092	4.675	15
16	9.447	8.851	7.824	6.974	6.265	5.954	5.669	5.162	4.730	16
17	9.763	9.122	8.022	7.120	6.373	6.047	5.749	5.222	4.775	17
18	10.059	9.372	8.201	7.250	6.467	6.128	5.818	5.273	4.812	18
19	10.336	9.604	8.365	7.366	6.550	6.198	5.877	5.316	4.844	19
20	10.594	9.818	8.514	7.469	6.623	6.259	5.929	5.353	4.870	20
21	10.836	10.017	8.649	7.562	6.687	6.312	5.973	5.384	4.891	21
22	11.061	10.201	8.772	7.645	6.743	6.359	6.011	5.410	4.909	22
23	11.272	10.371	8.883	7.718	6.792	6.399	6.044	5.432	4.925	23
24	11.469	10.529	8.985	7.784	6.835	6.434	6.073	5.451	4.937	24
25	11.654	10.675	9.077	7.843	6.873	6.464	6.097	5.467	4.948	25
26	11.826	10.810	9.161	7.896	6.906	6.491	6.118	5.480	4.956	26
27	11.987	10.935	9.237	7.943	6.935	6.514	6.136	5.492	4.964	27
28	12.137	11.051	9.307	7.984	6.961	6.534	6.152	5.502	4.970	28
29	12.278	11.158	9.370	8.022	6.983	6.551	6.166	5.510	4.975	29
30	12.409	11.258	9.427	8.055	7.003	6.566	6.177	5.517	4.979	30
35	12.948	11.655	9.644	8.176	7.070	6.617	6.215	5.539	4.992	35
40	13.332	11.925	9.779	8.244	7.105	6.642	6.234	5.548	4.997	40
45	13.606	12.108	9.863	8.283	7.123	6.654	6.242	5.552	4.999	45
50	13.801	12.233	9.915	8.304	7.133	6.661	6.246	5.554	4.999	50
∞	14.286	12.500	10.000	8.333	7.143	6.667	6.250	5.556	5.000	∞

Table 4 (Concluded)
PRESENT VALUE OF $1 RECEIVED (OR PAID)
AT THE END OF A PERIOD FOR n PERIODS*

$$P_n = A\left[\dfrac{1 - \dfrac{1}{(1 + i)^n}}{i}\right]$$

*To determine the present value of $1 received (or paid) at the beginning of a period for n periods, use the factor shown for one *less* period and *add* 1.000.

Periods (n)	22%	24%	25%	26%	28%	30%	35%	40%	45%	50%	Periods (n)
1	0.820	0.806	0.800	0.794	0.781	0.769	0.741	0.714	0.690	0.667	1
2	1.492	1.457	1.440	1.424	1.392	1.361	1.289	1.224	1.165	1.111	2
3	2.042	1.981	1.952	1.923	1.868	1.816	1.696	1.589	1.493	1.407	3
4	2.494	2.404	2.362	2.320	2.241	2.166	1.997	1.849	1.720	1.605	4
5	2.864	2.745	2.689	2.635	2.532	2.436	2.220	2.035	1.876	1.737	5
6	3.167	3.020	2.951	2.885	2.759	2.643	2.385	2.168	1.983	1.824	6
7	3.416	3.242	3.161	3.083	2.937	2.802	2.508	2.263	2.057	1.883	7
8	3.619	3.421	3.329	3.241	3.076	2.925	2.598	2.331	2.108	1.922	8
9	3.786	3.566	3.463	3.366	3.184	3.019	2.665	2.379	2.144	1.948	9
10	3.923	3.682	3.571	3.465	3.269	3.092	2.715	2.414	2.168	1.965	10
11	4.035	3.776	3.656	3.544	3.335	3.147	2.752	2.438	2.185	1.977	11
12	4.127	3.851	3.725	3.606	3.387	3.190	2.779	2.456	2.196	1.985	12
13	4.203	3.912	3.780	3.656	3.427	3.223	2.799	2.468	2.204	1.990	13
14	4.265	3.962	3.824	3.695	3.459	3.249	2.814	2.477	2.210	1.993	14
15	4.315	4.001	3.859	3.726	3.843	3.268	2.825	2.484	2.214	1.995	15
16	4.357	4.033	3.887	3.751	3.503	3.283	2.834	2.489	2.216	1.997	16
17	4.391	4.059	3.910	3.771	3.518	3.295	2.840	2.492	2.218	1.998	17
18	4.419	4.080	3.928	3.786	3.529	3.304	2.844	2.494	2.219	1.999	18
19	4.442	4.097	3.942	3.799	3.539	3.311	2.848	2.496	2.220	1.999	19
20	4.460	4.110	3.954	3.808	3.546	3.316	2.850	2.497	2.221	1.999	20
21	4.476	4.121	3.963	3.816	3.551	3.320	2.852	2.498	2.221	2.000	21
22	4.488	4.130	3.970	3.822	3.556	3.323	2.853	2.498	2.222		22
23	4.499	4.137	3.976	3.827	3.559	3.325	2.854	2.499			23
24	4.507	4.143	3.981	3.831	3.562	3.327	2.855	2.499			24
25	4.514	4.147	3.985	3.834	3.564	3.329	2.856	2.499			25
26	4.520	4.151	3.988	3.837	3.566	3.330	2.856	2.500			26
27	4.524	4.154	3.990	3.839	3.567	3.331	2.856				27
28	4.528	4.157	3.992	3.840	3.568	3.331	2.857				28
29	4.531	4.159	3.994	3.841	3.569	3.332					29
30	4.534	4.160	3.995	3.842	3.569	3.332					30
35	4.541	4.164	3.998	3.845	3.571	3.333					35
40	4.544	4.166	3.999	3.846	3.571	3.333					40
45	4.545	4.166	4.000								45
50	4.545	4.167									50
∞	4.545	4.167	4.000	3.846	3.571	3.333	2.857	2.500	2.222	2.000	∞

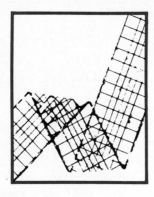

Index